W9-BPK-177

Switzerland

Nicola Williams
Damien Simonis, Kerry Walker

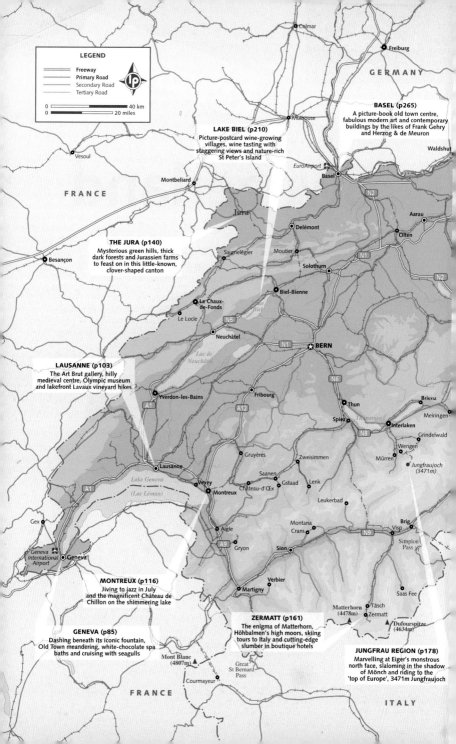

LEGEND

Freeway
Primary Road
Secondary Road
Tertiary Road

0   40 km
0   20 miles

GERMANY

BASEL (p265)
A picture-book old town centre,
fabulous modern art and contemporary
buildings by the likes of Frank Gehry
and Herzog & de Meuron

LAKE BIEL (p210)
Picture-postcard wine-growing
villages, wine tasting with
staggering views and nature-rich
St Peter's Island

FRANCE

THE JURA (p140)
Mysterious green hills, thick
dark forests and Jurassien farms
to feast on in this little-known,
clover-shaped canton

LAUSANNE (p103)
The Art Brut gallery, hilly
medieval centre, Olympic museum
and lakefront Lavaux vineyard hikes

MONTREUX (p116)
Jiving to jazz in July
and the magnificent Château de
Chillon on the shimmering lake

GENEVA (p85)
Dashing beneath its iconic fountain,
Old Town meandering, white-chocolate spa
baths and cruising with seagulls

ZERMATT (p161)
The enigma of Matterhorn,
Höhbalmen's high moors, skiing
tours to Italy and cutting-edge
slumber in boutique hotels

JUNGFRAU REGION (p178)
Marvelling at Eiger's monstrous
north face, slaloming in the shadow
of Mönch and riding to the
'top of Europe', 3471m Jungfraujoch

FRANCE

ITALY

Colmar
Freiburg
Mulhouse
EuroAirport
Basel
Waldshut
Vesoul
Montbéliard
Delémont
Aarau
Olten
N2
N1
N2
Jura
Besançon
Saignelégier
Moutier
Solothurn
Le Chaux-de-Fonds
Biel-Bienne
Le Locle
N5
Neuchâtel
N1
BERN
Luc de
Neuchâtel
Yverdon-les-Bains
Fribourg
Thun
Brienz
A1
A12
Spiez
Meiringen
Interlaken
N8
Grindelwald
Gruyères
Zweisimmen
Wengen
Jungfraujoch
(3471m)
Mürren
Saanen
Lausanne
Château-d'Œx
Gstaad
Lenk
Lake Geneva
(Lac Léman)
Vevey
Montreux
Leukerbad
Gex
Aigle
Montana
Crans
Brig
Visp
A9
Gryon
Sion
N9
Simplon
Pass
Geneva
International
Airport
Geneva
Verbier
Saas Fee
Martigny
Matterhorn
(4478m)
Täsch
Zermatt
Mont Blanc
(4807m)
Great
St Bernard
Pass
Dufourspitze
(4634m)
Courmayeur

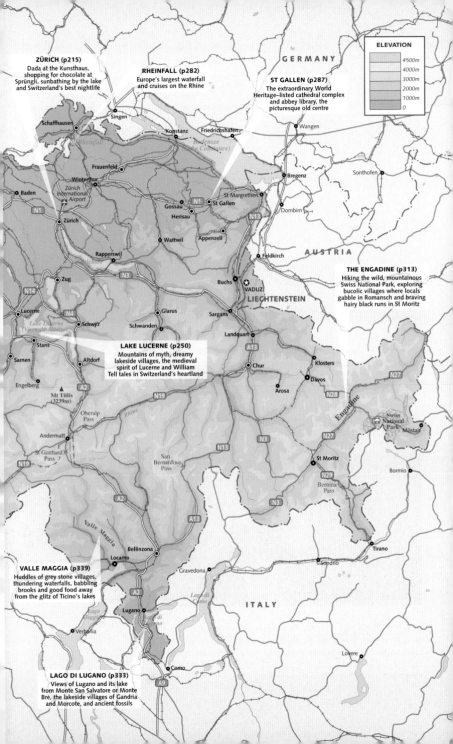

ELEVATION

	4500m
	4000m
	3000m
	2000m
	1000m
	0

ZÜRICH (p215)
Dada at the Kunsthaus,
shopping for chocolate at
Sprüngli, sunbathing by the lake
and Switzerland's best nightlife

RHEINFALL (p282)
Europe's largest waterfall
and cruises on the Rhine

ST GALLEN (p287)
The extraordinary World
Heritage–listed cathedral complex
and abbey library, the
picturesque old centre

THE ENGADINE (p313)
Hiking the wild, mountainous
Swiss National Park, exploring
bucolic villages where locals
gabble in Romansch and braving
hairy black runs in St Moritz

LAKE LUCERNE (p250)
Mountains of myth, dreamy
lakeside villages, the medieval
spirit of Lucerne and William
Tell tales in Switzerland's heartland

VALLE MAGGIA (p339)
Huddles of grey stone villages,
thundering waterfalls, babbling
brooks and good food away
from the glitz of Ticino's lakes

LAGO DI LUGANO (p333)
Views of Lugano and its lake
from Monte San Salvatore or Monte
Brè, the lakeside villages of Gandria
and Morcote, and ancient fossils

GERMANY

AUSTRIA

LIECHTENSTEIN

VADUZ

ITALY

Schaffhausen
Singen
Konstanz
Friedrichshafen
Wangen
Sonthofen
Frauenfeld
Winterthur
Bregenz
Zürich International Airport
Baden
Gossau
St Margrethen
St Gallen
Dornbirn
Zürich
Herisau
Rapperswil
Wattwil
Appenzell
Feldkirch
Zug
Buchs
N14
Lucerne
Glarus
Sargans
Schwyz
Schwanden
Landquart
Stans
Altdorf
Chur
Klosters
Sarnen
Davos
Arosa
Engelberg
Mt Titlis (3239m)
Oberalp Pass
Andermatt
St Gotthard Pass
San Bernardino Pass
St Moritz
Müstair
Swiss National Park
Bormio
Bernina Pass
Valle Maggia
Bellinzona
Tirano
Locarno
Gravedona
Sondrio
Lugano
Verbania
Como
Lovere

Rhein
Bodensee (Lake Constance)
Lago di Como
Lago Maggiore
Lake Lucerne (Vierwaldstättersee)
Rheinfall
Engadine

On the Road

NICOLA WILLIAMS Coordinating Author
The last leg home: I'd just spent a week skiing with the family in Bettmeralp (p168), a pearl of Swiss mountain charm where cars are banned, kids are towed about on picture-book Davos sledges and high-altitude slopes cruise next to the Aletsch Glacier. Cable car, Glacier Express, another train, now boat home across Lake Geneva to our lakeside village.

KERRY WALKER China-blue skies, glaciers and gold-tinged high moors – the Zmuttal on the Höhenweg Höhbalmen hike (p63) captures everything I love most about Switzerland. Close to Matterhorn yet a zillion miles away from Zermatt's bustle, this area is wild, serene and simply gorgeous in the diffused light of a September afternoon.

DAMIEN SIMONIS On a magnificent autumn day, we stopped to admire the scenery on the way from Glarus to Altdorf, a few kilometres short of the Klausenpass. After a long tour of the northeast, where scenery stops had been incessant, one could only smile at all the exuberant beauty in this little-travelled area.

For author biographies see p386.

EUPHORIC JOURNEYS

Switzerland honestly has it all: cities that happen, mountains that move, landscapes that uplift, art that inspires, and Alpine action stations that make hearts pound and souls spiral to heaven. Dash silk-smooth chocolate, cuckoo clocks, yodelling and feather-capped men in knickerbockers 'n braces: new-century Switzerland, Europe's forward-thinking land of four languages and cultural diversity, is all about being, sensing and living euphoric journeys.

Green Perspectives

No country begs outdoor escapades more than Switzerland, a God-like canvas of lush green peaks, wondrous white glaciers and hallucinatory natural landscapes etched so perfectly one could cry – or at least grab your boots, leap on your board, throw your hat in the air, toot your bike bell and let spirits soar from one euphoric green perspective to another.

① Aletsch Glacier
This glacier (p168) is among the world's natural marvels and for good reason: panoramic views of this 23km-long sea of ice, rock and snow from Jungfraujoch or, indeed, from the ski slopes of car-free Bettmeralp are joyous.

② Lake Geneva
The vivid emerald vines marching uphill in perfect unison from the shores of Lake Geneva in Lavaux (p115) are staggering. *The* urban viewpoint to admire Europe's largest lake (with Mont Blanc as the backdrop) is Geneva's Quai du Mont Blanc (p89).

③ Staubbach Falls, Lauterbrunnen
So moved were Goethe and Lord Byron by these wispy waterfalls (p185), fairy-tale threads of spray ensnaring the cliffside, they composed poems exalting their ethereal beauty. The Rheinfall (p282) are more crash-bang thunder.

④ Lake Lucerne
No view across this shimmering expanse of water (p250) to the green hillsides, meadows, valleys and tucked-away lake resorts disappoints; scale lookouts atop Mt Pilatus, Mt Rigi or the Stanserhorn to see it from a wider perspective.

⑤ Klöntal
Escape civilisation: roam one of the country's least touched valleys (p294), where majestic waterfalls slice clefts in the mountains and the mirror-still lake of Klöntaler See exudes perfect peace.

⑥ Hölloch Caves
Explore subterranean Switzerland with Europe's longest (and the world's third biggest) network of caves (p255). Hike along 170km of mapped-out tunnels and bivouac overnight.

⑦ Ruin' Aulta
Gawp at these weird limestone pinnacles in the glacier-gouged Rhine Gorge on foot (p75), afloat a white-water raft or – should you have the head for it – between *via ferrata* karabiners (p305).

Art & Architecture

From Roman to modern, Swiss architecture is dynamic, innovative and respectful of tradition when it comes to fusing iconic new with Heidi old – enchanting chalet farmsteads with paint-peeling shutters, a profusion of red geranium blossoms and metal milk churns on a bench waiting to be filled.

❶ Bern

Medieval cobbled streets, arcaded boutiques, a dancing clock and folk figures frolicking in fountains since the 16th century – not to mention the new millennium hills of Renzo Piano's Zentrum Paul Klee (p199, pictured) – make Switzerland's capital city a real art 'n architecture fest.

❷ Château de Chillon

This fairy-tale castle (p116), Switzerland's best, juts out across Lake Geneva and is everything a castle should be: romantic, historic, sumptuous and sugary sweet. Runner-ups: Château de Grandson on Lake Neuchâtel (p120) and Schloss Thun (p189).

❸ Le Corbusier

Trace the life of this iconic Swiss architect, from the White House he designed for his parents in La Chaux-de-Fonds (p138) to his very last creation, now a Le Corbusier Museum, in Zürich (p219, pictured).

❹ Sammlung Rosengart & KKL

Lucerne revels in the double whammy of a peerless Picasso collection, the Sammlung Rosengart, and inspired contemporary-art exhibitions in its striking Jean Nouvel–designed KKL (Arts & Congress Centre) (p245).

❺ Fondation Pierre Gianadda

Art and architecture kiss at Martigny's futuristic concrete creation (p147), where works by Picasso, Cézanne and van Gogh embrace inside, sculptures by Henri Moore and Niki de Saint Phalle outside.

❻ Fondation Beyeler

The long light-flooded building by Renzo Piano excites just as much as the vital collection of contemporary art – Switzerland's best – it showcases (p269).

❼ Therme Vals & Zervreilasee

Fuse a soak in the middle of cutting-edge quartzite design in the country's most famous spa (p306) with a trek to its neighbouring turquoise lake and you'll be Zen for weeks.

❽ Lugano

Catch Switzerland's most famous contemporary architect (p330) in the pink in his Italianate home town.

Urban Lifestyle

It is not all hiking, fondue dipping and off-piste hobnobbing. With four languages to pick from and a kaleidoscopic cultural variety to match, urban city-slicker Switzerland is a potent cocktail of street grit, shopping chic, after-hours Alpine adrenalin rush and – as the sun sinks across the lake – good old-fashioned romance.

❶ Zürich Nightlife
Europe's hippest city, an ode to urban renovation, screams party. Shop for fashion at
Freitag (p228) atop Kreis 5's first skyscraper,
quench your thirst in waterfront bars and
dance until dawn in Züri-West (p226).

❷ Genevan Seagulls
Zipping across Lake Geneva aboard Les Mouettes – canary-yellow Seagulls – is part and
parcel of daily life for the 180-odd nationalities living in Switzerland's most cosmopolitan
city, French-speaking Geneva (p85).

❸ Lucerne
Medieval bridge strolling is the soul of this irresistible Romeo. With sparkly lake vistas, alfresco café life, candy-coloured architecture
and Victorian curiosities too, this could well
be the start of a beautiful affair (p243).

❹ Lausanne
To this day a night watchman scales the bell
tower inside the Gothic cathedral in Lausanne
(p103) to call out the hour. On Switzerland's
national day (1 August), hire a pedalo and
watch fireworks light up this gorgeous lakeside town from the middle of the lake.

❺ Zug
Rock-bottom tax rates make lakefront Zug
(p260) a tycoon magnet. Play millionaire
over a slice of liqueur-soaked *Kirschtorte*
(cherry cake) in its medieval Old Town.

❻ St Gallen
What a feast: St Gallen (p287) has an extraordinary rococo library, a zany red square to
chill in and taverns in half-timbered houses –
all rooted in a deeply Germanic, rural world.

❼ Chur
Pure grunge is the after-dark vibe of the
Welschdörfli bar scene in Switzerland's oldest city (p298). Clear morning-after fuzzy
heads with a shot of Alpine action in Arosa,
365 stomach-churning hairpin bends away
(p302).

Madcap Merriment

From flag waving to yodelling, beard cutting to stone throwing, cow fighting to kid wrestling, the Swiss can party in the most unexpectedly madcap of manners. And with their bounty of patron saints to venerate, harvests to usher in, historic and folkloric traditions to honour, they need no excuse to do so. Every day is a festival.

1 Street Parade, Zürich
Zürich's wild, wacky, larger-than-life techno celebration in August is usually Europe's largest street party in any given year (p221).

2 Harder Potschete, Interlaken
Warty masked ogres dash through Interlaken on 2 January, cackling, hissing, clanging bells and causing mischief – as much mischief as they can – to the delight of fiendish merrymakers (p174).

3 L'Escalade, Geneva
Smash marzipan-filled chocolate cauldrons and gorge on the sweet broken pieces on the cobbled streets of Geneva's Old Town (p92).

4 Fasnacht, Lucerne
Stark raving bonkers is essentially what Lucerne's riot of a six-day pre-Lenten bash is (p247). Never dare call the Swiss Goody Two-Shoes again.

Contents

Regional Map Contents

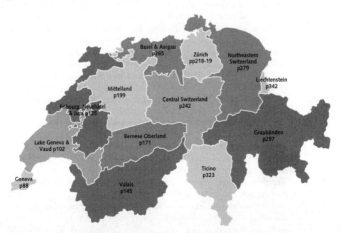

Basel & Aargau p265

Zürich pp218-19

Northeastern Switzerland p279

Liechtenstein p342

Mittelland p199

Central Switzerland p242

Fribourg, Neuchâtel & Jura p125

Graubünden p297

Lake Geneva & Vaud p102

Bernese Oberland p171

Geneva p88

Valais p145

Ticino p323

Destination Switzerland

What giddy romance and glamour Zermatt, St Moritz, Davos and other glitterati-encrusted names evoke: from the intoxicated chink of multimillionaires in Verbier hobnobbing over Champagne cocktails poured in ice-carved flutes to the comforting jangle of the cows coming home to sgraffito-blazoned farmsteads in the Engadine, seduction is head-over-heels complete. Ride a little red train between peak and pine, soak in mountain spa water, snowshoe to your igloo, fall madly in love with painted bridges in Lucerne and know life in this snug, smug, truly ravishing enclave in Europe is good.

This is after all *Sonderfall Schweiz* (literally 'special case Switzerland') – a rare and refined breed, a privileged neutral country set apart from others, borne out by its 1874 constitution (p29) and confirmed by the country's neutrality during both world wars (p30). Despite moves towards greater international cooperation (such as finally ditching border controls for Schengen countries in December 2008) coupled with the gargantuan presence of global institutions in Geneva, much about modern-day Switzerland is idiosyncratic, insular, parochial and unique. Few countries promote 'direct democracy' through referenda and practise 'armed neutrality' with a trained militia that will never find itself face to face with an enemy (given its neutrality).

No paradise is invincible. The world financial crisis in late 2008 took victims in Switzerland in the shape of the country's largest bank which would have gone belly up without state bailout (p33). Then there was the rumpus in August 2008 over the bid by the far-right Swiss People's Party (SVP) to ban building new minarets for Muslim calls of prayer. The same far-right political party published anti-immigrant posters featuring three white sheep kicking one black sheep off that striking white cross of the Swiss flag (p38 and p256), and tried – and failed – to make it even harder for noncitizens to get a Swiss passport (p37). A violation of human rights and the Swiss constitution according to the government, the minaret matter, in true Swiss style, will be decided in a national referendum that is likely to take years to happen.

Reinventing the Alps is the hot topic at higher altitudes. With great success world-class architects are respectfully weaving futuristic apartments clad in larch-wood tiles (Sir Norman Foster in St Moritz) and spiralling hotel towers of ecological dimensions (Herzog & de Meuron in Davos) into Switzerland's quintessential Heidi-postcard landscape of traditional wooden chalets and timeless church spires. But most pressing is not so much how to be green, how to be ecological, how to burn clean energy – Swiss eco-angels have that sorted (p235). Rather, it is what must be done to keep ski resorts sustainable as the globe warms: experts say forget sure-thing snow below 1500m by 2050.

The answer for Andermatt (p262) in central Switzerland lies in a mammoth Sfr1.08 billion investment by Egyptian billionaire Samih Sawiris set to turn the sleepy village of 1350 inhabitants into a luxury megaresort of appeal year-round with its tropical pool, sandy beach and 18-hole golf course alongside traditional high-altitude skiing. A burning question is how much one of its 700-odd apartments will cost when it opens in 2014. As James Blunt, Sir Richard Branson and a rash of other celebrities, entrepreneurs and nouveaux-riches Russians already snap up the best properties on the market, Alpine real-estate prices are rocketing through the roof – and out of the reach of less glam pockets.

Bollywood tourists tottering up Titlis premonsoon (p184), Geneva scientists playing God with big-bang experiments (p41): this small, smart, secretive country is as eclectic as the extraordinary linguistic and cultural diversity on which it rests.

FAST FACTS

Population: 7.59 million

Non-Swiss nationals: 20.7% of total population

Area: 41,285 sq km

GDP: Sfr480 billion (2007)

GDP per capita: Sfr65,830 (2007)

GDP growth: 1.9%

Inflation: 2%

Unemployment rate: 2.4% (2007)

Average life expectancy: 77.9 (men), 83.7 (women)

Highest point: Dufour-spitze (4634m)

Getting Started

Most know Switzerland as one of those historical, tried-and-tested luxury destinations that requires planning months in advance to snag a room (yes, any room) in one of its mythical grande-dame establishments. Less know that Swiss style can also say hell to opulence, fly by the seat of its pants in some circles and be up for grabs with very little or, depending on the season, no advance planning or booking to speak of.

While you won't get by on tuppence, travelling in Switzerland doesn't have to mean investing a small fortune. And the return – smooth, straightforward, famously reliable travel, generally well organised and free of bad surprises – is huge.

For climatic considerations and climate charts see p351.

WHEN TO GO

Summer, meaning June to September, offers the most pleasant climate for outdoor activities (p229), obviously with the exception of exclusively winter sports. Indeed, some extreme pursuits such as canyoning are only offered at this time. Peak months are July and August when prices soar, accommodation gets fully booked and most sights are rammed with tourists. Predictably, you'll find better deals and less people in summer's shoulder months: April, May and October.

Bar the busy Easter break, spring is a beautiful time to explore the countryside. In Ticino, flowers blossom as early as March. Hikers planning to walk at high altitudes should be equipped for snow and ice well into June (and, in some tricky spots, all year). Mid-August to late October generally has fairly settled weather, and is a good period for hiking trips. For more on when to walk, see p58.

In Alpine resorts the busy winter season kicks off mid-December and moves into full swing from Christmas onwards, closing down again when the snows start to melt around mid-April. Between the summer and winter seasons, Alpine resorts close down (except where year-round glacier skiing is on offer) or, at best, go into frustrating snooze mode.

Then, of course, there is Switzerland's fabulous fiesta of festivals around which to plan a trip: it parties year-round, although Switzerland's renowned international music festivals happen in summer, as do some of those lesser-known, decidedly eclectic local festivals that best express the country's deep-rooted Alpine culture (p34). See p21 for more.

COSTS & MONEY

No denying it: Switzerland is pricey – Geneva and Zürich were rated the world's seventh and eighth most expensive cities in 2008. Compared to other European countries, travellers from North America and Australia will feel it particularly keenly, and even those from the UK and Scandinavia will notice the difference, despite it lessening in recent years. One very good piece of news is that petrol in Switzerland is cheaper than in neighbouring countries Austria, France, Germany and Italy.

Your biggest expenses while in Switzerland are likely to be long-distance public transport, accommodation and eating out. In the most modest hotels, expect to pay at least Sfr80/120 per single/double. A full meal with 500ml of house wine for two can easily cost Sfr50 or more per person.

But there are ways to keep costs down. Travel passes (p367) immediately yield substantial savings on trains, boats and buses; while camping, and kipping in barns (p353) or hostels translate as cheap(er) sleeps. Self-catering,

HOW MUCH?

See also Lonely Planet Index, inside front cover.

Local newspaper Sfr2.50

Public-transport ticket Sfr2

10-minute taxi ride Sfr15

One-/six-day ski pass Sfr60/300

Half-/full-day bicycle hire Sfr25/35

100g Toblerone chocolate bar Sfr2.50

DON'T LEAVE HOME WITHOUT...

▪ Valid travel insurance (p354)

▪ Your ID card or passport and visa, if required (p358)

▪ Driving licence, car documents and car insurance (p364)

▪ Sunglasses and hat in both summer and winter – all that snow makes for sharp glare!

▪ If mountain bound, a head for heights and a sturdy set of hiking boots

▪ A sweet tooth and cheesy sense of taste (p42)

▪ Your party spirit and a thirst for something different (p21 & p34)

---

picnic lunches and skipping the alcohol with meals when dining out will keep your food budget under control. Likewise staying put in one place and taking the time to get beneath its skin means lower day-to-day living costs than if you flit fast, visiting lots of different places including big cities and major ski resorts. Other cent savers include restricting sightseeing to inexpensive sights (museum and gallery admission prices range from Sfr5 to Sfr10), and hiking if possible instead of taking cable cars: rarely covered by travel passes, count Sfr15 to Sfr30 for a short to medium ascent and Sfr80 to Sfr100 for a return trip up and down Mt Titlis or Schilthorn.

If budget travellers stick to all the above, they can expect to scrape by on about Sfr100 a day. Add at least another Sfr40 per day to stay in a budget hotel, and a further Sfr40 for a wider choice of restaurants and sightseeing options. Always allow extra cash for emergencies. Students, come armed with a discount-yielding student card (p353).

TRAVELLING RESPONSIBLY
Since our inception in 1973, Lonely Planet has encouraged our readers to tread lightly, travel responsibly and enjoy the magic independent travel affords. International travel is growing at a jaw-dropping rate, and we still firmly believe in the benefits it can bring – but, as always, we encourage you to consider the impact your visit will have on the global environment and local economies, cultures and ecosystems.

Sleeping in bed and breakfasts, farms, haylofts (p353) and eco-places bearing the Steinbock label (p353), opting for entertaining the kids with green nature-driven activities (p351) rather than huge theme parks, spurning domestic flights and the car for the train (p368) and trading in four wheels for two (p363) are immediate ways of minimising your impact and travelling sustainably within Switzerland.

Or trial **SwitzerlandMobility** (www.switzerlandmobility.ch), an innovative and pioneering green travel network that only the Swiss could dream up. Integrating the country's nonmotorised traffic routes, it maps out 22 national routes and 147 regional routes for walkers (6300km), cyclists (8500km), mountain bikers (3300km), rollerbladers/skaters (1000km) and canoeists (250km). Every route is perfectly signposted; sections suitable for families are flagged accordingly; and each comes with a list of relevant hire outlets, accommodation options, public-transport connections, striking landscapes and nature spots en route, digital maps and so on. **Swiss Trails** (☎ 044 450 24 34; www.swisstrails.ch) organises daily luggage transfers on national routes and can also arrange a package for you, be it for two or 10 days.

For a comprehensive list of green restaurants, hotels and other ecological and sustainable-tourism options reviewed in this guide, see p403. Tip-top green days out are listed on p19 and for help in planning that environmentally friendly ski trip, see p235.

TOP PICKS

FAVOURITE SKI RESORTS

- Andermatt (p262)
- Bettmeralp (p168)
- Crans-Montana (p157)
- Klosters and Davos (p309)
- Engelberg (p257)
- Champéry and Les Portes du Soleil (p146)
- Grindelwald, Wengen and Mürren, Bernese Oberland (p178)
- Arosa (p302)
- St Moritz (p317)
- Verbier (p150)
- Zermatt (p161) and Saas Fee (p165)

URBAN DESIGN

Contemporary-art and design buffs eat, sleep, drink and sightsee your heart out! Urban Switzerland positively bristles with striking cutting-edge creations.

- Vitra Design Museum (p269) and Herzog & de Meuron's Schaulager, Basel (p269)
- Renzo Piano's Fondation Beyeler, Basel (p269), and Zentrum Paul Klee, Bern (p203)
- City Lounge, St Gallen (p289)
- Mario Botta's Museum Jean Tinguely, Basel (p269), and his Lugano legacy (p330)
- KKL (p245) and The Hotel (p248), Lucerne
- Freitag, Zürich (p228)
- Therme Vals, Vals (p306)
- Giger Bar, Chur (p301)
- Matterhorn Museum (p162) and Vernissage Bar (p165), Zermatt
- Le Corbusier Pavilion & Heidi Weber Museum, Zürich (p219)
- La Cour des Augustins, Hôtel Auteuil and La Réserve, Geneva (p94)
- Auberge aux 4 Vents, Fribourg (p128)
- Le Corbusier's Maison Blanche, La Chaux-de-Fonds (p138)

GREEN DAYS

Go slow, go green and buzz sustainable with our pick of environmentally sweet travel experiences, each designed to do in a day.

- Lake lounging in Lugano with an overnight stop at Locanda del Giglio (p333).
- The pick of gentle day rambles from Restaurant St Martin, St Martin (p293).
- Village hopping and wine tasting in Klettgau; lunch on *Spätzli* (egg noodles) at Bad Osterfingen, Osterfingen (p283).
- Revelling in the Alpine joys of fresh cheese, buttermilk and sleeping on straw with a hike from Arosa (p302) to Lenzerheide via the Parpaner Rothorn (p78).
- Chilling in Engelberg (p257) with cheesemaking, biking, feasting on Stephan Oberli's organic gastronomy at Hess and flopping in a fabulous milky whey bath.
- Overcoming vertigo at Devil's Bridge near Andermatt (p262), with dinner afterwards at The River House Boutique Hotel (p263).
- Taking a St Bernard dog for a walk over the Great St Bernard mountain pass at the Fondation Barry near Martigny (p150).
- Travelling with a llama through the beautiful Engadine valley (p82) or with a horse and cart around the forgotten Jura (p143).
- Gulping in bags of old-fashioned fresh air with local farmers and winemakers near Murten; kipping the night at Owl Farm (p138).
- Taste what Switzerland is all about with a farm feast, alfresco in summer, at Auberge du Mont Cornu (p138) near Neuchâtel.

TRAVEL LITERATURE

A Perfect Waiter (Alain Claude Sulzer) Set in the Bernese Oberland's legendary, grand 19th-century Hotel Geissbach (p193), this recently published novel by the Basel-born writer is a love story entwined around a hotel waiter and a 1930s affair that broke his heart and returns to torment him.

The Rose of Bern (Paul Dasilva) Bern is the backdrop for this cliffhanging tale of espionage that will have the most avid of spy-thriller fans on the edge of their seats.

Zermatt (Frank Schaeffer) Set in 1966, *Zermatt* is the tale of a couple of Reformed Presbyterian missionaries from Kansas and their three teenage children on holiday in the Swiss Alpine resort. Family life is fundamentalist strict until their 14-year-old becomes aroused by a waitress.

Switzerland: A Village History (Paul Birmingham) Birmingham takes a different look at the balloon town of Château-d'Œx, tracing its history as a rural village, through impoverishment in the wake of the Napoleonic invasions and back to prosperity in the tourist age.

INTERNET RESOURCES

Lonely Planet (www.lonelyplanet.com) Summaries on Switzerland, links to Switzerland-related sites and traveller stories on the Thorn Tree.

Switzerland Tourism (www.myswitzerland.com) The national Swiss tourist board's website, loaded with just about everything you could possibly need, including particularly fine festivals and events listings.

SBB CFF FFS (www.sbb.ch) Check timetables and buy tickets online with Swiss Federal Railways.

Swiss Info (www.swissinfo.org) Swiss national news, politics, music, culture, podcasts and loads more to inform on this multilingual news site by public broadcaster Swiss Radio International.

Swiss World (www.swissworld.org) People, culture, history, geography, politics, chocolate and other background country info; subscribe to its digital newsletter.

The Swiss Portal (www.ch.ch) Government press releases, elections, portraits of every canton, traffic rules, laws and stacks more detailed information on political, economic and social affairs in contemporary Switzerland.

Festivals Calendar

Switzerland's rich cultural calendar is a magnetic, eclectic and, at times, downright wacky merry-go-round of age-old markets *(Märit)* and traditional fairs *(Chilbi)*, performing arts and music festivals, soulful Alpine rites of passage, gastronomic feasts and village celebrations with curious local traditions. Fireworks light up most of the country, particularly its lakes, on Swiss National Day on 1 August.

More events than we could possibly list happen; check www.switzerland.com. For key dates in Switzerland's sporting calendar, see p37.

JANUARY

HARDER POTSCHETE   2 Jan
Ogres plague Interlaken on this devilish day (p174).

VOGEL GRYFF   Late Jan
A griffin, a savage and a lion chase winter away from Basel during this folkloric celebration (p270).

WORLD SNOW FESTIVAL   Late Jan
Grindelwald is hot with creativity for six days as sculptors carve gargantuan ice sculptures at the foot of the Eiger glacier (p180).

FEBRUARY

CARNIVAL   Ash Wednesday
Dozens of communities, particularly in Catholic cantons, go street mad with pre-Lenten parades, costumes, music and all of the fun of the fair during their *Fasnacht* (carnival) in Lucerne (p247), Basel (p270), and Bellinzona (p326), among others.

APRIL

SECHSELÄUTEN   3rd Mon
Zürich celebrates winter's end with costumed street parades and the burning of a fireworks-filled 'snowman', aka the terrifying Böögg (p221).

LUGANO FESTIVAL   Apr-May
Lugano immerses itself in classical music (p330).

LUCERNE FESTIVAL   Easter
This world-class festival lures chamber orchestras, pianists and other musicians from all corners of the globe to Lucerne. True devotees can return in summer and November (p246).

JUNE

FESTI'NEUCH   Early Jun
Jazz, pop and rock alfresco around Lac de Neuchâtel (p136).

ST GALLER FESTSPIELE   Around 20 Jun–Early Jul
St Gallen's two-week opera season (p289).

JODLERFEST LUZERN   Late Jun
Thousands of Swiss yodellers, alphorn players and flag throwers rouse souls at Lucerne's fabulous Alpine festival (p246).

**WILLIAM TELL OPEN-AIR
THEATRE**   Jun–Early Sep
Actors take to the open-air stage in Interlaken to perform the tale of *William Tell* (p177).

JULY

MONTREUX JAZZ   Early Jul
A fortnight of jazz is reason enough to slot lakeside Montreux into your itinerary (p117).

PALÉO FESTIVAL   Late Jul
Billed as the king of summer music fests, this six-day open-air world-music extravaganza – a 1970s child – rips around Nyon (p112).

DAVOS FESTIVAL   Late Jul–Early Aug
Young talent performs at Davos' classical-music festival (p312).

AUGUST

FESTIVAL INTERNAZIONALE DI FILM
Locarno's two-week International Film Festival is a cinematic celebration in business since 1948 (p336).

**MONTREUX-VEVEY
MUSIC FESTIVAL**   Late Aug–Mid-Sep
Be moved by classical music at Montreux' annual classical-music fest (p117).

STREET PARADE   Mid-Aug
Be part of Europe's largest street party in Zürich (p221).

CHURER FEST   Mid-Aug
Three days of concerts, feasting and cow-milking marathons in Chur (p300).

SETTIMANE MUSICALI   End Aug–Mid-Oct
International musicians flock to lakeside Ascona to take part in this summer music festival (p338).

SEPTEMBER

FÊTE DES VENDANGES   Last weekend Sep
Wine is the thrust of Neuchâtel's grape-harvest celebration (p131).

OCTOBER

FOIRE DU VALAIS
Cows battle – at the last meeting of the season – for the title of bovine queen at this 10-day regional fair in Martigny (p148).

NOVEMBER

ONION MARKET   4th Mon Nov
Bern's open-air *Zibelemärit* – more carnival than straight market – is legendary (p204).

DECEMBER

CLAU WAU   1st weekend Dec
Men in red prove their Xmas factor at Samnaun's Santa Claus World Championships (p315).

L'ESCALADE   11 Dec
Torch-lit processions, fires, a run around town and chocolate cauldrons make Geneva's biggest festival of the year a real romp (p92).

Itineraries
CLASSIC ROUTES

GENEVA TO ZÜRICH
Two Weeks/Geneva to Zürich

This is a trip for urbanites keen to mix metropolitan fire with small-town charm, eminently doable by car or public transport. Fly into one airport, out the other, or zip back to your point of arrival by fast train in 2¾ hours. Geneva to Zürich can be done in either direction and plenty of variations suggest themselves en route.

Landing in **Geneva** (p85), explore the most cosmopolitan of Switzerland's big cities. From Geneva, trundle by road along the shore of Europe's largest Alpine lake to bustling **Lausanne** (p103), a hilly lakeside city and seat of the International Olympic Committee. Follow the same glorious route through the Lavaux wine terraces to **Montreux** (p116), from where you head north to the medieval fortress town of **Gruyères** (p132), known for its cheese and cream-smothered meringues. Further north still, you arrive in **Fribourg** (p125), on the French-German language frontier, which you cross to make for Switzerland's pretty national capital, **Bern** (p199). Later, drop down in the depths of Bern's cantons and the lakeside towns around **Interlaken** (p172). Nearby there is plenty of great skiing, hiking and other outdoor options. The route swings north to another bewitching lady of the lake, **Lucerne** (p243), before changing atmosphere completely by rolling onwards via **Zug** (p260) to Switzerland's most happening 'n hip city, **Zürich** (p215).

In order to give a little time to all the destinations on this route you will want at least two weeks, leaving two days apiece for places like Geneva, Lausanne, Bern, Lucerne and Zürich. The changes in scenery and culture on this 385km route are extraordinary.

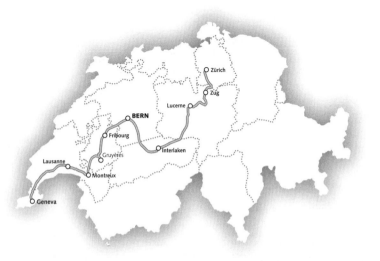

THE GLACIER EXPRESS   7½ Hours/Zermatt to St Moritz

Of the many remarkable railway trips on offer in Switzerland, this is the most breathtaking. The 272km trip through Alpine country, surrounded by icy peaks, high mountain pastures and pretty towns, winds its way through 91 tunnels and over 291 bridges.

It might not be as long as the Trans-Siberian, but this classic rail journey makes up for length in horizontal travel time with a vertical spectacle of stunning proportions. Switzerland sports several mountain rail trips, one of which is even on the Unesco World Heritage list (p320 and p313), but it is the Glacier Express, which runs from Zermatt northeast to St Moritz, that is the most mythical.

As Switzerland's Alpine resorts became popular with Europe's hoity-toity crowd in the early 20th century, the idea for a train linking Zermatt and St Moritz grew. In 1930, the inaugural steam-train journey between the two Alpine resorts took place and the 7½-hour trip – which can be done year-round – hasn't since lost its appeal. For practical details, see p368.

Starting in **Zermatt** (p161), the train winds slowly north down the valley to **Brig** (p167). From here it swings northeast along the pretty eastern stretch of the Rhône Valley towards the Furka Pass (which it circumvents by tunnel) and descends on **Andermatt** (p262) before again climbing up to the **Oberalp Pass**, the literal high point of the trip at 2033m.

From there it meanders alongside the Vorderrhein River, passing through **Disentis/Mustér** (p307) before arriving in **Chur** (p298). The main train continues to **St Moritz** (p317), with a branch line heading northeast to **Davos** (p311).

ROADS LESS TRAVELLED

LOST IN GRAUBÜNDEN & TICINO   Two to Three Weeks/Chur to Vals

With the exception of high-wilderness mountaineering, this is one of the best routes for getting away from it all (with occasional options to jump back into the tourist fray). As a circular route, you can kick off anywhere, but a convenient place to start is the Graubünden capital of **Chur** (p298), from where you head north for a quick detour to pretty **Maienfeld** (p309) and its vineyards. Make east for the skiing centres of **Klosters** (p309) and **Davos** (p311), where you leave the bustle behind to surge east into the lower Engadine Valley, with pretty towns to admire like **Guarda** (p314) and **Scuol** (p314). In the latter, hang about for some great bath treatment. From there the road ribbons east to the Austrian border, which you cross to then head south through a slice of Austria and Italy, before veering back west into Switzerland to contemplate the frescos at **Müstair** (p315). The road continues west and then southwest, passing through picture-postcard **Zuoz** (p316) before reaching chic **St Moritz** (p317). Then follow the Julier Pass mountain road that swings north and west, then drops down the gorges of the **Via Mala** (p307) to the hamlet of **Zillis** (p307), another key art stop.

The road continues south and crosses into Ticino and the medieval castles of **Bellinzona** (p324). From there, steam on past lakeside **Locarno** (p336) and up the enchanting **Valle Maggia** (p339). Backtracking to Bellinzona, the main route takes you along the Valle Leventina, with a stop in **Giornico** (p327) and any high valley hamlets you fancy, before crossing the **St Gotthard Pass** (p262) to **Andermatt** (p262) and then veering back east into Graubünden. Make a quick stop at the monastery of **Disentis/Mustér** (p307) before making one last highly recommended detour to the designer baths of **Vals** (p306), the last stop before Chur.

Get well off the beaten track on this circular road trip, taking in such gems as vivid Romanesque frescos, quaint Engadine towns, remote Ticino villages, medieval castles, high mountain passes and two tempting thermal baths. Give yourself two to three weeks for this 685km trail.

TAILORED TRIPS

WORLD TREASURES

In spite of all its natural wonders and overwhelming man-made beauty, Switzerland boasts only nine Unesco World Heritage Sites. Starting in the north, **St Gallen** (p287) is the seat of a grand abbey and church complex that safeguards one of the world's oldest libraries. On a similar note is the Kloster de St Johann (St John's Monastery) in **Müstair** (p315) in the far east of the country, graced with vivid Carolingian and Romanesque frescos.

Ticino has two heritage sites: the inspiring trio of defensive castles in **Bellinzona** (p324) and pyramid-shaped **Monte San Giorgio** (p335), a wood-covered mountain (1096m) south of Lago di Lugano with an extraordinary fossil record of Triassic marine life.

In southern Switzerland, the Jungfrau-Aletsch-Bietschhorn Alpine area is listed for its (sadly) receding glaciers, including the 23km-long **Aletsch Glacier** (p168). As the threats posed by global warming increase (p54), so does the Unesco-protected area, which was substantially enlarged in 2007.

In western Switzerland the old city centre of **Bern** (p199) with its enchanting arcaded streets is World Heritage precious. More recently, the steeply terraced vineyards of **Lavaux** (p115), along Lake Geneva's northern shore, became a world treasure; followed in 2008 by the **Sardona tectonic area** (p294) in the heart of the Glarus Alps in northeastern Switzerland, the magnificent **Albula railway** (p313) built in 1903 and the **Bernina mountain railway** (p320) that has crossed the Bernina Pass to link St Moritz with Tirano, Italy, since 1910.

A MOVEABLE FEAST

There's no better city to rev up taste buds than hip, urban **Zürich** (p223), with **Geneva** (p94) and its international cuisine and luxury spas cooking up baths of white chocolate (p94) coming up closely in the rear. If it's good old-fashioned Swiss you're after, flit east to **Gruyères** (p132) to watch Gruyère cheese being made, dip into a fondue and stuff yourself silly with meringues and cream. Serious cheese fiends should also prioritise the **Emmental Region** (p210), **Appenzell** (p291), the **Valais** (p144) for its AOC Raclette, and **Engelberg** (p257), where you can taste and buy creamy cheese in a Benedictine monastery.

Boarding the Chocolate Train in **Montreux** (p116) with a stop at the Nestlé factory in **Broc** (p134) is a sweet-toothed must, as is devouring a slice of *Zuger Kirschtorte* in **Zug** (p260) and eating feather-light meringues in their birthplace, **Meiringen** (p193).

Quench your thirst with beer in **Fribourg** (p125), absinthe aboard a steam train in the **Val de Travers** (p139) and wine from **Mont Vully** (p132). Ride a tractor train in the **Lavaux wine region** (p115) or a funicular in vineyards on the northern shore of **Lake Biel** (p211). Taste riesling and Sylvaner wines at source in **Spiez** (p190) and Pinot noir, Fendant (Chasselas) and dôle wines in **Salgesch** (p157). Then, of course, there are the full-bodied merlots and Italian cuisine of **Ticino** (p322).

History

Regardless of whether or not William Tell existed or was responsible for even half the deeds attributed to him (see p254), he is a key figure in Swiss identity. A national legend, the man who helped drive out Switzerland's foreign rulers by shooting an apple off his son's head has perfectly embodied the country's rather singular approach to independence throughout the ages.

PRE-CONFEDERATION

Modern Swiss history is regarded as starting in 1291, but people had already been living in the region for thousands of years.

The first inhabitants were Celtic tribes, including the Helvetii of the Jura and the Mittelland Plain and the Rhaetians near Graubünden. Their homelands were first invaded by the Romans, who had gained a foothold by 58 BC under Julius Caesar and established Aventicum (now Avenches) as the capital of Helvetia (Roman Switzerland). Then, Germanic Alemanni tribes arrived to drive out the Romans by AD 400.

The Alemanni groups settled in eastern Switzerland and were later joined by another Germanic tribe, the Burgundians, in the western part of the country. The latter adopted Christianity and the Latin language, laying the seeds for the division between French- and German-speaking Switzerland. The Franks conquered both tribes in the 6th century, but the two areas were torn apart again when Charlemagne's empire was partitioned in 870.

Initially, when it was reunited under the pan-European Holy Roman Empire in 1032, Switzerland was left to its own devices. Local nobles wielded the most influence, especially the Zähringen family – who founded Fribourg, Bern and Murten, and built a castle at Thun (see p189) – and the Savoy clan, who established a ring of castles around Lake Geneva, most notably Château de Chillon (see p116).

However, when the Habsburg ruler Rudolph I became Holy Roman Emperor in 1273, he sent in heavy-handed bailiffs to collect more taxes and tighten the administrative screws. Swiss resentment grew quickly.

SWISS CONFEDERATION

It was after Rudolph's death in 1291 that local leaders made their first grab for independence. It's taught in Swiss schools, although some historians see the tale – that the forest communities of Uri, Schwyz and Nidwalden met on the Rütli Meadow (p253) in Schwyz Canton on 1 August that year to sign an alliance vowing not to recognise any external judge or law – as slightly distorted. In any case, a pact does exist, preserved in the town of Schwyz (p255). It's seen as the founding act of the Swiss Confederation, whose Latin name,

An excellent source of information on Swiss history is www .geschichte-schweiz.ch. The site is divided into chronological sections and a series of thematic essays.

Learn about historical exhibitions being staged by the Swiss National Museum and its partners at www.musee-suisse .ch/e/. Many interesting themes from Swiss history are also discussed at length, although mainly in German or French.

TIMELINE

58 BC	AD 1032	1273
Julius Caesar establishes the Helvetii, a Celtic tribe, in the region between the Alps and the Jura to watch over the Rhine frontier and keep Germanic tribes out of Roman territory.	Clans in western Switzerland, together with the kingdom of Burgundy, are swallowed up by the Holy Roman Empire but left with a large degree of autonomy.	Habsburg ruler becomes Holy Roman Emperor Rudolph I and so takes control of much Swiss territory. As the Habsburgs increase tax pressure, resistance grows.

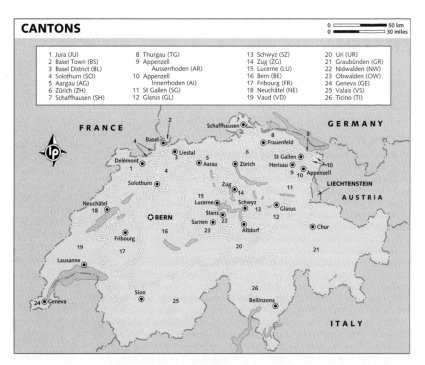

CANTONS

0 ⊏⊏⊏⊏ 50 km
0 ⊏⊏⊏⊏ 30 miles

1 Jura (JU)	8 Thurgau (TG)	13 Schwyz (SZ)	20 Uri (UR)
2 Basel Town (BS)	9 Appenzell	14 Zug (ZG)	21 Graubünden (GR)
3 Basel District (BL)	Ausserrhoden (AR)	15 Lucerne (LU)	22 Nidwalden (NW)
4 Solothurn (SO)	10 Appenzell	16 Bern (BE)	23 Obwalden (OW)
5 Aargau (AG)	Innerrhoden (AI)	17 Fribourg (FR)	24 Geneva (GE)
6 Zürich (ZH)	11 St Gallen (SG)	18 Neuchâtel (NE)	25 Valais (VS)
7 Schaffhausen (SH)	12 Glarus (GL)	19 Vaud (VD)	26 Ticino (TI)

Confoederatio Helvetica, survives in the 'CH' abbreviation for Switzerland (used on car number plates and in internet addresses, for example). The story of the patriotic William Tell, a central figure in the freedom struggle's mythology, also originates from this period.

In 1315, Duke Leopold I of Austria dispatched a powerful army to quash the growing Swiss nationalism. Instead, however, the Swiss inflicted an epic defeat on his troops at Morgarten, which prompted other communities to join the Swiss union. The next 200 years of Swiss history was a time of successive military wins, land grabs and new memberships. The following cantons came on board: Lucerne (1332), Zürich (1351), Glarus and Zug (1352), Bern (1353), Fribourg and Solothurn (1481), Basel and Schaffhausen (1501) and Appenzell (1513). In the middle of all this, the Swiss Confederation gained independence from Holy Roman Emperor Maximilian I after a victory at Dornach in 1499.

1291	1315	1476
Officially, modern Switzerland 'begins' with the independence pact signed at Rütli Meadow. Many historians consider the event, and the accompanying William Tell legend, to have actually taken place in 1307.	Swiss irregular troops win a surprise victory over Habsburg Austrian forces at the Battle of Morgarten. It was the first of several Swiss victories over imperial invaders.	Charles the Bold, Duke of Burgundy, is crushed at the Battle of Murten, one of three defeats at the hands of the Swiss Confederates and the French.

Then, having made it as far as Milan, the rampaging Swiss suddenly lost to a combined French and Venetian force at Marignano in 1515. This stinging defeat prompted them to withdraw from the international scene and declare neutrality for the first time. For several centuries afterwards, the country's warrior spirit was channelled solely into mercenary activity – a tradition still echoed in the Swiss Guard that protects the pope.

REFORMATION

The country's neutrality and diversity combined to give Switzerland some protection when the religious Thirty Years War broke out in 1618, although parts of it still suffered. The Protestant Reformation and the subsequent Catholic Counter-Reformation had caused deep divisions and upheaval throughout Europe. In Switzerland, too, preacher Huldrych Zwingli had started teaching the Protestant word in Zürich as early as 1519, as had Jean Calvin in Geneva. But Central Switzerland (Zentralschweiz) remained Catholic.

So, unable to agree even among themselves, the Swiss couldn't decide which side to take in the Thirty Years War and, fortunately for them, stuck to their neutrality.

However, religious disputes dragged on inside Switzerland. At first, the Catholic cantons were sucked into a dangerous alliance with France, before eventually agreeing to religious freedom. At the same time, the country was experiencing an economic boom through textile industries in the northeast.

The French invaded Switzerland in 1798 and established the brief Helvetic Republic. But they were no more welcome than the Austrians before them, and internal fighting prompted Napoleon (then in power in France) to restore the former Confederation of cantons in 1803 (the Act of Mediation), with France retaining overall jurisdiction. Further cantons joined the Confederation at this time: Aargau, St Gallen, Graubünden, Ticino, Thurgau and Vaud.

After Napoleon's defeat by the British and Prussians at Waterloo in 1815, the Congress of Vienna peace treaty for the first time formally guaranteed Switzerland's independence and neutrality, as well as adding the cantons of Valais, Geneva and Neuchâtel.

TOWARDS A MODERN CONSTITUTION

Civil war broke out in 1847, during which the Protestant army, led by General Dufour, quickly crushed the Sonderbund (Special League) of Catholic cantons, including Lucerne. In fact, the war lasted just 26 days, later leading the then German chancellor, Otto von Bismarck, to dismissively declare it 'a hare shoot'. Victory by Dufour's forces was rapidly consolidated with the creation of a new federal constitution in 1848 – largely still in place today – and the naming of Bern as the capital.

Protestant Swiss first openly disobeyed the Catholic Church during 1522's 'affair of the sausages', when a printer and several priests in Zürich were caught gobbling Würste on Ash Wednesday, instead of fasting as they should.

Jura is the youngest of Switzerland's cantons, having only gained independence from Bern in 1979. Of 23 cantons, three (Appenzell, Basel and Walden) are divided in two to make the usual total of 26.

1499	**1515**	**1519**
Swiss Confederation wins virtual independence from the Habsburg-led Holy Roman Empire after imperial forces are defeated in a series of battles along the Rhine and on Swiss territory.	After a campaign in 1512 that saw Swiss forces take Milan and Pavia in Italy, the Swiss are defeated at Marignano by a combined French-Venetian army. Thus chastised, the Swiss withdraw and declare neutrality.	Protestant Huldrych Zwingli preaches 'pray and work' in the Grossmünster in Zürich, promoting marriage for clerics and a new common liturgy to replace the Mass. In 1523, the city adopts his reform proposals.

The constitution was a compromise between advocates of central control and conservative forces wanting to retain cantonal authority. The cantons eventually relinquished their right to print money, run postal services and levy customs duties, giving these to the federal government. However, they retained legislative and executive control over local matters. Furthermore, the new Federal Assembly was established in such a way as to give cantons a voice. The lower national chamber, the *Nationalrat,* has 200 members, allocated from the 26 cantons in proportion to population size. The upper states chamber, the *Ständerat,* comprises 46 members, two per canton.

The 780-page *Dunant's Dream: War, Switzerland and the History of the Red Cross,* by Caroline Moorhead, examines the triumphs, ethical dilemmas and occasional moral failures of the world's leading humanitarian organisation.

Lacking in mineral resources, Switzerland developed cottage industries, and skilled labourers began to form guilds. Railways and roads were built, opening up Alpine regions and encouraging tourism. Between 1850 and 1860, six new commercial banks were established. In 1863, Henri Dunant established the International Red Cross in Geneva.

Opposition to political corruption sparked a movement for greater democracy. In 1874, the constitution was revised so that many federal laws had to be approved by national referendum – a phenomenon for which Switzerland remains famous today. A petition with 50,000 signatures can challenge a proposed law; 100,000 signatures can force a public vote on any new issue.

EARLY 20TH CENTURY

Despite some citizens' pro-German sympathies, Switzerland's only involvement in WWI lay in organising Red Cross units. After the war, Switzerland joined the League of Nations, but on a strictly financial and economic basis (which included providing its headquarters in Geneva), without military involvement.

Geneva sociologist Jean Ziegler's *The Swiss, the Gold and the Dead: How Swiss Bankers Financed the Nazi War Machine* offers a fascinating and controversial account of Switzerland's WWII history.

Although Swiss industry had profited during the war, the working classes had suffered as prices soared and wages fell. Consequently, a general strike was called in November 1918. With the country at a halt, the Federal Council eventually accepted some of the strikers' demands; a 48-hour week was introduced and the social security system was extended, laying the groundwork for today's progressive social state.

Switzerland was left largely unscathed by WWII. Apart from some accidental bombings (see Schaffhausen, p280), the most momentous event of the war for the country came when Henri Guisan, general of the civilian army, invited all top military personnel to the Rütli Meadow (site of the 1291 Oath of Allegiance) to show the world how determined the Swiss were to defend their own soil.

Although Switzerland proved a safe haven for escaping Allied prisoners, the country's banks have since been criticised for being a major conduit for Nazi plunder during WWII.

1590–1600	1847	1863
Some 300 women in Vaud are captured, tortured and burned alive on charges of witchcraft even as Protestants in other Swiss cantons strive to end witch hunts.	'Hare shoot' civil war between Protestants and Catholics lasts just 26 days, leaving 86 dead and 500 wounded, paving way for the 1848 federal constitution.	After witnessing slaughter and countless untended wounded at the Battle of Solferino in 1859 in northern Italy, the businessman and pacifist Henri Dunant founds the International Red Cross in Geneva.

THE SWISS WAY OF GOVERNMENT

▪ The make-up of Switzerland's Federal Council, the executive government, is determined not by who wins the most parliamentary seats, but by the 'magic formula', a cosy power-sharing agreement made between the four main parties in 1959.

▪ The Federal Council consists of seven ministers.

▪ The president is drawn on a rotating basis from the seven federal ministers, so there's a new head of state each year.

▪ Many federal laws must first be approved by public referendum; there are several of these every year.

▪ Until 2003, the 'magic formula' decreed the Socialists (left wing), Radical Party (conservative), and Christian Democrats (centre right) had two council members each, with one going to the right-wing Swiss People's Party (SVP). This was upset in 2003, when the SVP made hefty gains in national elections and took over the Christian Democrats' second seat.

POST-WWII

Since the end of WWII, Switzerland has enjoyed an uninterrupted period of economic, social and political stability.

While the rest of Europe was still recovering in the aftermath of the war, Switzerland was able to forge ahead from an already powerful commercial, financial and industrial base. Zürich developed as an international banking and insurance centre, while the World Health Organization and many other international bodies set up headquarters in Geneva. Switzerland's much-vaunted neutrality led it to decline to actually join either the UN (although it hosted from the outset its second seat after the main New York headquarters) or, more recently, the European Union, but the country became one of the world's richest and most respected.

Then, in the late 1990s, a series of scandals forced Switzerland to begin re-forming its famously secretive banking industry. In 1995, after pressure from Jewish groups, Swiss banks announced that they had discovered millions of dollars lying in dormant pre-1945 accounts, belonging to Holocaust victims and survivors. Three years later, amid allegations that they had been sitting on the money without seriously trying to trace its owners, the two largest banks, UBS and Crédit Suisse, agreed to pay $1.25 billion in compensation to Holocaust survivors and their families.

Banking confidentiality dates back to the Middle Ages and was enshrined in law in 1934, when numbered, rather than named, bank accounts were introduced. However, in 2004, the country made another concession to outside pressure, when it agreed to tax accounts held in Switzerland by EU citizens.

A comprehensive overview of the country's history, politics and society is provided by Jonathan Steinberg's *Why Switzerland?*

1918	1940	1979
With a sixth of the population living below the poverty line and 20,000 dead of a flu epidemic, workers stage a general strike, put down by the army after three days; the 48-hour week is among the long-term results.	General Guisan's army turns out at Rütli to warn off potential WWII invaders. Some 430,000 troops are placed on the borders but the core of the army is pulled back to Alpine fortresses to carry out partisan war in case of German invasion.	Five years after a first vote in favour in 1974, Jura (majority French-speaking Catholics), absorbed by Bern in 1815, leaves Bern (German-speaking Protestants) to become an independent canton.

INTO A NEW CENTURY

Switzerland made a hefty swing to the conservative right in parliamentary elections in 2003, when Christoph Blocher's SVP (Swiss People's Party) took 28% of seats in an unprecedented upsetting of the Swiss political apple cart. The anti-EU and anti-immigration SVP seemed to have struck a chord in Swiss society.

It promoted a referendum to toughen up immigration and political-asylum laws in 2006, which passed with an overwhelming majority. The following year, the SVP took 29% of seats in parliament (well ahead of their nearest rivals, the Socialists, on 19%) in national elections after a controversial campaign in which Blocher's party was accused by many of overt racism.

The party then seemed to become its own worst enemy, when Blocher was *not* elected by parliament to the Federal Council, the country's executive government. Instead, two other party members were elected, unleashing a storm within the SVP.

A series of expulsions and rebellions culminated, in mid-2008, in the creation of the splinter Bürgerlich-Demokratische Partei (BDP, Civil Democratic Party), centred on the cantons of Bern, Glarus and Graubünden, including the two, until then, SVP members of the Federal Council. Such a situation was a first: this tiny new party entered the national scene with two seats on the Federal Council, while the parliament's biggest party, the SVP, suddenly had none!

Blocher is a charismatic but controversial figure who rumpled many feathers during his stint on the Federal Council in 2003–2007. When the BDP's Samuel Schmid resigned from the Federal Council in late 2008, a spot was again opened up for the SVP. With only lukewarm support from his own party, Blocher had little chance and instead his party colleague Ueli Maurer got the job. Although closely associated with Blocher's hardline policies, Maurer made a public show of conciliatoriness. Time will tell how sincere he was.

As if to confirm a decline in Blocher's influence, another referendum aimed at further tightening immigration rules was soundly defeated in September 2008, just as the SVP's initiative to make acquiring Swiss citizenship tougher was voted down in Parliament.

In spite of the SVP's tough conservative line on many issues, there have been some concrete signs in the first years of the new century that Switzerland is opening up to the wider world. In 2002, it finally became the 190th member of the UN (a referendum on the issue had last been defeated in 1986). In 2005, it voted to join Europe's 'Schengen' passport-free travel zone (finally completing the process at the end of 2008) and, in theory, promised to open its borders to workers from the 12 new (mostly Eastern European) EU members by 2011.

Visit www.parliament.ch or www.admin.ch for more information on Switzerland's unusual political system, with its 'direct democracy', 'magic formula' and part-time politicians.

When Switzerland finally joined the UN in 2002, officials mistakenly ordered a rectangular Swiss flag to fly outside the organisation's New York headquarters. Swiss functionaries strenuously objected, insisting the UN run up the proper square flag pretty damn quick.

1989	2001	2005
The internet is 'born' at Geneva's CERN research centre, where Tim Berners-Lee develops HTML used to prepare pages for the World Wide Web and link text to graphics.	A bad year, in which national airline Swissair collapses, a gun massacre in Zug parliament leaves 14 politicians dead, 21 people perish in a canyoning accident and a fire in the Gotthard Tunnel kills 11 people.	A power surge brings the rail system to a halt for almost 24 hours as summer floods cause an estimated Sfr2 billion damage. Around 700 people are evacuated from Alpine regions and 300 from Bern.

In another 2005 referendum, the Swiss narrowly voted in favour of legalising civil unions for same-sex couples (but not marriage), in another defeat for the SVP.

Few expect the country to even consider joining either the EU or the euro single-currency zone any time soon (if ever). Traditionally, the western, French-speaking cantons have long desired both, while the German-speaking cantons (and Ticino) have generally been opposed. Many no doubt fear such integration would bring further damage to the country's privileged banking sector, where secrecy still reigns.

TREMBLING BANKS & MIXED SMOKE SIGNALS

In 2008, however, the banks themselves gave the Swiss a shock. As the US subprime-mortgage scandal sent shock waves through the world's financial markets, UBS and Crédit Suisse (the two giants of Swiss banking) had to admit heavy losses.

The government decided to wade in with massive support for the banking system, in particular a US$60 billion package to stabilise UBS (at a swingeing interest rate, however, of 12.5%). Crédit Suisse preferred to seek foreign funds to recapitalise in the tight lending market. The government's planned intervention, more or less in line with similar emergency plans in other Western countries, was unprecedented and unleashed howls of protest from the left, who denounced the imprudent history of huge bonuses paid to bank managers for risk taking in preceding years.

Possibly one of the most drawn-out debates in recent years in Switzerland concerns a particularly old habit – smoking. It was banned on public transport in 2005 and, in 2006, Ticino became the first canton to outlaw smoking in all public places. Since then, each of the cantons has wrangled over the subject, leading to a rainbow of laws and exceptions that is far from complete. Not a few citizens have been heard to grumble that they'd prefer a nationwide solution. Indeed, Bern passed a law in late 2008 that allows smoking in restaurants and bars no bigger than 80 sq metre (which means many of them). Just how this will resolve matters is unclear, as the cantons continue to go their own way. In late 2008, Vaud, Fribourg and Valais voted to ban smoking in public places but give restaurants, bars and so on the option of creating sealed off smoking sections (as in Ticino). These new cantonal laws were expected to come into effect by the end of 2009.

Combined with the atmosphere of economic uncertainty, it was all enough to make you reach for a smoke!

In its biggest military deployment abroad in modern times, Switzerland sent 220 volunteer army personnel to join the KFOR peace-keeping forces in Kosovo in 1999. Armed for self-defence, troops are due to stay until 2011.

2006	2008	2008
Ticino becomes the first canton to impose a smoking ban in public places. Other cantons follow suit in haphazard order in following years.	CERN, the European Centre for Nuclear Research in Geneva, inaugurates the LHC (Large Hadron Collider). A malfunction delays first experiments in the world's largest particle accelerator until mid-2009.	The world financial crisis affects Switzerland's two biggest banks, UBS and Crédit Suisse. The government bails out UBS with a US$60 billion package, while Crédit Suisse seeks funds elsewhere.

The Culture

SONDERFALL SCHWEIZ

Toblerone chocolate, cheese, cuckoo clocks, precision watches and banking secrecy, Heidi, William Tell, yodelling, the Alps – stereotypes envelope Switzerland and the Swiss like mad. Ruthlessly efficient, hard-working, supremely clean and organised, orderly, obedient and overly cautious are among the superlatives piled on this too-well-behaved people most mothers would adore as sons-in-law: no Swiss pedestrian dares cross the road unless the light is green.

Cultural diversity is this country's overwhelming trait, eloquently expressed in four languages and attitudes: German-, French- and Italian-speaking Swiss all, at one point or other, display similar characteristics to Germans, French and Italians respectively, creating an instant line-up of reassuringly varied, diverse and oftentimes surprising psyches. Then, of course, there are the handful in Graubünden (p296) who speak Romansch (p382), with its many dialects practically no one outside the valley concerned understands. Never say the Swiss are cookie-cutter dull.

Quite the contrary: the Swiss consider themselves different and they are. From centuries-old Alpine traditions, positively wild in nature, such as wrestling and stone throwing (p36), to new-millennium Zooglers who shimmy into work each morning down a fire pole (p215), to Geneva jewellers who make watches from moon dust (p99) or fashionable 30-somethings who strut savvy on recycled truck tarps and Cambodian fish sacks (p228 and p99), the Swiss know how to innovate.

Not just that: they have the determination to compliment their creativity, keenly demonstrated by both their restless quest to test their limits in the sports arena (p36) and the extraordinarily tough, independent spirit with which Swiss farmers resolutely work the land to mete out a sustainable lifestyle (p142). That *Sonderfall Schweiz* halo (p16) might not shine quite as brightly as it did a few decades back, but it definitely still glints.

HEALTHY, WEALTHY & WISE

'They are', wrote the UK's *Guardian* newspaper, 'probably the most fortunate people on the planet. Healthy, wealthy and, thanks to an outstanding education system, wise. They enjoy a life most of us can only dream about. For ease of reference we commonly refer to them as the Swiss.' This deadpan doffing of the cap from a nation that usually scorns 'dull' Switzerland was prompted by yet another quality-of-life survey listing Zürich, Geneva, and Bern among the planet's best cities. Those ratings haven't changed much since: Mercer Consultancy's 2008 quality-of-life report ranked Zürich number one for the seventh consecutive year, Geneva an equal second with Vienna and Bern ninth.

Urban Swiss don't enjoy a particularly different lifestyle from other Westerners; they just enjoy it more. They can rely on their little nation, one of the world's 10 richest in terms of GDP per capita, to deliver excellent health services, efficient public transport and all-round security. Spend a little time among them and you realise their sportiness, attention to diet and concern for the environment is symptomatic of another condition: they want to extract the most from life.

It's hardly surprising, then, that the Swiss have the greatest life expectancy in Europe: women live to an average 83.7 years, men to 77.9. Switzerland isn't immune to modern worries, including AIDS and drugs,

A one-stop digital shop for books in English about Switzerland is Bergli Publications at www .bergli.ch.

Assisted suicide is legal in Switzerland and international debate surrounds the role of Dignitas (www.dignitas.ch) in offering medical help to terminally or chronically ill foreign nationals who travel to the country.

To delve deeper into subterranean Switzerland, have a good root around *Fake Chalets* by photographer Christian Schwager.

but the distribution of wealth in Switzerland is more even than in many contemporary societies. Most people can afford to rate friends and family – not work – as their top priority.

Swiss lifestyle is not all sipping Champagne cocktails costing Sfr10,000 from carved ice glasses in Verbier (p151) and hobnobbing on the ski slopes during weekend visits to the chalets many Swiss own or rent for the season. In rural regions – particularly Appenzellerland, Valais and the Jura – it is traditional culture, not money-driven glam, that talks as people don folk costumes during festivals and mark the seasons with time-honoured Alpine rituals. Fathers teach their sons, as their fathers did when they were young, the fine art of alpenhorn playing (p39), while younger siblings learn how to wave the Swiss flag. In spring shepherds decorate their cattle with flowers and bells to herd them in procession to mountain pastures, where they both spend the summer.

ECONOMY

The Swiss are careful with money and conservative with their currency. Since the Swiss franc went into circulation in the 1850s, it has rarely been tampered with: the decision in 2005 to drop the five-cent coin because it cost six cents to make was a minor earthquake in a country where change tends to be viewed warily.

As the USA and EU countries lurched into recession at the end of 2008, Switzerland – despite its own twinset of troubled banks and UBS government rescue package (see p33) – appeared to be weathering the global financial crisis pretty well. The overall economy grew by 1.9% in 2008 and unemployment figures remain low compared to the rest of Europe – 2.5% in October 2008 and expected to rise, at worst, to 3.5% by the end of 2009. Inflation, 2.6% in mid-2008, will fall to 1.5% by 2009, say economists.

As a global financial centre and guardian to a substantial chunk of the world's offshore funds, Switzerland is synonymous with numbered accounts and financial secrecy. Every Swiss canton sets its own tax rates, prompting individuals and businesses to 'play' the canton market: Zug entices tycoons with Switzerland's lowest income and corporate tax rates and breaks, see p261. Obwalden meanwhile, in a bid to rejuvenate its rural economy, slashed its income tax in November 2008 to one flat rate (24.1%) for all, rich and poor alike.

Switzerland's pharmaceuticals industry is a major contributor to the economy, Swiss pharmaceutical giants Novartis and Roche being major players.

The Canton of Appenzell Inner Rhodes (p287) is Switzerland's cheapest place to live: low real-estate prices, and moderate taxes and healthcare premiums mean people here have the most disposable income. Appenzeller men are also Switzerland's shortest.

ON GUARD

'The Swiss are most armed and most free', wrote Machiavelli. Yet more than 400 years after their last major military excursion, even the Swiss are losing enthusiasm for 'armed neutrality'.

While Switzerland is the only Western nation to retain conscription, Switzerland's armed defences are diminishing. At the height of the Cold War, the country had more than 600,000 soldiers and 'universal militia' of reservists with a gun at home, comprising almost the entire male population. Today, every able-bodied Swiss man must still undergo military training and serve 260 days' military service between the ages of 20 and 36. However, community service is now an option, and the number of soldiers that can be mobilised within 48 hours has been scaled back to 220,000.

For many years, Switzerland maintained bunkers with food stockpiles to house just about the entire population underground in the event of attack. As army cost-cutting measures bite, however, some 13,000 military installations have recently been decommissioned – and, in true Swiss spirit, recycled as innovative tourist sights: the once top-secret bunkers disguised as farm houses at **Faulensee** (p192), the world's first **zero-star bunker hotel** (p292) and **La Claustra** (www.claustra.ch), a cutting-edge design equivalent beneath the Gotthard Pass at the other end of the market, are clearly but the start.

One piece of bad news for visitors: the rapid rise of the Swiss franc as a safe haven against all other main currencies.

POPULATION

Switzerland averages 176 inhabitants per square kilometre, with Alpine districts more sparsely populated and urban areas more densely populated: one-third of Switzerland's total population lives in the Zürich, Basel, Geneva, Bern and Lausanne agglomerations; another third lives in the countryside.

German speakers account for 64% of the population, French 19%, Italian 8% and Romansch under 1%. Swiss German speakers write standard (High) German, but speak their own language: Schwyzertütsch has no official written form and is mostly unintelligible to outsiders. Linguists have identified at least two Romansch dialects and three variants of Italian, sometimes varying from valley to valley.

SPORT

Sidestep mainstream sport: no country has better reinvented the sporting wheel than Switzerland.

Alpine Traditions

Hornussen, medieval in origin, is played by two teams, each 16 to 18 strong. One launches a 78g *Hornuss* (ball) over a field; the other tries to stop it hitting the ground with a *Schindel,* a 4kg implement resembling a road sign. To add to the game's bizarre quality, the *Hornuss* is launched by whipping it around a steel ramp with a flexible rod, in a motion that's a cross between shot putting and fly-fishing, while the *Schindel* can be used as a bat to stop the 85m-per-second ball or simply tossed into the air at it.

Verging on the vicious, *Schwingen* is a Swiss version of sumo wrestling, battled out between everyone from 10-year-old girls to brawny young farm lads. The pair, each wearing short hessian shorts, face off across a circle of sawdust. Each leans towards the other and grabs their opponent by the back of the shorts. Through a complicated combination of prescribed grips (including crotch grips), jerks, feints and other manoeuvres, each tries to wrestle their opponent onto his or her back. Go to any mountain fair or Alpine festival and there is sure to be a *Schwingen* with a very large crowd of cheering parents around it.

Other eclectic pursuits, all in good sport, include *Steinstossen* (stone throwing), famously practised at the Alpine Games (p175); cricket, polo and horse racing on ice (opposite); trotti-biking, whereby rural hipsters race down hills on an off-road version of the '90s urban microscooter; and *Waffenlaufen* (weapon running), whereby macho men don camouflage, military garb, rucksack and rifle and run up and down mountains.

Then there's cow fighting (p157) and *Chüefladefäscht* (cow-dung smashing; p168), which sees fired-up Swiss (is this possible?) wielding golf clubs and pitch forks as they leap around Alpine pastures polka-dotted with cow pats – 17,000 were laid out for Riederalp's 2008 competition in an attempt to beat the previous year's record of 2137 smashed cow pats.

Football & Tennis

No international sporting event was such a let-down for Switzerland as Euro 2008 (European Championship Cup) – the largest sporting event ever to take place in the country – which it cohosted with Austria…and got knocked out of in the very first round. The 23-day tournament did yield a couple of swanky designer stadiums for the country, though, to the joy of Swiss sports

Rural Switzerland is shrinking: urban development since 1935 has consumed as much land as it did over the course of the 2000 years previously, says a report published by the Swiss National Science Foundation.

A true superwoman, Swiss orienteer Simone Niggli-Luder (b 1978) has scooped 14 gold medals at world championships and was ranked number one in the world from 2002 until 2008 when she bowed out pregnant.

Switzerland's Prix Ecosport rewards sporting events (such as the Engadine Ski Marathon or Locarno Triathlon) that boost environmental awareness; read about past winners at www .prix-ecosport.ch, in German, French and Italian.

SPORTING DIARY

The Swiss move mountains to pit sporting prowess, ensuring a grand spectacle for lesser mortals happy to watch. Road marathons sprint around Geneva (p92), Lausanne (p108), Zermatt (p164) and Murten (p131), but it is September's **Jungfrau Marathon** (p174) around Switzerland's famous three peaks that is the most spectacular.

January ushers in Mürren's hell-for-leather **Inferno Run** (p187), a daredevil race, around since 1928. Wengen's **Lauberhorn downhill ski race** (p186) and Château-d'Œx' **International Hot Air Balloon Week** (p123) are equally world-famous.

All eyes are on the frozen lake in St Moritz (p318) in late January for the **Cartier Polo World Cup on Snow** and in February for the **White Turf** winter horse races and **cricket on ice**. March madness translates as the notoriously gruelling, 42.2km **Engadine Ski Marathon**, a fabulous sight as thousands upon thousands of cross-country skiers skate between pines and frozen water; watch in St-Moritz or Pontresina. The highlight of Verbier's sporting diary is March's **Xtreme Freeride Contest** (p151) when pro snowboarders brave the hair-raising Bec des Rosses North Face. April lands with a bump in Zermatt as freestylers fly between moguls during its **Bump Bash** (p164).

Summer ushers in tennis and July's **Swiss Open** (Allianz Suisse Open; p196) in Gstaad, and August's 90km-long **Eiger Bike Challenge** (p180). The game moves inside in October/November for one of Switzerland's biggest sporting events, Basel's **Swiss Indoors** (p270) tennis championship.

Roll on December and the **FIS Cross-Country World Cup** (p312) in Davos and its ski-jumping counterpart (p259) in Engelberg.

Check and buy tickets for sporting events in Switzerland at www.ticketcorner.com.

---

enthusiasts whose number-one spectator sport is football. On a national level FC Basel and Zürich Grasshoppers top the league.

Swiss tennis ace Roger Federer (b 1981) was world number one for a record 237 consecutive weeks between 2004 and 2008 (when Spain's Rafael Nadal knocked him to second place). In women's tennis Czech-born Swiss player Martina Hingis (b 1980) ranked world number one for 209 weeks before retiring from the game in 2006. Basel-born Patty Schnyder (b 1978), number seven in late 2008, is Switzerland's biggest current female player.

Winter Sports

Ice hockey is Switzerland's other big spectator sport and its men's national hockey side ranks number seven in the world. Zürich and Bern will cohost the IIHF World Championships in 2009.

Swiss Alpine ski champ Daniel Albrecht (b 1983) started the 2008–09 season in fine mettle by scooping the season-opening World Cup giant slalom – his third World Cup win and the first Swiss racer to win a season-opening event since Steve Locher (b 1967) in 1996. Off-piste the 25-year-old skier launched his own designer collection of skiwear, which sports his college nickname, Albright.

MULTICULTURALISM

Not counting seasonal workers, temporary residents and international civil servants, 20.7% of people living in Switzerland are not Swiss citizens – rather resident immigrants (54% of whom were either born in Switzerland or have lived in the country for at least 15 years). Many arrived after WWII, initially from Italy and Spain, and later the former Yugoslavia.

As anywhere else, part of the populace appreciates the cultural wealth and labour immigrants bring; others lean towards xenophobia. While obtaining Swiss citizenship remains notoriously difficult – foreigners must have lived in Switzerland for at least 12 years and approach the federal government, as well as their canton and commune – the process is not as ruthless as a few

World football's governing body, FIFA, has its headquarters (in a fabulous US$196-million glass-fronted complex no less) in Zürich.

THE SWISS FLAG

No national flag (p256) better lends itself to design than Switzerland's.

Take the **Swiss Army Recycling Collection** (Swissbags Beschreibung; www.swissbags.de), a hip line created by a Valais shoemaker and saddler, who makes eco-bags from rough wool blankets used by the Swiss Army until the 1960s when they switched to sleeping bags. Handles are recycled gun straps or soldiers' belts, but the icing on the cake is the bold white cross emblazoned across the front.

Then there's **Alprausch** (www.alprausch.ch), the last word in street- and snow-garb thanks in no small part to the gargantuan street cred of its hip Zürich creator, champion snowboarder Andy Tanner. But what is that emblazoned on his latest ski-jacket design (deemed so cool Victoria Beckham was snapped wearing an Alprausch jacket in St Moritz a few years back) or knitted hat? Why, a white cross on a red square…

---

years back when the final call on whether an applicant could become Swiss was down to the local community who voted in a secret ballot. Interestingly, a bid to revive this discriminatory system was rejected in a national referendum held in May 2008.

RELIGION

The split between Roman Catholicism (42%) and Protestantism (35%) roughly follows cantonal lines. Key Protestant areas include Zürich, Geneva, Vaud, Thurgau, Neuchâtel and Glarus; strong Catholic areas include Valais, Ticino, Uri, Unterwalden and Schwyz, as well as Fribourg, Lucerne, Zug and Jura.

Just over 4% of the population is Muslim.

Swissworld (www
.swissworld.org) offers a
quick rundown on most
aspects of Switzerland,
from people and culture
to science and economy.

ARTS

Many a foreign writer and artist, including Voltaire, Byron, Shelley and Turner, have waxed lyrical about Switzerland in words or on canvas – as have architects Sir Norman Foster, Renzo Piano and Jean Nouvel in steel and glass.

Architecture

Switzerland's contribution to modern architecture is pivotal thanks to Le Corbusier (1887–1965), born in La Chaux-de-Fonds. Known for his radical economy of design, formalism and functionalism, Le Corbusier spent most of his working life in France but did grace his country of birth with his first (p138) and last (p219) creations.

Images guaranteed
to raise a chuckle fill
*Football – Switzerland
1:1*, a photographic
match between Swiss
football and the country's
natural landscapes. Order
it online at www
.footballswitzerland.ch.

Contemporary Swiss architects continue to innovate. As creators of London's Tate Modern gallery, 2001 winners of the prestigious Pritzker Prize and designers of the main stadium for the 2008 Beijing Olympics, Basel-based partners Jacques Herzog and Pierre de Meuron (both b 1950) are the best known. Admire their work in Basel (p269) and in Davos – so far pie in the sky – in the form of a 105m-tall pencil twisting above the mythical Schatzalp (work was expected to start in 2009). The other big name is Ticino architect Mario Botta (b 1943; www.botta.ch) who basks in the international limelight as creator of San Francisco's Museum of Modern Art; his Church of San Giovanni Battista in Mogno (p340) and his cathedral-style Tschuggen Bergoase spa-hotel in Arosa (p302) are soul-soothing creations.

Then there is the award-winning Therme Vals (p306), cut from concrete and quartzite, by Basel-born Peter Zumthor (b 1943); Davos' Kirchner Museum (p311) by Zürich's Annette Gigon and Mike Guyer (www.gigon -guyer.ch); and a clutch of design hotels in Zermatt by resident avant-garde architect Heinz Julen (www.heinz-julen.com).

For an overview of rural Swiss architecture and its regional differences, visit the Freilichtmuseum Ballenberg (p193) near Brienz.

Literature

Thanks to a 1930s Shirley Temple film, Johanna Spyri's *Heidi* is the most famous Swiss novel. The story of an orphan living with her grandfather in the Swiss Alps who is ripped away to the city is unashamedly sentimental and utterly atypical for Swiss literature. Otherwise, the genre is quite serious and gloomy.

Take the German-born, naturalised Swiss Hermann Hesse (1877–1962). A Nobel Prize winner, he fused Eastern mysticism and Jungian psychology to advance the theory that Western civilisation is doomed unless humankind gets in touch with its own essential humanity – as in *Siddharta* (1922) and *Steppenwolf* (1927). Later novels such as *Narzissus und Goldmund* (1930) and the cult *The Glass Bead Game* (1943) explore the tension between individual freedom and social controls.

Similarly, the most recognised work by Zürich-born Max Frisch (1911–91), *Ich bin nicht Stiller* (1954; I'm Not Stiller/I'm Not Relaxed) is a dark, Kafkaesque tale of mistaken identity. More accessible is Friedrich Dürrenmatt (1921–90), who created a rich seam of detective fiction.

Green Henry (1854), by Gottfried Keller (1819–1900), is a massive tome revolving around a Zürich student's reminiscences and is considered one of the masterpieces of Germanic literature.

Music & Dance

Yodelling and alpenhorns are the traditional forms of Swiss 'music'. Yodelling began in the Alps as a means of communication between peaks, but became separated into two disciplines: *Juchzin* consists in short yells with different meanings such as 'it's dinner time' or 'we're coming', while *Naturjodel* sees one or more voices sing a melody without lyrics. Yodelling is fast becoming the trendy thing to do in urban circles thanks in part to Swiss folk singers like Nadja Räss who yodel with great success.

'Dr Schacher Seppli', a traditional song reyodelled by Switzerland's best-known yodeller, farmer and cheesemaker Rudolf Rymann (1933–2008), is an iconic iPod download. The other big sound is Sonalp (www.sonalp.com), a nine-man band from the Gruyères–Château-d'Œx region, whose vibrant ethno-folk mix of yodelling, cow bells, musical saw, classical violin and didgeridoo is contagious.

Max Frisch's *Homo Faber* (1957), the tale of an engineer's cold-hearted affair with what turns out to be his daughter and how it destroys them both, was adapted into the movie, *Voyager* (1991).

Catch Jack Nicholson in Sean Penn's love-it-or-loathe-it film *The Pledge* (2001), an adaptation of Friedrich Dürrenmatt's masterpiece *Das Versprechen* about how much sheer dumb luck (or lack of it) shapes our existence.

COMPLETELY DADA

Antibourgeois, rebellious, nihilistic and deliberately nonsensical, the Dada art movement grew out of revulsion to WWI and mechanisation of modern life. Its proponents paved the way for nearly every form of contemporary art by using collage, extracting influences from indigenous art, applying abstract notions to writing, film and performance and taking manufactured objects and redefining them as art.

Zürich was the movement's birthplace. Hugo Ball, Tristan Tzara and Emmy Jenning's creation of the Cabaret Voltaire in February 1916 kicked off a series of raucous cabaret and performance-art events in a bar at Spiegelgasse 1 (p219). The name Dada was allegedly randomly chosen by stabbing a knife through a French/German dictionary.

By 1923 the movement was dead, but its spirit lives on in the works of true Dadaists like George Grosz, Hans Arp and Max Ernst and of those infected with its ideas like Marcel Duchamp (whose somewhat damaged urinal-as-art piece conveys the idea succinctly) and photographer Man Ray. See Dadaist works in Zürich's Kunsthaus and Museum für Gestaltung (p217).

SWISS ROLL CALL

Switzerland has always attracted celebrities. Famous non-Swiss residents and former residents include Charlie Chaplin, Yehudi Menuhin, Audrey Hepburn, Richard Burton, Peter Ustinov, Roger Moore, Tina Turner, Phil Collins, the Aga Khan, Michael Schumacher, *Wallpaper* magazine founder Tyler Brûlé and Formula One star Lewis Hamilton. Yet plenty of native Swiss have made their mark on the world stage too, among them:

Ursula Andress (b 1936) Actress and '60s sex symbol, most famous for her bikini-clad appearance in the James Bond flick *Dr No*.

Sepp (Joseph) Blatter (b 1936) Outspoken president of FIFA, world football's governing body, who famously said of women's football that the shorts should be tighter.

Alain de Botton (b 1969) Zürich-born pop philosopher and globally best-selling author of *The Art of Travel* etc

Louis Chevrolet (1878–1941) Founder of the Chevrolet Manufacturing Company in 1911, producer of archetypal 'American' automobiles.

Le Corbusier (1887–1965) Architectural innovator, often confused as French.

Marc Forster (b 1969) Oscar-winning director of *Monster's Ball* and *Finding Neverland*.

Albert Hofmann (1906–2008) The first person to synthesise and experiment with lysergic acid diethylamide (LSD).

Jean-Luc Godard (b 1930) More-Swiss-than-French avant-garde film-maker.

Elisabeth Kübler-Ross (1926–2004) Psychiatrist whose *On Death and Dying* articulated the famous five stages of grief: denial, anger, bargaining, depression and acceptance.

Erich von Däniken (b 1935) Controversial expounder of far-fetched early-history theories in the 1970s bestseller *Chariots of the Gods?*

Should folk ballads be more your cup of tea, the fragile voice of 24-year-old Swiss singer Sophie Hunger (www.sophiehunger.com) will make it straight to your iPod: her second album *Monday's Ghost* (2008) won instant international acclaim.

The alpenhorn, a pastoral instrument used to herd cattle in the mountains, is a wind instrument, 2m to 4m long with a curved base and a cup-shaped mouthpiece: the shorter the horn the harder it is to play. Catch a symphony of a hundred-odd alpenhorn players blowing in unison on the 'stage' – usually alfresco and invariably lakeside between mountain peaks – and you'll be won over forever. Key dates include September's Alphorn In Concert festival (www.alphorninconcert.ch, in German) in Oesingen near Solothurn (p212) and July's International Alphorn Festival (www.nendaz.ch), emotively held on the Alpine shores of Lac de Tracouet in Nendaz, 13km south of Sion (p153) in the Valais; hike or ride the cable car up.

One performance group worth seeing is Öff Öff (www.oeffoeff.ch), an aerial-theatre and dance company from Bern which tours using a transportable 'Air Station' (rotating climbing frame) and has been described as a combination of dance and (how very Swiss!) mountaineering.

Painting, Sculpture & Design

Dada aside (see boxed text, p39), there have been few Swiss art movements. The painter who most concerned himself with Swiss themes was Ferdinand Hodler (1853–1918), who depicted folk heroes, like William Tell (see Kunstmuseum, p213), and events from history, such as the first grassroots Swiss vote (see Kunsthaus, p217). Hodler also remained resident in Switzerland, unlike many fellow Swiss artists.

Abstract artist and colour specialist Paul Klee (1879–1940) spent most of his life in Germany, including with the Bauhaus school, but the largest showcase of his work is in Bern (p203). Likewise, the sculptor Alberto Giacometti (1901–66) worked in Paris, but many of his trademark stick figures have made it back to Zürich's Kunsthaus (p217).

Quirky sculptures by Paris-based Jean Tinguely (1925–91) are clustered around Basel (p269) and Fribourg (p126).

Then there is Gianni Motti (b 1958), an Italian artist considered Swiss – he lives and works in Geneva – notorious for his 'artistic' stunts, such as selling bars of soap made from Silvio Berlusconi's liposuctioned fat for US$18,000 a piece. Yum.

The Swiss excel in graphic design. The 'new graphics' of Josef Müller-Brockmann (1914–96) and Max Bill (1908–94) are still extremely well regarded, as is the branding work by Karl Gerstner (b 1930) for IBM and the Búro Destruct (www.burodestruct.net) studio's typefaces, a feature of many music album covers.

Product design and installation art are Switzerland's other fortes. It gave the world Europe's largest urban lounge (p289) courtesy of Pipilotti Rist (b 1962) and Cow Parade whereby processions of life-size, painted fibreglass cows trot around the globe. The first 800-head herd had their outing in Zürich in 1998 and stray animals in different garbs continue to lurk around the country. Then there is its flag (see boxed text, p38).

Switzerland's two most world-famous music fests are the Lucerne Festival (p246) and Montreux Jazz Festival (p117).

SCIENCE

Not only do the Swiss have more registered patents and Nobel Prize winners (most in scientific disciplines) per capita than any other nationality, Albert Einstein coined the formula $E=mc^2$ while living in Bern (see Einstein Museum, p202) and the World Wide Web was born in Geneva at CERN (p91).

Then, of course, there's the latter's Large Hadron Collider, a machine that took 13 years to build and ranks as the world's biggest physics experiment as it attempts to recreate conditions minutes after the big bang (p16).

Food & Drink

This land of Heidi is the land of hearty. But there is far more to it than the iconic Swiss staples: chocolate, holey cheese and Swiss-German rösti.

Dining in Switzerland can be both excellent and varied, thanks not so much to a rich indigenous cuisine but to the trio of powerful neighbouring cuisines the country draws on: cooks in French-speaking cantons take cues from France, Ticino kitchens turn to Italy and a fair chunk looks to Germany and Austria for culinary clues (the result: fabulous desserts!). Immigrants to Switzerland have, meanwhile, enriched Swiss palates with a colourful array of imported cuisines, from Greek to Vietnamese.

Beer flows famously freely in German-speaking Switzerland, but it is lovers of wine whose taste buds get the biggest kick. Most Swiss wine is produced in the French-speaking cantons and little is exported, meaning it is just here that many Swiss wines can be sampled – an exquisite and increasingly rare gastronomic joy in this increasingly globalised world.

For culinary experiences around which to plan a trip, see p26.

STAPLES & SPECIALITIES

Rösti (crispy, fried, shredded potatoes) is German Switzerland's star dish. If only to prove they're different, Swiss French cook it in oil while Swiss Germans throw a lump of butter or lard in the frying pan. These days as common and cheap as chips, buy a pack to take home in a vacuum-sealed pack from any supermarket.

For the low-down on the feast served on Ticino's Italianate table, see p335.

TOP PICKS

It was no mean feat coming up with our favourite places to move mandibles, picked for palate pleasure over price consideration. In purely alphabetical order:

- **Alpenrose** (p225) Our man in Zürich's top choice, green to boot, on the country's most dynamic urban dining scene.
- **Auberge du Mont Conu** (p138) Autumnal game, air-dried meats and *cornet à la crème* on a farm with magnificent rural views: *this* is what Switzerland is all about.
- **Burestübli** (p304) Swiss soul food (gooey fondues, butter-soft steaks) in forested surrounds, followed by a star-lit toboggan race between trees.
- **Fletschhorn** (p167) Markus Neff interprets French cuisine with finesse at his Michelin-starred odyssey.
- **Hatecke** (p319) *Bündnerfleisch* (air-dried beef) and venison ham become edible art at this funky St Moritz café.
- **L'Adresse** (p96) The Genevan address for brunch and lunch between shops.
- **Michel's Stallbeizli** (p197) Back-to-nature dining on home-grown fare, with views of cud-chewing cows in the adjacent stable.
- **Montagnard** (p118) Hearty country fare in a farmhouse near Montreux.
- **Osteria Chiara** (p337) Go Italian beneath the pergola or by the fireside in a grotto.
- **Restaurant aux Trois Amis** (p211) Is there any Swiss village bistro with so startling a vineyard, lake and island view as this?
- **Restaurant Le Château** (p114) Dine fine with one of the biggest names in Swiss contemporary cooking at this 17th-century residence.

HOT BOXED TEXT

It's hot, it's soft and it's packed in a box. Vacherin Mont d'Or, an AOC-protected cheese, is the only Swiss cheese to be eaten with a spoon – hot. Only eaten between September and March, the Jurassien speciality derives its unique nutty taste from the spruce bark in which it's wrapped.

Connoisseurs dig a small hole in the centre of the soft-crusted cheese, fill it with finely chopped onions and garlic, pour white wine on top, wrap it in aluminium foil and bake it for 45 minutes to create a *boîte chaude* (hot box) – into which bread and other tasty titbits can be dunked to create an alternative fondue.

Cheese

Holey cheese (*Käse* in German; *fromage* in French; *formaggio* in Italian) is a quintessential Swiss image. Yet contrary to popular belief, not all Swiss cheese has holes in it. Emmental, the hard cheese from the Emme Valley east of Bern (p210), does. But most others, including the not dissimilar hard cheese Gruyère (p132), don't. Other fine cheeses include stinky Appenzeller from which a rash of stinky specialities are made (p291), L'Etivaz (p46), Vacherin and the curly-cut Tête de Moine (p141), first made at an abbey in the Jura.

No skier leaves Switzerland without dipping into a fondue (from the French verb *fondre,* meaning 'to melt'). The main French contribution to the Swiss table, a pot of gooey melted cheese is placed in the centre and kept on a slow burn while diners dip in cubes of crusty bread using slender two-pronged fondue forks. If you lose your chunk in the cheese, you buy the next round of drinks or, should you be in Geneva, get thrown in the lake. Traditionally a winter dish, the Swiss only eat it as long as there's snow around – unlike tourists who tuck in year-round.

The classic fondue mix is emmental and Gruyère cheese melted with white wine and/or a shot of kirsch (cherry-flavoured liquor), and thickened slightly with potato or corn flour. Boiled potatoes, gherkins and a basket of bread cubes accompany it. *Fondue moitié moitié* (half and half) mixes Gruyère with Vacherin Fribourgeois and *fondue savoyarde* melts equal proportions of Comté, Beaufort and emmental. Common variants involve adding ingredients such as mushrooms or tomato.

Drinking water while dipping is said to bring on unpleasant gut ache (not necessarily true) as it coagulates the warm cheese in your stomach. Rather, go for a local white wine like Fendant from Valais. Should you be feeling really stuffed, down a *trou normand* (Norman hole), a shot of high-octane liquor, often Calvados.

Raclette, Switzerland's other winter Alpine dish, is both the name of the dish and the cheese at its gooey heart. A half-crescent slab of Raclette is screwed onto a specially designed 'rack oven' that melts the top flat side. As it melts, so cheese is scraped onto plates for immediate consumption with boiled potatoes, cold meats and pickled onions or gherkins.

A delightful autumnal companion to any Alpine cheese board is *brisolée,* a dish of chestnuts from the Valais, crunchy on the outside and soft on the inside.

Meat, Fish & Game

Nothing beats a hearty platter of *Würste* (sausages) and rösti, topped with a fried egg perhaps and accompanied by a crisp green salad. Veal is highly rated and is served thinly sliced and smothered in a cream sauce to become *geschnetzeltes Kalbsfleisch* in Zürich. *Rippli,* a bubbling pot of pork rib meat cooked up with bacon, potatoes and beans, is the dish to try in and around Bern, while the canton of Vaud cooks up *taillé aux greubons,* a type of crispy

Müsli (muesli) was invented in Switzerland at the end of the 19th century. The most common form of this very healthy breakfast is *Birchermüsli,* sometimes served with less-than-slimming dollops of cream.

The Swiss have their own Marmite (Vegemite to Australians)! Cenovis is a dark spread made of beer yeast and vegetable extracts. Invented in 1931, it is high in vitamin B1.

TASTY TRAVELS: ENDANGERED EDIBLES

For the ultimate authentic dining experience, sample products featured on Slow Food's Ark of Taste (www.slowfoodfoundation.com), a list of endangered world food products threatened with extinction by industrialisation, globalisation, hygiene laws and environmental dangers.

In Switzerland travel taste buds with a dozen-odd endangered species, including the fiery **Berudge eau de vie** made from Berudge plums grown on the slopes of Mont Vully in the Fribourg canton, and sweet cherry **kirsch**: the real-McCoy Swiss version is feared for as fruit farmers replace ancient cherry varieties with less-aromatic modern equivalents. Cherries also make **chriesimues**, syrup as thick as honey used in baking or simply spread on bread. In Mittelland, the marked fall in the local Landrassen bee population could mean the end of **Landrassen bee honey**.

Sac (made from pork, liver, lard and spices aged for 12 months) and **fidighèla** (packed in veal intestine when straight, pork intestine if curved and aged for two to three weeks) are two types of salami worth a bite. Try them with the delightfully named, **hay-packed cheese**, a soft Alpine cheese which was indeed traditionally packed in hay, or grab a glass of wine and nibble **taillé** (a type of pork-speckled savoury bread) from the Vaud canton instead.

Ticino **farina bona** (flour made from toasted corn), **rye bread** from the Val Müstair in Graubünden, and **zincarlìn** (a raw-milk, cup-shaped cheese unusually made from unbroken curds on the Swiss–Italian border) also appear on the threatened-gastronomic-heritage list.

---

savoury pastry, soft and dotted with pork-lard cubes inside, and *papet vaudois* (a potato, leek, cabbage and sausage stew).

Beef is air-dried, smoked, thinly sliced and served in Graubünden as *Bündnerfleisch*, a truly sweet and exquisitely tender delicacy. It forms a key ingredient in *Capuns*, a rich mix of *Spätzli* dough, *Bünderfleisch*, ham and herbs, mixed together, cooked, cut into tiny morsels and wrapped with spinach in yet more *Spätzli*. *Pizokel* (also spelt *Bizochel*), from the same canton, are little globs of *Spätzli* boiled with herbs and served with a cheese *gratiné*. In the Engadine, onions are baked with potato and sausage to make *pian di pigna; Schaffhauser Bölletünne* is a savoury onion pie from Schaffhausen. Disturbingly perhaps for animal lovers, horse meat is another popular meat in Switzerland.

Autumn ushers in the hunt – fresh game, venison and wild boar in particular. Restaurants up and down the country advertise the *Wildspezialitäten/specialités de gibier* (or *chasse)/cacciagione*.

Fish is the speciality in lakeside towns. Perch (*perche,* in French) and whitefish fillets (*féra)* are common, although don't be tricked into thinking the *filets de perche* chalked on the blackboard in practically every Lake Geneva restaurant are from the lake: the vast majority cooked around its shores, Geneva included, come from Eastern Europe.

Sweets

Fruit finds its way into sweets and cakes such as Zug's to-die-for *Zuger Kirschtorte* (cake made from pastry, biscuit, almond paste and butter cream, infused with cherry liqueur). Vaudois *raisinée* or Fribourgois *vin cuit* is a dense, semi-hard concentrate used in tarts and other fruity desserts, made by cooking apple or pear juice for 24 hours; *Buttemoscht* is the less common rose-hip equivalent.

Apples and pears are notably grown in Thurgau and Aargau, two big fruit-production centres; Botzi pears grown around Gruyères in the canton of Fribourg even have their own AOC (p46).

Cuisses de dame (lady's thighs) are sugary deep-fried thigh-shaped pastries, found in French-speaking cantons next to *amandines* (almond

Chocolate-loving Swiss gobble down more of the sticky stuff than anyone else in the world – 11.3kg per person per year.

tarts). Bar the ubiquitous *Apfelstrudel* (apple pie), best served with vanilla sauce, German cantons propose *Vermicelles*, a chestnut-cream creation resembling spaghetti.

No cream is more famed than the extrathick calorie-killer variety made in Gruyères, where everything from a simple cup of coffee to one of the popular local meringues comes with a big fat serving of the stuff: sheer paradise for cream lovers. Meiringen in the Bernese Oberland is the other place in Switzerland to revel in such sweet kisses (p195).

Then, of course, there is chocolate (see boxed text, below)…

DRINKS

Tap water is fine to drink, but there is also plenty of locally produced mineral water. In the French cantons you will come across Henniez and, in Valais, Aproz. Various mineral waters are produced in Graubünden including Rhäzünser, Passugger and Valser.

Try the German-Swiss soft drink Rivella, uniquely made with lactose. The blue-label (reduced-fat) version is probably the best introduction, but it also comes with red (original) and green (mixed with green tea) labels. Swiss apple juice always comes with bubbles and *Süssmost* is a nonalcoholic cider made in German-speaking parts.

Coffee is more popular than tea – the latter comes milkless unless you ask otherwise. Hot chocolate is popular, although disappointingly it usually comes as a cup of hot milk and DIY sachet of coco powder.

Beer & Cider

Beer comes in 300ml or 500ml bottles, or on draught *(Bier vom Fass; bière à la pression; birra alla pressione)* with measures ranging from 200ml to 500ml in bars. Most beer guzzling is done in German-speaking Switzerland, although Feldschlösschen and Cardinal (p128) are well-known brands around for more than a century you'll encounter everywhere. Smaller breweries such as St Gallen's Schützengarten, the country's oldest brewery, dating to 1779, tend to be more closely identified with their area.

Sauermost is the alcoholic-cider version of *Süssmost*, found in German-speaking cantons.

Wine

The bulk of wine production takes place in the French-speaking part of the country where vineyards pirouette by lake shores to make quality reds, whites and rosés.

> Swiss like biscuits – eating an average 6kg a year according to the local biscuit industry body, Biscosuisse.

SWISS CHOCOLATE

In the early centuries after Christ's death, as the Roman Empire headed towards slow collapse on a diet of rough wine and olives, the Mayas in Central America were pounding cocoa beans, consuming the result and even using the beans as a system of payment.

A millennium later, the Spanish conquistador Hernando Cortez brought the first load of cocoa to Europe in 1528. He could not have anticipated the subsequent demand for his cargo – the Spaniards, and soon other Europeans, developed an insatiable thirst for the sweetened beverage produced from it. The solid stuff came later.

Swiss chocolate built its reputation in the 19th century, thanks to pioneering spirits such as François-Louis Cailler (1796–1852), Philippe Suchard (1797–1884), Henri Nestlé (1814–90), Jean Tobler (1830–1905), Daniel Peter (1836–1919) and Rodolphe Lindt (1855–1909). Cailler established the first Swiss chocolate factory in 1819 near Vevey. Daniel Peter added milk in 1875 and Lindt invented conching, a rotary aeration process that gives chocolate its melt-in-the-mouth quality.

WHAT THE LABEL SAYS

A system of quality-control labelling of wines, much like those in neighbouring France and Italy, has long been in place in Switzerland. The AOC (Appellation d'Origine Contrôllée) label denotes that a wine has been produced in its traditional area, by approved traditional methods and using approved ingredients. Anyone producing wine with the same name elsewhere is liable to prosecution.

Since the 1990s, AOCs have spread to other products, several cheeses included; see www.aoc-igp.ch for a full list with an illustrated map. L'Etivaz, a raw-milk Vaudois cheese made in the Pays d'Enhaut and ripened just eight months, was Switzerland's first nonwine product to receive the AOC label.

In 2007 the tangy round wheels of Raclette cheese produced in the Valais since the 16th century and used in the traditional dish (p43) were likewise awarded their own AOC – to the horror of dozens of cheesemakers in other cantons who vehemently argued, to no avail, that *raclette* (coming from the French verb *racler* meaning 'to scrape'), refers to the dish, not the cheese, and thus shouldn't be restricted to one region. Raclette du Valais AOC is made in wheels measuring 29cm to 31cm in diameter, weighing 4.8kg to 5.2kg, and using *lait cru* (unpasteurised milk). Any other Raclette-style cheese you might encounter, generically known as *raclette Suisse* (Swiss raclette) will be made industrially with pasteurised milk.

When ordering wine to accompany your meal, use the uniquely Swiss approach of *déci* (100ml) multiples – or order a bottle.

LAKE GENEVA & VAUD

There are plenty of small family *vignerons* (winemakers) to pay a *dégustation* (wine tasting) visit to on the fringes of Geneva, though the bulk of Lake Geneva *domaines viticoles* (winemaking estates) languish either side of Lausanne in Vaud.

The particularly precious terraced vineyards of Lavaux (p115), a Unesco world heritage site wedged between Lausanne and Montreux, produce riveting whites, most born of the Chasselas grape and occasionally combinations of this with other types. The two *grands crus* from the area are Calamin and Dézaley.

The generic Vaud red is the Salvagnin, divided into several labels and generally combining the Pinot noir and Gamay grapes. A home-grown offshoot is the Gamaret or Garanoir, created in the 1970s to produce a throaty red that ages well.

Straddling Vaud is the small Chablais winemaking area, best known for its Yvorne whites.

> For a short history and explanation of everything you ever wanted to know about chocolate, especially in Switzerland, browse www.chocolat.ch.

VALAIS

Much of the land north of the Rhône River in western Valais, which gets good sunlight from above the southern Alps, is given over to the grape. Indeed some of Switzerland's best wines come from here.

Two-thirds of Valais production is the dryish white Fendant, the perfect accompaniment to fondue and Raclette. Johannisberg is another excellent white, and comes from the Sylvaner grape. Petite Arvine and Amigne are sweet whites.

The principal red blend is dôle, made from Pinot noir and Gamay grapes, which is as full bodied as an opera singer with its firm fruit flavour. The Cadillacs of Valais reds are made with the Humagne rouge, Syrah, Cornalin and Pinot noir grape varieties.

Several Valais dessert wines, such as the Malvoisie (Pinot gris) and muscat, are also excellent.

LAC DE NEUCHÂTEL

Further north the fruity rosé, Œil-de-Perdrix, kicks in along the shores of Lake Neuchâtel. Against an industry tendency to filter out impurities in whites, some producers here are making unfiltered whites with considerable success. These need to be shaken up a little before serving and have a robust flavour.

TICINO

The favourite liquid for lunch in Switzerland's Italianate climes is merlot, which accounts for almost 90% of Ticino's wine production. Some white merlots are also made, as well as wines made from a handful of other grape varieties. The main winemaking areas are between Bellinzona and Ascona, around Biasca and between Lugano and Mendrisio.

GERMAN-SWISS WINES

Less known than their French-Swiss counterparts and produced in substantially smaller quantities, German-Swiss vintages are nonetheless worth tasting. About 75% are reds, predominantly Pinot noir (Blauburgunder), and the main white is Müller-Thurgau (a mix of riesling and Sylvaner). Gewürztraminer is a dry white variety.

The wine-growing villages staggered uphill from the western shore of Lake Biel (p211) are particularly enchanting and abound with wine-tasting opportunities. Graubünden produces some good Pinot gris white varieties, plus Blauburgunder in the Bündner Herrschaft region north of Chur.

Spirits & Schnapps

Locally produced fruit brandies are often served with or in coffee. Kirsch is made from the juice of compressed cherry pits. Appenzeller Alpenbitter (Alpine Bitters) is a liquor made from the essences of 67 different flowers and roots. Damassine, which you are more likely to find in the French cantons, is made of small prunes and makes a good postprandial digestive. A pear-based drop is the popular Williamine, and Pflümli is a typical plum-based schnapps in the German cantons.

After a century on the index of banned beverages, absinthe – aka the green fairy – is legal in Switzerland again to the joy of the valley in Neuchâtel canton where the wormwood drink was first distilled in the 18th century. For more on this aniseed-based rocket fuel with a typical alcohol reading approaching Richter-scale proportions of 56% or more, see p139. In bars and clubs look for absINt 56, aimed at a hip clubbing set and kissed with a smidgin of mint to take the aniseed edge off.

CELEBRATIONS

The intrinsically social nature of dipping into a pot of bubbling cheesy fondue with friends or sharing out abundant scrapings of melted Raclette lends itself to get-togethers – an easy dinner-party option at home or in restaurants.

One of the most impressive traditional feasts is St-Martin, celebrated in the Jura around the Fête de la St-Martin on the second Sunday after All Saints' Day in November. At this time of year, in Switzerland and elsewhere in Europe, pigs are traditionally slaughtered. Fattened over the summer, they are ready for the butcher. For centuries on farms and in villages, the slaughter would be followed by the salting of meat and the making of sausages. The work done, folk would then pass over to feasting to celebrate the day's toil. The main dish for the feast: pork.

In the Jura the feasting tradition very much lives on, with particular energy in and around Porrentruy (p142). Bars and restaurants in the region organise feasts for several weekends on the trot in October and November.

If you can read in one of Switzerland's national languages, then www .patrimoineculinaire.ch is the digital spot to find out everything there is to know about Swiss culinary history, prowess, products and much more

Enticing wine-and-food pairings, wine-tasting courses and vineyard walks are among the many viticultural discoveries waiting to be explored at www .campagnon.ch and www.vins-vaudois.com

To learn more about Swiss wines and see when the upcoming wine fairs are being staged, check out www.swisswine.ch.

A typical pork binge consists of eating up to seven copious courses, a feat few humans complete. You might start with *gelée de ménage,* a pork gelatine dish. This might be followed by *boudin, purée de pommes et racines rouges* (black pudding, apple compote and red vegetables), and piles of sausages accompanied by rösti and *atriaux* (a dish based on pork fat, sausage and liver, all roasted in sizzling fat). Next up is the main course, with *rôti, côtines et doucette* (roast pork, ribs and a green salad). A liquor-soaked sorbet might follow to aid digestion, followed by a serving of *choucroute* (boiled cabbage enlivened by, yum-yum, bacon bits). Finally, a traditional dessert, such as *striflate en sauce de vanille* (strings of deep-fried pastries in vanilla sauce), is served.

Around Fribourg the centuries-old festival, Le Bénichon – six hours of eating and drinking with gusto, held in thanks for the year's harvest each October – is another marathon affair. The traditional meal starts with *cuchaule,* a saffron-scented bread served with *moutarde de Bénichon* (a thick mustard condiment made of cooked wine must, spices, sugar and flour).

Wine is as good a reason as any to celebrate, with winemakers in Lausanne kicking off the party with their May-time Millésime. But the real cause for celebration is in September and October when the grapes are harvested.

Europe's highest vineyards (1150m) are in Visperterminen and the world's highest drystone walls ensnare lush green vines near Sion; find both in the Valais.

WHERE TO EAT & DRINK

For sit-down meals you will generally wind up in a restaurant (the same word in French and German, *ristorante* in Italian) or, in French-speaking cantons, a *brasserie* (beer bars) or café perhaps. In Ticino, the family-run, bistro-style *trattoria* and *osteria* are less-formal eateries; in rural Ticino, find a *grotto* (usually housed in a simple stone structure built in rocky mountain walls, often formerly used as a dwelling or storage room). Wine bars *(Weinstübli)* and beer taverns *(Bierstübli)* in the German-speaking cantons often serve meals too.

Lunch is usually eaten from noon onwards (a little later in the French- and Italian-speaking parts of Switzerland), the cheapest option usually being either the dish of the day *(Tagesteller; plat du jour; piatto del giorno)* or a fixed-menu comprising either starter and main course or main course and dessert.

Winter in the Alps: Food by the Fireside by Lugano-born Manuela Darling-Gansser instantly makes you want to bunk up in your chalet with a roaring fire. Packed with photos, stories, and recipes from the author's childhood, it paints an idyllic picture of Alpine life.

Come dusk, the Swiss dine – as early as 6.30pm in many places, especially in the German cantons and mountain resorts where it is hard to be served after 9.30pm. In cities, however, dining hours are more generous, with many places in the German cantons opening right through the day from 11am to 11pm.

Restaurants usually have a day off *(Ruhetag; jour de fermeture; giorno di riposo)*. For budget travellers self-service restaurants in the larger Migros and Coop outlets, and in department stores such as Manor, are a good deal; most open from around 11am to 6.30pm weekdays and until 4pm or 5pm Saturday.

Quick Eats

Be it a bag of piping hot chestnuts (autumn and winter only) or a freshly baked *Brezel* (pretzel) studded in rock salt or sunflower, pumpkin or sesame seeds, Switzerland cooks up some tasty street snacks to munch on the move. Practically every train station has kiosks selling such; indeed many quick eats, such as the sausages and bread sold at kiosks in St Gallen, are as much a regional speciality as fancy dishes.

The ubiquitous takeaway kebab joint is increasingly common in Swiss towns; Pittaria (p214), in small-town Solothurn, is one of Switzerland's most famed (and for good reason too).

VEGETARIANS & VEGANS

Dedicated vegetarian restaurants are common in cities, although practically every eating establishment will have a suitable pasta or rösti dish on its menu. *Fitnessteller* (literally 'fitness dishes') for the health conscious are increasingly offered in ski resorts.

A firm vegetarian favourite is *Älplermagronen,* a fancy version of macaroni cheese served with cooked apple and onion. Vegetarian soups are also popular and often contain little dumplings *(Knöpfli)*.

EATING WITH KIDS

Children are generally welcome in most restaurants. Some even offer smaller children's menus and servings. Toddlers are usually fed straight from their parents' plates and, if high chairs aren't available, staff will improvise a solution.

EAT YOUR WORDS
Useful Phrases

The following phrases are in German (G), French (F) and Italian (I).

A table for …, please.

Einen Tisch für …, bitte. (G)   *Une table pour …, s'il vous plaît.* (F)   *Un tavolo per …, per favore.* (I)

May I see the menu, please?

Darf ich die Speisekarte sehen, bitte? (G)   *Est-ce que je pourrais voir la carte, s'il vous plaît?* (F)   *Posso vedere, il menù, per piacere?* (I)

May I see the wine list, please?

Darf ich die Weinkarte sehen, bitte? (G)   *Est-ce que je pourrais voir la carte aux vins, s'il vous plaît?* (F)   *Posso vedere la carta dei vini, per piacere?* (I)

Bon appétit!

Guten Appetit! (G)   *Bon appétit!* (F)   *Buon appetito!* (I)

Cheers!

Prost! (G)   *Santé!* (F)   *Salute!* (I)

The bill, please.

Zahlen, bitte. (G)   *L'addition, s'il vous plaît.* (F)   *Il conto, per favore.* (I)

Is service included in the bill?

Ist die Bedienung inbegriffen? (G)   *Est-ce que le service est compris?* (F)   *È compreso il servizio?* (I)

I'm vegetarian.

Ich bin Vegetarier(in). (m/f; G)   *Je suis végétarien(ne).* (m/f; F)   *Sono vegetariano(a).* (m/f; I)

Food Glossary

These are some food terms that you may come across in German (G), French (F) and Italian (I):

boiled potatoes

Salzkartoffeln (G)   *pommes nature* (F)   *patate lesse* (I)

butter-fried trout

Forelle Müllerinart (G)   *truite à la meunière* (F)   *trota frittata al burro* (I)

fillet of beef

Rindsfilet (G)   *filet de bœuf* (F)   *filetto di manzo* (I)

flat pasta/noodles

Nudeln (G)   *nouilles* (F)   *tagliatelle* (I)

fruit salad

Fruchtsalat (G)   *macédoine de fruits* (F)   *macedonia di frutta* (I)

grilled salmon

grillierter Lachs (G)   *saumon grillé* (F)   *trota salmonata alla griglia* (I)

Read about the hunt, find out if kids really snack on a strip of chocolate stuffed inside bread and much more with Sue Style's beautifully illustrated *A Taste of Switzerland.*

ice cream
  Eis (G)   *glace* (F)   *gelato* (I)
pasta
  Teigwaren (G)   *pâtes* (F)   *pasta* (I)
pork
  Schwein (G)   *porc* (F)   *maiale* (I)
rice
  Reis (G)   *riz* (F)   *riso* (I)
sirloin steak
  Zwischenrippenstück (G)   *entrecôte* (F)   *costata di manzo* (I)
soup
  Suppe (G)   *potage* or *consommé* (F)   *zuppa* (I)
veal
  Kalb (G)   *veau* (F)   *vitello* (I)
vegetables
  Gemüse (G)   *légumes* (F)   *vedura* (I)
whitefish fillets (with almonds)
  Felchenfilets   *filets de féra*   *filetti di coregone*
  (mit Mandeln) (G)   *(aux amandes)* (F)   *(alle mandorle)* (I)

Environment

THE LAND

Landlocked Switzerland – sandwiched between Germany, Austria, Liechtenstein, Italy and France – is essentially an Alpine country. The magnificent Alps and Pre-Alps in the centre and south make up 60% of the modest 41,284 sq km that Switzerland clocks on the European map. The mightily less-known, mysterious Jura Mountains in the west comprise 10% and central Mittelland, otherwise known as the Plateau Central, makes up the rest. Farming of cultivated land is intensive, with cows being moved to upper slopes to graze on summer grass as soon as the retreating snowline allows.

Europe's highest elevations smugly sit here. The Dufourspitze (Dufour Peak; 4634m) of Monte Rosa in the Alps is Switzerland's highest point, but the Matterhorn (4478m) with its dramatic pyramidal cap is much better known. Then, of course, there's Mont Blanc (4807m), a hulk of a mountain – Europe's highest to boot – shared with France and Italy.

Southern Switzerland sports several high mountain passes crossing into Italy. Glaciers account for 2000 sq km in all. Most notable is the Aletsch Glacier, Europe's largest valley glacier, 23km long and covering 86 sq km at last count (p54). Several glaciers proffer summer skiing, memorably Les Diablerets' Glacier de Tsanfleuron (p122) at 3000m.

Lakes are dotted everywhere except in the gentle Jura where the substratal rock is too brittle and porous. The most prolific source of lakes and rivers, including the mighty Rhine and Rhône, is central Switzerland's St Gotthard Massif (p262). The Rhône remains a torrent from its source to Martigny, from where it then flows west to create Europe's largest Alpine lake and Switzerland's best known – Lake Geneva (Lac Léman in French).

The sole canton entirely south of the Alps is Ticino, home to the northern part of Lago Maggiore (193m), the lowest point in the country.

WILDLIFE

With some of Europe's largest mountains and lakes, and some of the strongest environmental legislation in its green fold, Switzerland's wildlife portfolio is rich, but not without risk. Experts reckon the last 150 years have blasted 200-odd plant and animal species in Switzerland into extinction, lark and otter included – and dozens more (such as the freshwater mussel, pretty purple monkey orchid and 81 bird species) hover on the brink.

Man meets Matterhorn in *Scrambles Amongst the Alps*, a mountaineering classic in which Edward Whymper describes his breathtaking ascent of Switzerland's most famous mountain in 1869 and the tragedy that befell his team coming down.

The Matterhorn might be the best known outside Switzerland, but the Swiss venerate the sacred trio of Eiger, Mönch and Jungfrau in the Bernese Oberland as their Holy Trinity of mountain peaks.

TOP PICKS: INCREDULOUS VIEWPOINTS

Zoom in on Switzerland's biggest and best natural features with these incredulous viewpoints.

- **Matterhorn** Best seen while skiing in its shadow, or aboard the Zermatt-Gornergrat cogwheel train (p162).
- **Mont Blanc** Enjoy the Swiss side with the Mont-Blanc Express (p149), Mont Blanc circuit (p150) or a simple stroll on a clear day along Geneva's Quai du Mont-Blanc (p89).
- **Jungfraujoch** Europe's highest railway takes you to the 'top of Europe' at 3454m, stopping en route inside the **Eiger** and **Mönch** (p183); or view the giant trio from the top of Mont Tiltis (p257) aboard the world's first revolving cable car.
- **Aletsch Glacier** Ski alongside Europe's largest valley glacier from the enchanting, car-free ski village of Bettmeralp (p168) or marvel at it from Jungfraujoch (see above).

RULES OF THE WILD

- Leave the rural environment as you found it.
- Stick to the marked paths when hiking. Short cuts straight down a slope could be transformed into a watercourse during the next heavy rainfall and cause soil erosion.
- Don't pick Alpine wildflowers; they really do look lovelier on the mountainsides.
- Farm gates should be left as you found them.
- Approach wildlife with discretion; moving too close will unnerve wild animals.
- Don't light fires, except in established fireplaces.
- Take everything you bring into the mountains out again: rubbish, used packaging, cigarette butts and used tampons included.
- If you really can't avoid leaving some memento of your visit, aka faeces, bury it in the ground at least 100m away from any watercourse.
- Don't camp in the national parks; it's strictly forbidden.

Animals

The bearded vulture, with its unsavoury bone-breaking habits and awe-inspiring 3m wing span, only remains in the wild thanks to reintroduction programs pursued by Alpine national parks, Swiss National Park (opposite) included. Extinct in the Alps by the 19th century, 21 captive-bred baby vultures in all were released into the park's Stabelchod Valley between 1991 and 2001, where they have since bred successfully and continue to prey. Since 2005 the park has tracked two young bearded vultures in live time using satellite telemetry as part of a European project aimed at better understanding the vulture.

The European kestrel and golden eagle are other majestic birds of prey to spot in protected Swiss Alpine skies. More plentiful than the vulture, the eagle nests with vigour in the Graubünden area and munches its way through marmots in summer, ungulate carcasses in winter. Markedly smaller is the Alpine chough *(Alpendohle)*, a relative of the crow; look for a flutter of jet-black feathers and yellow beaks around mountain tops.

The most distinctive Alpine animal is the ibex, a mountain goat with huge curved and ridged horns. Extinct in the Graubünden by 1650, an enterprising soul a couple of centuries back poached a couple from the Italian royal herd and in 1920 the first ibex bred from the pair was released into the Swiss National Park. Some 12,000 ibex inhabit Switzerland today, migrating up to altitudes of 3000m. The chamois (a horned antelope) is more timid but equally at home on the peaks – it can leap 4m vertically. Marmots (chunky rodents related to squirrels) are also famous residents, although they are hard to spot given they spend most of their lives darting in a maze of underground burrows to escape from hungry predators. Come September, marmots hibernate, their body temperatures bizarrely shooting every fortnight from between 3°C and 6°C to 38°C, where they remain for two days before plummeting back down to single digits.

The reintroduced European lynx, mountain hare, ermine, weasel and fox are other Alpine residents, as is the European brown bear. Hunted into extinction in Switzerland by 1904, the lumbering mammal has made a number of controversial appearances in recent years: the brown bear first crossed over the border from Italy in 2005, demolishing beehives and killing sheep in the Swiss National Park in summer 2007 and paying Lenzerheide (p301) a visit in 2008, bringing with it an appetite for sheep, local honey

Slow up with Bern-based Slow Up (www.slowup.ch, in German), a project that sees dozens of Swiss towns and cities ditch all forms of motorised transport for a day – walk or pedal instead; find dates online.

A classic of mountaineering literature, Heinrich Harrer's *The White Spider* tells the daring tale of a young climber and his ascent – the first ever – of the north face of the Eiger peak in 1938.

and nocturnal campsite escapades! One brown bear now wears a tracking device (p316).

The rutting season, September to early October, is the most impressive time to spot roe deer and larger red deer in forested regions and Alpine pastures. Fights can be fierce as stags defend their harem of hinds from other males. With the rutting season done and dusted, the deer abandon Alpine pastures in the Swiss National Park for the sunnier slopes of warmer valleys such as Engadine, Val Mustair and Vinschgau.

Just over 10% of Switzerland's agricultural land is farmed organically.

The noisy nutcracker with its distinctive sound and white-speckled brown plumage can be seen or heard practically everywhere you turn on pine-forest hiking paths, be it on a Swiss National Park information panel (the nutcracker is the park's symbol), high in a tree plucking out cone seeds with its long beak or stashing away nuts for the coming winter. Another ornithological treat – spot it on rocky slopes and in Alpine meadows above 2000m – is the rock ptarmigan, a chickenlike species that has been around since the last ice age and moults three times a year to ensure a foolproof camouflage for every season (brown in summer, white in winter).

Plants

Climatic variation means vegetation ranges from palm trees in Ticino to Nordic flora in the Alps. At higher altitudes, flowers bloom from April to July, depending on the species. The famous edelweiss, with star-shaped flowers, grows at up to 3500m altitude. Alpine rhododendrons (*Alpenrosen*) are numerous at 2500m. Spring gentians are small, violet-blue flowers. White crocuses bloom early (from March) at lower elevations.

Listen to the noise pollution of a jet plane, find out how much waste from households and small businesses is recycled annually, or hone in on an interactive air pollutant map at the Federal Office for the Environment (www.bafu .admin.ch).

Trees are a mixture of deciduous and coniferous varieties in the Mittelland. At an elevation of 800m conifers become more numerous. The red spruce is common at lower levels, while the arolla pine (*Arve* or *Zirbe* in German) and larch mostly take over higher up. At around 2000m, tall trees are replaced by bushes and scrub, which then finally give way to Alpine meadows.

NATIONAL PARKS

Switzerland has just one national park, predictably called **Swiss National Park** (www.nationalpark.ch). Created in 1914, it gives hard-core protection to 172.4 sq km of coniferous forest (28%), Alpine grassland (21%) and scree, rock or high mountains (51%) around Zernez (p315) in eastern Switzerland. Ibex, marmots and chamois are commonplace, 1800 to 2000 red deer roam around free as birds in summer, while the bearded vulture (reintroduced in 1991) is a rare treat for eagle-eyed visitors in the Stabelchod Valley. The main activity in the park is walking, although this is limited, with visitors being forbidden

---

SUPPORT THE LOCAL ECONOMY: LEASE A COW, MOTHER A CALF

Ramona, Ginette, Finette and a herd of other Alpine beauties with long curly eyelashes to die for are there for the milking at **Wylerhof** (☎ 033 951 31 60; www.kuhleasing.ch, in German & French; Stockmatte, Brienz), an Alpine dairy farm run by Helga and Paul Wyler in the Bernese Oberland. Lease the cow of your choice online for a month (Sfr200) or the whole season (June to September; Sfr380), or invest half a day's manual labour on the farm and get 70kg to 100kg of cheese from your cow at a reduced rate.

Should you prefer a calf, take your pick of 180 heads in 12 cantons with 'godparent dating agency' **Patenrind** (☎ 031 822 02 01; www.patenrind.ch, in German; Schaufelacker 3, Wohlen). Becoming a cattle godmother or godfather costs Sfr120 a year plus Sfr15 'agency' fees and godparents get the right to name their adopted offspring, a certificate and unlimited visiting and mucking-out rights.

to stray off the 80km of designated footpaths. November to May, the entire national park is off limits full stop.

A further 20% of Swiss land is protected to a substantially lesser degree by 600-odd regional nature parks, reserves and protected landscapes.

Since 2000, Swiss conservation group Pro Natura (see below) has been campaigning for the creation of another national park in Switzerland by 2010. State funding of Sfr10 million a year was approved in 2005 on the back of the completion of feasibility studies aimed at locating the new national park: nature-rich contenders include 600 sq km in Adula/Rheinwaldhorn near the San Bernardino Pass, a 349 sq km patch west of Locarno, 350 sq km snug against Matterhorn-proud Zermatt, and a pocket of the Muverans region.

Three natural gems feature on Unesco's list of precious World Heritage Sites: pyramid-shaped Monte San Giorgio (1096m; p335), south of Lago di Lugano in Ticino, which safeguards the world's best fossil record of Triassic marine life from 245 to 230 million years ago; southwest Switzerland's spectacular Jungfrau-Aletsch-Bietschhorn mountain region (extended from 539 sq km to 824 sq km in 2008; p168), where the Bernese Alps safeguard Europe's largest glacier and a rash of other equally stunning glacial creations; and, since 2008, the Sardona tectonic area in the heart of the Glarus Alps in northeastern Switzerland (p294).

In addition to the World Heritage Sites, Entlebuch, in the canton of Lucerne in central Switzerland, is watermarked by Unesco as a biosphere reserve (www.biosphaere.ch, in German), with 394 sq km of protected peat bogs, alluvial woodlands, forest and moorland.

> The first bearded vulture for more than a century was born in the wild, at a heady height of 2300m above the Olten Pass in eastern Switzerland, in April 2007; track the movements of the chick's transmitter-marked mates, Blick and Samuel, with On the Move at www.wild.unizh.ch/bg.

ENVIRONMENTAL ISSUES

Switzerland is extremely environmentally friendly: its citizens produce less than 400kg of waste each per year (half the figure of the USA), and that the Swiss are even more diligent recyclers than the Germans, with households religiously separating waste into different categories prior to collection, speaks volumes.

Hydroelectric power meets almost 60% of the country's energy demands and five Swiss nuclear power stations built between 1969 and 1984 provide the rest – and will continue to do so following the electorate's rejection in 2003 of an extension of a 10-year moratorium on the building of new plants that expired in 2000 and the *Strom ohne Atom* proposal calling for the closure of Switzerland's nuclear plants by 2014.

Air pollution caused by vehicle emissions is an issue, with larger cities like Geneva tackling the problem head on by introducing alternative circulation

---

GREEN CARD

Environmental and wildlife organisations in Switzerland include the following:

Alpine Initiative (☎ 041 870 97 81; www.alpeninitiative.ch; Herrengasse 2, Altdorf) Primarily concerned with Alpine transport routes.

Birdlife Switzerland (☎ 044 457 70 20; www.birdlife.ch; Wiedingstrasse 78, Zürich) Swiss birdlife protection; visitor centres near Zürich and Berne.

Greenpeace Switzerland (www.greenpeace.ch, in German & French); German-speaking (☎ 044 447 41 41; Heinrichstrasse 147, 8031 Zürich); French-speaking (☎ 022 731 02 09; Case Postale 1558, 1211 Geneva 1)

Pro Natura (www.pronatura.ch); French speaking (☎ 024 425 03 72; Champ Pittet, 1400 Yverdon les Bains); German speaking (☎ 061 317 91 91; Postfach, 4018 Basel) Switzerland's largest conservation NGO, founded in 1909 and responsible for national-park and nature-reserve management.

Wildlife Switzerland (☎ 044 635 61 31; www.wild.unizh.ch; Strickhofstrasse 39, Zürich)

WWF Switzerland (☎ 044 297 21 21; www.wwf.ch, in German, French & Italian; Hohlstrasse 110, 8010 Zürich)

of vehicles with odd/even number plates in summer, when ozone levels hit unacceptable highs. Reducing speed limits on freeways and encouraging motorists to leave their cars at home on chosen 'slow up' days is another means of controlling air pollution.

The biggest environmental concern for this predominantly Alpine country is naturally mountain protection. Fragile mountain ecosystems are particularly vulnerable to pollution and environmental damage, heavily contributed to by the 120 million–odd visitors a year tramping through its green pastures. Since the 1950s the federal government has introduced various measures to protect forests, lakes and marshland from environmental damage and in 1991 it signed the Alpine Convention, which seeks to reduce damage caused by motor traffic and tourism.

Then there is global warming, a burning global issue that is already seriously impacting Switzerland. 'Melting rapidly' is the verdict on Switzerland's 1800 glaciers which lost 18% of their surface between 1985 and 2000 and are expected to retreat another 30% by 2025 according to scientists. Switzerland's most famous mass of ice, rock and snow, the 23km-long Aletsch Glacier (p168), shrunk 114.6m in 2006 alone (65.6m in 2005, 32.4m in 2007) and could shrink 80% by 2100 if things don't change – hence the 600 or so people who famously posed naked on the melting ice to be photographed by New York artist Spencer Tunick in summer 2007 as part of a Greenpeace campaign calling for governments worldwide to act quickly.

The knock-on effect at lower altitudes is less snow, particularly in lower-altitude ski resorts, and erratic, unpredictable snowfalls at higher elevations (which, ironically works both ways – the 2008/09 season opened earlier than ever in Zermatt and other higher Alpine resorts where the first lifts opened in early November, a month earlier than usual). Artificial snow is one solution relied on by 19% of Swiss ski slopes despite its hefty energy and (even worse) water consumption.

Then, of course, there are the harsh implications on the mountain economy (p16).

Forget skiing! St Moritz' pioneering Clean Energy Tour (p318) shines light on the resort's use of solar and hydro power, Heidi's flower trail and the hotel where Switzerland's first electric light was switched on!

Walking in Switzerland

Soaring mountains and iridescent glaciers, sparkling rivers and karst gorges, remote moors and pastures drenched in shades of green – Switzerland has an almost indecent amount of natural splendour for its size. Guarding the best bits like a jealous lover, this topographic temptress flashes walkers a come-hither look. Only by slinging on a backpack and hitting the trail can you begin to appreciate just how *big* this tiny country really is. Dust off your boots and prepare to be seduced.

For purists, hiking in Switzerland means the Alps. The fixation becomes clear as you stride in the shadow of snow giants Eiger, Mönch and Jungfrau to the backbeat of cowbells, survey the pyramidal form of Piz Buin from a sheer precipice in the Swiss National Park, or gasp at 4000m peaks rising like jaws around the shark's fin of Matterhorn. Scratch the glacier-encrusted surface and you'll find yet more variety. Whether trudging past mist-shrouded outcrops in the canyonlike Ruin' Aulta, taking an intoxicating ramble through Valais' sun-dappled vineyards or tracing the icy curves of Aletsch Glacier, walking here will take your breath away. Literally.

If there is a sound more musical to Swiss ears than precision clockwork, it is rhythmic footsteps on a well-prepared trail. Come snow or shine, you'll find 30-somethings with Linford Christie thighs and strapping 70-year-olds traipsing up the heights as locals have done for eons. Take this as your cue to do likewise and you'll be richly rewarded. Witnessing the springtime wildflower blaze, overnighting in an Alpine hut to see dawn spotlight the summits one by one, crunching through larch woodlands cloaked gold in autumn – such experiences will ignite your passion for walking and spark your love affair with Switzerland.

GETTING STARTED

Stick to the path and it's almost impossible to get lost in Switzerland, which has one of the most extensive, best maintained and sign-posted walking networks on the planet. As the clued-up Swiss will tell you in admiring tones, the country's 62,500km of marked trails (*Wanderweg* in German; *sentier* in French) would be enough to stretch around the globe 1.5 times. Hardly surprising, then, that many locals are mad-keen walkers. Whether you're planning a gentle woodland ramble or a multi-day hike in the Alps, it's easy to join them.

Trails are cleverly colour-coded according to difficulty: yellow for easy (no previous experience necessary), white-red-white for mountain trails (you should be sure-footed as routes may involve some exposure) and white-blue-white for high Alpine routes (only for the physically fit; some climbing and/or glacier travel may be required). Pink signs and poles denote prepared winter walking trails.

INFORMATION
Information Sources

For interactive maps and inspiring walks searchable by region, difficulty, time and theme, get clicking on www.wanderland.ch and the excellent Switzerland Tourism website, www.myswitzerland.com. Avid snowshoe walkers should visit www.globaltrail.net.

Founded in 1863, the **Schweizer Alpen-Club** (SAC; Swiss Alpine Club; ☎ 031 370 18 18; www.sac-cas.ch) runs around 300 huts and shelters in the Swiss Alps. Annual membership costs between Sfr75 and Sfr130 depending on the branch you join, with substantial discounts for children and families. As well as reductions of up to 50% on rates at SAC huts (members pay a maximum of Sfr26), membership also covers mountain-safety courses, a monthly magazine and various discounts on maps and books.

Meals or cooking facilities are usually available and overnighting generally costs between Sfr28 and Sfr40 for a mattress on the floor or a bunk in a dorm. For more details, see the boxed text on hut-to-hut hiking (above).

For more specific information on walking in Switzerland, contact the **Swiss Hiking Federation** (Schweizer Wanderwege, SAW; ☎ 031 370 10 20; www.swisshiking.ch, in German & French; Monbijoustrasse 61, Bern), a national organisation that oversees the maintenance and waymarking of all official hiking routes, and organises excellent guided walks. Visit the website for walk suggestions and tips.

Maps

Surveying and cartography is something (else) the Swiss excel in: their maps are veritable works of precision, if not of art. Most comprehensive is the 1:50,000 series of walking maps published by the Swiss Hiking Federation (SAW; see Information Sources above). Distinguishable by their yellow covers and 'T' after the grid number (eg *Jungfrau* 264T), these sheets are drawn directly from the Federal Office of Topography maps. Generally the most accurate, durable and cheapest available, these maps retail at around

---

HUT-TO-HUT HIKING

Trade in your cushy hotel for a mattress in a SAC (Swiss Alpine Club) hut and you won't be disappointed. Spending the night at one of these mountain refuges, usually perched between 2000m and 3000m, is a highlight of hiking in Switzerland. When day trippers descend to the valley and silence descends on the heights, you are among the privileged few who can watch ibexes graze against the backdrop of Jungfrau at dusk or see the first light illuminate Matterhorn in the morning.

Dorms may be basic and hot showers sporadic, but the welcome is warm and the views outstanding at these high-altitude retreats. After a long day's hiking, there is nothing like curling up beside a tiled oven in a wood-panelled parlour, or chinking celebratory mugs of *Schoggi* (hot chocolate) and exchanging tips with fellow walkers. With a belly full of fondue, you are ready to hit the sack – just pray you haven't put yours next to a champion snorer.

The well-organised system means you're hardly ever further than a five- to six-hour trudge from the next hut, so there's no need to lug a tent, camping stove and other heavy gear. Most huts go with the snow, so to speak, and open from mid-June to mid-September. You can search for huts by region on the SAC website (see below). Blankets are often provided but you may need to bring your own sleeping sheet and towel. It's worth calling ahead to reserve a bed, especially in peak season (July and August).

Sfr22.50. Hallwag, Kümmerly + Frey (K+F) cover the country with 1:60,000 maps. See p355 for details.

Regional tourist authorities often produce useful walking maps of areas surrounding their resorts or valley, generally scaled at between 1:25,000 and 1:50,000. Depending on their size and quality, they normally cost between Sfr12 and Sfr20. See the individual walks for specific map requirements.

Large bookstores invariably have a wide selection of Swiss topographical and walking maps. Order SAW maps online at www.shop.wandern.ch and www.toposhop.admin.ch.

Books

For day hikes, pick up a copy of *Walking Easy in the Swiss & Austrian Alps* by Chet and Carolee Lipton. *Walking in the Alps* by Kev Reynolds has a varied selection of routes in the Alps, as does the informative *Trekking and Climbing in the Western Alps* by Hilary Sharp. Cicerone Press (www.cicerone.co.uk) publishes a wide range of walking guidebooks on Switzerland, which are particularly useful for multiday treks.

WHEN TO WALK

Summer is justifiably hailed the best time to hit the trail in the Alps, but real hikers will find some form of walking year-round. The trick is accessorising for the seasons: snowshoes are invaluable for stomping through deep powder, lightweight trekking poles for negotiating slippery leaves, waterproofs for spontaneous downpours. Where there's a will, there's a walk.

If you're planning on tackling high-altitude hikes, realistically June to September is your best bet. Skiers are still whizzing down the slopes in spring and, come October, snow levels creep lower and make certain passes inaccessible. Walking in summer sets senses on high alert – think melodic clanging of cowbells, pastures carpeted in gentians and shockingly pink *Alpenrosen,* and blue skies to make your heart sing. Alpine huts open their doors to weary walkers and tingling cold mountain lakes are a bracing alternative to a morning shower.

If dewy forests, mountains enshrouded in mist and the chance to spy rutting stags appeal, autumn it is. Quiet and enigmatic, this underrated season is full of gold and russet woodlands, mushrooms, crunchy leaves and smoke drifting from log huts. Many Swiss ski resorts now prepare winter walking trails and shuffling through the twinkling snow can be truly magical.

Wise locals will tell you never to take the weather for granted in the Alps, where conditions can skip from sunny to stormy to snowy to foggy in the course of a day. Check the forecast on www.meteoschweiz.ch before heading out.

WHAT TO TAKE

Light packs, happy backs… For day hikes, a 20L rucksack filled with a few essentials should suffice. Hikers need to keep up their blood-sugar levels, so here's your excuse to gorge on chocolate and cheese. High-energy foods such as nuts, dried fruits, bread and cured meats are also ideal. Pack at least 1L of water per person to avoid dehydration.

Take lightweight layers to warm up or cool down. The basics include a breathable T-shirt, polar-fleece jacket, loose-fitting trousers, sturdy walking boots and waterproofs. For high-altitude hikes, it may be worth adding a hat, gaiters, thermals, gloves and telescopic hiking poles.

Despite the air temperature, the sun can be incredibly powerful in the Alps; sunscreen is essential to avoid the lobster look. For emergency purposes, consider packing a flashlight, first-aid kit, compass, whistle and – of course – a Swiss army knife.

WALK DESCRIPTIONS

All indicated times are actual hiking times and do not include breaks for fondue lunches, Heidi-style photo shoots and midday catnaps. Factor these in when planning your walk. Read distances in conjunction with altitudes, as elevation can make as great a difference to your walking time as distance. Grading systems and times are always somewhat arbitrary; having an indication, however, may help you choose between walks. Easy denotes a short, well-marked walk on gentle terrain, medium refers to more challenging hikes with greater distances and tougher ascents, while hard is for serious hikers with long distances, significant elevation differences and possibly scrambling, climbing or glacier travel.

RESPONSIBLE WALKING

With just a little bit of respect for the environment, fragile Alpine ecosystems included,

WALKING IN SWITZERLAND

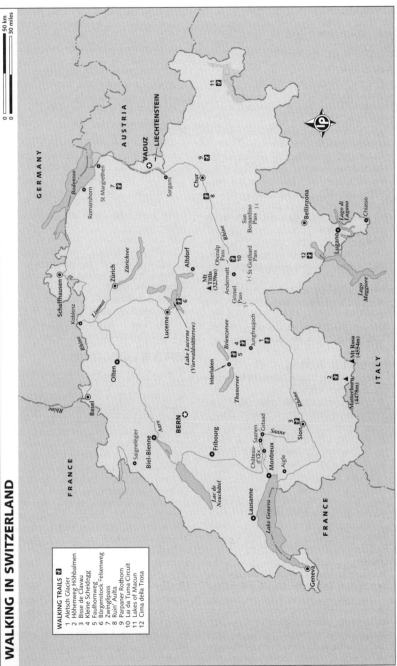

WALKING TRAILS 🚶
1 Aletsch Glacier
2 Höhenweg Höhbalmen
3 Bisse de Clavau
4 Kleine Scheidegg
5 Faulhornweg
6 Bürgenstock Felsenweg
7 Zwinglipass
8 Ruin' Aulta
9 Parpaner Rothorn
10 Lai da Tuma Circuit
11 Lakes of Macun
12 Cima della Trosa

walking can be a pursuit far more in tune with nature than other sports. To minimise your impact when walking, consider the following tips.

Trail Etiquette

- *Grüezi, bonjour, buongiorno* – greeting your fellow walkers with a cheery 'hello' in their native tongue will stand you in good stead.
- Ascending walkers have right of way over those descending on narrow paths.
- Leave farm gates as you find them. In summer low-voltage electric fences are set up to control livestock on the open Alpine pastures. Electric fences usually have hooks that can be easily unfastened to allow walkers to pass through without getting zapped.
- Edelweiss for your sweet? Forget it. Wildflowers look their blooming best, well, in the wild and many are protected species.
- Marmots prefer holes to camera lenses. Keep a considerate distance from wild animals so as not to unnerve them or distract them from fattening up for the long winter.

Human Waste Disposal

- Make an effort to use toilets in huts and refuges wherever possible.
- When nature calls outdoors, bury your waste. Dig a hole 15cm deep and at least 100m from any watercourse. Cover the waste and toilet paper with soil and a rock. In snow, dig down beneath the soil, otherwise your waste will be exposed when the snow melts.
- Contamination of water sources by human faeces can lead to the transmission of giardia, a nasty bacterial parasite. It can cause health risks to other walkers, locals and wildlife.

Rubbish

- As the old chestnut goes: take nothing but photos, leave nothing but footprints. Carry out what you have carried in, including easily forgotten items like tin foil, orange peels, cigarette butts, plastic wrappers and tampons. Empty packaging weighs little and can be stored as you go along in a dedicated rubbish bag.

- Burying rubbish is not recommended as digging disturbs soil, encourages erosion and may be dug up by animals. It also takes years to decompose, especially at high altitudes.
- Minimise waste by unpacking small-portion packages and combining their contents in one container before your trip. Take reusable containers or stuff sacks.

Erosion

- Mountain slopes and hillsides, especially at high altitudes, are prone to erosion. Stick to the trail and avoid short cuts that bypass a switchback, however tempting. If you blaze a new trail, it will turn into a watercourse with the next heavy rainfall and eventually cause soil loss and deep scarring.
- If the track passes through a muddy patch, get muddy – walking around the edge will increase the size of the patch.
- Avoid removing plant life, which keeps topsoil in place.
- To you it's a flower-strewn meadow or cornfield; to a farmer it's bread and butter. Refrain from stepping off paths that lead across cultivated land.

SAFETY & EMERGENCIES

Though avalanches and landslides spring to mind, walker injuries and fatalities are usually attributable to tiredness, hypothermia, dehydration and heat fatigue. Many falls result from sliding on leaves, scree or ice. On high-level routes rockfall can be a problem. In true Scout spirit, be prepared with suitable clothing and footwear. Factor in time for breaks and begin walks early enough to return before nightfall. The sight of Eiger towering above Grindelwald might make your feet itch, but common sense should prevail – know your limits, increase the difficulty of walks gradually, and be willing to turn back if proceeding becomes dangerous.

Sticking to marked trails is always advisable, but in heavy fog (and thus poor visibility) it is vital. Two is considered the minimum number for safe mountain hiking. Inform a responsible person, such as a hut warden or hotel receptionist of your plans, and let them know when you return.

The standard Alpine distress signal is six whistles, six calls or six smoke puffs – that is, six of whatever sign you can make – followed by a

FAMOUS FIVE LONG-DISTANCE TRAILS

If the day walks in this chapter give you wanderlust, consider hiking one of Switzerland's long-distance trails. Each is designed to show Switzerland from its most striking angles and provide an insight into the country's rich cultural diversity. If two weeks on the trail seems daunting, the treks can be broken down into shorter chunks, but there's nevertheless something satisfying about completing a great walk in its entirety.

■ **Alpine Pass Route** – The 350km Alpine Pass Route is Switzerland's classic long walk. The east–west route takes you right across the country, from Sargans near the Liechtenstein border to Montreux (p116) on Lake Geneva, traversing 16 passes and revealing some of the Swiss Alps' highest and most stunning mountainscapes. With rest days and time off for bad weather, walking the route takes three to four weeks. Cicerone's *Alpine Pass Route* guide covers the hike in detail.

■ **Tour Monte Rosa** – This challenging 10-day, 160km circuit of Switzerland's loftiest mountain massif, Monte Rosa, is varied and spectacular. Beginning in Zermatt (p161), the route goes via Grächen, Saas Fee and the Italian towns of Macugnaga, Gressoney and St-Jacques. Expect demanding passes (one involving glacier travel) and bewitching views of snowy 4000m giants including the iconic pyramid of Matterhorn and Switzerland's highest peak, 4634m Dufours-pitze. K+F has produced a 1:50,000 map, *Tour Monte Rosa*. For further details, see the website www.tmr-matterhorn.com.

■ **Tour des Combins** – This six- to eight-day circuit hike leads around the ice-encrusted 4000m peaks of the Grand Combins massif in Lower Valais. Verbier (p150) is traditionally the trail head. The route leads up through the Val de Bagnes over the Fenêtre de Durand to Barasson into the Val Pelline in Italy, then returns into Swiss territory via St-Rhémy, the Col du Grand St-Bernard and Val d'Entremont. For map and route descriptions, see www.tourdescombins.ch (in French).

■ **Senda Sursilvana** – Stretching from the wild Oberalp Pass (p304) down through the valley of the Vorderrhein as far as Chur (p298), this 110km, four- to five-day hike is one of the least strenuous long walks in Switzerland. The high-level route takes in dramatic scenery, enigmatic menhirs and culturally unique Romansch-speaking towns and villages. K+F's 1:40,000 walking map, *Senda Sursilvana* (Sfr8.50), fully covers the route.

■ **Haute Route** – Leading from Chamonix in France through southern Valais to Zermatt (p161), the Haute Route boasts some of the most astounding country accessible to walkers anywhere in the Alps. The trek is tough, involving long ascents, pass hopping and glacier travel, so experience is essential. Those with the skills to tackle this route are rewarded with unforgettable vistas of Mont Blanc, Dent Blanche and Matterhorn. The guidebook *Chamonix to Zermatt: The Walker's Haute Route* by Kev Reynolds (Cicerone) is recommended.

pause equalling the length of time taken before repeating the signal again. If you have a mobile phone, take it with you. **Swiss Mountain Rescue** (REGA; ☎ 14 14) is superefficient but remortgage-the-house expensive. Take out insurance that covers mountain sports.

VALAIS

ALETSCH GLACIER

Duration Five to six hours
Distance 17km
Difficulty Easy to medium
Nearest Towns Fiesch and Fiescheralp (p168)

Summary This high-Alpine walk takes in the epic scenery around the Aletsch Glacier, a nature-gone-wild spectacle of moors, jagged mountains and deeply crevassed glaciers.

Few places in the Alps, let alone Switzerland, can beat the Unesco-listed Aletsch Glacier (Grosser Aletschgletscher in German) for sheer visual impact. The seemingly never-ending 23km glacier is the longest and most voluminous in the European Alps and is fed by a number of other major glaciers from its source at the Jungfraujoch. A significant chunk of the walk follows a high-level ridge trail that commands peerless views of this glacial superhighway and the frosted peaks

WALKING IN SWITZERLAND

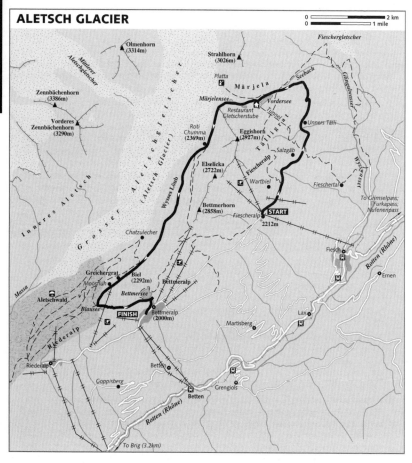

ALETSCH GLACIER

that razor their way above it. Taking in high moors, glittering tarns and pastures grazed by black-nosed sheep, the hike is as diverse as it is dramatic. Walkers are continuously rewarded with incredible views for minimal effort.

Bring drinks and snacks as there is only one restaurant between Fiescheralp and Bettmeralp. As the hike is above the treeline, it's sensible to check weather conditions before heading out. Quality maps covering the walk include the SAW 1:50,000 *Jungfrau 264T* (Sfr22.50) and the tourist office's 1:25,000 *Aletschgletscher* (Sfr13.50).

Getting to/from the Walk

The trail head is Fiescheralp, the middle station of the cable car from Fiesch to Eggishorn;

see p168 for details. The walk finishes at the vehicle-free mountain resort of Bettmeralp, where cable cars run roughly half-hourly down to Betten (one-way adult/child Sfr8/4). There are hourly train connections between Betten and Fiesch (Sfr4, 20 minutes).

The Walk

The views are immediately spectacular at 2212m **Fiescheralp** (Kühboden), with the distant peaks of Matterhorn and Weisshorn shimmering on the horizon. From the cable-car station, walk northeast along the flat dirt trail that contours open mountainsides streaked with wildflowers and commands long views down to the valley. On clear days, you will come across hang-gliders and paragliders launching themselves off these slopes and wheeling like birds of prey in the sky. Bear right past the path going up to the Eggishorn and the turn-off to Märjela via the small **Tälli** tunnel. The route can be shortened by an hour by walking through the tunnel – a decidedly unscenic alternative that requires a torch (flashlight) with plenty of battery power.

The route soon becomes a broad well-graded foot track, lined with bilberry bushes and tufty grass, which passes cow-grazed pastures and affords tantalising snapshot glimpses of the icy tongue of Fieschergletscher. Wind your way around the slopes high above the Fieschertal up through the grassy, rock-strewn gully of Unners Tälli. Begin a steeper climb in several switchbacks to a small wooden cross erected on a rock platform. This vertiginous natural viewing point offers giddying views across to the **Fieschergletscher**, which slithers down between the jagged 3905m Gross Wannenhorn and the thornlike peak of 4274m Finsteraarhorn.

Follow white-red-white markings westward across rocky ledges, listening out for the clanging of sheep bells and the shrill whistling of marmots. Head to the tiny valley of the **Märjela**, where a signpost marks the junction of trails coming from the Fieschertal and the Tälligrat. The path continues quickly down through high moorland, shadowing a brook that cuts a path through gold-tinged tussock grass and tufts of silky cotton grass to the turquoise Vordersee. Around two hours from Fischeralp, you reach **Restaurant Gletscherstube** (☎ 027 971 47 83; dm Sfr25, with breakfast Sfr32; ☺ early Jul-mid Oct). This cosy wooden hut sits below the Eggishorn at 2363m on an Alpine pasture grazed by sheep. It's a superb spot to refuel over lunch (mains around Sfr16) or spend a peaceful night close to the Aletsch Glacier. From here, you can already glimpse the peak of 3740m Geisshorn and the spindly Fusshörner that rise above the Aletsch Glacier.

Head down past several little tarns, crossing the small stream at a large cairn before making your way down through regenerating moraine slopes to the **Märjelensee** (2300m) after 30 to 35 minutes. Bordered by the icy edge of the Aletsch Glacier, this lake presents a dramatic picture. In the past the Märjelensee was higher and larger than its present form. At times the lake would rise and suddenly break through the ice wall, causing flooding downvalley,

but the glacier's steady retreat has solved that problem. From the polished-rock slabs above the Märjelensee you get a tremendous view northward across this amazingly broad, elongated expanse of glacial ice stretching right up to the pearl-white peaks of Eiger (3970m), Mönch (4107m) and Jungfrau (4158m).

Climb southward around a rocky ridge and sidle up to a signposted trail fork at **Roti Chumma** (2369m). Here, take the lower right-hand way, partly following an old aqueduct along a magnificent route high above what seems like an endless sweep of ice. The scenery is pure drama with uninterrupted views to the crevassed, moraine-streaked ice, thundering waterfalls and brooding peaks dominated by the 4193m Aletschhorn and the spiky Fusshörner. The shaggy black-nosed sheep that graze the slopes here seem tiny by comparison with the immense scale of the glacier.

After coming to Biel, a saddle on the Greichergrat at 2292m where a path turns down right to the Aletschwald, make your way southwest along a tarn-speckled ridge where it's often possible to sight chamois. Continue along the grassy slopes until you reach the restaurant and upper chairlift station at **Moosfluh** (2333m), 1¼ to 1¾ hours from the Märjelensee. From here the distinctive pyramid-shaped summit of the Matterhorn can be readily identified among the icy crags far away to the southwest.

The route continues along the ridge on a short section of marked foot track (not highlighted on some walking maps), cutting down leftward to the inky blue tarn of Blausee (2204m). Here duck under the chairlift and drop down eastward over verdant pastures to the attractive Bettmersee, where you might choose to take a refreshing dip. From here a dirt road leads on across the low dam wall to the upper houses of 2000m **Bettmeralp**, 40 to 50 minutes from Moosfluh. The upper station of the Betten–Bettmeralp cable car is 10 minutes' walk down through the village.

HÖHENWEG HÖHBALMEN

Duration 6½ to 7½ hours
Distance 18km
Difficulty Medium
Nearest Town Zermatt (p161)
Summary This long circuit day hike is pure Alpine fantasy, taking in wild glaciers, luscious Alpine pastures and the entrancing pyramidlike angles of Matterhorn.

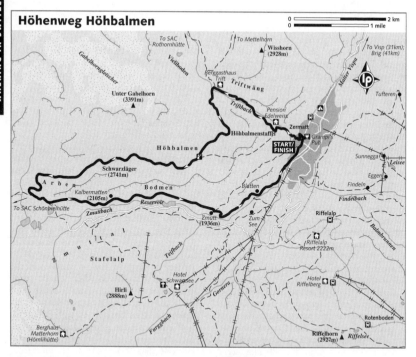

This outstanding hike embodies all that is unique about the Swiss Alps. Quickly leaving Zermatt behind, you enter another world of glittering streams, wildflower-cloaked slopes, crevassed glaciers and dagger-shaped peaks. At over 2600m, the rolling terraces of Höhbalmen provide one of the finest natural lookout points in Switzerland. The looming pyramidal form of the 4477m Matterhorn fixes your attention for much of the way, although the incredible vistas include almost two dozen other 'four-thousander' peaks.

Depending on snow and weather conditions, this route can normally be done from June until late October. As there are some very worthwhile side-trip options, the walk can be turned into an overnight outing by staying somewhere (preferably at the Berggasthaus Trift) en route. The local tourist authority's 1:25,000 *Wanderkarte Zermatt* (Sfr24.90) is recommended.

Getting to/from the Walk

This circuit walk begins and ends in Zermatt. See p165 for details on getting there and away.

The Walk

From Zermatt train station walk along the main street (Bahnhofstrasse) and turn right at **Grampi's Pub** onto a narrow cobbled footpath that leads up beside quaint wooden barns, winding its way more steeply up past holiday chalets and over hillside pastures, carpeted with thistles and wildflowers such as gentian, *Alpenrose*, monkshood and delicate cow wheat. The trail climbs quickly above Zermatt to enter a pristine Alpine wilderness. After crossing the gurgling Triftbach on a small wooden footbridge, climb on through shady larch forest to reach the turn-of-the-century **Pension Edelweiss** (☎ 027 967 22 36; s/d from Sfr42/84; ☼ Jun-Sep) after 40 to 50 minutes. Brimming with antique curios, this pension sits at 1961m on a balcony overlooking Zermatt and the upper Mattertal.

The path rises gently to recross the stream near a hydroelectricity diversion tunnel, then makes several broad switchbacks above the Triftbach Gorge and its crystal-clear falls (signs warn not to approach them). Jagged, snow-streaked peaks slide into view as you continue uphill past precariously perched boulders, scree patches and streamlets to reach the **Berggasthaus Trift** (p164) at 2337m, 50 minutes to one hour on. At the edge of a small grassy basin, this cosy mountain hut makes a great base if you want to split the hike into two leisurely days, or make strenuous yet rewarding side trips up to the 3406m Mettelhorn or the 3198m **SAC Rothornhütte** (☎ 027 967 20 48) on the rugged spur descending from the Zinalrothorn. Otherwise, the terrace is a fabulous spot to enjoy homemade apple tart and iced tea, with peerless views to the heavily crevassed Triftgletscher and a host of glistening peaks including Wellenkuppe, Trifthorn and Oberegabelhorn.

Cross the Triftbach a final time, quickly cutting southward across the tiny Alpine meadow, and begin a diagonal, zigzagging ascent up the grassy slopes flanked by rocky crags. Behind you the spiky 4221m Zinalrothorn comes into sight and, as you move up onto the high balcony of the **Höhbalmenstaffel**, a sensational panorama unfolds. The grandiose views sweep around from the Täschhorn to the Allalinhorn, the Rimpfischhorn, the Dufourspitze – at 4634m, Switzerland's highest peak – the Breithorn and the Klein Matterhorn, with great highways of ice creeping down from their glacier-encrusted summits. Directly ahead and demanding all the attention is the colossal toothlike shape of the Matterhorn (4478m).

The trail contours the rolling wildflower fields known as the Höhbalmen, where the extremely rare purple-yellow Haller's pasque flower grows, to reach a **signpost** at 2665m, 40 to 50 minutes from the Berggasthaus Trift. Here walkers are again held spellbound by the views of 4000m steel-grey peaks, rising like shark fins above a frothy white ocean. This is one of the best areas for wildlife, so keep your peepers open for golden eagles, chamois and ibex.

Head on westward into the Zmuttal. The route makes a high traverse around narrowing ledges opposite the fearsome north face of the Matterhorn, reaching the highest point of the walk at **Schwarzläger** (2741m) after 40 to 50 minutes. There are excellent views of the moraine-covered Zmuttgletscher, and more ice-bound peaks rising up at the glacier's head around the 4171m Dent d'Hérens.

Make a steady, sidling descent over the sparse mountainsides of Arben below shimmering hanging glaciers that spill over the high craggy cliffs on your right. The path snakes down to meet a more prominent walking track, which leads down from the easily reached **SAC Schönbielhütte** (☎ 027 967 13 54), alongside the high lateral moraine wall left by the receding Zmuttgletscher. Follow this down left in zigzags through the loose glacial rubble, before continuing along the gentler terraces above the icy cold Zmuttbach. The track heads on toward mighty horned peaks, passing a waterfall that plummets spectacularly over a precipice, to reach a tiny restaurant at **Kalbermatten** (2105m), one to 1¼ hours from Schwarzläger. Throughout the summer months, these grassy slopes are grazed by Valaisan black-nosed sheep.

Head on smoothly down above a small turbid-blue reservoir (whose water is diverted via long tunnels into the Lac des Dix in the adjacent Val d'Hérens), bearing right at a junction by the dam wall. This soon brings you down to the photogenic hamlet of **Zmutt** (1936m), a cluster of dark-timber, slate-roofed huts complete with pretty whitewashed chapel. From here a footpath descends on through hayfields dotted with neat farmhouses to intersect with a gravelled lane. Amble leisurely on past the Schwarzsee cable-car station, then take the next left turn-off leading up back into the thriving heart of Zermatt, 1¼ to 1½ hours from Kalbermatten.

BISSE DE CLAVAU

Duration Two to 2¼ hours
Distance 7km
Difficulty Easy
Nearest Town Sion (p153)
Summary This unstrenuous amble takes you along a beautiful stretch of the Chemin Vignoble, a long-distance trail leading through Valais' sun-drenched wine-growing district.

The Bisse de Clavau is a 550-year-old aqueduct that carries water 7.5km to the thirsty vineyards of the Rhône Valley. These steep, south-facing slopes are devoted almost entirely to the production of the fine red and white Valaisan wines known as dôle and Fendant. Here the vines are planted on narrow terraces supported by dry-stone retaining walls that defy the steep gradient.

The going can get very hot on these sunexposed slopes, so wear a hat and carry water in summer. Apart from the coldest days of winter, the walk can be done in all seasons,

WALKING IN SWITZERLAND

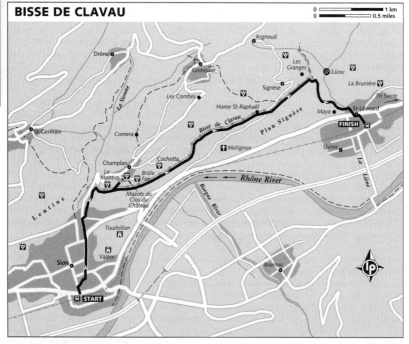

BISSE DE CLAVAU

although it's most spectacular in autumn when the gold-tinged vines hang heavy with ripe grapes. Come at the weekend to taste Valaisian wines and other specialities at one of the wineries.

SAW's 1:50,000 *Montana* (Sfr22.50) covers the region in detail, though a map is not essential as the walk is well signposted.

Getting to/from the Walk

For details on public transport services operating to/from Sion, see p155. The walk finishes in the tiny village of St-Léonard. Direct trains run hourly from St-Léonard to Sion (Sfr3, seven minutes).

The Walk

From Sion train station, walk 200m straight ahead, then turn right onto Rue des Creusets. Follow various small pedestrian laneways up through Sion's Old Town, proceeding north along Rue du Grand-Pont and Rue du Rawil. Just before you reach a roundabout, a signpost with some background information on the Bisse de Clavau points you off right onto the narrow **Chemin de Champlan** footpath,

which leads up between vine-clad stone walls and affords snapshot views of the first hillside vineyards.

Around 20 minutes from the trail head, the route signposted **Chemin Vignoble** begins an easy contouring traverse eastward beside the tiny aqueduct among steeply terraced vineyards. The grape vines have been planted in closely spaced rows in order to maximise the yield of this valuable crop. To your right Tourbillon and Valère, two rounded outcrops crowned by historic fortresses, will have you reaching for the camera. Towering above Sion, these craggy rock hills rise abruptly out of the built-up floor of the Rhône Valley. It seems remarkable that they survived the intense shearing action of the Rhône Glacier during past ice ages.

As you stroll, information panels (in German and French) provide some background on the region's unique microclimate and wine domains. The weather and vegetation here feel almost Mediterranean and you may well spy brightly coloured butterflies, lizards and dragonflies, fig trees and wildflowers like yellow dyer's woad. During the grape harvest, keep an eye out for the ingenious lifts vintners use to transport their crop up the vertiginous slopes.

With a large sunny terrace overlooking vineyards and the Alps, **Mazots du Clos du Château** (☎ 079 628 61 70; light meals Sfr13-25; ☺ 11am-9pm Sat, 11am-6pm Sun) makes a fine spot to taste Pinot blanc and Humagne wines at the source, together with some home-smoked salmon or Valaisan specialities such as Raclette.

Head on above a sweeping curve of the Rhône River, and enjoy stellar views of the Alps across the valley that, on a clear day, reach as far as the snowcapped peaks of Dent Blanche (4357m) and Bietschhorn (3934m). The route continues and crosses several small roads, passing below the tiny village of Signèse and the scattering of houses at Les Granges before turning down to the right away from the Bisse de Clavau. Make your way via a gravelled farm track along the edge of the vineyards above the gorge of the **Liène** (the waters of which are diverted subterraneously further upstream to feed the irrigation channels), short-cutting a few bends in the road.

Yellow arrows guide you quickly down past beech trees, sloe berries and vines to cobblestone Chemin de la Maya, dotted with stone villas. This lane brings you to a fast-flowing stream and the village of **St-Léonard** (508m), around 1½ hours from where you first met the Bisse de Clavau. The train station is 500m south on Ave de la Gare.

BERNESE OBERLAND

KLEINE SCHEIDEGG

Duration Six to seven hours
Distance 18km
Difficulty Easy to medium
Nearest Town Grindelwald (p179)
Summary This is unquestionably one of the most stunning walks in the Bernese Oberland, taking in Alpine meadows, forests and close-ups of Eiger, Mönch and Jungfrau.

Pick a clear day for this memorable hike, affording views of the chiselled Eiger north face and the glistening giants of the Jungfrau region that stir the soul. After an initial brisk uphill stride, the going is pretty smooth and there are Alpine huts aplenty en route, where you can kick back on a terrace and drink in some of the finest vistas in the Swiss Alps.

This broad saddle of the comparatively low Männlichen Range, dividing the two upper branches of the Lütschine River, makes a natural lookout, with incredible close-range views taking in Switzerland's most famous peaks. The walk involves a fairly gradual ascent of just over 1000m and a 1200m descent. It forms the seventh leg of the Alpine Pass Route. The best map for this walk is the SAW 1:50,000 *Interlaken* 254T (Sfr22.50).

Getting to/from the Walk

The walk sets off from Grindelwald (p179) and ends at Lauterbrunnen (p184); see regional chapters for information on getting to/from these towns. Since the walk largely traces the line of the Wengernalpbahn (WAB) narrow-gauge cog railway, hikers can cop out by boarding the train at any of the train stations passed en route. Wengen can be reached by cog railway from Lauterbrunnen (Sfr6.20, 17 minutes).

The Walk

From the main Grindelwald railway station, follow a signposted laneway leading down beside the Hotel Glacier and past undulating pastures dotted with timber chalets, reaching **Grindelwald-Grund** railway station after 15 to 20 minutes. Most trains to the Kleine Scheidegg and the Jungfraujoch leave from here.

Cross the railway tracks and take the footpath on the left marked for Kleine Scheidegg. Ascend steeply past log chalets ablaze with geraniums in summer, and marvel at the jaw-dropping vistas southeast to the jagged limestone turrets of Wetterhorn (3701m) and the crevassed ice of Unterer Grindelwaldgletscher. When you emerge at the broad road, continue to follow the signs and white-red-white markings uphill. The gentle gradient quickly steepens, but the completely arresting view of the chiselled, snow-encrusted north face of **Eiger** ahead, drawing nearer with each footstep, should spur you on.

Take the often-steep foot track that leads up beside the gin-clear stream of **Sandbach**. The trail soon dips in and out of a blissfully cool forest thick with larch and pine trees, ferns and lichen. This sylvan lushness is a startling contrast to the brooding limestone crags topped with sparkling glaciers that rise above. Pass under an arched stone rail bridge to reach **Restaurant Brandegg** (☎ 033 853 10 57; snacks & mains Sfr6-20; ☺ 9am-6pm Jun-Oct & Dec-Apr), which sits under the north face of the Eiger,

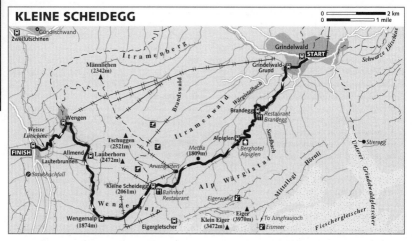

KLEINE SCHEIDEGG

about one hour from Grindelwald. Here you can enjoy a well-deserved break on the sunny terrace – the apple strudel is delicious.

The ascent is now easy going and the wrinkled north face of Eiger is your constant companion. When you reach the road, take the second left signposted to Alpiglen and head up a broad gravel path, which passes through the forest and then shadows the railway tracks of the Wengernalpbahn. The trail weaves through pastures ablaze with purple gentians and thistles in summer, then dips under a small rail tunnel just before reaching the **Berghotel Alpiglen** (☎ 033 853 11 30; www .alpiglen.ch; dm/s/d Sfr35/45/90), two to 2½ hours from Grindelwald-Grund. Inquisitive goats, cows and gloriously muddy pigs roam freely around this charming wooden hut. Unsurprisingly, organic meat features highly on the menu (mains Sfr18 to Sfr25), with specialities such as flavoursome goat sausage and schnitzel. If you're not in a hurry, this is a relaxing place to spend the night.

The path recrosses the rail lines a short way above the hotel, climbing more gently now and skirting below Eiger's north face. Following a gurgling stream, the trail leads past undulating pastures and clumps of bilberry bushes and *Alpenrosen;* the latter bloom pink in early summer. Head on past clusters of weather-beaten mountain pines and farmhouses in the hollow of **Mettla** (1809m).

Make your way up to the ski lifts of Arvengarten to a path contouring the mountainsides at roughly 2000m. This minor pass provides a tremendous close-range vantage point of the savage ice and rock walls of Eiger (3970m), Mönch (4107m) and Jungfrau (4158m), which soar almost 2000m above you, and glaciers that spill down the rock faces like froth on cappuccino cups: vistas that will have you burning up the pixels on your digicam. Sidling up around the slopes below the rail line you arrive at the **Kleine Scheidegg** (2061m), 1¼ to 1¾ hours from Berghotel Alpiglen.

From the bustling Kleine Scheidegg train station, walkers can opt to make the return trip by cog railway up to the Jungfraujoch – but don't expect the ticket price to be much cheaper than the expensive fare charged from Grindelwald itself! If you hike down, you'll be rewarded with yet more dazzling views to blindingly white peaks including the fin-shaped, icing-smooth Silberhorn (3695m). Also keep an eye out for the enigma of Kriegsloch, a mysterious permanent hole in the Giessengletscher.

Head gently down along the broad path to the left of the train line, dipping under the tracks shortly before you come to the station of **Wengernalp** at 1874m. There are more wonderful views ahead, including the Gspaltenhorn and Schilthorn beyond where the land plunges away into the deep glacial trough of the Lauterbrunnental. A track leads on northward through pockets of Alpine forest to cross the railway yet again, whereafter a well-formed roadway winds around the slopes via Allmend to reach the car-free mountain resort of Wengen (p186) at 1274m after 1½ to two hours.

From **Wengen** train station, follow the sign-posted walking track back under the rail lines onto a narrow road. The route soon begins a steep descent in short spirals through tall forests of spruce and maple, twice crossing the railway in quick succession. There are occasional glimpses through the foliage upvalley toward the 3785m Lauterbrunner Breithorn and the cascading Staubbach Falls. Drop on down through open slopes to cross the raging torrent of the Weisse Lütschine on a foot-bridge just before coming out at the main street in **Lauterbrunnen** (p184) at 796m after a final 40 to 50 minutes.

FAULHORNWEG

Duration 4¾ to 6¼ hours
Distance 15km
Difficulty Medium
Nearest Town Grindelwald (p179)
Summary With spellbinding views to the Jungfrau giants, this high-level panoramic route from Schynige Platte via Faulhorn to First is one of the Bernese Oberland's classic walks.

High above the treeline at elevations mostly over 2000m, this spirit-soaring ridgetop hike affords long views across turquoise Brienzersee and to the towering north faces of four of Europe's most famous peaks: Wetterhorn, Eiger, Mönch and Jungfrau. The Faulhornweg leads through the geologically fascinating range separating the Jungfrau region from the Brienzersee, with twisted and overlayed rock strata and karst fields as well as some of the most dramatic ridge formations you'll find anywhere in the Swiss Alps.

The Faulhornweg can easily be broken into two leisurely days by overnighting en route at Männdlenen or Berghotel Faulhorn, but you'll need to book ahead and bring a sleeping bag. The walk uses mountain transport to avoid any serious climbing yet still involves a gradual ascent totalling around 600m, which makes a rather tiring day. The final section of this trail between the Berghotel Faulhorn and First is a snow-cleared winter walking route.

Carry your own drinks as there's little running water up here. Given the high elevation, you should watch for signs of approaching bad weather. A recommended map is the SAW 1:50,000 *Interlaken* 254T (Sfr22.50).

Getting to/from the Walk

The trail head is Schynige Platte (1967m), accessible by the historic narrow-gauge cog railway from Wilderswil; see p177 for details. Trains run at least hourly from Grindelwald to Wilderswil (Sfr9, 29 minutes). The hike ends at First (2167m), from where the over-5km-long First-Bahn, one of Europe's longest gondola lifts, takes you down to Grindelwald. The First-Bahn runs daily from late May to late October; the one-way fare is Sfr32 and the last ride is at around 5pm.

The Walk

The arthritic old cog railway hauls walkers up some 1400m to the **Schynige Platte** station (1967m) in around 50 minutes. From this superb natural lookout, you get the first of the day's breathtaking vistas across to the perennially glaciated giants of the Jungfrau region. The views are utterly mesmerising – the iridescent peaks of Eiger, Mönch and Jungfrau rearing above rippling forests and wildflower-flecked pastures.

Before setting off for the day's hike, it is well worth visiting the Schynige Platte's **Alpengarten** (p177), showing typical Alpine blooms such as the elusive edelweiss. Walk northeast along a track over rolling pastures past the Alpine hut of Oberberg, heading gently upward above the green basin of Inner Iselten to reach **Louchera** (shown on some signposts as Laucheren) at 2020m. Not far from the Schynige Platte station, the Panoramaweg, a somewhat longer alternative route, diverges left and leads via the craggy 2069m Oberberghorn to Louchera, giving outstanding views down to Interlaken and glittering Brienzersee.

Head around scree slopes on the western side of the Loucherhorn (2230m) to cross over a low grassy crest. The way dips and rises as it sidles on through two gaps in rocky spurs on the mountain's southern flank before coming to **Egg**, a wide grassy pass at 2067m strewn with boulders and Alpine herbs, 1¼ to 1½ hours from Schynige Platte.

Egg opens out northeastward into the Sägistal, a tiny moorlike, sheep-grazed valley completely enclosed by ridges and without an above-ground outlet. Filling the lowest point within the basin, the aquamarine waters of the **Sägistalsee** (1937m) seep away subterraneously. Skirt up the Sägistal's southern side below the precipitous Indri Sägissa before swinging around southwest above the raw,

WALKING IN SWITZERLAND

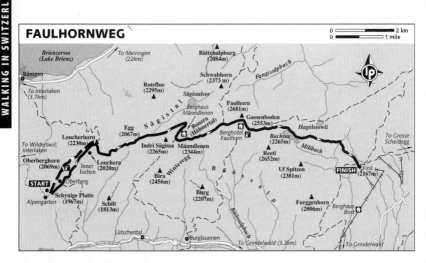

FAULHORNWEG

talus-choked gully of Bonera (or Hühnertal). The route picks its way up through an interesting landscape of rough karst slabs to arrive at the wood-shingled **Berghaus Männdlenen** (☎ 033 853 44 64; www.berghaus-maenndlenen.ch; dm with breakfast/half-board Sfr36/58; ⊗ mid-Jun–mid-Oct) on the little saddle of Männdlenen (2344m), one to 1½ hours on. This private restaurant/mountain hut has a small dorm for walkers. The sunsets here are spectacular and earlier risers stand a chance of spotting chamois grazing the surrounding slopes.

Make a steeply rising traverse along a broad ledge between stratified cliffs to gain the ridge of Winteregg, following white-red-white markings and metal posts northeastward. A short distance past a minor turn-off at 2546m, take a signposted foot track leading up left along the main range to arrive at the knobbly summit of 2681m **Faulhorn** (literally 'lazy rock'), one to 1¼ hours from Männdlenen. These lofty heights afford a spellbinding 360-degree panorama stretching from the grand trio of the Eiger, Mönch and Jungfrau to shimmering Brienzersee and Thunersee and, on clear days, as far as the Black Forest in Germany and Vosges in France.

Just below the summit sits the historic **Berghotel Faulhorn** (☎ 033 853 27 13; dm/s/d Sfr46/84/156; ⊗ late Jun–late Oct), which first opened for business in 1832 and is the oldest and highest mountain hotel in the Alps. Sit on the terrace to savour Valaisian specialities (mains Sfr18 to Sfr28) and views, or stay the night to appreciate a magical sunset and sunrise.

Keep an eye out for marmots as you descend the rounded, sparsely vegetated ridge to the little col of Gassenboden (2553m), then drop down eastward past an emergency shelter into the tiny grassy basin of the **Bachsee** (2265m). The gemstone-blue waters of this lake contrast starkly with the imposing, ice-shrouded peaks of (from left to right) the Wetterhorn (3701m), Schreckhorn (4078m) and Finsteraarhorn (4274m), which rise directly behind it – yet another marvellous view.

The path skirts the northern shore of the Bachsee, climbing gently past a smaller and slightly lower lake. A wide and well-trodden path now sidles gradually down through Alpine pastures high above the marshy streamlet of Milibach to the distant tinkling of cowbells, reaching the upper gondola-lift station at **First** (2167m) 1½ to two hours after leaving the Berghotel Faulhorn. First looks straight across to the narrow, snaking icefall of the Oberer Grindelwaldgletscher, and – unless you continue on foot to the Grosse Scheidegg, which adds another 1½ hours or so to the walk – this is the last high-level viewing point for what has been a particularly scenic walk.

CENTRAL SWITZERLAND

BÜRGENSTOCK FELSENWEG
Duration Two to 2½ hours
Distance 7.5km
Difficulty Easy
Nearest Town Lucerne (p243)

Summary This short walk with mild ascents and drops follows a spectacular route cut into sheer cliffs 500m above Lake Lucerne.

This panoramic half-day walk contours the Bürgenstock, often nicknamed the 'little brother of the Rigi', a high limestone ridge forming a peninsula that reaches across the cobalt waters of Lake Lucerne (Vierwaldstättersee). Although its upper heights reach a modest 1128m at the summit of Hammetschwand, Bürgenstock shows Lake Lucerne from its most beautiful angles, with tremendous views across the lake to Mt Pilatus, Lucerne and Mt Rigi.

Although some walkers prone to vertigo may find the *Felsenweg* (clifftop path) unnerving, the route is gentle, safe and suitable for families. The best available walking map is Nidwalder Wanderwege's 1:25,000 *Nidwalder Wanderkarte* (around Sfr20).

Getting to/from the Walk

The easiest (and most romantic) way to reach the trail head at Bürgenstock is to take a ferry to Kehrsiten-Bürgenstock (462m). From late May until late September, there are about a dozen boats daily from Lucerne (Sfr14.60, 30 to 50 minutes). From the Kehrsiten-Bürgenstock landing jetty, the funicular runs up to Bürgenstock during the same period; the one-way funicular fare is Sfr12.20/6.10 for adults/children (Half-Fare Card valid, see p367). Ennetbürgen, at the end of the walk, is also serviced by the Lake Lucerne ferries.

The Walk

From the upper funicular station at **Bürgenstock** (874m), walk east through the self-contained luxury resort of Bürgenstock Hotels, then turn left onto a broad gravelled walkway. Cut into the cliff face, the vertiginous path skirts around the limestone ridge above lushly forested cliffs that plummet 500m straight down to the lake. Head on through sun-dappled, ferny woodlands, where frequent breaks in the trees offer views across sparkling Lake Lucerne to rugged Mt Pilatus (2132m) behind you, the tilted form of Mt Rigi (1797m) ahead and northward as far as the Zugersee (Lake Zug) behind Lucerne. The walk is enchanting in autumn when the beech trees turn gold and mist swirls around the peaks.

After 30 to 35 minutes, you come to the **Hammetschwand-Lift**. This skeletal 160m structure was fixed onto the cliff face in 1905 and is still the highest free-standing lift in Europe. Now you face a choice: you can either take the minute-long ride (adult/child Sfr9/5.60) to Hammetschwand for a full panorama, stretching around from the Mittelland to the main peaks of the Central Swiss Alps in the south, or continue straight to Chänzeli. If you opt for the lift, listen for the oohs and ahs as you are catapulted up the cave-riddled cliff face and enjoy – albeit quickly – views stretching far over the lake and a patchwork of hills, valleys and forest. Savour the panorama over a drink on the terrace at **Hammetschwand Restaurant** (☎ 041 610 81 10; ◷ 9am-6pm May–mid-Oct) before walking to the lookout at 1128m. From here a trail leads through pastures and mixed woodlands to Chänzeli.

Alternatively, forgo the lift and take an alternative route through a series of short tunnels blasted into the vertical rock walls, with sturdy steel railings and frequent bench seats

---

SWISS PATH

Equipped with a decent pair of walking boots, you can circumnavigate Lake Uri (p253) on foot via the **Swiss Path** (Weg der Schweiz; www.weg-der-schweiz.ch, in German), inaugurated to commemorate the 700th anniversary of the 1291 pact and running from Brunnen to Rütli. As the spectacular views unfold, so too does the symbolism – the trail is divided into 26 sections, each representing a different canton, from the founding trio to Johnny-come-lately Jura (1979). As you stride, bear in mind that 5mm of track represents one Swiss resident, so populous Zürich spans 6.1km and rural Appenzell Innerrhoden a mere 71m.

The 35km, two-day walk over hill and dale takes in some of Central Switzerland's finest scenery, cutting through meadows flecked with orchids and ox-eye daisies, revealing classic Alpine panoramas, shimmying close to the lakeshore and then dipping back into ferny forest. You'll pass historically significant landmarks such as the Tellskapelle and the obelisk commemorating Schiller. To get a true sense of the area, it's worth completing the entire trail, although it can be broken down into shorter chunks. See the website for maps and distances.

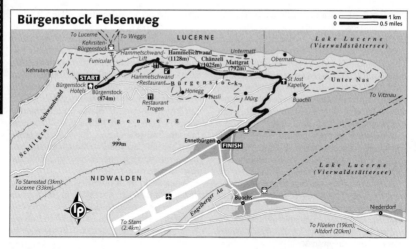

for the giddy. The *Felsenweg* passes under a final tunnel gate just before terminating at a junction, after which the white-red-white marked path (signposted 'Waldstätterweg') continues east along the wooded crest of the ridge via **Chänzeli** (1025m). The trail zigzags down through the forest, with rocks and tree roots forming a natural staircase at times, to reach Mattgrat (792m) 25 to 30 minutes on. The several houses here at the end of a gravelled road look down over open slopes toward the village of Ennetbürgen in a cove of Lake Lucerne.

Make your way gently up past a small private cableway (which services the isolated farmlet of Untermatt on the lakeshore), bearing left at a fork not far before you get to the historic **St Jost Kapelle** after 20 to 25 minutes. Situated at 690m on a grassy pasture high above the blue waters of the lake, this tiny whitewashed chapel was erected in 1733 as the final resting place of a medieval hermit who lived beneath a nearby granite boulder. During its renovation some years ago, original frescos were discovered under the interior plaster.

Cut diagonally down over the green fields past an enormous barnyard to some scattered farmhouses, then take a signposted path that doubles back briefly left alongside an overgrown fence. After crossing a minor road the route steers right again and sidles along the lightly forested lakeside to meet a sealed street at the edge of **Ennetbürgen**. Follow this straight down past the ferry dock to arrive at the village centre, 40 to 50 minutes from St Jost.

NORTHEASTERN SWITZERLAND

ZWINGLIPASS

Duration Two days
Distance 17.5km
Difficulty Medium
Nearest Town Appenzell

Summary This two-day hike leads through austerely beautiful karst scenery and rural valleys to cross a broad pass at the northern foot of the jagged Churfirsten.

Often overlooked in favour of obvious Alpine regions, the limestone peaks, fir-clad valleys and rustic farmhouses of this corner of Appenzellerland still feel like a well-kept secret. Leading past the Sämtisersee and Fälensee lakes, the route climbs through a remarkable karst landscape, which has sculpted sinkholes on the heights of the 2011m Zwinglipass. The perpendicular turrets and pinnacles of the Alpenstein Massif jut up so abruptly from gently contoured hills that they seem much higher than they actually are.

This two-day hike can normally be undertaken from around early June until early November. It is worth booking accommodation ahead. The SAW 1:50,000 *Appenzell* 227T (Sfr22.50) is a detailed map of the area.

Getting to/from the Walk

The walk begins in Brülisau, served by hourly postal buses from Appenzell (Sfr6.80, 15 minutes). For details of transport connections to Appenzell, see p291. The hike ends in Wildhaus, where it is advisable to spend the night – see the website www.wildhaus.ch for details – as return connections to Appenzell are irregular and lengthy (around two hours).

The Walk

DAY 1: BRÜLISAU TO BERGGASTHAUS BOLLENWEES

2½-3 hours / 7.5km / 548m ascent

From the lower Hoher Kasten cable-car station follow the signposted sealed road southeast, quickly crossing underneath the wires, past scattered wooden-shingled houses in the green fields to Pfannenstiel (940m). The quiet dirt road leads into the forested Brüeltobel Gorge, rising up over a watershed to reach **Gasthaus Plattenbödeli** (☎ 071 799 11 52; www .plattenboedeli.ch; snacks & mains Sfr8-28; ☉ May-Nov) after one to 1¼ hours. This rustic hut serves an array of tasty cheese dishes.

About 50m on take a path (signposted 'Waldabstieg') down left to the **Sämtisersee**,

making your way around the shoreline to meet the road again on flowery paddocks at the lake's upper side. Ringed by steep forested slopes and jagged peaks, the Sämtisersee is one of the most attractive natural spots in the Alpstein Massif, and in summer its shallow waters are generally warm enough for bathing.

Bear right at a fork at Appenzeller Sämtis, and head on toward the towering peaks of the Alpstein through a charming valley in which a stream flows through a terraced trench. The dirt track peters out at the farmlet of Rheintaler Sämtis (1295m), and a foot track marked with white-red-white paint splashes continues up to the grassy flats of Chalberweid below the canyonlike rock spikes of the Marwees Ridge.

Ignoring the trails going off right to the Bogartenlücke and the Widderalpsattel ahead, ascend southward via a steep gully onto a tiny saddle from where the stark, elongated form of the **Fälensee** (1446m) slides into view, around 1¼ to 1½ hours from the Gasthaus Plattenbödeli.

EVELYNE BINSACK, MOUNTAINEER & EXPEDITIONIST

The first Swiss woman to climb Everest, a trained helicopter pilot and mountain guide, an expeditionist who cycled, walked and skied 484 days from Innertkirchen to the south pole – the career of Evelyne Binsack (www.binsack.ch) reads like a gripping adventure novel. Modest in the flesh, the woman that has stunned Switzerland with her exploits takes time out after a morning's climbing in the Bernese Oberland to answer a few questions.

How do you feel in the mountains?

Free. Mountains don't prove your strength, they teach you how to fight and overcome weaknesses. When I confronted Everest in 2001, I was overwhelmed both physically and spiritually by the mountain – it has an incredible energy. To climb you need to respect the mountains and know your limits; people that rush headlong regardless usually end up hurting themselves. If I had to choose between two things in life, the mountains would always win. Even if it were a choice between a man or a mountain. My boyfriend knows he can never compete [laughs].

Tell us about Expedition Antarctica.

In 2006 I set out from Innertkirchen on a 25,000km expedition to Antarctica. Of course, there were special moments, such as meeting indigenous people in South America and seeing a huge full moon on the horizon, but often I was just thankful for basics like food, water and ending the day dry. In Antarctica I pushed my body to the limit, pulling 115kg on a sled in -40°C temperatures. My only thought was surviving the day, sometimes the hour ahead. Six days before the end, I had a physical breakdown, so I tapped into the energy of family at home, drew an imaginary cross above me and prayed. In retrospect I learned the real meaning of positive thinking. When I finally reached the south pole, I felt thankful, relieved and happy. Like 'whoa, here I am!'

Now you're back home in the Bernese Oberland, where do you climb?

Wendenstöcke is a dream area, as the limestone cliffs are physically and mentally challenging. I prefer limestone to granite as it's more tactile and playful. I enjoy high glacier tours on the north face of Mönch and the silence and grandeur of Wetterhorn. Life quality in Switzerland is fantastic, within 20 minutes I can be in 40 different areas.

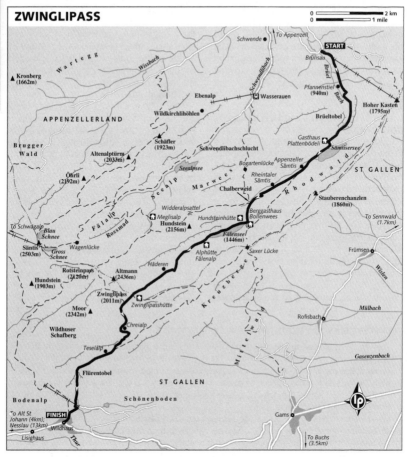

ZWINGLIPASS

A short way ahead at 1471m stands the scenic **Berggasthaus Bollenwees** (☎ 071 799 11 70; dm/s/ d Sfr35/68/120; ☼ mid-May–Oct), looking out across the deep-blue Fälensee, a typical karst lake, which drains away subterraneously to fill an enclosed glacial trough below towering craggy ranges. The pine-panelled rooms are a cosy place to spend the night. Breakfast is quite a spread, with fresh Alpine milk and cheese.

DAY 2: BERGGASTHAUS BOLLENWEES TO WILDHAUS
3½-4½ hours / 10km / 966m ascent

Head around the Fälensee's northern edge, sidling across broad scree fields that slide right into the water to reach the rustic Alphütte Fälenalp at the lake's far end. Braving

avalanches and rock fall, the Alpine huts of this romantic isolated pasture have dairy products for sale in season. Above you, spectacular needles protrude from the almost overhanging rock walls of the **Hundstein** (2156m). Continue on past marmot colonies in the tiny upper valley, before beginning quite a steep climb along a grassy ridge leading up to the three stone shelters of Häderen at 1738m, one to 1¼ hours from the Bollenwees.

The route now rises more gently through long fields of karst, with superb views ahead to the 2436m Altmann. Shaped like a bishop's mitre and rising dramatically above the valley, this is the Alpstein's second-highest summit. After passing through a drystone fence marking the Appenzell–St Gallen cantonal border, cross over the Zwinglipass (2011m), a rocky, grassy plateau full of depressions and sink-holes, then descend briefly leftward to arrive at the **Zwinglipasshütte** (☎ 071 988 28 02), 40 to 50 minutes on. This self-catering hut owned by the SAC is staffed only on summer weekends (but is always open), and sits at 1999m on a lookout terrace opposite the seven saw-blade peaks of the serrated Churfirsten.

Drop down the grassy mountainside, moving over to the left past Chreialp (1817m), a group of herder's huts standing below sheer cliffs opposite a prominent rock needle. The well-formed path now makes a much steeper descent in numerous switchbacks to reach **Teselalp** (1433m) at the end of a farm track in a pleasant upper valley, after 50 minutes to 1¼ hours.

Follow the dirt road for 1.25km to where a signposted foot track departs at the left. Make your way 400m down via the small dry chasm known as Flürentobel, before branching away to the right through little clearings in the spruce forest to meet another road near a gondola lift. Continue down, short-cutting the odd curve in the road to arrive at **Wildhaus**, 50 to 60 minutes from Teselalp. The village centre (1090m), a short way down to the right along the main road, has several hotels and restaurants.

GRAUBÜNDEN

RUIN' AULTA
Duration 3½ to four hours
Distance 12km
Difficulty Easy to medium
Nearest Town Chur (p298)
Summary This walk leads through the deep Ruin' Aulta, a remarkable limestone gorge where natural erosion has produced bizarre pillars and columns in the chalky white cliffs.

Affectionately dubbed the 'Swiss Grand Canyon', the fascinating ravine Ruin' Aulta is the result of one of Europe's largest-ever mountain landslides, the Flimser Bergsturz. Some 10,000 years ago, the enormous glacier filling the Surselva Valley retreated back to the headwaters of the Vorderrhein (Rein Anteriur in Romansch) and the mountains, where the skiing village of Flims now stands, collapsed. Over the following millennia, the Vorderrhein gradually cut its way through deposits of debris to shape this 400m-deep gorge, the Ruin' Aulta ('high quarry' in Romansch).

This half-day ramble takes you through pristine forests and fantastical landscapes of starkly eroded limestone pinnacles, caverns and pillars that border the snaking Vorderrhein. Still impassable for cars, the Ruin' Aulta is an important sanctuary for wildlife. In places, the continually eroding path calls for some sure-footedness. The SAW 1:50,000 *Sardona* 247T (Sfr22.50) covers the walk.

Getting to/from the Walk
The walk begins in Trin, a small village on the Tamins–Flims–Laax road. Trains run hourly from Chur (Sfr8.20, 20 minutes). There are also hourly rail connections from Ilanz (Sfr8.20, 18 minutes), where postal buses depart frequently for Flims and Falera. The walk ends at the Valendas-Sagogn train station on the Chur–Disentis line, where there are hourly trains back to Chur (Sfr11.80, 31 minutes) and Ilanz (Sfr4, 10 minutes).

The Walk
On the main road at the uphill side of **Trin** (876m), take the signposted footpath leading down through the lower village of Trin-Digg. A lonely country lane (the Senda Sursilvana, marked with yellow diamonds) winds south-west through farmland, rolling pastures and pockets of beech, fir and pine forest on a long, broad terrace overlooking the valley of the Surselva. The impressive rock formation ahead to the right is the unfortunately named Crap da Flem, whose massive cliffs rise up abruptly behind the Alpine resort of Flims, giving the mountain an awesome fortresslike appearance.

After the roadway swings around northward, follow route markings down left across the glacially cold Flem Stream and continue left up a farm track to pass a cluster of wooden chalets at **Pintrun** (832m). Walk on up the dirt road, punctuated by lovingly tended orchards and gardens, over a slight crest. The path leads through sun-dappled forest, where gaps in the trees reveal tantalising glimpses of the deep gorge below. Descend on to **Ransun**, a precipitous lookout point at 805m above the Vorderrhein about 50 minutes from Trin. The views are tremendous – reaching across the wild, glistening river to undulating wooded hills, which contrast dramatically with the chiselled limestone cliffs. It's a perfect spot for a picnic.

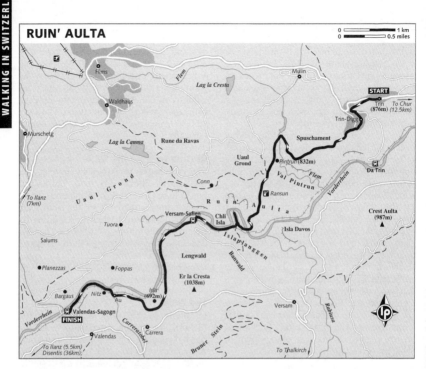

RUIN' AULTA

Steps and tree roots lead swiftly down through pine and larch woods, where the sound of rushing water and birds of prey are often your only companions. The white-red-white marked trail now zigzags down quite steeply, with several viewpoints on the way affording snapshots of the milky turquoise river below and close-ups of the knife-edge pinnacles that razor their way above the forest. Emerging into the gorge, the path crosses the river on the pedestrian section of the **railway bridge**, 1¼ to 1½ hours from Trin.

A worthwhile 15-minute side trip to the tip of the peninsula known as **Chli Isla** or Chrummwag can be made 200m after the rail bridge, where various rough trails lead rightward down through 'wild' campsites. Immediately opposite, the weirdly sculpted chalky white cliffs of the Ruin' Aulta tower above the river. After climbing over a small, steep ridge past the turn-off to Versam village, the main path drops down to the Chrummwag tunnel and traces the contours of the Vorderrhein upstream past small waterfalls and beaches. In places the swift-flowing river forms raging white-water rapids, and on summer days many inflatable rafts and kayaks float past.

Where the river makes another sweeping curve, cut straight ahead through more damp forest, rising slightly to cross over the rail tracks at the **Staziun Versam-Safien** (635m), another 30 to 40 minutes on. Versam train station, sitting high up on a glacial terrace at the mouth of the Safiental, looks across to another impressive cliff face of the Ruin' Aulta. Except in midsummer, this part of the valley receives little direct sunlight. **LinX-Beisl** (☎ 081 645 11 91; snacks Sfr9-18.50; ✆ 10am-7pm Sun-Thu, 9.30am-8pm Fri & Sat Apr-late Oct) makes a great pit stop for a salad or slice of homemade plum strudel. Wolfgang can arrange rafting and kayaking excursions here. There is also basic dorm accommodation (Sfr30 per night with own sleeping bag).

Continue on above the rail lines, in places following embankments that protect the railway from landslides. Here the route leads through an otherworldly eroded landscape of caverns, chasms and twirling columns formed in the unstable pulverised earth. Climb on leftward through pine forest to skirt above the farmlet of **Isla** (692m), from where the ski villages of Laax and Falera stand out on the slopes across the valley, then descend gently through the woods to reach the picturesque hamlet of Au after one to 1¼ hours. Cross the gushing Carreratobel via the rail bridge, and once again make your way upstream between the train tracks and the river. After passing final sections of chalk cliffs, the path arrives at the **Staziun Valendas-Sagogn** (669m) after a further 15 to 20 minutes.

PARPANER ROTHORN

Duration Five to seven hours
Distance 18km
Difficulty Medium
Nearest Town Arosa (p302)
Summary This popular day walk leads past sparkling Alpine lakes under some of the rawest crags in the Swiss Alps, culminating at the highest summit in the Plessur Massif.

The Parpaner Rothorn owes its striking 'red horn' formation to the brittle, copper-bearing rock typical of the Plessur Massif. From the early medieval period, the ore was mined high up on these bare mountainsides and carried down to Arosa for smelting. In places, the remains of shafts and mining huts are still visible. After the disastrous Plurs landslide of 1618 wiped out the owners of the mine, the Vertemati-Franchi family, the workings gradually fell into disuse.

Although there are few real difficulties, this is a serious high-Alpine walk with an ascent of over 1000m. The route is usually inaccessible before late June and after late October. Be sure to get an early start and check weather conditions before you head out, as this hike is not much fun when cloud descends or rain makes the loose rocks perilously slippery. Most recommended is the local tourist authority's 1:25,000 *Lenzerheide Wanderkarte* (Sfr15). Free maps at the Hörnli Express station also cover part of the hike.

Getting to/from the Walk

From Arosa train station there are free public buses at least half-hourly to the lower station of the Hörnli Express gondola lift, where the walk begins. The walk can be shortened by taking the **cable car** (Rothornbahn; ☎ 081 385 50 00) from Parpaner Rothorn to Lenzerheide, but the one-way fare is Sfr28/5 per adult/child and the roughly three-hour walk down is very pleasant. The cable car runs at least

half-hourly between June and October; the last downward ride is at 4.50pm. A one-day Wanderbillett covering cable car, train and postal bus travel (Lenzerheide–Rothorn–Arosa–Chur–Lenzerheide) is available from tourist offices for Sfr54 (Sfr62 including Hörnli Express). For details on how to reach Arosa, see p302.

The Walk

From the Hörnli Express gondola stop (1811m), a path (signposted 'Erzhornsattel') leads southwest below the cableway up to a narrow Alpine track that threads like a ribbon through the velvety pastures. Continue left gently out of the treeline on slopes overlooking Arosa to reach the inky green-blue **Schwellisee** (1933m) after just 15 to 20 minutes. Ringed by sheep-grazed meadows, this lake is a beautiful, if very popular, spot.

Cross the wooden footbridge over the babbling Plessur and continue up a track around the lake's eastern side above the meadows of the Arosa Alp past the isolated cluster of old arolla pines known as **Arven** (2060m). Several springs – to which locals once attributed magical powers – emerge just above here. The path recrosses the gravelly stream to meet routes going off to the Restaurant Alpenblick and Innerarosa. There is a large wooden emergency shelter (day use only) a few minutes down from this junction.

A short, steeper climb brings you up over a grassy crest above the exquisitely turquoise **Älplisee** (2156m), 30 to 45 minutes from the Schwellisee. This glassy Alpine lake fills a deep gully directly under the Schaftällihorn (2546m) and Älpliseehorn (2725m), whose rugged crags drop away into sweeping scree slides. There are also some last clear views north toward the Weisshorn (2653m) and the green, rolling Churer Alpen.

Head on above the Älplisee, following the white-red-white signs, and make a long sidling ascent through the Alpine pastures of Schafälpli, an area inhabited by hordes of whistling marmots. The path continues up through the sparse slopes of Gredigs Älpli high above the tiny Tötseeli, an often snow-filled tarn in the very head of the valley, to arrive at **Gredigs Fürggli** (2617m), one to 1½ hours from the Älplisee. This gap in the ridge gives views stretching northeast to the limestone peaks of the Rhätikon and northwest toward the snowcapped Glarner Alps. Below

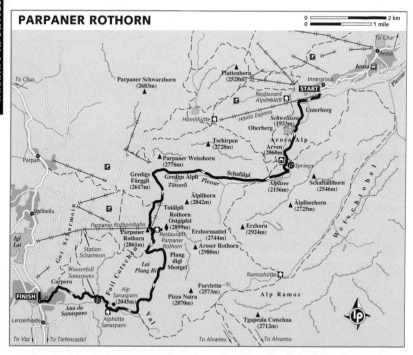

PARPANER ROTHORN

in the valley of Lenzerheide lies the idyllic Igl Lai (Heidsee).

Walk left along the narrow dirt road through a long wooden avalanche gallery (the curious 'box tunnel' visible on your ascent) to a winter chairlift. A geological path (with signs in German explaining local mineral phenomena) leads on up the red-rock ridge, barren but for sparse grasses, lichen and white marguerites, to the upper cable-car station on the summit of the **Parpaner Rothorn** (2861m), 45 minutes to one hour from Gredigs Fürggli. Here the Restaurant Parpaner Rothorn has a small terrace overlooking these raw ranges, but is rather pricey.

A marked path continues east along the ridge to the slightly higher summit of the Rothorn Ostgipfel at 2899m (40 minutes return).

A broad trail winds down steeply southward to a turn-off at a minor dip in the ridge. Here, cut down left (east) into the Plang digl Mestgel, a grassy bowl under the Aroser Rothorn (2980m). Continue along an old lateral moraine covered with bilberry heath past the tiny, shallow Lai Plang Bi. The route leads on smoothly down through the *Alpenrose* meadows and cow pastures of Val, crossing the deeply eroded Aua da Sanaspans just before reaching the farmlet of Alp Sanaspans (2045m), 1½ to two hours from the Parpaner Rothorn. Not far down is the cosy **Alphütte Sanaspans** (☎ 079 357 75 55; ✆ early Jul-late Sep), where the cheery owners serve refreshments to outside tables literally until the cows come home. Sample their homemade organic bread and creamy cheese, or nut tart with a glass of fresh-from-the-cow buttermilk.

A few paces down turn right and recross the stream on a footbridge above several springs gushing out of the mossy embankment. The path now descends in steep switchbacks through forest of spruce, larch and mountain pine past the **Wasserfall Sanaspans** (1840m), a spouting 20m cascade, to meet a narrow gravelled forest road. Follow this briefly right, then cut down left under power transmission cables before coming out onto the parklike meadow of Carpera (1545m) at the upper edge of Lenzerheide. The street called Voa Trotsch leads down past holiday houses to the main road through **Lenzerheide**, one to 1½ hours from Alp Sanaspans. The postal bus terminal is a few minutes along to the right.

LAI DA TUMA CIRCUIT

Duration Four to five hours
Distance 8.5km
Difficulty Easy to medium
Nearest Towns Andermatt (p262) and Disentis (p307)
Summary This delightful high-level route takes you through an Alpine nature reserve and along the crest of the Pazolastock Range to the source of the mighty Rhine.

The sparkling lake known to Romansch speakers as Lai da Tuma (Tomasee in German) is considered the ultimate source of the Rhine. Here Graubünden meets the Gotthard region, the central mountain hub of the Swiss Alps. Walkers often sight golden eagles soaring about the surrounding granite summits since these magnificent Alpine raptors were successfully reintroduced into the area during the early 1990s.

This is a circuit walk that returns to Oberalp Pass. Setting out from an altitude of over 2000m, you have a relatively modest ascent of less than 700m to negotiate. The top of the range around the Pazolastock is very exposed to the elements, however, so keep an eye on the weather. Recommended is the SAW 1:50,000 walking map *Disentis/Mustér 256T* (Sfr22.50).

Getting to/from the Walk

The walk begins and ends at the Oberalp Pass, the highest point on the narrow-gauge Furka–Oberalp Bahn (FOB) mountain railway (which links Disentis with Brig in the Valais). There are almost-hourly train connections to Andermatt (Sfr7.60, 20 minutes) and Disentis (Sfr10.20, 38 minutes). Private vehicles can be left at the free car park on the Oberalppass.

The Walk

Flanked by raw granite peaks and disappearing on the horizon like a natural infinity pool, the beautiful elongated Oberalpsee at the **Oberalp Pass** (2044m) is the starting point for the walk. From the small train station by the lake, walk 200m up to the Restaurant Alpsu. Take the dirt road opposite, then cut right over the open slopes above a cross mounted on a rock outcrop. The path climbs alongside a grassy and rocky spur, past classic high-

land moors dappled with anemones and gentians, in the tiny upper valley of Puozas. As you make your way up past clear streams, arrow-shaped peaks and slopes streaked with bilberry bushes and *Alpenrosen,* the whirr of traffic from the Oberalp Pass fades. Occasional marmot whistle aside, peace reigns on these lonely heights.

Negotiate a series of tight switchbacks uphill through scree-strewn slopes, where snow patches sometimes linger until summer. Looking back, you have fine views across pastures speckled with inky blue tarns.

Pass makeshift stone bunkers built by wartime soldiers, coming to a signpost on the exposed **ridgetop** at 2571m after one to 1½ hours. A side route from here goes down to the village of Andermatt, now visible to the west in the valley of the Reuss. Behind Andermatt, the 3500m summits of the ice-capped Winterberg Massif and fin-like Galenstock rise up on the Uri-Valais cantonal border.

There are more giddying perspectives down to the valley and twisting Oberalppass as you scale the mountain. The white-red-white

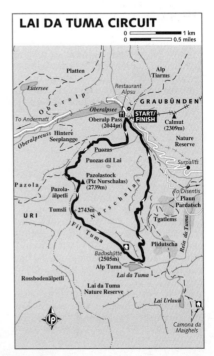

LAI DA TUMA CIRCUIT

marked route continues up the ridge past two rustic military buildings just under the 2739m **Pazolastock** (Piz Nurschalas), commanding a 360-degree panorama over the surrounding glaciated crags, which reaches as far as Innsbruck on a clear day. If you're lucky, you may spot a golden eagle. The trail now traverses the exposed crest of the craggy range with just enough rockhopping to make the going fun and unstrenuous for the sure-footed.

At point 2743 follow the Fil Tuma southeastward, and sidle steadily down along the grassy, rock-strewn right-hand side of the ridge to arrive at the **Badushütte** (☎ 032 512 83 84; dm Sfr25; ⏱ Jun-late Sep) a further one to 1½ hours on. This cosy SAC hut at 2505m is built against a low cliff face looking out toward the 2928m Badus (Six Madun). Snacks like soup and sausages are served in season. You can overnight in the simple dorms but, as the humorous owner will tell you, there's no breakfast except for the liquid kind – beer. Clued-up photographers often sleep here to catch the lake in the stillness of morning.

The path descends quickly over boulders to a signposted trail leading down to the shore of **Lai da Tuma** (2343m), 15 to 20 minutes from the hut. This dazzling blue-green lake lies in a cirque ringed by velvety green crags, formed by the grinding action of an extinct hanging glacier. The Vorderrhein, the true source of the Rhine, rises here. In hot weather its snow-fed waters are good for a speedy splash, and the lush natural lawns around the inlet are ideal for a midday picnic. Cotton grass, a species typical in waterlogged soils, thrives here. On the ungrazed slopes of the Alp Tuma just above you can find plants that are rare on cow-trodden pastures.

While the lake outlet, the **Rein da Tuma**, burbles out of sight to the northeast, the walk continues northward from the signpost above Lai da Tuma. Wind your way down the initially rocky hillside, past cow-grazed pastures and waterfalls, toward the multiple hairpin bends of the busy pass road, then turn left where you come onto the trail leading down from the Val Maighels. The path now sidles along flower-studded slopes, gradually moving around to meet the small stream flowing down from the pass. Follow the often-boggy banks gently up to arrive back at the Oberalp Pass, one to 1½ hours from the Lai da Tuma.

LAKES OF MACUN

Duration 7½ to 8½ hours
Distance 16km
Difficulty Hard
Nearest Town Zernez (p315)
Summary Unspoilt mountainscapes, wildlife encounters, exhilarating climbs, Piz Buin views – this challenging day trek through the remote Swiss National Park has the lot.

This highly rewarding, if rather strenuous, day walk leads up from the main valley of the Engadine into the magical lakeland of the Macun Basin. The Macun lies at around 2600m, and only the hardiest wildflowers and snow grasses survive its high-Alpine climate. Like a natural amphitheatre, the cirque is ringed by craggy peaks rising to over 3000m and sprinkled with almost two dozen Alpine lakes and tarns.

With a total ascent/descent of around 1400m, there is a lot of ground to cover in a day, so an early start is essential. Sure-footedness is a prerequisite, though avid hikers will find the scrambling just as stimulating as the scenery. Make sure you take enough water and snacks, as there is nothing en route. The highest part of the trek leads along an exposed ridge at nearly 3000m and may remain snow-bound into summer. Check the weather before heading out. Walking poles are recommended as is a decent map – try Lower Engadine tourist authority's 1:50,000 *Wanderkarte Scuol* (Sfr16).

Getting to/from the Walk

The walk begins in Lavin and ends in Zernez (p316). It is easiest to base yourself in Zernez, take an early morning train to Lavin and effectively walk back. There is free parking near the train station in Zernez. Hourly trains operate between Lavin and Zernez (Sfr5.60, 10 to 20 minutes).

The Walk

Situated directly south of Piz Buin above the Inn River, the achingly pretty Engadine village of **Lavin** (1412m), with its archetypal frescoed chalets, is the start of the hike. From the village square just below the train station, walk 250m down the main street to a barrel-like fountain, then proceed left to cross the turquoise Inn River on a roofed wooden bridge. Continue up to the right along the gravelled lane for 1.25km past a tight bend, before leaving off left on a track that twists up eastward through pine forest, affording snapshots of glaciated peaks through the foliage, to **Plan Surücha** (1577m).

A broad path rises on gently up the thickly forested slopes. The trail veers gradually southward to cross the fast-flowing Aua da Zeznina on a small wooden bridge. Views to the rugged 2889m Piz Macun and 2850m Fuorcletta da Barcli open up as you approach the stone cottage at **Alp Zeznina Dadaint** (1958m) around two hours from Lavin. Scenes from *Heidi* were shot at this idyllic spot and it's easy to see why – the Alpine meadows look out northward to the 3000m snowcapped peaks around the distinctively pyramid-shaped Piz Buin, on whose southern slopes the side valleys of Val Sagliains, the

Val Lavinuoz and the Val Tuoi drop steeply into the Engadine.

Make your way into the Val Zeznina past a trail going off left to Murtèra, then climb numerous steep switchbacks through Alpine pastures strewn with *Alpenrosen* and riddled with marmot holes. You'll feel your thighs as the steep ascent continues via a gully filled with loose old moraines, where it can be slippery underfoot. Snow patches often linger here well into summer. The gradient eventually eases as you rise up to a rustic shelter built against cliffs beside a tarn. Cross over the streamlet and continue along its rocky western banks to enter the national park. After passing a larger lake, the upper valley opens

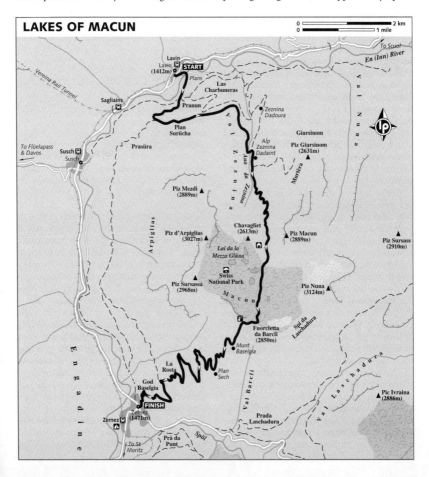

LAKES OF MACUN

LLAMA RAMA

Whether you've got kids in tow or just fancy a South American–style adventure, **Lama Trekking Engiadina** (☎ 079 601 55 77; www .lamatrekking-engiadina.ch; Baselgias, Lavin) has just the solution – doe-eyed, sure-footed llamas to accompany you on walks that take in the glorious forests, mountains and meadows of the Engadine. There's nothing like a camelid with impeccable eco credentials to motivate little 'uns to walk and love it. Half-day treks cost Sfr65 for adults and Sfr45 for children, while longer day and multiday treks are also available.

---

out into the undulating basin of **Macun**, 1½ to two hours from Alp Zeznina Dadaint.

'Wow' is the word that springs to mind at Macun, enclosed on three sides by a craggy mountain cirque. Unfurling before you like a crumpled cloak bejewelled with opal and topaz gemstones, the rippling, lake-studded landscape is set against a theatrical backdrop of glacier-topped mountains to the north, crowned by the 3312m Piz Buin. It's a terrific place to pack out a picnic and watch shafts of light pick out the contours of the rounded heights. The highest tarn is known in Romansch as the **Lai da la Mezza Glüna** (2631m).

Cross the stream and follow the white-red-white markings southward up sparsely vegetated ridges of glacial debris. As the track becomes fainter and steepens, greater concentration is required. Sure-footedness and a head for heights are essential on the next stretch of the route, which climbs steeply over slopes of coarse, loose rock, with occasional sections of scrambling that bring you up to the **Fuorcletta da Barcli**, a gap in the range at 2850m. From here traverse west along an exposed rocky ridgetop to reach a minor peak at 2945m one to 1½ hours from Macun. A sense of both relief and exhilaration is palpable as you reach the summit.

This sublime lookout commands top-of-the-world views. To the southwest the panorama stretches up the Engadine Valley from Zernez immediately below as far as the glistening white outline of 4049m Piz Bernina, and to the southeast across the park's wild valleys to the 3905m Ortler in South Tyrol, Italy. There is also a fine vista back to the Macun basin. From these giddy heights, eagles are often spotted above and grazing ibex and chamois on the slopes below.

In many ways, the descent is just as tough as the climb on tired knees. Trace a prominent spur running southwest directly from the summit, then drop away rightward out of the national park. The route leads down through rows of avalanche grids on the open slopes of Munt Baselgia to meet an Alpine track at **Plan Sech** (2268m). Apart from occasional short-cuts at some of the curves, keep to this (gradually improving) road, making a long serpentine descent into the mixed coniferous forest via La Rosta and God Baselgia. The final stretch leads out onto grassy fields just above the town, then down past the church to arrive at the main road in **Zernez** at 1471m after 2½ to three hours. The train station is a further 10 to 15 minutes' walk to the left.

TICINO

CIMA DELLA TROSA

Duration 3¾ to five hours
Distance 10km
Difficulty Easy
Nearest Town Locarno (p336)
Summary This short high-level route traverses the rounded mountaintops, affording eagle's-eye perspectives of the glittering Lago Maggiore and majestic Alpine peaks without the crowds.

Passing centuries-old hamlets and villages occupied only in summer and still only accessible on foot or horseback, this walk has a rustic flavour that shows how easy it can be to get off the beaten track in Ticino. Like in other parts of Ticino, many of the mountain farm cottages *(rustici)* in the tiny Valle di Mergoscia have long been disused and are falling into ruin.

Although this is essentially a short walk, spending a night on the mountain is a cheaper and more scenic alternative than staying down in Locarno. The walk can be done from the middle of spring right through to late autumn. Spring-fed drinking fountains along the route make carrying water unnecessary, except perhaps on the hottest of summer days, but you'll need protection from the elements – at least a hat and rain-jacket – regardless of when you do the Cima della Trosa. The most detailed map for this walk is Orell Füssli's 1:25,000 *Locarno/Ascona* (Sfr28.90).

Getting to/from the Walk

Take the funicular from near Locarno train station to Orselina, then the cable car up to the trail head at Cardada (1332m). From Locarno, the combined one-way fare is Sfr27/7 per adult/child to Cardada or Sfr27/8 to Cimetta. The cable car and chairlift stop for maintenance in November. From Mergoscia, there are about seven daily – don't laugh – FART buses back to Locarno; the last one leaves around 7pm.

The Walk

The walk begins from the upper cable-car station at Cardada at 1332m, high above Locarno. To get to Cardada, first take the funicular from near Locarno train station, or walk up the Via al Sasso to the famous 15th-century, ochre-hued **Madonna del Sasso** sanctuary. It's worth stopping to visit the interesting pilgrim church and museum here, before taking the cable car up to Cardada. For the less energetic, a chairlift continues up to the top of 1671m Cimetta.

Follow the dirt track up to the right, climbing around the mainly open slopes past Ristorante Capanna Cardada, with its panoramic terrace. Make your way on to reach **Capanna Lo Stallone** (☎ 091 743 61 46; dm Sfr42; ☺ May–early Oct) after 30 to 40 minutes. This large stone hut in the grassy hollow of Alpe Cardada (1486m) offers basic dorm accommodation. The restaurant serves typical Ticino dishes prepared with fresh organic ingredients.

From the Alpe, the track cuts back left up over the bracken-covered mountainsides, crossing under winter ski tows and the chairlift. It then swings up right, skirting the forest to arrive at the 1671m **Capanna Cimetta** (☎ 091 743 04 33; dm Sfr35, with half-board Sfr55), offering long views over Lago Maggiore from its sunny terrace. From just below the upper chairlift station, take the left-hand path leading quickly down to a tiny saddle (1610m) with a springwater fountain. Make a rising traverse of the southwestern slopes of Cima della Trosa, doubling around right to gain the ridge. A short side trail brings you to the large metal cross mounted on the windswept 1869m summit after a further 35 to 45 minutes. This lofty spot serves as a great lookout

CIMA DELLA TROSA

point, giving dreamy views stretch¹ng way across Lago Maggiore and the rippling peaks that frame the lake.

After signing the logbook, return to the main path. This soon begins winding down the northeastern sides of the Cima della Trosa to a minor col at 1657m. From here a side trip up to the rounded, often-snow-dusted peak of **Madone** (2039m) can be done in 1½ to two hours; the straightforward route follows white-red-white paint markings along the ridge, with some harmless rock-scrambling higher up, from where you get another striking overview of the rugged mountain and lake scenery.

Descend in broad zigzags through brush and bilberry heath to the goat dairy of Alpe di Bietri (1499m), pausing to try some of the creamy goat's cheese made there, and continue on an old mule trail running along the northern slopes of the tiny Valle di Mergoscia.

Dropping gently against the contour, the route passes dilapidated old houses and rustic hamlets built in local granite to reach the scattered village of **Bresciadiga** (1128m), 1¼ to 1¾ hours from the Cima della Trosa.

Bear right at a junction a short way on, where the path dips down into a lush forest of chestnuts and beech, leading past small shrines before coming into a car park at the end of a road. Stroll 600m downhill to intersect with the main road, then follow the sealed road left up steep hillsides planted out with vineyards to arrive at the little square beside the large baroque church of **Mergoscia** at 731m, after a final one to 1¼ hours.

This picturesque old village sits high above the Val Verzasca, looking out to the south across stone roofs and the Lago di Vogorno reservoir toward Monte Tamaro (identifiable by the telecommunications tower).

Geneva

Super sleek, slick and cosmopolitan, Geneva is a rare breed of city: it's one of Europe's priciest; its people chatter in every language under the sun; and it's constantly thought of as the Swiss capital – which it isn't. In fact this gem, superbly strung around the sparkling shores of Europe's largest Alpine lake, is only Switzerland's third-largest city.

Yet the whole world is here: the UN, International Red Cross, International Labour Organization, World Health Organization. You name it, they're in Geneva: 200-odd top-dog governmental and nongovernmental international organisations meting out world affairs with astonishing precision and authority. They fill the city's bounty of plush four- and five-star hotels with big-name guests. They feast on an incredible choice of international cuisine, cooked up by restaurants to meet 'local' demand. And they help prop up the overload of banks, luxury jewellers and chocolate shops for which the city is known. Strolling through manicured city parks, sailing on the lake and skiing in the Alps next door are hot weekend pursuits.

But, ask critics, where's the urban grit? Not in the lakeside with its tourist boats, silky-smooth promenades and a fountain of record-breaking heights. Not in its picture-postcard Old Town. No, if it's the rough-cut side of the diamond you're after, you need to dig into the Pâquis quarter, walk west along the Rhône's industrial shores or south into trendy Carouge, where rejuvenated factories, alternative clubs and humble neighbourhood bars hum with attitude. This is, after all, the Geneva of the Genevois...or as close as it's possible to get, at any rate.

HIGHLIGHTS

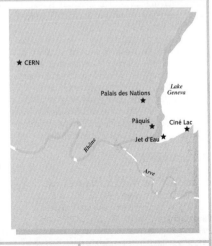

- Dashing like mad beneath the **Jet d'Eau** (p87), then plunging into the Old Town.
- Touring behind the scenes at **CERN** (p91) or the monumental **Palais des Nations** (p89).
- Splurging out on a shopping spree around Geneva's Old Town and **Pâquis boutiques** (p99), lunching at boutique L'Adresse (p94).
- Watching a box-office hit against the romantic backdrop of twinkling stars, boat lights and the rippling water of legendary Lake Geneva at **Ciné Lac** (p99).
- Spoiling yourself rotten at a hip urban spa with a good old soak in a **chocolate bath** (p94).

★ CERN

Palais des Nations ★

Lake Geneva

Pâquis ★   Ciné Lac ★

Jet d'Eau ★

Rhône

Arve

■ POPULATION: 178,603   ■ AREA: 282 SQ KM   ■ LANGUAGE: FRENCH

HISTORY

Occupied by the Romans and later a 5th-century bishopric, rich old Geneva has long been the envy of all. Its medieval fairs drew interest from far and wide, and in the 16th century John Calvin and his zealous Reformation efforts turned the city into 'Protestant Rome'. Savoy duke Charles Emmanuel took a swipe at it in 1602, but was repulsed by the Genevans who celebrate their victory each year on December 11 (p92).

French troops made Geneva capital of the French department Léman in 1798 but were chucked out in June 1814 and Geneva joined the Swiss Confederation. Watchmaking, banking and commerce prospered. A local businessman founded the Red Cross in 1864 and, as other international organisations adopted the strategically located city and birthplace of humanitarian law as their headquarters, Geneva's future as an international melting pot was secured. After WWI the League of Nations strived for world peace from Geneva and after WWII the UN arrived.

By the end of the 20th century, Geneva ranked among the world's 10 most expensive cities, relying heavily on international workers and world markets for its wealth. Foreigners (184 different nationalities) make up 45% of Geneva's population.

ORIENTATION

Geneva sits on the southwest lip of Lake Geneva (Lac Léman in French). The lakeside city is split by the westward progress of the Rhône, which meets the Arve River further west.

Central train station Gare de Cornavin is a few blocks north of the Rhône on the right bank *(rive droite)*. Northeast is seedy Pâquis and the international quarter Palais des Nations, home to most world organisations.

On the left bank *(rive gauche)* is Geneva's iconic Jet d'Eau fountain; the Rue du Rhône shopping district; pedestrian Old Town *(vieille ville)*; and museum-studded Plainpalais.

INFORMATION
Bookshops

Off the Shelf (Map p90; ☎ 022 311 10 90; www.offtheshelf.ch; Blvd Georges Favon 15; ☷ 9am-6.30pm Tue-Fri, 10am-5pm Sat) English-language bookshop.
Payot Libraire (Map p90; ☎ 022 731 89 50; www.payot.ch; Rue Chantepoulet 5; ☷ 9.30am-7pm Mon-Wed & Fri, to 8pm Thu, 9.30am-6pm Sat) Excellent choice of English books, fiction and reference.

Emergency

Police station (Map p90; ☎ 117; Rue de Berne 6)

Internet Access

Charly's Checkpoint (Map p90; ☎ 022 901 13 13; Rue de Fribourg 7; per hr Sfr5; ☷ 9am-midnight Mon-Sat, 2-11pm Sun) Forty machines.
Internet Café de la Gare (Map p90; ☎ 022 731 51 87; per hr Sfr10; ☷ 7.30am-10.30pm Mon-Fri, 8.30am-10.30pm Sat & Sun) In the train station.

Internet Resources

City of Geneva (www.ville-ge.ch)
Glocals (www.glocals.com) Globals and locals share their tips.
Spotted by Locals (http://geneva.spottedbylocals.com) English-language blog.

Laundry

Salon Lavoir (Map p88; Rue du 31 Décembre 12; ☷ 6am-midnight)

Medical Services

Hôpital Cantonal (Map p88; ☎ 022 372 33 11, emergency 022 372 81 20; www.hug-ge.ch, in French; Rue Micheli du Crest 24; ☷ 24hr)
SOS Médecins à Domicile (☎ 022 748 49 50; www.sos-medecins.ch, in French) Home/hotel doctor calls.

Post

Post Office (Map p90; Rue du Mont-Blanc 18; ☷ 7.30am-6pm Mon-Fri, 9am-4pm Sat)

Tourist Information

Information de la Ville de Genève (Map p90; ☎ 022 311 99 70; www.ville-ge.ch; Pont de la Machine; ☷ noon-6pm Mon, 9am-6pm Tue-Fri, 10am-5pm Sat) City information point; ticketing desk for cultural events.
Tourist Office (Map p90; ☎ 022 909 70 00; www.geneve-tourisme.ch; Rue du Mont-Blanc 18; ☷ 10am-6pm Mon, 9am-6pm Tue-Sat)

SIGHTS

Geneva's major sights are split by the Rhône, which flows through the city to create its greatest attraction: the lake.

To save a bob, visit Geneva's museums on the first Sunday of the month, when admission to most is free. On other days, the Swiss Museum Pass (p353) kicks in.

South of the Rhône

Get snapped in front of the **Horloge Fleurie** (Flower Clock; Map p90) in the **Jardin Anglais** (Map p90; Quai du Général-Guisan), Geneva's flowery lakeside garden, landscaped in 1854 on the site of an old lumber-handling port and merchant yard. Geneva's most photographed clock, crafted from 6500 living flowers, has ticked since 1955 and boasts the world's longest second hand (2.5m).

If it happens to be on the hour, nip into the Passage Malbuisson (off Rue du Rhône) to see 13 chariots and 42 bronze figurines dance to the chime of 16 bells on a fanciful 1960s clock. Then veer west for a coffee on **Île Rousseau**, one of five islands to pierce Europe's largest Alpine lake.

JET D'EAU

Landing by plane, this fountain is the first dramatic glimpse you get of Geneva. The 140m-tall lakeside **fountain** (Map p88; Quai Gustave-Ador) shoots up water with incredible force – 200km/h, 1360 horsepower – to create its sky-high plume, which is kissed by a rainbow on sunny days. At any one time, 7 tonnes of water is in the air, much of which sprays spectators on the pier beneath. Two or three times a year, it is illuminated pink, blue or some other vivid colour to mark a humanitarian occasion (World Suicide Prevention Day, Breast Cancer Awareness Month, World AIDS day etc). During Euro 2008, a 15m-wide helium-filled football danced on top of it.

The Jet d'Eau is Geneva's third pencil fountain: the first shot in the sky for 15 minutes each Sunday between 1886 until 1890 to release pressure at the city's water station; the second spurted 90m tall from the Jetée des Eaux-Vives on Sundays and public holidays from 1891 onwards; and the third and current was born in 1951. The time it functions – the 'on' button is pressed manually by one of five pensioners – was reduced by 10% (316 hours a year) in late 2008 as an energy-saving measure.

ESPACE ST-PIERRE

Started in the 11th century, **Cathédrale de St-Pierre** (St Peter's Cathedral; Map p90; Cour St-Pierre; admission free; 9.30am-6.30pm Mon-Sat & noon-6.30pm Sun Jun-Sep, 10am-5.50pm Mon-Sat & noon-5.30pm Sun Oct-May) is mainly Gothic with an 18th-century neoclassical facade. Atop its 157-step **northern tower** (adult/under 7yr/7-16yr Sfr4/free/2; 9am-7pm Jun-Sep, 10am-noon & 2-5pm Mon-Sat, 11am-12.30pm & 1.30-5pm Sun Oct-May), a stunning panorama of the city, Jet d'Eau and mountains fans out. June to September, organ and carillon **concerts** (www.concerts-cathedrale.com) fill the place with soul.

Protestant John Calvin preached here between 1536 and 1564; see his seat in the north aisle of the cathedral and trace his life in the neighbouring **Musée International de la Réforme** (International Museum of the Reformation; Map p90; 022 310 24 31; www.musee-reforme.ch; Rue du Cloître 4; adult/under 7yr/7-16yr/16-25yr Sfr10/free/5/7; 10am-5pm Tue-Sun).

Steps lead down from the cathedral square to the entrance of the **Site Archéologique** (Archaeological Site; Map p90; 022 311 75 74; www.site-archeologique.ch; Cour St-Pierre 6; adult/under 7yr/7-16yr Sfr8/free/4; 10am-5pm Tue-Sun), an interactive subterranean space displaying fine 4th-century mosaics and the tomb of an Allobrogian chieftain.

A ticket covering all these sights costs Sfr16/8/10 per adult/7-16yr/16-25yr.

MAISON TAVEL

Little is left to remind you of the age of Geneva's oldest house, 14th-century **Maison Tavel** (Map p90; 022 418 37 00; Rue du Puits St-Pierre 6; admission free; 10am-5pm), although its displays provide an intriguing account of 14th- to 19th-century urban life in Geneva.

ESPACE ROUSSEAU

The **Espace Rousseau** (Map p90; 022 310 10 28; www.espace-rousseau.ch; Grand-Rue 40; adult/under 7yr/7-18yr Sfr5/free/3; 11am-5.30pm Tue-Sun) is home to a 25-minute audiovisual display tracing the troubled life of Geneva's greatest thinker, born here in 1712.

MUSÉE BARBIER-MUELLER

Venerating world culture, the **Musée Barbier-Mueller** (Barbier-Mueller Museum; Map p90; 022 312 02 70; www.barbier-mueller.ch; Rue Jean Calvin 10; adult/under 12yr/student Sfr8/free/5; 11am-5pm) has objects from so-called primitive societies, including pre-Columbian South American art treasures, Pacific Island statues, and shields and weapons from Africa.

PARC DES BASTIONS & PLACE NEUVE

Four-and-a-half-metre-tall figures of Bèze, Calvin, Farel and Knox – in their nightgowns ready for bed – loom large in **Parc des Bastions** (Map p90). The park's northern entrance hugs **Place Neuve**, pierced by a statue of Red Cross cofounder Henri Dufour, who drew the first map of Switzerland in 1865. Geneva's theatre (p99) and the **Musée Rath** (Map p90; 022 418 33 40; Place Neuve), under renovation (to open in spring, 2009), are also here.

GENEVA

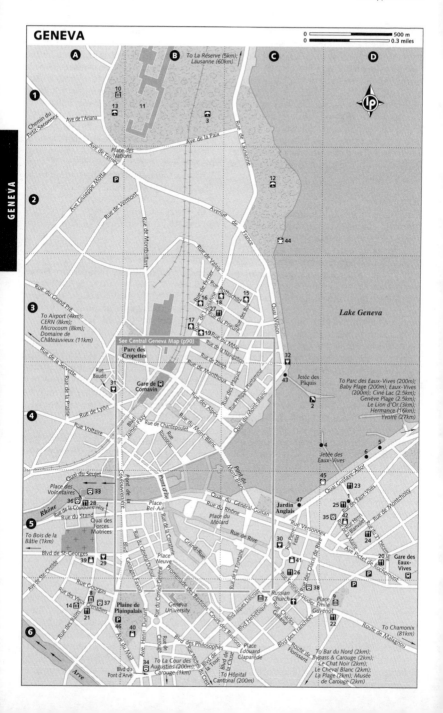

MUSÉE D'ART MODERNE ET CONTEMPORAIN

Set in an industrial 1950s factory, the **Musée d'Art Moderne et Contemporain** (MAMCO; Museum of Modern & Contemporary Art; Map p88; ☎ 022 320 61 22; www .mamco.ch, in French; Rue des Vieux Grenadiers 10; adult/under 18yr Sfr8/free, admission free from 6pm 1st Wed of month; 🕑 noon-6pm Tue-Fri, 11am-6pm Sat & Sun, noon-9pm 1st Wed of month) plays host to young, international and cross-media exhibitions.

PATEK PHILIPPE MUSEUM

A treasure trove of precision art, this **museum** (Map p88; ☎ 022 807 09 10; www.patekmuseum.com; Rue des Vieux Grenadiers 7; adult/under 18yr/18-25yr Sfr10/free/7; 🕑 2-6pm Tue-Fri, 10am-6pm Sat, free guided tour in English 2.30pm Sat) displays exquisite timepieces from the 16th century to the present.

OTHER LEFT-BANK MUSEUMS

Konrad Witz' *La pêche miraculeuse* (c 1440–44), portraying Christ walking on water on Lake Geneva, is a highlight of the **Musée d'Art et d'Histoire** (Art & History Museum; Map p88; ☎ 022 418 26 00; http://mah.ville-ge.ch; Rue Charles Galland 2; permanent/temporary collection admission free/variable; 🕑 10am-5pm Tue-Sun).

Kids adore the stuffed bears, tigers, giraffes and Swiss fauna in the **Musée d'Histoire Naturelle** (Natural History Museum; Map p88; ☎ 022 418 63 00; Rte de Malagnou 1; admission free; 🕑 9.30am-5pm Tue-Sun).

North of the Rhône

Cross the water aboard a seagull (p100); via Geneva's only road-traffic bridge **Pont du Mont-Blanc** (Map p88), notorious for traffic jams; or via pedestrian **Pont de la Machine** (Map p90), a footbridge that hugs an industrial building constructed in the 1840s to provide the city's public fountains with water. Recently converted into a striking exhibition space, **La Cité du Temps** (Map p90; ☎ 022 818 39 00; www.citedutemps .com; Pont de la Machine 1; 🕑 9am-6pm) hosts a lounge bar and restaurant (p96), contemporary art exhibitions, and **La Collection Swatch** where 1700 of the 4000 watches in the world's largest collection of the funky Swiss watches (1983–2006) are displayed. From Love Bite, made in 1998 for Valentine's Day, to the Skin collection, the world's thinnest plastic watches, created in 1997, or the specials created to mark the 20th anniversary of James Bond, these watches amuse. Two computer terminals allow you to design your own Swatch watch and there are always a few models for sale.

Flowers, statues and views of Mont Blanc (on clear days only) abound on Quai du Mont-Blanc, the northern lakeshore promenade which leads past the **Bains des Pâquis** (p92) to **Parc de la Perle du Lac** (Map p88), where Romans built ornate thermal baths. Further north, the peacock-studded lawns of **Parc de l'Ariana** (Map p88) ensnare the UN and the **Jardin Botanique** (Botanical Garden; Map p88; admission free; 🕑 8am-7.30pm Apr-Oct, 9.30am-5pm Nov-Mar).

PALAIS DES NATIONS

Home to the UN since 1966, the **Palais des Nations** (Map p88; ☎ 022 917 48 60; Ave de la Paix 14; adult/under 6yr/6-18yr Sfr10/free/5; 🕑 10am-noon & 2-4pm

GENEVA

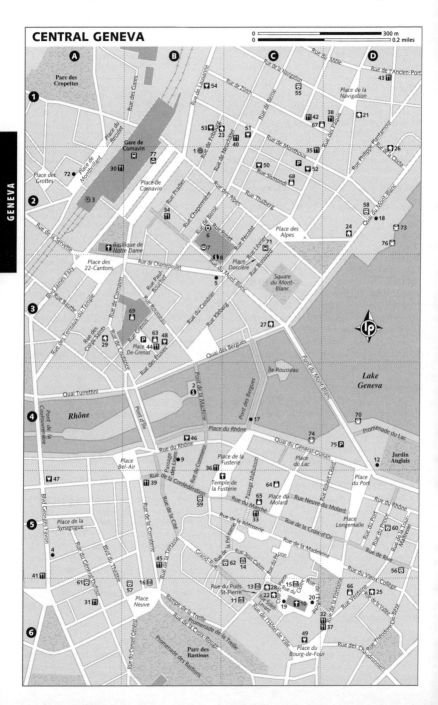

CENTRAL GENEVA

0 — 300 m
0 — 0.2 miles

GENEVA

Apr-Jun, Sep & Oct, 10am-5pm Jul & Aug, 10am-noon & 2-4pm Mon-Fri Nov-Mar) was built between 1929 and 1936 to house the now-defunct League of Nations. Admission includes an hour-long tour and entry to the gardens, where a grey monument sprouts, coated with heat-resistant titanium, donated by the USSR to commemorate the conquest of space. An ID card or passport is required for entry.

MUSÉE INTERNATIONAL DE LA CROIX ROUGE ET DU CROISSANT-ROUGE

Compelling multimedia exhibits at the **Musée International de la Croix Rouge et du Croissant-Rouge** (International Red Cross & Red Crescent Museum; Map p88; ☎ 022 748 95 25; www.micr.org; Ave de la Paix 17; temporary exhibition free, permanent exhibition adult/under 12yr/12-16yr Sfr10/free/5; 10am-5pm Wed-Mon) trawl through atrocities perpetuated by humanity. Against the long litany of war and nastiness, documented in films, photos, sculptures and soundtracks, are set the noble aims of the organisation created by Geneva businessmen and philanthropists Henri Dunant and Henri Dufour in 1864. Take bus 8 from Gare de Cornavin to 'Appia' stop.

CERN

Founded in 1954, **CERN** (European Organisation for Nuclear Research; off Map p88; ☎ 022 767 84 84; visits-service@cern.ch; free guided tours by advance reservation 9am & 2pm Wed & Sat), 8km west of Geneva near Meyrin, is a laboratory for research into particle physics. It accelerates electrons and positrons down a 27km circular tube (the Large Hadron Collider, the world's biggest machine) and the resulting collisions create new forms of matter. Three-hour guided visits need to be booked at least one month in advance and you need your ID or passport.

Microcosm (off Map p88; ☎ 022 767 84 84; http://microcosm.web.cern.ch; admission free; 8.15am-5.30pm Mon-Fri, 8.30am-5pm Sat), CERN's on-site multimedia and interactive visitors centre, runs physics workshops (9am and 3pm Wednesday, 3pm Saturday) for children aged 14 and older.

From the train station take tram 14 or 16 to Avanchet then bus 56 to its terminus in front of CERN (Sfr3, 40 minutes).

GENEVA FOR CHILDREN

On and around the lake, kids love the ducks and swans; the variety of slow pedal, speed motor and sleek sailing boats rented by **Les Corsaires** (Map p88; ☎ 022 735 43 00; www.lescorsaires.ch, in French; Quai Gustave-Ador 33); shooting down the water slide at **Genève Plage** (off Map p88; ☎ 022 736 24 82; www.geneve-plage.ch in French; Port Noir; ⏰ 10am-8pm Jun–mid-Sep), a 1930s lakeside swimming pool complex; and taking a dip at **Bains des Pâquis** (Map p88; ☎ 022 732 29 74; www.bains-des-paquis.ch, in French; Quai du Mont-Blanc 30; ⏰ 9am-8pm mid-Apr–mid-Sep), where Genevans have frolicked in the sun since 1872.

Other amusing options include an electric train tour (below); the Tarzan-inspired tree park with rubber tyres to swing from at **Baby Plage** (off Map p88; Quai Gustave-Ador); or the well-equipped playgrounds for toddlers in **Parc de la Perle du Lac** (p89) and **Bois de la Bâtie** (off Map p88; Bâtie Woods), where peacocks, goats and deer roam.

The exhibits and Wednesday-afternoon workshops at the **Musée d'Histoire Naturelle** (p86) mesmerise children, as do the many interactive exhibitions at MAMCO (p89).

For French or German speakers, www.genevefamille.ch is useful.

TOURS

DIY with an English-language audioguide from the tourist office (Sfr10) or sign up for one of its organised walking tours of the Old Town (Sfr15, two hours).

Key Tours (☎ 022 731 41 40; www.keytours.ch) runs trips to Yvoire (opposite) and various creative tours around town including a 45-minute **Old Town Tour** (Map p90; adult/child Sfr9.90/6.90; ⏰ 10.45am-6pm Mar-Dec) by old-fashioned tram departing up to 12 times daily from Place du Rhône; a 35-minute **Parks & Residences Tour** (Map p90; adult/child Sfr8.90/5.90; ⏰ 10am-dusk daily Mar-Oct, Sat & Sun Nov & Dec) aboard an electric white train

along the right bank from Quai du Mont-Blanc; or a 30-minute left-bank tour aboard the solar-powered, pillar-box-red **Mini-Train Electro-Solaire** (Map p88; adult/child Sfr8/5; ⏰ hourly 10.15am-10.15pm Apr-Sep) departing from just near the Jardin Anglais.

Year-round **CGN** (see p100) run one-hour lake cruises of Geneva's *belles rives* (beautiful shores), departing several times daily from its Jardin Anglais boat stop. Buy tickets (Sfr16) from the ticket office there. May to late October, memorable gastronomic cruises (lunch costs Sfr65, dinner Sfr85 or Sfr98), courtesy of chef Philippe Chevrier (www.savoie-philippe-chevrier.ch), set sail from the same stop. In winter, meanwhile, a meat or cheese fondue is the thing to dip into aboard a boat after dark (late September to mid-Jun; Sfr49/63).

May to October, on the other side of the lake, **Swissboat** (Map p88; ☎ 022 732 29 44; www.swissboat.com; 4-8 Quai du Mont Blanc) sells tickets for its various 40-minute to 2¾-hour thematic lake cruises and fascinating 2¾-hour nature cruise along the Rhône (adult/child Sfr24/17).

FESTIVALS & EVENTS

Smashing marzipan-filled *marmites en chocolat* (chocolate cauldrons) and gorging on the sweet broken pieces makes **L'Escalade** (www.escalade.ch, in French), Geneva's biggest festival on 11 December, loads of fun. Torch-lit processions enliven the Old Town and a bonfire is lit in the cathedral square to celebrate the defeat of Savoy troops in 1602. A tall tale says the assault was repelled by a housewife who tipped a pot of boiling soup over a trooper's head, whacked him with her cauldron, then raised the alarm.

A DETOUR INTO BOHEMIA

Geneva's bohemian streak strikes in Carouge, where the lack of any real sights – bar fashionable 18th-century houses overlooking courtyard gardens and **Musée de Carouge** (off Map p88; ☎ 022 342 33 84; muse@carouge.ch; Place de la Sardaigne 2; admission free; ⏰ 2-6pm Tue-Sun), displaying 19th-century ceramics – is part of the charm.

Carouge was refashioned by Vittorio Amedeo III, king of Sardinia and duke of Savoy, in the 18th century in a bid to rival Geneva as a centre of commerce – until 1816 when the Treaty of Turin handed it to Geneva. Bars, boutiques and artists workshops fill its narrow streets today.

Trams 12 and 13 link central Geneva with Carouge's plane tree–studded central square, Place du Marché, abuzz with market stalls Wednesday and Saturday morning. Horses trot along the streets during April's Fête du Cheval, and horse-drawn carriages line up on Place de l'Octroi in December to take Christmas shoppers for a ride.

DAY TRIPPER

Day trips from Geneva boil down to a boat trip on the lake, a mountain foray into the Jura or a meander into neighbouring France.

Oh-so-pretty French **Yvoire** (off Map p88), 27km northeast of Geneva on the lake's southern shore, is *the* spot where diplomats to dustmen while away weekend afternoons. The medieval walled village with a fishing port and fairy-tale castle (closed to visitors) has cobbled pedestrian streets to stroll, flowers to admire, a restored medieval vegetable garden, **Jardin des Cinq Sens** (Garden of the Five Senses; ☎ 72 82 04 50 80; www.jardin5sens.net; adult/4-16yr Sfr10/5.50; ☾ 11am-6pm Apr, 10am-7pm May–mid-Sep, 1-5pm mid-Sep–mid-Oct), and an overkill of souvenir shops and touristy lunchtime spots. The CGN (p100) boat ride from Geneva's Jardin Anglais (2nd-class day return Sfr37.80; 1¾ hours, May to September) or lakeside motor in a smart green old-fashioned bus (adult/child return costs Sfr49/24.50; daily May to October, Saturday and Sunday March, April, November and December), departing from Place du Rhône courtesy of Key Tours (opposite), is all part of the day out.

Quaint Swiss **Hermance** (off Map p88), 16km northeast of Geneva on the French-Swiss border, lures a more-discerning crowd with its narrow streets lined with medieval houses, the odd pricey art gallery and the legendary **Auberge d'Hermance** (☎ 022 751 13 68; www.hotel-hermance.ch; Rue du Midi 12; lunch menu Mon-Fri Sfr42, mains Sfr22-68), one of the region's most prestigious culinary addresses, where chickens are baked whole and served in a magical salt crust. TPG bus E (Sfr4.60, 30 minutes, at least hourly) links Hermance with Rue de Pierre Fatio on Geneva's left bank.

August's two-week **Fêtes de Genève** (www .fetes-de-geneve.ch, in French) ushers in parades, open-air concerts, lakeside merry-go-rounds and fireworks.

SLEEPING

Plug into a comprehensive list of accommodation at www.geneva-hotel.ch; the tourist office makes hotel reservations for Sfr5. When checking in, ask for your free public transport ticket covering unlimited bus travel for the duration of your hotel stay.

Budget

Auberge de Jeunesse (Map p88; ☎ 022 732 62 60; www.yh -geneva.ch; Rue Rothschild 28-30; dm Sfr29, d/q with toilet Sfr85/123, with shower & toilet Sfr95/135; ☾ reception 6.30-10am & 2pm-1am Jun-Sep, 6.30-10am & 4pm-midnight Oct-May; ▯) At this 350-bed apartment-block hostel rates include breakfast, dorms max out at 12 beds, bathrooms tout hairdryers, and there are facilities for disabled guests and a multimachine laundry.

Hôme St-Pierre (Map p90; ☎ 022 310 37 07; www .homestpierre.ch; Cour St-Pierre 4; dm Sfr29, s/d with washbasin Sfr46/68; ☾ reception 9am-noon & 4-8pm Mon-Sat, 9am-noon Sun; ▯) In the shade of the cathedral, this boarding house was founded by the German Lutheran Church in 1874 to host German women coming to Geneva to learn French. Women remain the primary clientele – just six dorm beds are up for grabs for six lucky

guys – and the rooftop terrace that crowns the place is magical.

City Hostel (Map p88; ☎ 022 901 15 00; www.city hostel.ch; Rue de Ferrier 2; dm Sfr32-36, s/d Sfr59/86; ☾ reception 7.30am-noon & 1pm-midnight; ☒ ℗ ▯) A spanking-clean and organised hostel, where two-bed dorms give travellers a chance to double up on the cheap; rates include sheets and towels, and use of the kitchen, TV room and a free locker.

ourpick Hôtel de la Cloche (Map p90; ☎ 022 732 94 81; www.geneva-hotel.ch/cloche; Rue de la Cloche 6; s with/ without bathroom from Sfr90/65, d with/without bathroom from Sfr110/Sfr95, q with bathroom from Sfr135; ☒) Elegant fireplaces, bourgeois furnishings, wooden floors and the odd chandelier add a touch of grandeur to this old-fashioned one-star hotel. Some rooms come with wrought-iron balconies and peep sweet at the Jet d'Eau.

ourpick Hotel St-Gervais (Map p90; ☎ 022 732 45 72; www.stgervais-geneva.ch; Rue des Corps Saints 20; s/d with washbasin Sfr109/119, d with shower & toilet Sfr140; ☾ reception 7am-11pm) Travellers with jumbo-sized suitcases beware: scaling the seven floors in the pocket-handkerchief lift of this quaint choice near the train station is a squash and a squeeze. Renovated rooms to kip in are on the 1st and 7th floors.

Midrange

Hôtel Bel'Esperance (Map p90; ☎ 022 818 37 37; www .hotel-bel-esperance.ch; Rue de la Vallée 1; s/d/tr/q from

THE ULTIMATE CHOCOLATE EXPERIENCE

Soothe urban body and soul at **After the Rain Spa** (Map p90; ☎ 022 819 01 50; www .spa-aftertherain.ch; Passage des Lions 4; ☘ 9am-9pm Mon-Sat), a haven of peace and tranquillity in downtown Geneva, where the icing on the cake for chocolate fiends has to be a body wrap in creamy milk chocolate (Sfr140, 45 minutes) or – even better – a good old soak in a milk or white chocolate bath (Sfr180, 30 minutes).

Sfr98/154/186/228; ☘ reception 7am-10pm; ✗ ▣) This two-star hotel is a two-second flit to the Old Town. Rooms are quiet and cared for, and those on the 1st floor share a kitchen. Ride the lift to the 5th floor to flop in a chair on a flower-filled rooftop terrace. Free wi-fi.

Hôtel At Home (Map p90; ☎ 022 906 19 00; www .hotel-at-home.ch; Rue de Fribourg 16; s/d Sfr130/170) Functionality is the driver of this stark hotel that aims to make guests feel 'at home' with its simple rooms and kitchen-equipped apartments, rented longer term. Neighbouring eateries whisk you around the world.

La Cour des Augustins (off Map p88; ☎ 022 322 21 00; www.lacourdesaugustins.com; Rue Jean-Violette 15; s/d from Sfr191/225; ▣ ▣) 'Boutique gallery design hotel' is how this slick contemporary space markets itself. Disguised by a 19th-century facade, its crisp white interior sports the latest technology and screams cutting edge. Before checking out, invest in a designer lamp or other household art object to take home at the hotel boutique.

Edelweiss (Map p90; ☎ 022 544 51 51; www.manotel .com; Place de la Navigation 2; d Sfr290-390) Plunge yourself into the heart of the Swiss Alps with this Heidi-style hideout, very much the Swiss Alps *en ville* with its big, cuddly St-Bernard lolling over the banister, fireplace and wildflower-painted pine bedheads. Its chalet-styled restaurant is a key address among Genevans.

Hôtel Jade (Map p88; ☎ 022 544 38 38; www.manotel .com; Rue Rothschild 55; d Sfr290-390) Elegant ebony and other dark woods contrast with mellow creams, beige and other natural hues to create a fashionably understated feel at this 'feng shui adventure', a stylish boutique hotel designed to soothe, revitalise and inspire with its ancient Chinese principles and Zen philosophy.

Hôtel Kipling (Map p88; ☎ 022 544 40 40; www .manotel.com; Rue de la Navigation 27; d Sfr290-390) What

The Jungle Book or its Bombay-born author has to do with Geneva is a question the staff at Hôtel Kipling can't answer. But what the heck! This stylish boutique hotel, created around the theme of British writer Rudyard Kipling, is a breath of fresh air.

Top End

Geneva is studded with four- and five-star hotels.

Hôtel Auteuil (Map p88; ☎ 022 544 22 22; www.manotel .com; Rue de Lausanne 33; d from Sfr350; ▣ ✗ ▩ ▣) The star of this crisp, design-driven hotel near the station is its enviable collection of B&W photos of 1950s film stars…in Geneva no less. Grab the book from reception to find out precisely who's who and where. Free wi-fi.

Hôtel Les Armures (Map p90; ☎ 022 310 91 72; www.hotel-les-armures.ch; Rue du Puits St-Pierre 1; s/d from Sfr395/605; ▣ ✗ ▩ ▣) This slumbering 17th-century beauty just oozes history from every last beam. Beautifully placed in the heart of the Old Town, it provides an intimate and refined atmosphere. Wi-fi costs Sfr25 per day.

our pick **La Réserve** (off Map p88; ☎ 022 959 59 59; www.lareserve.ch; Rte de Lausanne 301; d from Sfr500; ▣ ✗ ▩ ▣ ☎) Absolutely no reason to leave the premises: the handiwork of Parisian interior-design god, Jacques Garcia, this mythical lakeside spa hotel is an extravaganza of cutting-edge design, embracing everything from African colonialism to 1960s Barbarella-style pop and feng shui minimalism. 'Heaven on Earth' is a fair synopsis.

Hôtel des Bergues (Map p90; ☎ 022 908 70 00; www.bergueshotel.com; Quai des Bergues 33; d from Sfr760; ▣ ✗ ▩ ▣) Geneva's oldest hotel lives up to its magnificent heritage. Chandelier-lit moulded ceilings, grandiose flower arrangements, original oils in heavy gold frames and diamonds glittering behind glass is what this lakeside neoclassical gem from 1834 is all about. But how can a suite cost Sfr12,000 a night?

Hôtel Beau-Rivage (Map p90; ☎ 022 716 66 66; www.beau-rivage.ch; Quai du Mont-Blanc 13; d from Sfr790; ▣ ✗ ▩ ▣) Run by the Mayer family for four generations, the Beau-Rivage is a 19th-century jewel dripping in opulence.

EATING

Geneva flaunts ethnic food galore. For the culinarily curious with no fortune to blow, Pâquis cooks up cheapish eats from most corners of the globe.

Geneva's most legendary (read pricey) pan-Asian haunts are **Chez Kei** (Map p88; ☎ 022 346 47 89; Rte de Malagnou 6; mains Sfr30-37, lunch menu Mon-Fri Sfr28; ☺ lunch & dinner Mon-Fri, dinner Sat), the city's second-oldest ode to Chinese cuisine; **Jecks Place** (Map p90; ☎ 022 731 33 03; Rue de Neuchâtel 14; mains Sfr24-30; ☺ lunch & dinner Mon-Fri, dinner Sat & Sun), a moveable feast of Singaporean, Chinese, Malaysian and Thai; and **Little India** (Map p88; ☎ 022 731 11 71; www.littleindia.ch; Rue du Prieuré 20; mains Sfr15-30; ☺ Mon-Sun), which needs little explanation.

Restaurants – South of the Rhône

Filled to the brim much of the year, Place du Molard is perfect for lunch between shops. Or try one of the many eateries on Place du Bourg-de-Four, Geneva's oldest square.

Chez Ma Cousine (Map p90; ☎ 022 310 96 96; www .chezmacousine.ch; Place du Bourg-de-Four 6; lunch Sfr14.90; ☺ 11am-10pm) *'On y mange du poulet'* (we eat chicken) is the strapline of this student institution, which appeals for one good reason – generously handsome and homely portions of chicken, potatoes and salad at a price that can't possibly break the bank.

Omnibus (Map p88; ☎ 022 321 44 45; www.omnibus -cafe.ch, in French; Rue de la Coulouvrenière 23; lunch plat du jour Sfr18, mains Sfr25-40; ☺ 11am-2am Mon-Fri, 5pm-2am Sat & Sun) Don't be fooled or deterred by the graffiti-plastered facade of this Rhône-side bar and restaurant. Inside, a maze of retro rooms seduces on first sight. Particularly romantic is the back room (reservations essential) with carpet wall hangings and lots of lace. Its business card is a recycled bus ticket.

Café Prunier (Map p90; ☎ 022 781 09 24; www .caviarhouse-prunier.com; Place de la Fusterie 26; mains Sfr19-46, menu Sfr67; ☺ lunch & dinner Mon-Fri) One of the world's most prestigious caviar houses, founded in 1950, is at the heart of this up-market restaurant, tucked in a shopping mall behind the Caviar House & Prunier boutique. Pay Sfr50 for one precious spoon of caviar.

Café des Bains (Map p88; ☎ 022 321 57 98; www .cafedesbains.com; Rue des Bains 26; lunch plat du jour Sfr20, mains Sfr25-48; ☺ 11am-3pm & 6pm-1am Tue-Sat) No brand labels, beautiful objects and an eye for design are trademarks of this fusion restaurant opposite the contemporary art museum where Genevan beauties flock. Several dishes woo vegetarians.

Au Pied de Cochon (Map p90; ☎ 022 310 47 97; Place du Bourg-de-Four 4; mains Sfr23.50-36; ☺ 8am-midnight Mon-Fri, 11am-midnight Sat & Sun) It is a porky affair 'At the Pig's Foot' where fat stubby trotters – the house speciality – come stuffed, braised or pan fried. A zinc bar, noisy wine-quaffing clientele and plenty of game in season complete the classic bistro tableau.

Bistrot du Boucher (Map p88; ☎ 022 736 56 36; Ave Pictet de Rochemont 15; mains Sfr25-40; ☺ closed lunch Wed & Sat, all day Sun) Beef cuts are the mainstay of this feisty meat number, a Parisian-style bistro with lace curtains, stained glass and art-nouveau wood. *Entrecôte* (sirloin steak), *côte* (side), carpaccio or tartare are served with a choice of sauces, fries or risotto and salad. Baby-cow lovers will love or hate the sweet *tartare de veau* (Sfr30.50)

Au Grütli (Map p90; ☎ 022 328 98 68; www.cafedu grutli.ch; Rue du Général Dufour 16; mains Sfr28-35; ☺ 8am-11pm Mon-Fri, 4-11pm Sat & Sun) As much café as cutting-edge restaurant, this industrial-styled eating space with mezzanine seating is razor sharp. Indonesian lamb, moussaka, scallops pan fried with ginger and citrus fruits or

---

TOP PICKS: PICNIC SPOTS

With mountains of fine views to pick from, Geneva is prime picnicking terrain for those reluctant to pay too much to eat. Our top spots:

- In the contemplative shade of Henry Moore's voluptuous sculpture *Reclining Figure: Arch Leg* (1973) in the small quiet park opposite the Musée d'Art et d'Histoire (p89).
- Behind the cathedral (p86), in **Terrasse Agrippa d'Aubigné** (Map p90), a tree-shaded park with benches, a sand pit and see-saw for kids and a fine rooftop and cathedral view.
- On the shingly beach lacing the Pâquis pier, across from the entrance of Les Bains de Pâquis (p91).
- On a clear sun-filled day, a bench on Quai du Mont Blanc with majestic view of Mont Blanc.
- On the world's longest bench, measuring 126m, on chestnut-tree-lined Promenade de la Treille in Parc des Bastions (p87).

Provençal-inspired chicken are but some of its international flavours.

ù bobba (Map p90; ☎ 022 310 53 40; Rue de la Corraterie 21; mains Sfr29-47, menu Sfr49; ☾ 8am-3pm Mon, 8am-12.30am Tue-Thu, 8am-1am Fri, 10am-1am Sat) A cultured crowd gathers at this dining spot near the opera house, decked in red and gold, oozing attitude and flaunting what must surely be one of Geneva's hottest roof terraces.

Le Lion d'Or (off Map p88; ☎ 022 736 44 32; www.liondor.ch; Place Gautier 5, Cologny; mains Sfr78-95, 8-course tasting menu Sfr220; ☾ lunch & dinner Mon-Fri) Formal and packed with suits, the Golden Lion sits in the heart of Cologny, Geneva's most expensive 'burb. Mouth-watering fish and seafood creations honour a fine wine list. To avoid blowing a small fortune, dine in the cheaper bistro, which has a flowery garden.

Restaurants – North of the Rhône

Near the train station, Scandale (opposite) is as much a hot lunchtime spot as an evening drinking venue. For Swiss fondue (Sfr32) and yodelling, Edelweiss (p94) is *the* address.

Les 5 Portes (Map p90; ☎ 022 731 84 38; Rue de Zürich 5; brunch Sfr10, mains Sfr15-20; ☾ 9am-2am Mon-Fri, 11am-2am Sat, 11am-8pm Sun) The Five Doors – with indeed five doors – is a fashionable Pâquis port of call that successfully embraces the whole gambit of moods and moments.

Buvette des Bains (Map p88; ☎ 022 738 16 16; www.bains-des-paquis.ch, in French; Quai du Mont-Blanc 30; mains Sfr15; ☾ 8am-10pm) Meet Genevans at this earthy beach bar – rough and hip around the edges – at Bains des Pâquis (p92). Grab breakfast, a salad, the *plat du jour* or dip into a *fondue au crémant* (Champagne fondue). Dining is on trays and alfresco in summer.

ourpick **L'Adresse** (Map p88; ☎ 022 736 32 32; www.ladress.ch, in French; Rue du 31 Décembre 32; mains Sfr25-35; ☾ lunch & dinner Tue-Sat) Something of an urban loft with a fabulous rooftop terrace, it is all hip at The Address, a hybrid fashion/lifestyle boutique and contemporary bistro at home in renovated artists workshops. The Genevan address for lunch, brunch or Saturday slunch (a cross between tea and dinner, ie a casual evening 'meal' of cold and warm nibbles, sweet and savoury, shared between friends over a drink or three around 5pm)…

RestO by Arthur's (Map p90; ☎ 022 818 39 00; La Cité du Temps, 1 Pont de la Machine; mains Sfr35-46; ☾ 9am-midnight Mon-Thu, 9am-1am Fri, 11am-1am Sat) One of the city's trendiest addresses, this designer-driven dining space squats on the 1st floor of indus-

trial La Cité du Temps (p89). Cuisine is world, every dish has its own wine recommendation and water views are unbeatable.

Café de Paris (Map p90; ☎ 022 732 84 50; Rue du Mont-Blanc 26; green salad, steak & chips Sfr40; ☾ 11am-11pm) An impressive dining experience around since 1930, everyone here eats the same: green salad followed by *entrecôte* with a killer-calorie herb and butter sauce of legendary standing and as many supermodel-skinny fries as you can handle. Eat between wooden panels inside or on the buzzing heated pavement terrace.

Cafés

Gilles Desplanches (Map p90; ☎ 022 810 30 28; www.gillesdesplanches.com, in French; Rue de la Confédération 2; ☾ 7am-7pm Mon-Wed & Fri, 7am-8pm Thu, 8am-7pm Sat, 10am-6pm Sun) One for serious Swiss chocolate fiends: with its shocking-pink facade and exquisitely crafted cakes and chocolates alongside imaginative salads and savoury tarts, this is one address that bursts at the seams at lunchtime.

Café des Arts (Map p90; ☎ 022 321 58 85; Rue des Pâquis 15; ☾ 11am-2am Mon-Fri, 8am-2am Sat & Sun) As much a place to drink as a daytime café, this Pâquis hang-out lures a local crowd with its Parisian-style terrace and artsy interior. Foodwise, think meal-sized salads, designer sandwiches and other titillating lunch dishes (Sfr15 to Sfr20).

Le Pain Quotidien (Map p88; ☎ 022 736 36 90; Blvd Helvétique; breakfast Sfr10.50-16.50, tarts & salads Sfr12.50-17.50; ☾ 7am-6pm Mon-Fri, 8am-6pm Sat & Sun; ☒) Choose from a heap of breakfasts (continental, English etc) and brunches (classic, countryside etc) at this twinset of rustic daytime spots:

ICE ON THE MOVE

■ **Gelateria Arlecchino** (Map p88; ☎ 022 736 70 60; Rue du 31 Décembre 1; per scoop Sfr3.50, milkshakes Sfr7) Left-bank choice: chocolate and ginger, honey, peanut cream and mango are among the 40 flavours at this lip-licking parlour.

■ **Gelatomania** (Map p90; ☎ 022 741 41 44; Rue des Pâquis 25; per scoop Sfr3.50) Right-bank choice: a constant queue loiters outside this shop where ice-cream maniacs wrap their tongues around exotic flavours like carrot, orange and lemon, cucumber and mint, lime and basil or pineapple and basil.

the second branch is on Blvd Georges-Favon (Map p90).

Quick Eats

Rue de Fribourg, Rue de Neuchâtel, Rue de Berne and the northern end of Rue des Alpes (all Map p90) are loaded with kebab, falafel and quick-eat joints. Eat in or take out at the following:

Mikado (Map p90; ☎ 022 732 47 74; Rue de l'Ancien-Port 9; sushi per piece Sfr2.50, rice/hot main Sfr3/6.50; 🕙 10am-6.30pm Tue-Fri, 10am-6pm Sat) If it's authenticity, speed and tasty fast food on a red lacquered tray you want, this Japanese delicatessen with tables to sit down at hits the spot.

Piment Vert (Map p90; ☎ 022 731 93 03; www.pimentvert.ch, in French; Place De-Grenus 4; menu Sfr25, mains Sfr15-19; 🕙 11.30am-2.45pm & 5.30-10pm Mon-Fri, noon-4pm Sat) Fast, fresh and trendy sums up this hybrid Indian–Sri Lankan bar.

Globus (Map p90; ☎ 022 319 50 50; Rue du Rhône 50; 🕙 9am-10pm Mon-Sat) Snack-attack on sushi, sashimi, panini, tapas, antipasti, noodles and curry in the central department store.

Self-Catering

Shop for everything organic including cabbage juice, quince body lotion and seaweed tofu at **Le Marché de Vie** (☎ 022 735 44 34; Rue des Eaux-Vives 27). **Delicatessa Globus** (Map p90; Rue du Rhône 50) is the Harrods food hall of Geneva and **Boucherie Moulard** (Map p90; ☎ 022 311 71 66; www.boucheriemolard.ch; Rue du Marché 20) opposite has been around since 1921 and is a feast for the eyes and the senses.

Central supermarkets:

Aperto (Map p90; Gare de Cornavin; 🕙 6am-midnight)
Migros (Rue des Eaux-Vives 27; 🕙 8am-7pm Mon-Wed, 8am-7.30pm Thu & Fri, 8am-6pm Sat)

DRINKING

Paillote (Map p88; Quai du Mont-Blanc 30; 🕙 to midnight) With wooden tables inches from the water, this place is packed full in summer. By 11pm the grassy lawns, quay and walls within a 20m radius of the kiosk overflow with merry punters.

Scandale (Map p90; ☎ 022 731 83 73; www.scandale.ch; Rue de Lausanne 24; 🕙 11am-2am Tue-Fri, 5pm-2am Sat) Retro '50s furnishings in a cavernous interior bedecked with a fine choice of eclectic seating, including drop-dead-comfy sofas, ensure this lounge bar is never empty. Grub ranges from fully fledged mains (Sfr15 to Sfr20) to snack-attack salads, bruschetta and so on and

happenings include art exhibitions, Saturday-night DJs and bands.

Arthur's (Map p90; ☎ 022 810 32 60; www.arthurs.ch; Rue du Rhône 7-9; 🕙 7am-2am Mon-Fri, 11am-2am Sat) If Arthur was real, he'd be called 007 and drink vodka martinis shaken not stirred at this drop-dead gorgeous lakeside terrace where aperitif lovers linger.

La Bretelle (Map p90; ☎ 022 732 75 96; Rue des Étuves 17; 🕙 6pm-2am daily) Little has changed since the 1970s when this legendary bar opened. The Strap is just the place to tune into a good old accordion-accompanied French chanson. Indeed, there's live music most nights.

La Clémence (Map p90; ☎ 022 312 24 98; www.laclemence.ch; Place du Bourg-de-Four 20; 🕙 7am-1am Mon-Thu & Sun, 7am-2am Fri & Sat) Indulge in a glass of local wine (Sfr3.80 to Sfr6) or artisanal beer (Sfr7.40) at this more-than-veritable Genevois café-bar fronting the city's loveliest square.

La Plage (off Map p88; ☎ 022 342 20 98; Rue Vautier 19; 🕙 11am-1am Mon-Thu, 10am-2am Fri & Sat, 5pm-1am Sun) With bare wood tables, checked lino floor, green-wood shutters and tables outside, The Beach in Carouge is a timeless drinking hole.

Olé Olé (Map p90; ☎ 022 731 38 71; baroleole@yahoo.com; Rue de Fribourg 11; tapas Sfr10-20) An industrial tapas bar with giant street-facing windows and a bar lit by naked bulbs ensures a stop with a difference near the train station. The Italian place next door is a fine choice for dinner.

Boulevard du Vin (Map p90; ☎ 022 310 91 90; www.boulevard-du-vin.ch, in French; Blvd Georges-Favon 3; 🕙 4-11pm Mon-Fri) Wine sluggers will enjoy this excellent wine shop which doubles as a wine bar with its weekly *dégustation* sessions. Food platters add a gastronomic dimension.

Le Caveau de Bacchus (Map p88; ☎ 022 312 41 30; www.bacchus.ch, in French; Cours de Rive 5; 🕙 9.30am-7pm Mon-Fri, 9.30am-6pm Sat) Look out for the fantastic tasting *soirées* (Sfr70) run by this specialist wine shop; typically, nine different wines are tasted in an evening.

ENTERTAINMENT

Keep in the loop with www.nuit.ch and buy theatre and concert tickets at **Fnac Billetterie Spectacles** (Map p90; ☎ 022 816 12 30; Rue de Rive 16; 🕙 9.30am-7pm Mon-Wed, 9.30am-9pm Thu, 9.30am-7.30pm Fri, 9am-6pm Sat); **Service Culturel Migros Genève** (Map p90; ☎ 022 319 61 19; www.culturel-migros-geneve.ch, in French; Rue du Prince 5; 🕙 10am-6pm Mon-Fri); or the **box office** (🕙 noon-5pm Mon-Fri) in the tourist office (p86).

GENEVA

Edgy mixed-bag venues:

L'Usine (Map p88; ☎ 022 781 34 90; www.usine.ch, in French; Place des Volontaires 4) This grungy and youthful converted gold-roughing factory entertains with dance nights, art happenings, theatre, cabaret and club nights.

Le Chat Noir (off Map p88; ☎ 022 343 49 98; www.chat noir.ch, in French; Rue Vautier 13; concerts Sfr16-22; ☑ Tue-Sat) Nightly jazz, rock, funk and salsa gigs.

Clubs

Clubbing is not Geneva's forte (see below) but it does have a handful of ultratrendy dance floors where a drink easily sets you back Sfr20. Dress to kill.

White 'n Silver (Map p88; ☎ 022 735 15 15; www .whitensilver.ch; Rue des Glacis de Rive 15; ☑ 11pm-5am) Geneva beauties mingle at this Old Town designer nightclub in the space where the mythical Club 58 rocked Geneva in the '50s and '60s.

Bypass (off Map p88; ☎ 022 300 65 65; www.bypass.ch; Carrefour de l'Étoile; ☑ 10.30pm-5am Thu-Sat) The Carouge spot to mingle, rub shoulders and chink *verres* with Genevan socialites. In the words of a reliable source: 'Friday cheese, Saturday serious dance music'.

Java Club (Map p90; ☎ 022 908 90 88; www.javaclub.ch; Quai du Mont-Blanc 19; ☑ 11pm-5am Tue-Sat) Visiting international DJs spin tunes alongside resident music man Massimiliano at this *branché* (trendy) dance floor, inside the Kempinski hotel.

SIP (Map p88; www.lasip.ch; Rue des Vieux Grenadiers 10; ☑ 10pm-4am Thu, 10pm-5am Fri & Sat) Soul Influenced Product is 'not a nightclub', according to the propaganda of this design-led space, an 1860s factory that blasts out a wholly mainstream sound.

OUT ALL NIGHT

Far from being the 'nice but boring' city that many tag it as, Geneva is, as far as one Genevan-born-and-bred gal is concerned, a place that 'rocks, where you can party round the clock'. A 30-something Swiss urbanite reveals where to stay up all night.

So where do you start, which are 'the' bars?

Bar du Nord (off Map p88; ☎ 022 342 38 20; Rue Ancienne 66; ☑ 5pm-2am Thu-Fri, 9am-2am Sat), one of Carouge's oldest, was known in the '90s for its beach (yes, imported sand feature) and is now a stylish bar stuffed with Bauhaus-inspired furniture, the best whisky selection in town and a small courtyard terrace out back. It's young, trendy, unpredictable. Best nights are Thursday and Friday with good music, DJs, lots of electro.

L'Aiglon (Map p90; ☎ 022 732 97 60; www.laiglon.ch; Rue Sismondi 16; ☑ 10am-2am Mon-Sat) is a Pâquis institution where anything goes! It does good *steak frites* (steak and chips) but is better known for wild parties and a great alternative, gay-friendly atmosphere. Again good music, DJs, electro…

And later for clubbing, dancing?

Geneva doesn't have a club scene; Lausanne (p110) is definitely much better on this front.

One address is **Le Palais Mascotte** (Map p90; ☎ 022 800 33 33, reservations 079 820 33 33; www .palaismascotte.ch; Rue de Berne 43; mains Sfr15; ☑ to 5am daily), closed for over 10 years then reopened as a resto–cabaret bar for over 30s. It has a great atmosphere, quite selective. A restaurant is on the top floor; cabaret, '70s and '80s music on the ground floor; and concert followed by '90s music in the basement club, Le Zazou. Good fun!

And after, where do you move on to?

After hours, the well-known institution is **La Presse** (Map p88; ☎ 022 320 62 99; www.pubdelapresse.ch; Blvd de St-Georges 62-64) in Plainpalais, which closes at 2am and reopens for coffee and clubbers at 4am! Marez, the owner, knows how to keep people loyal…

OK, it's morning. The address for that quintessential brunch?

Le Cheval Blanc (off Map p88; ☎ 022 343 61 61; www.lechevalblanc.ch; Place de l'Octroi 15; ☑ 11.30am-1am or 2am Tue-Sat, 10.30am-1am Sun) in Carouge is a cosy, young, pretty-stylish bar with one of the best brunch offers in town – an all-you-can eat fresh buffet with hot and cold drinks – and Geneva's best tapas. And it has a club downstairs, Le Box, open for concerts.

Or there's **Melody's** (Map p90; ☎ 022 732 78 72; Rue des Pâquis 9; ☑ 8.30am-2.30pm & 5.30pm-midnight or 2am Mon-Fri, 7pm-2am Sat, 10am-6pm Sun), a new small bar in Pâquis with good DJs, tapas, after-hours parties and breakfast/brunch.

GAY & LESBIAN GENEVA

The key port of call is **Dialogai** (Map p90; ☎ 022 906 40 40; www.dialogai.org; Rue de la Navigation 11-13), which publishes a gay guide to the Geneva region and hosts candlelit dinners, Sunday brunch, film evenings, French-English discussion groups and club nights in its retro café; see its website for details.

The mainly male, expat **Gay International Group** (GIG; www.360.ch/espace/gig) brings together 80-odd nationalities for monthly drinks and dinners.

Key entertainment spots include **Nathan** (Map p88; ☎ 022 733 78 76; Rue Baudit 6; ⏰ 5pm-2am), a grungy bar heaving with Geneva's most hip; and nightclub **Le Déclic** (Map p88; ☎ 022 320 59 40; www.ledeclic.ch, in French; Blvd du Pont d'Arve 28; ⏰ 5pm-2am Mon-Fri, 9pm-2am Sat).

X-S Club (Map p90; ☎ 022 311 70 09; Grand-Rue 21, entrance at Rue de la Pelisserie 19; ⏰ 11pm-4am Thu, 11.30pm-5am Fri & Sat) R&B, disco, reggae, oriental; ladies' night Friday.

Cinemas

Watch films in English at **Rex** (Map p90; ☎ 0900 900 156; Confederation Centre, Rue de la Confédération 8) or **Les Scala** (Map p88; ☎ 022 736 04 22; www.les-scala.ch, in French; Rue des Eaux-Vives 23). Programs are online at http://geneve.cinemas.ch (in French).

Ciné Lac (off Map p88; www.cinelac.ch, in French; adult/under 14yr Sfr17/14; ⏰ Jul & Aug) Glorious summertime open-air cinema with a screen set up on the lakeside.

Theatre, Dance & Classical Music

Grand Théâtre de Genève (Map p90; ☎ 022 418 31 30; www.geneveopera.ch, in French; Blvd du Théâtre 11) Opera and ballet.

Victoria Hall (Map p90; ☎ 022 418 35 00; Rue du Général Dufour 14) Concert hall for both the Orchestre de la Suisse Romande (www.osr.ch) established in 1918 and the Orchestre de Chambre de Genève (www.locg.ch).

Bâtiment des Forces Motrices (Map p88; ☎ 022 322 12 60; www.bfm.ch; Place des Volontaires 4) Geneva's one-time riverside pumping station (1886) is now a striking space for classical music concerts, dance, ballet and other cultural events. Its Sunday-morning Musique sur Rhône concerts are particularly delightful.

Théâtre du Grütli (Map p90; ☎ 022 328 98 68; www.grutli.ch; Rue du Général Dufour 16) Experimental theatre and comedy.

SHOPPING

Designer shopping is wedged between Rue du Rhône and Rue de Rive. **Globus** (Map p90; Rue du Rhône 50) and **Manor** (Map p90; Rue de Cornavin) are the main department stores. For designer secondhand, try Rue des Étuves.

Grand-Rue in the Old Town and Carouge (p92) boast artsy boutiques, or try Geneva's twice-weekly **flea market** (Map p88; Plaine de Plainpalais; ⏰ Wed & Sat) for something different. Favourites:

L'Autre (p90; ☎ 022 738 34 60; Place De-Grenus 4; ⏰ 2-6.30pm Mon, 10am-6.30pm Tue-Fri, 10am-5pm Sat) Stylish and retro furniture and jewellery from the 1930s to 1980s.

L'Appart (p90; ☎ 022 732 12 80; Rue Sismondi 6; ⏰ 2-7pm Mon-Fri, 11am-5pm Sat) One-off fashion creations by young Swiss designers.

Collection Privée (p90; ☎ 022 738 75 69; Place De-Grenus 8; ⏰ 11.30am-6.30pm Tue-Fri, 11.30am-5pm Sat) Art-deco lamps, furniture and other 20th-century curiosities.

Great Outdoor Store (p88; ☎ 022 840 17 57; Cours de Rive 14; ⏰ 7am-7pm Mon-Fri, 9am-6pm Sat) Designer outdoor gear; everything you need for chic Swiss mountain forays.

La 3ème Main (The Third Hand; Map p90; ☎ 022 310 56 66; www.la3main.ch; Rue Verdaine 18) Designer items and accessories for the house, including Collpart bags – recycled Cambodian fish bags made by Lausanne-based designer Nina Raeber.

La Trouvaille (Map p88; ☎ 022 735 86 35; Rue de la Mairie 7; ⏰ 2-6.30pm Mon, 10.30am-6.30pm Tue-Fri, 10.30am-4.30pm Sat) Secondhand designer fashion for women.

Best Of (p88; ☎ 022 328 42 64; Rue des Bains 63; ⏰ 10.30am-6.30pm Mon-Fri) Secondhand designer clothing.

La Fringue-Halle (p90; ☎ 022 732 58 34; Rue de Zürich 2; ⏰ 11am-6pm Tue-Sat) For accessories, try Caritas' Pâquis *dépôt-vente* (sale shop).

GETTING THERE & AWAY
Air

Aéroport International de Genève (☎ flight information 0900 571 500; www.gva.ch), 4km from the centre of town, has connections to major European cities and many others worldwide. See p359.

Boat

The **Compagnie Générale de Navigation** (CGN; Map p90; ☎ 084 881 18 48; www.cgn.ch) operates a steamer service from its Jardin Anglais jetty to other villages on Lake Geneva. Many only sail from May to September, including those to/from Lausanne-Ouchy (adult 2nd-class single/return Sfr37.60/64, 3½ hours). Those aged six to 16 pay 50% less; under six years sail for free.

Check return-fare prices as a one-day Carte Journalière CGN pass can be cheaper: it allows unlimited boat travel and costs Sfr49/67 in 2nd/1st class. Eurail and Swiss rail passes (see the boxed text Swiss Travel Passes, p367) are also valid.

Bus

International buses depart from the **Gare Routière** (Bus Station; Map p90; ☎ 0900 320 320, 022 732 02 30; www.coach-station.com; Place Dorcière).

Car & Motorcycle

All the major car-rental agencies have a desk at the airport.

Train

More-or-less-hourly connections operate between Geneva's main train station, **Gare de Cornavin** (Place de Cornavin), and most Swiss towns, including Lausanne (Sfr20.60, 40 minutes), Bern (Sfr46, 1¾ hours) and Zürich (Sfr80, 2¾ hours). Pick up timetables at the station's **information office** (☎ 0900 300 300; 8.30am-6.30pm Mon-Fri, 9am-4.45pm Sat).

Trains running southeast to/from Annecy, Chamonix and other destinations in France use Geneva's French Railways (SNCF) train station, **Gare des Eaux-Vives** (Map p88; Ave de la Gare des Eaux-Vives).

For international connections see p362.

GETTING AROUND
To/From the Airport

The quickest way to/from Geneva airport is by train: some 200 trains per day link the airport train station with Gare de Cornavin (Sfr30, eight minutes). Slower bus 10 (Sfr3) also runs between the airport and Gare de Cornavin; get off at the '22 Cantons' stop. A metered taxi costs around Sfr30 to Sfr50.

Bicycle

Rent a bike from **Genève Roule** (Map p90; ☎ 022 740 13 43; www.geneveroule.ch, in French; Place de Montbrillant 17; 8am-6pm Mon-Sat) or its seasonal Jetée des Pâquis pick-up point (Map p88) for Sfr12/20 per day/weekend. May to October, borrow a bike carrying publicity for free.

Boat

Yellow shuttle boats dubbed Les Mouettes (The Seagulls) criss-cross the lake every 10 minutes between 7.30am and 6pm. Public-transport tickets dispensed by machines at boat bays are valid.

Car & Motorcycle

Much of the Old Town is off limits to cars. Street parking is hard to snag; head for a public car park such as **Parking du Mont Blanc** (Map p90; Quai du Général-Guisan; per 25 min Sfr1) or **Parking Plaine de Plainpalais** (Map p88; Ave du Mail; per 30 min Sfr1). Validate your parking ticket in an orange TPG machine before leaving the car park to get an hour's free travel for two people on buses, trams and boats.

Public Transport

Tickets for buses, trolley buses and trams run by **Transports Public Genevois** (TPG; ☎ 0900 022 021; www.tpg.ch, in French) are sold at dispensers at stops and at the **TPG office** (7am-7pm Mon-Fri, 7am-6pm Sat) at the train station. A one-hour ticket for multiple rides in the city costs Sfr3; a ticket valid for three stops in 30 minutes is Sfr2; and a city/canton day pass valid 9am to midnight is Sfr7/12. Schedules for **Noctambus night buses** (☎ 0900 022 021; www.noctambus.ch, in French) are online.

Taxi

Pick one up in front of the train station or call ☎ 022 331 41 33.

Lake Geneva & Vaud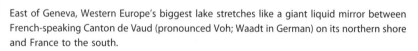

East of Geneva, Western Europe's biggest lake stretches like a giant liquid mirror between French-speaking Canton de Vaud (pronounced Voh; Waadt in German) on its northern shore and France to the south.

Known to most as Lake Geneva, to Francophones (except some in Geneva!) it is Lac Léman. Lined by the elegant city of Lausanne and a phalanx of pretty smaller towns, the Swiss side of the lake presents the marvellous emerald spectacle of tightly ranked vineyards spreading in terraces up the steep hillsides of the Lavaux area. These grapes and those grown to the west of Lausanne produce some fine tipples and it is possible to visit some *caveaux* (cellars). Modest beaches, often backed by peaceful woodland, dot the lake, and around Montreux the climate is mild enough for palm trees to thrive.

Jutting out over the waters of the lake near Montreux is the fairy-tale Château de Chillon, the first of many that await exploration a short way inland.

Lake-lovers can head north to Yverdon-les-Bains, which sits on the southern tip of Lac de Neuchâtel and offers the chance to relax in tempting thermal baths.

At its southeast corner, the canton rises into the magnificent mountain country of the Alpes Vaudoises (Vaud Alps), a hikers' paradise in spring and summer, and skiers' haven in winter. Those addicted to the white stuff can even indulge in moderate summer skiing across the impressive Les Diablerets glacier.

In July, music rocks the lake with Montreux' international jazz get-together and Nyon's multifaceted Paléo music fest.

LAKE GENEVA & VAUD

HIGHLIGHTS

- Marvelling at the fairy-tale **Château de Chillon** (p116) near Montreux
- Pondering the bizarre in Lausanne's unique **Musée de l'Art Brut** (p107)
- Touring the **Lavaux vineyards** (p115) east of Lausanne
- Hiking and skiing around **Les Diablerets** (p122) in the striking Alpes Vaudoises
- Grooving along to music festivals: jazz in **Montreux** (p117) and rock at the Paléo Festival in **Nyon** (p112)

| POPULATION: 672,040 | AREA: 3212 SQ KM | LANGUAGE: FRENCH |

History

As early as 58 BC, Caesar's troops had penetrated what is now southwest Switzerland. In the succeeding centuries a mix of Celtic tribes and Romans rubbed along in peace and prosperity. Aventicum (today Avenches) became the capital, with as many as 20,000 inhabitants, and numerous other towns (such as Lausanne) flourished.

By the 4th century AD, the Romans had largely pulled out of Switzerland and Germanic tribes stepped into the vacuum. Christianised Burgundians arrived in the southwest in the 5th century and picked up the Vulgar Latin tongue that was the precursor to French. Absorbed by the Franks, in 1032 Vaud became part of the Holy Roman Empire.

In the 12th and 13th centuries the Dukes of Savoy slowly assumed control of Vaud and embarked on the construction of impressive lakeside castles.

The Canton of Bern appreciatively took over those castles when, in 1536, it declared war on Savoy and seized Vaud. Despite the tendency of Bern's bailiffs to siphon off local wealth, by the 18th century Lausanne (the area's capital) was a thriving centre.

The French Revolution in 1789 had heavy consequences for its neighbours. On the urging of Fréderic-César de la Harpe, leader of the Liberal Party, the Directorate in Paris placed Vaud under its protection in December 1797. In 1803, Napoleon imposed the Act of Mediation that created the

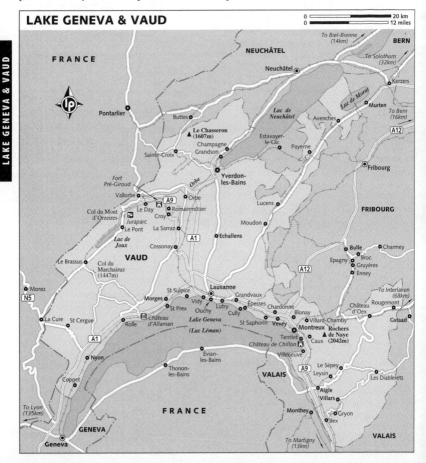

Swiss Confederation, in which Vaud, with Lausanne as its capital, became one of six separate cantons.

The second half of the 19th century was one of industrial development and comparative prosperity for the canton, later slowed by the turbulence of the two world wars.

Orientation & Information

Vaud straddles the three main geographical regions of Switzerland: the Jura mountains in the west, the relatively flat plain of the Plateau Central (Mittelland), and a smidgen of the Alps in the southeast.

Along its northern flank it is bordered by the Neuchâtel and Fribourg cantons. To the south lies France (briefly interrupted by the frontier with Geneva canton) and to the southeast Valais, while to the east German part of the country starts with the canton of Bern.

The **Canton de Vaud tourist office** (Map p104; ☎ 021 613 26 26; www.lake-geneva-region.ch; Ave d'Ouchy 60, 1006, Ouchy, Lausanne; ⏲ 8am-5.30pm Mon-Fri) provides hiking- and cycling-route brochures.

For information on Avenches and Payerne, which are part of Vaud, see p132.

In addition to the normal Swiss national holidays, the people of Vaud also take off St Basil's Day (2 January) and the Federal Day of Fasting (Lundi du Jeûne) on the third Monday in September.

Getting Around

The **Regional Pass** (7-day pass 1st/2nd class Sfr164/114) provides free bus and train travel throughout the canton three days in seven, and half-price travel on the other four days. It also gives 50% off CGN boat services as well as 25% off some cable cars (eg up to Les Diablerets glacier). There is a five-day version with two days of free travel (1st/2nd class Sfr136/94). Holders of one of the various Swiss rail passes (see p369) receive a 20% discount off the Regional Pass.

LAUSANNE

pop 119,180 / elevation 495m

This hilly city (loh-*san*), Switzerland's fifth largest, enjoys a blessed lakeside location. The medieval centre is dominated by a grand Gothic cathedral and, among the museums, the unusual Art Brut collection stands out, while sports fans will love the Musée Olympique. Throughout the year Lausanne's citizens are treated to a busy arts calendar. Strolling along the lake is itself a pure pleasure.

History

The Romans first set up camp on the lake at Vidy, a key halt on the route from Italy to Gaul that came to be known as Lousonna. In the face of an invasion by the Alemanni in the 4th century AD, Lousonna's inhabitants fled to the hilly inland site that became the heart of medieval Lausanne.

In 1529, Guillaume Farel, one of Calvin's followers, arrived in town preaching the Reformation but it wasn't until Bern occupied the city (not a shot was fired) seven years later that the Catholics were obliged to take notice.

From the 18th century, Lausanne exerted a fascination over writers and free-thinkers, attracting such characters as Voltaire, Dickens, Byron and TS Eliot (who wrote *The Waste Land* here).

Lausanne, with only 10,000 inhabitants, became capital of the Vaud canton in 1803. The city began to take on its present appearance with rapid development occurring from the latter half of the 19th century.

Today, Lausanne is a busy, vibrant city. And it competes with nearby Geneva as a cosmopolitan centre. If 43% of the latter's population have been foreigners since 1990, their number in Lausanne has risen from 28% to 39% in the same period.

Home to the Federal Tribunal, the highest court in the country, the International Olympic Committee (IOC), a high-flying international business school (IMD), Tetra Pak and the multinational tobacco conglomerate Philip Morris, it also boasts a fairly boisterous wining and dining scene.

Orientation

The Old Town (*vieille ville*), with its winding, hilly streets topped by the cathedral, is north of the train station. Rue Centrale runs along the valley that separates the *vieille ville* from another hill topped by Place St François and its church. This square is the main hub for local buses, and off it to the east runs the shopping street of Rue de Bourg. One of the country's top addresses in the 19th century (and on the Swiss version of Monopoly), it lost some of its class with the arrival of fast-food joints and

LAKE GENEVA & VAUD

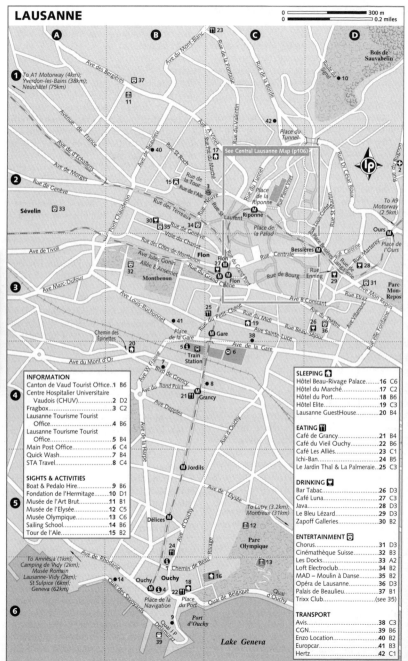

LAUSANNE

See Central Lausanne Map (p106)

INFORMATION
Canton de Vaud Tourist Office..**1** B6
Centre Hospitalier Universitaire
    Vaudois (CHUV).................**2** D2
Fragbox.................................**3** C2
Lausanne Tourisme Tourist
    Office...............................**4** B6
Lausanne Tourisme Tourist
    Office...............................**5** B4
Main Post Office....................**6** C4
Quick Wash...........................**7** B4
STA Travel.............................**8** C4

SIGHTS & ACTIVITIES
Boat & Pedalo Hire................**9** B6
Fondation de l'Hermitage....**10** D1
Musée de l'Art Brut.............**11** B1
Musée de l'Elysée...............**12** C5
Musée Olympique................**13** C6
Sailing School.....................**14** B6
Tour de l'Ale......................**15** B2

SLEEPING
Hôtel Beau-Rivage Palace.......**16** C6
Hôtel du Marché..................**17** C2
Hôtel du Port......................**18** B6
Hôtel Elite..........................**19** C3
Lausanne GuestHouse............**20** B4

EATING
Café de Grancy....................**21** B4
Café du Vieil Ouchy..............**22** B6
Café Les Alliés.....................**23** C1
Ichi-Ban..............................**24** B5
Le Jardin Thaï & La Palmeraie..**25** C3

DRINKING
Bar Tabac............................**26** D3
Café Luna............................**27** C3
Java...................................**28** D3
Le Bleu Lézard....................**29** D3
Zapoff Galleries...................**30** B2

ENTERTAINMENT
Chorus................................**31** D3
Cinémathèque Suisse............**32** B3
Les Docks...........................**33** A2
Loft Electroclub...................**34** B2
MAD – Moulin à Danse..........**35** B2
Opéra de Lausanne...............**36** D3
Palais de Beaulieu................**37** B1
Trixx Club...........................(see 35)

TRANSPORT
Avis...................................**38** C3
CGN...................................**39** B6
Enzo Location.....................**40** B3
Europcar............................**41** B3
Hertz.................................**42** C1

poor renovation. Just west and downhill from Place St François is Flon, an area of formerly derelict warehouses now transformed into a busy urban centre with a cinema complex, art galleries, trendy shops, restaurants and bars. The city long ago enveloped the picturesque lakeside village of Ouchy.

Information
BOOKSHOP
Librairie Payot (Map p106; ☎ 021 341 33 31; Place Pépinet 4) A broad selection of material on Switzerland and books in English; one of the best bookshop chains in French-speaking Switzerland.

INTERNET ACCESS
The city provides free wi-fi hotspots around town: Flon, Place de la Palud, Place St François, Place de la Riponne, Place du Port, Place de la Navigation and Montbenon.
Fragbox (Map p104; ☎ 021 311 89 69; www.fragbox.com; Rue de la Tour 3; per hr Sfr5; ⏲ 9am-11.30pm Mon-Fri, 1.30-11.30pm Sat, 1.30-10pm Sun) High-speed internet.

LAUNDRY
Quick Wash (Map p104; Blvd de Grancy 44; per load Sfr22; ⏲ 7.30am-8.30pm Mon-Fri, 9am-8.30pm Sat & Sun)

MEDICAL SERVICES
Centre Hospitalier Universitaire Vaudois (CHUV; Map p104; ☎ 021 314 11 11; www.chuv.ch; Rue du Bugnon 46) Lausanne's main hospital.

MONEY
Banque Cantonale Vaudoise (Map p106; Place St François 10) Has branches with ATMs all over town.
Exchange office (⏲ 8am-7pm) In the train station.

POST
Post office (Map p106; Place St François 15; ⏲ 7.30am-6.30pm Mon-Fri, 8-11.30am Sat) The house in which Edward Gibbon wrote much of *The History of the Decline and Fall of the Roman Empire* once stood on this site.
Post office (Map p104; Place de la Gare 1; ⏲ 8.30am-7pm daily) The main one; at the train station.

TOURIST INFORMATION
InfoCité (Map p106; ☎ 021 315 25 55; www.lausanne.ch /infocite; Place de la Palud 2; ⏲ 7.45am-noon & 1.15-5pm Mon-Fri) Run by city hall; has material on upcoming events in the city.
Lausanne Tourisme tourist office (☎ 021 613 73 73; www.lausanne-tourisme.ch; train station; Map p106; Place de la Gare 9; ⏲ 9am-7pm; Ouchy; Map p104; Place de la Navigation 4; ⏲ 9am-6pm Oct-Mar, to 8pm Apr-Sep)

TRAVEL AGENCIES
STA Travel (Map p104; ☎ 058 450 48 50; Blvd de Grancy 20) The budget travel agency has several branches in the city.

Sights & Activities
CATHEDRAL & AROUND
The Gothic **Cathédrale de Notre Dame** (Map p106; ⏲ 7am-7pm Mon-Fri, 8am-7pm Sat & Sun Apr-Aug, 7am-5.30pm Sep-Mar), arguably the finest in Switzerland, stands proudly at the heart of the *vieille ville*. Raised in the 12th and 13th centuries on the site of earlier, humbler churches, it lacks the lightness of French Gothic buildings but is remarkable nonetheless. Pope Gregory X, in the presence of Rudolph of Habsburg (the Holy Roman Emperor) and an impressive following of European cardinals and bishops, consecrated the church in 1275.

Although touched-up in parts in succeeding centuries (notably the main facade, which was added to the original to protect the interior against ferocious winds), the building is largely as it was. The most striking element is the elaborate entrance on the south flank of the church (which, unusually for Christian churches, was long the main way in). The painted statuary, partially restored and protected by glass, depicts Christ in splendour, the coronation of the Virgin Mary, the Apostles and other Bible scenes.

Inside, the 13th-century **rose window** in the south transept contains unusual geometric patterns comprising images relating to the seasons, signs of the Zodiac and the elements.

Just opposite the south flank of the cathedral are two minor museums. The **Musée**

TEN O'CLOCK AND ALL IS WELL!

Some habits die hard. From the height of the Cathédrale's bell tower, a *guet* (night watchman) still calls out the hours into the night, from 10pm to 2am. Four times after the striking of the hour he calls out: *C'est le guet! Il a sonné dix, il a sonné dix!* (Here's the night watchman! It's 10 o'clock, it's 10 o'clock!). In earlier times this was a more serious business, as the *guet* kept a look-out for fires around the town and other dangers. He was also charged with making sure the townsfolk were well behaved and the streets quiet during the solemn moments of church services.

CENTRAL LAUSANNE

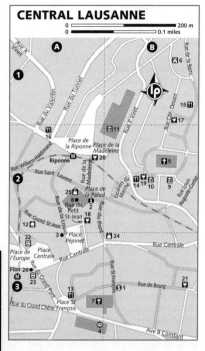

Historique de Lausanne (Map p106; ☎ 021 315 41 01; www.lausanne.ch/mhl; Place de la Cathédrale 4; adult/student Sfr8/free; ☼ 11am-6pm Tue-Thu, to 5pm Fri-Sun Sep-Jun, to 6pm Mon-Thu, to 5pm Fri-Sun Jul & Aug) traces the city's history, and the **Musée de Design et d'Arts Appliqués Contemporains** (Map p106; ☎ 021 315 25 30; www.mudac.ch; Place de la Cathédrale 6; adult/child/student Sfr10/free/5; ☼ 11am-6pm Tue-Sun Sep-Jun, to 6pm daily Jul & Aug) is a centre of modern design that frequently holds intriguing temporary exhibitions. Entry to both museums is free on the first Saturday of the month. A combined ticket for both costs Sfr15/free/8 (adult/child/student).

OLD TOWN (VIEILLE VILLE)

About 200m north of the Cathédrale stands the haughty, turreted **Château St Maire** (Map p106). This 15th-century castle was once the residence of the bishops of Lausanne and now houses government offices. In the streets between the cathedral and castle are several tempting eateries.

In front of the main entrance to the cathedral, a covered timber stairway leads down to Rue Pierre Viret, from where two more

stairways lead further downhill, one to the modern Place de la Riponne and the other to medieval **Place de la Palud** (Map p106). The latter's name suggests that this 9th-century market square was originally bogland. For five centuries it has been home to the city government, now housed in the 17th-century **Hôtel de Ville** (town hall; Map p106). The column with the allegorical figure of Justice that presides over the fountain dates from 1585, or rather it pretends to – the original is actually in the Musée Historique de Lausanne.

Rue du Pont descends from the eastern end of Place de la Palud to Rue Centrale, which you cross to climb Rue St François up to the square of the same name. The name comes from the church, **Église de St François** (Map p106), which today is a bit of a hybrid but in the beginning formed part of a 13th-century Franciscan monastery. You can admire some restored frescos inside. It is hard to imagine that the church and monastery once stood amid peaceful green fields!

About 200m west of Place de la Riponne stands the only surviving vestige of medieval Lausanne's defensive walls. The cylindrical **Tour de l'Ale** (Map p104), tucked away at the end of Rue de la Tour, was built in 1340 at the extreme western point of the medieval suburb of Ale. That we can admire the tower at all is due to those townspeople who opposed demolition plans in 1903.

MUSÉE DE L'ART BRUT

This extraordinary **collection** (Map p104; ☎ 021 315 25 70; www.artbrut.ch; Ave des Bergières 11-13; adult/child/student & senior Sfr10/free/5, free 1st Sat of month; ⏰ 11am-6pm Tue-Sun Sep-Jun, to 6pm Jul & Aug), put together by French artist Jean Dubuffet, opened in 1976 in what was a late 18th-century country mansion.

Brut means crude or rough, and that's what you get. None of the artists had training but all had something to express. A few were quite mad, many (justly or otherwise) spent time in mental asylums or were plain eccentric. Their works offer a striking variety, and at times surprising technical capacity and an often inspirational view of the world.

There are sculptures made out of broken plates and discarded rags, faces made out of shells, sculptures in wood, paintings, sketches and much more. To get there, take bus 2 or 3 to the Beaulieu stop.

PALAIS DE RUMINE

This neo-Renaissance pile was built to lord it over Place de la Riponne in 1904 and, aside from the parliament of the Vaud canton, is home to several museums. This is where the Treaty of Lausanne was signed in 1923, finalising the break-up of the Ottoman Empire after WWI.

The main museum is the **Musée Cantonal des Beaux-Arts** (Fine Arts Museum; Map p106; ☎ 021 316 34 45; www.beaux-arts.vd.ch; Place de la Riponne 6; adult/child/senior & student Sfr10/free/8, 1st Sat of the month free; ⏰ 11am-5pm Fri-Sun, to 6pm Tue-Wed, to 8pm Thu), with many works by Swiss and foreign artists, ranging from Ancient Egypt to Cubism. The core of the collection is made up of works by landscape painter, Louis Ducros (1748–1810), and three other locals. The permanent collection is closed during the frequent temporary exhibitions. It is mooted that the collection

will be moved to a new lakeside location in the coming years.

The other **museum collections** (admission to each adult/child/senior & student Sfr6/free/4, 1st Sat of the month free; ⏰ 11am-6pm Tue-Thu, to 5pm Fri-Sun) in the building cover natural history, zoology (with the longest – almost 6m – stuffed great white shark on show in the world), geology, coins, archaeology and history. The latter gives an overview of the history of the Vaud canton from the Old Stone Age to modern times. Tickets for any one of these museums are then valid for entry into the remaining three.

MUSÉE OLYMPIQUE & AROUND

This **museum** (Map p104; ☎ 021 621 65 11; www.museum.olympic.org; Quai d'Ouchy 1; adult/child/student & senior Sfr15/free/10; ⏰ 9am-6pm daily Apr-Oct, 9am-6pm Tue-Sun Nov-Mar) is surprisingly interesting given that its subject does not elicit universal interest. Housed in a lavish building in the Parc Olympique, atop a tiered landscaped garden, it tells the Olympic story from its inception under Pierre de Coubertin to the most recent competition. Videos, archival film (usually including footage of the most recent games), touch-screen computers and memorabilia (anything from the Olympic flame torches used since 1936 to a pair of sprinter Carl Lewis' track shoes) all help bring this sporting saga to life.

The **Musée de l'Elysée** (Map p104; ☎ 021 316 99 11; www.elysee.ch; Ave de l'Elysée 18; adult/child/student/senior Sfr8/free/4/6, free 1st Sat of month; ⏰ 11am-6pm) is worth keeping an eye on if you like photography. It stages temporary expositions that are often excellent.

THE LAKE

Lake Geneva (Lac Léman) provides plenty of sporting opportunities. Contact the **sailing school** (école de voile; ☎ 021 635 58 87; www.ecole-de-voile.ch; Chemin des Pêcheurs 7) at Ouchy for courses on windsurfing, water-skiing and sailing, and equipment rental for these activities. You can also rent pedalos (Sfr20 per hour) and motorboats (Sfr45 to Sfr50 per hour) at stands in front of the Château d'Ouchy.

CGN (see p111) offers a range of boat cruises.

In summer, head for the beach! The one at **Vidy** is one of the nicer beaches, backed by thick woods and parklands. Locals can be seen cycling, rollerblading (in-line skating) or just strolling along the waterfront on sunny

LAKE GENEVA & VAUD

weekends. Check out the remains of Roman Lousonna and the adjacent **Musée Romain Lausanne-Vidy** (☎ 021 315 41 85; www.lausanne.ch/mrv; Chemin du Bois de Vaux 24; adult/child/student Sfr8/free/5, free 1st Sat of the month; 11am-6pm Tue-Sun), housed on the site of a Roman villa and containing a modest collection of ancient artefacts.

BOIS DE SAUVABELIN

Lausanne is remarkably blessed with green spaces. Much of the lakeside is lined with thick woodland and spacious picnic areas. To the north stretches the bucolic expanse of the **Bois de Sauvabelin** (Map p104). This peaceful park is also home to the **Fondation de l'Hermitage** (Map p104; ☎ 021 312 50 13; www.fondation-hermitage.ch; Rte du Signal 2; adult/child/student/senior Sfr15/free/7/12; 10am-6pm Tue-Wed, to 6pm Fri-Sun & hols, to 8pm Thu). This charming 19th-century residence constantly hosts high-calibre temporary art expositions. Take bus 16 from Place St François.

Tours

A guided **walking tour** (☎ 021 321 77 66; adult/student & child/senior Sfr10/free/5; 10am & 2.30pm Mon-Sat May-Sep) of the *vieille ville*, lasting one to two hours and usually in French, leaves from the front of the Hôtel de Ville twice a day in spring and summer. From July to mid-September there are free guided visits of Cathédrale de Notre Dame four times a day, Monday to Saturday. Book a spot at least four days in advance.

Festivals & Events

In the first week of July the city hums with performances all over town in the week-long **Festival de la Cité** (www.festivalcite.ch).

For Switzerland's **national day** on 1 August, hire a pedalo (see p107) in the early evening and be ready on the lake for fireworks around 10pm.

The **Lausanne Marathon** (www.lausanne-marathon.com) is run towards the end of October.

Sleeping

In most hotels you will pay a one-off tourist tax of Sfr2.50 per person. In exchange, you'll be offered the Lausanne Transport Card, which entitles you to unlimited use of public transport.

BUDGET

Camping de Vidy (☎ 021 622 50 00; www.campinglausannevidy.ch; Chemin du Camping 3; campsites per adult Sfr7.50, per tent Sfr10-18, per car Sfr3.50; year-round) This camping ground is just to the west of the Vidy sports complex, on the lake. Take bus 2 from Place St François and get off at Bois de Vaux then walk underneath the freeway towards the lake. Throw a few francs on top for electricity, rubbish collection and local tourist tax.

Lausanne GuestHouse (Map p104; ☎ 021 601 80 00; www.lausanne-guesthouse.ch; Chemin des Épinettes 4; dm Sfr33-38, s/d Sfr94/115, without bathroom Sfr85/95; reception 7.30am-noon & 3-10pm; P) An attractive mansion converted into quality backpacking accommodation near the train station. Many rooms have lake views and you can hang out in the garden or terrace. Parking is Sfr10 and there's room to leave your bikes. Some of the building's energy is solar.

Hôtel du Marché (Map p104; ☎ 021 647 99 00; www.hoteldumarche-lausanne.ch; Rue Pré du Marché 42; s/d Sfr100/130, without bathroom Sfr70/110) For no-frills rooms in a pleasant-enough location, this is a good option. Rooms are kept nice and clean and there's a little terrace out the back.

MIDRANGE

The following hotels offer free wi-fi.

Hôtel Elite (Map p104; ☎ 021 320 23 61; www.elite-lausanne.ch; Ave Sainte Luce 1; s/d Sfr175/225; P) A central family-run hotel set in quiet grounds (dotted with sun loungers) with good-sized, comfortable (if a little dated) rooms, decorated in subtle colours and equipped with cable TV. Some have a shower, others a full bath. Those with balcony enjoy pleasant views across the city. Some have lake views (Sfr30 extra).

Hôtel du Port (Map p104; ☎ 021 612 04 44; www.hotel-du-port.ch; Place du Port 5; s/d Sfr180/230;) A perfect location in Ouchy, just back from the lake, makes this a good choice. The better doubles look out across the lake (Sfr20 extra) and are spacious (about 20 sq metres). Up on the 3rd floor are some lovely junior suites.

Hôtel des Voyageurs (Map p106; ☎ 021 319 91 11; www.voyageurs.ch; Rue Grand St Jean 19; s/d Sfr200/250; P) A handily located lodging for the historic centre of Lausanne, this hotel has 33 comfortable if plain rooms. Prices can fluctuate considerably, dropping as low as Sfr120/160 in slow periods.

TOP END

Hôtel Beau-Rivage Palace (Map p104; ☎ 021 613 33 33; www.beau-rivage-palace.ch; Place du Port 17-19; s/d Sfr450/520; P) Easily the most stunningly located hotel in town and one of only two five-star options, this place has it all. A beautifully maintained, early 19th-century mansion set in immaculate grounds, the hotel offers rooms with magnificent lake and Alp views, a wellness centre, three restaurants with terraces and two bars.

Eating

Café Romand (Map p106; ☎ 021 312 63 75; Place St François 2; mains Sfr18-28.50; ☺ 11am-11pm Mon-Sat) A tatty sign leads you into an equally unpromising looking arcade. A few steps in and a push of the door takes you out of the 21st century and back to another era. The broad, somewhat sombre dining area littered with timber tables attracts everyone from bankers to punks for traditional food, ranging from fine fondue to *cervelle au beurre noir* (brains in black butter). The kitchen operates all day, rare for this town.

our pick Café de Grancy (Map p104; ☎ 021 616 86 66; www.cafédegrancy.ch; Ave du Rond Point 1; mains Sfr18-35; ☺ 8am-midnight Mon & Wed-Thu, 8am-1am Fri, 10am-1am Sat, 10am-midnight Sun) An old-time bar resurrected with flair by young entrepreneurs, this spot has established itself as a hip hang-out with floppy lounges in the front, wi-fi, and a tempting restaurant out back. Brunch is offered on Saturday and Sunday (10am to 3pm).

Café du Vieil Ouchy (Map p104; ☎ 021 616 21 94; Place du Port 3, Ouchy; mains Sfr18.50-38.50; ☺ Thu-Mon) A simple but charming location for fondue (Sfr23.50), rösti and other classics. Follow up with a meringue smothered in *crème double de la Gruyère* (double thick Gruyère cream).

Le Jardin Thaï (Map p106; ☎ 021 555 59 99; Rue du Petit-Chêne 34; mains Sfr20-39; ☺ daily) With palms spreading overhead, low lights and rapid service, this is one of the better-value Thai eateries in town. There's a broad choice of rice, noodle, vegetarian, fish and meat options. The *curry de crevettes vertes au lait de coco* (green prawn curry in coconut milk) is good for those who don't like it hot. This hotel restaurant has La Palmeraie (same details) as its bed mate, a good spot for Swiss cooking and mussels.

Café-Restaurant du Vieux Lausanne (Map p106; ☎ 021 323 53 90; Rue Pierre Viret 6; mains Sfr25-42; ☺ lunch & dinner Tue-Fri, dinner Sat) An old stalwart, where good French and Swiss cooking comes in generous portions. Meat is the central theme, with dishes like *tartare de boeuf* (Sfr32) starring. In summer, sit beneath the narrow pergola.

Le Vaudois (Map p106; ☎ 021 331 22 22; www.levaudois.ch; Place de la Riponne 1; mains Sfr20-44; ☺ kitchen nonstop 11.30am-11.15pm daily) Classic local Swiss cuisine, concentrating on fondues and meat dishes like the nationwide fave, Zürich's *émincé de veau à la zurichoise* (thin slices of veal prepared in a creamy mushroom sauce, Sfr32.50).

Ichi-Ban (Map p104; ☎ 021 601 31 68; www.ichi-ban.ch; Ave d'Ouchy 58; mains Sfr35-45; ☺ Tue-Sun) Check out the most stylish and innovative of Lausanne's half-dozen or so Japanese eateries. Run by a George Clooney lookalike, this place offers especially good meat dishes (request how you want it cooked), fabulous sashimi and delicious *futto maki* (with seven ingredients mixed in, including avocado, shrimp and tuna).

La Pomme de Pin (Map p106; ☎ 021 323 46 56; Rue Cité-Derrière 11; mains Sfr40-56; ☺ lunch & dinner Mon-Fri, dinner Sat) Search out this beacon of French cuisine in the web of alleys in the medieval old town. During WWII, Winston Churchill and Charlie Chaplin ate here. The place is divided into *bistrot* and *gastro*, the latter a fancy restaurant setting. Local fish is a permanent fixture on a menu that is otherwise largely determined by seasonal goods.

our pick Café Les Alliés (Map p104; ☎ 021 648 69 40; www.lesallies.ch; Rue de la Pontaise 48; mains Sfr22-44; ☺ lunch & dinner Mon-Fri; ✗) It doesn't look like much on the outside but inside a cosy, warm restaurant with creaky timber floors winds out back towards a pleasant summer garden. At the front is the café. Some imaginative salads precede mains like *steak de veau poêlé au jus d'abricots* (pan-cooked steak in apricot sauce).

Drinking

XIIIeme Siècle (Map p106; ☎ 021 312 40 64; Rue Cité-Devant 10; ☺ 10pm-4am Tue-Sat) In a grand medieval setting with stone vaults and huge timber beams, this is a great place for a beer or six.

Giraf Bar (Map p106; ☎ 021 323 53 90; Escaliers du Marché; ☺ 8.30pm-1am Tue-Thu, to 2am Fri & Sat) This tiny, smoke-filled bar fills up on a Friday and Saturday night. The giraffe-skin motif is repeated inside on lampshades and the music can reach back to the 1980s.

Le Bleu Lézard (Map p104; ☎ 021 321 38 30; www.bleu-lezard.ch; Rue Enning 10; ☺ 7am-1am Mon-Thu, 7am-2am Fri, 8am-2am Sat, 9.30am-1am Sun) An oldie but a goodie, this corner bar-eatery with wooden tables and a chatty atmosphere remains a popular meeting place throughout the day and evening. If you feel like a dance, pop downstairs to its club-style section, Cave. This is also a good spot for Sunday brunch and they have wi-fi.

Java (Map p104; ☎ 021 321 38 37; www.lejava.ch; Rue Marterey 36; ☺ 7am-midnight Mon-Wed, 7am-1am Thu, 7am-2am Fri, 10am-2am Sat, 11am-midnight Sun) Similar in atmosphere to Le Bleu Lézard, this place spreads over two floors. Up on the first, a separate lounge area is perfect for a quiet one. Wall-length mirrors and thick lounge chairs dominate the decor.

our pick **Bar Tabac** (Map p104; ☎ 021 312 33 16; Rue Beau-Séjour 7; ☺ 7am-9pm Mon-Wed, 7am-1am Thu & Fri, 9am-2am Sat, 9am-3pm Sun) Like a spruced corner tavern of old, this is the kind of thing Hemingway probably had in mind when he spoke of a 'clean, well lighted place'. Squeaky timber floors lend warmth and punters engage in animated chat at tables around the L-shaped bar.

Café Luna (Map p104; ☎ 021 329 08 46; www.café-luna.ch; Place de l'Europe 7; ☺ 11am-midnight Mon-Wed, to 1am Thu, Fri & Sat) It's a spacious, modern bar, with angular dark furniture, huge, saucer-like lights hanging from the ceiling and DJs spinning all sorts of sounds from Thursday to Saturday.

Café du Pont (Map p106; ☎ 021 311 41 40; Rue Petit St Jean 7; ☺ 11am-2pm & 5pm-1am Tue-Thu, 11am-2pm & 5pm-2am Fri & Sat) This tiny upstairs bar, long a haunt for conspiratorial leftists to engage in long chats about the state of the nation (or the canton), is a curious little hideaway for sipping on Belgian beers.

The Great Escape (Map p106; ☎ 021 312 31 94; www .the-great.ch; Rue de la Madeleine; ☺ 11am-1am Sun-Thu, 2.30pm-2am Fri, 4.30pm-2am Sat) Beneath the whopping beams that hold up the roof of what could be a country house is a noisy pub with plenty of beers and ales on tap. At times a sports bar (claiming the best burgers in town), it heaves with an eclectic crew of punters on Friday and Saturday nights.

Entertainment

Lausanne is one of the busier night-time cities in Switzerland. In some bars you will find a handy free listings booklet, *What's Up* (www.whatsupmag.ch, in French and German). Tickets for many shows can be bought in advance from **Ticketcorner** (☎ 0900 800 800; www.ticketcorner.ch) or **Resaplus** (☎ 0900 552 333; www.resaplus.ch).

LIVE MUSIC
Le Bourg (Map p106; ☎ 021 625 07 07; www.lebourg.ch; Rue de Bourg 51; ☺ 7pm-1am Wed-Thu, 7pm-2am Fri-Sat)

What was once an old cinema is now one of central Lausanne's happening drink dens and live music stages. Squeeze upstairs past the bar for a good view down to the stage area. Music can be anything from Afro sounds to local jam sessions.

Chorus (Map p104; ☎ 021 323 22 33; www.chorus.ch; Ave Mon Repos 3; admission free-Sfr35; ☺ 8.30pm-2am Thu-Sat) The appropriately dark and sometimes smoky ambience is perfect for local and international stars at Chorus, one of Lausanne's top jazz venues.

Le Romandie (Map p106; ☎ 021 311 17 19; www .leromandie.ch; Place de l'Europe 1a; ☺ 10pm-4am Tue, Thu-Sat) Lausanne's premier rock club has taken up residence in this postindustrial location within the great stone arches of the Grand Pont. Expect live rock, garage and even punk, followed by DJ sounds in a similar vein.

Les Docks (Map p104; ☎ 021 623 44 44; www.lesdocks.ch; Ave de Sévelin 34; admission Sfr20-40; ☺ 9pm-2am Tue-Sun) This somewhat sombre semi-industrial and office-block zone is home to Les Docks, the tops spot for concerts of all descriptions. From hip-hop to heavy metal, singer-songwriters to reggae, the program can be quite eclectic.

CLUBS
MAD – Moulin à Danse (Map p104; ☎ 021 340 69 69; www.mad.ch; Rue de Genève 23; admission up to Sfr25; ☺ 11pm-4am Tue-Sun) With five floors of entertainment, MAD really is a crazy sort of place. Music themes can range from anything to trance to tranquil. Just behind it on Rue de Genève is Zapoff Galleries, a slick designer bar run by the same people. Snappy dressing is required and people under 25 don't get past the doorman – at least that's the policy.

Amnésia (☎ 021 619 06 50; www.amnesiaclub.ch; Ave E Dalcroze 9; admission Sfr20; ☺ 11pm-5am Fri-Sun) This place packs them in down on the lake. Apart from the club proper (with four dance floors) you can limber up in one of three attached bars beforehand and, in summer, get a snack in the restaurant on the beach (both open to 2am, May to October).

D-Club (Map p106; ☎ 021 351 51 40; www.dclub.ch; Place Centrale; admission Sfr10-25; ☺ 11pm-5am Wed-Sat) D-Club is a heaving club where local and guest DJs spin funk to house, especially the latter, in all its latest sub-forms. Friday night is electro night and Saturday the place shakes to humping house. To get here take the stairs down from Rue du Grand Pont and turn right before descending all the way into Place Centrale.

Loft Electroclub (Map p104; ☎ 021 311 63 64; www .loftclub.ch; Place de Bel-Air 1; admission up to Sfr20; ☺ 1-4am Wed, 11pm-5am Thu-Sat) Loft, a predominantly red bar and dance space just one level down the stairs of the Tour Bel-Air building, is another popular late-night option. DJs occasionally put on R & B nights, while Saturday is electro night.

GAY VENUES
Trixx Club (Map p104; admission free; ☺ 11.30pm-4am Sun) MAD hosts Trixx Club on Sunday night, *the* big club night for gays and lesbians throughout western Switzerland. Over the five floors is one dedicated to gals and another to guys.

CINEMA
Some of the cinemas around town show original language movies (watch for those marked 'vo' in the listings section of *24 Heures*).

Cinémathèque Suisse (Map p104; ☎ 021 315 21 70; www.cinematheque.ch; Allée E Ansermet 3, Casino de Montbenon) For classics and film cycles, head for this place, seat of the Swiss film archives and the location of a fine café and restaurant.

THEATRE, OPERA & CLASSICAL MUSIC
Lausanne has a rich theatre scene for most of the year. Listings appear in the local paper *24 Heures*. Otherwise, pick up information on upcoming events at the InfoCité (see p105).

Palais de Beaulieu (Map p104; ☎ 021 643 21 11; www .beaulieu.org; Ave des Bergières 10) This venue stages concerts, operas and ballets. Lausanne has its own chamber orchestra and the renowned Rudra Béjart Ballet company (www.bejart -rudra.ch).

Opéra de Lausanne (Map p104; ☎ 021 310 16 00; www.opera-lausanne.ch; Ave du Théâtre 12) Runs a season rich in events from September to May. Classics of opera alternate with classical music concerts and one-off presentations of world music. Tickets can cost from Sfr15 to Sfr130, depending on the performance and seats.

Shopping
Rue de Bourg is lined with boutiques and jewellery stores. Otherwise, head for Place de la Palud and the surrounding pedestrian streets, where you will find department stores, fashion boutiques, wine and food speciality stores.

La Ferme Vaudoise (Map p106; ☎ 021 351 35 55; Place de la Palud 5) This store sells an interesting array of cheeses, sweets, liqueurs and local farm produce from around Vaud.

Globus (Map p106; ☎ 021 342 90 90; www.globus.ch; Rue du Pont 5) The deli on the ground floor of Globus is full of costly Swiss and foreign goodies.

For grunge clothing and bargains away from the snooty central stores, hunt around the Flon, where you might also want to pop into the art galleries.

On Wednesday and Saturday mornings (6am to 2.30pm), produce markets set up on Rue de Bourg, Place de la Palud and a couple of the other pedestrian streets around the square.

Getting There & Away
BOAT
The company **CGN** (Map p104; ☎ 084 881 18 48; www .cgn.ch; Quai JP Delamuraz 17) runs boats from Ouchy to destinations around Lake Geneva. There are no car ferries.

Up to 14 boats daily shuttle to and from Evian-les-Bains (France) in July and August (Sfr17.20/29.40 2nd class one-way/return, 40 minutes), dropping to seven to nine boats the rest of the year. You can take less-frequent boats to places like Montreux (Sfr22.20/37.80 one-way/return, 1½ hours) and Geneva (Sfr37.60/64 one-way/return, about 3½ hours). A day pass to go anywhere on the lake costs Sfr49.

CAR & MOTORCYCLE
Several freeways link Lausanne to Geneva and Yverdon-les-Bains (A1), Martigny (A9) and Bern (A9 then A12). Car-rental companies include **Avis** (Map p104; ☎ 021 340 72 00; Ave de la Gare 50), **Hertz** (Map p104; ☎ 021 312 53 11; Place du Tunnel 17) and **Europcar** (Map p104; ☎ 021 319 90 40; Ave Louis Ruchonnet 2). **Enzo Location** (Map p106; ☎ 084 245 45 45; Ave de Beaulieu 8) offers a deal for Sfr20 a day plus Sfr0.20 per kilometre with a Fiat Panda bearing their logo.

TRAIN
As many as six trains an hour run to/from Geneva (Sfr20.60, 33 to 51 minutes) and up to four to its airport (Sfr25, 42 to 58 minutes). One or two an hour travel to/from Bern (Sfr31, 70 minutes). Up to four trains an hour run to Yverdon-les-Bains (Sfr14.80, 20 to 45 minutes).

Getting Around
Buses and trolley buses service most destinations (Sfr1.90 up to three stops, Sfr3 unlimited

LAKE GENEVA & VAUD

stops in central Lausanne for one hour, Sfr8.60 for 24-hour pass in central Lausanne).

The new m2 Métro line connects Ouchy with Gare (train station) and Flon and then heads on across town to Épalinges (Croisettes stop), in the northern suburbs. At Flon, the older m1 line heads west into the suburbs and on to Renens. Prices are the same as for the buses.

Parking in central Lausanne is a headache. In blue zones you can park for free (one-hour limit) with a time disk (see p366). Most white zones are meter parking. Costs vary but can rise to Sfr2 an hour with a two-hour limit. The lower end of Ave des Bains is one of the few streets with some free parking spots.

For a taxi, call ☎ 080 081 08 10. A short ride from the train station to a central hotel will cost Sfr12 to Sfr20.

You can 'hire' bicycles (which carry advertising) for free from **Lausanne Roule** (Map p106; ☎ 021 533 01 15; www.lausanneroule.ch; Place de l'Europe 1b) under the arches of Grand Pont in the Flon area. The bikes are available from 7.30am to 9.30pm. You leave a Sfr20 refundable deposit and ID. If you bring it back late, you pay Sfr1 an hour.

AROUND LAUSANNE
La Côte

The coast between Lausanne and Geneva (known simply as The Coast) is sprinkled with fantasy castles, imposing palaces and immaculately maintained medieval towns. More than half of the Canton de Vaud's wine, mostly white, is produced here. The towns along La Côte are on the train route between Lausanne and Geneva and some can be reached by CGN steamers (fares from Lausanne include: Morges Sfr13.60, Rolle Sfr21 and Nyon Sfr28.60).

LAUSANNE TO ROLLE

A pleasant walk west of Lausanne (about 6km from Ouchy) brings you to **St Sulpice**, a semi-suburban settlement whose jewel is the Romanesque church of the same name by the lake. A handful of restaurants are well placed to alleviate hunger. Take bus 2 from Place St François and change to bus 30 at Bourdonette.

Some 12km west of Lausanne, the first town of importance is the wine-growing centre of **Morges**. Dominating its port is the squat, four-turreted 13th-century **château** (☎ 021 316 09 90; Place du Port; adult/child/student/senior Sfr7/free/5/6;

☑ 10am-5pm Tue-Sun Jul & Aug, 10am-noon & 1.30-5pm Mon-Fri, 1.30-5pm Sat & Sun Sep-Jun), built by the Savoy Duke Louis in 1286 and today housing four museums on mostly martial subjects. Among them, the **Musée de la Figurine Historique** contains 8000 toy soldiers on parade!

The town hosts the **Fête de la Tulipe** (tulip festival) from April to mid-May along the lake in Parc de l'Indépendence. The views across the lake to the snowy hulk of Mont Blanc are impressive.

Lovers of exotic hot chocolate, teas and salads with an Asian twist should make a pilgrimage to **our pick** **Café de Balzac** (☎ 021 811 02 32; www.balzac.ch; Rue de Louis-de-Savoie 37; mains Sfr20-25, hot chocolate Sfr6.20-7.20; ☑ 8am-6.30pm Tue-Wed & Fri, 8am-10pm Thu, 9am-5pm Sat, 11am-5pm Sun), one block back from the lakeside promenade in the heart of the old centre.

Along the 26km stretch to the next major town, Nyon, are: the old village of **St Prex**, its centuries-old mansions bursting with the colour of creeping ivy and flower boxes, and **Rolle**, which also boasts a lakeside 13th-century Savoy castle (closed).

NYON TO COPPET

Nyon, of Roman origin but with a partly Celtic name (the 'on' comes from *dunon,* meaning fortified enclosure), is a busy lake town (population 17,615) at whose heart is a glistening-white, five-towered **château**. The castle was started in the 12th century and modified 400 years later. It houses the town's **Musée Historique** (History Museum; ☎ 022 363 83 51; ☑ 10am-5pm Tue-Sun Apr-Oct, 2-5pm Tue-Sun Nov-Mar), whose centrepiece is a collection of locally produced porcelain. Temporary art exhibitions are also held here. Nearby, in what was a 1st-century basilica, the multimedia display of the **Musée Romain** (☎ 022 361 75 91; www.mrn.ch; Rue Maupertuis; ☑ 10am-5pm Tue-Sun Apr-Oct, 2-5pm Tue-Sun Nov-Mar) lends insight into Nyon's Roman beginnings as Colonia Iulia Equestris. Nyon also offers a wealth of lakeside dining, from fondue to Thai.

About 2.5km northeast of central Nyon, the sprawling mansion of **Château de Prangins** houses a branch of the **Musée National Suisse** (☎ 022 994 88 90; www.musee-suisse.com; adult/child/senior & student Sfr7/free/5; ☑ 11am-5pm Tue-Sun). The permanent exhibition covers the period from 1730 to 1920 in Swiss history and there are regular temporary exhibitions.

The town's **Paléo Festival** (☎ 022 365 10 10; www .paleo.ch) is an outdoor international music extravaganza (the biggest in Switzerland) lasting six days in late July. Tickets cost about Sfr50 per day at the venue (cheaper in advance).

Coppet, halfway between Nyon and Geneva, is a tightly packed medieval village with a handful of cosy hotels and restaurants. A short walk uphill is the 18th-century **château** (☎ 022 776 10 28; adult/child/student & senior Sfr4/free/3; 2-6pm Easter-Oct), a rose-coloured stately home that belonged to the wily Jacques Necker, Louis XVI's banker and finance minister. The pile, sumptuously furnished in Louis XVI style, became home to Necker's daughter, Madame de Staël, after she was exiled from Paris by Napoleon. In her literary salons here she entertained the likes of Edward Gibbon and Lord Byron.

Lutry & Cully

About 4km east of central Lausanne, Lutry (population 8735) is a captivating village. Founded in the 11th century by French monks, it is perfect for an afternoon wander. The central **Église de St Martin et St Clément** was built in the early 13th century. A short way north is a modest **château**. Stroll along the pretty waterfront and, inland, the slightly twee main street, lined with art galleries, antique stores and the occasional bar. On the last weekend of September, the town celebrates the annual wine harvest with parades and tastings.

The **Caveau du Singe Vert** (Green Monkey Cellar; ☎ 021 866 16 26; www.jazzausingevert.ch; Grand Rue 41; admission Sfr25 for concerts) hosts a couple of live gigs a month. Another good place for concerts, especially *chanson française* (French classics) is **Esprit Frappeur** (☎ 021 793 12 01; www .espritfrappeur.ch; Villa Mégroz, Ave du Grand Pont 20; admission up to Sfr35; 7.30pm-2am Tue-Sat, 5pm-midnight Sun). Bus 9 runs to Lutry from Place St François in Lausanne.

Five kilometres east of Lutry, the wine town of Cully (population 1750) is home to a fine old hotel-restaurant. The **Auberge du Raisin** (☎ 021 799 21 31; www.aubergeduraisin.ch; Place de l'Hôtel de Ville 1; s/d Sfr180/220, apt Sfr380;) started taking in weary travellers in the 15th century. In the rotisserie you can sit down for a grand meaty meal or local fish (the set menu is Sfr120).

SWISS RIVIERA

Stretching east to Villeneuve, the Swiss Riviera rivals its French counterpart as a magnet for the rich and famous. The mild climate encourages palm trees and other subtropical flora to flourish barely an hour's drive from Alpine ski spots.

Lovers of panoramic train rides, steam trains and the like should inquire in either Vevey or Montreux about the many excursion options available in this area and to the Bernese Oberland.

VEVEY

pop 16,950 / elevation 385m

Lakeside Vevey exudes an understated swankiness and is well accustomed to welcoming celebrities, from Jean-Jacques Rousseau to Charlie Chaplin. Chaplin hung about for 25 years until his death in 1977. His former mansion in Corsier, the Manoir de Ban, is destined to become a Chaplin museum in 2010.

Orientation & Information

The hub of the town is Grande Place, 250m to the left of the train station. The **tourist office** (☎ 084 886 84 84; www.montreux-vevey.com; 9am-6pm Mon-Fri, 8.30am-12.30pm Sat mid-May–mid-Sep, 9am-noon & 1-5.30pm Mon-Fri, 9am-noon Sat mid-Sep–mid-May) is on the square in the former market building.

Sights

The old streets east of Grande Place and the lakeside promenades are worth exploring. Apart from that, the main entertainment comes from several museums.

The **Musée Suisse du Jeu** (Swiss Games Museum; ☎ 021 977 23 00; www.museedujeu.com; Rue du Château 11; adult/under 6yr/6-16yr/student & senior Sfr8/free/2/4; 11am-5.30pm Tue-Sun) is certainly the most amusing. The games are arranged according to themes – educational, strategic, simulation, skill and chance, and you can play several (explanations are in French). The museum is in the Château de la Tour de Peilz. To get there, take trolley bus 1 to Place du Temple.

Nestlé, with its headquarters located in Vevey since 1814, runs the **Alimentarium – Musée de l'Alimentation** (Food Museum; ☎ 021 924 41 11; www .alimentarium.ch; Quai Perdonnet; adult/child/student & senior Sfr10/free/8; 10am-6pm Tue-Sun), which takes an entertaining look at food and nutrition, past and present.

Musée Jenisch (☎ 021 921 29 50; www.musee jenisch.ch; Ave de la Gare 2; adult/child/student/senior Sfr15/free/7.50/13; 11am-5.30pm Tue-Sun) exhibits Swiss art from the 19th and 20th centuries, as well as a broad collection of drawings by international artists. Check out the special section on Oskar Kokoschka, the Viennese expressionist. Another section is dedicated to prints and engravings by artists ranging from Dürer and Rembrandt to Canaletto and Corot. Just behind the museum on Ave de la Gare is a cute little golden onion-domed 19th-century **Russian Orthodox church**. North across the railway line rises the imposing belltower of the 13th-century **Église de St Martin**. Part of the Gothic original remains and a peaceful, leafy cemetery spreads out to the north.

Musée Suisse de l'Appareil Photographique (☎ 021 925 21 40; www.cameramuseum.ch; Grande Place; adult/child/student & senior Sfr8/free/6; ◷ 11am-5.30pm Tue-Sun) concentrates on the instruments rather than the images they produce. Other museums in Vevey cover such topics as wine-growing and the history of the town.

Once every 20 to 25 years the Lavaux (see opposite) wine-growers descend on the town to celebrate a huge **summer festival**. The last time was in 1999, so we'll be waiting a while for the next one!

Sleeping

Yoba Riviera Lodge (☎ 021 923 80 40; www.rivieralodge .ch; Place du Marché 5; dm Sfr32, s/d Sfr88/95; 🅿 💻) This place is in a fun, central location, housed in a converted 19th-century mansion. The rooftop terrace offers great views and you can use the kitchen to keep eating costs down.

Hôtel des Négociants (☎ 021 922 70 11; www.hotel negociants.ch; Rue du Conseil 27; s/d Sfr115/182; ✴) Just inside the quiet and pretty old town of Vevey, this is a cheerful hotel with bright rooms and good restaurant. They have wi-fi throughout the building.

Hôtel des Trois Couronnes (☎ 021 923 32 00; www .hoteldestroiscouronnes.ch; Rue d'Italie 49; s/d from Sfr350/450; 🅿 ✴ 💻 🍴) An elegant pleasure dome in business since the mid-19th century, the 'Three Crowns' is Vevey's best. The hotel's three floors open onto interior galleries, and the decor – full of marble, period furniture and antiques – is all class.

Eating & Drinking

Le National (☎ 021 923 76 25; Rue du Torrent 9; mains Sfr25-32; ◷ 11am-midnight Mon-Tue, to 1am Wed-Thu, to 2am Fri & Sat) Run by a young and enthusiastic team, this is a great place to eat and drink. On one side is a hip bar and, on the other side, the restaurant, where you can enjoy a mix of international dishes and super salads (Sfr17).

On sunny days, take a seat in the back yard beneath the shade of a huge tree.

Le Mazot (☎ 021 921 78 22; Rue du Conseil 7; mains Sfr22-36; ◷ lunch & dinner Mon-Tue & Thu-Sat, dinner only Sun) In the heart of the old town, this is an institute of classic local cooking, dominated by steaks and horse meat filets in the special Mazot sauce (they're not letting out the secret recipe).

our pick **Restaurant Le Château** (☎ 021 921 12 10; www.denismartin.ch; Rue du Château 2; tasting menu Sfr260; ◷ dinner only Tue-Sun) Chef Denis Martin is one of the biggest names in Swiss contemporary cooking, inspired by the Catalan king of molecular kitchen wizardry, Ferran Adrià. The tasting menus involve a long list (some 20-odd) of tonsil-tickling taste sensations, some with such inscrutable names as *L'air de rien parmesan et cubisme de veau* (Parmesan looks like nothing with veal Cubism!). The restaurant is housed in a 17th century residence (that also houses the town's history museum) a block from the lake.

Getting There & Away

Vevey is 18 to 25 minutes from Lausanne by train (Sfr7) and five to 10 minutes from Montreux (Sfr3.40). Trolley bus 1 runs from Vevey to Montreux (Sfr3.20) and on to Villeneuve (Sfr4.60).

AROUND VEVEY

A steam train chugs along the 3km track (15 minutes) from Blonay to Chamby, where a **train museum** houses steam engines and machinery. Entry and the return trip cost Sfr18/9 per adult/child, but it only operates on Saturday afternoons and Sundays from early May to early October. On four or five Sunday afternoons in summer the steam train departs from Vevey (adult/child Sfr39/19.50). For more information, look up www.blonay-chamby.ch.

Spots near Vevey with good views and walks are Les Pléiades (1360m), accessible by train, Chexbres, a stop on the summer 'wine train' that runs to Puidoux, and Mont Pélerin (1080m) which is accessible by funicular and has a panoramic tower, Plein Ciel. En route to Les Pléiades is Lally, where **Les Sapins** (☎ 021 943 13 95; www.les-sapins.ch; Rte des Monts; s/d Sfr80/150, d with bathroom Sfr160; 🅿 💻 🍴) is a rambling and rustic choice for accommodation and food. Rooms are quite varied. They have a Jacuzzi and sauna on site and can arrange massages. The views south to the Alps are fabulous.

LAKE GENEVA & VAUD

LAVAUX WINE REGION

The serried ranks of lush, green, vine terraces that carpet the steep slopes above Lake Geneva between Lausanne and Montreux belong to the Lavaux wine region, which produces 20% of the Canton de Vaud's wine and has been a Unesco World Heritage site since 2007.

The villages of Lutry, Villette, Cully, Calamin, Epesses (which, by the way, hosts one of the lake's few nudist beaches), Dézaley, St Saphorin, Chardonne and Riex are among the wine centres. The two main wine types are Calamin and Dézaley and most of the whites (about three-quarters of all production) are made with the Chasselas grape.

It is possible to walk through much of the Lavaux wine country. Starting in Lutry, you can follow trails that lead you through hamlets

---

FRANZ WEBER, CHAMPION OF LAVAUX

Born in Basel in 1927, Franz Weber studied at the Paris Sorbonne from 1948 and was for years a roving journalist. He fell in love with the Lavaux wine region in 1956 and took up his first environmental cause in the fight to preserve the village of Surlej, in Graubünden, in 1965. It was the first of more than 150 conservation battles. He set up the Fondation Franz Weber (www.ffw.ch) in 1975 and is still fighting today.

You prefer the term 'defender of nature' to 'ecologist'.
When I see something beautiful, which could be enjoyed by our descendents, being destroyed, it makes me sick. I was an ecologist before the word even existed!

When did you give up journalism?
In 1974, I was late with 15 stories – impossible!

You have a special fondness for Lavaux…
In Paris, when I wanted to show foreigners something beautiful, I would bring them down to see Lavaux. I created the Save Lavaux association in 1972 (to fight development plans). But, with the exception of some winemakers, everyone was against me, including the government! They said, 'No Parisian from Basel is going to tell us what to do!' Even many of the winemakers wanted to speculate. In Lausanne, however, the press backed me.

The region was finally protected under the constitution of the Vaud Canton and in 2007 became a Unesco World Heritage site. Is the battle over?
No, we have to fight constantly against construction projects. It's dreadful. In 2003, a new constitution was adopted and the Lavaux article was dropped. We launched another fight and in the referendum we had a crushing victory. This time 80% of the Lavaux winemakers were behind us! And almost 100% in Lausanne!

You are backing the fight against moving Lausanne's Musée de Beaux Arts.
Its present building (Palais de Rumine) is magnificent! And they (Lausanne City Hall) want to build a bunker right on the lake, destroying the lake's beauty! It's terrible. There is absolutely no need for this. It's a beautiful belle époque building.

Are you still in touch with Brigitte Bardot?
Of course.

In the 1970s, was it you who got Bardot involved in the campaign against hunting baby seals in Canada?
I was shocked by the hunt and began talking about it on the radio and in the press. Some people from Greenpeace came to ask for help. I lent them US$5000, which was never returned. But it was I who started the international campaign. Bardot had written to me and I said to her, 'Come along!' (To the ice floes in Canada, where Weber organised for 75 journalists to witness the hunt.)

Does one need to be angry to conduct these campaigns? Do you never tire of fighting?
Anger is necessary. I've always been a rebel against injustice.

You are still campaigning?
Oh yes, there are many fights. There are those in Zürich who would like to turn St Gallen into Geneva, to create a forest of skyscraper…it's awful.

And the future?
I don't know. In Switzerland, many think only of themselves. When something beautiful in the world dies, something in us dies too.

like Grandvaux and down to lakeside Cully. In each it is often possible to visit *caveaux*. They tend to open between 5pm to 9pm Friday through Sunday. You could even walk all the way to Chardonne, about four hours' walk depending on what sort of detours you make along the way. From there head to a lakeside town to pick up a train back to Lausanne.

The **Lavaux Express** (www.lavaux.com, in French & German; adult/under 4yr/4-12yr Sfr10/free/5; ☑ Mar-Oct) is a tractor-driven tourist train that does several circuits along wine trails between Lutry and Cully.

MONTREUX & AROUND
pop 23,200 / elevation 385m

In the 19th century, writers, artists and musicians (Lord Byron and the Shelleys among them) flocked to this pleasing lakeside resort. It has remained a magnet ever since, its main drawcards being peaceful waterfront walks, mild microclimate and the Château de Chillon.

Montreux is known to music lovers for its annual summer jazz festival (going since 1967). In 1971, Montreux casino was the stage for a rather different kind of gig. Frank Zappa was doing his thing when the casino caught fire, casting a pall of smoke over Lake Geneva and inspiring the members of Deep Purple to pen their classic rock number, *Smoke on the Water*.

Orientation & Information

The lakeshore is fronted by a mix of 19th-century hotels, restaurants and shops, while the *vieux quartier* (Old Town) is a small cluster of quiet streets around Rue du Pont, high uphill. From the train station, on Ave des Alpes, take the lift or stairs from opposite the post office down to the shore. Here you'll find the **tourist office** (☎ 084 886 84 84; www.montreux -vevey.com; ☑ 9am-6pm Mon-Fri, 10am-5pm Sat & Sun mid-May–mid-Sep, 9am-noon & 1-5.30pm Mon-Fri, 10am-2pm Sat & Sun mid-Sep–mid-May), whose staff will help book hotels – a must at festival time.

Sights & Activities
CHÂTEAU DE CHILLON

This extraordinary, oval-shaped **castle** (Map p102; ☎ 021 966 89 10; www.chillon.ch; Ave de Chillon 21; adult/child/student & senior Sfr12/6/10; ☑ 9am-6pm Apr-Sep, 9.30am-5pm Mar & Oct, 10am-4pm Nov-Feb) was brought to the world's attention by Lord Byron, and the world has been filing past ever since.

Occupying a stunning position on Lake Geneva, the 13th-century fortress is a maze of courtyards, towers and halls filled with arms, period furniture and artwork. The landward side is heavily fortified but lakeside it presents a gentler face. Chillon was largely built by the House of Savoy and then taken over by Bern's governors after Vaud fell to that canton. In the **Chapelle St Georges** are medieval frescos. And don't miss the spooky Gothic dungeons.

Byron made the place famous with *The Prisoner of Chillon,* his 1816 poem about François Bonivard, thrown into the dungeon for his seditious ideas and freed by Bernese forces in 1536. Byron carved his name into the pillar to which Bonivard was supposedly chained. Painters William Turner and Gustave Courbet captured the castle's silhouette on canvas, while Jean-Jacques Rousseau, Alexandre Dumas and Mary Shelley were all moved to write about it.

The castle is a 45-minute walk along the lakefront from Montreux. Otherwise take trolley bus 1 (Sfr2.30), which passes by every 10 minutes.

OLD MONTREUX

The **Musée de Montreux** (Montreux Museum; ☎ 021 963 13 53; www.museemontreux.ch; Rue de la Gare 40; adult/child/student & senior Sfr6/free/4; ☑ 10am-noon & 2-5pm mid-Mar–early Nov) recounts the history of the town and locality. Displays range from a handful of Roman finds and coins through to period furniture, bathtubs and street signs. The steep streets around the museum and further uphill are the core of the original Old Town of Montreux and merit a wander. The charming **Maison Visinand** (☎ 021 963 07 26; www .montreux.ch/visinand; Rue du Pont 32; ☑ 3-6pm Wed-Sun) is a cultural centre and theatre with regular exhibitions.

AUDIORAMA

Thousands of radios and TVs of all vintages are held in what is also known as the **Musée National Suisse de l'Audiovisuel** (☎ 021 963 22 33; www.audiorama.ch; Ave de Chillon 74; Territet; adult/ child/student & senior Sfr10/free/6; ☑ 1-6pm Tue-Sun). Throwing more light on the history of radio and TV are audiovisual archives from around the world. The whole is housed in the former Grand Hôtel, a belle époque gem whose star room is the Salle Sissi, an art-nouveau marvel with lake views.

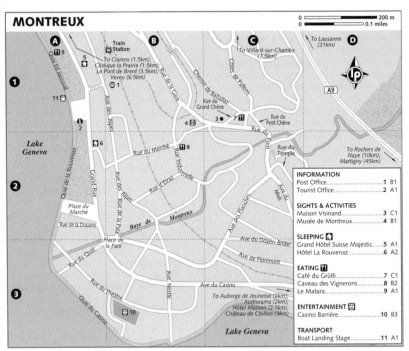

MONTREUX

INFORMATION
Post Office.......................................1 B1
Tourist Office...................................2 A1

SIGHTS & ACTIVITIES
Maison Visinand..............................3 C1
Musée de Montreux........................4 B1

SLEEPING 🏠
Grand Hôtel Suisse Majestic............5 A1
Hôtel La Rouvenaz.........................6 A2

EATING 🍴
Café du Grütli................................7 C1
Caveau des Vignerons...................8 B2
Le Matara......................................9 A1

ENTERTAINMENT 🎭
Casino Barrière.............................10 B3

TRANSPORT
Boat Landing Stage.......................11 A1

LAKE GENEVA & VAUD

ROCHERS DE NAYE
A scenic railway from Montreux leads to this natural platform (2042m), from where you have remarkable lake and Alpine views. MOB trains cost Sfr59 return.

SPAS
Montreux is a good place for a relaxing bath and beauty session.

Clinique la Prairie, Clarens-Montreux (☎ 021 989 33 11; www.laprairie.ch; Chemin de la Prairie, Clarens; beautymed programs from Sfr8400 a week) is Switzerland's most famous spa. Specialising in 'scientific rejuvenation', or 'beautymed' treatments, it offers everything from whirlpool baths to cosmetic surgery.

Festivals & Events
Montreux' best-known festival is **Montreux Jazz** (☎ 021 966 44 44; www.montreuxjazz.com) lasting two weeks in early July. Many free concerts take place every day, but count on spending around Sfr40 to Sfr100 for one of the big gigs. The music is not only jazz; past performers have included BB King, Paul Simon, Jamiroquai and Marianne Faithful.

The **Montreux-Vevey Music Festival** (☎ 021 962 80 00; www.septmus.ch; admission Sfr20-115) is a classical music fest (also known as Septembre Musical) held from late August to mid-September.

Sleeping
Auberge de Jeunesse (☎ 021 963 49 34; Passage de l'Auberge 8, Territet; dm from Sfr32; 🕑 7.30-10am & 5-10pm mid-Feb–mid-Nov; 🖥) This modern, chirpy hostel is a 30-minute walk along the lake clockwise from the tourist office (or take the local train to Territet or bus 1). Dorms have two to eight beds.

Hôtel La Rouvenaz (☎ 021 963 27 36; www.montreux .ch/rouvenaz-hotel; Rue du Marché 1; s/d Sfr130/190; 🖥) A simple, family-run spot with its own Italian restaurant downstairs, you cannot get any closer to the lake or the heart of the action. The 12 rooms are simple but pleasant and bright, and most have at least a lake glimpse.

ourpick Hôtel Masson (☎ 021 966 00 44; www.hotel masson.ch; Rue Bonivard 5; s/d Sfr180/240 🅿) In 1829, this vintner's mansion was converted into a hotel. The old charm has remained intact and the hotel, set in magnificent grounds, is on the Swiss Heritage list of the most beautiful hotels in the country. It lies southeast of Montreux and back in the hills, and is best reached by taxi. It also has a small sauna and Jacuzzi for guests.

Grand Hôtel Suisse Majestic (☎ 021 966 33 33; www.suisse-majestic.com; Ave des Alpes 45; s/d Sfr240/340, with lake views Sfr290/390; ✗ 🖳) With its two-tiered frontage and ranks of bright yellow awnings sheltering the balconies of those rooms looking out over the lake, this historic hotel (built in 1870) remains one of the most atmospheric on the waterfront. Rooms with parquet floors and muted decor are warm and inviting.

Eating

Café du Grütli (☎ 021 963 42 65; Rue du Grand Chêne 8; mains up to Sfr30; ✗ Wed-Mon) This cheerful little eatery is hidden away in the old part of town and provides good home cooking, ranging from rösti with ham to hearty meat dishes, salads and the inevitable fondue.

Caveau des Vignerons (☎ 021 963 25 70; Rue Industrielle 30bis; mains Sfr23-38; ✗ lunch & dinner Mon-Fri, dinner Sat) This is the classic locale for traditional Swiss cooking. Various fondue options (Sfr23 to Sfr31) are tempting, as are the meat dishes, done on *ardoise* (hot stone).

Le Matara (☎ 021 966 22 20; www.eurotelriviera.ch; Grand Rue 81; mains Sfr30-48; ✗ 11am-11pm) For well-prepared lake catch of the day, Matara is one of the better lakeside choices. It has a slightly dated feel but the outdoor terrace is very pleasant.

our pick **Montagnard** (☎ 021 964 83 49; www.montagnard.ch; mains Sfr22-28; ✗ Wed-Sun) For a taste of hearty country fare in a one-time timber farmhouse that has been operating as a restaurant since 1928. It sits amid gardens in the village of Villard-sur-Chamby, a 9.5km taxi ride from central Montreux.

Le Pont de Brent (☎ 021 964 52 30; www.lepontdebrent.com; Rte de Blonay, Brent; tasting menus Sfr85-285, mains Sfr40-80; ✗ Tue-Sat) Set in a pretty country house, this is one of Switzerland's top restaurants and has three Michelin stars (one of only two in the country). A changing and imaginative menu is complemented by a fine wine list. It's northwest of Montreux in the hamlet of Brent, accessible by train.

Entertainment

Casino Barrière (☎ 021 962 83 83; www.casinodemontreux.ch; Rue du Théâtre 9; ✗ 11-3am Sun-Thu, to 5am Fri & Sat) This casino has everything from slot

machines to a pool (to cool off after burning through your millions).

Getting There & Away

From Lausanne, three trains an hour (Sfr10.20) take 20 to 35 minutes to reach Montreux. Scenic trains head up into the Bernese Oberland and Alps from Montreux (see p368). For boat services, see p100.

NORTHWESTERN VAUD

The Jura mountain chain closes off the northwest of Vaud, running roughly parallel in the north to Lac de Neuchâtel, at whose southern tip sits Yverdon, a pleasant low-key town where you can take the waters.

YVERDON-LES-BAINS

pop 24,700 / elevation 437m

The Romans were the first to discover the healthy qualities of Yverdon's hot spa waters and since then the town has made its living from them. It's an enjoyable lakeside resort and Canton de Vaud's second-largest town.

Information

The **tourist office** (☎ 024 423 61 01; www.yverdon-les-bains.ch/tourisme; Ave de la Gare 1; ✗ 9am-6pm Mon-Fri, 9.30am-3.30pm Sat & Sun Jul & Aug, 9am-noon & 1.30-6pm Mon-Fri, 9.30am-3.30pm Sat & Sun May, Jun & Sep-Oct, 9am-noon & 1.30-6pm Mon-Fri Nov-Apr) has information on the town and surrounding area.

Sights & Activities

The Old Town core is clustered around the 13th-century **château**, built by Peter II of Savoy. Inside, the **Musée du Château** (Musée d'Yverdon-les-Bains et Région; ☎ 024 425 93 10; adult/child/student & senior Sfr8/4/7; ✗ 11am-5pm Jun-Sep, 2-5pm Oct-May) contains local prehistoric artefacts, arms, clothing and a Ptolemaic Egyptian mummy.

Opposite the castle, the **Maison d'Ailleurs** (House of Elsewhere; ☎ 024 425 64 38; www.ailleurs.ch; Place de Pestalozzi 14; adult/child/student & senior Sfr9/5/7; ✗ 2-6pm Wed-Fri, noon-6pm Sat & Sun) is a science-fiction museum that features a mock-up of a spaceship, a room dedicated to HR Giger (of *Alien* fame) and masses of material dealing with the science-fantasy worlds of figures ranging from Homer to Jules Verne. The latter section is separate and contains models of the fantastical vehicles Verne dreamt up

YVERDON-LES-BAINS

INFORMATION	
Post Office	1 B2
Tourist Office	2 B2

SIGHTS & ACTIVITIES	
Centre Thermal	3 B3
Château	4 B2
Maison d'Ailleurs	5 B2
Musée du Château	(see 4)
Temple	6 A2

SLEEPING ⌂	
Grand Hôtel des Bains	7 C3
Hôtel de l'Ange	8 C2
Hôtel L'Ecusson Vaudois	9 B2

EATING ⊞	
Café/Restaurant du Château	10 B2

TRANSPORT	
Bus Stop	11 B2

in his novels. The museum only opens when a temporary exhibition is on.

At the west end of the same square stands the ochre, rounded and rather unique baroque facade of the mid-18th-century **temple**. This central church has a strange trapezoid form dictated by the medieval street plan.

The lake offers the opportunity for various boat rides and other water activities, including windsurfing, water-skiing and sailing. Beaches stretch along 5km of the lakeside. One company that rents out boats, windsurfing kits and the like is **Les Vikings** (www.lesvikings.ch; Chemin des Colons 16) at Yvonand, east of Yverdon along the lake.

SPAS

The water from the 14,000-year-old mineral springs starts 500m below ground. By the time it hits the surface it has picked up all sorts of salubrious properties from the layers of rock, and is particularly soothing for rheumatism and respiratory ailments.

The **Centre Thermal** (☎ 024 423 02 32; www.cty.ch; ☺ 8am-10pm Mon-Fri, 9am-8pm Sat, Sun & hols), the health complex off Ave des Bains, offers a

wide range of treatments. Even if you feel fine you can enjoy bathing in indoor and outdoor pools (temperature 28°C to 34°C) for Sfr19 for adults and Sfr11.50 for children (three to 16 years). For Sfr30 you get access to the pools, saunas, *hammam* (Turkish bath), a tropical shower, Japanese baths and a giant Jacuzzi.

Sleeping & Eating

Hôtel L'Ecusson Vaudois (☎ 024 425 40 15; www.ecusson vaudois.ch; Rue de la Plaine 29; s/d Sfr90/130, without bathroom Sfr70/110; ⊠) This hotel, with a ground-floor café, is the only central place. It has a handful of fresh, modernised rooms, some of which do not have their own bathroom and are a little cheaper. The nonsmoking1st-floor restaurant (mains Sfr21 to Sfr32) is worth stopping by for traditional local cooking (perch filets, horsemeat steaks) and a range of vegetarian options. You can opt for a three-course set vegetarian (Sfr38) or fish (Sfr45) meal.

Hôtel de l'Ange (☎ 024 425 25 85; Rue de Clendy 25; s/d Sfr85/140; Ⓟ ⊠) A sprawling old house about a 15-minute walk east of the train station, the 'Angel Hotel' has 22 straightforward rooms. The restaurant is also good for moderately priced local cooking. Lake fish, trout and flambéed scampi are among the house specialities.

Grand Hôtel des Bains (☎ 024 424 64 64; www .grandhotelyverdon.ch; Ave des Bains 22; s/d to Sfr350/440; P 🍴 🖥 🕿) The big daddy of the luxury bath hotels, it offers all imaginable comforts and free entry to the thermal pools.

Café/Restaurant du Château (☎ 024 425 49 62; Place de Pestalozzi 13; mains Sfr23-42) With its heavy dark timber beams and fine traditional meat and fish dishes, this classic mixes in a more modern tone with discreet furniture and lounge music. It also offers a limited pizza and pasta menu.

Getting There & Away

Regular trains run from Lausanne (Sfr14.80, 20 to 45 minutes). One or two an hour run to Neuchâtel (Sfr13.80, 20 minutes). An hourly train heads for Estavayer-le-Lac (Sfr7, 17 minutes).

AROUND YVERDON-LES-BAINS

Grandson

Grandson's stout, grey, 13th-century **château** (☎ 024 445 29 26; www.chateau-grandson.ch; adult/ child/student & senior Sfr12/5/9; 🕗 8.30am-6pm Apr-Oct, to 5pm Nov-Mar) fell briefly to Charles the Bold in early 1476, but Swiss Confederate troops soon turned the tables and strung some of his routed Burgundian troops from the apple trees in the castle orchard.

The castle's **Musée d'Histoire** recounts the story of 1476 and other battles with dioramas, while the prize exhibit at its **Musée de l'Automobile** is Greta Garbo's white Rolls Royce.

Regular buses connect Yverdon with Grandson (Sfr3, 13 minutes). Or you could walk the 5km around the lake.

Sainte-Croix

pop 4305 / elevation 1066m

High in the Jura Mountains, Sainte-Croix has been hailed for its music boxes since the mid-19th century. The art of making these intricate items is documented in the **Centre International de la Méchanique d'Art** (☎ 024 454 44 77; www.musees .ch; Rue de l'Industrie 2; guided tour in French adult/child/ student & senior Sfr13/7/11; 🕗 10.30am, 2pm, 3.30pm & 5pm Tue-Sun Jun-Aug, 2pm, 3.30pm & 5pm Tue-Sun Feb-May & Sep-Oct, 3pm Tue-Fri, 2pm, 3.30pm & 5pm Sat & Sun Nov-Jan). Music boxes contain a rotating spiked cylinder that bends and releases metal prongs, causing

---

> **DAVID AND GOLIATH**
>
> As far as France is concerned, Champagne, a hamlet 3km northeast of Grandson, may as well not exist. Eager to protect the sacred name of Champagne, French courts ruled in early 2008 that the Cornu biscuit company, based in the Swiss village, could not sell one of its biscuit varieties as *flûtes de Champagne* (which could also be understood to mean Champagne glasses) in France. The courts also banned the company's website name: www.champagne.ch. Months later, the company was planning to appeal and the website was still up and running. A few years earlier, Switzerland had ceded to French demands and agreed that Champagne's winemakers could not label their wine as coming from…Champagne.

them to vibrate and hum melodiously. Some of the more elaborate boxes also incorporate miniature drums, bells and accordions. The best exhibits are the musical automata, such as the acrobats and a tiny Mozart.

The town is otherwise none too scintillating, but makes a handy base for local winter sports. The highest point in the area is **Le Chasseron** (1607m), the focus for the area's downhill skiing and a two-hour walk from Sainte-Croix. It provides a marvellous 360-degree panorama of the Alps, Lac de Neuchâtel and the Jura.

A local train runs from Yverdon (Sfr10.20, 36 minutes).

TO LAC DE JOUX

This little-visited corner of the canton to the north of Lac de Joux and its valley hides several gems. By car you could easily tour the area from Lausanne or Geneva in a day.

La Sarraz to Romainmôtier

From Lausanne take the N9 highway (not the freeway) towards La Sarraz. Its **castle** (☎ 021 866 64 23; adult/child/student & senior Sfr9/5/8; 🕗 1-5pm Tue-Sun Jun-Aug & Oct, 1-5pm Sat & Sun & hols Easter-May & Sep), some of it dating from the 11th century, contains a museum devoted to the horse and carriage. From there follow a side road north to **Orbe** (where Nescafé was invented in 1938), which is interesting for the 13th-century **Tour Bernard** defensive tower and the **Musée de Mosaïques Romaines** (☎ 024 441 52 66; adult/child

Sfr4/3; ☻ 9am-noon & 1.30-5pm Mon-Fri, 1.30-5.30pm Sat & Sun Easter-Oct). The museum is a series of pavilions containing mosaics on the site of a 3rd-century Gallo-Roman villa, 1.5km north of town. In the first pavilion is the beautiful polychrome *mosaïque aux divinités*, which depicts the seven planetary gods (Jupiter, Saturn and co). The second one contains the *mosaïque du cortège rustique*, with several rural scenes, including a man driving an ox-drawn cart.

Eight kilometres southwest, **Romainmôtier** is cupped in a lush green bowl of vegetation and wholly dominated by the Cluny order's **Abbatiale** (☎ 024 453 14 65; admission free; ☻ 7am-8pm), a remarkable sandstone church whose origins reach back to the 6th century. Upon and around its 11th-century Romanesque core were added new layers in higgledy-piggledy fashion over the ensuing centuries. Through the mixed Romanesque-Gothic entrance you step into the proud interior of the church, with its powerful pillars and faded frescos. It is frequently the setting for concerts and recitals (www.concerts-romainmotier.ch). Of the couple of hotels and restaurants here, the pick is the delightful 17th-century ⌜our pick⌟ **Hôtel au Lieutenant Baillival** (☎ 024 453 14 58; www.romain motier.ch/~baillival; s Sfr110-180, d Sfr160-260; (P) (X) (🖳)), full of antique furniture and rustic charm. It has its own restaurant and wi-fi throughout.

Vallorbe to Lac de Joux

About 12km west along the N9 is the industrial town of **Vallorbe**. Its pleasant old centre astride the Orbe River is home to the **Musée du Fer et du Chemin de Fer** (Iron & Railway Museum; ☎ 021 843 25 83; adult/child/student Sfr12/6/10; ☻ 9.30am-noon & 1.30-6pm Tue-Sun, 1.30-6pm Mon mid-Mar-Oct, 1.30-6pm Tue-Fri Nov-mid-Mar), where you can see a blacksmith working at a traditional forge. Power for the furnace is derived from four large paddlewheels turning outside in the river. The railway section includes models and memorabilia. An hourly regional train from Lausanne to Vallorbe (Sfr16.80, 45 minutes) travels via La Sarraz. It makes a stop at Croy, from where it is just a short postal bus ride on to Romainmôtier (total trip Sfr3, five minutes).

A few kilometres outside Vallorbe is the underground **Fort Pré-Giroud** (Map p102; ☎ 021 843 25 83; adult/child/student & senior Sfr12/7/11; ☻ 10.30am-4pm daily Jul-late Aug, 11am-3.45pm Sat & Sun & hols May-Jun & late Aug-Oct), built in 1937 to ward off a possible attack from France. The seemingly unremarkable mountain chalet commands views across the Orbe Valley into France and below ground could accommodate 130 men. In its dormitories, canteens, kitchen, telephone exchange and infirmary now stand around 40 military mannequins. Bring warm clothing, as the underground temperature is 8°C. The fort is a 40-minute walk from Vallorbe (follow the Fort 39-45 signs) or a nice drive through forests on a minor back road leading over the mountain ridge to Vaulion.

About 2km south of Vallorbe on the road to Lac de Joux at Mont d'Orzeires is **Juraparc** (☎ 021 843 17 35; www.juraparc.ch; adult/child Sfr5/3.50; ☻ 9am-dusk), where North American bison cavort in the company of bears and wolves.

Shortly afterwards you reach the Col du Mont d'Orzeires pass and descend to Le Pont, a sleepy village at the northern end of the **Lac de Joux**, a delightfully peaceful spot and source of your dinnertime perch filets.

The main road south follows the Orbe river through Le Brassus and skirts the border on the French side (bring your passport). You could turn east at Le Brassus to climb to the Col du Marchairuz pass (1447m) and descend through pretty villages towards Lake Geneva.

ALPES VAUDOISES

The southeast corner of Vaud extends into a captivating Alpine nook. A five-day regional ski pass for the Alpes Vaudoises (Vaud Alps), including Les Diablerets glacier and Gstaad (see p196), costs Sfr249. Glacier skiing is an option in June and July and the hiking in summer is a dream.

AIGLE

pop 8160 / elevation 405m

A many-turreted castle surrounded by vineyards is the highlight of Aigle, the capital of the Chablais wine-producing region in southeast Vaud. The Chablais, which extends into neighbouring Valais, produces some of the country's best whites.

The castle, on a gentle rise, is itself enough to induce you to stop by. Anyone with even a vague interest in wine will want to visit its **Musée de la Vigne et du Vin** (☎ 024 466 21 30; adult/child/student & senior Sfr9/5/6; ☻ 11am-6pm daily Jul-Aug, to 6pm Tue-Sun Apr-Jun & Sep-Oct). Two thousand years of wine-making are explained across 17 rooms. Opposite the castle gates, the Maison de la Dîme houses the **Musée de l'Etiquette**, in which some 800 wine-bottle labels from around the world are displayed and explained. The naughty labels misappropriating names like 'Champagne' are at times quite a laugh. You enter with the ticket from the Musée de la Vigne et du Vin.

There are several hotels should you wish to stay. Regular trains operate from Lausanne (Sfr14.80, 30 minutes) to Aigle via Montreux.

LEYSIN
pop 3480 / elevation 1350m

Leysin started life as a tuberculosis centre but is now a sprawling ski resort with 60km of runs. Many other sports are on offer, including a *via ferrata* – a vertical 'footpath' negotiated via cables and rungs. The **tourist office** (☎ 024 493 33 00; www.leysin.ch; Place Large) is based in the New Sporting Centre. Take in the Alpine scenery from the revolving restaurant atop **Mt Berneuse** (2048m). The cable car costs Sfr21 return in summer, or Sfr43 for the lift and a day's skiing in winter.

Hiking Sheep (☎ 024 494 35 35; www.hikingsheep .com; dm/d Sfr30/80; P ⊠ ▣) gets floods of accolades from happy backpackers. This tall, art-deco house is two minutes' walk from Grand Hotel station. It has a kitchen and good communal facilities. **Les Orchidées** (☎ 024 494 14 21; www.lesorchidees.ch; s/d Sfr80/140; P ⊠), a family hotel by Vermont station, has 18 crisp rooms, Alpine views and a decent restaurant. It is one of more than a dozen options.

To get to Leysin take the hourly cogwheel train that goes from Aigle (Sfr9, 22 to 30 minutes).

LES DIABLERETS
elevation 1150m

Overshadowed by the mountain of the same name (3209m), Les Diablerets is one of the key ski resorts in the Alpes Vaudoises. A number of fairly easy ski runs are open during June and July at **Glacier de Tsanfleuron** (3000m), which gives the Diablerets resort its recent official name, Glacier 3000. Whether you plan to ski or not, the views are fabulous.

Two cable cars run up to the glacier from the valley floor, both are linked to the village by bus: starting from Reusch or Col du Pillon you get to Cabane des Diablerets, where a further cable car whisks you almost to the summit at Scex Rouge. To ski from here all the way back down to Reusch is an exhilarating 2000m descent over 14km.

A one-day ski pass that takes in Les Diablerets, Villars and Gryon and the glacier costs Sfr58.

The town's **tourist office** (☎ 024 492 33 58; www .diablerets.ch), to the right of the train station, has more information.

Auberge de la Poste (☎ 024 492 31 24; www.auberge delaposte.ch; Rue de la Gare; s/d Sfr100/200; P ⊠ ⊠) is a grand, inviting, timber hotel oozing mountain charm. It has wi-fi.

From Aigle take the hourly train via Le Sépey (Sfr10.80, 50 minutes).

VILLARS & GRYON

Villars (1350m) and nearby Gryon share the same local ski pass with Les Diablerets and in winter are linked by a free train for holders of the ski pass. For information on the area check out each village's website: www.villars .ch and www.gryon.ch. If you want to buy ski passes in advance at reduced rates, check out www.easyski.ch.

The skiing is mostly intermediate but the runs are varied, making it ideal for families. In summer, the country is perfect for hiking. One great walk starts at the Col de Bretaye pass (reached by BVB train from Villars), takes you past the pretty Lac de Chavonnes and on through verdant mountain country to Les Diablerets. The walk takes about fours hours, and from Les Diablerets you could catch a train to Aigle. The views from around the Col de Bretaye are magnificent, taking in the Dents du Midi and Mont Blanc.

Early risers can easily get in a day's skiing here from Geneva or Lausanne. Staying overnight is, generally, not a terribly cheap option.

In Villars, **Hôtel Ecureuil** (☎ 024 496 37 37; Rue Centrale; s/d Sfr125/210) offers pleasant and mostly spacious rooms, with plenty of timber. It also has a tempting little restaurant (mains Sfr17-43; ⊗ Wed-Mon; ⊠), specialising in grilled meats.

Much of Villar's nightlife revolves around **El Gringo** (www.elgringo.ch; ⊗ 11pm-4am Fri & Sat low season, nightly ski season). Aside from the club, the same people run a couple of bars in the same complex, along with the perfectly acceptable **La Toscana** (☎ 024 495 79 21; Rte des Hôtels; meals Sfr50-60; ⊗ 7-11pm Wed-Mon), which does good Italian grub.

From Aigle you can reach Villars by an hourly bus (Sfr8.20, 40 minutes). Otherwise, mainline trains continue to **Bex** (known for its nearby **salt mines** – www.mines.ch) and connect with local trains to Gryon (Sfr6.20, 25 to 30 minutes) and Villars (Sfr8.20, 40 minutes). The train running from Gryon to Villars is free with the ski pass. Occasional postal buses connect Villars with Les Diablerets via the Col de la Croix pass (closed in winter).

PAYS D'ENHAUT

The 'High Country' rises in the northeast corner of Vaud about midway between Aigle and Gruyères. In winter it could almost be considered the Francophone extension of the swank Gstaad ski scene, just over the cantonal frontier.

Château-d'Œx is an attractive family resort with a nice selection of moderate ski runs, but the place is best known for all its hot air. Bertrand Piccard and Brian Jones launched their record-breaking, round-the-world, 20-day hot-air balloon ride from here in March 1999 (they landed in Egypt). For one week in the second half of January the place bursts into a frenzy of floating colour as the town hosts the annual **Semaine Internationale de Ballons à Air Chaud** (www.ballonchateaudoex.ch) involving around 100 hot-air balloons ranging from the standard floater to odd creatures such as a massive Scottish bagpipe player! Entry just to see and feel all the hot air up close is Sfr9 on the weekend (free on weekdays). If you want to fly up, up and away, steady your nerves for fiscal turbulence. It costs up to Sfr350 per adult (half for children) for about one hour. Cheese and sweets lovers should make a beeline for **Le Chalet** (☎ 026 924 66 77; www.lechalet-fromagerie .ch; mains Sfr15-23; 9am-6pm Tue-Sun). This grand old cheesemaker is the place to gorge yourself on creamy fondue or Raclette and dreamy meringues with double cream. And they make the cheese before your eyes (from 1.30pm to 3.30pm Wednesday to Sunday)!

Less than 10km east is **Rougemont**, the other main centre. Both villages offer a variety of accommodation throughout the year. Summer activities include rafting and hiking.

The Château-d'Œx **tourist office** (☎ 026 924 25 25; www.chateau-doex.ch; La Place) is in the centre, below the hilltop clock tower. There are about 20 places to stay, ranging from chalets to a handful of rather overbearing big hotels.

The village is on the scenic Montreux-Spiez train route serviced by MOB trains. From Montreux it takes one hour and costs Sfr18.20.

LAKE GENEVA & VAUD

Fribourg, Neuchâtel & Jura

A far cry from the staggering Alpine scenes more readily associated with Switzerland, this gentle corner in the west of the country remains a 'secret'. From the evocative medieval cantonal capitals of Fribourg and Neuchâtel to the mysterious green hills and thick dark Jura forests, from the land of three lakes to gorgeous medieval villages like Gruyères and St Ursanne, it proffers a wealth of sights and scapes off the tourist track.

Be it listening to frogs singing in lakeside bogs, marvelling at palatial ice creations between pine trees or following the call of the devilish green fairy into the Val de Travers, travelling here is a brilliant sensory experience…and that includes the taste buds: savour monks' heads (strong, nutty-flavoured cheese), see how one of Switzerland's best-known AOC cheeses is made and sample sweet feather-light meringues smothered in rich, thick double cream. When it all gets too much, thousands of kilometres of waistline-saving walking, cycling and cross-country skiing trails – not to mention sailing, skiing and wakeboarding on lake water – kick in.

This chapter covers (from south to north) the cantons of Fribourg, Neuchâtel and Jura, and the northwestern tip of the Bern canton. The trio of lakes wedged between the Fribourg and Neuchâtel cantons – Lac de Neuchâtel, Lac de Morat and Bieler See – and the Fribourg canton fall mostly within the Plateau Central (Mittelland) plain. French rules everywhere bar the eastward edge of the latter canton, where German predominates.

HIGHLIGHTS

- Stuffing yourself silly on cheese, meringues and thick cream in **Gruyères** (p132)
- Stamping on the big red button to make the creations of modern artistic prodigy Jean Tinguely (p269) tick in **Fribourg** (opposite) and revelling in the town's industrial nightlife
- Taking a big hearty gulp of Vully wine, *saucisson du marc* and old-fashioned fresh air at **Owl Farm** (p132) near Murten
- Being enchanted by medieval **Neuchâtel** (p134) and the Val de Travers' (p139) green fairy
- Delving deep into the **Jura** (p140) to discover local life on a Jurassien farm and its Jurassic past at Préhisto Parc (p143)

★ Jura

★ Neuchâtel

★ Val de Travers   ★ Owl Farm

★ Fribourg

★ Gruyères

| POPULATION: 496,500 | AREA: 3311 SQ KM | LANGUAGE: FRENCH |

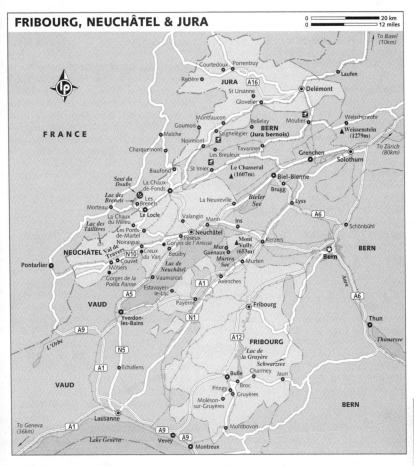

FRIBOURG, NEUCHÂTEL & JURA

Getting There & Around

Rail connections to/from the main cities, Fribourg and Neuchâtel, make light work of getting around. By road, the A12 freeway linking Bern with Lausanne and Geneva roars down the Canton de Fribourg's central spine.

CANTON DE FRIBOURG

The southernmost of the three cantons, Canton de Fribourg (population 258,250) tots up 1671 sq km on the drawing board. Pre-Alpine foothills rise grandly around its cold craggy feet; Gruyères with its sprinkling of small mountain resorts pierces its heart; and Fribourg heads the canton up north, where

pretty lakeside villages slumber between vineyards and fruit orchards.

What makes this canton most fascinating is its *Röstigraben* (linguistic divide): west speaks French, east speaks German.

FRIBOURG

pop 33,420 / elevation 629m

Nowhere is Switzerland's language divide felt more keenly than in Fribourg (Freiburg) or 'Free Town', a medieval city where inhabitants on the west bank of the Sarine River speak French, on the east bank of the Sanne speak German. Throw Catholicism and a notable student population into the cultural cocktail and you get a fascinating town with a feisty nightlife and a healthy waft of originality.

Its greatest moment in history saw a messenger sprint from Murten to Fribourg in 1476 to relay the glad tidings that the Swiss had defeated Charles the Bold…only to drop dead with exhaustion on arrival. Onlookers, saddened by this tragic twist, took the linden twig from the messenger's hat and planted it.

Information

BOOKSHOPS
Librairie Albert le Grand (☎ 026 347 35 35; Rue du Temple 1; ☼ 1-6.30pm Mon, 8.30am-6.30pm Tue, Wed & Fri, 8.30am-8pm Thu, 8am-4pm Sat) English section and maps on the 1st floor.
Payot Librairie (☎ 026 322 46 70; www.payot.ch; Rue de Romont 21; ☼ 1-6.30pm Mon, 9am-6.30pm Tue, Wed & Fri, 9am-8pm Thu, 9am-4pm Sat) English-language fiction.

INTERNET RESOURCES
Pays de Fribourg (www.pays-de-fribourg.ch) Low-down on Fribourg land.

POST
Post Office (Ave de Tivoli 3; ☼ 7.30am-6.30pm Mon-Fri, 8am-4pm Sat)
Post Office (Rue des Chanoines; ☼ 7.30am-noon & 1.45-6pm Mon-Fri, 8-11am Sat)

TOURIST INFORMATION
Tourist Office (☎ 026 321 31 75; www.fribourgtourism.ch; Ave de la Gare 1; ☼ 9am-6pm Mon-Fri, to 3pm Sat May-Sep, to 6pm Mon-Fri, to 12.30pm Sat Oct-Apr)

Sights
The 12th-century **Old Town** was laid out in simple fashion, with Grand-Rue as the main street and parallel Rue des Chanoines/Rue des Bouchers devoted to markets, church and civic buildings. The settlement later spread downhill into Auge. The bridges here – quaint stone **Pont du Milieu** and cobbled, roof-covered **Pont du Berne** – proffer great views. Pont de Zaehringen, Rte des Alpes and Chemin de Lorette are other prime vantage points.

Fribourg's famous **Tilleul de Morat** (Morat Linden Tree) stands in front of the Renaissance **town hall** (Grand-Rue).

CATHÉDRALE DE ST NICOLAS DE MYRE
Before entering this brooding 13th-century Gothic **cathedral** (☎ 026 347 10 40; www.cathedrale-fribourg.ch, in French; Rue des Chanoines 3; ☼ 9am-6pm Mon-Fri, 9am-4pm Sat, 2-5pm Sun), contemplate the main portal with its 15th-century sculptured portrayal of the Last Judgment. On your right upon entering, inside the **Chapelle du Saint Sépulcre**, is a sculptural group (1433) depicting Christ's burial with exceptional lifelikeness and movement.

A 368-step hike up the cathedral's 74m-tall **tower** (adult/child Sfr3.50/1; ☼ 10am-noon & 2-5pm Mon-Fri, 10am-4pm Sat, 2-5pm Sun Apr-Oct) is a highlight.

ESPACE JEAN TINGUELY – NIKI DE SAINT PHALLE
Jump on the button to watch the *Retable de l'Abondance Occidentale et du Mercantilisme Totalitaire* (1989–90) make its allegorical comment on Western opulence. Created in memory of Fribourg's modern artistic prodigy, Jean Tinguely (1925–91), in a tramway depot dating to 1900, the **Espace Jean Tinguely – Niki de Saint Phalle** (☎ 026 305 51 40; Rue de Morat 2; adult/child/student Sfr6/free/4; ☼ 11am-6pm Wed & Fri-Sun, to 8pm Thu) showcases his machines alongside wacky creations by French-American artist Niki de Saint Phalle (1930–2002) who worked with him from the 1950s until his death.

ÉGLISE DES CORDELIERS
Inside 13th-century **Église des Cordeliers** (Rue de Morat 6; ☼ 7.30am-7pm Apr-Sep, to 6pm Oct-Mar) the triptych (1480) above the high altar depicts the Crucifixion. Next door, the **Basilique de Notre-Dame** (Rue de Morat 1) shelters an 18th-century **Crèche Napolitaine** featuring 75 figurines re-enacting the nativity, annunciation and scenes from daily life. Drop Sfr2 in the slot to illuminate it for eight minutes.

FRIBOURG, NEUCHÂTEL & JURA

THE FRIBOURG FUNICULAR
Nowhere else in Europe does a funicular lurch up the mountainside with the aid of good old stinky sewage water; indeed on certain days it smells as such too. Constructed in 1899 and managed by the Cardinal Brewery until 1965 (when the municipality took over), the **Funiculaire de Fribourg** (ticket valid 30 min Sfr2.30; ☼ 7-8.15am & 9.30am-7pm Mon-Sat, 9.30am-7pm Sun) links the lower part of the town with the upper every six minutes. The ride in one of two counterbalancing water-powered carriages from the lower Pertuis station (121m; place du Pertuis) to the upper station (618m; Rte des Alpes) takes two minutes and includes bags of great Old Town views.

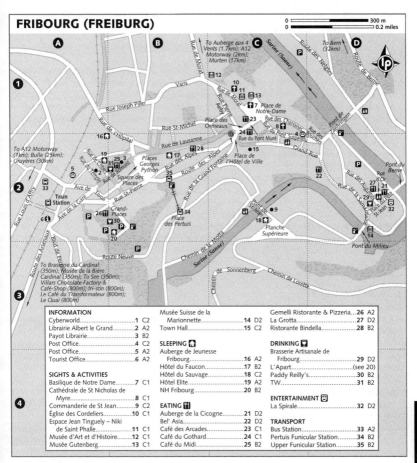

FRIBOURG (FREIBURG)

INFORMATION		
Cyberworld	1	C2
Librairie Albert le Grand	2	A2
Payot Librairie	3	B2
Post Office	4	C2
Post Office	5	A2
Tourist Office	6	A2

SIGHTS & ACTIVITIES		
Basilique de Notre Dame	7	C1
Cathédrale de St Nicholas de Myre	8	C1
Commanderie de St Jean	9	C2
Église des Cordeliers	10	C1
Espace Jean Tinguely – Niki de Saint Phalle	11	C1
Musée d'Art et d'Histoire	12	C1
Musée Gutenberg	13	C1

Musée Suisse de la Marionnette	14	D2
Town Hall	15	C2

SLEEPING		
Auberge de Jeunesse Fribourg	16	A2
Hôtel du Faucon	17	B2
Hôtel du Sauvage	18	C2
Hôtel Elite	19	A2
NH Fribourg	20	B2

EATING		
Auberge de la Cicogne	21	D2
Bel' Asia	22	D2
Café des Arcades	23	C1
Café du Gothard	24	C1
Café du Midi	25	B2

Gemelli Ristorante & Pizzeria	26	A2
La Grotta	27	D2
Ristorante Bindella	28	B2

DRINKING		
Brasserie Artisanale de Fribourg	29	D2
L'Apart	(see 20)	
Paddy Reilly's	30	B2
TW	31	B2

ENTERTAINMENT		
La Spirale	32	D2

TRANSPORT		
Bus Station	33	A2
Pertuis Funicular Station	34	B2
Upper Funicular Station	35	B2

MUSÉE GUTENBERG

Duck behind the Basilique de Notre-Dame and embark on a voyage of the printed word in the **Musée Gutenberg** (Gutenberg Museum; ☎ 026 347 38 28; www.gutenbergmuseum.ch; Place Notre Dame 16; adult/child Sfr10/6; 11am-6pm Wed, Fri & Sat, 11am-8pm Thu, 10am-5pm Sun), a printing and communication museum in a 16th-century granary. A multimedia show brings the historical exhibition up to 21st-century speed.

MUSÉE D'ART ET D'HISTOIRE

Fribourg's **Musée d'Art et d'Histoire** (Art and History Museum, MAHF; ☎ 026 305 51 40; Rue de Morat 12; adult/child/student Sfr6/free/4; 11am-6pm Tue, Wed & Fri-Sun, to 8pm Thu), with an excellent collection of late-Gothic sculpture and painting, is housed in

the Renaissance Hôtel Ratzé, with annexes in the former slaughterhouse and armoury. Gothic meets Goth in the underground chamber, where religious statues are juxtaposed with some of Tinguely's sculptural creations combining animal skulls with metal machine components. The bench-clad museum garden, overlooking the river and pierced by a Niki de Saint Phalle sculpture, is a lovely picnic spot.

MUSÉE SUISSE DE LA MARIONNETTE

Puppets prance on the stage of the **Musée Suisse de la Marionnette** (Swiss Puppetry Museum; ☎ 026 322 85 13; www.marionnette.ch, in French; Derrière-les-Jardins 2; adult/child Sfr5/3; 2-5.30pm Sat & Sun) for performances and Saturday-afternoon puppetry workshops.

INDUSTRIAL FRIBOURG

A 10-minute stroll south from the train station along Rte des Arsenaux ushers in Fribourg's most exciting quarter – the old industrial zone.

Duck west under the train tracks along Passage du Cardinal and visit local brewery, **Brasserie du Cardinal** (www.cardinal.ch, in French & Dutch; Passage du Cardinal), which has brewed one of Switzerland's best-known lagers since 1788. Two-hour **brewery tours** (☎ 058 123 42 58; adult Sfr12; ☺ advance reservation required) demonstrate how water, malt and hops are turned into nine different types of Cardinal beer and include the **Musée de la Bière Cardinal** (☎ 084 812 50 00; www.cardinal.ch; Passage du Cardinal; adult/child Sfr10/5; ☺ 2-6pm Tue & Thu).

Continue south along Rte des Arsenaux, following the waft of chocolate (no, you're not dreaming) along its continuation, Rte Wilhelm Kaiser, and at the end of the street backtrack onto Rte de la Fonderie. Fribourg's hippest DJ bars, band venues and daytime cafés – Le Quai (opposite), Le Café du Transformateur (opposite) and fri-son (p130) – hide in tatty warehouses here.

But the burnt red- and caramel-brick **Villars chocolate factory**, in business at No 2 since 1901, is the sweetest. Known for its slabs of Swiss chocolate made from Alpine-rich Gruyère milk and kid-loved *têtes au choco* (chocolate-covered marshmallow heads), the factory can't be visited. But its **café-shop** (☺ 8.30am-5.30pm Mon-Fri, 9am-noon Sat) can, much to the joy of locals, who flock here to stock up on chocolate at factory prices (Sfr6 for a 300g bar) and flop on leather sofas over a hot chocolate topped with whipped cream and Villars chocolate shavings.

PLANCHE SUPÉRIEURE

Cross Pont du Milieu and head west towards this broad sloping square dominated by the former **Commanderie de St Jean**, erected by the Knights of the Order of St John in the 13th century.

Sleeping

Auberge de Jeunesse Fribourg (☎ 026 323 19 16; Rue de l'Hôpital 2; dm/s/d incl breakfast Sfr31.50/59/95; reception ☺ 7.30-10am & 5-10pm Mar–mid-Oct; P ✗) The rules are clear at this city hostel in one wing of the 17th-century Hôpital des Bourgeois, opposite Fribourg University. No smoking, no cooking or eating in rooms, and night owls must ring to enter after 10pm.

Hôtel du Faucon (☎ 026 321 37 90; www.hotel-du -faucon.ch, in French; Rue de Lausanne 76; s/d/ste Sfr85/95/200; reception ☺ 9am-9pm) A golden eagle marks the spot: well-placed on Fribourg's main pedestrian street, this contemporary hideout offers an exceptional price-quality ratio. Furnishings are right up to date, a fridge hides inside a large cupboard and there are channels galore – BBC and CNN included – on the flat-screen TV. Or watch a DVD. Free wi-fi.

Hôtel Elite (☎ 026 322 22 60; elitefribourg@bluewin .ch; Rue du Criblet 7; s/d/tr/q incl breakfast Sfr90/140/160/215) Nothing to look at – indeed rather drab – from the outside, Hôtel Elite does have well-maintained rooms and competitive half-board rates (add Sfr25 per head) should you wish to dine in its neighbouring (again rather drab) restaurant.

NH Fribourg (☎ 026 351 91 91; www.nh-hotels.com; Grand-Places 14; d incl breakfast Sfr160-235; P ✗ ✗ 🖳) Notably modern in a lumbering apartment block, upmarket NH lures suits in the main with its business facilities, modern decor, classy restaurant and Jacuzzi-clad suites. Frustratingly for those not on a corporate account, rates fluctuate daily, depending on availability. Wi-fi is available.

Hôtel du Sauvage (☎ 026 347 30 60; www.hotel -sauvage.ch, in French; Planche Supérieure 12; s/d from Sfr195/260; menu from Sfr34) Another medieval veteran, this Old Town house boasts 17 charming rooms above a restaurant in a twinset of 16th-century houses. Find it mere footsteps from the river, flagged with a medieval sign featuring a savage caveman and his club. Free wi-fi.

ourpick Auberge aux 4 Vents (☎ 026 347 36 00; www.aux4vents.ch; Res Balzli Grandfrey 124; s/d incl breakfast Sfr140/200, s/d/tr/q with shared bathroom Sfr50/100/140/180; P 🐾) 'Stylish' scarcely does justice to this imaginative eight-room country inn, 2km north of town, where wacky design rules. Its four-bedded *dortoir* is Switzerland's most luxurious dorm, and the dreamy Blue Room sports flowery period furnishings and a bathtub that rolls out on rails through the window for a soak beneath stars. To find the '4 Winds', drive north along Rue de Morat and turn right immediately before the train bridge.

Eating

Café des Arcades (☎ 026 321 48 40; www.cafedesarcades
.ch, in French; Rue des Ormeaux 1; mains Sfr15; ⏱ 7am-
11.30pm Tue-Thu, 7-1am Fri, 8-1am Sat, 10am-10pm Sun)
Alive and kicking since 1861, this café is an
authentic address for breakfast, brunch or
lunch. Sit beneath the kids frolicking on the
swing hung in the tree outside and watch the
Fribourg world go by.

Café du Gothard (☎ 026 322 32 85; Rue du Pont Muré
16; mains Sfr15-35, fixed lunch menu Sfr17.50; ⏱ 9am-
11.30pm Tue-Fri, 8am-11.30pm Sat & Sun) Tinguely's
favourite eating haunt is a kitsch mix of
19th-century furnishings, Niki de Saint Phalle
drawings and art nostalgia. Take your pick
from the feisty day's specials chalked on the
multiple blackboards, sit back and revel in this
legendary bistro.

Gemelli Ristorante & Pizzeria (☎ 026 321 59 10;
www.gemelli-fr.ch; Grand-Places 10; pizza Sfr15-24; ⏱ 8am-
11.30pm Sun-Thu, to midnight Fri & Sat) The pizza, ice-
cream sundaes and Sardinian specialities such
as squid-studded black risotto served inside
this glass shoebox are handsome. But it is the
garden terrace out back that really lures the
punters. End your meal with a stroll across
the lawn to the Tinguely fountain, created by
the Fribourg artist for his mate, Swiss racing
driver Jo Siffert, months before his fatal car
accident in 1971.

Café du Midi (☎ 026 322 31 33; www.lemidi.ch; Rue de
Romont 25; mains Sfr15-25, fondues Sfr23-30; ⏱ lunch & dinner daily) Unchanged for decades, Fribourg's old
boy pulls the punters onto its busy pavement
terrace with dozens of types of fondue (ever
tried a goats' cheese one?), a steal of a Sfr18.50
menu du jour and loads of other cheesy and
not-so-cheesy dishes.

our pick **Ristorante Bindella** (☎ 026 322 49 05;
www.bindella.ch, in French; Rue de Lausanne 38-40; pasta
Sfr25, mains Sfr40; ⏱ lunch & diner Tue-Fri, dinner Sat)
This authentic Italian oozes elegance. From
the polished wooden tables to the flickering
candles, olive-oil soaked *bruschetta* and cries
of *'ciao bella!'* emanating from the kitchen,
you could quite easily imagine that you were
in Florence.

Auberge de la Cicogne (☎ 026 322 68 34; www.la
-cigogne.ch, in French; Rue d'Or 24; mains Sfr30-60, menus
Sfr115 & Sfr130; ⏱ lunch & diner Tue-Sat) Eastern aromas waft over a couple of mains and desserts
are divine at this highly revered establishment, constructed in 1771 in riverside Auge.
Its *menu du midi* (fixed lunch menu; Sfr29)
renders it pleasantly affordable.

Also recommended:

Bel' Asia (☎ 026 323 44 68; www.belasia.ch; Grand-Rue
36; mains Sfr20-30; ⏱ dinner Tue-Fri, lunch & dinner Sat
& Sun) Thai restaurant with staggering views from its Old
Town roof terrace.

La Grotta (☎ 026 322 81 00; www.lagrotta.ch, in
French; Rue d'Or 5; pasta Sfr25, mains Sfr31-36, lunch
menu Sfr49; ⏱ lunch & dinner Tue-Fri, dinner Sat) Tastebuds pirouette in heaven at this upmarket Italian splurge
between exposed stone and transparent Kartell chairs.

Drinking

For a candle-lit aperitif in elegant but earthy
surrounds, try Ristorante Bindella (left).

Le Quai (☎ 026 424 22 23; http://lequai.ch, in French; Rte
de la Fonderie 6; ⏱ 9am-11.30pm Mon-Wed, 9am-12.30pm
Thu, 9am-3am Fri, 2pm-3am Sat) Brilliantly placed
near the mythical Villars chocolate factory,
this postindustrial lounge-bar seethes with
soul and a healthy dose of attitude. DJs spin
sets Friday and Saturday evening.

Le Café du Transformateur (www.myspace.com
/letransformateur; Rte de la Fonderie 11; ⏱ 8-11.30pm Tue
& Wed, 3.30pm-3am Thu & Fri, 8pm-3am Sat) Across the
road is this gargantuan space, another tatty
warehouse with a hip interior of metallic
pipes and sofas to lounge on. Weekend DJs
and bands.

L'Apart (☎ 026 321 53 50; www.lapart.ch; Grand-Places
14; ⏱ 4pm-3am Mon-Sat) Ignore the concrete tower
on top and take your pick of 1950s seating
in this loft-style bar made by Séb and JC. In
summer its slick wooden-deck terrace gets
packed and DJs fill the place to bursting at
weekends. Free wi-fi.

TW (☎ 026 321 53 82; www.tmcafe.ch; Rue de Romont
29-31; ⏱ 7am-11.30pm Mon-Wed, 7am-midnight Thu, 7-2am
Fri, 9-2am Sat, 2-11.30pm Sun) Trendies drink and
dance, shots are hot and DJs spin bastard
electro to breakbeat and bop at Talk Wine, a
chic café and lounge bar above a shoe shop.
Oysters are shucked in winter during that
all-essential after-work *apéro*.

Paddy Reilly's (☎ 026 321 18 28; www.paddys.ch;
Grand-Places 12; ⏱ 4.30pm-1.30am Mon-Thu, to 3am Fri &
Sat, to 1am Sun) If it's football, beef and Guinness
pie, a fry-up late or pints of the hard stuff
you're after, Irish Paddy's your man. Student
night (cheap beer) is Monday.

Brasserie Artisanale de Fribourg (☎ 026 322
80 88; Rue de la Samaritaine 19; ⏱ 8am-5pm Sat) This
tiny microbrewery run by a couple of mates
who began the enterprise as an amusing pastime (and now run it as a Saturday hobby!)
brews just 50 hectolitres a year – of golden

Barbeblanche, Barberousse with subtle caramel and honey aromas, and black Old Cat stout.

Entertainment

The buzziest DJ clubs and band venues are in the industrial zone, west of the train station where late-night happenings pack Le Quai (p129) and Le Café du Transformateur (p129).

La Spirale (☎ 026 322 66 39; www.laspirale.ch, in French; Place du Petit St-Jean 39; 5 entries Sfr80; ☺ Wed-Sun) Jazz, blues, world fusion, Swiss yodelling, Spanish flamenco et al create a potent musical cocktail in this cellar club by the river. Wednesday is strictly local Fribourg sounds. Look for the inconspicuous blue door.

fri-son (☎ 026 424 36 25; www.fri-son.ch, in French; Rte de la Fonderie 13; admission Sfr5-Sfr40; ☺ 8pm-late Wed-Sun) DJs spin varied sounds inside this graffiti-covered warehouse – one of western Switzerland's biggest stages for live concerts. Buy tickets online.

To See (☎ 026 424 46 53; www.toseeclub.com, in French; Passage Cardinal 2c; admission Sfr15, often free before 11pm; ☺ 10pm-3am Wed, 11pm-3am Thu, 11pm-4am Fri & Sat) Three dance floors, a select gallery and frenetic clubbing crowd flock to this vast space opposite the Cardinal brewery.

Getting There & Away

Trains travel hourly to/from Neuchâtel (Sfr19.60, 55 minutes), and more frequently to Geneva (Sfr32, 1½ hours) and Bern (Sfr12.80, 20 minutes). Regular trains run to Yverdon-les-Bains (Sfr17.40, 55 to 80 minutes) and Lausanne (Sfr23, 45 to 55 minutes).

Buses depart from behind the **bus station** (☎ 026 351 05 79), accessible from the train station, for Avenches (Sfr8.20, 25 minutes), Bulle (Sfr14.40, 55 minutes) and Schwarzsee (Sfr14.40, one hour).

ESTAVAYER-LE-LAC

pop 4500 / elevation 455m

A charming manicured lakeside enclave that has largely preserved its medieval core, Estavayer-le-Lac is a lovely hideout known for frogs – dead or alive.

Orientation & Information

From the train station walk 400m along Rue de la Gare to town and the **tourist office** (☎ 026 663 12 37; www.estavayer-le-lac.ch, in French; Rue de l'Hôtel de Ville 16; ☺ 8.30am-noon & 1.30-5.45pm Mon-Fri, 10am-noon

& 2-4pm Sat), on the corner of Rte du Port that leads downhill to the lake.

Sights & Activities

Frogs star at the **Musée des Grenouilles** (Frog Museum; ☎ 026 663 24 48; www.museedesgrenouilles.ch; Rue du Musée 13; adult/child Sfr5/3; ☺ 10am-noon & 2-5pm Tue-Sun Mar-Jun, Sep & Oct, 10am-noon & 2-5pm daily Jul & Aug, 2-5pm Sat & Sun Nov-Feb), caught, stuffed and 'modelled' by François Perrier, a retired Swiss military fellow, in the 1860s. Weapons, Roman coins, 17th-century kitchen utensils et al focus on local history.

Château de Chenaux (1285–90), home to the prefecture and police station, cannot be visited but its ramparts can be strolled. Ask the tourist office for its **Circuit des Remparts** brochure that maps out a 1½ hour stroll along the original 40m-long and 35m-wide rectangle interspersed with 16 gates and turrets galore. The largest tower, 32m-tall **Grand Tour**, could only be accessed via a door that stood 9m above ground level and was reached by a drawer bridge in medieval times.

Lac de Neuchâtel reins in a buoyant crowd with Alphasurf's **Téléski** (☎ 026 663 50 52; www.alphasurf.ch; 30/60/120 min Sfr22/35/60; ☺ 1-7pm daily May-Sep) that tows waterskiers and wakeboarders around a cableway circuit from the end of a jetty at **Nouvelle Plage**. You can swim, sail and surf on the gravelly beach here…or listen to a frogs' chorus in the nearby **Grande Cariçaie** (www.grande-caricaei.ch). This chain of marshy reed-fringed lakes strung along the southern edge of Lac de Neuchâtel is a stronghold for common green frogs, pool frogs, tree frogs and common toads. Watchtowers provide a bird's-eye view of the unique frog land.

Sleeping & Eating

L'Abri-Côtier (☎ 026 663 50 52, 079 653 40 14; www.abri-cotier.ch, in French; Grande Gouille 1; dm/breakfast Sfr20/5, s/d Sfr75/110) Alphasurf's accommodation arm, this functional shoebox rolling-out-of-bed distance from all the lakeside action gets packed with outdoor enthusiasts. Guests sleep in a dorm with four or 12 beds and share a kitchen/summer grill.

Hôtel du Port (☎ 026 664 82 82; www.hotelduport.ch, in French; Rte du Port; s/d/tr/q from Sfr80/130/150/160, mains Sfr30; Ⓟ) Old-style Hôtel du Port sits plump between lake and Old Town. Fish lovers make up the jovial crowd that dines here, and lunch in the garden, kitted out with swings and trampolines, is a family choice. Free wi-fi.

Les Lacustres (☎ 026 663 11 96; www.leslacustres.ch, in French; Rte des Lacustres 22; mains Sfr20-35; ☒ Thu-Tue) For beach buzz hit this waterfront café-restaurant where boarders eat, drink, play *pétanque* (French bowls) and lounge. Brunch is dished up Sunday, beach sushi is a Friday speciality and weekends usher in a rash of party-mad themed *soirées* (sexy blue jeans, western, rock & roll etc) on the sand.

Au Château (☎ 026 663 10 49; www.auchateau.info, in French; Rue des Granges 2; mains Sfr20-30; ☒ 8am-11.30pm or midnight, closed Tue evening & Wed in winter) Eat well on the pretty tree-shaded terrace or up top in the more formal restaurant at this ode to regional cuisine – perch filets fresh from the lake?

Getting There & Away
Estavayer-le-Lac is on the road/rail route between Fribourg (Sfr11.80, 40 minutes) and Yverdon (Sfr7, 17 minutes). Boats call in too (see p137).

MURTEN
pop 5650 / elevation 450m
This fortified German-speaking medieval village on the eastern shore of Murten See (Lac de Morat) isn't called Murten (Morat) – derived from the Celtic word *moriduno* meaning 'fortress on the lake' – for nothing. In May 1476 the Burgundy duke Charles the Bold set off from Lausanne to besiege Murten – only to have 8000 of his men butchered or drowned in Murten Lake during the Battle of Murten. The fortifications that thwarted the duke (who escaped) create a quaint little lakeside town well worth an afternoon stroll today.

Canals link Murten See with Lac de Neuchâtel (west) and Bieler See (north) to form the Pays des Trois Lacs (Land of Three Lakes) – a lake district crisscrossed with some 250km of marked roller-skating, cycling and walking paths.

Information
Tourist Office (☎ 026 670 51 12; www.murten.ch, in German; Französische Kirchgasse 6; ☒ 9am-noon & 1-6pm Mon-Fri Oct-Mar, 9am-noon & 1-6pm Mon-Fri, 10am-2pm Sat Apr-Sep).

Sights & Activities
Murten is a cobbled three-street town crammed with arcaded houses. A string of hotel-restaurants culminating in a 13th-century **castle** (closed to visitors) line Rathausgasse;

shops and eateries stud parallel Hauptgasse, capped by the medieval **Berntor** city gate at its eastern end; while parallel Deutsche Kirchgasse and its western continuation, Schulgasse, hug the city ramparts. Don't miss **Boutique Noël** (☎ 026 670 67 37; www.christmasbynoel .com; Rathausgasse 19), a Pandora's box of a boutique, where it is Christmas year-round.

Scale the wooden **Aufstieg auf die Ringmauer** (rampart stairs) behind the **Deutsche Kirche** (German Church; Deutsche Kirchgasse) to reach the covered walkway traversing part of the sturdy medieval walls.

In a mill beyond the castle, the **Museum Murten** (☎ 026 670 31 00; www.museummurten.ch, in French & German; Ryf 4; adult/child Sfr6/2; ☒ 2-5pm Tue-Sat, 10am-5pm Sun Apr-Oct, 2-5pm Tue-Sun Nov-Apr) displays artefacts discovered during the dredging of the Broye Canal in 1829 and cannons used in the Battle of Murten.

From late April to mid-October **Navigation Lacs de Neuchâtel et Morat** (p137 for details) runs tours of Lake Murten (70 minutes, Sfr18).

Festivals & Events
Murten's three-day **carnival** is in early March and its 8000-runner **marathon**, the Murten–Fribourg race on the first Sunday of October, commemorates the dash by the messenger who relayed news of the Battle of Murten.

Sleeping & Eating
Hotel Murtenhof & Krone (☎ 026 672 90 30; www.murten hof.ch; Rathausgasse 1-5; economy d Sfr75-95, superior 100-140; ☒ ☒) The Murtenhof, in a 16th-century patrician's house, mixes old and new to create a spacious space to eat and sleep. Fancy a round bed? Its terrace restaurant (mains Sfr21 to Sfr25) cooks up 1st-class lake views and a traditional cuisine with a worldly hint of fusion. Its cosy Wein und Käse Lounge opposite entices with *wein* (wine) and *käse* (cheese).

Des Bains (☎ 026 670 23 38; www.desbains-murten.ch, in German; Ryf 35; mains Sfr25-35; ☒ 11am-11.30pm Wed & Thu, 11am-midnight Fri, 10am-midnight Sat, 10am-10pm Sun) For lakeside dining, the Baths are prime. A green lawn tumbles from its tabled terrace down to the water where swans gag for crumbs. Try the *filets de perche* (perch filets) in Vully wine.

Hôtel Le Vieux Manoir (☎ 026 678 61 61; www.vieux manoir.ch; Rue de Lausanne 18, Meyriez; s/d from Sfr300/430, mains from Sfr50; ☒ mid-Feb–Dec; ☒ ☒ ☒) This unabashedly luxurious timber Normandy house, built as a whim on the lakeside in the early 1900s, is *the* ultimate splurge. For woo-ers wanting their loved one to say yes, opt for the solitary table for two at the end of a long jetty, where you can dine at sunset for a huge amount of money. Find the Old Lake Manor 1km south of Murten in Meyriez.

Getting There & Around

From the train station (Bahnhofstrasse), 300m south of the city walls, hourly trains run to/from Fribourg (Sfr10.80, 30 minutes), Bern (Sfr12.80, 35 minutes) via Kerzers (Sfr3.50, nine minutes), and Neuchâtel (Sfr11.80, 25 minutes). Hourly trains to/from Payerne (Sfr7.40, 20 minutes) stop at Avenches (Sfr3.20, seven minutes).

Murten train station rents **bicycles** (☎ 051 221 15 52; per day Sfr33; ☼ 9am-4pm).

Navigation Lacs de Neuchâtel et Morat runs seasonal boats to/from Neuchâtel; see p137. By car, Murten is on the N1 linking Lausanne with Bern.

AROUND MURTEN

Overwhelmingly agricultural with bags of green fields and hay barns (see p353) to roll around in, the countryside around Murten offers a gulp of old-fashioned fresh air. Farmers trustingly pile up carrots on the roadside for motorists to buy and open their lettuce fields and apple orchards to the agriculturally curious as part of the **Inforama Seeland** (www.inforama .ch, in German) green tourism project. On the western side of the lake, Vully wine is made from grapes grown on the gentle slopes of Mont Vully (653m).

For a real taste of this rural neck of the woods stay at `our pick` **Eulenhof** (Owl Farm; ☎ 026 673 18 85; www.fermeduhibou.ch; Rue du Château 24, Mur; camping on straw incl breakfast adult/child Sfr30/20, dm incl breakfast adult/child Sfr43/26, d incl breakfast Sfr96-120, dinner & Sun lunch mid-Mar–mid-Sep Sfr27; ☼ Jan-Oct; P ✗), a farm on the cycling and hiking **Sentier du Vins de Vully** (Vully wine trail). Farmer Willy and wife Nadja cook up regional cuisine in a terraced garden with lake view; reserve in advance. To find Eulenhof, 13km north of Murten, follow the lake road north to Guénaux, then head 1km inland to Mur village.

Avenches

Roman Aventicum, 8km southwest of Murten, grew on the site of the ancient capital of the Celtic Helvetii tribe and was a major centre in the 2nd century AD, with a population 10 times what it is today. But in the late 3rd century its 5.6km of defensive ramparts failed to withstand attacks by the Alemanni tribe and by the 5th century the town had tumbled into obscurity.

Its Roman glory days are evoked in its **amphitheatre**, host to a **Musée Romain** (Roman Museum; ☎ 026 675 17 27; Ave Jomini; adult/child Sfr4/free; ☼ 10am-noon & 1-5pm Tue-Sun Apr-Sep, 2-5pm Tue-Sun Oct-Mar) and an audience of 12,000 during its July **Opera Festival**; contact the **tourist office** (☎ 026 676 99 22; www.avenches.ch, in French; place de l'Église 3) for tickets.

Payerne

Payerne, 10km southwest, is dominated by the 11th-century five-apse Romanesque **Abbatiale de Payerne** (Abbey Church; ☎ 026 662 67 04; Place du Marché; admission without/with exhibition Sfr3/8-12; ☼ 10am-noon & 2-6pm Tue-Sun May-Sep, to 5pm Oct-Apr). The sandstone complex boasts fine sculptural decoration and frescos, hosts art exhibitions and classical concerts. Find details at www .mepayerne.ch or ask the neighbouring **tourist office** (☎ 026 660 61 61; www.payerne.ch, in French; Place du Marché 10; ☼ 8am-noon & 1.30-6pm Mon-Fri).

Kerzers

Tropical butterflies flutter alongside hummingbirds and other exotic birds 11km northeast of Murten at **Papiliorama** (☎ 031 756 04 60; www.papiliorama.ch; adult/child Sfr16/8; ☼ 9am-6pm Apr-Oct, 10am-5pm Nov-Mar). Indigenous butterflies flit about in the **Swiss Butterfly Garden**, tarantulas creep and crawl in **Arthropodarium**, night creatures from Latin America hide in **Nocturama** (☼ 10am-6pm Apr-Oct, to 5pm Nov-Mar), and in **Jungle Trek** – a recreation of a Belize nature reserve complete with mangroves, tropical dry forest and 7m-high panorama bridge – intrepid explorers do just that.

Papiliorama is 80m from Kerzers train station, linked to Murten by train.

GRUYÈRES

pop 1490 / elevation 830m

Cheese and featherweight meringues drowned in thick cream are what this village, so dreamy even Sleeping Beauty wouldn't wake up, is all about. Named after the emblematic *gru* (crane) brandished by the medieval Counts of Gruyères, it is a riot of 15th- to 17th-century houses tumbling down a hillock. Its heart is cobbled, a castle is its crowning glory and hard AOC Gruyère cheese has been made for centuries in its surrounding Alpine pastures.

Information

Tourist Office (☎ 026 921 10 30; www.gruyeres.ch, in French; Rue du Bourg 1; ☻ 10.30am-noon & 1.30-4.30pm Mon-Fri year-round, 9am-5pm Sat & Sun Jul–mid-Sep)

Sights

CHÂTEAU DE GRUYÈRES

This bewitching turreted **castle** (☎ 026 921 21 02; www.chateau-gruyeres.ch; adult/child Sfr9.50/3; ☻ 9am-6pm Apr-Oct, 10am-4.30pm Nov-Feb), home to 19 different Counts of Gruyères who controlled the Sarine Valley from the 11th to 16th centuries, was rebuilt after a fire in 1493. Inside, view period furniture, tapestries and modern 'fantasy art' and watch a short multimedia film. Don't miss the short footpath that weaves its way around the castle.

MUSEUM HR GIGER

Biomechanical art fills the **HR Giger Museum** (☎ 026 921 22 00; www.hrgigermuseum.com; adult/child Sfr12/5; ☻ 10am-6pm Mon-Fri, 10am-6.30pm Sat & Sun May-Oct, 11am-5pm Nov-Apr), dedicated to the man behind the sci-fi uniforms in the *Alien* movies – Chur-born, Zürich-based Giger (b 1940). The museum bar opposite, **Bar HR Giger** (☻ 10am-8.30pm Tue-Sun), is kitted out in the same weird, wacky surrealist style.

A combined museum and château ticket costs Sfr17.

CHEESE DAIRIES

The secret behind Gruyère cheese is revealed at **La Maison du Gruyère** (☎ 026 921 84 00; www.lamaison dugruyere.ch; adult/child Sfr7/3; ☻ 9am-7pm Apr-Sep, to 6pm Oct-Mar) in Pringy, 1.5km from Gruyères. Cheese-making takes place four times daily between 9am and 11am and 12.30pm to 2.30pm.

At the **Fromagerie d'Alpage de Moléson** (☎ 026 921 10 44; ☻ 9.30am-10pm mid-May–mid-Oct), a 17th-century Alpine chalet 5km southwest of Gruyères in Moléson-sur-Gruyères (elevation 1100m), cheese is made a couple of times a day in summer using old-fashioned methods.

Both dairies sell cheese (Sfr2 to Sfr2.40 per 100g) and serve fondue, *soupe du chalet* (a thick and hearty vegetable and potato soup topped with Gruyère double cream and cheese), *soupe à l'oignon au Gruyère* (Gruyère-topped onion soup) and other typical mountain dishes in their dairy restaurants.

Cheese is still produced in a couple of traditional mountain chalets along the **Sentier des Fromageries**, a trail that takes walkers through green Gruyères pastures. Ask at the Maison du Gruyère for the brochure outlining the two-hour walk (7km to 8km).

Eating

Cheese fondue is the natural star of every menu, irrespective of season (locals only eat fondue in winter); *moitié-moitié* is a mix of Gruyère and soft local vacherin.

Chalet de Gruyères (☎ 026 921 21 54; www.chalet -gruyeres.ch, in French; Rue du Château 53; fondues & Raclettes Sfr30; ☻ lunch & dinner daily) The quintessential Gruyères address, this cosy wooden chalet strung with cow bells oozes Alpine charm – and fodder (fondue, Raclette, grilled meats).

Auberge de la Halle (☎ 026 921 21 78; Rue du Château; menus Sfr32 & Sfr43.50, cheese fondue per person

---

GRUYÈRE: FAST FACTS

- The village is called Gruyères; its cheese is called Gruyère (no s).

- A cow consumes 100kg of grass and 85L of water a day to produce 25L of milk.

- Cheese-makers need 400L of milk to make one 35kg wheel of Gruyère.

- There are allegedly 75 different Alpine scents in Gruyère cheese. Vanilla, orchid, violet, chestnut, mint, wood shavings, hazelnuts, fresh grass…you name it, it's there.

- Approximately 330 million litres of milk are processed into 27,500 tons of cheese in 200-odd dairies in the Fribourg, Neuchâtel, Jura and Vaud cantons; Gruyères cows yield 5.7 million litres a year.

- A mild (*doux*) Gruyère is left to mature for five to six months, a semi-salted (*mi-salé*) for seven to eight months, a salted (*salé*) for nine to 10 months, a reserve (*réserve au surchoix*) for at least 10 months, and a deliciously strong-tasting mature (*vieux*) for at least 15 months.

- Two-thirds of Gruyère production is consumed in Switzerland; the EU and North America eat the rest.

Sfr24.50; ⊗ lunch & dinner Wed-Mon) Snag a seat at one of two tables outside this inn, a granary in medieval times where the wheat would be weighed in stone urns – still there today! Try the meal-sized *soupe du chalet* (soup of mushrooms, pasta, cheese etc), *croûte au fromage* (baked cheese on bread) and *sérac* (*fromage frais* made from the whey of Gruyère).

Getting There & Around
Gruyères can be reached by hourly bus or train (Sfr17.20, 40 minutes to one hour) from Fribourg to Bulle, where you need to hop on another hourly bus or train (Sfr3.50, 15 to 20 minutes). Gruyères is a 10-minute walk uphill from its train station.

BROC & BULLE
Experience chocolate thrills and spills at **Cailler** (☎ 026 921 51 51; Rue Jules Bellet 7; admission free; ⊗ 9.30am-4pm May-Oct), one of Switzerland's oldest chocolate makers, in business since 1825. Don't expect to get anywhere near the production line; visits comprise a video of how chocolate is made – and free samples. Find the factory 2km north of Gruyères, in Broc.

Bulle, the area's main transport hub 5km northwest of Gruyères, is worth a stop for its 13th-century **château** (now administrative offices) and **Musée Gruérien** (☎ 026 912 72 60; www.musee-gruerien.ch, in French; Rue de la Condémine 25; adult/child Sfr8/free; ⊗ 10am-noon & 2-5pm Tue-Sat, 2-5pm Sun).

CHARMEY & THE SCHWARZSEE
From Broc it is a pretty climb into the Pre-Alps of Canton de Fribourg. **Charmey** (elevation 876m) is the centre of local skiing, with 30km of downhill slopes (1630m). In summer, it's a haven for walkers and mountain bikers. The **tourist office** (☎ 026 927 55 80; www.charmey.ch; ⊗ 2-6pm Tue-Sun), across the car park from its cable car, has trail details, including around Vanil Noir (2389m), the region's highest point.

Head east for another 11km and you hit German-speaking territory and the hamlet of **Jaun** with its twinset of churches. The older one with wood shingle roof shelters **Cantorama** (☎ 026 929 81 81; tourismus@jaun.ch; admission Sfr4, concerts Sfr20 or Sfr30; ⊗ 2-5pm Sat & Sun mid-Jun–mid-Oct), a music centre with displays on traditional Fribourgeois chants and host to choral concerts. The newer church (1910) has an unusual cemetery where

wooden crosses dating from the 1980s to present feature carvings of the deceased's job in life.

North of Charmey is the solitary 13th-century **Chartreuse de la Valsainte**, Switzerland's only still-functioning Carthusian monastery where 26 monks lead a silent life dedicated to prayer and manual work. It can't be visited, unlike the small chapel outside the walled compound.

Nearby is the mountain lake of **Schwarzsee** (Black Lake; www.schwarzsee.ch), set for winter skiing and summertime hiking. About 2km north of the village is Karl Neuhaus' **Eis Paläste** (Ice Palace; www.eispalaeste.ch; adult/child Sfr8/4; ⊗ 2-9pm Wed-Sun Dec-Mar), a magical construction of turrets, bridges, domes, grottoes and crystal palaces between pine trees – built solely from ice. Illuminated at night, an evening stroll along the sand paths (not to mention a picnic in an igloo) is quite fairy tale–like.

CANTON DE NEUCHÂTEL

The focus of this heavily forested 800 sq km canton (population 168,910), northwest of its Fribourg counterpart, is Lac de Neuchâtel – the largest lake entirely within Switzerland. Canton capital Neuchâtel sits plump on its northern shore and the gentle Jura Mountains rise to the north and west. Watch-making has been a mainstay industry since the 18th century and the canton's two other large towns – La Chaux-de-Fonds and Le Locle – remain firmly on the much-marketed 'Watch Valley' tourist trail.

Together with Biel and Murten lakes, Neuchâtel falls into the Pays de Trois Lacs. With France bang next door, French is *the* language of this rural land.

NEUCHÂTEL
pop 32,330 / elevation 430m
Its Old Town sandstone elegance, the airy Gallic nonchalance of its café life and the gay lakeside air that breezes along the shoreline of its glittering lake makes Neuchâtel disarmingly charming. The small university town – complete with spirited *commune libre* (free commune) – is compact enough to discover on foot, while the French spoken here is said to be Switzerland's purest.

Neuchâtel's town observatory gives the official time-check for all of Switzerland.

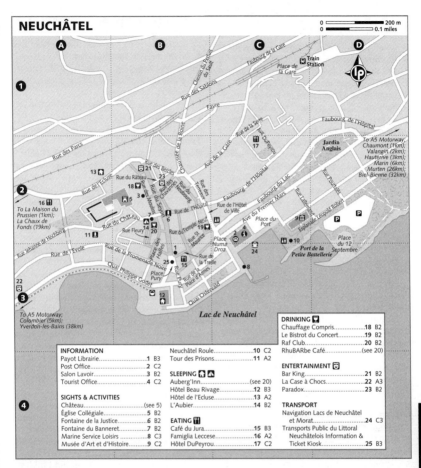

NEUCHÂTEL

0 — 200 m
0 — 0.1 miles

Lac de Neuchâtel

INFORMATION		
Payot Librairie	1	B3
Post Office	2	C2
Salon Lavoir	3	C2
Tourist Office	4	C2

SIGHTS & ACTIVITIES		
Château	(see 5)	
Église Collégiale	5	B2
Fontaine de la Justice	6	B2
Fontaine du Banneret	7	B2
Marine Service Loisirs	8	C3
Musée d'Art et d'Histoire	9	C2

Neuchâtel Roule	10	C2
Tour des Prisons	11	A2

SLEEPING		
Auberg'Inn	(see 20)	
Hôtel Beau Rivage	12	B3
Hôtel de l'Ecluse	13	A2
L'Aubier	14	B2

EATING		
Café du Jura	15	B3
Famiglia Leccese	16	A2
Hôtel DuPeyrou	17	C2

DRINKING		
Chauffage Compris	18	B2
Le Bistrot du Concert	19	B2
Raf Club	20	B2
RhuBARbe Café	(see 20)	

ENTERTAINMENT		
Bar King	21	B2
La Case à Chocs	22	A3
Paradox	23	B2

TRANSPORT		
Navigation Lacs de Neuchâtel		
et Morat	24	C3
Transports Public du Littoral		
Neuchâtelois Information &		
Ticket Kiosk	25	B3

Information

BOOKSHOP

Payot Librairie (Rue du Seyon; ⏲ 1.30-6.30pm Mon, 9am-6.30pm Tue-Fri, 8.30am-5pm Sat) Maps, guidebooks & English-language fiction.

LAUNDRY

Salon Lavoir (Rue des Moulins 27; ⏲ 8am-8pm)

POST

Post Office (Pl du Port; ⏲ 7.30am-6.30pm Mon-Fri, 8.30am-noon Sat)

TOURIST INFORMATION

Tourist office (☎ 032 889 68 90; www.neuchatel tourism.ch; Hôtel des Postes, place du Port; ⏲ 9am-noon

& 1.30-5.30pm Mon-Fri, 9am-noon Sat Sep-Jun, 9am-6.30pm Mon-Fri, 9-4pm Sat, 10am-2pm Sun Jul & Aug)

Sights

OLD TOWN & CHÂTEAU

The streets are lined by fine, shuttered 18th-century mansions and studded with fanciful gold-leafed fountains topped by anything from a banner-wielding knight, **Fontaine du Banneret** (Rue Fleury), to a maiden representing Justice, **Fontaine de la Justice** (Rue de l'Hôpital); see a copy on the street and the original in the Musée d'Art et d'Histoire (p136).

Heading uphill along Rue du Château, walk through the medieval city gate to view the **Tour des Prisons** (☎ 032 717 71 02; Rue Jehanne de Hochberg 5; admission Sfr1; ⏲ 8am-6pm Apr-Sep). Scale it for lake

---

LIFE IN THE COMMUNE

Neuchâtel's so-called **Commune Libre du Neubourg et Alentours** (Free Commune of Neubourg & Surroundings; www.leneubourg.ch, in French) – a good mate of Paris' Montmartre (a self-declared free commune since 1920) – boils down to a good excuse to party. Founded in 1979, it embraces a trio of Old Town streets – Rue de Neubourg, Rue des Fausses-Brayes and colourfully frescoed Rue des Chavannes, otherwise dubbed Rue des Peintres (Painters' St) with the free-thinking motto *'voir d'un œil, sentir de l'autre'* (look with one eye, feel with the other). The hot-air balloons painted underfoot say it all.

---

and Alpine views. Inside the largely Gothic **Église Collégiale** a mix of Romanesque elements (notably the triple apse) looms large. Facing the main entrance is a statue of Guillaume Farel, who brought the Reformation to town, after which the cathedral was obliged to swap sides.

Behind the church is the 15th-century **château** (☎ 032 889 60 00; admission free; ☻ guided tours hourly 10am-noon & 2-4pm Mon-Sat, 2-4pm Sun Apr-Sep) with a pretty courtyard made for meandering. Summertime guided tours (45 minutes) allow you to poke your nose around the castle's innards.

MUSÉE D'ART ET D'HISTOIRE

The **Musée d'Art et d'Histoire** (Art and History Museum; ☎ 032 717 79 25; www.mahn.ch, in French; Esplanade Léopold Robert 1; adult/child Sfr8/free, free Wed; ☻ 11am-6pm Tue-Sun) is notable for three clockwork androids made between 1764 and 1774 by watchmaker Jaquet Droz. The Writer can be programmed to dip his pen in an inkpot and write up to 40 characters, while the Musician plays up to five tunes on a real organ. The Draughtsman is the simplest, with a repertoire of six drawings. The androids are activated on the first Sunday of the month at 2pm, 3pm and 4pm.

Activities

The port buzzes with summer fun. Place du 12 Septembre is one big playground, while **Marine Service Loisirs** (☎ 032 724 61 82; www.msloisirs.ch, in French; Port de la Ville; ☻ Apr-Oct) rents motor boats (Sfr5 to Sfr70 per hour), pedalos (Sfr25 to Sfr35 per hour) and two- or four-seated pedal-powered buggies (Sfr25 to Sfr35 per hour) and

bicycles (Sfr25/38 per half-/full day) to cruise along the silky-smooth quays.

Alternatively pick up a set of wheels for free from the seasonal **portside kiosk** (Esplanade Léopold Robert; ☻ 7.30am-9.30pm late Apr–early Nov) run by **Neuchâtel Roule** (☎ 032 717 77 75; www.neuchatelroule.ch, in French).

For a lake cruise contact the **Navigation Lacs de Neuchâtel et Morat** (see opposite).

Festivals & Events

Parades, costumes and drunken revelry ensure fun at the **Fête des Vendanges** (Grape Harvest Festival), the last weekend in September. Jazz, pop and rock set the lakeside jiving during June's open-air **Festi'Neuch** (www.festineuch.ch, in French).

Sleeping

Auberg'Inn (☎ 078 615 84 21; www.auberginn.ch, in French; Rue Fleury 1; s/d/tr/q/5-person r Sfr100/150/160/190/210; ☻ reception 8am-6pm Mon-Sat, to noon Sun) An atmospheric hostel-style place to stay next to a chivalrous fountain, this trend-setting inn flouts five design-driven rooms on the upper floors (no lift) of a late Renaissance townhouse. Draw on the walls of the Blackboard room, sleep green in the Bamboo room or chill before a flat screen in the Cinema room. The place is above a bar (read: noisy). Winter rates are Sfr10 per room cheaper. There's free wi-fi.

L'Aubier (☎ 032 710 18 58; Rue du Château 1; s/d with sink Sfr80/110, with shower & toilet Sfr130/180; ☻ reception 11.45am-7pm Mon, 7.30am-7pm Tue-Fri, 8am-6pm Sat) Soulful sleeping above one of Neuchâtel's greenest eating spaces is what this lovely café-hotel is all about. Find it in an old building with diagonal-striped shutters peeping down on a sword-wielding knight.

Hôtel de l'Ecluse (☎ 032 729 93 10; www.hoteldelecluse.ch; Rue de l'Ecluse 24; s/d incl breakfast Sfr139/184; ☻ reception 11am-7pm; P) Set back off a busy road, this three-star house with blue wooden shutters has modernised rooms with brass beds, kitchenettes and a cute little stone-clad courtyard out back to lounge in. Free wi-fi.

Hôtel Beau Rivage (☎ 032 723 15 15; www.beau-rivage-hotel.ch, in French; Esplanade du Mont Blanc 1; s/d from Sfr295/370, mains from Sfr45; P X X ⬚ ⬚) Overlooking the lake and sculpture-studded gardens, this majestic ship of a hotel is ab fab – as is its spa, veranda bar and the culinary wonders of its chef Jean-Baptiste Molinari.

Eating

Local specialities include tripe and *tomme neuchâteloise chaude* (baked goat's-cheese starter). Casual eating places line Rue des Moulins or join the in-crowd at Le Bistrot du Concert (right).

L'Aubier (☎ 032 710 18 58; Rue du Château 1; ✆ 11.45am-7pm Mon, 7.30am-7pm Tue-Fri, 8am-6pm Sat) Perfectly placed in the Old Town shade of Fontaine du Banneret, this green-thinking café cooks up a healthy smattering of salads, quiches, tarts and so on – ideal for a spot of lunch.

our pick **Famiglia Leccese** (☎ 032 724 41 10; Rue de l'Ecluse 49; pasta/mains Sfr15/20; ✆ dinner Tue-Sat, lunch & dinner Sun) Never was there a slice of Italy – Lecce in southern Italy to be precise – outside of Italy so authentic as this earthy, friendly, brilliant and *bellissimo* Italian-run joint. With an entrance resembling a private apartment, it is impossible to find unless you're local and know about it. Look for the fairy lights behind Claude Cordey Motos.

Café du Jura (☎ 032 725 14 10; Rue de la Treille 7; lunch menu Sfr16.50, mains Sfr25-35; ✆ lunch & dinner Mon-Sat) Food is cooked to fill and despite meaty mains such as *tripes à la Neuchâteloise* (Neuchâtel-style tripe) and *tête et langue de veau* (calf head and tongue), vegetarians are well catered for at this bistro.

La Maison du Prussien (☎ 032 730 54 54; www.hotel-prussien.ch; Au Gor du Vauseyon, Rue des Tunnels 11; mains from Sfr30; ✆ lunch & dinner Mon-Sat) This one-time brewery in a grand old house, enclosed by woods and cradled by the impetuous babbling of a nearby brook, is a treat – and it has great rooms too. Hop aboard Cormondrèche-bound bus 1 from Place Pury, alight at Beauregard and head down the stairs to your right following the signs.

Hôtel DuPeyrou (☎ 032 725 11 83; www.dupeyrou.ch, in French; Ave Du Peyrou 1; mains Sfr30-60, menus Sfr89, Sfr100 & Sfr140; ✆ lunch & dinner Tue-Sat) DuPeyrou presides like a mini-Versailles over manicured gardens. Built between 1765 and 1770, it regales with gastronomic dining in an 18th-century ambience. Come autumn, its game dishes are not to be missed.

Drinking

New places are constantly cropping up on pedestrian Rue des Moulins and nearby Rue des Chavannes in the commune (opposite). Lots of noise emanates from the **Raf Club** (Rue Fleury 1; ✆ 10am-1am Mon-Thu, 10am-2am Fri & Sat, 4pm-

1am Sun), a grungy cellar bar with dart board and overwhelming pub feel.

Le Bistrot du Concert (☎ 032 724 62 16; Rue de l'Hôtel de Ville 4; mains Sfr20-25; ✆ 8am-midnight Mon-Thu, 8am-1am Fri & Sat, 3pm-midnight Sun) One of those great all-round addresses, this industrial-styled bar with busy pavement terrace has a soulful spirit, zinc bar and family-friendly menu chalked on the blackboard.

RhuBARbe Café (☎ 032 721 44 20; www.rhubarbecafe.ch, in French; Rue Fleury 1; ✆ 8-11am & 3-8pm Mon-Wed, 8-11am & 3-10pm Thu, 8-11am & 3pm-midnight Fri & Sat, 8-11am Sat) Armchairs and sofas to lounge on beneath wooden beams adds instant appeal to this 2nd-floor hang-out. Light snacks to compliment the drink menu include French *croques monsieurs* and Mexican nachos.

Chauffage Compris (Rue des Moulins 37; ✆ 9am-1am Mon-Thu, 9am-2am Fri & Sat, 3pm-1am Sun) Its name – Heating Included – speaks volumes. This retro bar with a decorative tiled entrance that translates as 'heating and kitchen equipment' is one cool place to loiter, be it for morning coffee, evening aperitif, night-owl drink or laid-back weekend brunch (Sfr10).

Entertainment

Paradox (☎ 032 721 33 77; www.paradoxclub.com in French; Rue du Râteau; ✆ 10.30pm-4am Thu-Sat, À l'Étage 5pm-1am or 2am Tue-Sun) Paradox is a trio of trendy, steely spaces: À l'Étage (1st-floor bar), Para (club with entrance at Rue des Terreaux 7) and Dox (entrance at Rue de Chavannes 19).

La Case à Chocs (☎ 032 721 20 56; www.case-a-chocs.ch, in French; Quai Philippe Godet 20; admission free-Sfr25; ✆ 9.30 or 10pm-2am Fri-Sun) Alternative venue in a converted brewery with live music.

Bar King (☎ 032 724 27 07; www.barking.ch, in French; Rue du Seyon 38; ✆ 6pm-1am Mon-Thu, 6pm-2am Fri, 7pm-2am Sat) Buzzing venue for bands, concerts, fringe theatre, jazz and various other gigs.

Getting There & Away

BOAT

Late April to mid-October, **Navigation Lacs de Neuchâtel et Morat** (☎ 032 729 96 00; www.navig.ch; Port de la Ville) runs boats to/from Estavayer-le-Lac (Sfr19.60, 1¾ hours), Yverdon-les-Bains (Sfr34, 2½ hours), Murten (Sfr23, 1¾ hours) and Biel (Bienne; Sfr33, 2½ hours). Buy tickets on board; return fares are double one-way fares quoted.

TRAIN

From the **train station** (Ave de la Gare), a 10-minute walk northeast of the Old Town, hourly trains run to/from Geneva (Sfr38, 1¼ to 1½ hours), Bern via Kerzers (Sfr18.20, 35 minutes), Basel (Sfr35, 1½ hours), Biel (Sfr11.80, 20 minutes) and other destinations. Two per hour serve Yverdon (Sfr13.80, 20 minutes).

Getting Around

Local buses hit transport hub Place Pury and **Transports Public du Littoral Neuchâtelois information & ticket kiosk** (☎ 032 720 06 58; www.tnneuchatel .ch, in French; Place Pury; ⏱ 7am-6pm Mon-Fri, 8.30-11.30am Sat). Journeys less than 30 minutes cost Sfr1; otherwise buy a Sfr1.70/2.50 valid for a short/ long journey. Bus 6 links the train station and Place Pury.

AROUND NEUCHÂTEL
Inland

Soak up views across the three lakes to the Alps in **Chaumont** (1160m), a ride on bus 7 from Neuchâtel to La Coudre then a 12-minute ride up the mountain on a panoramic **funicular** (☎ 032 720 06 00; one-way/return Sfr3.60/7.20; ⏱ 7.15am-7pm year-round).

Pushing north along the N20, **Vue-des-Alpes** (1283m) is popular with mountain-bikers who fly along two circular 7.3km and 11km vtrails. The pass also makes an exhilarating stop for kid-clad motorists whose young passengers go bananas over the 700m-long **Toboggan Géant** (☎ 032 761 08 00; www.toboggans .ch; adult/under 8yr/child Sfr4/free/3, three descents Sfr11/ free/7; ⏱ 1-6pm Mon-Fri, 10am-6pm Sat & Sun), a luge track that rips down the mountain. In winter, locals sledge, snow-shoe and ski down the gentle slopes (three drag lifts) or along 53km of cross-country trails.

The place to feast on seasonal produce is **our pick** **Auberge de Mont Cornu** (☎ 032 968 76 00; Mont Cornu 116; menus Sfr48 & Sfr78, mains Sfr25-35; ⏱ lunch & dinner Wed-Sun Mar-Nov), a chalet at 1152m, well-endowed with flower blossoms and surrounded by cow-spotted fields. The pride and joy of the Lüthi family, the inn oozes intimacy; has a menu built solely from local cheese, mushrooms, air-dried meats, autumnal game and so on; and serves a *cornet à la crème* (crunchy homemade ice-cream cornet filled with thick double cream!) to die for. This is what Switzerland is all about. Drive 2km north of Vue-des-Alpes along the N20 then turn right to Mont Cornu, following signs for the latter for 3km along a country lane, partly unpaved.

Le Corbusier and art-nouveau architecture is the reason to push northwest to **La Chaux-de-Fonds** (pop 36,710), the canton's largest city and

---

THE CONCRETE KING

Few know that Le Corbusier (1887–1965, see p38), often perceived as French, was born in La Chaux-de-Fonds at Rue de la Serre 38. Charles Edouard Jeanneret (the ground-breaking architect's real name) spent his childhood in the clock-making town whose concrete, Soviet-style grid-plan clearly found its way somewhere into his young psyche.

After brief stints in the Orient and Berlin, Le Corbusier returned to La Chaux in 1912 to open an architectural office and build Villa Jeanneret for his parents. The architect who, a few years later would become a serious pal of Germany's Walter Gropius and the Bauhaus movement, lived in the house until 1917, when he left Switzerland for Paris' bright lights. Two years later his parents sold up and left town.

The neoclassical house with white facade and shiny roof, now known as **La Maison Blanche** (The White House; ☎ 032 910 90 30; www.maisonblanche.ch; Chemin de Pouillerel 12; adult/under 12yr/12-18yr Sfr10/free/5; ⏱ 10am-5pm Fri & Sat), is prized as Le Corbusier's first independent piece of work – and a notable break from the regional art nouveau. Architecturally unrecognisable as Le Corbusier to anyone familiar with his later work, it sat derelict in the leafy hilltop neighbourhood above La Chaux until 2004, when the modern architecture treasure was renovated, refurnished (with some original furnishings, such as the green canapé in the sitting room) and opened to the public.

The house is one of 11 points on a DIY Corbusier itinerary around several villas designed by the young Le Corbusier in La Chaux, including the Mediterranean-inspired **Villa Turque** (☎ 032 912 31 31; www.ebel.ch, in French; Rue du Doubs 167; ⏱ free guided tour 11am-4pm 1st & 3rd Sat of month). Thematic **art-nouveau walking tours** (2hr, adult/child/student Sfr12/free/9; ⏱ 10.30am Sat mid-Jun–mid-Sep) departing from the tourist office also take in the Corbusier sights.

FAIRYLAND ABSINTHE

It was in the deepest darkest depths of the Val de Travers – dubbed the **Pays des Fées** (Fairyland) – that absinthe was first distilled in 1740 and produced commercially in 1797 (although it was a Frenchman called Pernod who made the bitter green liqueur known with the distillery he opened just a few kilometres across the French-Swiss border in Pontarlier).

From 1910, following Switzerland's prohibition of the wickedly alcoholic and ruthlessly bitter aniseed drink, distillers of the so-called 'devil in the bottle' in the Val de Travers moved underground. In 1990 the great-grandson of a pre-prohibition distiller in Môtiers came up with Switzerland's first legal aniseed liqueur since 1910 – albeit one which was only 45% proof alcohol (instead of 50% to 75%) and which scarcely contained thujone (the offensive chemical found in wormwood, said to be the root of absinthe's devilish nature). An *extrait d'absinthe* (absinthe extract) quickly followed and in 2005, following Switzerland's lifting of its absinthe ban, the **Blackmint – Distillerie Kübler & Wyss** (☎ 032 861 14 69; www.blackmint.ch; Rue du Château 7) in Môtiers distilled its first true and authentic batch of the mythical *fée verte* (green fairy) from valley-grown wormwood. Mix one part crystal-clear liqueur with five parts water to make it green.

Swilling the green fairy, aka absinthe, at the bar aboard an old steam train as it puffs the length of the Val de Travers is particularly evocative. Jump aboard in Neuchâtel with **Vapeur Val de Travers** (VVT; ☎ 032 863 24 07; www.rvt-historique-ch; Rue de la Gare 19, Travers; day trips with lunch Sfr75).

Switzerland's highest. In the 18th and 19th centuries the drab grid-plan town was a household name in Europe as the centre of precision watch-making and still manufactures timepieces today. Get the full story in its **Musée International d'Horlogerie** (International Museum of Watchmaking; ☎ 032 967 68 61; www.mih.ch, in French; Rue des Musées 29; adult/under 12yr/12-18yr Sfr15/free/10; ☽ 10am-5pm Tue-Sun), a well thought-out museum in a leafy park with history and fine arts museums as neighbours and a huge steel **carillon** behind it that plays on the quarter, half-hour and hour. The **tourist office** (☎ 032 889 68 95; Espacité 1, Place Le Corbusier; ☽ 9am-noon & 1.30-5.30pm Mon-Fri, 9am-noon Sat), a five-minute walk north of the train station along Ave Léopold Robert, has details.

Hourly trains run from Neuchâtel to/from La Chaux-de-Fonds (Sfr10.80, 30 minutes).

Along the Lake

Family-scale vineyards have dressed the hilly northwest shore of Lac de Neuchâtel since the 10th century.

At Hauterive, 3km northeast of Neuchâtel, **Laténium** (☎ 032 889 69 17; www.latenium.ch; adult/under 7yr/7-16yr Sfr9/free/4; ☽ 10am-5pm Tue-Sun) is an archaeological trip back in time from local prehistory to the Renaissance. Take bus 1 from Place Pury to the Musée d'Archéologie stop.

Southbound, **Château de Vaumarcus** (☎ 032 836 36 10; www.chateauvaumarcus.ch, in French; guided tour adult/child Sfr12/free; ☽ advance reservation only) is a keep with witch-hat turrets and vineyards rescued

from ruin in the 1980s. It now houses the excellent restaurant that serves lunch, **La Cour du Peintre** (mains Sfr25-38, menu Sfr62). Charles the Bold allegedly slept here in March 1476, and you can take his room, the only guest space in the house (doubles Sfr290). Guided castle tours include admission to the castle-based Fondation Marc Jurt, an art foundation that hosts art, sculpture and installation exhibitions.

Val de Travers

From **Noiraigue**, plump in the Travers Valley 22km southwest of Neuchâtel, it is a short walk to the enormous abyss of **Creux du Van** (Rocky Hole – *van* is a word of Celtic origin meaning rock). A product of glacial erosion, the spectacular crescent moon wall interrupts the habitually green rolling countryside hereabouts in startling fashion: imagine an enormous gulf 1km long and 440m deep.

Continuing along the N10 or on the same train from Neuchâtel (Sfr10.80, 35 minutes), you reach **Môtiers** with its pretty castle, **absinthe distillery** (above) and **Maison des Mascarons** (☎ 032 861 35 51; Grande Rue 14; adult/child Sfr5/2; ☽ 2.30-5.30pm Tue, Thu, Sat & Sun May–mid-Oct), a local arts, crafts and history museum. Immediately south from here a 4½ ring walk leads through the **Gorges de la Poëta Raisse** to high green plains, forest and a 1448m crest.

A spirit-soothing green sleep in this valley is ecologically sound **L'Aubier** (☎ 032 732 22 11; www.aubier.ch; s/d/tr/q incl breakfast from Sfr125/160/280/330), a small eco-hotel on a biodynamic farm in

Montézillon, a hamlet at 750m, 8km south-west of Neuchâtel. Thoroughly contemporary, light-flooded rooms overlook fields of grazing cows, whose milk is mixed with carrot juice to make carrot cheese; buy it alongside chestnut pasta, farm-baked bread and other organic products in the hotel's well-stocked eco-shop.

MONTAGNES NEUCHÂTELOISES

The west of the canton is dominated by the low mountain chain of the Jura, which stretches from the canton of the same name to the northeast and into Canton de Vaud in the southwest. Cross-country skiers, hikers and bikers love the locals hills, the Montagnes Neuchâteloises.

Le Locle

pop 10,150 / elevation 950m

Incredibly, the whole lucrative Swiss watch business began ticking in this straggly town when Daniel Jean-Richard (1665–1741) established a cottage industry in the manufacture of timepieces. His name is still lent to luxury watches manufactured by Jean Richard (www.danieljeanrichard.ch) in La Chaux-de-Fonds. Drive along the N20 from one town to another past dozens of factories emblazoned with big-name watchmakers Cartier, Tissot, Tag Heuer, Dior, Breitling et al.

Grand 18th-century rooms filled with all manner of clocks make the **Musée de l'Horlogerie du Locle** (Watchmaking Museum; ☎ 032 931 16 80; www.mhl-monts.ch, in French; Rte des Monts 65; adult/under 10yr/10-18yr Sfr8/free/4; ☒ 10am-5pm Tue-Sun May-Oct, 2-5pm Tue-Sun Nov-Apr) tick. The manor house, Château des Monts, was built for an 18th-century watchmaker atop a hill 3km from the town centre. Bus 1 links the train station with the 'Monts' stop, 150m from the museum.

A timely place to sleep is stylish *maison d'hôtes* **Maison Du Bois** (☎ 079 342 25 37; www.maisondubois.ch; Grande Rue 22; s/d incl breakfast Sfr100/140; ☒ reception 8.30am-1.30pm & 3.30-6pm Mon, Tue, Thu & Fri, 8am-1.30pm Wed, 8am-noon Sat), across from the church in the town centre. Not only is the old watchmaker's house dating to 1785 hugely historic; its interior oozes soul, reflected in the line-up of old-fashioned syrups colouring one shelf in the retro breakfast room to the fabulous weekend brunches (10am to 1pm Saturday and Sunday) cooked for guests and non-guests (reserve in advance). Free wi-fi.

About 2km west, a series of underground mills carved out of the rock to exploit subterranean water flowing into the Doubs River makes for an unusual day out at the 17th-century **Moulins Souterrains du Col-des-Roches** (☎ 032 931 89 89; www.lesmoulins.ch, in French; admission by guided tour adult/child/family Sfr12.50/7/28; ☒ 10am-5pm May-Oct, 2-5pm Tue-Sun Nov-Apr), 2km west of Le Locle.

Le Locle is 8km by train (Sfr3.50, six minutes, at least hourly) from La Chaux-de-Fonds.

Les Brenets & Saut du Doubs

Le Doubs River, which springs forth inside France, widens out at the peaceful village of **Les Brenets**, 6km from Le Locle. For the next 45km on its serpentine northwestern course from here, the river forms the border between the two countries before making a loop inside Switzerland and then returning to French territory.

About a one-hour walk along **Lac des Brenets** (Lac de Chaillexon on the French side) the river brings you to the **Saut du Doubs**, a splendid crashing waterfall where the river cascades 27m to a natural pool. For non-walkers, **Navigation sur le Lac des Brenets** (NLB; ☎ 032 932 14 14; www.nlb.ch) runs regular boats from Les Brenets to the waterfall up to 11 times a day from June to September (adult single/return Sfr8/13), and three daily in April, May and October.

Le Locle–Les Brenets trains (Sfr3.50, seven minutes) are frequent.

CANTON DE JURA

Clover-shaped Canton de Jura (840 sq km, population 69,290) is a rural, mysterious peripheral region that few reach. Its grandest towns are no more than enchanting villages, while deep forests and impossibly green clearings succeed one another across its low mountains. While the Jura mountain range proper extends south through Canton de Neuchâtel and Canton de Vaud into the Haut-Jura in neighbouring France, it is here that its Jurassic heart lies.

Getting around is impossible without your own wheels – two or four – or hiking boots. Travelling between the main towns by pretty red mountain train, look for the set of 13 walking and cycling brochures published by local train company **Chemins de Fer du Jura** (www.cj-transports.ch, in French & German); train schedules and fares are online.

FRANCHES MONTAGNES

Settlers only began trickling into these untamed 'free mountains' in the 14th century. Heavily forested hill country marking the northern end of the Jura range, the area – undulating at roughly 1000m – is sprinkled with hamlets and is ideal for walking, mountain biking and cross-country skiing. The Doubs River kisses its northern tip.

Saignelégier (population 2140, elevation 1000m), the Jura's main town on the train line between La Chaux-de-Fonds (Sfr13.80, 35 minutes, almost hourly) and Basel (Sfr27, 1½ with a change at Glovelier), is of little interest unless you're around for its August horse show or keen to try your hand at *trottinette* trekking (Sfr37/42 per half-/full day including equipment hire): rent a chunky micro-scooter and helmet at the train station and follow one of three marked trails, 14.4km to 20km long.

The tourist office, **Jura Tourisme** (☎ 032 420 47 70; www.juratourisme.ch; Rue de la Gruère 1; ◷ 9am-noon & 2-6pm Mon-Fri, 10am-4pm Sat), covers the whole Jura and has ample info on farm accommodation.

Cross-country skiers can skate around tiny **Montfaucon**, 5km northeast or **Les Breuleux**, 7km south. **Le Noirmont**, 6km southwest, has the summer bonus of a **Tipi Village** (☎ 079 449 12 32; www .tipivillage.ch; Le Creux des Biches; 2/3/4-6 people incl firewood Sfr50/70/100; ◷ May-Sep) to kip beneath the stars and one of Switzerland's best chefs, **Georges Wenger** (☎ 032 957 66 33; www.georges-wenger.ch; Rue de la Gare 2; d from Sfr320, mains Sfr75, tasting menus Sfr165-245; **P** 🖳), who cooks up incredible Michelin-starred culinary creations at his self-named restaurant and hotel, opposite the hamlet's tiny train station. In summer, canoe and raft in **Goumois**, 8km west of Saignelégier on the Swiss-French border.

For panoramic Jurassien views, scale 199 steps up **Tour de Moron** (www.tourdemoron.ch, in French & German) in **Malleray**, a designer concrete tower by contemporary Swiss architect Mario Botta (p38) that spirals 30m up into the sky. Dozens of footpaths lead to it from surrounding hamlets; count 25 minutes from its designated car park on the northern fringe of Malleray, a few kilometres east of Bellelay.

Alternatively, for an eagle-eye view across the Jura, Bieler See and Alps, head to **St-Imier**, 18km south of Saignelégier, then follow the minor road south towards Villiers. The first turn left (east) takes you along a winding (in winter snowbound) road to **Le Chasseral** (1607m), a launch pad for hang-gliders.

NORTHERN JURA

Three towns within easy reach of one another are strung out across northern Jura, never far from the French frontier.

Delémont
pop 11,320 / elevation 413m

Canton de Jura's capital moored alongside the Scheulte River is modest. Its Old Town preserves a whiff of years gone by, with uneven houses topped by improbably tall tiled roofs peeping over 18th-century **Église St-Marcel** and **château** (1716–21). The **Musée Jurassien d'Art et d'Histoire** (☎ 032 422 80 77; www.mjah.ch, in French; Rue du 23 Juin 52; adult/child Sfr6/free; ◷ 2-5pm Tue-Sun) displays a hodgepodge of paintings, religious art and so on.

Motorists can follow the signs 3km north out of town to the ruined **Chapelle de Vorbourg**,

FRIBOURG, NEUCHÂTEL & JURA

MONKS' HEADS

For eight centuries, villages around the **Abbaye de Bellelay** (www.domaine-bellelay.ch, in French), 8km north of Tavannes between Moutier and St Imier, have produced a strong, nutty-flavoured cheese known until the French Revolution as *fromage de Bellelay*, or monks' cheese. In 1792 revolutionary troops marched in, obliging the monks at the abbey to leave and abandon the cylindrical cheese maturing in their cellars. Troopers, so the story goes, instantly dubbed the cheese Tête de Moine (Monk's Head), perhaps after the curious way tradition demands it is sliced. Shavings are scraped off the top in a circular motion to create a pretty rosette, done since the 1980s with a nifty handled device called a *girolle*.

Tête de Moine is no longer made at the abbey (now a psychiatric hospital) but the semi-hard AOC-protected cheese is made all over the Jura, including at Saignelégier's **Fromagerie de Tête de Moine** (☎ 032 952 42 40; visites.saigne@emmi.ch; Chemin du Finage 19; ◷ guided visits 3-5pm Fri Mar-Oct).

JURASSIEN FARM LIFE

Sleeping with a herd of goats is not as rough as it sounds. In fact, our night spent kipping in the eaves between bales of hay and spiky straw stacked like sugar cubes was disarmingly romantic. It was far too nippy to stick so much as a little finger out of the sleeping bag and getting dressed in the morning felt like a race against frost bite. But we are talking late October, when the remote Jura hills sit lost in swirling mist until 10am when the autumnal blue sky suddenly breaks through in crystal-clear song.

Elizabeth runs Ferme Montavon (opposite) – home to four generations, 150 heads of cattle and a menagerie of other animals – with her husband, son and just one hired hand. She is a quietly unassuming but firm lady who mothers five children and an 86-year-old father-in-law in between tending land, livestock and farmhouse built in 1812.

'My father-in-law bought the farm in 1952. It is hard. He didn't have a car until 1964, just horses. We work every day but recently decided that every 15 days one of us has a day off,' says Elisabeth as she welcomes us with two bottles of homemade apple juice, one hot off the press and cloudy, the other 'cooked' and clear. We sit at the table with a Swiss family from Zürich who rolled up at dusk in a horse and cart. It's their second *aventure sur la paille* (p353) and the loo hidden between bales in one corner of the mammoth hay barn we'll share is sheer luxury for them.

The farm has two donkeys, dozens of ducks, hens and chickens, a twinset of great big dogs called Asta and Baloue, and too many cats to count. First and foremost it breeds cows for meat – which we eat that night, impossibly tender and pan-fried pink to perfection, as *entrecôte de veau* (veal steak).

'I prefer to cook a roast but this veal just came back from the abattoir today, so it really is fresh,' says Elizabeth, explaining how calves in Switzerland are slaughtered young, when they are

a dramatically located centre of pilgrimage. Contemporary art and installation lovers will enjoy **La Balade de Séprais** (www.balade-seprais.ch), an open-air sculpture park, 12km northwest, around which you can freely wander. Trails range from 30 minutes to three hours.

St Ursanne
pop 870 / elevation 430m
A pretty 30-minute drive west from Delémont wends through beautiful countryside to the Jura's most enchanting village, medieval riverside St Ursanne. As early as the 7th century a centre of worship existed on the site of 12th-century **Église Collégiale**, a grand Gothic church with a splendid Romanesque portal on its southern flank and intriguing crypt.

Ancient houses, the 16th-century town gates, a lovely stone bridge and bevy of eating options on miniature central square, Place Roger Schaffter, tumble down towards the Doubs River from the church. The thin crisp *tartes flambées* (Sfr17.50) cooked over flames followed by to-die-for apple cake are the icing on the cake at 10-room **Hôtel-Restaurant de la Demi Lune** (☎ 032 461 35 31; Place Roger Schaffter; s/d from Sfr95/100). Its riverside terrace is fab.

The **tourist office** (☎ 032 420 47 73; Place Roger Schaffter; 10am-noon & 2-5pm Mon-Fri, 10am-4pm Sat

& Sun) has mountains of information on river kayaking, canoeing and walking.

Trains link St Ursanne train station, 1km east of the centre, with Delémont (Sfr6.80, 20 minutes) and Porrentruy (Sfr4.80, 12 minutes).

Porrentruy
pop 6750 / elevation 425m
From Col de la Croix, the road dips through forest and into a plain to the last Jura town of importance before heading into France – pretty Porrentruy. Fine old buildings, now shops, line the main street, Grand Rue, against a backdrop of bulky **Château de Porrentuy**, now occupied by the cantonal tribunal and various government offices. Scale 44m-tall **Tour de Réfous** (1270; admission free; 8.45-11.45am & 1.15-6pm), the oldest part of the 13th- to 18th-century hilltop complex, for a fine rooftop view. The walls at its sturdy base are 4.5m thick.

Everything from books and clocks to pharmaceutical objects are displayed in the **Musée de l'Hôtel Dieu** (☎ 032 466 72 72; www.museehoteldieu .ch, in French; Grand Rue 5; adult/child Sfr5/free; 2-5pm Tue-Sun Easter–mid-Nov), Porrentuy's former hospital, worth a meander for its gorgeous baroque building with cobbled courtyard, home to the **tourist office** (☎ 032 466 59 59; www.porrentruy.ch, eight to 10 months old, following which the meat hangs in a cold room for a couple of weeks. Images of the doe-eyed, long-lashed calves suckling their mothers on the ground floor of the barn we're sleeping in meddle with each bite.

Ironically, this farmer's wife doesn't eat meat, hence the herd of goats she introduced to the farm. They are milked twice a day (so that's what all the bell-jangling was at some ungodly hour this morning) and give the farmer 2L or so with each milking, hence the delicate white, fresh Elizabeth-made *chèvre* (goats cheese) we savour at breakfast along with just-baked bread, jam loaded with cherries and redcurrants, and a golden yellow, almost cheesy-tasting pat of butter, scratched on the top with a childish flower and made from the rich creamy milk of Elizabeth's solitary Jersey cow.

Later we tour the farm, admiring the old stone farmhouse facing the hills – a profusion of red-geranium flower boxes in summer (next year's cuttings sat with us at dinner) – and glancing across at the neighbouring wood to search out the border marker, a boulder dated 1817 and engraved with a Swiss boar and a French lily of the valley. We walk past a moss-covered chair and a flower-pot lady with two straw plaits and a felt-pen smile to the vegetable patch, planted with lettuces, cabbages, parsley, onions and all sorts. While the cows in their stalls – now in for the winter – feast on hay and fermented silage, we ramble to the pig sty.

'Most farmers in this region kill their pig for St-Martin,' explains Elizabeth, referring to the Fête de la Saint Martin, a centuries-old feast that falls the second Sunday after All Saints' Day in November to celebrate the end of the rural working year, 'but we'll wait until later to put ours in the casserole,' she says, smiling as the kids, one by one, are lifted up to admire the three pink curly-tailed porkers. A fabulous excuse to gorge on all sorts of sausages, cold meats and puddings, the festival is *the* gastronomic date in the Jura. Shame we're a month too early.

---

in French; Grand Rue 5; ☽ 9am-noon & 2-5.30pm Mon-Fri, 9am-noon Sat).

The best place to sleep, eat, drink and lounge in town is next door: **Chez Steph** (☎ 032 466 88 30; www.chezsteph.ch; Grand Rue 1; d from Sfr90; ☽ 5-11pm Wed, 10am or 11am-2pm & 5-11pm or midnight Thu-Sat, 11am-3pm Sun) is a thoroughly contemporary lounge bar with a Spanish-fuelled tapas menu and very satisfying weekend brunches (Sfr18 to Sfr25).

Towards France

From Porrentuy one road leads west into France, 16km away. Pick up a mount to canter through the gorgeous green cow-speckled countryside here in **Courtedoux**, one of just a couple of villages along this gently scenic stretch. Not only do David and Veronique Protti at **Tourisme Équestre** (☎ 032 466 74 52; www .tourismeequestre.net; La Combatte 79a; ☽ Easter-Oct) organise guided horse treks (Sfr30/80/100 per hour/half-/full day); they also rent horse-drawn carriages equipped with BBQ, picnic table and chairs, plates and so on, allowing you to explore the Jura by horse and cart – at a delightfully green average go-slow speed of 5km/h.

Two- to six-day itineraries include overnights in hay barns on farms such as **Ferme Montavon** (☎ 032 476 67 23; www.fermemontavon.ch; Réclère; sleeping in straw incl breakfast & shower adult/under 12yr/12-16yr Sfr24/8/14, d incl breakfast Sfr80; ☽ Easter-Oct), on the Swiss-French border in Réclère with one room in the farmhouse and a bed of straw in the eaves of a huge hay barn – stable to goats and cows in winter. Advance reservations, including for a hearty dinner of farm produce (Sfr20 to Sfr30), are essential.

Hike or drive the 1.5km from the farm to **Préhisto Parc** (☎ 032 476 61 55; www.prehisto.ch; in French; adult/under 5yr/5-15yr Sfr8/free/6; ☽ 10am-noon & 1-5.30pm Easter-Jun & Sep–mid-Nov, 9.30am-6pm Jul & Aug), a well put-together dinosaur park with a 2km-long footpath in woods that passes 45 different prehistoric creatures lurking between trees. Underfoot are the **Grottes de Réclère** (same tel & opening hr; admission by 50min guided tour adult/under 5yr/5-15yr Sfr9/free/6), stalagmite-filled caves discovered in 1886. A combined ticket for both costs Sfr14/10 per adult/child.

FRIBOURG, NEUCHÂTEL & JURA

Valais

As melt-in-your-mouth as the chocolate-box angles of Matterhorn, as cool as the slopes in Verbier, as intoxicating as the wines of Salgesch – Valais is a salacious natural beauty. Wedged into a remote corner of southern Switzerland, this is where farmers were so poor they didn't have two francs to rub together a century ago and where today luminaries sip Sfr10,000 champagne cocktails at Coco Club.

This fickle canton can be as earthy as a vintner's boots in September and as clean as the aesthetic in Zermatt's lounge bars, as splintery as a blackened barn and as smooth as velvet ropes in Verbier. Although united in matters of cantonal pride, wine and glorious *fromage* (cheese), the French- and German-speaking towns reveal idiosyncrasies. To the west Martigny hides Henry Moore sculptures and slobbery St Bernards, while tracing the curves of the Rhône east brings you to castle-topped vineyards in Sion and the baroque grandeur of Brig.

Marvellously eccentric and deeply traditional, Valais is a one-off. In snowbound winters of yore, locals amused themselves with feats of weirdness. Today you'll still find friendly cow fights and dung-whacking festivals, hairy Tschäggättä prowling the lonesome Lötschental come carnival time and dreadlocked, black-nosed sheep patrolling pastures in summer. Even the ubiquitous granaries are unique – built on stilts with stone slabs to outwit thieving rodents.

Peculiarities aside, Valais' landscapes will leave you dumbstruck: from the unfathomable Matterhorn (4478m) that defies trigonometry, photography and many a karabiner to the Rhône valley's tapestry of vineyards, the polished teeth of Dents du Midi rising above Champéry to the shimmering 23km Aletsch Glacier. Valais is a tale of rags to riches, of changing seasons and celebrities, of an outdoors so great it never goes out of fashion.

HIGHLIGHTS

- Striding, climbing or schussing in the shadow of Switzerland's pyramid-perfect **Matterhorn** (p162)

- Getting gooey over the tribe of slobbery St Bernards at **Musée et Chiens du Saint-Bernard** (p148) in Martigny

- Quaffing Pinot Noir at the source and strolling sun-dappled vineyards in **Salgesch** (p157)

- Melting over the views of 4000m peaks rearing above the seemingly never-ending **Aletsch Glacier** (p168)

- Drifting in the thermal baths of **Leukerbad** (p160) set against a canyon-like backdrop

| ■ POPULATION: 298,500 | ■ AREA: 5224.5 SQ KM | ■ LANGUAGE: FRENCH & GERMAN |

VALAIS

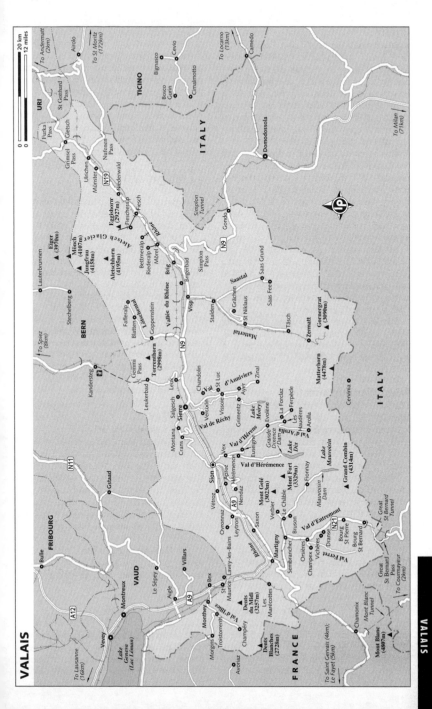

History

As in neighbouring Vaud, Julius Caesar was an early 'tourist' in these parts. The Roman leader brought an army to conquer the Celtic community living in the valley, penetrating as far as Sierre. Once under Roman domination, the four Celtic tribes of Valais were peaceably integrated into the Roman system. Archaeological remains attest to the passage of the rambling general and his boys from Rome.

Sion became a key centre in the valley when the Bishop of Valais settled there from AD 580. By 1000, the bishop's power stretched from Martigny to the Furka Pass. That authority did not go uncontested. A succession of Dukes of Savoy encroached on the bishops' territory and a Savoyard army besieged Sion in 1475. With the help of the Swiss Confederation, the city was freed at the battle of Planta. Internal opposition was equally weighty and Valais' independently minded communes stripped the bishops of their secular power in the 1630s, shifting control to the Diet, a regional parliament.

The Valais was not invaded again until Napoleon Bonaparte stopped by in 1798, determined to dominate the routes into Italy. Valais joined the Swiss Confederation in 1815.

Orientation & Information

The Rhône carves a broad, sunny valley between the Bernese Alps to the north and the Valaisan Alps marking the southern frontier with France and Italy. French dominates the lower (western) valley and German the upper (eastern) half of the canton.

Information is available at the regional tourist office, **Valais Tourisme** (☎ 027 327 35 70; www.valais.ch; Rue de Pré-Fleuri 6, Sion; ⏰ 8am-noon & 1.30-5.30pm Mon-Fri).

Getting There & Around

The smoothest routes are from Italy to Martigny (via the Great St Bernard Pass and Tunnel) and Brig (via the Simplon Pass and Tunnel). The most direct route from Chamonix, France, to Valais is by road from Martigny. The N19 highway enters the canton in the east via the Furka Pass and passes through main junctions like Brig. In Sierre it becomes the A9 freeway, continuing to Sion, Martigny and then north to Geneva. The same route is served by a major rail line, with a branch route into Italy via Domodossola.

The Erlebniskarte Wallis is a transport card for Upper Valais and entitles holders to two, three or five days' (Sfr95/125/175) unlimited travel on trains and buses within a one-month period. It gives you 50% off on most lifts and sporting activities on those days too.

The three-day Mont Blanc Pass, covering Mont Blanc Express/St Bernard Express trains between Chamonix, Martigny and Aosta, costs adult/child Sfr75/38. Ask at the towns' tourist offices about the passes.

LOWER VALAIS

Stone-walled vineyards, tumbledown castle ruins and brooding mountains create an arresting backdrop to the meandering Rhône valley in western Valais. Running west to east, the A9 freeway links towns such as Roman-rooted Martigny and vine-strewn Sion and Sierre, where the French influence shows not only in the lingo but also in the locals' passion for art, wine and pavement cafés.

Glitzy resorts like Verbier and Crans-Montana have carved out reputations for sunny cruising, big panoramas and celebrity style, but there's more. Narrow lanes wriggle up to forgotten valleys such as Val d'Anniviers and Val d'Arolla, packed with rural charm and crowd-free skiing in the shadow of ice-capped mountains.

CHAMPÉRY

pop 1260 / elevation 1055m

Champéry still feels like a well-kept secret. Stuck between the pointy jaws of Dents du Midi and Dents Blanches, this hidden Swiss chocolate box is worth seeking. Small but beautiful, the resort exudes authenticity, with its cosy log chalets and friendly locals. Les Portes du Soleil region offers larger-than-life skiing with a whopping 650km of pistes to play on.

The **Champéry tourist office** (☎ 024 479 20 20; www.champery.ch; ⏰ 8am-noon & 2-6pm), 50m from the station, can help arrange activities such as canyoning.

Activities

Champéry is at the heart of slalom wonderland **Les Portes du Soleil** (Gateway to the Sun; www.portesdusoleil.com), straddling the Franco-Swiss border, a downhill heaven for intermediate, backcountry skiers and snowboarders. Cross-country skiers can explore 243km of trails.

THE WALL

For speed demons, skiing in Champéry means one thing: the Swiss Wall at Chavanette, a heart-stopping, hell-for-leather mogul run, famed as one of the world's toughest. Accomplished skiers with the bottle to throw themselves off the edge should check conditions first, as ice can make the run treacherous. Otherwise Chavanette is the ultimate scream, a mad downhill bump over moguls the size of small cars, with gradients of up to 50 degrees. It's fast, steep and there's no going baaaaaaack…

Morzine and Avoriaz in France are just a lift ride away. Day ski passes for the whole area cost Sfr55/46/44/37 per adult/student or under 26 years/senior/child.

A short walk from the top of Planachaux cable car, **Croix de Culet** (1963m) affords an eagle's-eye perspective of serrated limestone pinnacles.

In summer, the 40km trail around the Dents du Midi is a memorable multi-day hike. Easier but equally scenic is the amble along Galerie Défago, hewn out of the implausibly sheer rock face. The tourist office can provide details on walking, biking and climbing.

Sleeping & Eating

Hôtel des Alpes (☎ 024 479 12 22; www.hotel-desalpes.ch; Rue du Village 9; s/d 135/230; **P**) Go traditional or modern in rooms with wi-fi and sunny balconies at this family-run chalet. You'll soon warm to the place swaddled in a sheepskin by the open fire or savouring crumbly croissants at breakfast.

Hôtel Beau-Séjour (☎ 024 479 58 58; www.bo-sejour .com; Rue du Village 114; s/d Sfr145/250) Robert and Hélène run this cutesy pad, a joyous ski-boot hop from the lifts. With fluffy duvets and painted furniture, the pine-filled rooms are incredibly snug, and the balconies afford dreamy mountain views. Nice touch: homemade cakes served by a log fire.

Mitchell's (☎ 024 479 20 10; mains Sfr18-40; ☼ 11am-midnight) Nordic sylvan chic and laid-back vibes make Mitchell's a must. That and the après-ski *glögg* (mulled wine), and Swedish treats like home-smoked reindeer carpaccio with lingonberries, and eye-candy staff.

Getting There & Away

From Aigle (20 minutes along the train track from Martigny to Lausanne), a train runs via Monthey hourly to Champéry (Sfr12.80, one hour).

MARTIGNY

pop 15,375 / elevation 476m

Once the stomping ground of Romans in search of Swiss wine and sunshine en route to Italy, Martigny is Valais' oldest town. Look beyond its less lovable elements (namely concrete high-rises) and the rewards are many; among them a world-class gallery showcasing works by Henry Moore and Rodin, an intact Roman amphitheatre, and a posse of droopy St Bernards at the Musée et Chiens du Saint-Bernard.

Fresh, youthful and arty, Martigny isn't always pretty, but it *is* interesting and an antidote to Alpine cuteness overkill. It's also the perfect base for vineyard strolls and two-wheeled adventures along the Rhône.

Orientation & Information

Most action spirals around Place Centrale, where you'll find the **tourist office** (☎ 027 720 49 49; www.martignytourism.ch; Place Centrale; ☼ 9am-noon & 1.30-6pm Mon-Fri, 9am-noon & 1.30-4.30pm Sat summer, plus 10am-noon & 4-6pm Sun Jul & Aug, closed Sun & Sat afternoon rest of year), 500m south of the train station along Ave de la Gare.

Sights & Activities

Set in a spacey concrete edifice, the **Fondation Pierre Gianadda** (☎ 027 722 39 78; www.gianadda.ch; Rue du Forum; adult/student/family Sfr15/12/42; ☼ 9am-7pm Jun-Nov, 10am-6pm Dec-May) harbours a star-studded art collection. A copy of Rodin's *The Kiss* sculpture by the entrance promises great things and the gallery delivers with works by Picasso, Cézanne and van Gogh, occasionally shifted to make space for blockbuster exhibitions. A highlight is the garden where Henry Moore's organic sculptures and Niki de Saint Phalle's buxom *Bathers* peek above the foliage.

Entry covers two other permanent exhibitions. Upstairs the **Musée Archéologique Gallo-Romain** is a treasure-trove of Roman milestones, vessels and jewellery. Fine pieces include the titchy statuette of Celtic horse goddess Epona. Downstairs the **Musée de l'Auto** gleams with chrome-plated nostalgia, showing classic cars from vintage Fords to Swiss Martinis (the kind you drive, not drink).

VALAIS

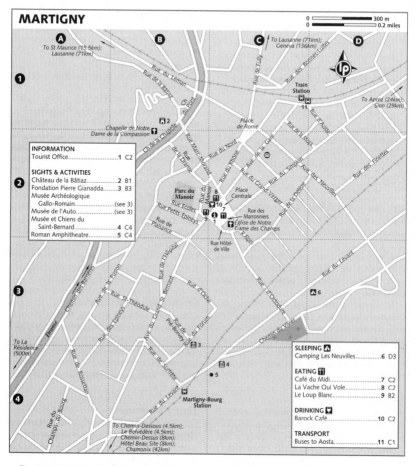

MARTIGNY

INFORMATION
Tourist Office..........................1 C2

SIGHTS & ACTIVITIES
Château de la Bâtiaz...............2 B1
Fondation Pierre Gianadda.......3 B3
Musée Archéologique
  Gallo-Romain.....................(see 3)
Musée de l'Auto.....................(see 3)
Musée et Chiens du
  Saint-Bernard.....................4 C4
Roman Amphitheatre...............5 C4

SLEEPING 🛏
Camping Les Neuvilles...............6 D3

EATING 🍴
Café du Midi.............................7 C2
La Vache Qui Vole.....................8 C2
Le Loup Blanc..........................9 B2

DRINKING 🍷
Barock Café............................10 C2

TRANSPORT
Buses to Aosta.......................11 C1

Revisit Martigny's fascinating Roman past at the meticulously restored **Roman Amphitheatre** (admission free) nearby.

Next to the amphitheatre is the town's new tail-wagging attraction, **Musée et Chiens du Saint-Bernard** (☎ 027 720 49 20, www.museesaintbernard.ch, Rte du Levant 34; adult/child/under 8yr Sfr10/8/free; ☼ 9am-7pm Jun-Nov, 10am-6pm Dec-May). A tribute to the lovably dopey St Bernard, this museum would merit but a sniff if it weren't for the real-life fluff bundles in the kennels. If you're lucky, you might be able to stroke them; all together now, ah… Upstairs an exhibition traces the role of St Bernards in hospice life, on canvas (note Ernst Otto Leuenberger's oil paintings), in advertising and on film. From Suchard to Peter Pan, these pooches have serious star quality.

Clinging to a crag above Martigny, **Château de la Bâtiaz** (Bâtiaz Castle; ☎ 027 721 22 70; admission free; ☼ 11am-6pm Fri-Sun mid-May–mid-Oct) is worth the uphill pant for its far-reaching views over the surrounding vineyards and Rhône valley. Less appealing is the gruesome collection of medieval torture instruments inside.

Nip into the tourist office for details on vineyard walks or a free cycling map of the famous 320km Rhône Route from Andermatt to Lake Geneva. Bike hire is available at the train station.

Festivals & Events
Pigs don't fly, but cows certainly fight in Martigny. The 10-day October **Foire du Valais** (Valais Regional Fair) ends with a bovine

bash-about of epic proportions (see Close Cow Encounters, p157).

If the idea of watching crunch-tackle cows doesn't appeal, there's sizzling action at the **Foire du Lard** (Bacon Fair) in December. Local residents have been picking on the prize porkers since the Middle Ages.

Sleeping

Martigny's tutti-frutti tower-block hotels have all the charm of prefab '70s bedsits. Yet scratch the surface and you'll find attractive deals, particularly if you go the extra 2km (five-minute train ride) south to Martigny-Croix. The tourist office has a list of B&Bs and apartments.

Camping Les Neuvilles (☎ 027 722 45 44; Rue du Levant 68; sites per adult/tent Sfr8.80/9.20; ❧) This countrified campsite is a half-hiking boot's distance from the centre. Its first-rate facilities include a restaurant and swimming pool.

La Résidence (☎ 027 723 16 00; www.residence -martigny.ch; Les Creusats, Martigny-Croix; s/d Sfr70/120) Sitting pretty amid vineyards, this rosy guest house has big sunny rooms with garden-facing terraces. Chantal and Jean-François will feed you tips over a delicious breakfast with homemade jam, local cheese and ham.

Hôtel Beau Site (☎ 027 722 81 64; www.chemin.ch; Chemin-Dessus; s/d Sfr110/140) Perched on wooded slopes, this retreat oozes art-nouveau flair with stained-glass windows and classically elegant rooms. Follow the road from Rue des Champs-du-Bourg roundabout north to Chemin-Dessus. Local bus 5 heads up here hourly (25 minutes).

Eating & Drinking

Plane tree-flanked Place Centrale is Martigny's life, soul and party, framed by pavement cafés and bistros serving everything from pizza to sugary crêpes.

our pick **La Vache Qui Vole** (☎ 027 722 38 33; Place Centrale 2b; mains Sfr18-40; ❧ 10.30am-1am Mon-Sat) Martigny's 'Flying Cow' is a theatrical gallery-style restaurant with Boho ambience and cult cow kitsch: from the angelic bovine beauty suspended from the ceiling to snazzy cow-bell lights. Check out the quirky Virgin Mary collection upstairs. Salads, pasta, risotto, Sri Lankan curries – it's all uniformly delicious.

Le Belvédère (☎ 027 723 14 00; Chemin-Dessus; mains Sfr26-43; ❧ closed Mon & Tue, dinner Sun) A country lane snakes up to this dapper mansion, where you can savour long views over the Rhône

valley and regional treats like Val d'Hérens beef tournedos in creamy chanterelle sauce in the pine-panelled dining room. See the directions for Hôtel Beau Site.

Café du Midi (☎ 027 722 00 03; Rue des Marronniers 4; mains Sfr20-35; ❧ closed Tue) This shabby-chic café near the church emits an inviting glow. You too will radiate warmth when you sit at one of the well-worn wooden tables to guzzle Trappist brews and gorge on fondue with mountain herbs. There's free wi-fi.

Le Loup Blanc (☎ 027 723 52 52; Place Centrale 12; mains Sfr18-30; ❧ 8am-1am) Warm colours and a Med-style menu make this avant-garde café popular. Everything from calamari to pizza is beautifully cooked and artfully presented.

Barock Café (☎ 027 722 71 60; www.barock-café.com, in French; Place Centrale 8; ❧ 10am-1am) With a design born in the USA – think Pepsi placards and pics of rock-and-roll legends – this groovy bar doubles as a venue for gigs. By night it's as loud and lively as it gets in Martigny.

Getting There & Away

Martigny is on the main rail route from Lausanne (Sfr23, 50 minutes) to Brig (Sfr25, 50 to 60 minutes). Buses go from Martigny via Orsières and the Great St Bernard Tunnel to Aosta in Italy (Sfr31.80, at least two departures per day).

The private **Mont-Blanc Express** (☎ 027 721 68 40; www.tmrsa.ch) usually goes hourly to Chamonix (Sfr32, 1½ hours) in France, with up to 12 trips daily in the high season. Martigny is also the departure point for the St Bernard Express to Le Châble (Sfr10.20, 26 minutes; ski lift or bus connection for Verbier) and Orsières (Sfr10.20, 26 minutes) via Sembrancher.

AROUND MARTIGNY
Val d'Entremont & Great St Bernard Pass

Emblazoned with its canine mascot, the St Bernard Express train from Martigny to Orsières branches south at Sembrancher, chugging south to the Italian border through classic Alpine scenery in the Val d'Entremont. **Orsières**, just off the main road to the Col du Great St-Bernard, marks the beginning of pine-brushed **Val Ferret**. Here you could pause for lunch at **Hôtel les Alpes** (☎ 027 783 11 01; lunch menus Sfr65, dinner menus Sfr180; ❧ closed dinner Mon), a former inn where today Michelin-starred chef Jean-Maurice Joris conjures seasonal delicacies, from juicy Burgundy snails to freshly hunted game.

A branch road leads to **Champex**, which sits by a glassy lake. From Orsières it's a 1¾-hour walk. A chair lift operates in winter and summer to La Breya (2194m), where views reach to snowcapped Grand Combin (4314m).

Wildlife spotters with their own wheels could follow the N21 road further south towards Drance, then turn off for Vichères. Look out for a footpath a couple of kilometres before reaching the hamlet. This trail leads along La Combe de l'A nature reserve, which is particularly beautiful on golden autumn days when you may well spy rutting stags.

The N21 dips south to the Italian border, which you can cross by tunnel or twisting mountain road, depending on your preferences and weather conditions.

High on a col overlooking a petrol-blue lake, the **hospice** (☎ 027 787 12 36; dm/d Sfr21/66) at Great St Bernard Pass is snowed in for up to six months of the year. In winter, the only way up or down is on foot (snowshoes or skis) from the entrance to the tunnel 7km downhill. Call ahead to find out if it's open and if there's space. Dorms are spartan, but the monks are welcoming and the setting is magical.

Monks have kept the hospice since the 11th century to give spiritual succour and rescue travellers lost in the snow. And so the legend of the **St Bernard dogs** was born, as they frequently found the lost souls and did the rescuing. No nose was finer tuned than that of doggie legend Barry (1800–1814), who saved 40 lives. Fondation Barry runs the **kennels and museum** (adult/senior/child Sfr8/6.50/5.50; ⏰ 9am-7pm Jul & Aug, 9am-noon & 1-6pm Jun & Sep), which you can visit in summer.

LET ME DO THE WALKING

Big softie or not, everyone loves a St Bernard, so **Fondation Barry** (☎ 027 722 65 42; www.fondation-barry.ch) has come up with a clever plan to please visitors to the Great St Bernard Pass and ensure the dogs get regular exercise. From July to mid-September, you can accompany the doe-eyed woofers on a 1½-hour walk over the pass. These guided strolls are a one-off chance to lap up the Alpine scenery and, of course, give the dogs much-needed strokes. Walks depart daily at 10am (brisk) and 2pm (gentle) and cost Sfr48 for adults and Sfr8 for children.

To get to the hospice from Martigny in summer, take the St Bernard Express train to Orsières (see p149) and change for the connecting bus (45 minutes). The total cost from Martigny is Sfr25. Otherwise the bus won't go past Bourg St Pierre.

MONT BLANC
elevation 4810m

Yes, you read the elevation right. Despite the fact textbooks say 4807m, Mont Blanc is, ironically, growing because of global warming, with more snow massing on its summit than previously. Although it's not actually in Switzerland, the giant of the Alps feels close enough to touch at times. The main resort in France is Chamonix, famous for its hair-raising chutes and steep off-piste terrain. It's easily reached by road from Geneva or by train from Martigny. The must-ski for the fit is Europe's longest run, **Vallée Blanche**, an epic 22km glacier descent that starts at the 3880m spike of Aiguille du Midi and finishes in Chamonix. On the Italian side, the big resort is Courmayeur. For information on both resorts, see www.chamonix.com and www.courmayeur.com. Hikers can tackle the stunning 170km **Mont Blanc circuit**, about a third of which passes through Switzerland. The high-level route climbs above 2500m and typically takes 10 to 14 days. In Switzerland trailheads include Champex (left) and Col de la Forclaz pass, reached by bus from Martigny.

VERBIER
pop 2800 / elevation 1500m

Verbier is the diamond of the Valaisan Alps: small, stratospherically expensive and cut at all the right angles to make it sparkle in the eyes of accomplished skiers and piste-bashing stars. British royals have flocked here for years, but the snow just got hotter with the likes of Sir Richard Branson playing hotelier and new resident James Blunt practising yodelling (oh dear) from his balcony.

Yet despite its ritzy packaging, Verbier is that rare beast of a resort – all things to all people. It swings from schnapps-fuelled debauchery to VIP lounges, bunker hostels to design-oriented hotels, burgers to Michelin stars. Here ski bums and celebs slalom in harmony on powder that is legendary.

Orientation & Information

Verbier sits on a southwest-facing ledge above Le Châble, the rail terminus. The

---

YOU'RE BEAUTIFUL, VERBIER, IT'S TRUE...

Luminaries who have adopted Verbier as their holiday retreat or home have caused a snowstorm in an Alpine teacup recently by sending property prices sky-high. The resort is swiftly reinventing itself as one of the hottest in the Swiss Alps. Fergie once boogied at Farm Club, Prince William and Kate Middleton love the steaks at Chez Dany and Sir Richard Branson – always quick to spot a nice little earner – has opened the Lodge (www.thelodge.virgin.com) complete with Jacuzzi and ice-rink. Yours for Sfr86,000 a week. Ouch.

Other regulars include Posh and Becks, Al Pacino, Diana Ross and Michael Schumacher. And now that the ice-white, ubercool Coco Club has opened, they have somewhere to drink. Owned by entrepreneur Harvey Sinclair and former footballer Ramon Vega, the VIP club serves the champagne-based Coco Chalet cocktail in a carved ice glass for a cool Sfr10,000. Why not have two? James Blunt is one of the latest to sprinkle celebrity stardust on Verbier by snapping up a chalet here. To honour his presence, authorities have named a ski lift after his warble-ness. Beautiful indeed.

---

resort proper is uphill from Verbier village. Verbier's hub is Place Centrale home to the **tourist office** (☎ 027 775 38 88; www.verbier.ch; 8am-6.30pm Mon-Fri, 9am-noon & 3-7pm Sat, 9am-noon & 3-6.30pm Sun). Just off the square is the post office and postal bus terminus. Verbier is mostly shut between seasons, including the cable cars. The resort has a free bus service in the high season.

Activities

Verbier's skiing is justifiably billed as some of Europe's finest. The resort sits at the heart of the **Quatre Vallées** (Four Valleys), comprising a cool 412km of runs and 94 ski lifts. A regional ski pass costs Sfr65. Cheaper passes excluding Mont Fort are also available.

The terrain is exciting and varied, with beginners on gentle slopes at **Le Rouge** and intermediates carving long slopes at **La Chaux**. Boarders make for the latter to catch big air on kickers and rails. Experts can tackle short blacks like Savoleyres Nord and the heart-stoppingly steep, mogul-speckled **Mont-Fort** run. The broad, well-groomed runs from Les Attelas to Verbier are ideal for cruising. Real challenges lie off-piste in the virgin powder for accomplished skiers. It's wise to hire a guide. **Adrenaline** (☎ 079 205 95 95; www.adrenaline -verbier.ch) arranges freeride tours from Médran lift for around Sfr100.

Verbier Sport + (☎ 027 775 33 63; www.verbier booking.com), behind the post office, offers ski instruction, paragliding and other activities, including a six-day trek along the Haute Route to Zermatt.

The **hiking** here is superb. From Les Ruinettes, it takes 1½ hours to ascend to the ridge at Creblet, and down into the crater to Lac des Vaux. Other worthwhile walks include the seven-hour trek to Corbassière glacier, which snakes down from 4314m Grand Combin, and the five-hour Sentier des Chamois trail, popular with wildlife lovers as it offers chances to spot chamois, marmots and eagles. The tourist office regional map costs Sfr8.

Downhill freaks can flaunt their expertise on routes from Les Ruinettes and Médran or hone their skills at **Kona Bike Park** (☎ 027 775 25 11; www.verbierbikepark.ch; adult/child Sfr28/14; 9am-4.30pm Jul-Sep). The tourist office organises free guided mountain bike tours every Wednesday afternoon in July and August; contact them for details.

If being on the top of a mountain isn't high enough, you can take to the air hang-gliding or paragliding. **Centre de Parapente** (☎ 027 771 68 18; www.flyverbier.ch) offers 30-minute tandem flights from Sfr190.

Festivals & Events

The biggest bash is the **Verbier Festival & Academy** (☎ 027 925 90 60; www.verbierfestival.com) in July, a high-profile classical music festival.

A highlight on the winter sports calendar is the **Xtreme Freeride Contest** (www2.xtremeverbier.com) in March, when pro snowboarders brave the hair-raising Bec des Rosses North Face.

Sleeping

Verbier is doable for ski bums on a budget with a little preplanning. If money isn't an issue, there are posh digs that will help you fritter away your francs – fast. Rates nosedive by 30% to 50% in summer.

VALAIS

Le Stop (☎ 079 549 72 23; www.le-stop.ch; Villa Des Dames; Le Châble; dm Sfr29-45) This former bunker has a new raison d'être with no-frills dorms. What you'll get is four walls, a queue for the loo and a rickety bunk, but at Sfr29 a night, with Verbier just a cable-car ride away, frankly it's a gift. Bring your own sleeping bag.

our pick Cabane du Mont-Fort (☎ 027 778 13 84; www.cabanemontfort.ch; dm Sfr42-52) Above the clouds with mesmerising vistas to the Massif des Combins, this 2457m-high Alpine hut is brilliant for walkers in summer and skiers in winter, with direct access to La Chaux. Expect cosy slumber in pine-panelled dorms, panoramas that will motivate you to rise at dawn and a restaurant serving tasty mountain grub.

Les Touristes (☎ 027 771 21 47; www.hoteltouristes -verbier.ch; s/d Sfr70/140; ℗) If you think *le chic c'est freak,* try this rustic chalet. Rooms are modest yet comfy with pine trappings, floral bedding and washbasins. The restaurant (mains Sfr19 to Sfr39) will fill your belly with cheese or buy farm-fresh *fromage* next door. It's a 15-minute walk from the centre.

Ermitage (☎ 027 771 64 77; www.ermitage-verbier .ch; Place Centrale; s/d Sfr150/310; ℗ 🖳 🕭) This central chalet has smiley service and perks like free internet and wi-fi. Though a tad poky, rooms are modern and spotless. Quiet south-facing doubles with views to the Massif des Combins are a better deal.

Nevaï (☎ 027 775 40 00 www.nevai.ch; s/d/ste Sfr300/490/1350; ℗ 🖳) There's not a whiff of Alpine kitsch in Nevaï's minimalist chic rooms – think earthy hues, beds dressed in Egyptian cotton, balconies with Alpine views, and gadgets like iPods and DVD players. Penthouses come with log fires and outdoor whirlpools. The hip restaurant (mains Sfr30 to Sfr60) serves Asian–Med fusion cuisine, the spa has Elemis treatments and the boudoir-style bar offers decadent cocktails beside a 4m-long fireplace.

Eating

Milk Bar (☎ 027 771 67 77; Rue de Médran; snacks & light meals Sfr8-20) This mellow hut is famous for its *grands crus de cacao* (hot chocolate) and toasty atmosphere. Sit under the cowbells for scrummy homemade tarts, pancakes and other sugar-loaded treats to put a whoosh in your schuss.

Harold's (☎ 027 771 62 43; Place Centrale; burgers around Sfr10; 🕭 10am-1.30am high season, 11am-11pm low season) Thumping music mixes with hissing grills at Harold's, where the menu is sweet and simple: 100% homemade burgers slathered in cocktail sauce. Check emails while you wait.

Chez Dany (☎ 027 771 25 24; Clambin; mains Sfr26-54) On a sunny plateau between Les Ruinettes and Médran, this buzzy chalet is Prince William's favourite place to tuck into a juicy steak. The terrace affords sweeping views to the Massif des Combins. Revive snow-sore eyes over hot chocolate or cheesy *croûte au fromage.* It's fun to take a skidoo up here in the evening and sledge back down.

Le Caveau (☎ 027 771 22 26, Place Centrale; mains Sfr27-42; 🕭 10am-midnight Wed-Sun) Behind the barrel door lies a cave-like den strewn with cuckoo clocks and lanterns. It's a cosy spot for Raclette or posh fondue with champagne and truffles.

Drinking

Like the skiing, the après-ski scene in Verbier is full throttle, kicking off on the slopes before sliding down to Place Centrale.

Pub Mont Fort (☎ 027 771 48 98; Chemin de la Tinte 10; 🕭 3pm-1.30am) All hail this après-ski heavyweight for its lively vibe, pulsating beats and half-price tipples at happy hour (4pm to 5pm). Try a vodka-cranberry Swiss Kiss. In winter, it sells the most beer in Switzerland – enough said.

Farinet (☎ 027 771 66 26; Place Centrale; 🕭 4pm-1.30am) Young, loud and fun (if your idea of fun is bootylicious snow-boot jiggling), Farinet is another wild après-ski haunt. The conservatory brims with ruddy-faced ski bums guzzling shakers and dancing on tables, while the chill-out lounge offers rest for the wicked.

Farm Club (☎ 027 771 61 21; Rue de la Poste) Looking gorgeous following a complete makeover, the Farm has been going strong for 35 years. You'll need to dress up to slip past the velvet rope but it's worth it. The swanky club heaves with socialites out spending daddy's (or sugar daddy's) pension on Moët magnums.

Getting There & Away

Trains from Martigny run hourly year-round, take 30 minutes and terminate at Le Châble. From there you either get a bus or, when it's running, the cable car. The full trip costs Sfr15.80 and takes about an hour.

VAL DE BAGNES

From Le Châble it's a 19km drive south to Lac de Mauvoisin (Lake Mauvoisin), an eye-popping 250m-high dam. Several hiking trails set out from here, including one that crosses the mountain frontier with Italy over the Fenêtre du Durand pass (2797m) and down into the Valpelline valley in the Val d'Aosta region. Three daily buses run on weekends from Le Châble (Sfr13.80, 45 minutes).

OVRONNAZ

Few people cotton on to this petite but attractive family-friendly ski resort with thermal baths. From Martigny, head east up the A9 as far as the Leytron turn-off, where a mountain road zigzags 10km north to Ovronnaz. The **tourist office** (☎ 027 306 42 93; www.ovronnaz .ch; 8.30am-noon & 1.30-6pm Mon-Fri, 9am-6pm Sat, 9am-noon Sun mid-Dec–mid-Apr, 8.30am-noon & 1.30-6pm Mon-Fri, 9am-noon & 2-5pm Sat, closed Sun mid-Apr–mid-Dec), at the north end of the village near Coop supermarket, can advise on B&Bs and apartments.

The limited skiing here is geared towards intermediates and makes for a queue-free day cruising. What makes it especially fun is combining the slopes with bath time. A combined lift pass and entry to the **Thermalp baths** (☎ 027 305 11 11; www.thermalp.ch; 8am-8.30pm) costs Sfr57 (a saving of Sfr5 on paying for them separately).

Buses run from Martigny (change at Leytron) hourly (Sfr13.80, about one hour). You have similar options from Sion.

SION

pop 28,870 / elevation 490m

Sion has a bewitching backdrop: ringed by vineyards, bisected by the serpentine Rhône and watched over by twin pop-up hills crowned with ruined castles that glow by night. The Valaisan capital moves to a relaxed beat, with pavement cafés lining the helter-skelter of lanes that thread down from Château de Tourbillon to the medieval Old Town.

Castles and cobbles aside, much of Sion's appeal lies in the surrounding vine-strewn hills inviting languid strolls and foaming rivers perfect for adrenalin-pumping pursuits like white-water rafting and hydrospeeding.

Orientation

The French-speaking town sits north of the Rhône. The train station is downhill and south of the Old Town, facing the modern, commercial heart of Sion. Most areas of interest are within walking distance of the station, along Ave de la Gare and Rue de Lausanne.

Information

Sion has a **post office** (Place de la Gare 11; 8am-6.15pm Mon-Fri, 9am-4pm Sat) and a **tourist office** (☎ 027 327 77 27; www.siontourism.ch; Place de la Planta; 9am-noon & 1.30-6pm Mon-Fri, 9am-12.30pm Sat).

Sights

CHURCHES & TOWERS

Graced with a sturdy Romanesque tower, Gothic **Notre Dame du Glarier** and its smaller 16th-century sidekick **Église de St Théodule** vie for your attention on a leafy square in the Old Town. Up Rue de la Tour from the churches is a reminder of Sion's medieval past, the **Tour des Sorciers** (Wizards' Tower), one of the watchtowers in the one-time city walls.

CHÂTEAU DE TOURBILLON

Lording it over the fertile Rhône valley from its hilltop perch above Sion, this ruined **castle** (☎ 027 606 47 45; Rue des Châteaux; admission free; 10am-6pm mid-Mar–mid-Nov) is worth the trudge alone for the postcard views. It's a short climb from the centre to the crumbling remains of this medieval stronghold, destroyed by fire in 1788.

CHÂTEAU DE VALÈRE

Slung on a hill above the centre opposite Château de Tourbillon is fortified Château de Valère, sheltering a 12th-century **basilica** (Rue des Châteaux; adult/child/family Sfr3/2/6; hourly visits 10am-6pm Mon-Sat, 2-6pm Sun Jun-Sep, 10am-5pm Mon-Sat, 2-5pm Sun Oct-May). The world's oldest playable organ juts out from the wall opposite the apse like the stern of a medieval caravel. Concerts are held on Saturday afternoons (from 4pm) from mid-July to mid-August.

The church interior reveals beautifully carved choir stalls and a brightly frescoed apse. From the basilica you have a commanding panoramic view across the city. Downhill from the basilica is **Musée Cantonal d'Histoire** (☎ 027 606 47 15; adult/child/family Sfr8/4/15; 11am-6pm daily Jun-Sep, 11am-5pm Tue-Sun Oct-May), spelling out Sion's history in artefacts.

MAISON SUPERSAXO

Squirreled away in a cobbled courtyard in the Old Town, this grand **residence** (Passage de Supersaxo; admission free; 8am-noon & 2-5pm Mon-Fri) was built by Georges Supersaxo in 1505 to provoke his friend-turned-enemy, the bishop of Sion. Exhibits tracing the city's history are eclipsed by the beautiful faded frescos,

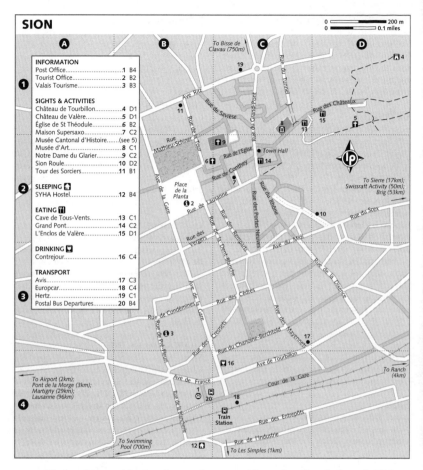

SION

0 —————— 200 m
0 —————— 0.1 miles

INFORMATION
Post Office.....................1 B4
Tourist Office...................2 B2
Valais Tourisme.................3 B3

SIGHTS & ACTIVITIES
Château de Tourbillon............4 D1
Château de Valère...............5 D1
Église de St Théodule............6 B2
Maison Supersaxo...............7 C2
Musée Cantonal d'Histoire......(see 5)
Musée d'Art...................8 C1
Notre Dame du Glarier...........9 C2
Sion Roule....................10 D2
Tour des Sorciers..............11 B1

SLEEPING
SYHA Hostel...................12 B4

EATING
Cave de Tous-Vents.............13 C1
Grand Pont...................14 C2
L'Enclos de Valère.............15 D1

DRINKING
Contrejour...................16 C4

TRANSPORT
Avis........................17 C3
Europcar.....................18 C4
Hertz.......................19 C1
Postal Bus Departures..........20 B4

cross-ribbed vaulting and intricately carved
ceilings of the building itself.

MUSÉE D'ART

Lodged in a vine-strewn 13th-century castle,
the well-curated **Musée d'Art** (Museum of Fine Art;
☎ 027 606 46 90; Place de la Marjorie 19; adult/child/family
Sfr5/2.50/10; ☼ 11am-5pm Tue-Sun) showcases works
by Swiss artists including Ernest Bieler and
Caspar Wolf, alongside star pieces by Austrian
Expressionist Oskar Kokoschka.

Activities

Sion's terraced vineyards yield highly quaffable dôle and Fendant wines. You can ramble through the vines and taste tipples at the
source on the gentle 7km walk along 500-

year-old aqueduct **Bisse de Clavau** (p65) from
Sion to St-Léonard.

Alternatively, explore the vineyards and the
banks of the Rhône by bike. The eco-friendly
initiative **Sion Roule** (Place du Scex; ☼ 9am-7pm mid-
May–mid-Sep) offers free bike hire, but you'll
need to show ID and leave a Sfr50 deposit.

Hugging the Rhône, Sion is a terrific base
for splashy adventures. **Swissraft Activity** (☎ 027
475 35 10; www.swissraft-activity.ch; Rue du Scex 28; ☼ office 10am-6pm May-Oct) takes thrill-seekers white-
water rafting (Sfr75 to Sfr95), hydrospeeding
(Sfr140) and canyoning (Sfr160).

Sleeping

If Sion's cookie-cutter chain hotels don't
appeal, there are attractive chalets, farms

and B&Bs in the area. Pick up a list at the tourist office.

Ranch (☎ 027 203 13 13; www.ranch.ch; per person Sfr25; ⊗ May-Oct) Snooze in a straw-filled barn, breakfast on bacon and eggs, then canter off into the countryside at the Ranch. The friendly owners arrange horse-riding treks and sell home-grown jam and juice. It's 5km from the train station. Take a postal bus towards Evolène and get off at Les Fontaines.

SYHA Hostel (☎ 027 323 74 70; www.youthhostel.ch; Rue de l'Industrie 2; dm/d Sfr31.50/82; ⊗ 8-10am & 5-10pm closed Jan–mid-Mar, late Oct-Dec) This hostel behind the train station won't bowl you over with personality, but dorms are bright and clean, and facilities include a garden, games room and bike rental.

Les Simples (☎ 027 398 10 37; www.lessimples.ch; Chemin des Gardes de Nuit 36; r per person Sfr40) Scenically poised on the banks of the Rhône, this chalet-style B&B offers no-frills pine-panelled rooms. There's a fruit tree-shaded garden and a restaurant serving local organic fare. It's 10 minutes' stroll from the station.

Eating & Drinking

Rue du Grand-Pont is peppered with restaurants and bars, many with alfresco seating.

Grand Pont (☎ 027 322 20 96; Rue du Grand-Pont 6; mains Sfr25-42; ⊗ Mon-Sat) Art-slung walls, space-age lighting and bubbly staff make this café a top pick. The menu skips from Thai-style papaya salad to sushi. Sit on the terrace when the sun's out.

L'Enclos de Valère (☎ 027 323 32 30; Rue des Châteaux 18; mains Sfr30-45; ⊗ Tue-Sat) Up the cobbled lane to Tourbillon, this cottagey restaurant offers a taste of rural France with seasonal flavour bombs, from garlicky fish soup to venison with chestnut risotto. The garden bristles with vines and fruit trees (check out the kiwis!).

Cave de Tous-Vents (☎ 027 322 46 84; Rue des Châteaux 16; mains Sfr22-43; ⊗ 5pm-midnight) Flickering candles illuminate the brick vaults of this medieval cellar, where loved-up couples dine in cosy nooks. Just as gooey is the fondue, including varieties with saffron or chanterelles.

Contrejour (☎ 027 323 21 11; Ave de la Gare 6; ⊗ 6pm-1am Mon-Thu, 6pm-2am Fri & Sat) Brushed gold walls and choc-mint velvet stools define Sion's hippest hangout, which also has a courtyard for summertime tipples. DJs spin house at the weekend.

Getting There & Away

AIR

The **airport** (☎ 027 329 06 00; www.sionairport.ch; Rte de l'Aéroport) is 2km west of the train station; bus 1 goes there (Sfr3.60). There are year-round flights to Edinburgh, London and Corsica. During the ski season shuttle buses operate direct from the airport to resorts such as Crans-Montana, Verbier and Zermatt.

BUS

Postal buses leave from outside the train station. For information, call ☎ 027 327 34 34 or ask at the train station.

TRAIN

All trains on the express route between Lausanne (Sfr29, 50 to 70 minutes) and Brig (Sfr18.20, 35 to 45 minutes) stop in Sion.

CAR & MOTORCYCLE

The A9 freeway passes by Sion. There's free parking by the swimming pool, five minutes' walk west of the youth hostel.

Europcar (☎ 027 323 88 88; Place de la Gare 1) is at the train station. **Hertz** (☎ 027 322 37 42; Ave Ritz 33) is at Garage du Nord, and there's also **Avis** (☎ 027 322 20 77; Ave de Tourbillon 23-25).

AROUND SION

Lac Souterrain St-Léonard

Tiny St-Léonard hides Europe's biggest **underground lake** (☎ 027 203 22 66; www.lac-souterrain.com; adult/child/under 5yr Sfr10/5/free; ⊗ 9am-5pm mid-Mar-Oct, to 5.30pm Jun-Aug). To see the emerald waters shimmer, join a 30-minute guided tour (available in English). Trains run at least hourly from Sion to St-Léonard (Sfr3.40; four to 18 minutes).

Val d'Hérémence

Out of earshot of tourist footsteps, this valley remains mystifyingly unknown, despite harbouring one of the world's greatest hydraulic marvels, the 285m-high **Grande Dixence dam**. From Sion, follow the signs for this valley and the Val d'Hérens, which share the same road as far as Vex, where you branch right and follow a twisting road 30km to the dam.

You can't miss the quirky Cubist-style church in **Hérémence** that caused uproar when it was erected in the 1960s. The heavily wooded valley narrows as you gain altitude, finally opening up into a plain before the road becomes a country lane. It then makes a series

VALAIS

of dizzying switchbacks to the base of the dam, which will force you to look up in wonder.

Just before heading down that road you'll see a huddle of houses called **Pralong**, home to a couple of bijou hotel-restaurants that make convenient bases for walkers. Try woodsy **Val des Dix** (☎ 027 281 12 13; www.val-des-dix.ch, in French; r per person Sfr60), which has spotless, timber-lined rooms and a snug restaurant (mains Sfr15 to Sfr38) for gorging on *croûte au fromage* (Alpine cheese on toast). You can rent snowshoes or cross-country skis here in winter.

From the dam base, it's a 45-minute hike or a speedy **cable car** (adult/child return Sfr9/4.50; 9.30am-12.20pm & 1.15-6.20pm) ride to the top. Framed by snow-dusted crags, the milky green waters abruptly vanish like a giant infinity pool. Collecting the meltwater of 35 glaciers, weighing 15 million tonnes and supplying a fifth of Switzerland's energy, the dam impresses with both its scale and statistics. Its sheer magnitude prompts little gasps and comments along the lines of 'what if it burst?' Fear not, this is Switzerland.

Hikers can do a circuit of the lake or cross over into the next valley and make for Arolla, a six-hour trek for the fit.

Val d'Hérens & Val d'Arolla

Just like neighbouring Val d'Hérémence, these thickly wooded valleys hide many peculiarities and pastures mown by silky black Hérens cattle. The road wriggles up from Sion through Vex and then **Euseigne**. Before reaching the latter, the road ducks under the wondrous Gaudí-esque rock pinnacles **Pyramides d'Euseigne**. Nicknamed the *cheminées des fées* (fairy chimneys), these needle-thin, bouldertopped spires have been eroded by glaciers into their idiosyncratic forms over millennia.

Edging 8km further south is the valley's main town, **Evolène**, where you'll find most of the valley's accommodation and restaurants. Popular among walkers and cyclists, **Hôtel Arzinol** (☎ 021 283 16 65; www.hotel-arzinol.ch; s/d Sfr60/120) offers cheerful rooms in a timber chalet. On winter nights you can snuggle by the fire in the lounge.

Another 5km and you reach the deeply traditional hamlet of **Les Haudères**. Here the road forks. To the left, one leads 7km up to another pretty mountain settlement, **Ferpècle**, the end of the road and the start of some mountain hiking in the shadow of the pearly white tooth of Dent Blanche (4356m).

The other road veers right, rising steeply onto a wooded ridge before dropping down into another remote valley, the **Val d'Arolla**. After 11km you roll into a modest ski resort. To the east you can decipher Dent Blanche and to the southwest the glaciated Pigne d'Arolla (3796m), one of half a dozen 3600m-plus peaks that encircle Arolla. The village is a stop on the classic multi-day Haute Route from Chamonix to Zermatt. A seasonal dump of snow makes for crowd-free downhill and cross-country skiing in winter.

Set in gardens thick with larch trees, the stone lodge **Grand Hotel & Kurhaus** (☎ 027 283 70 00; www.kurhaus.arolla.com; r per person Sfr71-92; closed btwn seasons) stands in blissful isolation a couple of kilometres beyond Arolla and has been in business since 1896. Cheaper rooms come without bathroom.

Four to seven daily buses from Sion run up the valley to Evolène (Sfr13.80, 45 minutes) and some roll on to Arolla (change at Les Haudères, Sfr20.60, 1½ hours), which is 40km from Sion.

SIERRE

pop 15,400 / elevation 581m

One of Switzerland's sunniest towns, Sierre is where French-speaking residents say (rather tipsily) *bonjour* to their German-speaking neighbours. Indeed there's nothing like a glass of the local Pinot noir to loosen linguistic boundaries in the château-dotted vines rising above the town centre.

The **tourist office** (☎ 027 455 85 35; www.sierre -salgesch.ch; 8.30am-6pm Mon-Fri, 9am-5pm Sat, 9am-1pm Sun) is in the train station. Pick up the guide on local vineyards and walks called *Promenade des Châteaux*.

Sights & Activities

The big draw is 17th-century manor **Château de Villa** (☎ 027 455 18 96; www.chateaudevilla.ch; Rue Ste-Catherine 4), a 20-minute uphill trudge from the train station along Ave du Marché, leading through the older part of town and past postage stamp-sized vineyards. The turreted château houses the **Musée du Vin** (2-5pm Tue-Fri Apr-Nov), displaying presses and wine-related curios. It was closed for renovation at the time of research, but should reopen in late 2009.

Wine lovers can sample local tipples at the **Oenothèque** (wine store; 10.30am-1pm & 4.30-8.30pm), whose cellar bulges with 500 different bottles.

LOWER VALAIS •• Salgesch **157**

CLOSE COW ENCOUNTERS

It might sound like a load of bull, but cow fights known as the *Combats de Reines* (*Kuhkämpfe* in German) are serious stuff in Val d'Hérens, organised to decide which beast is most suited to lead the herd to summer pastures. These Moo-Hammad Ali wannabes charge, lock horns then try to force each other backwards. The winner, or herd's 'queen', can be worth Sfr20,000. Genetic selection and embryo freezing are used to get effective contenders to the field of combat. Once selected, they are fed oats concentrate (believed to act as a stimulant) and sometimes wine. Contests take place on selected Sundays from late March to May and from August to September. Combatants rarely get hurt so visitors shouldn't find the competition distressing. There is a grand final in Aproz (a 10-minute postal bus ride west of Sion) in May on Ascension Day, and the last meeting of the season is held at Martigny's Foire du Valais in early October.

If you'd rather enjoy a glass over Valaisan specialities, visit the restaurant at Château de Ville (see below).

A 10-minute walk, partly past vineyards, from the Château de Villa is the **Château Mercier**, set with a series of other villas, an orangery and former stables in a pretty park. It's used for receptions and events, but you can wander the grounds any time.

Sleeping & Eating

Bois de Finges (☎ 027 455 02 84; www.tiscover.ch /camping-bois-de-finges; sites per adult/child/tent/car & tent Sfr7.20/3.60/11.50/18.50; ♾ late Apr-Sep; P ♿) Set in protected pine woodland near the Rhône, this back-to-nature campsite is east of the centre. It's brilliant for families with a playground and heated outdoor pool.

our pick Hôtel Terminus (☎ 027 455 13 51; www .hotel-terminus.ch; Rue du Bourg 1; s/d Sfr120/190; P ✗) Recently transformed into one of the region's top addresses, this is a gourmet mecca with snazzy digs. Pared-down chic describes the contemporary rooms with plasma TVs and wi-fi. In the smart restaurant (tasting menus Sfr140 to Sfr210, open Tuesday to Saturday), Didier de Courten has been awarded two Michelin stars for cuisine that allows the freshness and flavour of each ingredient to shine through.

Le Thaï (☎ 027 456 84 56; mains Sfr12-16; ♾ 11am-8pm Mon-Sat) For a cheap Thai feed, pop into this hole-in-the-wall snack bar. The coconut-infused curries, tom yam and chilli beef are authentically spicy.

Château de Villa (☎ 027 455 18 96; www.chateaude villa.ch; Rue Ste-Catherine 4; Raclette Sfr31) All turreted towers and centuries-old beams, this château rolls out a Raclette feast with five types of cheese, washed down with full-bodied local wines.

Getting There & Away

Around two trains an hour stop at Sierre on the Geneva–Brig route. The town is the leaping-off point for Crans-Montana; a red SMC shuttle bus (*navette;* free) from outside the station runs to the nearby funicular station for Montana (Sfr11.80, 20 minutes).

SALGESCH
pop 1345 / elevation 540m

As dreamy as a Turner watercolour in the golden autumn light, the wine-growing hamlet of Salgesch produced the first-ever Swiss grand cru in 1988. Blessed with sunshine and chalky soil, Salgesch yields spicy Pinot Noirs, fruity dôles and mineral Fendants. Many cellars open their doors for tastings. If your passion for wine goes beyond drinking it, you can even help a local wine grower tend vines for the day from April to October (see the website www.salgesch.ch for details).

A scenic trail leads from Château de Villa in Sierre through vineyards to Salgesch, where the gabled **Weinmuseum** (☎ 027 456 45 25; adult/ student & senior Sfr5/4; ♾ 2-5pm Tue-Sun Apr-Nov) turns the spotlight on wine growing in the region.

If you've ever dreamed of sleeping in a wine barrel or press, make for the quirky **Hotel Arkanum** (☎ 027 451 21 00; www.hotelarkanum.ch; s/d Sfr115/180), where each of the beamed rooms has a different wine-related theme. The restaurant (mains Sfr18 to Sfr38) serves delicious Valaisan specialities and Salgesch wines. Trains run hourly to Salgesch from Sierre (Sfr3, three minutes).

CRANS-MONTANA
pop 7000 / elevation 1500m

Crans-Montana has been on the map ever since Dr Théodore Stéphani took a lungful of crisp Alpine air in 1896 and declared it

---

DAMIAN CINA

Since inheriting the family vineyard at 17, Damian has strived to achieve excellence in his wines. His efforts were rewarded in 2005 when **Caves Fernand Cina** (www.fernand-cina.ch) won the first-ever gold medal for Switzerland at the Vinalies Internationales in Paris.

Why is Salgesch ideal wine-growing territory? Salgesch has made a fantastic name for itself since producing the first grand cru in 1988. The conditions here are ideal. When I wake up the sun nearly always shines! High cliffs trap heat and the limey soil dries quickly even after heavy rain. It's like a little Saint-Émilion.

I judge a good wine by its... Finish. The aftertaste should linger on the tongue at least 30 seconds after swallowing. Wine is my life and passion. I'd never sell a bottle I wouldn't personally like to drink myself.

So what makes your wines special? When my brother and I took over the vineyard in 1987, there were four different wines – today there are 40. As well as classic Pinot Noirs, you'll find interesting ones like Maîtresse de Salquenen, an assemblage of 13 grape varieties. We looked for a niche with exclusive wines and found it. To ensure quality, we handpick the grapes from our 12 hectares of vines, working in harmony with nature, not against it. Our demand is greater than our supply and I'm never happier than when my cellar is empty.

---

splendid for his tuberculosis patients. Full of sparkling cheer in winter, the twin resort is now the much-loved haunt of luminaries like Roger Moore and nouveaux-riches Russians.

But there's more to Crans-Montana than Prada and posing. The skiing is intermediate paradise, with cruising on sunny slopes and 360-degree vistas reaching from the Matterhorn to Mont Blanc, which makes it a favourite for hosting downhill championships. In summer, golfers practise their swing on an 18-hole course designed by Seve Ballesteros.

Orientation & Information

The modern, sprawling resort is set along a string of lakes. The **tourist office** (☎ 027 485 04 04; www.crans-montana.ch; ☿ 8.30am-6.30pm Mon-Sat, 10am-12.30pm & 2-5pm Sun Dec-Apr & mid-Jun-Aug, 8.30am-noon & 2-6pm Mon-Fri, 8.30am-noon Sat rest of the year) has branches on Rue Centrale in Crans and Ave de la Gare in Montana.

Activities

Almost exclusively south-facing, the ski area comprises 160km of slopes and 50km of cross-country trails. On Friday nights, 4km of slopes are floodlit. Boarders should check out the quarter-pipes and rails at Aminona terrain park. Crans-Montana day ski passes cost Sfr63/54/38 per adult/youth/child. For about 20% more you can include the **Plaine-Morte Glacier** (3000m). There's plenty to amuse non-skiers and families, such as snowshoeing, winter walking and a 6km toboggan run.

Crans-Montana golf courses include nine and 18 holes. Prices range from Sfr40 to Sfr80. Contact the **golf club** (☎ 027 485 97 97; www.golfcrans .ch; ☿ May-Oct). The resort hosts the Omega European Masters in September.

Adrenatur (☎ 027 480 10 10; www.adrenatur.ch) packs in adventure, offering rafting (Sfr80), canyoning (Sfr160) and zip-line thrills in the Fun Forest (Sfr30).

Worthwhile **walks** include the vertigo-inducing 3½-hour hike to Bisse du Ro and an eight-hour trudge from Plaine-Morte Glacier down to Chermignon-d'en-Bas. A basic walking map is available for Sfr5 at the tourist office.

The region boasts 135km of first-rate **mountain biking** terrain. Downhill freaks are catered for with marked trails and a bike park at Crans Cry d'Er cable car base station, where 16 obstacles are graded according to difficulty. **Crans Mountain** (☎ 027 480 30 30; www.crans-mountain.ch; Rue Centrale 15; ☿ 9am-noon & 2-6pm Mon-Sat, closed Thu) rents top-of-the-range wheels.

Sleeping & Eating

You can book online through the resort website (www.crans-montana.ch). The tourist office hands out a list of apartments and chalets.

Auberge du Petit Paradis (☎ 027 481 21 48; www .petit-paradis.com; s/d Sfr80/150; P) Nestled below Crans in the hamlet of Bluche, this rustic family-run retreat offers brilliant value. The cosy pine-panelled rooms have balconies with mountain views.

La Diligence (☎ 027 485 99 85; www.ladiligence.ch; Rte de la Combaz; s/d 125/175; **P**) Backed by forest, this serene and inviting chalet, 1km east of Montana, has well-kept rooms with either balconies or terraces.

Hostellerie du Pas de l'Ours (☎ 027 485 93 33; www .pasdelours.ch; Rue du Pas de l'Ours; ste Sfr600-1650; **P ☎**) This character-filled timber-and-stone mountain hideaway is fairy-tale stuff. A roaring fire and web-like vaulting in the lobby bar set the tone. The rest meets initial expectations: nine suites with whirlpools and fireplaces, an outdoor pool framed by manicured lawns, a spa and a restaurant (tasting menus Sfr65 to Sfr175) where Michelin-starred chef Franck Reynaud creates Provençal taste sensations. All at a price, of course.

Le Plaza (☎ 027 481 20 83; Rue Centrale; tapas Sfr6-20, mains Sfr20-50; ☻ 7.30am-1am Mon-Fri, 10am-1am Sat & Sun) As quirky as it gets in Crans, this lounge reveals a razor-sharp eye for detail – note the bold cow paintings and chairs draped with Swiss army blankets. Electro-jazz plays at the bar, where you can sip wines and graze on garlicky chorizo and inventive salads.

Le Pavillon (☎ 027 481 24 69; Rte de Rawyl; mains Sfr29-48; ☻ daily high season, Wed-Mon low season) With a sunny terrace overlooking Lac Grenon, this old-world restaurant attracts in-the-know locals. Eat whatever is fresh that day, be it salmon or Zürich-style veal with rösti. It's halfway between Crans and Montana (bus stop Pavillon).

Getting There & Away

See p157 for information on getting to Crans-Montana. Free shuttles move around the resort area.

VAL D'ANNIVIERS

Brushed with pine and larch, scattered with dark timber chalets and postcard villages and set against glistening 4000m peaks, this strikingly beautiful, little-explored valley beckons skiers eager to slalom away from the crowds for fresh powder and hikers seeking big nature.

The road south from Sierre corkscrews precipitously past postage-stamp orchards and vineyards, arriving after 13km in the medieval village of **Vissoie**, a valley crossroads for five ski stations (www.sierre-anniviers.ch). You can get a ski pass for the whole area (adult/child/student Sfr47/28/40), which totals 220km of ski runs. About 11km along a narrow road winding back north towards Sierre is **Vercorin**

(☎ 027 455 58 55; www.vercorin.ch), geared up for families with gentle skiing on 35km of pistes and a handful of places to stay and eat. It's also accessible direct from Sierre via Chippis. On a one-hour walk south to the wildlife-rich **Val de Réchy**, it's often possible to spot sizeable groups of deer in September.

Closer and more enticing for skiers are the combined villages of **St Luc** (☎ 027 475 14 12; www.saint-luc.ch) and **Chandolin** (☎ 027 475 18 38; www.chandolin.ch), with 75km of broad, sunny runs, a half-pipe for boarders and fairy-tale panoramas. St Luc is 4km east of Vissoie, up a series of switchbacks, and Chandolin another 4km north. The latter is the more attractive of the two, a huddle of timber houses hanging on for dear life to steep slopes at around 2000m. While here, visit **Espace Ella Maillart** (admission free; ☻ 10am-6pm Wed-Sun), dedicated to the remarkable Swiss adventurer who lived in Chandolin when she wasn't exploring remote Afghanistan and Tibet, or winning ski races and regattas. Solar system models punctuate the Chemin des Planètes (Planets Trail), an uphill amble from Tignousa (above St Luc) to the **Weisshorn Hotel** (☎ 027 475 11 06; www.weisshorn.ch; s/d with half-board Sfr140/275; ☻ closed btwn seasons). Sitting at 2337m, the grand 19th-century hotel is accessible on foot or by mountain bike only (or on skis in winter, when luggage is transported for you from St Luc).

Back down in Vissoies you could continue to bucolic **Zinal** (☎ 027 475 13 70; www.zinal.ch), via the hamlet of Ayer, for 70km of fine skiing in the shadow of 4000m giants like Weisshorn, Zinal Rothorn and tooth-like Dent Blanche.

Prettier still is storybook **Grimentz** (☎ 027 476 20 01; www.bendolla.ch), where Valaisan granaries built on stilts (originally to keep thieving mice out!) and burnt-timber, geranium-bedecked chalets huddle over narrow lanes. The village makes a charming base for walking or skiing. **Hotel de Moiry** (☎ 027 475 11 44; www.hoteldemoiry.ch; s/d with half-board Sfr136/232) has comfy digs with all the trappings of a warm mountain chalet. Eat heartily in the restaurant downstairs. Central **Le Mélèze** (☎ 027 475 12 87; www.lemeleze.ch; r per person Sfr51) shelters humble pine-panelled rooms and a barn-style restaurant.

The 8km road south along La Gougra stream to cobalt **Lac de Moiry** (2249m) is only open in summer. Another 3km brings you to a smaller dam, where the road peters out. Before you, the Glacier de Moiry sticks out its dirty white tongue, a 1½-hour hike away.

VALAIS

Up to eight postal buses a day run from Sierre to Vissoie for connections to Chandolin (Sfr14.80) via St Luc, Zinal (Sfr15.80) and Grimentz (Sfr13.80). All these trips take about one hour from Sierre. In summer three buses run the 20 minutes from Grimentz to Lac de Moiry (Sfr10.20).

UPPER VALAIS

In a xylophone-to-gong transition, the soothing loveliness of vineyards in the west gives way to austere beauty in the east of Valais. Bijou villages of woodsy chalets stand in collective awe of the drum-roll setting of vertiginous ravines, spiky 4000m pinnacles and monstrous glaciers. The effervescent thermal waters of Leukerbad, the dazzling 23km Aletsch Glacier and the soaring pyramid of Matterhorn are natural icons that invite spontaneous applause.

LEUK

pop 3460 / elevation 750m

Most people overlook Leuk in their hurry to reach Leukerbad and, oops, miss one of Valais' best-kept secrets. Celts, Romans and Burgundians wore the cobbles smooth in this clifftop village. Stuck in a medieval time warp, the centre is small enough to explore on foot and drink in all the details. Narrow lanes twist past gurgling fountains, timber granaries and vine-clad manors. Architect Mario Botta has put his stamp on Romanesque **Schloss Leuk**, which has, over the centuries, been a bishop's residence, torture chamber and the scene of witch trials. The main square, Hauptplatz, is home to a butcher, baker and a smattering of cafés.

Escapist fantasy **Hotel Schloss** (☎ 027 473 12 13; www.schlosshotel-leuk.ch; Leukerstrasse 14; s/d Sfr60/100) is humbler and more affordable than its stately exterior suggests, with simple and spotless wood-panelled rooms.

Leuk is on the main rail route from Lausanne to Brig, with half-hourly trains to Sierre (Sfr4, seven minutes) and Brig (Sfr10.80, 20 minutes).

LEUKERBAD

pop 1565 / elevation 1411m

The road that zigzags up from Leuk past breathtakingly sheer chasms and wooded crags is a spectacular build-up to Leukerbad. Gazing up to an amphitheatre of towering rock turrets and canyon-like spires, Europe's largest thermal spa resort is pure drama. Beauty-conscious Romans once took Leukerbad's steamy thermal waters, where today visitors soak after clambering up the Gemmi Pass, braving Switzerland's longest *via ferrata* or carving the powder on Torrenthorn.

Orientation & Information

Leukerbad is 14km north of Leuk. The **tourist office** (☎ 027 472 71 71; www.leukerbad.ch; 9am-noon & 1.15-6pm Mon-Fri, 9am-6pm Sat, 9am-noon Sun Jul-Nov & Dec-Apr, 9am-noon & 1.15-5.30pm Mon-Sat rest of year) in the centre can advise on therapies. In the same complex you'll find the town hall, post office, parking garage and bus station. Leukerbad is car-free by night.

Sights & Activities

The biggest of Leukerbad's four public baths is **Burgerbad** (☎ 027 472 20 20; www.burgerbad.ch; Rathausstrasse; 3hr bath adult/student/child/under 8yr Sfr20/16/12/free; 8am-8pm), with indoor and outdoor tubs, whirlpools, massage jets, steam grottoes and waterslides.

Its posher rival is **Lindner Alpentherme** (☎ 027 472 10 10; www.alpentherme.ch; Dorfplatz; 3hr baths adult/child/under 6yr Sfr20/14/free, Roman-Irish bath with/without massage Sfr74/54, sauna village Sfr19; baths 8am-8pm, to 10pm Fri, Roman-Irish bath & sauna village 10am-8pm), where those who dare to bare can try the Roman–Irish bath – two hours of blissful bathing, mud scrubs and soapy rubs. Otherwise, you can book treatments like underwater massages and wildflower wraps, or drift in 40°C thermal waters. The latest attraction is a Valaisan sauna village complete with mill, ice-cold stream and herbal steam rooms.

A cable car ascends the sheer mountain ridge to **Gemmi Pass** (2350m), a fantastic area for hiking. The ride is Sfr19/28 one-way/return, or a steep two-hour climb. For more of a challenge, traverse the pass on an eight-hour trek to **Kandersteg** (p195). A gentler option is the so-called thermal canyon walk through a gorge that emerges at a cascading waterfall. Surefooted thrill-seekers can tackle Switzerland's longest *via ferrata* to **Dauberhorn** (2941m), a dizzying eight-hour scramble up the cliffs. The mesmerising views of the Valaisan and Bernese Alps make the sweating and swearing worthwhile. Enquire about equipment rental and guides at the tourist office.

The **skiing** at Torrenthorn (2998m) is mostly easy and intermediate aside from one demanding run descending 1400m. One-day ski passes cost Sfr49/29/39 per adult/child /student and senior.

Sleeping & Eating

Weisses Rössli (☎ 027 470 33 77; www.rossli.net; Tuftstrasse 4; s/d Sfr60/120) Just off Dorfplatz, this belle-époque hotel is run with *passione* by Italian-speaking Paolo and his son Jean-Pierre. The old-style rooms with washbasins and teeny balconies are basic but comfy.

Hôtel de la Croix Fédérale (☎ 027 472 79 79; www .croix-federale.ch; Kirchstrasse 43; s/d Sfr95/180) The welcome is heartfelt at this geranium-strewn chalet. The all-pine, snug-as-a-bug rooms have downy duvets and flatscreen TVs. Downstairs Walliser Kanne (mains Sfr20 to Sfr35) has delicious wood-fired pizzas and occasionally upbeat yodelling sessions.

Lindner Hotel Leukerbad (☎ 027 472 10 00; www .lindnerhotels.ch; Dorfplatz; s/d Sfr229/459; P ⊒ ⊠) Smack in the centre, this is quite a complex. The spacious rooms are starting to show their age, but are due for a makeover soon. Anyway, you won't be awarding design points with direct access to the thermal baths and saunas. Grab your bathrobe and go.

Café Leukerbad (Rathausstrasse; light meals Sfr5-15.50; ⊗ 11am-9pm) No airs, no graces, just locals contentedly slurping goulash soup and scoffing cakes at what you'll find at this gem of a tea house. Expect old-fashioned service with a smile.

Getting There & Away

From Leuk an hourly postal bus goes to Leukerbad; last departure is 7.20pm (Sfr10.80, 30 to 35 minutes).

LÖTSCHENTAL

A remote wilderness of gin-clear brooks, larch forests and glaciers, the Lötschental is an engaging and little-visited foretaste of the valleys that make up the Aletsch region, mostly accessible east of Brig (see p168). Most people who venture here make it only as far as Goppenstein, 9km north of the N9 road, to load their cars onto the half-hourly Lötschbergtunnel train that whisks them to Kandersteg in the Bernese Oberland (Sfr20 to Sfr25 per car, 15 minutes).

Beyond Goppenstein, the road swings northeast along an isolated valley through a string of quiet hamlets to **Fafleralp** (1787m), little more than a huddle of chalets. **Hotel Fafleralp** (☎ 027 939 14 51; www.fafleralp.ch, in German; r per person Sfr75-90) is a delightful rustic getaway with rooms made of local wood and not a telephone or TV in sight. Snow often cuts off the road in winter, but if you reserve they will pick up your luggage from Blatten and you will walk the 4km in snowshoes.

The icy finger of the **Langgletscher** glacier stretches down towards the village and is an easy 1½-hour hike from the main car park. Other walks into the mountains, creased by glacial waterfalls and largely bereft of any vegetation but a touch of Alpine grass, are also possible; see www.loetschental.ch (in German) for the low-down.

Cross-country skiing is popular and there's even a little downhill action on the **Lauchneralp** at **Wiler**, 3km southwest of Blatten.

Up to 12 postal buses run from Goppenstein to Blatten, and on to Fafleralp (32 minutes) from June to October.

VISP

pop 6670 / elevation 650m

All most visitors see of Visp is the station as they board a train to Zermatt or Saas Fee, yet the Old Town is attractive with its cobbled streets and shuttered windows. Wine lovers can work up a thirst on a 2½-hour uphill hike to **Visperterminen**, famously home to Europe's highest vineyard at 1150m. An hourly bus (Sfr6.20) does the same trip in 20 minutes.

Should you get stuck here, there is a cluster of hotels near the train station. Trains run every hour or so to Zermatt (Sfr33, 65 minutes). An hourly postal bus runs to Saas Fee (Sfr15.80, 45 minutes).

BRIGERBAD

Make a summertime splash at Brigerbad's open-air **thermal baths** (☎ 027 946 46 88; www .brigerbad.ch; adult/child Sfr15/7; ⊗ 9.30am-6pm early May-Sep), ranging from rapid rivers to curative grotto-style pools. The baths are halfway between Visp and Brig but more easily accessible from the former by postal buses (Sfr3, 10 minutes) that leave more or less hourly.

ZERMATT

pop 5785 / elevation 1605m

You can almost sense the anticipation on the train from Täsch: couples gaze wistfully out of the window, kids fidget and stuff in Toblerone,

VALAIS

folk rummage for their cameras. And then, as they arrive in Zermatt, all give little whoops of joy at the pop-up book effect of one-of-a-kind **Matterhorn** (4478m). Trigonometry at its finest, topographic perfection, a bloody beautiful mountain – call it what you will, Matterhorn is hypnotic. Like a shark's fin it rises above the town, like an egotistical celebrity it squeezes into every snapshot, like a diva it has moods swinging from pretty and pink to dark and mysterious.

Since the mid-19th century, Zermatt has starred among Switzerland's glitziest resorts. Today it attracts intrepid mountaineers and hikers, skiers who cruise at snail's pace spellbound by the scenery, and style-conscious darlings flashing designer togs in the lounge bars. But all are smitten with Matterhorn, an unfathomable monolith you can't quite stop looking at.

Information

Go online for free or bring your laptop for wi-fi at **Papperla Pub** (p165; ☎ 027 967 40 40; www .papperlapub.ch). The **tourist office** (☎ 027 966 81 00; www.zermatt.ch; Bahnhofplatz 5; ☒ 8.30am-6pm Mon-Sat, 8.30am-noon & 1.30-6pm Sun mid-Jun-Sep, 8.30am-noon & 1.30-6pm Mon-Sat, 9.30am-noon & 4-6pm Sun rest of year) has stacks of brochures on the area.

Sights

Views from the cable cars and gondolas are uniformly breathtaking, especially from the cogwheel train to 3090m **Gornergrat** (one-way Sfr38), which takes 35 to 45 minutes

with two to three departures per hour. Sit on the right-hand side to gawp at Matterhorn. Alternatively, you can hike from Zermatt to Gornergrat in around five hours.

Hinterdorf is the oldest corner of the village, crammed with archetypal Valaisan chalets and timber storage barns with stone discs and stilts to keep out the rats. It's a world away from the flashy boutiques on Bahnhofstrasse.

The **cemetery** is a sobering experience for any would-be mountaineer, as numerous monuments tell of deaths on Monte Rosa, Breithorn and Matterhorn.

The crystalline, state-of-the-art **Matterhorn Museum** (☎ 027 967 41 00; www.matterhornmuseum.ch; Kirchplatz; adult/student/child/under 10yr Sfr10/8/5/free; ☒ 11am-6pm Dec-Sep, 2-6pm Oct, closed Nov) centres on an authentically recreated Valaisan village. It provides a fascinating insight into mountaineering, the dawn of tourism and the lives Matterhorn has claimed. Must-sees include Roosevelt's letters, Raymond Lambert's reindeer-skin boots (made to measure after his toes were amputated) and the infamous rope that broke in 1865 and turned the first ascent of Matterhorn into a tragedy.

Activities

Zermatt is cruising heaven, with mostly long, scenic red runs, plus a smattering of blues for ski virgins and knuckle-whitening blacks for experts. The three main skiing areas are **Rothorn**, **Stockhorn** and **Klein Matterhorn**. In all, there are 300km of ski runs and free buses between areas. February to April is peak time. Snow can be sketchy in early summer but lifts are significantly quieter. Snowboarders make for Klein Matterhorn's freestyle park and half-pipe, while mogul fans enjoy a bumpy glide on Stockhorn.

Klein Matterhorn is topped by Europe's highest cable-car station (3820m), providing access to the highest skiing on the continent, Switzerland's most extensive summer skiing (25km of runs) and deep powder at the Italian resort of Cervinia. Broad and exhilarating, the No 7 run down from the border is a must-ski. Don't forget your passport. If the weather is fine, take the lift up to the summit of Klein Matterhorn (3883m) for top-of-the-beanstalk views over the Swiss Alps (from Mont Blanc to Aletschhorn) and deep into Italy.

A day pass for Zermatt (excluding Cervinia) costs Sfr71/36/65 per adult/child/

FEBRUARY'S FREAKY MONSTERS

Come Fasnacht time, hairy Tschäggättä monsters flit about the Lötschental. Wearing sheep or goat pelts and fat cowbells, these fellows don scary wooden masks and gloves dipped in soot. Traditionally they would stalk villagers from noon to 6pm, rubbing the soot into anyone they could lay their hands on. Nowadays they tend to prowl in the evening and are more considerate towards their soot-loathing victims. Opinion is divided on how the tradition was born; some say it was to ward off the vestiges of winter and evil spirits, while others believe it has its origins in a band of masked thieves that operated in the valley in the 11th century.

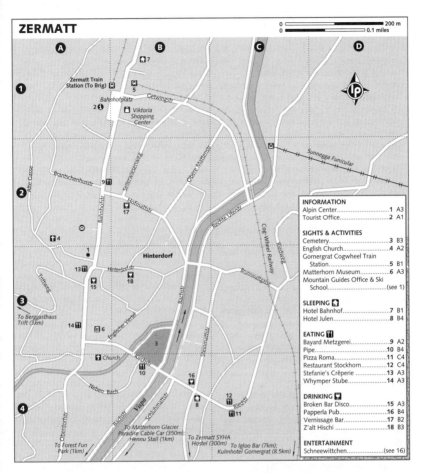

ZERMATT

senior and student and Sfr80/40/74 including Cervinia. From September to late November, budget skiers can save on weekend packages that involve testing the latest skis on a limited number of runs around Klein Matterhorn Glacier. Prices including breakfast, ski passes and test-ski rental vary from Sfr315 per person in a one-star hotel to Sfr439 in a four-star.

Zermatt lures hikers in summer with 400km of trails through some of the most incredible scenery in the Alps. For Matterhorn close-ups, the ultimate day trek is **Höhenweg Höhbalmen** (p63). The tourist office website provides details on other great walks such as the 2¼ hour Matterhorn glacier trail and the four-hour Hörnli trail.

The **Alpin Center** (☎ 027 966 24 60; www.alpincenter -zermatt.ch; Bahnhofstrasse 58; ☼ 8.30am-noon & 3-7pm mid-Nov-Apr & Jul-Sep) houses the ski school and mountain guides office. They arrange guided climbs to major 4000ers, including Breithorn (Sfr165), Riffelhorn (Sfr257) and, for experts willing to acclimatise for a week, Matterhorn (Sfr998). Their program also covers multi-day hikes, glacier hikes to Gorner (Sfr120), snowshoeing (Sfr140) and ice climbing (Sfr175).

For a Tarzan-style adventure, head for the **Forest Fun Park** (☎ 027 968 10 10; adult/child/under 7yr Sfr31/21/15; 9am-6.30pm Apr-Nov), a gigantic above-the-treetops playground of zip-lines, platforms, river traverses and bridges graded according to difficulty.

MAN OR MATTERHORN

On 13 July 1865 Edward Whymper led the first successful ascent of Matterhorn via Hörnli ridge, but the descent was marred by tragedy when four team members crashed to their deaths in a 1200m fall down the North Wall. The catastrophe haunted Whymper, who lamented: 'Every night, do you understand, I see my comrades of the Matterhorn slipping on their backs, their arms outstretched, one after the other, in perfect order at equal distances.'

Ironically, the tragedy put Zermatt on the map, and soon other plucky souls came to climb Matterhorn and the surrounding giants, including a 20-year-old Winston Churchill, who scaled Monte Rosa (4634m) in 1894. In 1881 Franklin D Roosevelt climbed Matterhorn and wrote to his sister that 'the mountain is so steep that snow will not remain on the crumbling, jagged rocks', but that after the ascent he 'felt as fresh as ever after a cup of tea and a warm bath'.

As you wander Hinterdorfstrasse, note the fountain commemorating Ulrich Inderbinen (1900–2004), who climbed Matterhorn a staggering 370 times, the last time age 90. Nicknamed the King of the Alps, the Zermatt-born mountaineer was the oldest active mountain guide in the world when he retired at the ripe old age of 95.

Festivals & Events

Fun-loving freestylers do the **Bump Bash** (www.bumpbash.com), a mogul race around Triftji Glacier in April. In July, the super fit compete in the (literally) breathtaking **Zermatt Marathon** (www.zermatt-marathon.ch) from St Niklaus to Riffelberg. The **Folkloreumzug** (Folklore Parade) on 10 August brings Alpine music, merrymaking and feasting to Zermatt. In September, the **Zermatt Festival** welcomes world-famous chamber orchestras.

Sleeping

Zermatt has recently upped the ante in the slumber stakes with a flurry of new boutique hotels. Book ahead in winter, and bear in mind that nearly everywhere closes from May to mid-June and from October to mid-November.

Zermatt SYHA Hostel (☎ 027 967 23 20; Staldenweg 5; dm/d with half-board Sfr47.50/100; ☺ 7-10am & 4-10.30pm; ☐) Question: how many hostels have Matterhorn peeking through the window in the morning? Answer: one. And if that doesn't convince you, the modern dorms, sunny terrace and first-rate facilities should.

Hotel Bahnhof (☎ 027 967 24 06; www.hotelbahnhof .com; Bahnhofstrasse; dm/s/d Sfr43/78/98; ☺ 8am-noon & 4-8pm) Opposite the station, these spruce budget digs have proper beds that are a godsend after scaling or schussing down mountains all day. There's a lounge, a snazzy open-plan kitchen and free wi-fi.

ourpick Berggasthaus Trift (☎ 079 408 70 20; dm/d with half-board Sfr63/150 ☺ Jul-Sep) It's a long trudge up to this 2337m-high mountain hut but the hike is outstanding. At the foot of Triftgletscher,

this Alpine haven is run by Hugo (a whiz on the alphorn) and Fabienne. The rooms are cosy and the views – ah the views! – to the frosted 4000ers mesmeric. Kick back on the terrace for treats like home-cured beef and oven-warm apple tart. Have your camera handy as the sun sets over Monte Rosa.

Kulmhotel Gornergrat (☎ 027 966 64 00; Gornergrat; s/d180/310) Above the clouds at 3000m, Switzerland's highest hotel appeals to those who like the atmosphere and views of an Alpine hut but shiver at the thought of thin mattresses and icy water. The sleek rooms with downy duvets afford views to Monte Rosa or Matterhorn. When the crowds leave at dusk, savour the solitude and panoramas of glowing 4000m peaks.

Hotel Julen (☎ 027 966 76 00; www.julen.com; Riedstrasse 2; s/d with half-board Sfr265/530; ☒) Part of the Swiss romantic hotel clan, Julen is woodcutter's cottage meets Parisian boudoir – think ornately carved ceilings, red velvet and thick sheepskins. The pine-filled rooms are little love nests with Christmassy red-and-green fabrics and mountain views. There's also a spa and restaurant.

Eating

Stefanie's Crêperie (☎ 079 772 99 66; Bahnhofstrasse 60; snacks Sfr5-16; ☺ 11am-midnight) Such perfectly thin, light crêpes are worth the wait. Through the hatch you'll spy Stefanie the crêpe fairy, working her magic with a frying pan. Dig into varieties with chocolate or homemade preserves.

Bayard Metzgerei (☎ 027 967 22 66; Bahnhofstrasse 9; sausages around Sfr6; ☺ noon-6.30pm Jul-Sep, 4-6.30pm Dec-Mar) Follow your nose to this butcher's grill for to-go bratwurst, chicken and other carnivorous bites.

Pizza Roma (☎ 027 967 32 29; Riedstrasse 20; mains Sfr16-26; ☯ dinner) For crisp wood-oven pizza, hearty pasta dishes and the silkiest tiramisu this side of Bellinzona, head to this low-slung haunt.

Pipe (☎ 079 758 53 24; Kirchstrasse 38; mains Sfr27-39; ☯ dinner) This jammin' Afro-Asian den promises to 'spice up your life'. Your tastebuds will do somersaults over hot and fruity springbok curry or apricot-glazed Karoo lamb paired with a liquoricey Shiraz. Surfboards on the ceiling, tribal masks on the wall and elbow-to-elbow tables create an original, intimate vibe.

Whymper Stube (☎ 027 967 22 96; Bahnhofstrasse 80; mains Sfr23-42) Named after intrepid explorer Edward Whymper, who made the first ascent of Matterhorn in 1865, this Alpine classic serves the tastiest fondue in Zermatt, including variations with pears and gorgonzola. The mantra: gorge today, climb tomorrow.

Restaurant Stockhorn (☎ 027 967 17 47; Riedstrasse 11; mains Sfr35-40; ☯ dinner) A snug chalet to make you feel all warm and fuzzy, Stockhorn does just-right fondues, Raclettes and wood-fired meat specialities. The fall-off-the-bone lamb is divine.

Drinking

Still fizzing with energy after schussing down the slopes? Zermatt pulses in party-mad après-ski huts and suave lounge bars. Most close (and some melt) in low season.

Papperla Pub (☎ 027 967 40 40; Steinmattstrasse 34; ☯ 11am-11.30pm) Rammed with sloshed skiers in winter, this pub blends pulsating music with lethal Jägermeister bombs and good vibes. Squeeze in, slam shots, then shuffle downstairs to Schneewittchen club (open to 4am) for more of the same.

Hennu Stall (☎ 027 966 35 10; Klein Matterhorn; ☯ 2-7pm) Last one down to this snow-bound 'chicken run' is a rotten egg. Hennu is the wildest après-ski shack on Klein Matterhorn. Order a caramel vodka and take your ski boots grooving to live music on the terrace. A metre-long 'ski' of shots will make you cluck all the way down to Zermatt.

Igloo Bar (Gornergrat; www.iglu-dorf.ch; ☯ 10pm-4pm) Subzero sippers make for this igloo bar to guzzle glühwein amid the ice sculptures, sunbathe and stare wide-mouthed at Matterhorn. It's on the run from Gornergrat to Riffelberg.

Z'alt Hischi (☎ 027 967 42 62; Hinterdorfstrasse 44; ☯ 9pm-2am) Finding this watering hole, tucked away in Zermatt's most charming street, is a challenge best left to the sober. It's a warm, woody affair, serving generous measures and local gossip.

Broken Bar Disco (☎ 027 967 19 31; Bahnhofstrasse 41; ☯ 10pm-4am) In Hotel Post's vaulted cellar, you can jive on a wine barrel to '80s cheese and Europop till 4am.

Vernissage Bar (☎ 027 967 66 36; Hofmattstrasse 4; ☯ 5pm-2am) The ultimate après-ski antithesis, Vernissage exudes grown-up sophistication. Local artist Heinz Julen has created a theatrical space with flowing velvet drapes, film-reel chandeliers and candlelit booths. Catch an exhibition, watch a Bond movie in the decadent cinema, then practice your 007 martini pose in the lounge bar.

Getting There & Away

CAR

Zermatt is car-free. Dinky electric vehicles are used to transport goods and serve as taxis around town. Drivers have to leave their vehicles in one of the garages or the open-air car park in Täsch (Sfr13.50 per day) and take the train (Sfr7.60, 12 minutes) into Zermatt.

TRAIN

Trains depart roughly every 20 minutes from Brig (Sfr35, 1½ hours), stopping at Visp en route. Zermatt is also the starting point of the Glacier Express to Graubünden, one of the most spectacular train rides in the world.

SAAS FEE

pop 1665 / elevation 1800m

Hemmed in by a menacing grey amphitheatre of 13 implacable peaks over 4000m and backed by the threatening tongues of nine glaciers, little Saas Fee looks positively feeble in the revealing light of summer. Until 1951, only a mule trail led to this isolated outpost and locals scraped a living from farming. Although the village centre has kept its rustic feel, dotted with timber chalets and barns on stilts, the rest is largely a modern creation. The resort is less charming than neighbouring Zermatt, but equally full of twinkling cheer in the ski season.

Orientation & Information

Saas Fee is a sprawling resort. The village centre and ski lifts are southwest of the bus station.

The **tourist office** (☎ 027 958 18 58; www.saas -fee.ch; ✆ 8.30am-noon & 2-6.30pm Mon-Sat, 10am-noon & 3-5pm Sun) is opposite the post office and bus station. Opening hours are slightly shorter in shoulder seasons. The local Guest Card offers various discounts.

Sights & Activities

Saas Fee's slopes are snow-sure, with most **skiing** taking place above 2500m and the glacier act- ing like a deep freeze. The 140km of groomed, scenic pistes are more suited to beginners and intermediates, though experts willing to take a guide to go off-piste will find bottomless powder. Ski-mountaineering is possible along the famous Haute Route to Chamonix. The resort is a snowboarding mecca and regularly hosts world championships. Boarders gravitate towards the kickers, half-pipe and chill-out zone at Mittelallalin freestyle park. A lift pass costs Sfr65/36 per adult/child for one day and Sfr370/205 for one week.

Non-skiers can stomp along 20km of marked **winter footpaths** or hurtle down Hannig on a toboggan. For a twilight downhill dash through glittering woodlands, check out night sledding every Tuesday and Thursday from 6pm to 9pm. Other winter activities include ice climbing, husky sledding and air boarding.

The tourist office has a map of 350km of summer **hiking** trails in the Saas Valley. There are gentle strolls along the fast-flowing Vispa and through the forest to Saas-Almagell. Worthwhile high-level routes include a five- hour hike to Gspon, affording jaw-dropping mountain vistas, and the 3½-hour walk from Mattmark to Macugnaga in Italy. Kids in tow? Take them to Spielboden to feed and pet the tame marmots.

An underground funicular operates year- round to **Mittelallalin** (3500m), where you'll find the world's highest revolving restaurant, offering 360-degree views of the 4000m gla- cial giants. It gives access to Feegletscher, a centre for summer skiing (July and August) with 20km of runs above 2700m. Wrap up warm at the subzero **Eispavillion** (adult/child Sfr5/3), 10m below the ice surface. From Saas Fee to Mittelallalin by cable car then funicular costs Sfr69 return (children are half-price).

Sleeping

Ask the tourist office for a brochure list- ing good-value chalets and apartments.

Most hotels and restaurants close in May and November.

Unique Hotel Dom (☎ 027 958 77 00; www.uniquedom .com; dm Sfr45-60; ✆ reception 8am-9pm winter, 9am-6pm summer) Young, hip and totally chilled, this is the go-to hostel if you want to snowboard and party till you crash. It's full of dudes in baggy Gore-Tex who dig the Smartie-bright dorms with PlayStations and wi-fi, and the gigs downstairs in Popcorn. The restaurant is run by a tribe of 'am I bovvered?' teens who, frankly, would rather pound powder than pander to your whims.

Hotel Elite (☎ 027 958 60 60; www.elite-saas-fee.ch; s/d Sfr140/266) Cheery and family-run, this homely chalet has pine-panelled rooms with snowy white duvets, mountain-facing balconies and free wi-fi. There's a kids' play area.

Hotel Waldesruh (☎ 027 958 64 64; www.hotel waldesruh.ch, in German; s/d Sfr164/308) Next to the for- est and an ecstatic I'll-be-first-in-the-queue hop from the ski lifts, this chalet is a find. The owners are affable and the old-style rooms comfy, with balconies overlooking the slopes. There's a sauna, whirlpool and regular alphorn and glockenspiel playing performances.

Romantik Hotel Beau-Site (☎ 027 958 15 60; www .beausite.org; s/d Sfr230/405; 🐾) Beau-Site receives glowing recommendations for its polished service and classically elegant rooms with antique furnishings. On wintry days, you'll find it hard to drag yourself away from the fireplace in the bar and the spa's steam baths, grotto-like pool and saunas.

Eating

Zur Mühle (☎ 027 957 26 76; mains Sfr15-30) Sheepskins, cow-print curtains and cop- per pans create a snug feel at this riverside restaurant. Rösti is the mainstay and comes in various guises, such as with ham, onions and cheese.

La Ferme (☎ 027 958 15 69; mains Sfr19-49; ✆ 9.30am-midnight) Dirndl-clad maidens bring traditional Valaisan specialities to the table at this barn-style restaurant, decked out with hops, cowbells and farming implements. Try tender lamb loin cooked in Alpine hay or fresh river trout.

Holzwurm (☎ 027 957 24 84; mains Sfr20-40; ✆ 3.30pm-1.30am winter, 8pm-1.30am summer) The laid-back 'woodworm' serves up live music, a laid-back atmosphere and super *fondue chinoise* and Raclette. It's near the church in the village centre.

VALAIS

ourpick **Fletschhorn** (☎ 027 957 21 31; www.fletsch
horn.ch; tasting menu Sfr175-205; ☒ 10am-midnight)
Nestled in a forest glade with dramatic mountain views, this Michelin-starred restaurant
is one of Switzerland's top addresses. Chef
Markus Neff interprets French cuisine with
finesse, with signatures such as crispy, rose-
mary-infused suckling pig and roast pigeon
with black truffles. The sommelier will help
you choose a bottle of wine from the 30,000
on the list. Call ahead and staff will pick
you up.

Drinking
About a dozen lively après-ski bars vie for
attention on the main drag.

Popcorn Bar (☎ 027 958 19 14; ☒ 8am-4am)
Work on that snow-goggle tan, rehearse
your grungy boarder pose and check out the
scene at this snowboard shop-cum-après-
ski dive. By late afternoon, Popcorn is fit to
burst with rowdy riders united in their love
of Jägermeister and hip-hop.

Nesti's Ski Bar (☎ 027 957 42 11; ☒ 3.30am-2am)
Always packed, Nesti's is a buzzy après-ski
favourite. Stop by for a spiced glühwein or
three.

Getting There & Away
Buses depart half-hourly from Brig (Sfr21,
1¼ hours) and Visp (Sfr15.80, 45 minutes).
From Brig it's marginally faster to take the train
and change at Visp. You can transfer to/from
Zermatt at Stalden Saas.

Saas Fee is car-free. Park at the entrance
to the village, where the first 24 hours in
winter costs Sfr16 (covered parking). It gets
cheaper after the first day and if you use the
Guest Card.

BRIG
pop 11,900 / elevation 688m
Close to the Italian border and bisected by
the Rhône and Saltina rivers, Brig has been
an important crossroads since Roman times.
Though often overlooked en route to Mont
Blanc or Milan, it's worth lingering to see
the cobbled Stadtplatz, framed by alfresco
cafés and candy-hued townhouses, and the
fantastical baroque palace.

Orientation & Information
The centre is south of the Rhône and east of
its tributary, the Saltina. The train station is
on the 1st floor of the **tourist office** (☎ 027 921

60 30; www.brig-tourismus.ch; Bahnhofplatz 1; ☒ 8.30am-
noon & 1.30-6pm Mon-Fri). Postal buses leave from
outside the train station. Directly ahead,
Bahnhofstrasse leads to the town centre.

Sights
STOCKALPERSCHLOSS
Kaspar von Stockalper (1609–91), a shrewd
businessman who dominated the Simplon
Pass trade routes, built this whimsical palace
and dubbed himself the 'Great Stockalper'.
Locals didn't think he was so great and sent
him packing to Italy. His **palace** (☎ 027 921 60
30; Alte Simplonstrasse 28; adult/child/under 7yr Sfr7/3/free;
☒ hourly 50min guided visit 9.30-4.30pm Tue-Sun May-Oct)
remains with its baublelike onion domes and
arcaded inner courtyard. It's free to wander
the main court (open 6am to 10pm April
to October and 6am to 8pm November to
March) and the baroque gardens with their
quintessential parterres, fountains and
clipped hedges.

Sleeping & Eating
When the weather warms, locals fill the
cafés and restaurants on pedestrian-only
Hauptplatz.

Schlosshotel (☎ 027 922 95 95; Am Schlosspark; www
.schlosshotel.ch; s Sfr85-98, d Sfr120-160; ℙ ▢) So close
to the palace you can almost polish the domes,
this is the best choice in Brig, with terrific
views and a cheery welcome. Many of the
light, spacious rooms have balconies facing
Stockalperschloss. There's free internet in
the lounge.

Hotel de Londres (☎ 027 922 93 93; www.hotel
-delondres.ch; Bahnhofstrasse 17; s/d Sfr85/140) Sure
the decor is a blast from the '70s, but this
hotel's friendly service, inviting atmosphere
and prime location are timeless. It's a five-
minute walk from the train station on the
main square.

Zum Eidgenossen (☎ 027 923 92 07; Zum Eidgenossen;
mains Sfr16-36; ☒ Wed-Mon) Travel your tastebuds
with adventurous grill specialities such as wild
boar and bison in this warm, Valaisan mountain chalet-style setting.

Getting There & Away
Brig is on the Glacier Express line from Zermatt
to St Moritz and the main line between Italy
(Milan via Domodossola) and Geneva (Sfr57,
two to 2¾ hours). Trains from Brig also run
to Locarno (Sfr51, 2½ hours) in Ticino, via
Domodossola (take your passport).

THE GOMS & ALETSCH GLACIER

Bidding Brig farewell, you enter another world. As you approach the source of the mighty Rhône and gain altitude, the deep valley narrows and the verdure of pine-clad mountainsides and south-facing vineyards that defines the west of the canton switches to rugged wilderness. Known as the Goms, a string of bucolic villages (one of the first invitingly named Bitsch) of geranium-bedecked timber chalets and onion-domed churches stretches northeast, waiting to be counted off like rosary beads. On either side of the turquoise torrent that is the Rhône stretch billiard table-green fields scattered with farmhouses.

Aletsch Glacier

Go behind the scenes in the Goms for real Alpine drama. Out of view from the valley floor lies the 23km Aletsch Glacier (Aletschgletscher), a seemingly never-ending swirl of deeply crevassed ice that slices past thundering falls and jagged spires of rock that stab at the sky. The longest glacier in the Alps and a Unesco World Heritage site, it stretches from Jungfrau in the Bernese Oberland to a plateau above the Rhône. Its southern expanse is fringed by the 2000m Aletschwald, one of Europe's highest pine forests.

ORIENTATION & INFORMATION

Three car-free resorts border the southern rim of the glacier, separated from the forest by a ridge of hills. The westernmost is **Riederalp** (☎ 027 928 60 50; www.riederalp.ch), followed by **Bettmeralp** (☎ 027 928 60 60; www.bettmeralp.ch) and **Fiescheralp** (☎ 027 970 10 70; www.goms.ch), all at an altitude of just under 2000m. Each has a tourist office, as do the towns in the valley floor from where cable cars depart.

ACTIVITIES

Most people get their first tantalising glimpse of Aletsch Glacier from Jungfraujoch (p183), but this is the best place to visit it. If you do nothing else in the Goms, stop at Fiesch and take two **cable cars** (☎ 027 971 27 00; www.eggishorn.ch; adult/child return Sfr42.80/21.40; ☉ every 30 min 8.15am-6.15pm Jun-mid-Oct) up to **Eggishorn** (2927m). As you float up over the velvety fields and then, above the tree line, the stark olive, brown and grey Alpine landscape, nothing can prepare you for what awaits on exiting the gondola.

Streaming down in a broad curve around the Aletschhorn (4195m), the glacier looks like a frozen six-lane freeway. In the distance, to the north, rise the glistening summits of Jungfrau (4158m), Mönch (4109m), Eiger (3970m) and Finsteraarhorn (4274m). If you scamper up the loose and rocky rise, topped by an antenna, to the west of the cable car exit, you might spy Mont Blanc and Matterhorn in the distance.

While gawping at this wonder of nature, consider the statistics. The main glacier (the Grosser Aletschgletscher) covered 163 sq km in 1856, 128 sq km in 1973 and just 85 sq km today. In a couple of generations it may well be gone.

There's no better way to appreciate the drop-dead gorgeous scenery of the Aletsch region than by hitting the trail in summer. One of Switzerland's finest walks is the **Aletsch Glacier** hike (p61) from Fiescheralp to Bettmeralp. An easier option is to take the cable car up to the glacier and then walk back down to Fiescheralp, the midway station. For an adrenalin rush, tackle the dizzying *vie ferrate* at Eggishorn (2½ hours) and Aletsch (4 hours).

In winter, there is great skiing in the three hamlets, each with accommodation and eating options. Family-friendly Bettmeralp is the handiest and prettiest. Alternatively, stay in one of the three access towns in the Rhône valley, Mörel, Betten and Fiesch. In the Aletsch region there are 99km of ski runs and 35 lifts. The skiing is mostly intermediate or easy. Ski passes cost Sfr50/25 per adult/child per day, or Sfr56/28, including the lifts up from the valley towns.

PULVERISING COW PATS

Recently the good folk of Riederalp have put their own twist on a centuries-old tradition. In the old days, farmers leading cattle down from the high Alpine plains at the end of summer would smash up the dung and spread it as fertiliser. Inspired by this rural ritual, locals held their first-ever Chüefladefäscht (cow pat festival) in 2005. The aim of the game: to give as many cow pats as possible a proper thumping with a golf club–style instrument. For those who like a flutter, the villagers had another idea. They demarked 49 squares on a field and let the cows out. Bet on the square in which you think one of the cows will first drop a pat...

Paragliders and hang-gliders take advantage of the excellent thermals and grandiose glacier views at Fiescheralp. To join them, contact **Good Flight** (☎ 027 971 20 85; www.good-flight.ch), offering tandem flights from Sfr120.

SLEEPING & EATING

Tourist offices provide a list of chalets and apartments. Expect discounts of up to 50% in summer on the high-season rates given below.

Camping Eggishorn (☎ 027 971 03 16; Fiesch; sites per adult/child/tent/car Sfr13/6/12/3; ✆ year-round; ☒) On the banks of a babbling stream, this pleasantly green site's top-notch facilities include a restaurant, heated outdoor pool and playground. Just 10 minutes' stroll from the cable car to Eggishorn, it's a peaceful spot to pitch a tent.

Hotel Eggishorn (☎ 027 971 14 44; www.hotel -eggishorn.ch; dm Sfr35-45, d Sfr130-200) Whether you opt for the no-frills dorms or woody rooms drenched with natural light, you share the same views to the frosted peaks of Matterhorn and Weisshorn. The restaurant (mains Sfr15 to Sfr35) dishes up Valaisan fare and the sunny terrace breathtaking panoramas. Fiescheralp is near Eggishorn cable car, so well placed for the skier or hiker eager to get up to the glacier.

Hotel Alpina (☎ 027 927 24 24; www.alpinafiescher alp.ch, in German; s/d Sfr135/250; ☒) Another great choice at Fiescheralp, the Alpina has light, pine-filled rooms with balconies. Unwind in the sauna and whirlpool or over mulled wine in the tepee bar. The restaurant (mains Sfr15 to Sfr25) serves delicious rösti with salmon and horseradish.

Bettmerhof (☎ 027 928 62 10; www.bettmerhof.ch; s/d with half-board Sfr162/315; ☒) Near the lifts in Bettmeralp, this chalet is brilliant for skiers itching to be first on the slopes. You'll sleep like a babe in the snug pine-panelled rooms. Fork out an extra Sfr10 and you'll get a view of Matterhorn. There's a restaurant, spa and playroom.

GETTING THERE & AWAY

The base stations for these resorts are on the train route between Brig and Andermatt. Cable-car departures are linked to the train arrivals. Mörel to Riederalp costs Sfr9 each way,

the same as from Betten up to Bettmeralp. Some versions of the ski pass include these cable cars.

From Fiesch to the Furka Pass

The trail out of Valais weaves northeast from Fiesch, with more postcard-cute villages along the way, including **Niederwald**, where Cäsar Ritz (1850–1918), founder of the luxury hotel chain, was born and is now buried. Of them all, **Münster** is easily the most charming. Tightly packed chalets drop down the hill from its bright white church. A brook babbles contentedly through the village heart, and weary travellers delight in the **Hotel Croix d'Or et Poste** (☎ 027 974 15 15; www.hotel-post muenster.ch; s/d Sfr100/200), the extraordinarily flower-laden hotel on a tiny square in the main road. Goethe slept in here in 1779. The traditional rooms are comfy but with a granny's love of pastels, florals and frilly doilies.

At **Ulrichen** you must make a decision. You can turn southeast down a narrow road that twists its way south out of the Valais and into the mountains that separate the canton from Ticino. Impressively barren country that at times recalls the stark beauty of the Scottish Highlands and Spanish Pyrenees leads you to the **Nufenen Pass** (Passo di Novena) at 2478m, probably the most remote gateway into Switzerland's Italian canton. Dropping down the other side, the first major town is **Airolo** (p328), 24km east of the pass along the quiet, almost gloomy Val Bedretto.

Should you decide to push on east of Ulrichen, you will head slowly upwards towards **Gletsch**. From here the mighty **Grimsel Pass**, with its spectacular views west over several lakes in Bern canton and eastern Valais, lies a short, steep drive north, but it is often closed, even in summer.

Marking the cantonal frontier with Uri is the vertiginous **Furka Pass** (2431m), the run up to which offers superlative views over the fissured Rhône glacier to the north. Open in summer only, it is the gateway into southeast Switzerland. Car trains in **Oberwald** negotiate the trip underground when the pass is shut. The train surfaces at Realp near Andermatt (p262).

VALAIS

Bernese Oberland

The Bernese Oberland should come with a health warning – caution: may cause trembling in the north face of Eiger, uncontrollable bouts of euphoria at the foot of Jungfrau, 007 delusions at Schilthorn and A-list fever in Gstaad. And it's highly addictive. Mark Twain wrote that no opiate compared to walking through this landscape (and he should know), but even when sober the electric-green spruce forests, so-big-they'll-swallow-you-up mountains, surreal china-blue skies, swirling glaciers and turquoise lakes seem the products of hallucination.

After an adrenalin fix in Interlaken, the Jungfrau Region beckons. Feel the spray of the wispy Staubbach Falls, savour chocolate-box Mürren, slalom the Lauberhorn and feel humbled by the original pearly kings and queens: Eiger, Mönch and Jungfrau. Up at Europe's highest station, Jungfraujoch, husky yapping mingles with Bollywood beats. Yet just paces away, the serpentine Aletsch Glacier flicks out its tongue and you're surrounded by 4000m turrets and frosty stillness.

From Interlaken, head east to Meiringen for Sherlock Holmes eccentricities and meringues, or west for medieval flair at Thun's turreted castle. Down south you enter wilder territory in Kandersteg, where the dress-code is muddy walking boots. Not so in nearby Gstaad, where Paris Hilton pouts in the paparazzi's lens and the nouveaux riches flash porcelain smiles whiter than snow.

But though photographers might capture celebs at their best, the landscape defeats them. Listen carefully for the tutting of tourists at the postcard carousels trying – and failing – to find something to match their memories. An inevitable side effect, surely, of a place so outrageously beautiful it has to be seen to be believed.

HIGHLIGHTS

- Getting dizzy on zip-wires, hanging bridges and Eiger views on the *via ferrata* in **Mürren** (p188)

- Hiking the heavenly **Faulhornweg** (p69) from Schynige Platte to Grindelwald-First

- Whizzing past 4000m mountains and glaciers on a husky-driven sleigh at **Jungfraujoch** (p183)

- Gliding above the peaks on a tandem paragliding flight from **Interlaken** (p174)

- Discovering Sherlock Holmes mysteries and divine meringues in **Meiringen** (p193)

| ▬ POPULATION: 897,500 | ▬ AREA: 5907 SQ KM | ▬ LANGUAGE: GERMAN |

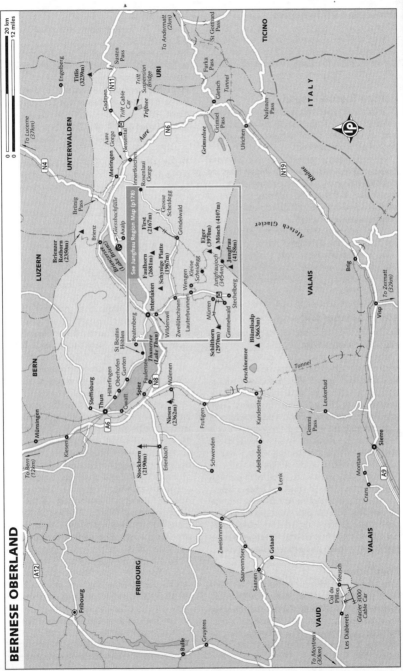

BERNESE OBERLAND

Orientation & Information

This region covers the southern part of the canton of Bern, stretching from Gstaad in the west to the Susten Pass (2224m) in the east. **Berner Oberland Tourismus** (www.berneroberland.ch) offers online information only.

Getting There & Around

The Bernese Oberland is easily accessible by road and train from major Swiss airports, including Basel, Bern, Geneva and Zürich, as well as from Lucerne.

If you intend spending most of your holiday here, investigate the **Berner Oberland Regional Pass** (www.regiopass-berneroberland.ch; 7/15 days Sfr224/270; ☯ May–Oct), offering free travel on three/five days on certain routes, plus discounts on others.

Alternatively, the Jungfrau Region, at the heart of the Bernese Oberland, has its own **Jungfraubahn Pass**. Note that a Swiss or Eurail Pass alone will take you only so far into the Jungfrau Region. See p179 for more information.

INTERLAKEN

pop 5280 / elevation 570m

Once Interlaken made the Victorians swoon with mountain vistas from the chandelier-lit confines of grand hotels; today it makes daredevils scream with adrenalin-loaded adventures. Straddling the glittering Lakes Thun and Brienz and dazzled by the pearly whites of Eiger, Mönch and Jungfrau, the scenery here is mind-blowing. Particularly, some say, if you're abseiling waterfalls, thrashing white water or gliding soundlessly above 4000m peaks.

Though the streets are filled with enough yodelling kitsch to make Heidi cringe, Interlaken still makes a terrific base for exploring the Bernese Oberland. Its adventure capital status has spawned a breed of funky bars, party-mad hostels and restaurants serving flavours more imaginative than fondue.

Orientation

Interlaken has two train stations: Interlaken West and Interlaken Ost; each has bike rental, money-changing facilities and a landing stage for boats on Lake Thun and Lake Brienz. The main drag, Höheweg, runs between the two stations. You can walk from one to the other in less than 30 minutes.

Information

Hospital (☎ 033 826 25 00; Weissenaustrasse 27) West of the centre.

Kikireon Internet (☎ 033 823 32 32; Postgasse 6; per min Sfr0.30; ☯ noon-10.30pm) Computer shop with internet connection, including for laptops.

Post office (Postplatz; ☯ 8am-noon & 1.45-6pm Mon-Fri, 8.30-11am Sat) Telephones and stamp machines outside.

Rocco's Latino Bar (☎ 033 827 87 83; City Hotel Oberland, Am Marktplatz; per min Sfr0.30; ☯ 8am-12.30pm) Internet access.

Tourist office (☎ 033 826 53 00; www.interlaken tourism.ch; Höheweg 37; ☯ 8am-7pm Mon-Fri, 8am-5pm Sat, 10am-noon & 5-7pm Sun Jul–mid-Sep, 8am-noon & 1.30-6pm Mon-Fri, 9am-noon Sat rest of year) Halfway between the stations. There's also a hotel booking board outside its office and at both train stations.

Sights & Activities

With snowy behemoths Eiger, Mönch and Jungfrau in the backyard, it's impossible to stay in Interlaken for more than a day or two without getting seriously itchy feet to hike, climb or throw yourself off something.

Still, it's worth crossing the turquoise Aare River for a mooch around Interlaken's old quarter, **Unterseen**. Here the humble **Tourist Museum** (☎ 033 822 98 39; Obere Gasse 26; adult/child Sfr5/2; ☯ 2-5pm Tue-Sun May-Oct) presents a romp through tourism in the region with costumes, carriages and other curios.

When the sun's out, take the nostalgic **funicular** (adult/child return Sfr12/9) up to family-friendly **Heimwehfluh** (☎ 033 822 34 53; toboggan run Sfr6; ☯ 9.30am-5pm Apr-Oct) for long views across Interlaken. Kids (and big 'uns) love the whizzy toboggan ride down the hill – lay off the brakes to pick up speed.

For far-reaching vistas to the 4000m giants, ride the funicular to **Harder Kulm** (☎ 033 828 71 11; one-way/return Sfr15/Sfr25; ☯ 8am-6.30pm Apr-Oct). Many hiking paths begin here if you want to stretch your legs. The wildlife park near the valley station is home to furry Alpine critters, including marmots and ibex.

Not ready to climb Eiger north face *just* yet? Squeeze in some climbing practice at **K44** (☎ 033 821 28 21; www.k44.ch; Jungfraustrasse 44; adult/child Sfr19/12; ☯ 4-10pm Mon, 9am-10pm Tue-Fri, 9am-8pm Sat, 9am-6pm Sun Oct-Apr, 9am-6pm Tue-Fri & 9am-4pm Sat, closed Sun & Mon May-Sep). The 14.5m-high hall offers a variety of wall types. There's equipment rental in the sports shop downstairs.

INTERLAKEN

EXTREME SPORTS

Tempted to hurl yourself off a bridge, down a cliff or along a raging river? You're in the right place. Switzerland is the world's second-biggest adventure-sports mecca, nipping at New Zealand's sprightly heels, and Interlaken is its busiest hub.

Almost every heart-stopping pursuit you can think of is offered here (although the activities take place in the greater Jungfrau Region). You can white-water raft on the Lütschine, Simme and Saane rivers, go canyoning in the Saxetet, Grimsel or Chli Schliere gorges, and canyon jump at the Gletscherschlucht near Grindelwald (see p180). If that doesn't grab you, there's paragliding, glacier bungee jumping, skydiving, ice climbing, hydrospeeding and, phew, much more. The latest craze, which you have to be crazy to try, is zorbing, where you're strapped into a giant plastic ball and sent spinning down a hill.

The major operators able to arrange most sports include the following:

Alpinraft (☎ 033 823 41 00; www.alpinraft.ch; Hauptstrasse 7)

Outdoor Interlaken (☎ 033 826 77 19; www.outdoor-interlaken.ch; Hauptstrasse 15)

Swissraft (☎ 033 821 66 55; www.swissraft-activity.ch; Obere Jungfraustrasse 72)

Bohag (☎ 033 822 90 00; www.bohag.ch, in German; Gsteigwiler) and **Scenic Air** (☎ 033 821 00 11; www.scenicair.ch, www.skydiveswitzerland.com) conduct scenic flights, skydiving and other activities. **Hang Gliding Interlaken** (☎ 079 770 0704; www.hanggliding interlaken.com) organises hang-gliding flights above Interlaken.

Prices are from Sfr90 for rock climbing, Sfr95 for zorbing, Sfr110 for rafting or canyoning, Sfr120 for hydrospeeding, Sfr130 for bungee jumping, Sfr160 for paragliding, Sfr195 for hang-gliding, and Sfr430 for skydiving.

Most excursions are without incident, but there's always a small risk and it's wise to ask about safety records and procedures.

Festivals & Events

Cackling, clanging bells and causing mischief, the *Potschen* dash through Interlaken on 2 January or **Harder Potschete** (www.harderpotschete .ch). These warty masked ogres apparently scare away evil mountain spirits, though you might quite get a fright if one takes a fancy to you and drags you off through the streets. The

revelry spills into the night with upbeat folk music and fiendish merrymaking.

Established and emerging brass bands and orchestras take centre stage at the **Jungfrau Music Festival** (www.jungfrau-music-festival.ch) in July.

Eiger, Mönch and Jungfrau are always breathtaking but never more so than for runners competing in September's **Jungfrau Marathon** (www.jungfrau-marathon.ch) from Lauterbrunnen to Kleine Scheidegg.

Sleeping

Ask your hotel for the useful Guest Card for free bus transport plus discounts on attractions and sports facilities. Call ahead during the low season, as some places close.

BUDGET
Camping & Farmhouses

RiverLodge & Camping TCS (☎ 033 822 44 34; Brienzstrasse 24; sites per adult/tent/car Sfr9/7/4, dm/s/d Sfr28/64/88; ☼ May–mid-Oct) Facing the Aare River and handy for Interlaken Ost train station, this campsite and hostel duo offer first-class facilities including a kitchen, laundry and wi-fi. You can rent bikes and kayaks here.

Schlaf im Stroh (☎ 033 822 04 31; www.uelisi.ch; Lanzenen 30; per person Sfr28; ☼ May-Sep; **P**) Our readers sing the praises of this friendly farm. Bring your sleeping bag to snooze in the straw and wake up to a hearty breakfast. Kids adore the resident cats, goats and rabbits. It's 15 minutes' walk from Interlaken Ost station along the Aare River (upstream). Otherwise, take the bus to Interlaken Geissgasse and then walk 500m along Sendlistrasse.

Hostels

Balmer's Herberge (☎ 033 822 19 61; www.balmers.ch; Hauptstrasse 23; dm Sfr27-30, d Sfr74-80; ☼ reception 24hr; **P** 🖳) Adrenalin junkies hail Balmer's for its fun frat-house vibe. These party-mad digs offer beer-garden happy hours, wrap lunches, a pumping bar with DJs, and chill-out hammocks for nursing your hangover. But when somewhere blows its own alphorn so loudly, there's often a catch; some think Balmer's should invest backpacker dosh in longer, thicker mattresses and ditch the theme-park feel.

Backpackers Villa Sonnenhof (☎ 033 826 71 71; www.villa.ch; Alpenstrasse 16; dm/d Sfr37/98; Jungfrau view extra Sfr5; ☼ reception 7am-11pm; 🖳) While most Interlaken hostels are charged with more energy than a Duracell bunny, this homely place

ROCKY HORROR

The rivalries between Switzerland's linguistic communities are usually low-key, but when they do erupt it's often over the most unlikely things. Take the German-speaking canton of Bern and French-speaking Jura separatists as an example. They've been tussling over a 83.5kg piece of rock for more than 20 years.

The 200-year-old Unspunnen Stone (*Unspunnenstein*) is a focal point of Switzerland's Alpine Games, which since 1805 have symbolically asserted national unity and are now held about once every 12 years. The stone was first kidnapped from an Interlaken museum in 1984 by the French-speaking 'Beliers', who lay claim to part of Bern's territory. They kept it hostage for 17 years, while also demanding Jura's devolution from Switzerland and entry into the European Union.

In 2001, the stone was suddenly given back in mysterious circumstances, and engraved with the EU flag. Just four years later there was another theft, again from Interlaken, where the travelling games were due to be held that year.

The **Alpine Games** (Unspunnenfest; ☎ 033 826 53 53; www.unspunnen-schwinget.ch) feature yodelling, alphorn playing, *Schwingen* wrestling and stone-throwing, preferably of the historic Unspunnen Stone. The next Interlaken games are planned for 2017. At the time of writing, the stone still hadn't reappeared.

recharges your batteries. The olive-fronted villa exudes Victorian flair with stucco and vintage steamer trunks. Dorms are immaculate, and some have balconies with Jungfrau views. There's also a lounge, a well-equipped kitchen, and a leafy garden.

Funny Farm (☎ 033 828 12 81; www.funny-farm.ch; Hauptstrasse 36; dm Sfr30-38.50, s/d Sfr90/110; ⏰ reception 24hr; P ☐ 🐕) Funny Farm is halfway between a squat and an island shipwreck. The ramshackle art-nouveau house, surrounded by makeshift bars and a swimming pool, is patrolled by Spliff, the lovably dopey St Bernard. Dorms are a bit faded and musty, but guests don't care; they're here for the party and revel in such anachronism.

Other budget digs include:

Happy Inn Lodge (☎ 033 822 32 25; www.happy-inn .com; Rosenstrasse 17; dm/s/d/tr Sfr22/40/80/96, breakfast Sfr8) OK central hostel, recently spruced up a little. Expect rock-bottom rates, a noisy bar below and chip-shop smells throughout.

SYHA hostel (☎ 033 822 43 53; www.youthhostel.ch /boenigen; Aareweg 21, Bönigen; dm Sfr29-35; ⏰ reception 7-10am & 2-11.30pm, hostel closed late Oct–Dec; ☐) Quite a way from town with a garden on the waterfront. Has bike and kayak rental. Take bus 1.

Hotels & Pensions

our pick **Hotel Rugenpark** (☎ 033 822 36 61; www.rugen park.ch; Rugenparkstrasse 19; s/d/tr/q Sfr65/105/140/175, with bathroom Sfr85/130/165/200; ⏰ closed Nov–mid-Dec; P ✗ ☐) Chris and Ursula have worked magic to transform this into an incredibly sweet B&B. Rooms remain humble, but the

place is spotless and has been enlivened with colourful butterflies, beads and travel trinkets. There's free internet, a big garden where Monty the dog roams, and a kitchen for preparing a snack. You'll feel right at home, and your knowledgeable hosts are always ready to help with local tips.

Hotel Lötschberg/Susi's B & B (☎ 033 822 25 45; www.lotschberg.ch; General Guisan Strasse 31; B&B s/d Sfr95/135, hotel s/d Sfr120/165; P ✗ ☐) The picture of faded grandeur, this hotel and B&B offer reasonable value. The old-style rooms are bright and clean, though bathrooms are microscopic. Cheery Fritz serves breakfast and feeds guests tips on the area. Other pluses include a kitchen and free internet.

MIDRANGE

Post Hardermannli (☎ 033 822 89 19; www.post -hardermannli.ch; Hauptstrasse Unterseen 18; s/d Sfr100/155; P) An affable Swiss–Kiwi couple, Andreas and Kim, run this rustic chalet. Rooms are simple yet comfy, decorated with pine and chintzy pastels. Cheaper rooms forgo balconies and Jungfrau views. The home-grown farm produce at breakfast is a real treat.

Gasthof Hirschen (☎ 033 822 15 45; www.hirschen -interlaken.ch, in German; Hauptstrasse 11; s/d Sfr110/180; P) With its dark wood, geranium-clad facade, this heritage-listed chalet radiates 17th-century charm. Low ceilings and wafts of smoke add to the cosiness. Rooms are 'rustic modern', with parquet floors, downy duvets, bathroom pods and wi-fi. The restaurant (mains Sfr20 to Sfr30) rustles up local favourites.

Hotel Splendid (☎ 033 822 76 12; www.splendid
.ch; Höheweg 33; s/d Sfr145/240) Right on the main
drag, this 100-year-old family-run hotel shelters large, sunny rooms with parquet floors
and lots of pine. Light sleepers might have
problems nodding off, though. Check out
the zebra-stripe stools and stag-antler book-
shelves in the quirky bar downstairs.

Hôtel du Lac (☎ 033 822 29 22; www.dulac-interlaken
.ch; Höheweg 225; s/d Sfr160/280; 🖳) Smiley old-
fashioned service and a riverfront location
near Interlaken Ost make this 19th-century
hotel a solid choice. It has been in the same
family for generations and, despite the mish-
mash of styles, has kept enough belle époque
glory to remain charming.

Hotel Royal St Georges (☎ 033 822 75 75; www.royal
-stgeorges.ch; Höheweg 139; s/d Sfr190/290) Catapulting
you back to Victorian times, this hotel has
preserved some original pizzazz in the high-
ceilinged public areas with stucco and chandeliers. Rooms are comfortable despite the
dated furnishings. There's a small sauna and
steam room.

Metropole Hotel (☎ 033 828 66 66; www.metropole
-interlaken.ch; Höheweg 37; s/d Sfr198/305, breakfast Sfr25;
🅿 🖳 🕭) As the tallest concrete high-rise
on Interlaken's horizon, this is impossible
to miss. However, with an exterior this ugly,
staying here is a boon: you enjoy lofty views
of the town and Jungfrau, and are saved from
looking at the Metropole.

Hotel Krebs (☎ 033 826 03 30; www.krebshotel
.ch; Bahnhofstrasse 4; s/d/ste 238/312/490; 🅿 🕱 🖳)
Looking stylish after a complete facelift,
this hotel sports rooms in earthy tones with
bold splashes of scarlet, black-and-white
photos of mountains, and designer flourishes a-plenty. All feature glam bathrooms,
flatscreen TVs and wi-fi. Downstairs there's
a self-consciously trendy bar and a superb
Asian–French restaurant.

TOP END

Victoria-Jungfrau Grand Hotel & Spa (☎ 033 828 28 28;
www.victoria-jungfrau.ch; Höheweg 41; s/d from Sfr560/680,
d with Jungfrau views from Sfr780; 🅿 🕱 🖳 🕭) The
reverent hush and impeccable service here
(as well as the prices) evoke an era when
only royalty and the seriously wealthy trav-
elled. A perfect melding of well-preserved
Victorian features and modern luxury make
this Interlaken's answer to Raffles – with plum
views of Jungfrau to boot.

Eating

Am Marktplatz is scattered with bakeries and
bistros that have alfresco seating.

Sandwich Bar (☎ 033 821 63 25; Rosenstrasse 5;
snacks Sfr4-8; 🕒 7.30am-7pm Mon-Fri, 8am-5pm Sat) This
crimson-walled snack bar is an untouristy
gem. Choose your bread and get creative with
fillings (our favourite is *Bündnerfleisch*, sun-
dried tomatoes and parmesan). Otherwise
try tasty soups, salads, toasties and locally
made ice cream.

My Little Thai (☎ 033 821 10 17; Hauptstrasse 19;
mains Sfr12.50-22, lunch menus Sfr10.50-15.50; 🕒 closed
Tue) Next to Balmer's, this hole-in-the-wall den
is authentically Thai, festooned with pics of
the King of Thailand, kitschy fairy lights and
lucky cats. Snag a table to chomp on Eddie's
freshly prepared spring rolls, curries and spicy
papaya salads.

Pizzeria Horn (☎ 033 822 92 92; Hardererstrasse
35; pizzas Sfr14-22, mains Sfr25-35; 🕒 dinner Thu-Mon)
Exposed brick, chunky tables and photos of
Don Camillo set the scene at this inviting pizzeria. Find a cosy nook to feast on antipasti and
delicious wood-oven pizza. There's alfresco
dining on the garden terrace in summer.

Belvédère Brasserie (☎ 033 828 91 00; Höheweg 95;
mains Sfr18-36) Yes it's attached to the boring-
look Hapimag, but this brasserie has upbeat
modern decor and a terrace with appetising
Jungfrau views. It serves international favourites such as veal in merlot sauce, alongside a handful of Swiss stalwarts like fondue
and rösti.

Benacus (☎ 033 821 20 20; www.benacus.ch;
Stadthausplatz; mains Sfr20-30; 🕒 closed Sun, lunch Sat)
Super-cool Benacus is a breath of urban
air with its glass walls, slick wine-red sofas,
lounge music and street-facing terrace. The
TV show *Funky Kitchen Club* is filmed here.
The menu stars creative flavours like potato
and star anis soup and Aargau chicken with
caramelised pak choi.

Goldener Anker (☎ 033 822 16 72; www.anker.ch,
in German; Marktgasse 57; mains Sfr18-38; 🕒 dinner daily)
Even fussy eaters will find tastebud pleas-
ers at this beamed restaurant, which, locals
will whisper in your ear, is the best in town.
The globetrotting menu tempts with everything from sizzling fajitas to red snapper
and ostrich steaks. It also has a roster of live
bands.

For coffee and cake, or a cocktail, try **Top o'
Met** (☎ 033 828 66 66; Höheweg 37) on the top floor of
the Metropole Hotel, which has stellar views.

Schuh (☎ 033 822 94 41; Höheweg 56; ☼ 9am-11.30pm) is a Viennese-style coffee house with can't-stop-at-one pastries and pralines. Skip dinner, however, as the tinkling, Barry Manilow–style piano and sickly pink interior can feel like being trapped in a 1970s B-movie.

Good cheap eats include **Tamil Asian Shop & Takeaway** (☎ 033 822 23 30; Uniongasse 1; all menus Sfr12.90; ☼ 10.30am-10.30pm).

There's a supermarket opposite each train station and another, **Coop Pronto** (Höheweg 11; ☼ 6am-10.30pm daily), in between them.

Drinking

The bars at Balmer's and Funny Farm are easily the liveliest drinking holes for revved-up 20-something travellers. You'll find a mixed crowd in the Happy Inn.

Buddy's Pub (☎ 033 822 76 12; Höheweg 33) Pull up a stool, order a draft Rugenbräu or a 'sex on the mountain' (for want of a beach) cocktail and enjoy a natter with the locals. Switzerland's first pub is loud, smoky and convivial.

Hooters (☎ 033 822 65 11; Höheweg 57) Yes, it's part of a chain and, yes, the girls in hot pants and too-tight tank tops make feminists rant, but – ooh er, missus – Hooters remains popular. It serves beer, big-screen sports and fine Jungfrau views from the terrace, though most punters seem to have their eyes fixed on bumps of a different kind…

Per Bacco (☎ 033 822 97 92; Rugenparkstrasse 2; ☼ 9am-midnight Mon-Sat) A slightly more sophisticated and well-dressed clientele props up the horseshoe bar at Per Bacco, which serves antipasti and Italian wines by the glass.

Entertainment

There are twice-weekly performances of Schiller's *Wilhelm Tell* (William Tell) between late June and early September, staged in the open-air theatre in Rugen Forest. The play is in German but an English synopsis is available. Tickets are available from **Tellspielbüro** (☎ 033 822 37 22; www.tellspiele.ch; Höheweg 37; tickets Sfr26-48) in the tourist office.

Getting There & Away

Trains to Lucerne (Sfr30, two hours), Brig via Spiez (Sfr41, one hour) and Montreux via Bern or Visp (Sfr57 to Sfr67, 2¼ to three hours) depart frequently from Interlaken Ost train station.

The A8 freeway heads northeast to Lucerne and the A6 northwest to Bern, but the only way

south for vehicles without a big detour round the mountains is to take the car-carrying train from Kandersteg, south of Spiez.

Should you wish to hire a car in Interlaken for trips further into Switzerland, big-name rental companies **Avis** (☎ 033 822 19 39; Waldeggstrasse 34a), near a 24-hour petrol station, and **Hertz** (☎ 033 822 61 72; Harderstrasse 25), are both reasonably central.

Getting Around

You can easily get around Interlaken on foot, but taxis, buses and even horse-drawn carriages (around Sfr40) are found at each train station. Alternatively, you can pick up scooters and cars for zipping around town at **Daniel's** (☎ 033 822 01 75; www.daniels-rental.ch; Hauptstrasse 19), among others.

AROUND INTERLAKEN

SCHYNIGE PLATTE

The must-do day trip from Interlaken is Schynige Platte, a 1967m plateau where the **Alpengarten** (admission Sfr4) nurtures 600 types of Alpine blooms, including snowbells, arnica, gentian and edelweiss. The biggest draw up here, however, is the hiking. The **Panoramaweg** is an easy two-hour circuit, while the high-level 15km **Faulhornweg** (p69) trail is a truly memorable trudge, affording out-of-this-world views to Eiger, Mönch and Jungfrau. If you're here in July or August, don't miss the **moonlight hikes** that follow the same route.

You reach the plateau on a **cog-wheel train** (www.schynigeplatte.ch, www.jungfraubahn.ch; one-way/return Sr33/54; ☼ closed late Oct–late May) from Wilderswil. Trains run up to Schynige Platte at approximately 40- to 50-minute intervals until around 5pm, although the period of operation varies, depending on weather and snow conditions. If you don't have your own boots with you, there is, amazingly, free Lowa boot-testing on Schynige Platte (see the website for details).

ST BEATUS-HÖHLEN

Sculpted over millennia, the **St Beatus Caves** (St Beatus-Höhlen; ☎ 033 841 16 43; adult/child/student Sfr18/10/16; ☼ 10.30am-5pm mid-Mar–late Oct) are great for a wander through caverns of dramatically lit stalagmites, stalactites and underground lakes. Lore has it that in the 6th century they sheltered St Beatus, monk, hermit and first apostle of Switzerland, who apparently did battle with a dragon here. They are a 1½-hour walk or a short Sfr9.60 boat ride from Interlaken.

JUNGFRAU REGION

If the Bernese Oberland is Switzerland's Alpine heart, the Jungfrau Region is where yours will skip a beat. Presided over by glacier-encrusted monoliths Eiger, Mönch and Jungfrau (Ogre, Monk and Virgin), the scenery stirs the soul and strains the neck muscles. Whether trekking through luxuriantly green pastures and deep ravines in Grindelwald, rising in a cable car to Schilthorn, or lounging in a hotel in Mürren, you're faced with epic beauty everywhere you turn. Hundreds of kilometres of walking trails allow you to capture the landscape from many angles, but it never looks less than astonishing.

The 'big three' peaks have an enduring place in mountaineering legend, particularly the 3970m Eiger, whose fearsome north wall claimed many lives and remained uncon-quered until 1938. Reaching great heights is easier today; it takes just hours to whiz up by train to Jungfraujoch (3454m), the highest station in Europe.

Orientation & Information

Two valleys branch southwards from Interlaken. The broad valley curving east is dominated by Grindelwald. The valley running directly south leads to Lauterbrunnen, from where you can reach car-free resorts on the hills above – Wengen on the eastern ridge, or Mürren and Gimmelwald on the west via mountainside Grütschalp or Stechelberg farther along the Lauterbrunnen Valley floor. Schilthorn lookout point is reached via Mürren.

Between the two valleys stands the holy grail of Jungfraujoch. It's usual to travel in a loop, say, from Interlaken to Grindelwald, to Kleine Scheidegg at the bottom of the Eiger, to Jungfraujoch, back to Kleine Scheidegg and on to Wengen, Lauterbrunnen and Interlaken. However, you could travel in the opposite, anticlockwise direction, or retrace your steps.

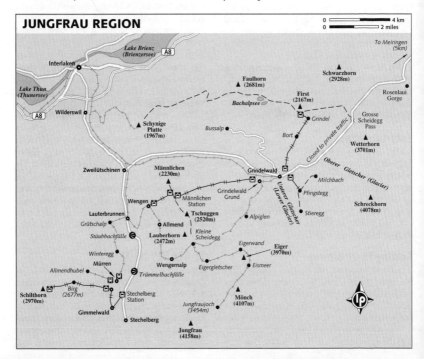

JUNGFRAU REGION

Summit journeys are really worth making only on clear days. Conditions are volatile in the mountains, so it's worth checking webcams – such as the ones on www.jungfraubahn.ch and www.swisspanorama.com – before you leave.

Staying in resorts entitles you to a Gästekarte (Guest Card), good for discounts throughout the entire region. Ask your hotel for the card if one isn't forthcoming.

Getting There & Around

Hourly trains depart for the region from Interlaken Ost station. Sit in the front half of the train for Lauterbrunnen or the back half for Grindelwald. The two sections of the train split up where the two valleys diverge at Zweilütschinen. The rail tracks loop around and meet up again at Kleine Scheidegg at the base of the Eiger, from where the route goes up and back to Jungfraujoch.

Swiss Passes are valid as far as Grindelwald in one direction and Wengen and Mürren in the other; beyond that, holders get a 25% discount. Eurail and InterRail Passes are not valid beyond Interlaken, although they are good for a 25% discount on Jungfrau journeys. The Swiss Half-Fare Card is valid within the entire region.

Jungfraubahnen (Jungfrau Railways; ☎ 033 828 72 33; www.jungfraubahn.ch) offers its own pass, providing six days of unlimited travel throughout the region for Sfr195 (Sfr145 with Swiss Pass, Swiss Card or Half-Fare Card), though you still have to pay Sfr52 from Eigergletscher (just past Kleine Scheidegg) to Jungfraujoch.

Sample fares include the following: Interlaken Ost to Grindelwald Sfr10.20; Grindelwald to Kleine Scheidegg Sfr31; Kleine Scheidegg to Jungfraujoch Sfr107 (return); Kleine Scheidegg to Wengen Sfr23; Wengen to Lauterbrunnen Sfr6.20; and Lauterbrunnen to Interlaken Ost Sfr7. Check out the website for a complete and up-to-date list.

Many of the cable cars close for servicing in late April and late October.

GRINDELWALD

pop 3810 / elevation 1034m

Grindelwald's sublime natural assets are film-set stuff – the chiselled features of Eiger north face, the glinting tongues of Oberer and Unterer glaciers and the ruggedly beautiful Wetterhorn will make you stare, swoon and lunge for your camera. Skiers and hikers

cottoned onto its charms in the late 19th century, which makes it one of Switzerland's oldest resorts. And it has lost none of its appeal over the decades, with archetypal Alpine chalets and verdant pastures set against an Oscar-worthy backdrop.

Orientation & Information

The centre is east of the train station. At either end of the village, Terrassenweg loops north off the main street and takes a scenic, elevated east–west course. Below and south of the main street is the Schwarze Lütschine river.

Postal buses and local buses depart from near the train station, and a post office is nearby.

The **tourist office** (☎ 033 854 12 12; www.grindelwald.ch; Dorfstrasse; ⊙ 8am-noon & 1.30-6pm Mon-Fri, 9am-noon & 1.30-5pm Sat & Sun summer & winter, 8am-noon & 1.30-5pm Mon-Fri, 9am-noon Sat rest of year) in the Sportzentrum hands out brochures and maps. There's an accommodation board with a phone and a coin-operated internet terminal outside. The post office is next to the main train station.

Sights & Activities

The shimmering, slowly melting **Oberer Gletscher** (Upper Glacier; adult/child Sfr6/3; ⊙ 9am-6pm mid-May–Oct) is a 1½-hour hike east from the village, or catch a bus (marked Terrasen Weg–Oberer Gletscher) to Hotel-Restaurant Wetterhorn. Walk 10 minutes from the bus stop, then pant up 890 log stairs to reach a terrace offering dramatic vistas. A new crowd-puller is the vertiginous hanging bridge spanning the gorge.

Turbulent waters carve a path through the craggy **Gletscherschlucht** (Glacier Gorge; admission Sfr7; ⊙ 10am-5pm May-Oct, to 6pm Jul & Aug), a 30-minute walk south of the centre. A footpath weaves through tunnels hacked into cliffs veined with pink and green marble. It's justifiably a popular spot for canyon- and bungee-jumping expeditions.

HIKING

Grindelwald is outstanding hiking territory, criss-crossed with trails that afford bewitching views to massive north faces and glaciated peaks. One of the best day hikes for close-ups of mighty Eiger, Mönch and Jungfrau is the 18km **Kleine Scheidegg** (p67) walk from Grindelwald to Lauterbrunnen. Other high-altitude walks – around Männlichen, First and Pfingstegg – can be reached by taking cable cars up from the village. Some of these areas can just as easily be approached from Wengen or Schynige Platte, so see p182 for details. Anyone craving a challenge can tackle the Schwarzhorn's *via ferrata,* a giddying 5½-hour scramble from First to Grosse Scheidegg.

WINTER SPORTS

Stretching from Oberjoch at 2486m right down to the village, the region of First (see p182) presents a fine mix of cruisy red and challenging black **ski** runs. From Kleine Scheidegg or Männlichen there are long, easy runs back to Grindelwald, with Eiger demanding all the attention. For a crowd-free swoosh, check out the 17km of well-groomed **cross-country skiing** trails in the area. Grindelwald Sports includes the skiing school.

OTHER ACTIVITIES

In the tourist office, **Grindelwald Sports** (☎ 033 854 12 90; www.grindelwaldsports.ch) arranges mountain climbing, canyon jumping, glacier bungee jumping at the Gletscherschlucht and

skydiving. **Paragliding Jungfrau** (☎ 079 779 90 00; www.paragliding-jungfrau.ch) organises jumps from 1200m at First (from Sfr170).

Festivals & Events

In late January, artists get chipping at the **World Snow Festival** to create extraordinary ice sculptures. **SnowpenAir** (www.snowpenair.ch) rocks Kleine Scheidegg in early April with a star-studded concert line-up. **Schwingen** (Swiss Sumo-style wrestling), stone-throwing and other Alpine frivolities enliven Grosse Scheidegg in July, while the 90km **Eiger Bike Challenge** races over hill and dale in August.

Sleeping

Grindelwald is full of character-filled B&Bs and holiday chalets; pick up a list at the tourist office. Nearly everywhere closes in April and from mid-October to mid-December. Local buses and the sports centre swimming pool and ice rink are free with the Guest Card.

CAMPING

Gletscherdorf (☎ 033 853 14 29; www.gletscherdorf.ch; sites per adult/child/tent Sfr7.50/3.50/6-18; ⌛ May-Oct)

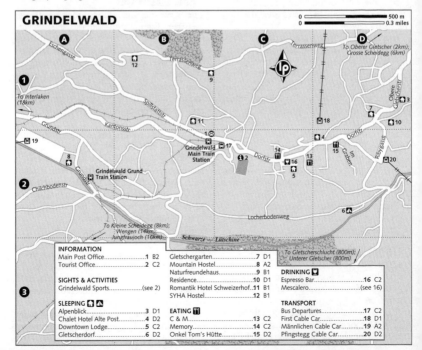

GRINDELWALD

INFORMATION		
Main Post Office	1	B2
Tourist Office	2	C2

SIGHTS & ACTIVITIES		
Grindelwald Sports	(see 2)	

SLEEPING		
Alpenblick	3	D1
Chalet Hotel Alte Post	4	D2
Downtown Lodge	5	C2
Gletscherdorf	6	D2
Gletschergarten	7	D1
Mountain Hostel	8	A2
Naturfreundehaus	9	B1
Residence	10	D1
Romantik Hotel Schweizerhof	11	B1
SYHA Hostel	12	B1

EATING		
C & M	13	C2
Memory	14	C2
Onkel Tom's Hütte	15	D2

DRINKING		
Espresso Bar	16	C2
Mescalero	(see 16)	

TRANSPORT		
Bus Departures	17	C2
First Cable Car	18	D1
Männlichen Cable Car	19	A2
Pfingstegg Cable Car	20	D2

It isn't until you wake up with icicles hanging from your nostrils that you realise why this campsite is called glacier village. Yet despite trapping cold like a deep freeze (pack an expedition sleeping bag), this riverfront campsite near Pfingstegg cable car is among Switzerland's most stunning, with awesome views of Unterer Gletscher and Eiger. Facilities include a common room, laundry and free wi-fi.

HOSTELS

The first two hostels are reached by buses to Bussalp, Terrassenweg and Waldspitz. Services run at least hourly from 9am to 5pm. The 30-minute uphill walk sets off from the road that follows the rail tracks on the northern side. Look for the sign indicating the steep footpath up to the right.

SYHA hostel (☎ 033 853 10 09; www.youthhostel .ch/grindelwald; Terrassenweg; dm Sfr31.50-38.50, d Sfr80, with bathroom Sfr108; ☺ reception 7.30-10am & 4-10pm; 💻) High on a hill with spectacular views, this hostel is spread across a cosy wooden chalet and a modern annexe. As well as large, airy dorms, there's an open fire and a sunny terrace.

our pick Naturfreundehaus (☎ 033 853 13 33; www .naturfreundehaeuser.ch; Terrassenweg; dm/s/d Sfr36/46/72, breakfast Sfr8; ☺ reception closed 1-3pm, closed low season; 💻) Perched above the village, this eco-friendly chalet is a gem. Most folk have a cat or dog, but Vreni and Heinz have Mono, a six-year-old pet trout in the garden pond. Creaking floors lead up to cute pine-panelled rooms with check curtains, including a shoebox single that's apparently Switzerland's smallest. Try an Eiger coffee with amaretto or a homemade mint cordial in the quirky café, downstairs. The garden has wonderful views to Eiger and Wetterhorn.

Downtown Lodge (☎ 033 828 77 30; www.downtown -lodge.ch; Dorfstrasse; dm/d Sfr36/82; ☺ reception 7.30am-noon & 4.30-9.30pm; 💻) Grindelwald's most central digs are modern, clean and welcoming. Dorms are nothing flash, but the facilities are above-par with a bistro, shared kitchen, games room and free internet.

Mountain Hostel (☎ 033 854 38 38; www.mountain hostel.ch; Grundstrasse; dm Sfr37-42, d Sfr 92-102; ☺ reception 4-9pm) Near Männlichen cable-car station, this rambling turquoise complex is an ideal base for sports junkies, with well-kept dorms and a helpful crew. There's a courtyard and a lounge with cable TV and wi-fi.

HOTELS & PENSIONS

Alpenblick (☎ 033 853 11 05; www.alpenblick.info; Obere Gletscherstrasse; dm Sfr48, d Sfr148-190; 🅿) In a quiet corner of town, 10 minutes' stroll from the centre, Alpenblick is a great budget find, with squeaky-clean, pine-filled rooms. Basement dorms are jazzed up with bright duvets. There's free parking, wi-fi, an American-style diner (mains Sfr15 to Sfr19) and a terrace with glacier views. Edi and Vreni ensure everything runs like Swiss clockwork.

Residence (☎ 033 854 55 55; www.residence-grindelwald .ch; Dorfstrasse; s/d Sfr105/180; 🅿 ✂) This homey chalet is tucked away in a serene part of the village with brilliant views to Wetterhorn. Decorated in neutral hues with '70s-style trappings, rooms aren't special but they are spotless. The best rooms have geranium-smothered balconies.

Chalet Hotel Alte Post (☎ 033 853 42 42; www .altepost-grindelwald.ch; Dorfstrasse; s/d from Sfr115/200; 🅿 💻) To be first on the slopes, stay at this quaint chalet next to First lift. Bright and spacious, rooms are decorated in light pine and earthy colours. Chocolates on the pillows are a nice touch. Relax in the whirlpool and sauna or beside the fire in the lounge in winter.

Gletschergarten (☎ 033 853 17 21; www.hotel-gletscher garten.ch; Dorfstrasse; s/d from Sfr120/220; 🅿 ✂ 💻) The sweet Breitenstein family make you feel at home in their rustic timber chalet, brimming with heirlooms from landscape paintings to snapshots of Elsbeth's grandfather who had 12 children (those were the days…). Decked out in pine and flowery fabrics, the rooms have balconies facing Unterer Gletscher at the front and Wetterhorn (best for sunset) at the back.

Romantik Hotel Schweizerhof (☎ 033 854 58 58; www.hotel-schweizerhof.com; Dorfstrasse; s/d/ste with half-board Sfr270/490/690; 🅿 💻 🎿) The granddaddy of Grindelwald, this plush Victorian-era hotel has stylish rooms with gleaming slate-floored bathrooms. The spa is a big draw, with massage jets, treatment rooms, a teeth-chattering ice grotto and a pool with wide-screen mountain vistas. The first-class restaurant uses home-grown vegetables and herbs.

Eating

Onkel Tom's Hütte (☎ 033 853 52 39; Im Graben 4; pizzas Sfr13-33; ☺ 6pm-midnight Thu, noon-midnight Fri-Tue) Tables are at a premium in this incredibly cosy barn-style chalet. Yummy pizzas are prepared fresh in three sizes to suit any appetite. The encyclopaedic wine list flicks from Switzerland to South Africa.

Memory (☎ 033 854 31 31; mains Sfr16-28; Dorfstrasse; 11.30am-10.30pm) Always packed, the Eiger Hotel's unpretentious restaurant rolls out tasty Swiss grub like rösti and fondue. Try to bag a table on the street-facing terrace.

C & M (☎ 033 853 07 10; mains Sfr20-36; 8.30am-11pm Wed-Mon) Just as appetising as the menu are the stupendous views to Unterer Gletscher from this gallery-style café's sunny terrace. Enjoy a salad, coffee and cake, or seasonally inspired dishes like venison stew with dumplings and bilberry-stuffed apple.

Drinking

Full to the gills in winter, the misleadingly named **Espresso Bar** (☎ 033 954 88 88) in the Spinne Hotel draws a boisterous beer-guzzling crowd. It also harbours kitschy Mexican-themed **Mescalero** (admission free; Mon-Sat winter, Thu-Sat summer) with a DJ and occasional live music.

Getting There & Away

See p179 for train fares. Grindelwald is off the A8 from Interlaken. A smaller road continues from the village over the Grosse Scheidegg Pass (1960m). It's closed to private traffic, but from mid-June to early October postal buses (one-way/return Sfr49/95, two hours) travel this scenic route to Meiringen roughly hourly from 7am to 4.30pm.

AROUND GRINDELWALD
First

A cable car zooms up to **First** (☎ 033 828 77 11; one-way/return Sfr31/51), the trailhead for 100km of paths, half of which stay open in winter. From here, you can trudge up to **Faulhorn** (2681m; 2½ hours) via the cobalt Bachalpsee (Lake Bachalp). As you march along the ridge, the unfolding views of the Jungfrau massif are entrancing. Stop for lunch and 360-degree views at Faulhorn. From here, you can either continue on to Schynige Platte (another three hours) and return by train, or you can hike to Bussalp (1800m; 1½ hours) and return by bus to Grindelwald (Sfr20.60).

Other great walks head to Schwarzhorn (three hours), Grosse Scheidegg (1½ hours), Unterer Gletscher (1½ hours) and Grindelwald (2½ hours). Early birds can catch a spectacular sunrise by overnighting in a rustic dorm at **Berggasthaus First** (☎ 033 853 12

84; dm with half-board Sfr79) by the First cable-car summit station.

First has 50km of well-groomed pistes, which are mostly wide, meandering reds suited to intermediates. The south-facing slopes make for interesting skiing through meadows and forests. Freestylers should check out the kickers and rails at **Bärgelegg** or the superpipe at **Schreckfeld** station.

Männlichen

On the ridge dividing the Grindelwald and Lauterbrunnen valleys, Männlichen (2230m) is one of the region's top viewpoints. Europe's longest **cable car** (☎ 033 854 80 80; www.maenn lichen.ch) connects Grindelwald Grund to Männlichen (Sfr31/Sfr51 one-way/return, Sfr31 return 3pm to 5pm). Another cable car comes up the other side of the ridge, from Wengen (Sfr23/Sfr38 one-way/return).

From Männlichen top station, walk 10 minutes up to the crown of the hill to enjoy the view. At the southern end of the ridge are Tschuggen (2520m) and Lauberhorn (2472m), with the 'big three' looming behind. From here, you notice the difference between the two valleys – the broad expanse of the Grindelwald Valley to the left, and the glacier-carved, U-shaped Lauterbrunnen Valley to the right. To the north you can see a stretch of Thunersee.

If you wish to stay overnight, try cosy **Berggasthaus Männlichen** (☎ 033 853 10 68; berg gasthaus@maennlichen.ch; s/d Sfr80/170) in summer. A snow bar lures skiers here in winter. Affording long views across the frosted peaks, the sunny terrace is the perfect spot to kick back with a glühwein.

Männlichen's broad cruising terrain is perfect for skiing in the shadow of Eiger, Mönch and Jungfrau. An alternative for non-skiers is the speedy 45-minute sled run down to **Holenstein**, negotiating steep bumps and hairpin bends.

A classic hike from Männlichen is the scenic **Panoramaweg** to Kleine Scheidegg, which heads south to Honegg, and skirts around the Lauberhorn ridge to reach Rotstöckli and Kleine Scheidegg in 1½ hours.

Pfingstegg

Another cable car rises up to **Pfingstegg** (☎ 033 853 26 26; www.pfingstegg.ch; one-way/return Sfr12/Sfr18; ☺ May-Oct), where short hiking trails lead to Stieregg, near the deeply crevassed Unterer Gletscher. Check to see whether the trail to **Hotel Wetterhorn** (☎ 033 853 12 18; www.grosse -scheidegg.ch) at the base of the Oberer Gletscher (1½ hours) via the Restaurant Milchbach (one hour) is open. Along this, you pass the **Breitlouwina**, a geologically fascinating rock terrace scarred with potholes caused by moving ice.

There's also a summer **bobsled** (adult/child Sfr5/3; ☺ 11am-6pm).

KLEINE SCHEIDEGG

Eiger, Mönch and Jungfrau soar almost 2000m above you at Kleine Scheidegg (2061m), where restaurants huddle around the train station. Most people only stay for a few minutes while changing trains for Jungfraujoch, but it's worth lingering to appreciate the dazzling views, including those to the icing-smooth, fang-shaped peak of Silberhorn (3695m).

Kleine Scheidegg is a terrific base for hiking. There are short, undemanding trails, one hour apiece, to Eigergletscher, down to Wengernalp, and up the Lauberhorn behind the village. These areas become intermediate ski runs from December to April. Alternatively, you can walk the Eiger Trail from Eigergletscher to Alpiglen (2¼ hours).

Basic digs can be found in **Restaurant Bahnhof Röstizzeria** (☎ 033 828 78 28; dm/d Sfr51.50/133, half-board extra Sfr19.50) and the more recently renovated **Restaurant Grindelwaldblick** (☎ 033 855 13 74; dm Sfr40, half-board extra Sfr25; ☺ closed Nov & May), eight minutes' walk towards Grindelwald. Clued-up hikers bed down at **Guesthouse Eigergletscher**

GLIDING GREAT

Not only skiers love the deep powder at First. You can also stomp through the snow on the No 50 trail to Faulhorn in winter. The 2½-hour walk takes in the frozen Bachalpsee and the Jungfrau range in all its wintry glory. But the trail offers more than just a fab view. Faulhorn is the starting point for Europe's longest toboggan run, accessible only on foot. Bring your sled to bump and glide 15km over icy pastures and through glittering woodlands all the way back down to Grindelwald via Bussalp. Nicknamed 'Big Pintenfritz', the track lasts around 1½ hours, depending on how fast you race.

(☎ 033 828 78 66; d/tr with half-board Sfr138/207) to hike the Eiger Trail in the peace of morning.

Rambling, creaky and atmospheric, **Hotel Bellevue des Alpes** (☎ 033 855 12 12; s/d Sfr250/410) is a formerly grand Victorian hotel. It has a world-beating location and a rather macabre history of people using its telescopes to observe mountaineering accidents on the Eiger.

JUNGFRAUJOCH

Sure, everyone else wants to see Jungfraujoch (3454m) and yes, tickets are expensive, but don't let that stop you. It's a once-in-a-lifetime trip that you need to experience firsthand. And there's a reason why two million people a year visit Europe's highest train station. The icy wilderness of swirling glaciers and 4000m turrets that unfolds at the col is truly enchanting.

The last stage of the train journey from Kleine Scheidegg burrows through the heart of Eiger before arriving at the sci-fi Sphinx meteorological station. Opened in 1912, the tunnel took 3000 men 16 years to drill. Along the way, you stop at Eigerwand and Eismeer, where panoramic windows offer tantalising glimpses across rivers of crevassed ice.

Good weather is essential for this journey; check on www.jungfrau.ch or call ☎ 033 828 79 31. Don't forget to take warm clothing, sunglasses and sunscreen, as there's snow and glare up here all year. Within the Sphinx weather station, where trains disgorge passengers, there's an ice palace gallery of otherworldly sculptures, restaurants, indoor viewpoints and a souvenir shop, where you can purchase your very own chunk of Eiger

---

THE HILLS ARE ALIVE WITH THE SOUND OF HINDI

Confused by the curry buffet and Shahrukh Khan snapshots at Jungfraujoch? The answer is simple really. India's huge movie industry just adores a mountain, a waterfall or a lake as the backdrop to its shamelessly escapist song-and-dance sequences. So when the traditional location of Kashmir became too risky for Bollywood film crews to venture into, Switzerland began acting as its stand-in.

As a result, more Bollywood movies are now shot here than in any other country, and thousands of loyal fans are following in their movie idols' footsteps. Since *Dilwale Dulhania Le Jayenge* was filmed here in 1995, dozens of other Indian blockbusters have followed, and the number of Indian tourists to Switzerland has more than doubled. Huge tour groups arrive in the pre-monsoon months of May and June to visit their favourite locations, including Gstaad (p196), Engelberg/Titlis (p257) and Geneva (p85).

---

to grace the mantelpiece. Somehow not *quite* as impressive as the mountain itself.

Outside there are magical vistas of the serpentine, moraine-streaked 23km tongue of the **Aletsch Glacier** (see p168), the longest glacier in the European Alps and a Unesco World Heritage site. The views across sparkly peaks, stretching as far as the Black Forest in Germany, will have you burning up the pixels in your digicam.

When you tire (as if!) of the view, you can dash downhill on a snow disc (free), zip across the frozen plateau on a flying fox (Sfr20), enjoy a bit of tame skiing or boarding (Sfr33), drive a team of Greenland dogs (see opposite) or do your best Tiger-Woods-in-moon-boots impersonation with a round of glacier golf. It isn't cheap at Sfr10 a shot, but get a hole-in-one and you win the Sfr100,000 jackpot. Mysteriously, nobody has won yet.

If you cross the glacier along the prepared path, in 50 minutes you reach the **Mönchsjochhütte** (☎ 033 971 34 72; ☻ mid-Mar–mid-Oct) at 3650m. Here you'll share your dinner table and dorm with hardcore rock climbers, psyching themselves up to tackle Eiger or Mönch. It's worth tumbling out of your bunk at dawn to catch sunrise.

From Interlaken Ost, the journey time is 2½ hours each way and the return fare is Sfr177.80 (Swiss Pass/Eurail Sfr133). The last train back is at 5.50pm in summer and 4.40pm in winter. However, there's a cheaper 'good morning' ticket of Sfr153.80 (Swiss/Eurail Pass discounts available) if you take the first train (6am from Interlaken Ost) and leave the summit by 12.30pm. From 1 November to 30 April the reduction is valid for both the 6am and 7.05am trains, and the 12.30pm restriction doesn't apply.

Getting these early trains is easier if you start from deeper in the region. Stay overnight at Kleine Scheidegg to take the excursion-fare train at 7.35am in summer and at 7.35am or 8.30am in winter. From here, the 'good morning' return is Sfr83, instead of Sfr107. The farthest you can walk is up to Eigergletscher (2320m), which saves you only Sfr7.60/12.60 one-way/return from Kleine Scheidegg.

Even the ordinary return ticket to Jungfraujoch is valid for one month, so you can use that ticket to form the backbone of your trip, venturing as far as Grindelwald and stopping for a few days' hiking, before moving on to Kleine Scheidegg, Jungfraujoch, Wengen and Lauterbrunnen.

LAUTERBRUNNEN
pop 2480 / elevation 796m

Lauterbrunnen's wispy Staubbach Falls (Staubbachfall) inspired both Goethe and Lord Byron to pen poems to their ethereal beauty. Today Lauterbrunnen attracts a less highfalutin crowd. Laid-back and full of unpretentious lodgings, the town is a great base for nature-lovers wishing to hike or climb. It is also a magnet to thrill-seeking base-jumpers.

The **tourist office** (☎ 033 856 85 68; www.myjung frau.ch; ☻ 9am-noon & 1-6pm daily May-Sep, 9am-noon & 1-6pm Mon-Fri rest of year) is opposite the train station, while the post office, bank, most hotels and sights are to the left of the station (as you face the tourist office).

If you're travelling to the car-free resorts of Wengen and Mürren, there's a multistorey **car park** (☎ 033 828 71 11; www.jungfraubahn.ch; per day/week Sfr12/65) by the station, but it's advisable to book ahead. There is also an open-air car park by the Stechelberg cable-car station, charging Sfr5 for a day.

Sights & Activities

Especially in the early-morning light, it's easy to see how the vaporous, 300m-high **Staubbach Falls** (admission free; ☺ 8am-8pm Jun-Oct) captivated prominent writers with its threads of spray floating down the cliffside. What appears to be ultra-fine mist from a distance, however, becomes a torrent when you walk behind the falls. Be prepared to get wet.

The **Trümmelbachfälle** (☎ 033 855 32 32; www .truemmelbach.ch; adult/child Sfr11/4; ☺ 9am-5pm Apr-Nov, 8.30am-6pm Jul & Aug) are more of a bang-crash spectacle. Inside the mountain, up to 20,000L of water per second corkscrews through ravines and potholes shaped by the swirling waters. The 10 falls drain from 24 sq km of Alpine glaciers and snow deposits. A bus (Sfr3.40) from the train station takes you to the falls, which are along the valley floor towards Stechelberg. Take a raincoat, as you get quite damp – making this an ideal excursion in poor weather.

The valley floor is also good for **cross-country skiing** during the winter.

Sleeping

Camping Jungfrau (☎ 033 856 20 10; www.camping-jung frau.ch; sites per adult/tent/car Sfr11.60/10/3.50, dm Sfr27-30; ☺ reception 8am-noon & 2.30-6.30pm winter, 7am-noon & 3-8pm summer; 🖳) This Rolls Royce of a campsite also offers cosy dorms and huts for those craving more comfort. The top-notch facilities include a kitchen, kiosk, bike rental and wi-fi. There's even a dog shower for messy pups! It's a few minutes' walk south of the centre, right near the Staubbach Falls.

Valley Hostel (☎ 033 855 20 08; www.valleyhostel.ch; dm/tw/d Sfr25/60/70; ☺ reception 8am-noon & 3-10pm; 🅿 🖳) Flying the Korean flag from the back garden, this chilled hostel has an open-plan kitchen, a garden with waterfall views, a laundry, free wi-fi and a cat, Tiggy. Most of the spacious, pine-clad dorms have balconies. The chirpy team can help organise activities.

Gästehaus im Rohr (☎ 033 855 21 82; r per person Sfr27) Ablaze with scarlet geraniums in summer, this 400-year-old chalet is a bargain. Creaky floorboards and small windows add to its cosy, old-world charm. The '70s-style rooms are humble but spotless, and there's a huge communal balcony overlooking the falls.

Hotel Staubbach (☎ 033 855 54 54; www.staubbach .com; s/d/tr/f Sfr110/150/180/250, s/d without bathroom from Sfr70/90; 🖳) Nothing is too much trouble for the kindly owners of this grand old hotel. The bright rooms with downy duvets are immaculately kept; the best have balconies with Staubbach Falls views. There's a sociable

---

THOMAS KERNEN, MUSHER AND HUSKY BREEDER

Yelps and howls resonate across the blindingly white frozen plain at Jungfraujoch. The Greenland dogs (a husky-like breed) are eager to be off and tug frantically at their chains. Before they dash, musher and sled-dog racing world champion Thomas Kernen takes time to answer a few questions.

How long have the Greenland dogs been here? The first were brought over from Greenland about 100 years ago to deliver provisions to Eigergletscher and prepare the pistes, and then later for sledge rides on the Aletsch Glacier. We now offer rides at Jungfraujoch in summer and Eigergletscher in winter; a spin costs Sfr8 for adults and Sfr5 for children.

What is your role? Leader of the pack, I guess [laughs], as I feed and exercise the dogs. Snow conditions are great up here, but the sun is more powerful than in Nordic countries, so I have to ensure they don't get sunburn or blisters by providing shade in igloos or under parasols. Even if it's too warm for sled rides, visitors can still stroke and photograph the Greenland dogs in the Sphinx Hall.

How do you feel when you race with the Greenland dogs? Exhilarated. I bought my first Greenland dog seven years ago. Then one became two, two four, four 12… I gradually built up stamina and speed and won the world championships in 2005 and 2006 with these dogs. The real reward for me was knowing that I had done my job well, by treating the dogs fairly and responding to their needs instinctively.

Any tips for visitors to Jungfraujoch? Autumn is my favourite season, as there are fewer tourists and better views because the weather is clearer. To really get a feel for the area, it's definitely worth staying overnight at Mönchsjochhütte. Visitors should remember to dress warmly, too. It can be 30°C in Interlaken yet 0°C up here.

vibe in the lounge with free coffee and a kids' play area.

Eating & Drinking

Airtime (☎ 033 855 15 15; www.airtime.ch; 🕙 9am-8pm summer, 9am-noon & 4-8pm winter; 🖳) Inspired by their travels in New Zealand, Daniela and Beni have set up this funky café, book exchange, laundry and extreme sports agency. Munch homemade pies or sip hot chocolate as you check your email (Sfr12 per hour) or crack the spine on a novel. You can book adrenalin-fuelled pursuits like ice climbing, canyoning and bungee jumping here.

Hotel Oberland (☎ 033 855 12 41; mains Sfr16.50-36) The street-facing terrace at this traditional haunt is always humming. On the menu: Swiss and international favourites from fondue to pizza, vegetable curry and hybrid dishes like Indian-style rösti.

Hotel Horner (☎ 033 855 16 73; 🖳) Base-jumpers tell hair-raising parachute tales at this buzzy pub, as they come back down to earth over a pint or four. The vibe gets clubbier as the night wears on. Internet costs Sfr12 per hour (15 minutes are free when you buy a drink).

WENGEN

pop 1330 / elevation 1274m

Photogenically poised on a mountain ledge, Wengen's 'celestial views' have lured Brits here since Edwardian times. The fact you can only reach this chocolate-box village by train gives it romantic appeal. From the bench in front of the church at dusk, the vista takes on watercolour dreaminess, peering over to the misty Staubbach Falls, down to the Lauterbrunnen Valley and up to glacier-capped giants of the Jungfrau massif. In winter, Wengen morphs into a ski resort with a low-key, family-friendly feel.

The **tourist office** (☎ 033 855 14 14; www.myjung frau.ch; 🕙 9am-6pm daily, closed Sat & Sun Nov & Mar-Apr) is minutes from the train station, taking a left at Hotel Silberhorn and continuing 100m farther on. Next door is the **post office**. Internet access is available a few steps along, at **Rock's Bar**.

The highlight in Wengen's calendar is the world-famous **Lauberhorn downhill ski race** in late January, where pros reach speeds of up to 160kmph. Mere mortals can pound powder by taking the cable car to Männlichen or train to Allmend, Wengernalp or Kleine Scheidegg. Skiing is mostly cruisy blues and reds, though experts can brave exhilarating black runs at Lauberhorn and the aptly named 'Oh God'. There's trickier off-piste terrain, such as the legendary White Hare, at the foot of the daunting Eiger north face.

The same areas are excellent for hiking in the summer (see p182 for details on walking from Männlichen). Some 20km of paths stay open in winter too. The hour-long forest trail down to Lauterbrunnen is a beauty.

Sleeping

Expect summer rates to be roughly 30% cheaper than those quoted below. The tourist office has a list of holiday apartments in the area.

Hotel Bären (☎ 033 855 14 19; www.baeren-wengen.ch; s/d from Sfr90/180; 🖳) Loop back under the rail track and head down the hill to this snug log chalet with bright, if compact, rooms. The affable Brunner family serves a hearty breakfast and the extra Sfr20 for half-board is incredible value. Free internet is another bonus.

Hotel Berghaus (☎ 033 855 21 51; www.berghaus -wengen.ch; s/d from Sfr135/270) Sidling up to the forest, this family-run chalet is a five-minute toddle from the village centre. Rooms are light, spacious and pin-drop peaceful – ask for a south-facing one for dreamy Jungfrau views. Call ahead and they'll pick you up from the train station.

Hotel Caprice (☎ 033 856 06 06; www.caprice -wengen.ch; d Sfr430; 🖳) If you're looking for design-oriented luxury in the Jungfrau mountains, this boutique gem delivers with discreet service and authentically French cuisine. Don't be fooled by its cute Alpine trappings; inside it exudes Scandinavian-style simplicity with chocolate-cream colours, slick rooms and a lounge with an open fire.

Eating & Drinking

Santos (☎ 078 67 97 445; snacks Sfr6-9; 🕙 10am-midnight) Popular with ravenous skiers coming down from the slopes, this Portuguese TV-and-tiles place is the real deal. Mrs Santos whips up burgers, calamari, sandwiches and divine *pastéis de nata* (custard tarts).

Café Gruebi (☎ 033 855 58 55; snacks & mains Sfr7-16; 🕙 8.30am-6pm Mon-Sat, 1-8pm Sun) Run by a husband-and-wife team, Gruebi offers cheap eats like rösti and goulash. The yummy homemade cakes are baked almost daily by the…husband.

Da Sina (☎ 033 855 31 72; pizzas Sfr16-25, mains Sfr14-42; 🕑 11.30am-11.30pm high season, 11.30am-2pm & 6-11.30pm rest of year) This inviting pizzeria is filled with cosy nooks, copper pans and candlelight. DJs or karaoke notch up the decibels in the adjacent pub, perennially popular with the après-ski crowd.

Hotel Bären (☎ 033 855 14 19; mains Sfr18-42; 🕑 lunch & dinner Tue-Sat, dinner Sun & Mon) This family-run hotel puts a creative, international spin on Swiss dishes, and its restaurant is well worth visiting, even if you're not staying.

Crystal Bar (Haus Crystal; 🕑 8am-2am) Pumping tunes and occasionally hosting gigs, this relaxed bar draws fun-loving après-ski types. It's opposite Männlichen cable car.

STECHELBERG
pop 260 / elevation 922m

To witness the drama of the waterfall-gone-mad Lauterbrunnen Valley, where a staggering 72 falls cascade over perpendicular walls of rock, make for Stechelberg. The valley takes its name from *lauter* (clear) and *Brunnen* (spring). To see the cataracts at their thundering best, visit in spring when the snow thaws or after heavy rain. Though long a bolthole for savvy hikers, this tiny village still feels like a well-kept secret.

Blissfully rural **Alpenhof Stechelberg** (☎ 033 855 12 02; www.alpenhof-stechelberg.ch; r per person Sfr28; 🕑 closed Nov) harbours light-filled, neat-and-tidy rooms that offer fantastic value for your franc. A hearty breakfast with local dairy products is served for Sfr12.

MÜRREN
pop 430 / elevation 1650m

Arriving on a clear evening, as the train from Grütschalp floats along the horizontal ridge towards Mürren, the peaks across the valley feel so close that you could reach out and touch them. And that's when you'll think you've died and gone to Heidi heaven. With its low-slung wooden chalets and spellbinding views of Eiger, Mönch and Jungfrau, car-free Mürren is storybook Switzerland.

The **tourist office** (☎ 033 856 86 86; www.myjung frau.ch; 🕑 8.30am-7pm Mon-Sat, to 8pm Thu, 8.30am-6pm Sun high season, 8.30am-7pm Mon-Sat, 8.30am-5pm Sun shoulder seasons, 8.30am-noon & 1-5pm Mon-Fri low season) is in the sports centre.

In summer, the **Allmendhubel funicular** (one-way/return Sfr12/7.40) takes you above Mürren to a panoramic restaurant. From here, you can set out on many walks, including the famous **Northface Trail** (1½ hours), via Schiltalp to the west, leading through wildflower-strewn meadows with views to the glaciers and waterfalls of the Lauterbrunnen Valley and the monstrous Eiger north face – bring binoculars to spy intrepid climbers. There's also a kid-friendly **Adventure Trail** (one hour).

In winter, there are 53km of prepared ski runs nearby, mostly suited to intermediates, and a **ski school** (☎ 033 855 12 47). Mürren is famous for its hell-for-leather **Inferno Run** down from Schilthorn in late January. Daredevils have been competing in the race since 1928 and today the course attracts nearly 2000 amateur skiers. It's also the reason for all the devilish souvenirs.

Sleeping & Eating

Eiger Guesthouse (☎ 033 856 54 60; www.eigerguest house.com; dm Sfr40-70, d without/with bathroom from Sfr120/160; 💻) Run by a fun-loving, on-the-ball Swiss–Scottish couple, this abode offers great value. Besides clean, spruced-up rooms, you get a generous buffet breakfast. The pub downstairs serves tasty grub and a peerless selection of single malts.

Hotel Jungfrau (☎ 033 856 64 64; www.hotel jungfrau.ch; s Sfr88-110, d Sfr270-300; 💻) Set above Mürren and overlooking the nursery slopes, this welcoming family-run hotel dates to 1894. Despite '70s traces, rooms are tastefully done in warm hues; south-facing ones have Jungfrau views. Downstairs there's a beamed lounge with an open fire.

Hotel Alpenruh (☎ 033 856 88 00; www.alpenruh -muerren.ch; s/d Sfr145/270; ❌ 💻) Lots of loving detail has gone into this much-lauded chalet. Grimacing masks to ward off evil spirits and knick-knacks enliven the place, while the light-flooded rooms feature lots of chunky pine. Guests praise the service, food and unbeatable views to Jungfrau massif.

Hotel Eiger (☎ 033 856 54 54; www.hoteleiger.com; s/d Sfr198/325; ❌ 💻 🐾) Sleek and contemporary, this hotel has plush rooms, first-rate service and amazing views from its (phew!) 32°C swimming pool – the picture-windows frame Eiger, Mönch and Jungfrau.

Tham's (☎ 033 856 01 10; mains Sfr15-28; 🕑 dinner) Tham's serves Thai and other Asian dishes cooked by a former five-star chef who's literally taken to the hills to escape the rat race. The Sichuan beef and Singapore fried noodles are authentically spicy.

CLIFFHANGER

Feel like an adventure? Little beats Mürren's vertigo-inducing **Klettersteig** (☎ 033 856 86 86; www.klettersteig-muerren.ch; ☿ mid-Jun–Oct). Sure to get the adrenalin pumping, this high-altitude 2.2km *via ferrata* is one of Switzerland's most astonishing, wriggling across breathtakingly steep limestone cliffs to Gimmelwald. Equipped with harness, helmet and karabiner, you can flirt with mountaineering on ladders that snake across the precipices and bring you to a zip-line – whoa there goes Eiger! – and an 80m-high suspension bridge. Equipment can be rented for Sfr20 per day from Intersport opposite the tourist office. Or you can go with a guide for Sfr95 by contacting **Bergsteigen für Jedermann** (☎ 033 821 61 00; www.be-je.ch).

Restaurant La Grotte (☎ 033 855 18 26; mains Sfr16.50-35; ☿ 11am-2pm & 5-9pm) Brimming with cowbells, cauldrons and Alpine props, this kitsch-meets-rustic mock cave of a restaurant is touristy but fun. Fondues and flambées are good bets.

GIMMELWALD
pop 110 / elevation 1370m
If you think Mürren is cute, wait until you see Gimmelwald. This pipsqueak of a village has long been a hideaway for hikers and adventurers tiptoeing away from the crowds. The secret is out, though, and this mountainside village is swiftly becoming known for its drop-dead-gorgeous scenery, rural authenticity and sense of calm.

The surrounding hiking trails include one down from Mürren (30 to 40 minutes) and one up from Stechelberg (1¼ hours). Cable cars are also an option (Mürren or Stechelberg Sfr5.60).

Sleeping & Eating
Pension Berggeist (☎ 033 855 17 30; www.berggeist.ch; dm/d Sfr15/40; ☿ reception 9am-10pm) Even the owners describe this as simple and rustic, but few want more in back-to-nature Gimmelwald. Rooms are a bargain, views are priceless and sandwiches are sold by the centimetre to please every pocket. You can book all kinds of activities here, from skydiving to llama trekking.

Mountain Hostel (☎ 033 855 17 04; www.mountain hostel.com; dm Sfr20; ☿ Apr-Nov, reception 8.30am-noon & 6-11pm; ▣) A backpacking legend, this basic, low-ceilinged hostel has a sociable vibe. After a sweaty day's hiking, there's nothing like a soak in the outdoor whirlpool with stunning mountain views.

ourpick Esther's Guest House (☎ 033 855 54 88; www.esthersguesthouse.ch; s/d Sfr45/100, apt Sfr140-220; ▣) Esther runs this charming B&B with love. Drenched with piny light, the rooms are spotless, while the apartments are ideal for families. The attic room is a favourite with its slanted roof and star-gazing window. For an extra Sfr15, you'll be served a delicious breakfast of homemade bread, cheese and yoghurt. There's also a tiny shop by the entrance where you can stock up on local goodies like Gimmelwald salami and Stechelberg honey.

SCHILTHORN
There's a tremendous 360-degree panorama from the 2970m **Schilthorn** (www.schilthorn.ch). On a clear day, you can see from Titlis around to Mont Blanc, and across to the German Black Forest. Yet some visitors seem more preoccupied with practising their delivery of the line, 'The name's Bond, James Bond', than taking in the 200 or so peaks. That's because a few scenes from *On Her Majesty's Secret Service* were shot here in 1968–69 – as the fairly tacky **Touristorama** below the **Piz Gloria** revolving restaurant will remind you.

From Interlaken, take a Sfr116 excursion trip (Half-Fare Card and Eurail Pass 50% off, Swiss Pass 65% off) going to Lauterbrunnen, Grütschalp, Mürren, Schilthorn and returning through Stechelberg to Interlaken. A return from Lauterbrunnen (via Grütschalp) and Mürren costs Sfr100, while the return journey via the Stechelberg cable car costs Sfr91.80. A return from Mürren is Sfr71.40. Ask about discounts for early-morning trips.

En route from Mürren, the cable car goes through the Birg station (2677m), where you can stop to take in marvellous views.

THE LAKES

Anyone who travels to Interlaken for the first time from Bern will never forget the moment they clap eyes on Thunersee (Lake Thun). As the train loops past pastures and tidy villages on the low southern shore, some people literally gasp at the sight of the Alps rearing above the petrol-blue waters.

Flanking Interlaken to the east Brienzersee (Lake Brienz) has just as many cameras snapping with its surreal turquoise colour and rippling mountains. The lake is widely touted as Switzerland's cleanest (quite some feat), so if you've ever fancied swimming in mineral water, this comes pretty close.

Steamers ply both lakes from late May to mid-September. There are no winter services on Brienzersee, whereas special cruises continue on Thunersee. For more information contact **BLS** (☎ 033 334 52 11; www.bls.ch). A day pass valid for both lakes costs Sfr55 (children half-price). Eurail Passes, the Regional Pass and the Swiss Pass are valid on all boats, and InterRail and the Swiss Half-Fare Card get 50% off.

THUN

pop 41,650 / elevation 559m

Ringed by mountains, hugging the banks of the Aare River and squatting beneath a castle that looks every bit the Disney blueprint with its dreaming turrets, Thun (pronounced toon) is a medieval town full of youthful spirit. Hedonistic crowds sun themselves at waterfront pavement cafés and kooky shops fill the unusual arcades. Despite these charms, most Swiss associate it more readily with football. Having unexpectedly felled several European Goliaths in recent years, minnows FC Thun have won a place in the nation's heart.

Orientation

The town sits on the northern tip of its namesake lake, along the Aare River. The river separates the train station (which has bike rental and money-exchange counters) from the medieval core around the castle. A sliver of land midstream, linked to both banks by footpaths and roads, has the pedestrianised street Bälliz running along it.

Information

Post office (Bahnhofplatz; ◷ 7.30am-7pm Mon-Fri, 8am-noon Sat) Opposite the train station.

Manor (☎ 033 227 36 99; Bahnhofstrasse 3; ◷ 9am-6.30pm Mon-Fri, 9am-9pm Thu, 8am-4pm Sat) Internet access is available on the 1st floor of this supermarket.

Tourist office (☎ 033 225 90 00; www.thunersee.ch; Bahnhofplatz; ◷ 9am-6pm Mon-Fri, 9am-noon & 1-4pm

Sat Jul & Aug, 9am-noon & 1-6.30pm Mon-Fri, 9am-noon Sat rest of year)

Sights & Activities

It's a pleasure simply to wander Thun's attractive riverfront, plazas and lanes punctuated by 15th- and 16th-century townhouses in candy colours.

One unmissable street is the split-level, cobblestone **Obere Hauptgasse**, hiding quirky shops selling everything from spices to jewellery to Moroccan *babouches* (slippers). A pedestrian footpath runs along the top of these shops' roofs.

Hogging the limelight, the 12th-century hilltop **Schloss Thun** is pure fairy-tale stuff with its red turrets, soaring towers and Alpine backdrop. It once belonged to Duke Berchtold V of the powerful Zähringen family. Now it houses a **historical museum** (☎ 033 223 20 01; www.schlossthun.ch; adult/under 6yr/6-16yr/student Sfr7/ free/2/5; ◷ 10am-5pm daily Apr-Oct, 1-4pm Sun Nov-Jan, 1-4pm daily Feb & Mar), showcasing prehistoric and Roman relics, tapestries, majolica and plenty of shining armour.

Set in lakefront gardens, rosy **Schloss Schadau** is now a swish restaurant and bar. Should you wish to pedal out here, free city bikes are available for hire from **Thun Rollt** (Aarefeldstrasse; passport & deposit of Sfr20; ◷ 7.30am-9.30pm May-Oct).

Sleeping & Eating

Herberge zur Schadau (☎ 033 222 52 22; www.herberge .ch; Seestrasse 22; dm Sfr39; ◷ check-in 5-7pm) You can't miss this sky-blue hostel, a five-minute stroll along the riverfront south of the train station. The pine-walled dorms are basic but clean.

Hotel zu Metzgern (☎ 033 222 21 41; Untere Hauptgasse 2; s/d without bathroom Sfr55/110) Sitting on Thun's prettiest square is this 700-year-old guild house. Bold artworks glam up the well-kept, parquet-floored rooms. Downstairs the chef uses local organic ingredients to prepare dishes like lavender-rosemary marinated lamb shanks and vegetable dhal (mains Sfr27 to Sfr44).

Hotel Emmental (☎ 033 222 01 20; Bernstrasse 2; s/d Sfr90/180) This Swiss farmhouse of sorts catches your eye with its ornately carved eaves. Though furnishings and bathrooms are a '70s flashback, rooms are airy and spacious and not too much noise floats up from the bar below.

Kaffee und Kuchen (☎ 079 79 254 02; Obere Hauptgasse 34; cakes & snacks Sfr5-12; ◷ 8am-10.30pm Tue-Wed,

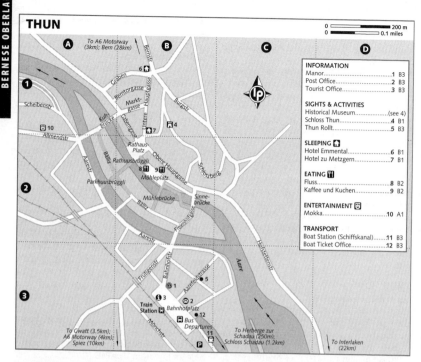

THUN

INFORMATION
Manor...1 B3
Post Office....................................2 B3
Tourist Office................................3 B3

SIGHTS & ACTIVITIES
Historical Museum......................(see 4)
Schloss Thun................................4 B1
Thun Rollt....................................5 B3

SLEEPING
Hotel Emmental...........................6 B1
Hotel zu Metzgern.......................7 B1

EATING
Fluss...8 B2
Kaffee und Kuchen.......................9 B2

ENTERTAINMENT
Mokka...10 A1

TRANSPORT
Boat Station (Schiffskanal).........11 B3
Boat Ticket Office........................12 B3

8am-midnight Thu-Sat, 10am-6pm Sun) Art-slung walls and funky jazz give this candlelit vaulted cellar a Boho vibe. Gabrielle's homemade *Kuchen* prompt squeals of delight. Gorge on nutty brownies or rich white-chocolate cake. The atmosphere invites lazy days spent reading papers, guzzling coffee and lingering over brunch.

Fluss (☎ 033 222 01 10; Mühleplatz 9; mains Sfr18-49; ⏰ 11am-12.30am, closed Sun & Mon winter) This uberhip glass-walled lounge bar attracts trendy types who come for the beautifully prepared sushi, sashimi and grill specialities. The Med-style waterfront deck is perfect for sundowners and people-watching.

Entertainment
Each Thursday in July and August there are free folklore performances on Rathausplatz. Thun's most famous club is **Mokka** (www.mokka .ch, in German; Allmendstrasse 14), with a line-up of top DJs, gigs and festivals.

Getting There & Away
Thun is on the main north–south train route from Frankfurt to Milan and beyond. From

Interlaken West, Thun is Sfr14.80 each way by train, Sfr33 by boat. Thun is on the A6 freeway, which runs from Spiez north to Bern.

SPIEZ
pop 12,410 / elevation 628m
Hunched around a horseshoe-shaped bay, with a medieval castle rising above tumble-down vineyards, the oft-overlooked town of Spiez makes a great escape. The vibe is low-key but the setting magical, with views to conical Niesen (2362m) and a fjord-like slither of the lake. Its vines yield quaffable Riesling and Sylvaner wines.

Orientation & Information
The **tourist office** (☎ 033 655 90 90; www.thunersee.ch; ⏰ 8am-6pm Mon-Fri, 9am-noon & 2-6pm Sat summer, 8am-noon & 2-6pm Mon-Fri winter) is outside the train station. It is open shorter hours in the shoulder seasons. Seestrasse, the main street, is down to the left, and leads to the castle (15 minutes).

Sights & Activities
Turreted **Schloss Spiez** (☎ 033 654 15 06; adult/child Sfr7/2; ⏰ 2-5pm Mon, 10am-5pm Tue-Sun Easter–mid-Oct,

10am-6pm Jul–mid-Sep) is smothered in oil paintings of its former masters, the influential von Bubenburg and von Erlach families. But it's the view that will grab you, whether from the lofty tower (which also sports 13th-century graffiti) or the banqueting hall.

Nearby sits the **Heimat und Rebbaumuseum** (admission free; ☽ 2-5pm Wed, Sat & Sun May-Oct), an 18th-century chalet with exhibits on wine cultivation. The best time to actually taste local tipples is at the **Läset-Fescht** wine festival in late September.

Freibad Spiez (☎ 033 654 15 76; adult/child Sfr6/3; ☽ 7.30am-8pm mid-May–Aug, 8am-7pm Sep) attracts sun-worshipping locals and families who come to frolic in the lake or swim laps in the Olympic-sized swimming pool. It has volleyball and tennis courts, minigolf and – wait for it – the longest waterslide in the Bernese Oberland.

Sleeping & Eating

Hotel Bellevue (☎ 033 654 84 64; www.bellevue-spiez .ch; Seestrasse 36; s/d Sfr85/150; **P**) The '70s-style rooms at this hotel won't bowl you over but they are adequate and some have fab lake views. The restaurant serves tasty homemade grub.

Strandhotel Belvédère (☎ 033 655 66 66; www .belvedere-spiez.ch; Schachenstrasse; s/d from Sfr130/270; ☽ Mar-Jan; **P** 🖳 🐾) Whisking you back 100 years, the chandelier-lit public areas at this genteel hotel exude art-nouveau flair. Some rooms overdo the Laura Ashley–style pastels and florals but they are comfy, especially those with lake-facing balconies. To justify the price tag, there's a spa and a Gault Millau–rated restaurant (mains Sfr39 to Sfr55).

You'll find many, rather ordinary, pizza and pasta places located around the boat station.

Getting There & Away

From Interlaken West, Spiez is Sfr9.60 each way by train. By boat it's Sfr16.20 from Thun and Sfr21 from Interlaken West.

LAKE THUN
Castles & Museums

For a right royal day out, the grand castles and palaces dotted around Thunersee (Lake Thun) can easily be reached boat.

Schloss Oberhofen (☎ 033 243 12 35; Oberhofen; adult/child Sfr7/2; ☽ 2-5pm Mon, 10am-5pm Tue-Sun mid-May–mid-Oct) was wrested from Habsburg control after the Battle of Sempach (1386) and now traces Bernese life from the 16th to the 19th centuries. A spin takes in the medieval chapel, ornate Napoleonic drawing room and Turkish smoking room. You can almost picture aristocrats swanning around its manicured English landscaped **gardens** (admission free; ☽ 10am-dusk mid-Mar–mid-Nov), bristling with exotic foliage.

Oberhofen is 25 minutes by boat from Thun (services approximately hourly), or you can take a bus (14 minutes, every quarter hour).

The plaything of a Prussian baron, silver-turreted **Schloss Hünegg** (☎ 033 243 19 82; Staaststrasse 52, Hilterfingen; adult/under 6yr/6-16yr Sfr8/free/3; ☽ 2-5pm Mon-Sat & 11am-5pm Sun mid-May–mid-Oct) is a feast of art-nouveau and neo-Renaissance styles, with fabulous 19th-century bathrooms and stuccoed salons.

Water Sports

When the mercury rises, Thunersee lures water babies with splashy activities from swimming and messing around in boats to scuba diving and sailing. **Wakeadventure** (☎ 078 635 88 33; Gunten) arranges windsurfing, waterskiing and wakeboarding, plus light-hearted fun with ringos, banana boats and sumo tubes. Thun tourist office has a complete list of centres and schools in its *Thunersee* brochure, or see www.thunersee.ch.

Camping Gwatt (☎ 033 336 40 67; camping .gwatt@tcs.ch; Gwattstrasse 103; sites per adult/child/tent Sfr8.40/4.20/10.50, Modulhotel r per person Sfr65-80; ☽ May-Oct) offers lakefront camping and top facilities including a restaurant, shop and wi-fi. For a unique snooze, check out the bizarre Modulhotel, five giant tubes kitted out with bunk beds.

BRIENZ
pop 2980 / elevation 566m

Quaint and calm, Brienz peers across the exquisitely turquoise waters of its namesake lake to rugged mountains and thick forests beyond. The deeply traditional village has a stuck-in-time feel with its tooting steam train and wood-carving workshops. When you've had your nostalgia fill, explore worthy nearby attractions such as the Freilichtmuseum Ballenberg and Giessbach Falls.

Orientation & Information

The train station, boat station, Rothorn Bahn and post office all huddle in the compact

---

BUNKER MENTALITY

Ever wondered why the radio plays on deep in the heart of a tunnel? What lies above the surface in Switzerland is only half the story. Riddled with more holes than an Emmental cheese, this country is full of subterranean surprises, including the formerly top-secret bunkers at **Faulensee** (☎ 033 654 25 07; artfort@bluewin.ch; adult/child Sfr9/5; ☼ 2-5pm 1st Sat of month Apr-Oct) built to house troops defending Thun, Spiez and the Lötschberg railway. During summer, they're open to the public once a month. Cleverly disguised as farmhouses, the entrances to the bunkers are guarded by cannons and connected by underground tunnels in which you'll find offices, laboratories, kitchens and cramped sleeping quarters. Tours last 1½ to two hours, and you'll need warm clothing and sturdy shoes. To ask about English explanations, call or email ahead.

Faulensee can be reached by bus from Spiez train station and from Interlaken West by boat (Sfr21/36 one-way/return).

---

centre. The **tourist office** (☎ 033 952 80 80; www.alpenregion.ch; ☼ 8am-6pm daily mid-Jun–Oct, 8am-noon & 2-6pm Mon-Fri Nov–mid-Jun) is in the train station.

Sights & Activities

The **Rothorn Bahn** (☎ 033 952 22 22; www.brienz-rothorn-bahn.ch; one-way/return Sfr48/74, 50% discount with Swiss Pass; ☼ hourly 7.30am-4.30pm May-Oct) is the only steam-powered cogwheel train still operating in Switzerland, climbing 2350m, from where you can set out on hikes or enjoy the long views over Brienzersee to snow-dusted 4000m peaks. Walking up from Brienz takes around five hours.

Back in town, mosey down postcard-perfect **Brunngasse**, a twisting cobbled lane dotted with stout wooden chalets, each seemingly trying to outdo its neighbour with window displays of vines, twee gnomes and billowing geraniums.

Shops selling touristy kitsch and locally carved statues, music boxes and cuckoo clocks line Hauptstrasse.

Several outlets open their attached workshops, including **Jobin**, which has been in business since 1835. You can see the craftsmen chipping and painting away in its **Living Museum** (☎ 033 952 13 00; Hauptstrasse 111; admission Sfr5, guided tour Sfr15; ☼ 8am-6.30pm daily May-Oct, 8am-noon & 1.30-6.30pm Mon-Fri, 9am-5pm Sat, closed Wed & Sun Nov-Apr).

Sleeping & Eating

Camping Aaregg (☎ 033 951 18 43; Seestrasse 22, sites per adult/car & tent Sfr12/10; ☼ Apr-Oct) Set on a little peninsula, this is a peaceful lakeside campsite with excellent facilities including a restaurant and playground. It's a 10-minute walk east of the train station.

SYHA hostel (☎ 033 951 11 52; www.youthhostel.ch /brienz; Strandweg 10; dm/d Sfr26.90/62.80; ☼ 7.30-10am & 5-10pm mid-Apr–mid-Oct) Overlooking the lake, this chalet-style hostel is a decent budget pick, though some dorms are impersonally large. Still, the superb views, garden and barbecue area make up for the mass snoring sessions.

Hotel Lindenhof (☎ 033 952 20 30; www.hotel-lindenhof.ch; Lindenhofweg 15; s Sfr130-160, d Sfr160-240) Perched on a hill and surrounded by rambling gardens, this quirky place comprises several chalets. The individually themed rooms are certainly fun – you can snooze in a tree-trunk bed, under a bale of hay or in an Alpine-style hut. The giggly staff is less of a novelty, though.

Hotel Steinbock (☎ 033 951 40 55; www.steinbock-brienz.ch; Hauptstrasse 123; s/d Sfr150/200; P ✗) Since its facelift, this pine chalet is looking better than ever. Decorated in warm terracotta hues, the plush, immaculate rooms have organic mattresses, wi-fi, flatscreen TVs and slick bathrooms with pebble-floored showers for a spot of DIY reflexology. There's a cosy restaurant and wine cellar downstairs.

Tea-Room Hotel Walz (☎ 033 951 14 59; Hauptstrasse 102; mains Sfr18-30; ☼ 8am-10.30pm daily, 8am-6.30pm Thu-Tue winter) Dirndl-clad waitresses bring hearty meals and cakes to the table at this old-fashioned tea room. Try the unfortunate-sounding but tasty speciality Brienzer Krapfen, pastries filled with dried pears.

Seerestaurant Löwen (☎ 033 951 12 41; Hauptstrasse 8; mains Sfr21-46; ☼ mid-Mar–late Dec) Sit on the lakeside terrace to choose from a vast array of fish dishes, including beer-battered perch, catfish in wholegrain mustard, and monkfish in green curry. Meat-lovers and vegetarians are also catered for.

Getting There & Away

From Interlaken Ost, Brienz is accessible by train (Sfr7.60) or boat (Sfr23, April to mid-October). The scenic Brünig Pass (1008m) is the road route to Lucerne.

AROUND BRIENZ
Freilichtmuseum Ballenberg

For a fascinating insight into the rural Switzerland of yore, visit **Ballenberg Open-Air Museum** (☎ 033 952 10 30; www.ballenberg.ch; adult/under 6yr/6-16yr Sfr18/free/9; ☉ buildings 10am-5pm daily, grounds 9am-6pm mid-Apr–end Oct), set in 80-hectare grounds east of Brienz. Authentically reconstructed farming hamlets take you on an architectural stroll around Switzerland, with 100 century-old buildings from humble wooden huts in Valais to hip-roofed farmhouses in the Bernese Oberland. Demonstrations from bobbin lace–making to cow herding showcase Swiss crafts and traditions. Woodlands, medicinal herb gardens and animals (check out the shaggy black-nosed sheep) are also on site. Picnickers can buy wood-oven bread, homemade cheese and sausage at the shop.

Ballenberg is too big to absorb in one day. Instead, pick up a map at the entrance, check the times of special demonstrations on the board, and plan your itinerary.

There are two entrances and car parks at each. The nearest train station is Brienzwiler. A good option is to take the bus (Sfr4 each way) from Brienz train station. It's often packed, but you can get off at one entrance and leave by the other, without having to retrace your steps.

Giessbachfälle

Illuminating the fir forests like a spotlight in the dark, the misty **Giessbachfälle** (Giessbach Falls) plummet 500m over 14 rocky ridges. Europe's oldest funicular, dating to 1879, creaks up from the boat station (one-way/return Sfr5/7), but it's only a 15-minute walk up to the most striking section of the falls. Giessbach is easily reached by boat (return from Brienz Sfr16.40, from Interlaken Ost Sfr32).

Overlooking Brienzersee and the thundering falls from its hilltop perch, the lavish 19th-century **Grand Hotel Giessbach** (☎ 033 952 25 25; www.giessbach.ch; s Sfr140-180, d Sfr210-380; ☉ late Apr–Oct) is a romantic retreat with antique-filled rooms, polished service and a restaurant with far-reaching views from its terrace.

EAST BERNESE OBERLAND

Grab your walking boots, do a little Sherlock Holmes–style detective work and you'll unearth natural wonders in the Hasli Valley (Haslital), east of the Jungfrau Region, from slot-like gorges to Europe's highest hanging bridge over the Trift glacier. Base yourself here if you want to embark on tours across the Grimsel and Susten passes.

MEIRINGEN
pop 4530 / elevation 595m

When the writer Arthur Conan Doyle left his fictional detective Sherlock Holmes for dead at the base of the Reichenbach Falls near Meiringen, he ensured that a corner of Switzerland would forever remain English eccentric. Every 4 May, fans in tweed deerstalker hats and capes gather here for the anniversary of Holmes' 'death'.

Espionage aside, Meiringen's claim to fame is as the birthplace of those airy egg-white marvels that grace sweet trolleys from Boston to Brighton – meringues. They provide just the sugar fix needed to hike to nearby gorges and glaciers.

Orientation

The town is north of the Aare River. As you exit the train station (bike rental available), you'll see the post office and bus station opposite. Head straight past Hotel Meiringen, turn right onto the main thoroughfare and in a few minutes you'll reach the tourist office.

Information

Haslital Pass (3/6 days Sfr100/160; ☉ Apr-Oct) Offers unlimited use of local buses, Brienz-Meiringen-Brünig trains, BLS boats and Meiringen-Hasliberg lifts. Children receive free passes when accompanied by their parents.

Tourist office (☎ 033 972 50 50; www.alpenregion.ch; Bahnhofstrasse; ☉ 8am-noon & 2-6pm Mon-Fri year-round, 9am-noon & 1.30-5pm Sat late Apr–mid-Oct, 3-5pm Sun Jul- Aug)

Sights & Activities

Gazing over the mighty **Reichenbachfälle** (Reichenbach Falls), where the cataract plunges 250m to the ground with a deafening roar, you can see how Arthur Conan Doyle thought them perfect for dispatching his increasingly burdensome hero, Sherlock

Holmes. In 1891, in *The Final Problem*, Conan Doyle acted like one of his own villains and pushed both Holmes and Dr Moriarty over the precipice here. Fans have flocked to the site ever since.

Reichenbach funicular (☎ 033 972 90 10; www.reichenbachfall.ch; one-way/return adult Sfr6/9, child Sfr3/5; 9am-6pm Jul & Aug, 9-11.45am & 1.15-5.45pm May, Jun, Sep & Oct) rises from Willigen, south of the Aare River, to the top. It takes an hour to wander back down to Meiringen. Alternatively, take the steep path up the side of the falls to the village of Zwirgi. At Gasthaus Zwirgi, you can rent trotti-bikes (adult/child Sfr19/15) to scoot back down to Meiringen.

Zwirgi is the start of the mountainous **Reichenbach Valley**, which runs towards Grindelwald. A path leads to Rosenlaui and the **Gletscherschlucht** (Glacier Gorge; ☎ 033 971 24 88; www.rosenlauischlucht.ch; adult/under 7yr/7-16yr Sfr7 /free/3.50; 9am-6pm Jun-Sep, 10am-5pm May & Oct). The walk back to Meiringen takes at least two hours, but hourly buses also ply the route from June to September.

Real fans won't want to miss the **Sherlock Holmes Museum** (☎ 033 971 41 41; www.sherlockholmes.ch; Bahnhofstrasse 26; adult/child Sfr4/3, combined with Reichenbachfall funicular Sfr11/7; 1.30-6pm Tue-Sun May-Sep, 4.30-6pm Wed-Sun rest of year) in the basement of the English church back in Meiringen. The highlight is a recreated sitting room of 221b Baker Street. Multilingual audio guides are available.

Otherwise, keep exploring the region. Less than 2km from the town is the narrow **Aareschlucht** (Aare Gorge; ☎ 033 971 40 48; www.aareschlucht.ch; adult/7-16yr/under 7yr Sfr7.50/free/4; 8am-6pm daily Jul & Aug, plus 9-11pm Wed & Fri, 9am-5pm Apr-Jun & Sep-Oct), where tunnels and galleries lead past milky blue torrents and limestone overhangs. The **MIB** (☎ 033 982 10 11; one-way/return Sfr3.40/6.80; 6am-7pm) is a train running half-hourly on weekdays, less frequently at weekends, from Meiringen to Aareschlucht East, near the eastern entrance.

The Hasli Valley is laced with 300km of signposted walking trails. A huge hit since opening in 2005 is the 102m-long **Triftbrücke** (Trift Bridge; www.trift.ch, in German), Europe's longest and highest suspension bridge. Hikers come to balance above the majestic Trift glacier, as it becomes melt-water more swiftly than it once did. To reach the glacier from Meiringen, take a train to Innertkirchen, then a bus to Käppel bei Nessental, Trift (Sfr5.60, 35 minutes). Here a

cable car (☎ 033 982 20 11; www.grimselwelt.ch; one-way/return Sfr12/20; 9am-4pm Jun-Oct) takes you up to 1022m, from where it's a 1½-hour walk to the bridge (1870m).

Meiringen tourist office can provide details on the Triftbrücke, as well as on mountaineering and paragliding. The 60km of skiing in the region is well suited to beginners and intermediates; a day pass costs Sfr54.

Sleeping & Eating

Hasli Lodge (☎ 033 971 59 00; www.haslilodge.ch; Kirchgasse 11; s/d Sfr80/120; P ⌨) Though the style is granny's bedroom (net curtains, soft beds, love of beige) meets kids' playroom (cartoon trains on duvets), rooms here offer reasonable value. The popular bar downstairs serves tasty rösti and steaks (mains Sfr14 to Sfr28).

Park Hotel du Sauvage (☎ 033 971 41 41; www.sauvage.ch; Bahnhofstrasse 30; s/d Sfr115/205) Arthur Conan Doyle once stayed in this belle époque classic, but today it's pensioners on whodunit weekends who spy on the breakfast buffet. There's a whiff of former glory downstairs, but in the rooms flat-pack '70s furniture clashes spectacularly with pastels sicklier than half a dozen meringues. Real detectives, however, will find its merits: friendly service, superb views and perhaps a tweed hat in the wardrobe…

our pick **Hotel Victoria** (☎ 033 972 10 40; www.victoria-meiringen.ch; Bahnhofplatz 9; s/d Sfr140/190; P ⌨) Undoubtedly the best hotel in town, Victoria is looking posher than Beckham following a top-to-toe makeover. The sleek rooms, decorated with blonde wood and local artworks, offer perks beyond their modest rates such as fresh fruit, flowers and free room service. Downstairs, Simon tempts with delicacies like homemade venison and ricotta ravioli in his Gault Millau–rated restaurant (mains Sfr29 to Sfr47). Pull up a funky log stool by the fire to nurse a glass of red after dinner.

Hotel Alpbach (☎ 033 971 18 31; Kirchgasse 17; mains Sfr24-52; 8.30am-midnight) Festooned with cowbells and accordions, this traditional pine-panelled haunt serves seasonally inspired cuisine. Flavoursome dishes such as perch with risotto and roast duck liver with chutney pair nicely with Swiss wines.

Frutal (☎ 033 971 10 62; Bahnhofstrasse 18; cakes Sfr3-6; 7am-6.30pm) A kitsch plastic meringue licks its lips in the window of this old-fashioned tea room. You'll do likewise when you taste the melt-in-your mouth meringues here.

SWEET KISSES

Though France doth protest, Meiringen claims to be the rightful birthplace of the meringue, apparently created by Italian confectioner Gasparini in 1600. The crisp, sugary shells soon took Europe by storm – Queen Elizabeth I described it as 'a kiss' and sweet-toothed King Louis XV couldn't get enough of them. Yet the standard shell served with a dollop of cream seems modest by comparison with Frutal's (opposite) magnum opus. In 1985 they took on the challenge to make the world's biggest meringue, whisking up 2500 eggs and 120kg of sugar. Baked in a specially adapted sauna, the giant meringue, served with 80L of cream, was polished off by locals in less than three hours, but the success stuck in the *Guinness Book of Records*.

Getting There & Away

Frequent trains go to Lucerne (Sfr21.60, 80 minutes; with a scenic ride over the Brünig Pass) and Interlaken Ost (Sfr11.80, 30 minutes, via Brienz). In summer, buses and cars can take the pass southeast (to Andermatt), but the road southwest over Grosse Scheidegg (to Grindelwald) is closed to private vehicles.

WEST BERNESE OBERLAND

At the western side of the Jungfrau are Simmental and Frutigland, dominated by two wildly beautiful river valleys, the Simme and the Kander. Further west is Saanenland, famous for the ritzy ski resort of Gstaad.

KANDERSTEG

pop 1190 / elevation 1176m

Turn up in Kandersteg wearing anything but muddy boots and you'll attract a few odd looks. Hiking is this town's raison d'être, with 550km of surrounding trails. An amphitheatre of spiky peaks studded with glaciers and aquamarine lakes creates a sublime natural backdrop to the rustic village of dark timber chalets.

The **tourist office** (☎ 033 675 80 80; www.kander steg.ch; ⏰ 8am-noon & 1.30-6pm Mon-Fri, 8.30am-noon & 3-6pm Sat Jun-Sep, 8am-noon & 2-6pm Mon-Fri, 8.30am-noon & 3-6pm Sat Dec-Mar, 8am-noon & 2-5pm Mon-Fri rest of year) can suggested hiking routes and other activities in the area.

Jagged mountains frame the impossibly turquoise **Oeschinensee** (Lake Oeschinen; www.oeschinen see.ch). A brand-new lift takes you to within 20 minutes of the lake by foot. Once there, it takes an hour to hike back down to Kandersteg.

Kandersteg has some first-rate hiking in its wild backyard on the cantonal border with Valais. A superb trek is the high-level **Gemmi Pass** (2314m) to Leukerbad (p160), involving a steep descent. Alternatively, you could walk through flower-strewn pastures in the wildlife-rich Üschenetäli, or trudge 5km up to **Blausee** (☎ 033 672 33 33; admission Sfr5) and its nature park to eat fresh trout by the shore. For more of a challenge, test the 3½-hour *via ferratta* at **Allmenalp**. Equipment can be hired at the valley station for Sfr20.

In winter there are more than 50km of **cross-country ski** trails, including the iced-over Oeschinensee. The limited 15km of downhill skiing is suited to beginners, and day passes cost Sfr37. Kandersteg's frozen waterfalls attract ice climbers. **Bergsteigen Kandersteg** (☎ 079 604 40 59; www.bergsteigen-kandersteg.ch) offer instruction, with Wednesday taster sessions starting at Sfr50.

Sleeping & Eating

Kandersteg's popularity with hikers means there's lots of cheaper accommodation, but many places close between seasons. Ask for the Guest Card for reductions on activities.

Camping Rendez-vous (☎ 033 675 15 34; www .camping-kandersteg.ch; sites per adult/child/car/tent Sfr7.50/4.20/3/8-16; ⏰ year-round) This green and pleasant site is at the foot of Oeschinen. Its restaurant dishes up hearty Swiss fare.

Hotel zur Post (☎ 033 675 12 58, www.hotel-zur-post .ch, s Sfr50-70, d Sfr100-120) Cheery and central, these good-value digs offer simple rooms with balconies. Downstairs the restaurant has a menu packed with Swiss staples like fondue and rösti (mains Sfr18 to Sfr35). Sit on the terrace when the sun's out.

Hotel Victoria Ritter (☎ 033 675 80 00; www.hotel -victoria.ch; s/d from Sfr125/210; P ☒) This one-time coach tavern is now an elegant hotel, expertly run by the Platzer family. The Victoria side has traditional 19th-century décor, while the snug wood-panelled rooms in the Ritter are more rustic. There's a restaurant, pool, kids' playroom and even a tennis court.

BERNESE OBERLAND

Waldhotel Doldenhorn (☎ 033 675 81 81; www
.doldenhorn-ruedihus.ch; s/d from Sfr140/240; **P** 🖳) Less
unique than its sister Ruedihus, the modern
rooms here aren't as plush as you would expect for the price. That said, the glam new spa,
well-regarded restaurant and free afternoon
tea sweeten the deal.

Ruedihus (☎ 033 675 81 81; www.doldenhorn-ruedihus
.ch; s/d from Sfr140/260; **P**) Oozing 250 years of
history from every creaking beam, this archetypal Alpine chalet is a stunner. Romantic
and warm, the cottage-style rooms feature low
ceilings, antique painted furniture and four-
poster beds. Home-grown herbs are used to
flavour dishes served in the cosy restaurant
(mains Sfr34 to Sfr40).

Hari (☎ 033 675 12 59; Bahnhofstrasse; ⏰ 8am-noon
& 2-6.30pm Mon-Sat) Stock up on picnic goodies
at this tiny grocery store selling fresh bread,
homemade yoghurt, and local cheese, honey
and wine.

Getting There & Away
Kandersteg is at the northern end of the
Lötschberg Tunnel, through which trains
trundle to Goppenstein (30km from Brig)
and onwards to Iselle in Italy. See www.bls
.ch/autoverlad for more details. The traditional way to head south is to hike; it takes a
little over five hours to get to the Gemmi Pass
and a further 1¾ hours to reach Leukerbad.

GSTAAD
pop 3600 / elevation 1100m
Synonymous with the glitterati and fittingly
twinned with Cannes, Gstaad appears smaller
than its reputation – too little for its designer ski
boots, as it were. Michael Jackson, Roger Moore,
Paris Hilton and even Margaret Thatcher have
flexed platinum cards to let their hair down
here. While the principal competitive sports are
seeing and being seen and gazing wistfully into
Gucci-filled boutiques, mere mortals might
enjoy the fine hiking and skiing.

Orientation & Information
The train station is in the centre, parallel to
the main street, Hauptstrasse. Walk straight
ahead to Hauptstrasse, turn right and go 200m
east along the pedestrian-only section to reach
the tourist office.

Information
The three-day Easyaccess card (Sfr33) offers
some free transport, guided tours and swim-

ming and discounts on many activities from
May to October.

The **tourist office** (☎ 033 748 81 81; www.gstaad.ch;
Promenade; ⏰ 8.30am-6.30pm Mon-Fri, 9am-noon & 1.30-
5pm Sat & Sun Jul-Aug & Dec-Mar, 8.30am-noon & 1.30-6.30pm
Mon-Fri, 10am-noon & 1.30-5pm Sat rest of year) has stacks
of info on the area.

Activities
'Where does one actually ski in Gstaad?' is
an oft-repeated complaint. There is some **skiing**, but lifts around the village only go up to
around 2200m, meaning you can't be sure
of snow. Runs tend to be blue or easy red.
For more varied skiing, head to neighbouring
resorts like Saanen, Saanenmöser, St Stephan
and Zweisimmen. These are only some of the
places included in the Super Ski Region, totalling 250km of runs. In all, 62 lifts are covered,
some as far afield as Château-d'Œx and Les
Diablerets glacier (see p122). The regional
pass is available for a minimum of two days
(Sfr116); for single days, buy specific sectors
(Sfr29 to Sfr58).

Snowboarding is better, especially above
the Eggli cable car, where there are snow
-making machines. From here, you can reach
the Videmanette area by chair lift, where pistes offer more of a challenge.

Hiking is possible in four valleys radiating
out from Gstaad. A scenic, undemanding
walk is to Turbach, over the Reulisenpass,
and down to St Stephan or to Lenk in the
adjoining Simmen Valley (around 4½ hours
total). From either resort, a train runs back to
Gstaad (change at Zweisimmen).

There's **rafting** on the Saane and nearby
rivers, from May to September, for around
Sfr98. One reliable operator is **Absolut Activ**
(☎ 033 748 14 14; www.absolut-activ.ch), which
also organises tubing, canyoning, glacier
tours, ice climbing and paragliding. **Swiss
Adventures** (☎ 084 816 11 61; www.swissadventures.ch)
arranges similar activities, plus winter pursuits such as igloo building, airboarding and
snowshoeing.

Festivals & Events
Gstaad hosts the **Allianz Suisse Open** (☎ 033 748 08
60; www.allianzsuisseopengstaad.com) tennis tournament in July and the classical **Menuhin Festival**
(☎ 033 748 83 38; www.menuhinfestivalgstaad.ch) in
August. Big hair, Stetsons and the sounds of
Nashville come to **Country Night** (www.countrynight
-gstaad.ch) in mid-September.

Sleeping

The following rates are for winter high season; expect discounts of 30% to 50% in summer. The tourist office has a list of campsites and self-catering chalets. Many places close from mid-October to mid-December and from April to mid-June.

SYHA hostel (☎ 033 744 13 43; www.youthhostel.ch /saanen; dm Sfr34; ☻ reception 8-10am & 5-9pm; ⬚) Situated in Saanen, just four minutes away by train, this is a peaceful chalet hostel with bright, clean dorms, a games room and kiosk.

Hotel Alphorn (☎ 033 748 45 45; www.gstaad -alphorn.ch; Gsteigstrasse; s/d Sfr130/240; ⓟ ⬚) A traditional Swiss chalet with a 21st-century twist, Alphorn has smart rooms with dark parquet floors, chunky beds, and balconies with country views. Downstairs there's a restaurant (mains Sfr16 to Sfr38) and a coin-operated whirlpool big enough for two.

Hotel Christiania (☎ 033 744 51 21; www.christiania .ch; Hauptstrasse; s/d from Sfr145/246) Smack in the centre of Gstaad, this homely, family-run chalet has inviting rooms in warm colours. The Egyptian owner cooks aromatic Middle Eastern fare in the restaurant.

Iglu-Dorf Gstaad (☎ 041 612 27 28; www.iglu-dorf .com; per person Sfr149-179; late Dec–Easter) 'Brr!' best describes Gstaad's igloo hotel, perched at 1550m on Eggli mountain and affording sweeping views over the Alps and Les Diablerets glacier. Fondue and schnapps pave the way to subzero slumber land.

Gstaad Palace (☎ 033 748 50 00; www.palace.ch; s/d from Sfr620/1020; ⓟ ✗ ✗ ✗) Opulent, exclusive and (in case you were wondering) accessible by helicopter, this hilltop fairy-tale palace casts its haughty gaze over Gstaad. Michel Jackson, Robbie Williams, Liza Minnelli, you name it – they've stayed here. And who can blame them with the penthouse a steal at Sfr14,000 per night? Retro disco Green Go is also up here.

Eating & Drinking

If Gstaad's ritzy restaurants aren't for you, head for the woodsy mountain restaurants at the summit stations of the cable cars. Otherwise keep an eye out for Günther's stall on Promenade at the weekend, selling delicious homemade bread, tarts and doughnuts.

Apple Pie (☎ 033 744 46 48; Promenade; light meals Sfr10-22; ☻ 8.30am-10pm) Just as nice as its name suggests, Apple Pie has given Gstaad an injection of cool with bubbly young staff and a Boho vibe. The saliva-inducing French menu skips from crêpes to thick onion soup and crisp apple tart.

Shumi (☎ 033 748 15 00; Promenade; sushi & sashimi Sfr19-42) This self-consciously trendy sushi bar, lounge and club is partly owned by Roger Moore's son, Geoffrey. Celebrities and wannabes come here to nibble sashimi, sip cocktails and shimmy on the dance floor.

Michel's Stallbeizli (☎ 033 744 43 37; mains Sfr22-29; ☻ 9.30am-6pm mid-Dec–Mar) Dining doesn't get more back to nature than at this converted barn. In winter, you can feast away on fondue, drink Alpine herbal tea, or munch home-cured meat and cheese, with prime views to the cud-chewing cows and goats in the adjacent stable. Kids love it.

Blun Chi (☎ 033 748 88 44; Hotel Bernerhof; mains Sfr30-44) When Alpine cheese begins to pall, try this convivial spot for authentic Asian food from Chinese crispy duck to Thai-style red snapper. There's a bamboo-flanked terrace for sunny days.

Rialto (☎ 033 744 34 74; Promenade; mains Sfr42-65) Rialto is ever so Italian and refreshingly unpretentious despite its gleaming Murano chandeliers and polished service. The menu goes way beyond pizza – think freshly made pasta, thinly sliced beef carpaccio and Med-style sea bass. The pavement terrace is great for people watching.

Chesery (☎ 033 744 24 51; Lauenenstrasse; tasting menus Sfr150-168; ☻ noon-2pm & 6.30-9.30pm Tue-Sun Dec-Apr & Jun-Oct) Founded by the Aga Khan in the 1960s, this Gault Millau award-winning restaurant is excellent – and boy, does it know it. Signature dishes such as wild sea bass with aubergine caviar are served with full-bodied wines, French finesse and a smidgen of arrogance.

Getting There & Away

Gstaad is on the Golden Pass route between Montreux (Sfr24, 1½ hours) and Spiez (Sfr25, 1½ hours; change at Zweisimmen). You can get to Geneva airport (Sfr51, three hours) via Montreux. A postal bus goes to Les Diablerets (Sfr12.40, 50 minutes) about five times daily. N11 is the principal road connecting Aigle and Spiez, and it passes close to Gstaad at Saanen.

Mittelland

It is quite extraordinary really that this flat, unassuming 'middle ground', as its mince-no-words name states so unabashedly, should have Switzerland's capital at its heart. If it's bright lights, urban action and big-city cosmopolitan chic you're expecting, think again: few even realise that riverside Bern is the Swiss capital as the city is so delightfully languid, laid-back and – dare one say – provincial and middle sized. *So* nonpowerhouse …

Yet Bern's middling is precisely what makes it so politically savvy. An important city-state during the medieval era, Bern lost territory when the French invaded in 1798 and, a century on as politicians picked a capital for the troubled Swiss Confederation (p29), it leapt out as the only unthreatening choice: Geneva was simply too French, Zürich too German. But Bern, with its subtle linguistic plurality – Bernese are largely German-speaking with an infamously slow, lilting dialect, but French has equal footing along the region's western border, home to Switzerland's so-called Röstigraben (German–French linguistic divide) – was just right.

And what joy! Hands down one of the most understated, charming capitals on the planet, its 15th-century Old Town is fairy-tale-like with its terraced stone buildings, covered arcades, clock towers, church spires and cobbled streets. The surrounding countryside is just as benignly beautiful, with centuries-old traditional villages and farm upon farm speckling the rolling green hills. Cows, with bells jangling, are put out to pasture each spring, their milk being carted off to the local dairy in churns each morning to make Emmental – a holey cheese that could not be more Swiss if it tried.

HIGHLIGHTS

- Fountain hopping through fairy-tale **Bern** (p201) and getting hammered at its onion market (p204).
- Surfing the delights of the stunningly wave-shaped **Zentrum Paul Klee** (p203).
- Revelling in wine tasting on another plane in **Ligerz** (p211), a postcard-pretty lakefront hamlet on the northern shore of Lake Biel.
- Being cheesy in **Emmental**: taste it, roll it, watch it being made at the show dairy, then take your pick of local farms and inns for an evening feast (p210).
- Meandering lazily around Old Town **Solothurn** (p212), allowing bags of time for its baroque cathedral and creative dining and drinking spaces by the water.

■ POPULATION: 1.2 MILLION   ■ AREA: 842 SQ KM   ■ LANGUAGES: GERMAN, FRENCH

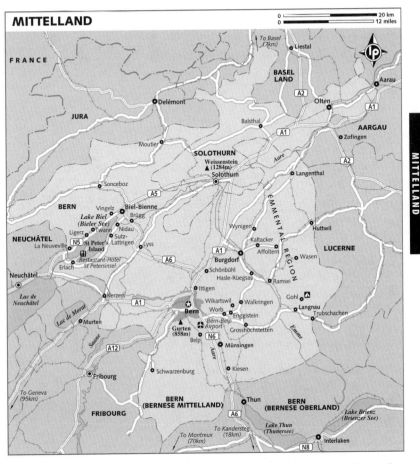

Orientation & Information

Switzerland's Mittelland (Schweizer Mittelland/Le Plateau Central) is a flat plain between the Alps and the Jura, comprising mainly the northern part of the canton of Bern (Berner Mittelland/Le Plateau Bernois) and the canton of Solothurn (Soleure).

The Bern-based regional tourist office is **Schweizer Mittelland Tourismus** (☎ 031 328 12 12; www.smit.ch, in German), but Bern's **tourist office** (p201) dispenses regionwide information to personal callers.

Getting There & Around

Although Bern has only a small airport, road and rail links into the region are excellent in every direction. Some train services within the region are operated by smaller, private companies.

BERN

pop 122,422/ elevation 540m

Wandering its picture-postcard Old Town, with 6km of arcaded stone streets and a provincial, laid-back air, it is hard to believe that Bern (Berne in English and French) is the capital of Switzerland – but it is, plus a Unesco World Heritage Site to boot.

Indeed, on the city's long, curving and cobbled streets, lined with tall, 15th-century terraced buildings and fantastical folk figures frolicking on fountains since the 16th century, you feel as if you're in some kind of dizzying

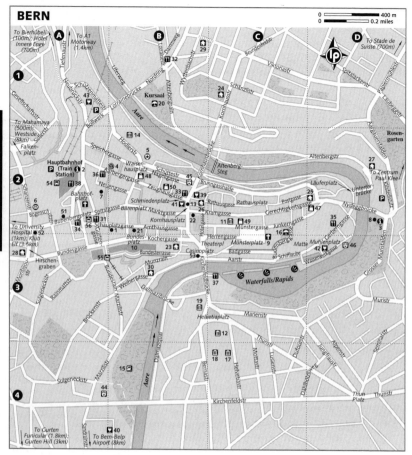

architectural canyon. From the surrounding hills, you're presented with an equally captivating picture of red roofs crammed on a spit of land within a bend of the Aare River.

Yet despite the provincial air, Bern captivates. Its drinking scene is dynamic, its alternative arts scene is happening and one only has to take in the shocking-pink bicycles planted around town to advertise the latest film fest or Daniel Libeskind's striking new architectural creation to know there's more to Bern than a bunch of parliamentary bureaucrats.

Information

BOOKSHOPS

Atlas Travel World (☎ 031 311 90 44; Schauplatzgasse 21; 🕑 noon-6pm Mon, 9am-6.30pm Tue, Wed & Fri,

10am-8pm Thu, 9am-5pm Sat) Travel books and backpacking accessories; walking and street maps in the basement.

Stauffacher (☎ 031 311 24 11; Neuengasse 25; 🕑 9am-7pm Mon-Wed & Fri, 9am-9pm Thu, 9am-5pm Sat) A labyrinth of a bookshop, with a brilliant range of English-language fiction, nonfiction, travel literature and books about Switzerland on the 3rd floor.

EMERGENCY

Police Station (☎ 031 321 21 21; Waisenhausplatz 32)

INTERNET ACCESS

Surf on a terminal in the train-station tourist office for Sfr12 per hour.

Internet Café (☎ 031 311 98 50; www.pokerhill.ch; in German; Aarbergergasse 46; internet access per hr Sfr8-10; 🕑 9.30am-12.30am Mon-Fri, noon-12.30am Sat)

MITTELLAND

MEDICAL SERVICES
Medical Emergency Service (☎ 0900 57 67 47;
☽ 24hr)
Pharmacy Emergency Service (☎ 0900 98 99 00;
☽ 24hr)
University hospital (☎ 031 632 21 11; Fribourgstrasse;
☽ 24hr) West of the centre; has a casualty department.

POST
Post Office (Schanzenstrasse 4; ☽ 7.30am-9pm Mon-Fri,
8am-4pm Sat, 9am-4pm Sun)

TOURIST INFORMATION
Bern Tourismus (www.berninfo.com) train station
(☎ 031 328 12 12; Bahnhofplatz; ☽ 9am-8.30pm
Jun-Sep, 9am-6.30pm Mon-Sat, 10am-5pm Sun Oct-May);
bear pits (☎ 031 328 12 12; Bärengraben; ☽ 9am-6pm
Jun-Sep, 10am-4pm Mar-May & Oct, 11am-4pm Nov-Feb)
Located on the street-level floor of the train station and by
the bear pits. City tours, free hotel bookings, internet access.

Sights
If you're around for a day or so and you're
intent on sightseeing, buy a **BernCard** (per
24/48/72hr adult Sfr20/31/38, child Sfr16/24/29), covering
admission to the permanent collections of
27 museums and the Bern Show, free public
transport and a 25% discount on city tours.

OLD TOWN
Bern's flag-bedecked medieval centre is
an attraction in its own right, with 6km of
covered arcades and cellar shops and bars
descending from the streets. After a devastating fire in 1405, the wooden city was rebuilt
in today's sandstone.

A focal point is Bern's **Zytglogge** (clock
tower), once part of the city's western
gate (1191–1256). It's reminiscent of the
Astronomical Clock in Prague's old town
square in that crowds congregate to watch
its revolving figures twirl at four minutes before the hour, after which the actual chimes
begin. Tours enter the tower to see the clock
mechanism from May to October; contact
the tourist office.

The clock tower supposedly helped Albert
Einstein (p202) hone his theory of relativity,
developed while working as a patent clerk
in Bern.

The great scientist surmised, while travelling on a tram away from the tower, that if
the tram were going at the speed of light, the
clock tower would remain on the same time,
while his own watch would continue to tick –
proving time was relative.

Another Bern landmark is its 11 decorative **fountains** (1545), which depict historic
and folkloric characters. Most are along
Marktgasse as it becomes Kramgasse and
Gerechtigkeitsgasse, but the most famous
lies in Kornhausplatz: the **Kindlifresserbrunnen**
(Ogre Fountain) of a giant snacking…on
children.

MITTELLAND

BERNER MÜNSTER

The high point of the 15th-century Gothic cathedral **Berner Münster** (Bern Minster; audioguide Sfr5, tower admission adult/7-16yr Sfr4/2; ☺ 10am-5pm Tue-Sat, 11.30am-5pm Sun Easter-Nov, 10am-noon & 2-4pm Tue-Fri, to 5pm Sat, 11.30am-2pm Sun rest of year, tower closes 30 min earlier) is its lofty spire. At 100m, it's Switzerland's tallest, and those with enough energy to climb the dizzying 344-step spiral staircase are rewarded with vertiginous views of the Bernese Alps on a clear day. Coming down, take a breather by the **Upper Bells** (1356), rung at 11am, noon and 3pm daily, and the three **Lower Bells**, each weighing 10 tonnes, making them Switzerland's largest bells.

Back on terra firma, look at the decorative **main portal** depicting the Last Judgment. The mayor of Bern is shown going to heaven, while his Zürich counterpart is being shown into hell.

Afterwards, wander behind the cathedral to the **Münster Plattform**, a bijou park of boxed hedges and benches, which drops away into a steep cliff. Spoil yourself with a coffee in the sunshine at the pavilion café in the park, then ride the **public lift** (admission Sfr1.20) down to the quarter of **Matte** on the river plain. A medieval district of craftsmen, dockworkers and artisans, it had its own distinctive variety of Bernese German. More recently, floods in 1999 and 2005 saw Matte suffer extensive damage.

EINSTEIN HAUS

The world's most famous scientist developed his special theory of relativity in Bern in 1905. Find out more at the small **museum** (☎ 031 312 00 91; www.einstein-bern.ch; Kramgasse 49; adult/student Sfr6/4.50; ☺ 10am-5pm Mon-Fri, 10am-4pm Sat Feb–mid-Dec) inside the humble apartment where Einstein lived with his young family between 1903 and 1905 while working as a low-paid clerk in the Bern patent office. Multimedia displays now flesh out the story of the subsequent general equation – $E=mc^2$, or energy equals mass times the speed of light squared – which fundamentally changed our understanding of space, time and the universe. Upstairs, a 20-minute biographical film tells his life story.

BUNDESHÄUSER

Home of the Swiss Federal Assembly, the **Bundeshäuser** (Houses of Parliament; ☎ 031 322 85 22; www.parliament.ch; Bundesplatz), built in Florentine style in 1902, contain statues of the nation's founding fathers, a stained-glass dome adorned with cantonal emblems and a 214-bulb chandelier. When the parliament is in recess, there are 45-minute **tours** (admission free; ☺ hourly 9am-4pm Mon-Sat). During parliamentary sessions, watch from the public gallery. Bring your passport to get in.

On the vast square in front of parliament spout 26 illuminated **water jets**, representing every Swiss canton. The perfect playground for kids in warmer weather, the square gently hums with city dwellers hanging out – plop yourself down on the pavement and do the same.

BÄRENGRABEN

A popular folk etymology is that Bern got its name from the bear (*Bär* in German), when the city's founder, Berthold V, duke of Zähringen, snagged one here on a hunting spree. To the dismay of some, there is still a bear pit in the city today, which, by autumn 2009, will take the shape of a spacious, riverside park, in which one bear, or perhaps a family of bears, will roam. The 'perhaps' rests on whether Pedro, the 28-year-old bear that arrived in Bern as a mere babe, makes it into 2009 – something the entire city, not to mention Walter, his loving keeper, is holding out for (bears in captivity usually only live until 25 or so).

Should you be in Bern before the new bear pit opens, join the crowds ogling Pedro in his lifelong home at the eastern end of the Nydeggbrücke. Don't feed him your lunch; rather buy a paper cone of mixed fresh fruit (Sfr3) from Walter who, at night, shepherds Pedro into his subterranean stables beneath the current circular stone-walled **Bärengraben** (bear pit; www.baerenpark-bern.ch, in German; ☺ 9.30am-5pm), 3.5m deep.

Behind the pit, in the tourist office, is the **Bern Show** (☎ 031 328 12 12; Tourist Center Bärengraben; adult/12-16yr Sfr3/1; ☺ 9am-6pm Jun-Sep, 10am-4pm Mar-May & Oct, 11am-4pm Nov-Feb), a 20-minute multimedia show on Bern's history in English, French or German.

ROSENGARTEN & UNIVERSITY BOTANICAL GARDEN

Uphill from the Bärengraben is the fragrant **Rosengarten** (rose garden), known more for its stupendous view over town than its sweet-smelling blooms, although both are worth the climb.

A flight of steps leads from the northern end of Lorrainebrücke to the **University Botanical Garden** (☎ 031 631 49 45; Altenbergrain 21; admission free; ☺ 8am-5.30pm May-Sep, to 5pm Oct-Apr), a riverside garden with plenty of green specimens to admire and a couple of greenhouses.

ZENTRUM PAUL KLEE

Bern's answer to the Guggenheim, the fabulous **Zentrum Paul Klee** (Paul Klee Centre; ☎ 031 359 01 01; www.zpk.org; Monument in Fruchtland 3; adult/6-16yr Sfr16/6, audioguides Sfr5; ☺ 10am-5pm Tue-Sun) is an eye-catching 150m-long building filled with popular modern art. Renzo Piano's curvaceous building swoops up and down like waves to create a trio of 'hills' in the agricultural landscape east of town. Shame about the busy A6 freeway whizzing by right next to it.

The middle hill houses the main exhibition space, showcasing 4000 rotating works from Paul Klee's prodigious and often-playful career. Interactive computer displays built into the seating mean you can get the low-down on all the Swiss-born artist's major pieces, while music-driven audioguides (Sfr5) take visitors on a one-hour DIY musical tour of his work. In the basement of another 'hill' is the fun-packed **Kindermuseum Creaviva**, an inspired children's museum, where kids can experiment with hands-on art exhibits (included in admission price) or sign up for a one-hour art workshop (Sfr15); young artists can take their creations home with them.

In the museum grounds, a walk through fields takes visitors past a stream of modern and contemporary sculptures, including works by Yoko Ono and Sol Lewitt.

Take bus 12 from Bubenbergplatz to Zentrum Paul Klee (Sfr3.80). By car the museum is right next to the Bern-Ostring exit of the A6.

HISTORICHES MUSEUM BERN

Tapestries, diptychs and other world treasures vividly illustrate Bernese history from the Stone Age to the 20th century in the marvellous **Bern Historical Museum** (☎ 031 350 77 11; www .bhm.ch; Helvetiaplatz 5; adult/child Sfr24/12, Einstein Museum only Sfr18/8; ☺ 10am-5pm Tue-Sun, 10am-8pm Wed). Part of the history museum is devoted to a superb permanent exhibition on Einstein.

KUNSTMUSEUM

The permanent collection at the **Kunstmuseum** (Museum of Fine Arts; ☎ 031 328 09 44; www.kunst museumbern.ch, in German; Hodlerstrasse 8-12; adult/student

permanent collection Sfr8/5, temporary exhibitions Sfr8-18; ☺ 10am-9pm Tue, 10am-5pm Wed-Sun) includes works by Italian artists such as Fra Angelico, Swiss artists like Ferninand Hodler (p38) and others like Picasso and Dali.

OTHER MUSEUMS

The **Schweizerisches Alpines Museum** (Swiss Alpine Museum; ☎ 031 351 04 40; www.alpinesmuseum.ch; Helvetiaplatz 4; adult/6-16yr Sfr10/3; ☺ 2-5.30pm Mon, 10am-5.30pm Tue-Sun) outlines the history of Alpine mountaineering and cartography with the help of impressive relief maps.

The mounted moth-eaten remains of famous Barry, a St Bernard rescue dog, steal the show at the **Naturhistorisches Museum** (Natural History Museum; ☎ 031 350 71 11; www.nmbe.unibe.ch, in German; Bernastrasse 15; adult/child Sfr8/free; ☺ 2-5pm Mon, 9am-5pm Tue, Thu & Fri, 9am-6pm Wed, 10am-5pm Sat & Sun).

The **Museum für Kommunikation** (Communication Museum; ☎ 031 357 55 55; www.mfk.ch; Helvetiastrasse 16; adult/6-16yr Sfr12/3; ☺ 10am-5pm Tue-Sun) houses items from antique phones and stamps to electronic communication devices.

ACTIVITIES

In summer, the open-air **Marzili pools** (www .aaremarzili.ch, in German; admission free; ☺ May-Sep), beside the Aare River, are the perfect place to get a tan. Only strong swimmers should dip in the river itself.

Scenic bike paths on the riverside and in the Bernese hills are plentiful; for free bike hire see p207.

Some 3km south of town is **Gurten Hill** (☎ 031 970 33 33; www.gurtenpark.ch), whose peak boasts two restaurants, a miniature railway, fun trails for bikers, a summer circus, winter sledge runs, an adventure playground and all sorts of other seasonal outdoor fun. Enjoy fine views as you hike down the mountain (about one hour), following the clearly marked paths. To get there, take tram 9 towards Wabern, alight at Gurtenbahn and change to the **Gurten funicular** (www.gurtenbahn.ch, in German; adult one-way/ return Sfr6/10, child Sfr3/5; ☺ 7am-11.30pm), which goes to the top.

Bern for Children

With its dancing clock tower, fairy-tale Old Town, story-book fountains (p201) and bears (opposite), Bern enchants kids. Particularly tailor-made for younger children are Gurten Hill (p203) and the Zentrum Paul Klee (left).

MITTELLAND

HAMMER HEAD

Market traders take over Bern on the fourth Monday in November during the legendary **onion market** *(Zibelemärit)*, a riot of 600-odd market stalls selling delicately woven onion plaits, wreaths, ropes, pies, sculptures and so on alongside other tasty regional produce. Folklore says the market dates to the great fire of 1405 when farmers from the canton of Fribourg helped the Bernese recover and were allowed to sell their produce in Bern as a reward. In reality, the market probably began as part of Martinmas, the medieval festival celebrating winter's start. Whatever the tale, the onion market is a fabulous excuse for pure, often crazy revelry as street performers surge forth in the carnival atmosphere and people walk around throwing confetti and hitting each other on the head with – bizarrely – squeaky plastic hammers.

Older kids could pedal around with Bern Rollt (p207), tour the Stade de Suisse (p207) or play chess on one of two giant outdoor chessboards, immediately behind the parliament buildings (Bundeshäuser) on the leafy Bundesterrasse.

Festivals & Events

Bern canton has a public holiday on 2 January (Berchtoldstag), a **jazz festival** (www.jazzfestivalbern .ch) in May and the **Gurten Rock Festival** (www.gurten festival.ch, in German) in mid-July. August's **Aare swimming race** (www.aareschwuemme.ch, in German) is a lively spectacle. But nothing beats getting hammered at its onion market (see boxed text, above)…

Sleeping

The tourist office makes hotel reservations (free) and has information on 'three nights for the price of two' deals, in which many hotels in town participate.

BUDGET

SYHA hostel (☎ 031 326 11 11; www.youthhostel.ch/bern; Weihergasse 4; dm incl breakfast Sfr33-44.50, lunch or dinner Sfr15.50; reception ☺ 7am-noon & 2pm-midnight; 🖥 ✂) Prettily set just across from the river, this well-organised hostel sports spotlessly clean dorms and a leafy terrace with pillar-box-red seating and a ping-pong table. To get there, follow the paths downhill from the parliament building or ride the funicular (p207). Free bike rental from May to October (Sfr20 deposit).

Hotel Glocke Backpackers Bern (☎ 031 311 37 71; www.bernbackpackers.com; Rathausgasse 75; dm incl breakfast Sfr33-41, s/d without bathroom Sfr69/104, d with bathroom Sfr140; ☺ reception 8-11am & 3-10pm; 🖥 ✂) Modern bedrooms, clean bathrooms, a kitchen and a sociable lounge – all in the Old Town – make this many backpackers' first choice, although

street noise might irritate light sleepers. Dorms sport two or six beds and are mixed occupancy. Free wi-fi.

Hotel Landhaus (☎ 031 331 41 66; www.landhaus bern.ch; Altenbergstrasse 4; dm without/with pillow & quilt Sfr33/38, breakfast Sfr8, d without/with bathroom Sfr120/160; 🖥 ✂ P) In a pretty part of town backed by the grassy slope of a city park and fronted by the river and Old Town spires, this historic hotel with an apricot facade and a witch's-hat roof oozes character. Its buzzing ground-floor restaurant, a tad bohemian, is its soul – and draws a staunchly local crowd.

our pick **Marthahaus Garni** (☎ 031 332 41 35; www.marthahaus.ch; Wyttenbachstrasse 22a; dm Sfr45, s/d/tr without bathroom Sfr69/99/135, s/d/tr with bathroom Sfr110/135/165; 🖥 ✂) Plum in a leafy residential location, this five-storey building feels like a friendly boarding house. Clean, simple rooms have lots of white and a smattering of modern art, plus there's a kitchen.

Hotel National (☎ 031 381 1988; www.nationalbern.ch, in German; Hirschengraben 24; s/d without bathroom from Sfr60/120, s/d with bathroom Sfr95/140; 🖥) A quaint, charming hotel, the National wouldn't be out of place in Paris with its wrought-iron lift, lavender sprigs and Persian rugs over creaky wooden floors. Family rooms sleep five (Sfr220 to Sfr280).

MIDRANGE

Hotel Allegro (☎ 031 339 55 00; www.allegro-hotel.ch; Kornhausstrasse 3; s/d Sfr230/285; ✂ 🖥 ✂) Cool and modern, this curved sliver of a building across the river offers excellent views from its front rooms. Jam-packed with dining and drinking spaces, it is a one-stop shop for business travellers, yet its interior design is far from being cookie cutter. The best room in the house – the 7th-floor penthouse suite – is an ode to the life and times of Bern's favourite artist, Paul Klee. Cheaper weekend rates.

our pick Hotel Innere Enge (☎ 031 309 61 11; www
.zghotels.ch; Engestrasse 54; d from Sfr240; 🖥 ✕ 🅿) It
might not be bang-slap city centre, but this
historic inn – a jazz hotel – is unique. Owned
and run with a hands-on passion by Bern
Jazz Festival organiser Hans Zurbrügg and
wife Marianne Gauer, a top Swiss interior
designer, the place oozes panache. Don't miss
its cellar jazz bar.

Hotel Belle Epoque (☎ 031 311 43 36; www.belle
-epoque.ch; Gerechtigkeitsgasse 18; s/d from Sfr250/350;
🖥 ✕) A romantic Old Town hotel with
opulent art-nouveau furnishings, the Belle
Epoque's standards are so exacting it even
cleverly tucks away modern aberrations – like
the TV – into steamer-trunk-style cupboards,
so as not to spoil the look.

TOP END

Bellevue Palace (☎ 031 320 45 45; www.bellevue-palace.ch;
Kochergasse 3-5; s/d from Sfr360/390; ✕ 🖥 ✕ 🅿)
Bern's power brokers, and international states-
men like Nelson Mandela, gravitate towards
Bern's only five-star hotel. Near the parliament, it's the address to impress. Cheaper
weekend rates.

Eating

If it's waterside you want to dine, you won't
get closer than stylish **Cinématte** (p207).

Sassafraz (☎ 031 311 79 50; www.sassafraz.ch;
Aarbergergasse 57; pasta Sfr16.50-35, mains Sfr25-40;
🕑 8.30am-11.30pm Mon, to 12.30am Tue-Fri, 10am-
12.30am Sat, 10am-11.30pm Sun) A lovely address
for wine lovers, this contemporary lounge
and *vinothèque* cooks up the whole gamut
of cuisines, English fish and chips (Sfr25.50)
included, but it is the Italian mozzarella bar
that steals the culinary show. In summer
tempting smells waft across the teak tables
outside.

Altes Tramdepot (☎ 031 368 14 15; Bärengraben;
mains Sfr18-38, menus Sfr16-20; 🕑 11am-12.30am, from
10am Sat & Sun) Even locals recommend this
cavernous microbrewery tucked in the attractive tourist-office building by the bear
pits. Swiss specialities snug up to wok-cooked
stir-fries, pasta and international dishes on its
bistro-styled menu.

Fugu Nydegg (☎ 031 311 51 25; www.fugu-nydegg
.ch; Gerechtigkeitsgasse 16; mains Sfr19-25; 🕑 lunch &
dinner Mon-Fri, 10am-12.30am Sat, 10am-10pm Sun) If
it's Bangkok-style pad thai, fried noodles or
Thai fish you're craving, then crisp, cool Fugu
hits the spot. The dining area is lime-green,

stainless steel and raw concrete inside, or in
the sun outside.

Du Nord (☎ 031 332 23 38; www.dunord-bern.ch;
Lorrainestrasse 2; mains Sfr20-35; 🕑 8am-11.30pm Mon-Thu,
to 12.30am Fri, 4pm-12.30am Sat) It might be a short
walk across the bridge from the Old Town,
but this gay-friendly space, with a good-value
international kitchen and bar that buzzes with
Bern's hippest and the occasional gig, is one
of Bern's hottest addresses. Find it crowned
by a pretty pink, fairy-tale turret in the leafy
Lorraine quarter.

Terrasse & Casa (☎ 031 350 50 01; www.schwellen
maetteli.ch; Dalmaziquai 11; mains Sfr28-45; 🕑 Terrasse 9am-
11.30pm Mon-Sat, Sun 9am-10pm, Casa lunch & dinner Tue-Fri,
11.45am-11.30pm Sat & Sun) Dubbed 'Bern's Riviera',
this twinset of classy hang-outs on the Aare
is an experience. Distinctly St-Tropez in feel,
Terrasse is a glass shoebox with wooden decking over the water, sun lounges overlooking
a weir (illuminated at night) and comfy sofa
seating – a perfect spot for Sunday brunch or
a drink at any time of day. Casa, by contrast,
cooks up Italian food in a cosy, country-style
timber-framed house.

Kornhauskeller (☎ 031 327 72 72; Kornhausplatz
18; mains Sfr32-52; 🕑 lunch & dinner Mon-Sat, dinner Sun,
bar 5pm-1am Mon-Wed, 5pm-2am Thu-Sat, 5pm-12.30am
Sun) Dress well and dine fine beneath vaulted
frescoed arches at Bern's surprisingly ornate
former granary, now a stunning cellar restaurant serving Mediterranean cuisine. Beautiful
people sip cocktails alongside historic stained-
glass windows on the mezzanine above, and
across the street in its neighbouring café
(lunch *menu* Sfr18.50), punters lunch in the
sun on the busy pavement terrace.

Also recommended:

Santorini (☎ 031 312 18 12; www.santorini.ch; Ger-
berngasse 34; mains Sfr25-40; 🕑 lunch & dinner Tue-Fri,
dinner Sat & Sun) Greek restaurant on a pretty street in the
riverside Matte quarter.

Casa Della (☎ 031 311 21 42; Schauplatzgasse 16;
mains Sfr25-38; 🕑 10.30am-11.30pm Mon-Fri, 9am-3pm
Sat) Paul Klee was here in 1890; wholly traditional fare.

Mahamaya (☎ 031 301 01 01; www.mahamaya.ch;
Länggassstrasse 43; 🕑 lunch Mon-Fri, dinner Tue-Sat)
Indian restaurant, takeaway and the odd hip happening;
loads of flyers posted in the window.

Drinking

Bern has a healthy nightlife. For an earthy
drink with old-generation locals, order at the
marble-topped bar inside the **Markthalle** (see
boxed text, p206).

MITTELLAND

MITTELLAND

TOP PICKS: QUICK EATS

This city, busy with students, has some super quick-eat options, oozing atmosphere and even a table thrown in for a highly affordable price.

■ For a munch between meals, nothing beats the **Brezels** (pretzels) smothered in salt crystals or sunflower, pumpkin or sesame seeds from kiosks at the train station, or a bag of piping **hot chestnuts** crunched to the tune of the astronomical clock striking.

■ **Markthalle** (Bubenbergplatz 9; ☺ 6.30am-11.30pm Mon-Wed, 6.30am-12.30am Thu & Fri, 7.30am-12.30am Sat) Buzzing in atmosphere and quick-snack action, this covered market arcade is jam-packed with cheap eateries from around the world: curries, vegetarian, wok stir-fries, *bruschette*, noodles, pizza, southern Indian, Turkish, Middle Eastern. You name it, it's here – to be eaten standing at bars or around plastic tables.

■ **Sous le Pont** (below) Grab fries, falafel or a schnitzel from the graffiti-covered hole in the wall next to the café-bar of the same name and dine at the graffiti-covered table in the graffiti-covered courtyard. Beer costs Sfr3.80/5.20 per 3/5dl glass.

■ **Tibits** (☎ 031 312 91 11; Bahnhofplatz 10; ☺ 6.30am-11.30pm Mon-Wed, 6.30am-midnight Thu-Sat, 8am-11pm Sun) This vegetarian buffet restaurant inside the train station is just the ticket for a quick healthy meal of any size, at any time of day. Serve yourself, get it weighed and pay accordingly.

BARS & LOUNGES

Several clubs and eating spaces, such as Kornhauskeller and Altes Tramdepot (p205), are as much drinking as dining spots. A few bright and busy after-work aperitif bars stud Gurtengasse near the Bundeshäuser.

Silo Bar (☎ 031 311 54 12; www.silobar.ch, in German; Muhlenplatz 11; ☺ 10pm-3.30am Thu-Sat) Plum by the water in the increasingly hip Matte quarter, Bern's monumental 19th-century corn house throbs with mainstream hits and a lively predominantly student set – the place to drink, dance and party.

Sous le Pont (☎ 031 306 69 55; www.souslepont.com; Neubrückstrasse 8; ☺ 11.30am-2.30pm & 6-11.30pm Tue-Thu, 11.30am-2.30pm & 7pm-2am Fri, 7pm-2.30am Sat) Delve into the grungy underground scene around the station, with this bar in the semichaotic alternative-arts centre, the Reitschule, an old stone, graffiti-covered building – an old riding school built in 1897 – by the railway bridge.

Pery Bar (☎ 031 311 59 08; Schmiedenplatz 3; ☺ 5pm-1.30am Mon-Wed, 5pm-2.30am Thu, 5pm-3.30am Fri, 6pm-3.30am Sat) A popular venue with a young crowd, the Pery Bar boasts a good-time atmosphere and pavement tables in summer.

Café des Pyrénées (☎ 031 311 30 63; Kornhausplatz 17; ☺ Mon-Sat) With its mix of wine-quaffing trendies and beer-loving students, this lovely Bohemian joint feels like a Parisian café-bar. 'An essential stop on any bar crawl' was the verdict of most magazines writing about Bern in the lead-up to Euro 2008.

CLUBS

Pick up flyers for clubbing events at **Olmo Shoes** (opposite); **Olmo Ticket** (☎ 031 318 18 18; ☺ 9.30am-7pm Mon-Wed, Fri & Sat 9.30am-9pm Thu) inside sells tickets. **Midnight Lounge** (☺ 11.30pm-2am Fri & Sat) is the chic clubbing arm of Kornhauskeller (p205).

Bierhübeli (☎ 031 301 92 92; www.bierhuebeli.ch; Neubrückstrasse 43; ☺ 7pm-12.30am Mon-Thu, 9.30pm-3.30am Fri & Sat) This huge old hall with a balcony hosts mainstream international bands and club nights. Its chic DJ lounge throbs most nights – as does its summer beer garden. Take bus 11 to Bierhübeli from the train station.

Wasserwerk (☎ 031 312 12 31; www.wasserwerkclub .ch; Wasserwerkgasse 5; ☺ 10pm-late Thu-Sat) Bern's main techno venue with bar, club and occasional live music – Moby and the Prodigy, it boasts, played here in their heydays.

Klub Elf (www.myspace.com/klubelf; Ziegelackerstrasse 11a; ☺ 11pm-late Fri & Sat) House, techno, trance and minimal form the dance beat at this popular weekend club, where the real Saturday-night party kicks off after midnight and continues with an 'after' party from 5am on Sunday. Find flyers on their website.

Gaskessel (☎ 031 372 49 00; www.gaskessel.ch; Sandrainstrasse 25; ☺ 7.30pm-3.30am Thu-Sat) Inside this graffiti-covered domed building in Marzili is another counter-cultural centre, with lots of trance, rap and some gay evenings.

Dampfzentrale (☎ 031 310 05 40; www.dampf zentrale.ch, in German; Marzilistrasse 47; ☺ variable) Host to far more than its action-packed Friday-night club (from 10pm), this industrial red-brick riverside building hosts concerts, festivals and contemporary dance, and has a riverside restaurant terrace (☎ 031 312 33 00; open for lunch and dinner Monday to Friday, and dinner Saturday and Sunday)

Entertainment
CINEMA
Sous le Pont (opposite) screens alternative films in its cinema, as does **Cinématte** (☎ 031 312 21 22; www .cinematte.ch; Wasserwerkgasse 7; ☺ 6pm-11.30pm Mon, Thu & Sun, 6pm-12.30am Fri & Sat), a riverside address with a bamboo-ensnared wooden-decking restaurant terrace (mains Sfr28 to Sfr42) and a riveting line-up of film screenings.

PERFORMING ARTS & CLASSICAL MUSIC
Buy theatre and music-concert tickets at **Bern Ticket** (☎ 031 329 52 52; www.bernbillett.ch, in German; Nageligasse 1a; ☺ noon-6.30pm Mon-Fri, 10am-2pm Sat), near the theatre.

Stadttheater Bern (☎ 031 329 51 51; www.stadttheater bern.ch, in German; Kornhausplatz 20) Opera, dance, classical music and plays (in German).

SPORT
Bern's 32,000-seat **Stade de Suisse** (www.stadede suisse.ch, in German & French; tours adult/child Sfr20/15), built over the demolished Wankdorf Stadium (host to the 1954 World Cup final), northeast of the Old Town, is home to the local Young Boys team and hosts international matches.

Outside match times, tour the complex, which is topped by the world's largest expanse of solar panelling (8000 sq metres) and contains shops and restaurants.

Shopping
Revel in the lively atmosphere at Bern's open-air **vegetable, fruit & flower markets** (Bärenplatz, Bundesplatz, Schauplatz & Münstergasse; ☺ 6am-noon Tue & Sat) and the **general market** (Waisenhausplatz; ☺ 8am-6pm Tue, 8am-4pm Sat Jan-Nov).

Mooching around the Old Town boutiques, many tucked below the street in bunker-style cellars or above in covered arcades, is delightful. Allow extra time for quaint Gerechtigkeitsgasse with its myriad of art and antique galleries, antiquarian bookshops, small shops specialising in funky house design and darling fashion boutiques, such as **Alpin** (Gerechtigkeitsgasse 19), which sells gorgeous knitwear and mix 'n match dresses by Zürich designer Nathalie Schweizer. Nearby **Olmo Shoes** (Zeughausgasse 14)

sells funky footwear and **Holz Art** (Münstergasse 36) sells exquisite hand-carved wooden toys, ornamental chalets and clocks.

Bern's snappiest dresser is **Westside** (www .westside.ch; Riedbachstrasse 100; ☺ shops 9am-8pm Mon-Thu, 9am-10pm Fri, 8am-5pm Sat), a state-of-the-art leisure and shopping centre – 55 shops, a cinema, restaurants, a water park and spa – designed by internationally renowned architect Daniel Libeskind. It opened west of the city centre in 2008; take bus 14 from Bubenbergplatz (Sfr3.80).

Getting There & Away
AIR
Bern-Belp airport (☎ 031 960 21 21; www.alpar.ch) is a small airport with direct flights to/from Munich (from where there are onward connections to pretty much everywhere) with Lufthansa (p359) and Southampton in the UK with Flybe (p360).

BUS & TRAIN
Postal buses depart from the western side of the **train station** (Bahnhoftplatz). By rail, there are services at least hourly to most destinations, including Geneva (Sfr46, 1¾ hours), Basel (Sfr37, 70 minutes), Interlaken Ost (Sfr26, 50 minutes) and Zürich (Sfr46, one hour).

Getting Around
TO/FROM THE AIRPORT
An **airport shuttle bus** (☎ 031 971 28 88, 079 651 70 70) links Bern-Belp airport with the train station (one-way Sfr15, 20 minutes), coordinated with flight arrivals/departures.

A **taxi** (☎ 031 333 55 55, 079 702 89 77) costs Sfr40 to Sfr50.

BICYCLE & SCOOTER
Bicycle is *the* way to get around as the dozens of bike lanes wedged alongside car and tram routes attest. Borrow a bike from one of the three kiosks of **Bern Rollt** (☎ 079 277 28 57; www .bernrollt.ch; 1st 4hr free, then Sfr1 per hr; ☺ 7.30am-9.30pm May-Oct), located inside the train station, on Casinoplatz and just off Bubenbergplatz on Hirschengraben. You'll need ID and Sfr20 as a deposit; ditto for its micro-scooters and skateboards.

BUS, TRAM & FUNICULAR
Get around on foot – perfectly manageable – or hop on a bus or tram run by **Bern Mobil** (☎ 031 321 88 44; www.bernmobil.ch, in German;

Bubenbergplatz 17; 7am-7pm Mon-Fri, 8am-5pm Sat, noon-5pm Sun). Tickets, available from the Bern Mobil office or ticket machines at stops, cost Sfr2 for journeys up to six stops (valid 30 minutes) or Sfr3.80 for a single journey within zones 1 and 2 (valid one hour). A day ticket is Sfr12.

Moonliner (☎ 031 321 88 12; www.moonliner.ch, in German) night buses transport night owls from Bahnhofplatz two or three times between midnight and 3.30am on Friday and Saturday nights. Fares cost Sfr5 to Sfr20 depending on the journey length; discount passes are invalid.

The **Stadt Bern-Drahtseilbahn Marzili funicular** (one-way Sfr1.20; 6.15am-9pm) runs from behind the parliament building downhill to the riverside Marzili quarter.

BIEL-BIENNE

pop 49,038 / elevation 429m

Slap bang on the *Röstigraben*, Switzerland's French–German divide, double-barrelled Biel-Bienne is the country's most bilingual town. Locals switch language in mid-conversation; indeed much of the time it is a tad tricky to know which one to use.

In nobody's language is this Switzerland's most picturesque town. Despite a reasonably well-preserved historic centre, its only drawcards are the lake that laps Biel-Bienne's shores and the vineyards that stagger up steeply from it. Other than that, you might well change trains here.

Orientation & Information

Biel-Bienne is at the northern end of Lake Biel (Bieler See, Lac de Bienne). The train station lies between the lake and the Old Town and has bicycle-rental and money-exchange counters. The Old Town is a 10-minute walk north of the station (or take bus 1).

Post Office (Bahnhofplatz 2; 7.30am-6.30pm Mon-Fri, 8am-4pm Sat)

Tourist Office (☎ 032 329 84 84; www.biel-seeland .net; Bahnhofplatz 12; 8am-12.30pm & 1.30-6pm Mon-Wed & Fri, to 8pm Thu, 9am-3pm Sat) Kiosk in front of the train station; Old Town tours (Sfr10) and public-transport tickets and info.

Sights & Activities

Biel-Bienne's concrete A-line-shaped **Kongresshaus** (Palais des Congrès; Zentralstrasse 60), built in the

1950s with a sports centre and a pool, sums up most people's first impression of this town – ungainly, drab and not worth a special trip.

Yet delve into the minute Old Town, huddled around the so-called **Ring**, a plaza whose name harks back to bygone days when justice was dispensed here as community bigwigs sat in a semicircle passing judgment on unfortunate miscreants brought before them, and you might just decide to linger a while.

Leading from the Ring, past its colourful 16th-century fountain, is **Burggasse**, home to the stepped-gabled town hall and theatre, Fountain of Justice (1744) and several shuttered houses.

The best of Biel-Bienne's museums are the **Museum Schwab** (Musée Schwab; ☎ 032 322 76 03; Seevorstadt 50; admission Sfr5; 2-6pm Tue-Sat, 11am-6pm Sun), displaying prehistoric relics found around Biel, Murten and Neuchâtel lakes; and the **Omega-Museum** (Musée Omega; ☎ 032 344 92 11; Stämpflistrasse 96; admission free; Mon-Fri by appointment) where dozens of watches are showcased behind glass, including a pocket-watch worn by Lawrence of Arabia and another that's been to the moon.

Outside town, the **Magglingen Funicular** (Seilbahn Magglingen, Funiculaire Macolin; ☎ 032 322 45 11; www.funic.ch, in German & French; Seevorstadt; adult/child Sfr5/2.50) scales Magglingen hill, riddled with hiking trails and photogenic views. Ask at the tourist office for its leaflet outlining five short walks.

Roughly a 30-minute walk along the road to Solothurn (or take bus 1) is the **Taubenloch Gorge** (Taubenlochschlucht, Gorges du Taubenloch). A path runs along its 2.5km length (no entry charge, but there's a donation box).

Festivals & Events

The **Bieler Braderie** in June is among Switzerland's biggest markets.

Sleeping

Lago Lodge (☎ 032 331 37 32; www.lagolodge.ch; Uferweg 5; dm Sfr28-34, d with bathroom Sfr80, breakfast/lunch/dinner Sfr8/17/17; reception 7-11.30am & 2-10pm;) Between the train station and the lake, this Swiss Backpackers–affiliated hostel resembles an American motel with its small dorms – just three to six beds in each – laid out in a row over two storeys. Reception is in the bistro bar (open Wednesday to Monday), which cooks food and, more notably, brews four types of very delicious organic beer.

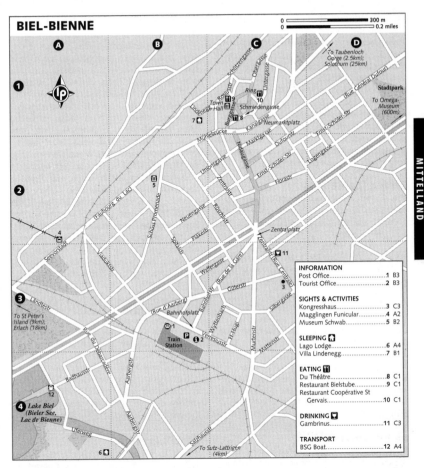

BIEL-BIENNE

MITTELLAND

Villa Lindenegg (☎ 032 322 94 66; www.lindenegg.ch; Lindenegg 5; s Sfr90-180, d Sfr150-250; P) Languishing in a pleasant park minutes from the centre, this lovely 19th-century country villa with garden offers elegance and personal service at a very affordable price. Its eight rooms mix modern with historic, some have balconies and there is a bistro to dine in or enjoy an early evening aperitif.

Eating & Drinking

our pick **Restaurant Coopérative St Gervais** (☎ 032 322 48 22; www.stgervais.ch; Untergasse/Rue Basse 21; mains Sfr15-20; ☷ 9.30am-12.30am Mon & Wed-Sat, 9.30am-3pm Tue, 2-11.30pm Sun) Beneath vaulted arches or at its enchanting, always-packed tables beneath trees, this hip and alternative restaurant,

bar and gallery cooks up wholesome, often organic dishes and has a fabulous range of cultural events – concerts, gigs and so forth. Find its program online.

Restaurant Bielstube (☎ 032 322 65 88; Rosiusstrasse 18; mains Sfr28-36; ☷ 11am-2.30pm & 6pm-midnight Mon-Fri, from 9am Sat) Peppermint-green walls pierced by pea-green shutters flag this historic restaurant plum in the heart of the Old Town. Cuisine is equally age-old: think various types of *Rösti* and lots of beef, veal, pork and horse (yes!) steaks 'n cutlets, often in a creamy sauce.

Du Théâtre (☎ 032 325 50 50; Schmiedengasse/Rue des Maréchaux 1; mains Sfr28-40; ☷ 8am-11.30pm Tue-Sun) Natural daylight streams into this contemporary bistro with high ceilings, changing art installations in the window and sofa seating to lounge on between meals. Cuisine is Italianate; its mixed plate of *antipasti* (small/medium Sfr12/18) makes an alternative lunch. Sunday brunch costs Sfr25.

Gambrinus (☎ 032 322 41 89; www.gambrinus -loungeria.ch; Zentralstrasse 57; ◷ 7.30am-midnight Tue & Wed, 7.30am-1.30am Thu & Fri, 9am-2am Sat, 6pm-midnight Sun) Cream sofas, lime-green walls and tons of cocktails woo a beautiful set. Somewhat pretentiously it calls itself Switzerland's first 'loungeria' – a bar, lounge and Italian *trattoria* rolled into one. You decide.

Getting There & Away

Biel-Bienne is served by train from Bern (Sfr14.80, 30 minutes), Solothurn (Sfr10.80, 15 to 30 minutes) and Neuchâtel (Sfr11.80, 15 to 30 minutes).

A more enjoyable, if pricier, summer connection is by daily **BSG boat** (☎ 032 329 88 11; www.bielersee.ch, in German & French) to/from Murten (single/return Sfr51/102, four hours) and Neuchâtel (Sfr34/68, 2½ hours).

Solothurn (single/return Sfr44/88, 2½ hours, five daily Tuesday to Sunday) can be reached along the Aare River; see also p214.

Getting Around

Rent bicycles and rollerblades from the **left-luggage counter** (☎ 051 226 22 81; www.rentabike.ch; half-/full day bike Sfr18/26, rollerblades Sfr20/25) at the train station.

AROUND BIEL-BIENNE

Wine-growing villages line the western shore of Lake Biel, and the nature reserve of **St Peter's Island** (St Petersinsel/Île de St Pierre) sits in the middle. Actually, falling water levels mean this is no longer an island proper but a long, thin promontory jutting out into the lake from the southwest shore near Erlach. It is possible to take a 1¼-hour stroll along this causeway from Erlach, but because of the difficulties in reaching Erlach from Biel-Bienne (you need to catch a train to La Neuveville and an infrequent bus to Erlach), it's easiest to catch a boat from Biel-Bienne (single/return Sfr20.60/41.20, 50 minutes).

Political theorist Jean-Jacques Rousseau spent, he said, the happiest time of his life on St Petersinsel. The 11th-century monastery where he resided is now the renowned **Restaurant-Hotel St Petersinsel** (☎ 032 338 11 14; www.st-petersinsel.ch, in German & French; d Sfr225, ste Sfr285-305; ✗).

Visiting the island makes a relaxing day trip, and you can hop off and on as you like, including at the drop-dead gorgeous wine-growing villages of **Twann** (Douanne in French) and **Ligerz** (Gléresse in French); see the boxed text, opposite, for memorably scenic wine tasting in both villages. If you're more interested in swimming, take a dip from Erlach, St Peter's Island or La Neuveville.

Neighbouring Lac de Neuchâtel and Lac de Morat (Lake Murten) are connected to Lake Biel (Bieler See) by canal, and day-long cruises of all three (around Sfr77 including lunch) are run year-round by Biel-based **BSG** (☎ 032 329 88 11; www.bielersee.ch, in German & French) and **Navigation Lacs de Neuchâtel et Morat** (☎ 032 729 96 00; www.navig.ch) in Neuchâtel. Other regular lake services operate only in spring and summer, though there are special cruises (eg fondue evenings) in winter and autumn.

EMMENTAL REGION

One of Switzerland's most famous dairy products – holey Emmental cheese – is what this rural idyll east of Berne is all about. Think a mellow patchwork of quiet villages, grazing cows, fields of sugar beet and fabulous farm chalets with vast barns and overhanging roofs, all strung out along the fertile banks of the River Emme.

Sights & Activities

Watch Emmental cheese being made into 95kg wheels and taste it at the **Emmentaler Schaukäserei** (Emmental Show Dairy; ☎ 034 435 16 11; www.showdairy.ch; admission free; ◷ 8.30am-6.30pm) in Affoltern. Short videos explain the modern production process and how Emmental gets its famous holes, while cheese-making as it was done in the 18th century happens once a day over an open fire in the 18th-century herdsman's cottage. The dairy processes 6 million litres of milk a year, brought each morning at 6am or 7am by farmers in the surrounding area. In summer try your hand at cheese rolling – yes, just that.

The road from Burgdorf to **Affoltern**, 6km to the east, is a scenic drive past lumbering old farmsteads, with farmhouses proudly bedecked with flower boxes, winter wood neatly stacked and kitchen garden perfectly

WINE TASTING WITH A VIEW

The lush green vines that stagger down the steep hillside in strictly regimented lines towards the northern shore of Lake Biel are spectacular.

And there is no better spot to savour this viticultural magnificence, heavy with grapes prior to the autumnal harvest, than **Ligerz** (Gléresse in French), a quaint lakeside hamlet with a small **wine museum** (☎ 032 315 21 32; www.vinsdulacbienne.ch; Le Fornel; adult/child Sfr6/free; ⏱ 1-4.30pm Sat & Sun May-Oct) and an old-fashioned **funicular** (☎ 032 315 12 24; www.vinifuni.ch, in German & French; adult one-way Sfr5.40) that climbs through vines to hilltop **Prêles**. On clear days views across the vines and beyond to the snowcapped Bernese Alps are breathtaking.

A twinset of to-die-for addresses, both uphill from the water, make Ligerz an enviable place to lunch or taste local wine as an early evening aperitif. Start at the thoroughly modern **Wein Lounge/Lounge à Vin** (☎ 032 315 23 24; www.schernelz-village.ch, in German; Untergasse 22; ⏱ 5-9pm Jun–mid-August), where you can taste chardonnay, Pinot noir and other varieties produced on the Domaine de Schernelz Village on a stylish decking terrace above vines. Contemporary designer sofas make it a particularly comfortable place to hang, glass in hand, as the sun drops behind St Peter's Island. In keeping with its beautiful setting, this wine lounge opens only in beautiful weather.

Next up is `our pick` **Restaurant Aux Trois Amis** (☎ 032 315 11 44; Untergasse 17), a quintessential village bistro with a centuries-old facade up which a vine creeps. The place really comes into its own in summer, when its tree-shaded terrace heaves with punters purring contentedly as they eat, drink and gaze at the tumbling vines, just centimetres away, and the slate-blue water rippling towards St Peter's below.

Try overnighting at Ligerz' lakefront **Hotel Restaurant Kreuz** (☎ 032 315 11 15; www.kreuz-ligerz.ch; Hauptstrasse 17; s/d from Sfr105/205), an old patrician's house with painted shutters, a Renaissance soul and a garden by the water's edge, from where you can take a dip. Its garden bistro serves wine produced from its own vines that march uphill in lines behind. In January and February, don't miss *Treberwurst (saucisse du marc* in French), a sausage traditionally made by winegrowers as they distilled leftover grape skins and pulp to make *Marc* (a fiery type of brandy), hence the sausage's distinct kick.

Hands down the most idyllic way of getting to Ligerz is on foot along the **Sentier du Viticole**, a trail that follows the northern shore of Lake Biel from Vingelz (in the east) to Twann and beyond to La Neuveville (in the west). In Twann taste and buy 300-odd vintages by Lake Biel winegrowers at the **Vinethek Viniterra Bielersee** (☎ 032 315 77 47; Im Moos 4; ⏱ 5-9pm Tue-Fri, 2-8pm Sat & Sun).

tended. Stop in Kaltacker for a hunk of rustic pumpkin bread smothered in melted cheese and sun-dried tomatoes (Sfr14) or *rösti* sprinkled with calf kidneys (Sfr27) at traditional farmhouse restaurant, **Landgasthof zum Hirschen** (☎ 034 422 32 16; Kaltacker; mains Sfr15-30; ⏱ lunch & dinner Thu-Mon, closed Mar & Nov).

By public transport take the train from Burgdorf to Hasle-Rüegsau, then postal bus 195 (Sfr6) or, better still, rent a bike from Burgdorf train station (Sfr33 per day) and pedal. The **tourist office** (☎ 058 327 50 92; www .burgdorf.ch; Bahnhofstrasse 44; ⏱ 9am-noon & 1.30-6pm Mon-Fri) at the station has route maps.

Burgdorf itself (literally 'castle village') is split into two: the Upper Town and the Lower Town. The natural highlight of the quaint old *Oberstadt* (Upper Town), the 12th-century

Schloss (castle), is straight out of a book with its drawbridge, thick stone walls and trio of museums focusing on castle history, Swiss gold and ethnology. By contrast, in the new Lower Town, the works of Switzerland's foremost photorealist painter steal the show at the **Franz Gertsch Museum** (☎ 034 421 40 20; Platanenstrasse 3; adult/child Sfr12/5; ⏱ 10am-6pm Tue, Thu & Fri, 10am-7pm Wed, 10am-5pm Sat & Sun).

The small town of **Langnau**, 20km to the south, is known for its ornamental crockery and has a couple of demonstration potteries *(Schautöpfereien)*. Emmental's quaintest hamlet, where 16th-century Anabaptist villagers were persecuted for their religious beliefs, slumbers 6km southeast of here: **Trubschachen** with its serene square and church steeple is a world away.

TOO MUCH CHEESE

When all that cheese gets too much, flit to the mountain hamlet of Rüttihubelbad for an alternative sensory experience at **Sensorium** (☎ 031 700 85 85; www.sensorium.ch; adult/child/family Sfr17/9/50; ☺ 9am-5.30pm Tue-Fri, 10am-5.30pm Sat & Sun), an interactive museum aimed at exploring four of the five senses (no taste involved!). A disconcerting stroll in the dark through a maze, a thump on a deafening gong, a back massage with a bowl, a swing in a wicker basket and a barefoot stroll across sand, bricks and tree stumps are among the playful experiences. Once or twice a month, the adjoining hotel hosts **Sensonero** (☎ advance reservations 031 700 81 81; Sfr60), a three-course meal in the dark.

Sensorium is a pleasant 45-minute hike from Worb train station or one hour from Walkringen; follow yellow 'Berner Wanderwege' signs. By car, drive east from Worb to the tiny hamlet of Enggistein, then bear north towards Wikartswil to Rüttihubelbad.

Sleeping & Eating

Langnau has a handful of traditional chalet-style hotels, window boxes bursting with red geraniums; its tourist office covers the entire Emmental region.

SYHA Hostel (☎ 034 402 45 26; www.youthhostel.ch /langnau; Mooseggstrasse 32, Langnau; dm inc breakfast Sfr27, d Sfr68, packed lunch Sfr9; ☺ reception 7-9am & 5-8pm, closed early Feb & late Sep–mid-Oct) This Langnau hostel, a 10-minute walk from the station but still well off the beaten track, is a farmhouse-style chalet built in 1768 with a huge overhanging roof, basic rooms and a notably cheery, convivial atmosphere.

Landgasthof Löwen (☎ 034 495 53 04; Löwenplatz, Trubschachen; s/d Sfr45/90; ☺ lunch & dinner Fri-Tue) This typical Emmental village inn, with a creamy facade, a giant steep roof, green shutters and flower boxes, gazes sleepily at the hills from its central-square perch. Rooms are simple with shared bathrooms, and dining (*menus* Sfr25.50 and Sfr29.50) is local and fireside cosy.

our pick Möschberg (☎ 031 710 22 22; www.hotel moeschberg.ch, in German; Grosshöchstetten; s/d without bathroom Sfr90/120, dinner Sfr28; ☒) This green hotel and cultural centre, 100% organic, situated between fields of cows and gentle walking trails, is a quintessential slice of the Emmental. Rooms are simple but stylish; dinner is a vibrant homemade affair packed with vegetables – no meat here – and organic wine. Find this friendly house, an agricultural school for women in the 1930s, 14km west of Langnau in the rolling green hills above dairy-farming hamlet Grosshöchstetten. Before leaving, be sure to knock on the door of the neighbouring cheese farm to taste (and buy) its *Alpkäse* and more mature *Hobelkäse*.

our pick Gasthaus Bäregghöhe (☎ 034 495 70 00; www.baeregghoehe.ch; Trubschachen; s/d Sfr90/150;

☺ Wed-Sun Mar-Jan) Well and truly in the sticks is what this five-room family-run inn is – or, rather, atop a green hill lolling down to the valley below against a fabulous backdrop of snow-covered peaks. The view from the south-facing terrace is divine; the style art nouveau and stylishly hip; and the cuisine (mains Sfr15 to Sfr30) in part organic and absolutely raved about for miles around. One not to be missed; find it signposted 2.8km uphill along a wiggly country lane from the eastern end of Langnau.

Hotel Stadthaus (☎ 034 428 80 00; www.stadthaus.ch, in German; Kirchbühl 2, Burgdorf; s/d Sfr210/250, weekend rate Sfr140/200; ☒ Ⓟ) Try this option for unadulterated luxury. The only five-star hotel for miles, this former city hall has every amenity as well as brilliant views.

Getting There & Around

Hourly trains run by **BLS** (www.bls.ch) link Bern and Burgdorf (Sfr8.40, 15 minutes). Langnau can be reached by direct train from Bern (Sfr13) or Burgdorf (Sfr8.40).

SOLOTHURN

pop 15,184 / elevation 440m

Solothurn (Soleure in French) is an enchanting little town with a mellow stone-cobbled soul, creative dining and one very big cathedral: the imposing, 66m-tall facade of St Ursus may take you by surprise as it looms up out of the pavement at one end of the dinky main street. Without it, this could almost be a French village – an impression that makes more sense when you learn of confirmed Catholic Solothurn's long-standing links to France.

But the presence of the cathedral standing majestically alongside fountains, churches and city gates gives weight to Solothurn's claim to be Switzerland's most beautiful baroque town. Buy a paper cone of *heissi Marroni* (hot chestnuts) from a street stall, don your meandering shoes and prepare to be thoroughly charmed.

Orientation & Information

Exit the train station and walk in a straight line north along Rötistrasse and across the Aare River to the Old Town, less than a 10-minute walk away and easily spotted by the cathedral spire spiking Kronenplatz, the central square.

Tourist Office (☎ 032 626 46 46; www.solothurn-city .ch; Hauptgasse 69; ☼ 8.30am-12.30pm & 1.30-6pm Mon-Fri, 9am-noon Sat) By the cathedral; ATM next door.

Sights & Activities

Architect Gaetano Matteo Pisoni restrained himself with the classical Italianate facade of Solothurn's monolithic 18th-century **Kathedrale St-Ursen** (☎ 032 622 87 71; admission free; Kronenplatz; ☼ 8am-noon & 2-7pm Easter-Sep, to 6pm Oct-Easter) but went wild inside with a white-and-gilt trip of wedding-cake baroque.

Two minutes east, **Baseltor** is the most attractive city gate and the one most enter through. A stone's throw west down Hauptgasse is a **Jesuit Church** (1680–89) whose unprepossessing facade disguises an interior of baroque embellishments and stucco work. All the 'marble' in here is fake – mere spruced-up wood and plaster.

A little further west ticks the 12th-century **Zeitglockenturm**, an astronomical clock where a knight, a king and a grim reaper jig on the hour. Its clock hands are reversed so the smaller one shows the minutes.

Nearby on Hauptgasse, the **Justice Fountain** (1561) – a blindfolded representation of Justice, holding aloft a sword, while the four most important contemporary figures in Europe sit at her feet – will likewise produce a wry smile. The Holy Roman Emperor, in red and white robes, is by Justice's right foot, then proceeding anticlockwise, you'll see the Pope, the Turkish Sultan and…the mayor of Solothurn!

MUSEUMS

The centrepiece of the **Kunstmuseum** (Museum of Fine Arts; ☎ 032 622 23 07; www.kunstmuseum-so.ch, in German; Werkhofstrasse 30; admission by donation; ☼ 11am-5pm Tue-Fri, 10am-5pm Sat & Sun) is Ferdinand Hodler's famous portrait of William Tell. Before arriving in Switzerland, you might never have imagined the national hero as a red-haired, bearded goliath in a white hippy top and short pants, but you'll see this personification repeated many times. The *Madonna of Solothurn* (1522), by Holbein the Younger, is one of only a small number of other major works, but the museum hosts interesting temporary exhibitions.

The early 17th-century rust-coloured facade of the vast, multi-windowed **Museum Altes Zeughaus** (Old Arsenal Museum; ☎ 032 623 35 28; Zeughausplatz 1; adult/under 8yr/family Sfr6/4/10; ☼ 10am-noon & 2-5pm Tue-Sat, 10am-5pm Sun May-Oct, 2-5pm Tue-Fri, 10am-noon & 2-5pm Sat & Sun Nov-Apr) is a reminder that Solothurn was once a centre for mercenaries, many of whom fought for French kings. Break for a cup of coffee between canons and suits of armour in the museum café.

Sleeping

For a tiny town, Solothurn surprises with funky sleeping spaces.

SYHA Hostel (☎ 032 623 17 06; www.youthhostel.ch /solothurn; Landhausquai 23; dm incl breakfast Sfr29.50-47, d with shower & toilet Sfr94, lunch or dinner Sfr15; ☼ reception 7.30-10am & 4.30-9.30pm Mar–mid-Dec; ▯ ✕ ⌂) Hands down one of Switzerland's most contemporary hostels, this centuries-old building by the river is a striking waterside mix of glass,

MITTELLAND

GREEN SLEEP

Mountains of fresh air are a sure thing at the **Cornfield Openair Hotel** (☎ 032 622 39 53, 079 439 20 74; www.maishotel.ch, in German; Rütihof 111, Nennigkofen; d/q Sfr80/160, breakfast adult/4-14yr Sfr15/7; ☼ Jun–early Sep), Solothurn's greenest sleep, in a cornfield 4.5km west of town in Nennigkofen. 'Rooms' for two or four are equipped with one or two canopied wrought-iron double beds, straw mattresses, mosquito nets, wood-log stools and 'walls' of green corn sheaths – all you need to bring is your sleeping bag and a mood for romance. Prior to candles out, meals, music concerts and film screenings woo guests beneath twinkling stars.

stainless steel and raw concrete. Dorms sport three to 10 beds, and are sometimes mixed gender, and the place is equipped for travellers in wheelchairs.

our pick **Gasthaus Kreuz & Café Landhaus** (☎ 032 622 20 20; www.kreuz-solothurn.ch, in German; Kreuzgasse 4; s/d/tr/q without bathroom Sfr50/90/120/140) Another riverside choice, this youthful guest house–cum–cultural centre exudes a definite funk with its cherry-red shower block shared by 13 rooms, each minimalist in soul with creaky wooden floors and crisp white linens. Simple dining with friends is the lure of its street-level café-bar (lunch costs Sfr15; dinner Sfr20 to Sfr30), host to bands, concerts, cultural happenings and Solothurn's biggest dance party of the year on 1 January.

Baseltor (☎ 032 622 34 22; www.baseltor.ch; Hauptgasse 79; s/d Sfr95/160; ✗) Charmingly set in the shade of the cathedral, this atmospheric old inn with steel-grey wooden shutters and an attractive minimalist interior is as much traditional dining spot (mains cost Sfr28 to Sfr40) as bed to rest one's weary head. Three of its nine simple but handsome rooms slumber in a separate annexe.

Hotel an der Aare (☎ 032 626 24 00; www.hotel aare.ch, in German; Berntorstrasse 2; s/d from Sfr130/165; ▢ ✗ Ⓟ) The riverside nursing quarters of the 18th-century Solothurn hospital, itself built in 14th-century style, have found new life as a superstylish, ultramodern hotel with beautiful designer fittings and brightly coloured walls interspersed with exposed stone and brick. Taste and buy local *Wein* in the wine cellar opposite.

Eating & Drinking

Café Landhaus (see above) is an atmospheric option, or try one of the following:

our pick **Pittaria** (☎ 032 621 22 69; Theatergasse 12; filled pita Sfr12-15; ✆ 10am-3pm & 5.30-9pm Tue-Fri, 10am-6pm Sat) The natural charisma, charm and creative talents of Palestinian owner Sami Daher fused with his extraordinarily tasty mint tea, homemade mango chutney, hummus and falafel is a winning combination. This kebab shop has excellent food, a friendly intimate atmosphere and bench seating laid with Persian rugs. In 2004 Pittaria was named Switzerland's best takeaway.

Sol Heure (☎ 032 625 54 34; Ritterquai 10; menus Sfr17.50-20.50, mains Sfr15-25; ✆ 5.30-11.30pm Mon, 11.30am-12.30am Tue-Thu, 10am-2am Sat, 2-11.30pm Sun) Old stone walls, modern furniture, lifestyle magazines and a sun-flooded terrace facing the water ensures that half of Solothurn can be found at this riverside bar in a trendy former warehouse. Food is casual: think red chicken curry, New Mexico burgers.

Cantinetta Bindella (☎ 032 623 16 85; Ritterquai 3; pasta Sfr15-20, mains Sfr30-44; ✆ 10am-12.30am Mon-Sat) Across the road from Sol Heure is this refined Italian with a quaint candlelit interior and white tablecloths beneath trees in its leafy walled garden (try to nab the old stone table if you can). Authentic *primi piatti* of pasta come in small, Italian-sized portions or as a larger main course.

Getting There & Away

Solothurn has two trains per hour to Bern on the private RBS line (www.rbs.ch, in German; Sfr15.20, 40 minutes, rail passes valid). Regular trains also run to Basel (Sfr26/25 via Olten/Moutier-Delemont, one to 1½ hours) and Biel (Sfr10.80, 15 to 30 minutes).

Boats also connect Solothurn to Biel-Bienne (see p210).

AROUND SOLOTHURN

The grand **Schloss Waldegg** (☎ 032 622 38 67; www .schloss-waldegg.ch, in German; Feldbrunnen-St Niklaus; adult/7-16yr Sfr6/4; ✆ 2-5pm Tue-Thu & Sat, 10am-5pm Sun Mar-Oct), a few kilometres north of town, was built in the 17th century and displays period furniture and paintings. Take bus 4 from the station to the St Niklaus stop, then walk north past the church for a further 10 minutes.

The **Weissenstein** (1284m), north of Solothurn, is a mountain that's good for hiking, cross-country skiing or a scenic drive.

Zürich

Zürich is an enigma. It is the epitome of Swiss efficiency: a savvy financial centre with possibly the densest public transport system in the world, but it also has a gritty, post-industrial edge that would seem more at home in a German Ruhr Valley town.

Once famed for its hard-drug problem, Switzerland's biggest city is undeniably hip – and efficient – why else would Google (whose local employees are called Zooglers) have located its European engineering centre here? With a grungy, wacky, art-world freedom one associates with Berlin, it has grubby(ish) districts alongside posh quarters. The locals may be earnest, hard-working early risers but, come clock-off time, they throw themselves wholeheartedly into a festive vortex – its summer Street Parade is one of Europe's largest street parties.

Much of the ancient centre, with its winding lanes and tall church steeples, has been kept lovingly intact. The city, however, is no stick-in-the-mud stranger to contemporary design trends. Nowhere is that clearer than in abandoned industrial Kreis (district) 5 and adjacent Kreis 4, long the near-exclusive domain of drug dealers, street mafiosi and prostitutes, which have been caught up in an urban renovation revolution since the mid-1990s. Züri-West, as the whole area is dubbed, is the epicentre of the city's nightlife.

Beyond the city, in the rest of the canton of the same name, the heights of Uetliberg are inviting to walkers and there are countless pretty spots, such as Rapperswil, along the lake. Winterthur, to the northeast, is a cultural powerhouse, with major art and science museums.

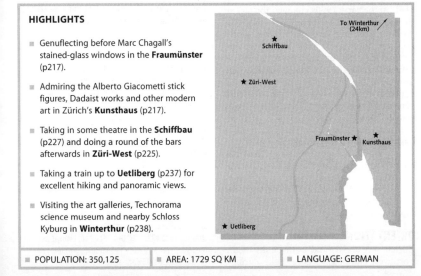

HIGHLIGHTS

- Genuflecting before Marc Chagall's stained-glass windows in the **Fraumünster** (p217).

- Admiring the Alberto Giacometti stick figures, Dadaist works and other modern art in Zürich's **Kunsthaus** (p217).

- Taking in some theatre in the **Schiffbau** (p227) and doing a round of the bars afterwards in **Züri-West** (p225).

- Taking a train up to **Uetliberg** (p237) for excellent hiking and panoramic views.

- Visiting the art galleries, Technorama science museum and nearby Schloss Kyburg in **Winterthur** (p238).

★ Schiffbau
★ Züri-West
To Winterthur (24km)
Fraumünster ★ ★ Kunsthaus
★ Uetliberg

■ POPULATION: 350,125 ■ AREA: 1729 SQ KM ■ LANGUAGE: GERMAN

ZÜRICH

HISTORY

Today frequently voted Europe's most liveable city, Zürich started life as a Roman encampment called Turicum. Germanic tribes moved in by AD 400 and, in 1336, the already prosperous town underwent a minor revolution as craftsmen and traders took power, expelling the nobles and creating the 13 *Zünfte* (guilds), which for long after directed the city's fortunes. Many still exist today and come out to play for the Sechseläuten festival (p221). Only locals can join and many a city bigwig is a *Zunft* member.

In 1351, Zürich joined the Swiss Confederation and, in the early 16th century, became a key player in the Reformation under Zwingli (opposite). In the following centuries, it grew rich on textiles and banking.

Due to Switzerland's neutrality during both world wars, Zürich attracted all sorts of personalities both in wartime and peace. James Joyce and Vladimir Lenin hung out here. And in the wake of the horrors of WWI, the counter-cultural Dada art movement was born in Zürich. By 1923 the movement was dead, but its spirit lived on in the works of Georg Grosz, Hans Arp and Max Ernst. Dadaist works are on display in Zürich's Kunsthaus (opposite) and the Plakatraum (Poster Collection) of the Museum für Gestaltung (opposite).

Politicians *can* make all the difference: the switch from conservative rule to a Social Democrat regime in the Rathaus (Town Hall) in the early 1990s changed the face of the city. The Zürich of before was known for its dour Protestant work ethic and wealth and startlingly overt heavy drug problem. In 1995 the drug supermarket at Letten was dismantled. The heroin addicts haven't gone away, but the city is keeping a lid on the problem with supervised public injection centres. Of course, the city's wealth remains intact.

More visible has been the Town Hall's backing for the city's awakening as a cool town. Relaxed laws governing bars and clubs and active support for a plethora of cultural activities have transformed the grey lakeside city of the 'gnomes' (Brit parlance for Zürich's bankers) into one of central Europe's hippest hang-outs.

ORIENTATION

Zürich spreads around both banks of the northwest end of Zürichsee (Lake Zürich).

The Limmat River runs further north still, splitting the medieval city centre in two. The narrow streets of the Niederdorf quarter on the river's east bank are crammed with restaurants, bars and shops; down the west bank runs the hoity-toity shopping avenue of Bahnhofstrasse, capped at the north by the Hauptbahnhof (main train station).

The reborn hip part of the city, known as Züri-West and stretching west of the Hauptbahnhof, is primarily made up of two former working-class districts: Kreis 4 and Kreis 5.

Kreis 4, still a red-light district and centred on Langstrasse, is lined with opportunity shops, eateries, bars and peep shows.

Langstrasse continues north over the railway lines into Kreis 5, where it quietens down a little but still offers plenty of options. The main focus of Kreis 5 action is, however, along what the city fathers have dubbed the Kulturmeile (culture mile; www.kulturmeile.ch), Hardstrasse.

The bulk of the canton of Zürich spreads east and north of the city. Winterthur, to the northeast, has some remarkable museums. Zürichsee drops away to the southeast like a juicy fat *Kalbswurst* (veal sausage), where it runs into the eastern cantons of St Gallen and Schwyz.

INFORMATION
Bookshops
Orell Füssli (Map p220; ☎ 044 211 04 44; www.books.ch; Bahnhofstrasse 70; ☺ 9am-8pm Mon-Fri, 9am-6pm Sat) English-language bookshop.

Discount Card
ZürichCard (per 24hr adult/child Sfr17/12, per 72hr Sfr34/24) Available from the tourist office and the airport train station, this provides free public transport, free museum admission and more.

Emergency
Police station (Map p220; ☎ 044 216 71 11; Bahnhofquai 3)

Internet Access
Internetcafe (Map p220; ☎ 044 210 33 11; www.e-cafe .ch; Uraniastrasse 3; per min Sfr0.30; ☺ 7am-11pm Mon-Fri, 8am-11pm Sat, 10am-10pm Sun) You can connect your laptop (Swiss power points, p349).
Quanta (Map p220; ☎ 044 260 72 66; Limmatquai 94, Niederdorf; per hr Sfr10; ☺ 9am-midnight) Noisy but central. Enter via Mühlegasse.

Medical Services

Bellevue Apotheke (Map p220; ☎ 044 266 62 22; www.bellevue-apotheke.com; Theaterstrasse 14) A 24-hour chemist.

UniversitätsSpital Zürich (University Hospital; Map pp218-19; ☎ 044 255 11 11, 044 255 21 11; www.usz.ch; Rämistrasse 100).

Post

Hauptbahnhof post office (Map p220; Hauptbahnhof; ☿ 7am-9pm daily)

Sihlpost (Map pp218-19; Kasernenstrasse 97; ☿ 6.30am-10.30pm Mon-Fri, to 8pm Sat, 10am-10.30pm Sun)

Tourist information

Zürich Tourism (Map p220; ☎ 044 215 40 00; www .zuerich.com; Hauptbahnhof; ☿ 8am-8.30pm Mon-Sat & 8.30am-6.30pm Sun May-Oct, 8.30am-7pm Mon-Sat & 9am-6.30pm Sun Nov-Apr) For hotel reservations through the tourist office, call ☎ 044 215 40 40. Offers excellent city walking tours.

SIGHTS
Churches

The 13th-century **Fraumünster** (Map p220; ☎ 044 221 20 63; www.fraumuenster.ch, in German; Münsterhof; ☿ 10am-6pm Mar-Oct, 10am-4pm Nov-Feb) is renowned for its distinctive stained-glass windows, designed by the Russian-Jewish master Marc Chagall (1887–1985). He did a series of five windows in the choir-stalls area in 1971 and the rose window in the southern transept in 1978. The rose window in the northern transept is by Augusto Giacometti (1945).

More of Augusto Giacometti's work is on show across the river in the twin-towered **Grossmünster** (Map p220; ☎ 044 251 38 60; www .grossmuenster.ch; Grossmünsterplatz; ☿ 9am-6pm daily mid-Mar–Oct, 10am-5pm Nov–mid-Mar, tower closed Sun morning mid-Mar–Oct & all Sun Nov–mid-Mar). Charlemagne founded this landmark cathedral in the 9th century.

The firebrand preacher from the boon-docks, Huldrych Zwingli (1484–1531), began speaking out against the Catholic Church here in the 16th century, and thus brought the Reformation to Zürich. You can climb the southern tower, the **Karlsturm** (admission Sfr2; ☿ 9.15am-5pm Mar-Oct). **Zwingli's house**, where he both lived and worked, is nearby at Kirchgasse 3.

From any position in the city, it's hard to overlook the 13th-century tower of **St Peterskirche** (St Peter's Church; Map p220; St Peterhofstatt;

☿ 8am-6pm Mon-Fri, 8am-4pm Sat, 11am-5pm Sun). Its prominent clock face, 8.7m in diameter, is the largest in Europe. Inside, the choir stalls date from the 13th century but the bulk of the rest of the church is an 18th-century remake.

Museums

Compact Zürich has 43 museums; the tourist office has a list. To keep in touch with the city's art scene, check out www.artinzurich.ch.

KUNSTHAUS

Zürich's impressive **Kunsthaus** (Museum of Fine Arts; Map pp218-19; ☎ 044 253 84 84; www.kunsthaus.ch; Heimplatz 1; adult/child/student & senior Sfr18/free/8, free Sun; ☿ 10am-8pm Wed-Fri, 10am-6pm Tue, Sat & Sun) boasts a rich collection that includes Alberto Giacometti stick-figure sculptures, Monets, Van Goghs, Rodin sculptures and other 19th- and 20th-century art. Swiss artist Ferdinand Hodler is also represented. The clumpy cement building itself is a bit of a horror.

SCHWEIZERISCHES LANDESMUSEUM

Housed in a cross between a mansion and a castle, the big **Schweizerisches Landesmuseum** (Swiss National Museum; Map pp218-19; ☎ 044 218 65 11; www.musee-suisse.ch; Museumstrasse 2; permanent collection adult/concession Sfr5/3; ☿ 10am-5pm Tue-Sun) is a large cream cake of a museum. The permanent collection includes a tour through Swiss history, plus there are usually enticing special exhibitions.

MUSEUM FÜR GESTALTUNG

Consistently impressive and wide-ranging, the exhibitions at the **Museum für Gestaltung** (Design Museum; Map pp218-19; ☎ 043 446 67 67; www.museum -gestaltung.ch; Ausstellungstrasse 60; adult/concession Sfr9/6; ☿ 10am-8pm Tue-Thu, 10am-5pm Fri-Sun) include anything from Bollywood to 'short stories in photography'. The Museum für Gestaltung's nearby **Plakatraum** (Poster Collection; Map pp218-19; Limmatstrasse 55; ☿ 1-5pm Tue-Sat) draws on a huge archive of vintage tourism, Dada and other posters.

MUSEUM RIETBERG

Set in three villas in a leafy park, the **Museum Rietberg** (off Map pp218-19; ☎ 044 206 31 31; www.rietberg .ch; Gablerstrasse 15; permanent collection adult/concession Sfr12/10, special exhibitions Sfr16/12; ☿ 10am-5pm Tue & Fri-Sun, 10am-8pm Wed & Thu) houses a fine collection of African, Oriental and ancient-American art.

ZÜRICH

INFORMATION
Sihlpost	1	D3
UniversitätsSpital Zürich	2	F4

SIGHTS & ACTIVITIES
Bad Utoquai	3	E6
Giessereihalle	(see 11)	
Johann Jacobs Museum	4	E6
Kunsthalle Zürich	(see 8)	
Kunsthaus	5	E4
Letten	6	D2
Männerbad	7	D4
Migros Museum	8	C1
Museum für Gestaltung	9	D2
Plakatraum	10	D3
Puls 5	11	B1
Schiffbau	12	B1
Schweizerisches Landesmuseum	13	D3
Seebad Enge	14	D6

SLEEPING
Dakini	15	B3
Hotel Foyer Hottingen	16	F5
Hotel Greulich	17	B3
Hotel Plattenhof	18	F4
Hotel Rothaus	19	C3
Hotel Seegarten	20	F6
Lady's First	21	F6
Romantik Hotel Florhof	22	E4

EATING
Alpenrose	23	C2
Fribourger Fondue-Stübli	24	C4
Lade	25	C3
les halles	26	A1
Restaurant Reithalle	27	D4
Restaurant Rosso	28	B2
Sankt Meinrad	29	B3
Seidenspinner	30	C4
Tibits by Hiltl	31	E6

DRINKING
Acapulco	32	C2
Daniel H.	33	C4
Hard One	34	B1
Liquid	35	C3
Longstreet Bar	36	C3
Riff Raff	37	C2
Rimini Bar	(see 7)	
Sphères	38	B1

ENTERTAINMENT
Adagio	39	D5
Club Q	40	A1
Dynamo	41	D2
Helsinki Hütte	42	B2
Indochine	43	B1
Kanzlei	44	C4
Kino Xenix	(see 44)	
Labor Bar	45	B1
Le Bal	46	D6
Mascotte	47	E5
Moods	(see 12)	
Opera House	48	E6
Schauspielhaus	(see 12)	
Supermarket	49	B2
Tonhalle	50	D5
Zukunft	51	C3

SHOPPING
Bürkliplatz Market	(see 54)	
Flohmarkt Kanzlei	(see 44)	
Freitag	52	B2

TRANSPORT
Avis	53	B4
Bürkliplatz Riverboat & Lake Steamer Landing Stage	54	E5
Europcar	55	C3
Hertz	56	C5
International Buses	57	D3
Schweizerisches Landesmuseum Riverboat Landing Stage	58	E3
Velogate	59	D3

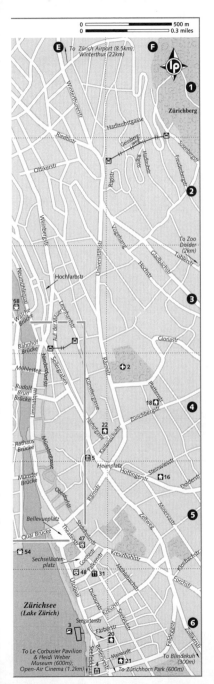

MODERN ART MUSEUMS

Cabaret Voltaire (Map p220; ☎ 043 268 57 20; www
.cabaretvoltaire.ch; Spiegelgasse 1; admission varies, free to
café/bar; ☿ exhibitions noon-6.30pm Tue-Fri & Sun, 11am-
5pm Sat, bar noon-midnight Tue-Sat, 12.30-6.30pm Sun) is
the birthplace of the Dada movement (see
p39) and since 2004 has again been putting
on exhibitions and shows, frequently with a
dose of vitriolic social criticism.

Migros Museum (Map pp218-19; ☎ 044 277 20 50; www
.migrosmuseum.ch; Limmatstrasse 270; adult/concession
Sfr8/4, combined admission with Kunsthalle Zürich Sfr12/6;
☿ noon-6pm Tue & Wed-Fri, to 8pm Thu, 11am-5pm Sat &
Sun), displaying contemporary art, is one of two
main museums in the converted Löwenbräu
brewery, which also houses several galleries, a
bookshop, a fitness centre and offices.

Kunsthalle Zürich (Map pp218-19; ☎ 044 272 15 15; www
.kunsthallezurich.ch; Limmatstrasse 270; same prices & hr as
Migros Museum), like the Migros Museum, features
changing exhibitions of contemporary art.

OTHER MUSEUMS

Johann Jacobs Museum (Map pp218-19; ☎ 044 388
61 51; www.jacobsfoundation.org; Seefeldquai 17; adult/
concession Sfr5/3; ☿ 2-7pm Fri, 2-5pm Sat, 10am-5pm Sun)
is as addictive as the coffee to which it is
devoted. The permanent collection includes
everything from coffee pots to paintings of
coffee houses.

Beyer Museum (Map p220; ☎ 043 344 63 63; www
.beyer-chronometrie.ch; Bahnhofstrasse 31; adult/child Sfr5/
free; ☿ 2-6pm Mon-Fri) is a small museum chroni-
cling the rise of timekeeping, from striated
medieval candles to modern watches. It is
inside a shop, whose display of precision time
instruments is almost as extraordinary as the
museum collection.

The **Le Corbusier Pavilion & Heidi Weber museum**
(off Map pp218-19; www.centrelecorbusier.com; Zürichhorn
park; ☿ 2-5pm Sat & Sun Jul-Sep), the last item designed by the iconoclastic Swiss-born (naturalised French) architect, looks like a Mondrian
painting set in parkland. Completed after his
death, it contains many of his architectural
drawings, paintings, furniture and books –
collected by fan and friend Heidi Weber.

James Joyce spent much of WWI in
Zürich and wrote *Ulysses* here. The **James
Joyce Foundation** (Map p220; ☎ 044 211 83 01;
www.joycefoundation.ch; Augustinergasse 9; admission
free; ☿ 10am-6pm Mon-Fri) hosts regular public
readings in English from *Ulysses* (5.30pm to
7pm Tuesday) and *Finnegan's Wake* (7pm to
8.30pm Thursday).

ZÜRICH

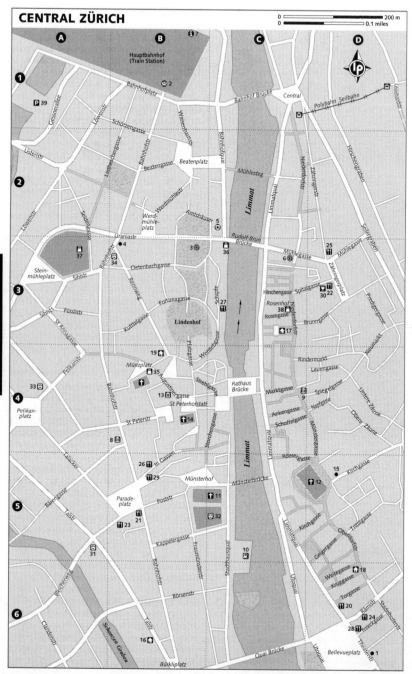

CENTRAL ZÜRICH

ZÜRICH

Waterfront

Zürich comes into its own in summer, when the green parks lining the lake are overrun with bathers, sun seekers, in-line skaters, footballers, lovers, picnickers, party animals and preeners. Police even patrol on rollerblades!

From May to mid-September, official swimming areas are open around the lake and up the Limmat River. Of course, there are plenty of free, unofficial places to take a dip, too.

Official swimming areas are usually wooden piers with a pavilion and most offer massages, yoga, saunas and snacks. Admission is Sfr6, and swimming areas are generally open from 9am to 7pm in May and September and 9am to 8pm from June to August. At trendy **Seebad Enge** (Map pp218-19; ☎ 044 201 38 89; www.seebadenge .ch; Mythenquai 95; ☺ mid-May–mid-Sep), the bar opens until midnight when the weather is good. In the cooler months (September to April), it operates a **sauna** (Sfr25; ☺ 11am-11pm daily, women only Mon). On the opposite shore, adjacent to the Zürichhorn park, is **Bad Utoquai** (Map pp218-19; ☎ 044 251 61 51; Utoquai 49).

Along the river, the 19th-century **Frauenbad** (Map p220; Stadthausquai) is only open to women during the day. In the same way, **Männerbad** (Map pp218-19; Schanzengraben) is men only by day. The two baths open their trendy bars to both sexes at night (see p226).

Letten (Map pp218-19; ☎ 044 362 92 00; Lettensteg 10; admission free), a bathing area further north up the river, is where Züri-West trendsetters swim, barbecue, skateboard, play volleyball, or just drink at the bars and chat on the grass and concrete. You'd never know that this was the focus of Zürich's street drug scene and a virtual no-go area until 1995.

For a month from mid-July, there's an extremely popular waterside **open-air cinema** (off Map pp218-19; ☎ 080 007 80 78; www.orangecinema.ch; Zürichhorn).

Zoo

Zoo Dolder (off Map pp218-19; ☎ 044 254 25 05; www .zoo.ch; Zürichbergstrasse 221; adult/under 6yr/6-16yr/student Sfr22/free/11/16; ☺ 9am-6pm Mar-Oct, 9am-5pm Nov-Feb), up on the Zürichberg, has an expansive location, 1800 animals and a recreated rainforest. Take tram 6 to Zoo station.

FESTIVALS & EVENTS

The following are just the most important; for a full list of events, see www.zuerich.com.

Sechseläuten (www.sechselaeuten.ch, in German) During this spring festival on the third Monday of April, guild members parade down the streets in historical costume and a fireworks-filled 'snowman' (the *Böögg*) is ignited to celebrate the end of winter.

Street Parade (☎ 044 215 40 00; www.street-parade .ch) This techno celebration in the middle of August is one of Europe's largest street parties.

Knabenschiessen (www.knabenschiessen.ch, in German) Huge shooting competition for 12- to 17-year-olds in late September.

SLEEPING

Finding a room on the weekend of the Street Parade is tough and prices skyrocket. They also sometimes head upwards for various major trade fairs (including those in Basel!).

Budget

Not many hotels fall into the budget category. You'll be relying mostly on hostels and B&Bs (check the relevant page on the tourist-office website, www.zuerich.com).

HOSTELS

City Backpacker (Hotel Biber; Map p220; ☎ 044 251 90 15; www.city-backpacker.ch; Niederdorfstrasse 5; dm Sfr34, sheets extra Sfr3, s/d Sfr71/104; ☷ reception closed noon-3pm; ☐) Friendly and well equipped, if a trifle cramped. In summer, you can always overcome the claustrophobia by hanging out on the rooftop terrace. Be warned, this is a bit of a youthful party hostel.

SYHA hostel (off Map pp218-19; ☎ 043 399 78 00; www.youthhostel.ch; Mutschellenstrasse 114, Wollishofen; dm Sfr42, s/d Sfr106.50/127; ☐) This bulbous, purple-red hostel features a swish 24-hour reception/dining hall, flat-screen TVs and sparkling modern bathrooms. Dorms are quite small. Take tram 7 to Morgental, or S-Bahn to Wollishofen.

B&BS

Dakini (Map pp218-19; ☎ 044 291 42 20; www.dakini.ch; Brauerstrasse 87; s Sfr75-95, d Sfr130; ☐ ✗) This relaxed B&B attracts a bohemian crowd of artists and trendy tourists. Four double rooms and two singles are spread across a couple of apartments over two floors, sharing the kitchen and bathroom on each.

HOTELS

Hotel Foyer Hottingen (Map pp218-19; ☎ 044 256 19 19; www.hotel-hottingen.ch; Hottingerstrasse 31; dm Sfr40, s/d without bathroom Sfr110/145; s with bathroom Sfr125-145, d Sfr165-185; ✗) This place is a good deal better inside than outside appearances would suggest. Rooms are clinical but good value and some have a balcony. Each floor has showers and a communal kitchen and on the top floor is a dorm for women only with a rooftop terrace.

Hotel Rothaus (Map pp218-19; ☎ 043 322 10 58; www.hotelrothaus.ch; Sihlhallenstrasse 1; s Sfr82-88, d Sfr110-195; ✗) Smack in the middle of the Langstrasse action, you'd never guess this cheerful red-brick place was once a brothel. A variety of fresh, airy rooms are complemented by a busy little eatery-bar downstairs.

CAMPING

Camping Seebucht (off Map pp218-19; ☎ 044 482 16 12; www.camping-zurich.ch; Seestrasse 559; Sfr27 for two people, tent & car; ☷ May-Sep) Four kilometres from the city centre and on the western shore of the lake, this has good facilities: a restaurant with lake views, a children's play area, hot showers and even a party tent if you want to organise an event. Take bus 161 or 165 from Bürkliplatz.

Midrange

Hotel Otter (Map p220; ☎ 044 251 22 07; www.wueste.ch; Oberdorfstrasse 7; s Sfr115, d Sfr150-175) A true gem, the Otter has 17 rooms variously decorated with pink satin sheets and plastic beads, raised beds, wall murals and, in one instance, a hammock. A popular bar, the Wüste, is downstairs.

Uto Kulm Uetliberg (off Map pp218-19; ☎ 044 457 66 66; www.utokulm.ch; Uetliberg; s Sfr150-200, d Sfr250-490) Luxurious Uto Kulm is perfect for a romantic retreat with its spa baths and big beds. Rooms come in all shapes and sizes, with timber or parquet floors. Take the S10 to Uetliberg (p237) and staff will collect you.

Hotel Greulich (Map pp218-19; ☎ 043 243 42 43; www.greulich.ch; Hermann Greulich Strasse 56; s Sfr190-270, d Sfr255-360; ✗) The curving blue-grey walls lend this designer digs in a quieter part of Kreis 4 a retro art-deco touch. The minimalist, off-white rooms are laid out in facing bungalows along two sides of an austere courtyard.

Hotel Seegarten (Map pp218-19; ☎ 044 388 37 37; www.hotel-seegarten.ch; Seegartenstrasse 14; s Sfr190-275, d Sfr240-325) Rattan furniture and vintage tourist posters give this place a rustic Mediterranean atmosphere, which is reinforced by the proximity to the lake and the on-site Restaurant Latino.

our pick Hotel Plattenhof (Map pp218-19; ☎ 044 251 19 10; www.plattenhof.ch; Plattenstrasse 26; s Sfr205-245, d Sfr245-285; ℗) This youthful minimalist design hotel in a quiet residential area has low, Japanese-style beds, Molteni furniture and oak parquet floors, plus mood lighting in some rooms. It's cool without being pretentious, and even the 'old' rooms are stylishly minimalist. Downstairs in the same building is a hip little café.

Lady's First (Map pp218-19; ☎ 044 380 80 10; www.ladysfirst.ch; Mainaustrasse 24; s Sfr215-255, d Sfr270-320; ☐)

Immaculate and generally spacious rooms provide a pleasant mixture of traditional parquet flooring and designer furnishings. The hotel spa and its accompanying rooftop terrace are reserved for female guests only. There is free wi-fi.

Romantik Hotel Florhof (Map pp218-19; ☎ 044 250 26 26; www.florhof.ch; Florhofgasse 4; s Sfr220-290, d Sfr330-380) This traditional hotel nestles in a lovely garden, a stone's throw from the Kunsthaus (p217).

Top End

Hotel Widder (Map p220; ☎ 044 224 25 26; www.widder hotel.ch; Rennweg 7; s/d from Sfr523/725; P ⊠ ▣) A stylish hotel in the equally grand district of Augustiner, the Widder is a pleasing fusion of modernity and traditional charm. Rooms and public areas across the eight town houses that make up this place are stuffed with art and designer furniture.

Baur au Lac (Map p220; ☎ 044 220 50 20; www.baurau lac.ch; Talstrasse 1; s/d from Sfr523/825; P ⊠ ⊠ ▣) This family-run lakeside jewel is set in a private park and offers all imaginable comforts and a soothing sense of privacy. Rooms are decorated in classic colours, adding to the sense of quiet well-being. Throw in the spa, restaurants and faultless service and you can see why VIPs flock here.

EATING

Denizens of Zürich have the choice of an astounding 2000-plus places to eat and drink. Traditional local cuisine is very rich, as epitomised by the city's signature dish, *Zürcher Geschnetzeltes* (sliced veal in a creamy mushroom sauce).

Cafés

Café Odeon (Map p220; ☎ 044 251 16 50; www.odeon.ch; Am Bellevueplatz; ⊗ 9am-2am Sun-Thu, 9am-4am Fri & Sat) This one-time haunt of Lenin and the Dadaists is still a prime people-watching spot for gays and straights alike. Come for the art-nouveau interior, the OTT chandeliers and a whiff of another century. They serve food too.

Café Sprüngli (Map p220; ☎ 044 224 47 31; www .spruengli.ch; Bahnhofstrasse 21; ⊗ 7am-6.30pm Mon-Fri, 8am-6pm Sat, 9.30am-5.30pm Sun) Sit down for cakes, chocolate and coffee at this epicentre of sweet Switzerland, in business since 1836. You can have a light lunch too, but whatever you do, don't fail to check out the heavenly chocolate shop around the corner on Paradeplatz.

> ### SMOKING OUT THE SMOKERS
>
> In a referendum in September 2008, Zürich voted to ban smoking in bars and restaurants that don't have separate smoking areas. The change is due to come into effect by mid-2009.

Budget

Tibits by Hiltl (Map pp218-19; ☎ 044 260 32 22; www.tibits .ch; Seefeldstrasse 2; meals per 100g Sfr3.60-4.10; ⊗ 6.30am-midnight Mon-Fri, from 8am Sat, from 9am Sun) Tibits is where with-it, health-conscious inhabitants of Zürich head for a light bite. There's a tasty vegetarian buffet, fresh fruit juices, coffee and cakes.

Sternen Grill (Map p220; Bellevueplatz/Theatrestrasse 22; snacks Sfr5-12; ⊗ 11.30am-midnight) This is the city's most famous – and busiest – sausage stand; just follow the crowds streaming in for a tasty grease fest. The classic *Kalbsbratwurst mit Gold Bürli* (veal sausage with bread roll) costs Sfr6.50. They have a few vegetarian options too.

Schipfe 16 (Map p220; ☎ 044 211 21 22; Schipfe 16; menus Sfr16-20; ⊗ 10am-4pm Mon-Fri) Overlooking the Limmat River from the historic Schipfe area, Schipfe 16 is a good-natured canteen-style spot for a humble lunch, from Mediterranean to Indian to Swiss.

Café Zähringer (Map p220; ☎ 044 252 05 00; Zähringerplatz 11; mains Sfr18-32; ⊗ 6pm-midnight Mon, 9am-midnight Tue-Sun) This very-old-school alternative café serves up mostly organic, vegetarian food around communal tables. They have huge vegetarian and carnivores' breakfasts (Sfr20.50 and Sfr22.50).

Lade (Map pp218-19; ☎ 043 317 14 34; www.nietengasse .ch; Nietengasse 1; mains Sfr20-32; ⊗ lunch & dinner Tue-Fri, lunch Mon) Set on a leafy back lane of Kreis 4, this is the kind of spot you might find in London's Stoke Newington or Berlin's Prenzlauer Berg. A modest former general store with a mellow ambience, they serve a short menu of dishes, ranging from salads to pasta.

les halles (Map pp218-19; ☎ 044 273 11 25; www .les-halles.ch; Pfingstweidstrasse 6; mains Sfr22-29; ⊗ 11am-midnight Mon-Wed, 11am-1am Thu-Sat) This joyous scrum of timber tables in Kreis 5 is the best place in town to sit down to *Moules mit Frites* (mussels and fries). Hang at the bustling bar and shop at the market. It is one of several chirpy bar-restaurants in formerly derelict factory buildings in the area.

ZÜRICH

COOKING UP A STORM IN ZÜRICH

Lucerne-born Tobias Meinrad Buholzer, at just 28 years of age, runs one of Zürich's up-and-coming restaurants, **Sankt Meinrad** (opposite). Awarded a high 15 (of 20) points by the prestigious Swiss Gault-Millau restaurant guide for 2009, he also has his eye on a possible future Michelin star.

How important is this kind of recognition?

It's the best advertising you can get. Since this news we have been fully booked as much as two weeks in advance.

Are there different food cultures in Switzerland?

I grew up at a time when everything was mixed together. Everything is relatively *multi-kulti* now.

What is modern Swiss cooking?

Personally, I try not to set myself any limits. Except for Asian cooking – the Asians already do that much better! I grew up with Italian, French and German food and that's how I cook. I take elements from all three and mix them up.

What about traditional rules?

There aren't any rules any more: Ferran Adrià (the Catalan superchef) has broken all of them. Nowadays, pretty much anything goes.

Is traditional cooking disappearing?

No, I don't think so. There are always chefs who return to classic cuisines, who say 'enough with all the fancy-shmancy stuff'. I think it's great. You can't eat creative cuisine all the time. Meatloaf still tastes great!

Do you only use local products?

I'd love to, but that's impossible. Wherever I can, yes, I do. But we get most of our vegetables from Italy, for instance. In Switzerland, we've got lots of potatoes. Oh, and carrots too.

How many people work here?

Five.

That's not many.

No… I've been thinking about getting someone else in the kitchen, but there's not much room. It'd have to be a small person!

Do you ever get sick of cooking?

Sure, there are times when you're up to your ears with work and you think, 'I've got to get out!' But, after a couple of weeks' holiday, I always look forward to getting back into the kitchen.

What's your favourite food?

I love crêpes more than anything else. Whenever I'm in France, I've got to eat a couple. You can put anything in them!

How do you like Zürich?

It's my adopted home town. There is so much going on here and people from all over.

Do you go out much?

I love to eat out. A great place is Coco (opposite). They do grilled meats and fish with simple side dishes – fantastic!

Midrange

Zeughauskeller (Map p220; ☎ 044 211 26 90; www .zeughauskeller.ch; Bahnhofstrasse 28a; mains Sfr17.50-33.50; 🕑 11.30am-11pm) The menu (in eight languages) at this huge, atmospheric beer hall offers 20 different kinds of sausages, as well as numerous other Swiss specialities, including some of a vegetarian variety.

Fribourger Fondue-Stübli (Map pp218-19; ☎ 044 241 90 76; www.fondue-stuben.ch; Rotwandstrasse 38; mains Sfr20-25; 🕑 lunch & dinner Mon-Fri, dinner Sat & Sun) One of three branches of this minichain located

around town, this is a cosy, warm spot for indulging in your fondue fantasy. Bright gingham adorns the timber tables and matches the steaming red pots of delicious hot melted cheese.

Restaurant Zum Kropf (Map p220; ☎ 044 221 18 05; www.zumkropf.ch; In Gassen 16; mains Sfr21.50-45.50; 🕑 11.30am-11.30pm Mon-Sat) Notable for its historic interior, with marble columns, stained glass and ceiling murals, Kropf has been favoured by locals since 1888 for its hearty Swiss staples and fine beers.

Restaurant Rosso (Map pp218-19; ☎ 043 818 22 54; Geroldstrasse 31; mains Sfr21.50-46; ☺ Sun-Fri) In what was a gas-factory canteen, backing onto the railway line, now lurk the best pizzas (only seven options at Sfr16 to Sfr26) in town. They are thin, crispy and tasty, just as their contented Italian customers like them.

Restaurant Reithalle (Map pp218-19; ☎ 044 212 07 66; www.restaurant-reithalle.ch; Gessnerallee 8; mains Sfr23.50-33.50; ☺ lunch & dinner Mon-Fri, dinner Sat & Sun) Fancy eating in the stables? The walls are still lined with the cavalry horses' feeding and drinking troughs. Straw has been replaced by a menu of Swiss and international dishes, including vegetarian options. Part of a former barracks complex, it's a boisterous, convivial location but keep in mind that tables are cleared at 11.30pm to turn the place into a dance club.

our pick Alpenrose (Map pp218-19; ☎ 044 271 39 19; Fabrikstrasse 12; mains Sfr24-42; ☺ Mon-Sat) With its timber-clad walls, 'No Polka Dancing' warning and fine cuisine from regions all over the country, the Alpenrose makes for an inspired meal out. You could try risotto from Ticino, or *Pizokel* (aka *Bizochel*, a kind of long and especially savoury *Spätzli*) from Graubünden or freshly fished local perch filets.

Coco (Map p220; ☎ 044 211 98 98; www.coco-grill.ch; Bleicherweg 1a am Paradeplatz; mains Sfr25-45; ☺ lunch & dinner Mon-Fri, dinner Sat) For straightforward, juicy grilled meats and fish, this is the place to be. Secreted down a short alley just off Paradeplatz, you first encounter a teeny front bar, good for a predinner wine. The almost conspiratorial dining area is out the back.

Giesserei (off Map pp218-19; ☎ 044 205 10 10; www.die giesserei.ch; Birchstrasse 108; mains Sfr25-40; ☺ lunch & dinner Mon-Fri, dinner Sun, brunch Sun) This former factory in Oerlikon is a winner with its scuffed postindustrial atmosphere and pared-down menu (three starters, three mains and three desserts). The abundant brunch (Sfr49) is renowned across town. Take tram 11 to Regensbergbrücke from the Hauptbahnhof.

Blindekuh (Blind Man's Bluff; off Map pp218-19; ☎ 044 421 50 50; www.blindekuh.ch; Mühlebachstrasse 148; mains Sfr27-41; ☺ lunch & dinner Tue-Fri, dinner Mon, Sat & Sun) Eat and drink in total darkness. Run by people with impaired vision as a means of sharing their experience, this restaurant is booked out months in advance for dinner, but lunch (plus some last-minute evening) reservations are possible.

Raclette Stube (Map p220; ☎ 044 251 41 30; www .raclette-stube.ch; Zähringerstrasse 16; mains Sfr27.50-43.50;

☺ dinner) For the quintessential Swiss cheese experience, Raclette, pop by this welcoming *Stube*, which feels like a warm country restaurant. Aside from Raclette (Sfr36.50), they do fondue too.

Top End

Sankt Meinrad (Map pp218-19; ☎ 043 534 82 77; www .sanktmeinrad.ch, in German; Stauffacherstrasse 163; mains Sfr29-54; ☺ lunch & dinner Tue-Fri, dinner Sat) Soft, creamy decor in this one-time corner bistro allows you to concentrate on the creative cooking emerging from the partly open kitchen run by Tobias Meinrad Buholzer (see boxed text, opposite). Just thinking about the *Toggenburger Rindsfilet in Kakaobohnen rosa gebraten mit Pastinaken-Karotten-Gemüse und Petersilien-spätzli* (medium-rare Swiss filet steak in cocoa-bean sauce with parsnips, carrots and parsley *Spätzli*) gets the mouth watering.

Seidenspinner (Map pp218-19; ☎ 044 241 07 00; www .seidenspinner.ch; Ankerstrasse 120; mains Sfr29-56; ☺ lunch & dinner Tue-Fri, dinner Sat) A favourite with the media and fashion crowd, the Silk Spinner boasts an extravagant interior, with huge flower arrangements and shards of mirrored glass covering the walls. Broadly European cooking dominates, with such dishes as *Hirsch-Entrecote Calvados mit Eierspätzli und typischen Herbstbeilagen* (Deer steak in Calvados with *Spätzli* and autumn vegetables). Lunch menus start at Sfr22.

Kronenhalle (Map p220; ☎ 044 251 66 69; Rämistrasse 4; mains Sfr30-80; ☺ noon-midnight) A haunt of city movers and shakers in suits with an old-world feel, the Crown Hall is a brasserie-style establishment, with white tablecloths and lots of dark wood. Impeccably mannered waiters move discreetly below Chagall, Miró, Matisse and Picasso originals.

DRINKING

Of course there are options all over town, but the bulk of the more-animated drinking options congregate in the happening Kreis 4 and Kreis 5 districts, together known as Züri-West. Langstrasse is the main scene in Kreis 4, with more bars clustered along its side streets. There's plenty more happening in Kreis 5, mainly along and near Hardstrasse. Heading south from Escher-Wyss-Platz, there's a gaggle of bars on the right-hand (west) side.

our pick Longstreet Bar (Map pp218-19; ☎ 044 241 21 72; www.longstreetbar.ch; Langstrasse 92; ☺ 8pm-3am

ZÜRICH

WATERSIDE TIPPLING

The Frauenbad and Männerbad public baths (see p221) open their doors to some refreshing nocturnal bar action. At the former, up to 150 men are allowed into the **Barfussbar** (Barefoot Bar; Map p220; ☎ 044 251 33 31; www.barfussbar.ch; Stadthausquai; 🕑 from 8.30pm Wed-Sun mid-May–mid-Sep). You leave shoes at the entrance – drink while you dip your feet in the water! At the Männerbad, women come in the evenings to the **Rimini Bar** (Map pp218-19; ☎ 044 211 95 94; www .rimini.ch; Schanzengraben; 🕑 7.30pm-midnight Sun-Fri, 5pm-midnight Sat), open in good weather only.

Tue-Thu, 8pm-4am Fri & Sat, 8pm-2am Sun) Run by the guy who seems to be behind half the city's nightlife, Yves Spink, the Longstreet is a music bar with a varied roll-call of DJs coming in and out. Try to count the thousands of light bulbs in this purple-felt-lined one-time cabaret.

Liquid (Map pp218-19; ☎ 079 446 73 66; www.liquid-bar .ch; Zwinglistrasse 12; 🕑 5pm-1am Mon-Thu, 5pm-3am Fri, 7pm-3am Sat) With its striped wallpaper and moulded plastic chairs in the form of boiled eggs broken in half, this is a kitsch kinda setting, with mostly lounge-oriented music nights. A groovy way to get ready for the latter half of the night.

Sphères (Map pp218-19; ☎ 044 440 66 22; www .spheres.cc; Hardturmstrasse 66; 🕑 8am-midnight Mon-Fri, 9.30am-7.30pm Sat & Sun) An intimate, candle-lit bar-bookshop, you could start a Kreis 5 evening here with some wine, a book reading and perhaps some short films.

Also recommended:

Acapulco (Map pp218-19; ☎ 044 272 66 88; Neugasse 56; 🕑 5pm-1am Mon-Tue, 3pm-2am Wed-Thu, 5pm-3am Fri, 3pm-3am Sat, 3pm-2am Sun) A retro hang-out.

Hard One (Map pp218-19; ☎ 044 444 10 00; www .hardone.ch; Hardstrasse 260; admission free-Sfr15; 🕑 6pm-2am Tue-Thu, 6pm-4am Fri & Sat) A glass cube of a lounge bar with great views and gigs on weekends.

Riff Raff (Map pp218-19; ☎ 044 444 22 05; Neugasse 57; 🕑 from 8am Mon-Fri, from 10am Sat & Sun) This cinema-cum-bistro is a counter-cultural way to start the evening.

ENTERTAINMENT

Züritipp is the city's events magazine, available around town and from the tourist office. Also look for the quarterly *Zürich Guide*. Tickets for events are available from the **Billettzentrale**

(Map p220; ☎ 044 221 22 83; Stadthausquai 9; 🕑 10am-6.30pm Mon-Fri) in the riverside Stadthaus or individual venues.

Clubs

Generally dress well and expect to pay Sfr15 to Sfr30 admission.

ZÜRI-WEST

Zukunft (Map pp218-19; www.zukunft.ch; Dienerstrasse 33; 🕑 11pm-late Thu-Sat) Having resolved the problem of the complaining neighbour by finding him another apartment, this literally underground dance bar is back in full swing. Look for a modest queue (there's no sign) and head downstairs. A broad range of electronic and other dance music keeps a mixed crowd happy. Heaven knows what the literature reading near the entrance is all about.

our pick **Club Q** (Map pp218-19; ☎ 044 444 40 50; www .club-q.ch; Förrlibuckstrasse 151; admission up to Sfr30; 🕑 11pm-7am Fri, 11pm-8am Sat, 10pm-4am Sun) In a car park, this club is for those who take their dancing – to house, hip hop and R&B – more seriously than seeing and being seen. It's at the back of the car park, on Mühleweg. Although its Ibiza nights don't quite match the Spanish rave island's megaclub vibe, Zürich's club crowd see it as the next best thing. Also in the car park is Club Q's minor cousin, the smaller club BBQ.

Supermarket (Map pp218-19; ☎ 044 440 20 05; www.supermarket.li; Geroldstrasse 17; 🕑 11pm-late Thu-Sat) Looking like an innocent little house, Supermarket boasts three cosy lounge bars around the dance floor, a covered back courtyard and an interesting roster of DJs playing house. The crowd tends to be mid-20s.

Labor Bar (Map pp218-19; ☎ 044 272 44 02; www.laborbar .ch; Schiffbaustrasse 3; 🕑 7pm-late Tue, 10pm-late Fri & Sat) The epitome of retro chic, with lots of Plexiglas and diffuse coloured light. Always filled with beautiful people, Friday is Celebreighties and Saturday '80s and '90s night.

Indochine (Map pp218-19; ☎ 044 448 11 11; www.club -indochine.ch; Limmatstrasse 275; 🕑 10pm-late Thu-Sat) Models and rich kids mingle between the dimly lit fat Buddhas of this faux opium den. It's Zürich's answer to Paris's Buddha Bar.

CENTRAL ZÜRICH

Kaufleuten (Map p220; ☎ 044 225 33 22; www.kaufleuten .com; Pelikanstrasse 18; 🕑 11pm-late) An opulent art-deco theatre with a stage, mezzanine floor and bars arranged around the dance floor, Zürich's 'establishment' club plays house, hip hop and Latin rhythms to a slightly older crowd.

Saint Germain (Map p220; ☎ 044 215 90 00; www .saintgermain.ch; Bahnhofstrasse 66; ☿ 11pm-4am Fri & Sat) This is about as hip as it gets in an uptown way these days. After impeccably turned out folks have finished dining on designer blini and smoked salmon, the tables are whisked away to turn this into a heaving dance den. Enter from Rennweg.

Alte Börse (Map p220; www.alteboerse.com; Bleicherweg 5; ☿ 10pm-late Thu-Sat) In a respectable town-centre building, hundreds of dance fanatics cram in to this recently opened club for intense electronic sessions with DJs from all over the world. They also get in occasional live acts.

Mascotte (Map pp218-19; ☎ 044 260 15 80; www .mascotte.ch; Theaterstrasse 17; ☿ 9.30pm-2am Mon-Thu, 9.30pm-5am Fri & Sat, 9.30pm-midnight Sun) The old variety hall 'Corso' is now a popular club with huge windows facing Sechseläutenplatz and the lake. It's renowned for Tuesday's Karaoke from Hell, where punters sing punk or metal songs accompanied by a live band.

Two adjacent clubs for a well-dressed over-25 crowd lie just back from the northwest end of the lake. **Adagio** (Map pp218-19; ☎ 044 206 36 66; www.adagio.ch; Gotthardstrasse 5; ☿ 9pm-2am Tue-Wed, 9pm-late Thu, 9pm-4am Fri & Sat) seems like a scene from a medieval thriller with its vaulted and frescoed ceiling. They play a broad range of dance music, while neighbouring **Le Bal** (Map pp218-19; ☎ 044 206 36 66; www .lebal.ch; Beethovenstrasse 8; ☿ 9pm-2am Tue-Wed, 9pm-late Thu-Sat) swings predominantly between Latin and house nights.

Cultural Centres

Rote Fabrik (off Map pp218-19; ☎ for music 044 481 91 21, for theatre 044 482 42 12; www.rotefabrik.ch; Seestrasse 395; ☿ 9.30pm-late Tue-Sun) This once counter-cultural and now largely mainstream institution stages rock concerts, original-language films, theatre and dance performances. There's also a bar and a restaurant. Take bus 161 or 165 from Bürkliplatz.

Kanzlei (Map pp218-19; ☎ 044 291 63 11; www.kanzlei.ch; Kanzleistrasse 56; ☿ 10pm-late Fri & Sat, 6pm-late Sun) Kanzlei is similar to Rote Fabrik. What is a school playground by day morphs into an outdoor bar session by night, especially in summer. Kanzlei's club action happens downstairs, underground.

Kino Xenix (Map pp218-19; ☎ 044 242 04 11; www .xenix.ch; Kanzleistrasse 52) Located in the same spot as Kanzlei, Kino Xenix is an art-house cinema with a bar.

Gay & Lesbian Venues

Zürich has a lively gay scene, encompassing Café Odeon (p223).

Barfüsser (Map p220; Spitalgasse 14; ☿ noon-1am Sun-Thu, noon-2am Fri & Sat) One of the first gay bars in the country and still going strong, Barfüsser now incorporates a sushi bar.

Daniel H (Map pp218-19; ☎ 044 241 41 78; www.danielh .ch; Müllerstrasse 51; ☿ 3pm-midnight Mon-Thu, 3pm-2am Fri, 11am-2am Sat) An easygoing lounge-bar arrangement (with a tiny courtyard at the side), the 'Dani H' is a cruisy place to start the night. It is very hetero friendly.

Live Music

Aside from the high-brow stuff, Zürich has an effervescent live-music scene. Many of the bars and clubs mentioned earlier in this chapter offer occasional gigs.

CLASSICAL & OPERA

Tonhalle (Map pp218-19; ☎ 044 206 34 34; www.tonhalle -orchester.ch; Claridenstrasse 7) An opulent venue used by Zürich's orchestra and chamber orchestra.

INDUSTRIAL CONVERSION

Symbolic of the renaissance of once-industrial western Zürich is the **Schiffbau** (Schiffbaustrasse). Once a mighty factory churning out lake steamers and, until 1992, turbine-engine parts, this enormous shell has been turned (at considerable cost) into the seat of the **Schauspielhaus** (www.schauspielhaus.ch), a huge theatre, with three stages. It is worth just having a look inside. It is also home to a stylish restaurant (LaSalle), upstairs bar (Nietturm) and jazz den (Moods, see Live Music above).

Pop around also to **Giessereihalle** in **Puls 5** (Technoparkstrasse). This one-time foundry is being converted into a multiuse centre, with restaurants, bars and offices. The impressive main hall, with industrial accoutrements intact, is used for events.

Opera House (Opernhaus; Map pp218-19; ☎ 044 268 66 66; www.opernhaus.ch; Falkenstrasse 1) Enjoys a worldwide reputation.

ROCK, POP & JAZZ

our pick **Helsinki Hütte** (Map pp218-19; www.helsinki klub.ch; Geroldstrasse 35; ☼ 8pm-2am Thu-Tue) Little more than a leftover hut from the area's industrial days, the Helsinki attracts people of all walks and ages for its low-lit, relaxed band scene. Sip on Sfr5 beer and settle in for anything from the regular country nights on Sundays to soul and funk.

Moods (Map pp218-19; ☎ 044 276 80 00; www.moods .ch; Schiffbaustrasse 6; ☼ 7.30pm-midnight Mon-Thu, 7.30pm-late Fri & Sat, 6-10pm Sun) One of the city's top jazz spots, although other musical genres such as Latin and world music grab the occasional spot on its busy calendar.

Dynamo (Map pp218-19; ☎ 044 365 34 44; www .dynamo.ch; Wasserwerkstrasse 21; admission free-Sfr18; ☼ 8pm or 9pm-late) Various spaces here lend themselves to concerts with powerful sound, anything from rock through reggae to lashings of heavy metal. There's usually something every night.

Sport

Local football team, FC Zurich, plays at **Letzigrund Stadium** (off Map pp218-19; cnr Herden & Baslerstrasse). Bus 31 to Letzipark will get you there.

SHOPPING

For high fashion, head for Bahnhofstrasse and surrounding streets. Funkier boutiques are dotted about the lanes of Niederdorf across the river. For grunge, preloved gear and some none-too-serious fun young stuff, have a stroll along Langstrasse in Kreis 4.

Freitag (Map pp218-19; ☎ 043 366 95 20; www.freitag.ch; Geroldstrasse 17) The Freitag brothers turn truck tarps into water-resistant carry-all chic in their factory. Everything is recycled and every item is original. Their outlet is equally impressive – a pile of containers; they call it Kreis 5's first skyscraper and shoppers may climb to the top.

Fidelio (Map p220; ☎ 044 211 13 11; www.fidelio-kleider .ch; Münzplatz 1) One of the city's best clothes boutiques, Fidelio sells a wide range of men's and women's wear, from designer labels to street fashions.

Heimatwerk (Map p220; ☎ 044 222 19 55; www.heimat werk.ch; Uraniastrasse 1) Good-quality, if touristy,

souvenirs are found here, including fondue pots, forks, toys and classy handbags.

Jelmoli (Map p220; ☎ 044 220 46 00; www.jelmoli .ch; Seidengasse 1) The basement food hall is the highlight of this legendary department store, Zürich's first, biggest and best.

The leading markets include the flea market at **Bürkliplatz** (Map pp218-19; ☼ 8am-4pm Sat May-Oct), the year-round **Flohmarkt Kanzlei** (Map pp218-19; www.flohmarktkanzlei.ch; Kanzleistrasse 56; ☼ 8am-4pm Sat) and **Rosenhof** (Map p220; ☼ 10am-8pm Thu, 10am-5pm Sat Mar-Dec), but the tourist office has details of more options.

GETTING THERE & AWAY
Air

Zürich airport (off Map pp218-19; ☎ 043 816 22 11; www .zurich-airport.com) is 9km north of the centre, with flights to most European capitals and to some in Africa, Asia and North America.

Car & Motorcycle

The A3 approaches Zürich from the south along the southern shore of Lake Zürich. The A1 is the fastest route from Bern and Basel. It proceeds northeast to Winterthur.

Europcar (Map pp218-19; ☎ 044 271 56 56; Josefstrasse 53), **Hertz** (Map pp218-19; ☎ 084 882 20 25; Morgartenstrasse 5) and **Avis** (Map pp218-19; ☎ 044 296 87 87; Gartenhofstrasse 17) all also have airport branches.

Train

Direct trains run to Stuttgart (Sfr76), Munich (Sfr104), Innsbruck (Sfr79) and other international destinations. There are regular direct departures to most major Swiss towns, such as Lucerne (Sfr23, 46 to 50 minutes), Bern (Sfr46, 57 minutes) and Basel (Sfr31, 55 minutes).

GETTING AROUND
To/From the Airport

Up to nine trains an hour go to/from the Hauptbahnhof between around 6am and midnight (Sfr6, nine to 14 minutes).

Bicycle

City bikes (www.zuerirollt.ch) may be borrowed or rented from various locations, including **Velogate** (Map pp218-19; ☼ 8am-9.30pm year-round) at the Hauptbahnhof. ID and Sfr20 must be left as a deposit. Rental is free if you bring the bike back after six hours for a pit stop; otherwise it costs Sfr5 a day.

(Continued on page 237)

Action
Stations

Switzerland boasts some of the maddest black runs around, such as this one in Engelberg (p257)

CHRISTIAN ASLUND

In a land where the average 65-year-old calls a four-hour hike over a 2500m mountain pass a *Sonntagsspaziergang* (Sunday stroll), where giggly three-year-olds ski rings around you on the slopes and where locals bored with 'ordinary' marathons run races backwards, up mountains, for fun – to call Switzerland sporty would be an understatement. It's hyperactive.

And the national passion for everything that involves sweat, stamina, clingy Lycra and salopettes is contagious. Why? Just look around you. The landscapes are lyrical: glacial brooks and thundering waterfalls, colossal peaks and dexterously folded valleys. The water is mineral pure, the sky a brighter shade of blue, the air piny fresh. No wonder the Swiss can't keep still with that phenomenal backyard.

ON AIR
Paragliding & Hang-Gliding

Where there's a beautiful breeze and a mountain, there's tandem paragliding and hang-gliding in Switzerland. Strap into your harness, take a run, jump and be blown away by the rippling mountains, velvety pastures and forests unfolding beneath you. There's no better way to soak up the scenery of this fabled land than by taking to the skies, some say. And they're right.

In the glacial realms of the Unesco-listed Aletsch Glacier, Fiescheralp (p168) is a prime spot to catch thermals, as is First (p180) for spirit-soaring vistas to mighty Jungfrau. If lake scenery is more your style, glide like a bird over glittering Lake Lucerne (p253) and Lago di Lugano (p336).

'For a buzz, nothing beats throwing yourself out of an aeroplane at 4000m with (phew!) a qualified instructor strapped to your back'

Bungee Jumping

As gravity pulls you down, there's no time for nail biting. Feel the rush free falling towards the frothing Lütschine in Grindelwald's glacier-gouged Gletscherschlucht (p179) or hurtling 134m from Stockhorn near Interlaken (p174). Fancy yourself as a bit of a Bond? Here's your chance to do a 007 leaping from the 220m Verzasca Dam (p340) in Locarno, which starred in the opening scene of *GoldenEye* and is the world's second-highest bungee jump. For more fantastic Swiss elastic, visit www.bungy.ch.

Skydiving & Base Jumping

When paragliding no longer thrills, O intrepid one, get yourself to Interlaken (p174) sharpish for heart-stopping skydiving moments. For a buzz, nothing beats throwing yourself out of an aeroplane at 4000m with (phew!) a qualified instructor strapped to your back. Free fall past the vertical face of Eiger then, as the pro opens the parachute, drink in the scenery in glorious slow motion.

Paragliding is a great way to take advantage of Switzerland's spectacular mountain vistas

MARTIN MOOS

Hard-core adrenalin junkies with the guts and know-how can test their mettle base jumping by the Staubbach Falls (p185) in Lauterbrunnen. The risky business of free falling and opening the parachute just before you splat is, however, not for the uninitiated. Hotel Horner (p186) is a popular base-jumping gathering place.

Hot-Air Ballooning

If skydiving and bungee jumping sound *way* too scary, how about drifting noiselessly over hill, dale and forest against the backdrop of the ice-covered Alps? There's a basket ready and waiting in Château-d'Œx (p123), which hosts the Hot-Air Balloon Week in January and arranges passenger flights year-round. The 360-degree views stretching to Mont Blanc and Eiger are most mesmerising in the dusky glow. Bonus: your hands are free for legendary photo ops.

ON LAND
Cycling

Criss-crossed with 3300km of signposted routes, this enviously green land is an efficiently run paradise for the ardent cyclist. Reliable wheels are available in all major towns and – hurrah! – many now offer free bike hire from May to October as part of the eco-friendly initiative **Schweiz Rollt** (www.schweizrollt.ch), including Bern, Lausanne, Zürich and Geneva. For detailed maps, route descriptions and the low-down on Switzerland's nine national routes, visit **Veloland** (www.veloland.ch).

Switzerland is riddled with bike trails
ROBERTO GEROMETTA

Andermatt (p262) makes a terrific base if you're keen to test your stamina on the hairpins of leg-achingly mountainous passes such as Furka, Oberalp and Gotthard. Two striking national routes begin here: a 320km pedal to Geneva via the Rhône Glacier and pastoral Goms and a heart-pounding 430km stretch along the Rhine to Basel. Serious bikers craving back-breaking inclines and arresting views flock to Lenzerheide (p301) and Klosters-Davos (p309).

Shorter, flatter trails that avoid the slog but sacrifice none of the splendour circumnavigate the country's lakes and shadow its rivers. To combine pedalling with wine tasting, free-wheel through the sunny terraced vineyards around Sion (p154) or Lavaux (p115).

Speed-mad downhill bikers flock to Alpine resorts in summer, where cable cars often allow you to take your wheels for free or for a nominal fee. The verdant meadows and craggy peaks become a blur as you rattle and roll down summits in resorts like Arosa (p303) and Lenzerheide (p301). To hone your skills on obstacles, check out the terrain parks in Crans-Montana (p158) and Verbier (p151).

Climbing

Switzerland has been the fabled land for mountaineers ever since Edward Whymper made the first successful ascent of Matterhorn in 1865 (see p164), albeit a triumph marred with rope-breaking tragedy. Within reach for hard-core Alpinists are some of Europe's most gruelling climbs: Monte Rosa (4633m), Matterhorn (4478m), Mont Blanc (4807m), Eiger (3970m) – the names of these fearsome giants alone connote high-altitude adventure.

If you're eager to tackle the biggies, Zermatt's Alpin Center (p163) arranges some first-class climbs to surrounding 'four-thousanders'. Wildly scenic Kandersteg (p195) hooks proficient ice climbers with its spectacular frozen waterfalls, while glaciated monoliths like Piz Bernina make Pontresina (p320) a climbing mecca. For information on Switzerland's top 33 mountain-sport schools, contact **Verband Bergsportschulen Schweiz** (☎ 027 948 13 45; www.bergsportschulen.ch). The **Swiss Mountain Guides' Association** (www.4000plus.ch) lists qualified guides.

ULTIMATE ADRENALIN RUSHES

- Feeling your heart pound and boots quake as you ski into the void on the Swiss Wall (p147).
- Giving a jubilant Tarzan cry as you zip above Jungfraujoch on a flying fox (p183).
- Gliding, bouncing and growing icicles on your bum sledding the 15km 'Big Pintenfritz' toboggan run (p183).
- Hurtling head-first and hitting speeds of up to 140km/h on the icy Cresta Run (p316).
- Cartwheeling downhill hamster-style in a giant plastic sphere, aka zorbing (p174).

Get to know your karabiner from your harness at the superb climbing halls in Chur (p299) and Interlaken (p172). Read our interview with famous Swiss mountaineer Evelyne Binsack (p73) for more mountaineering tips.

Vie Ferrate

Anyone who fancies flirting with mountaineering but with the security of being attached to the rock face should clip onto a *via ferrata* (*Klettersteig* in German). Though safer and easier for the uninitiated than climbing, these vertigo-inducing fixed-cable traverses involving ladders, zip-lines and tightrope-style bridges are not for the faint-hearted. This hiking-and-climbing hybrid is currently all the rage in Switzerland. **Via Ferrata** (www.viaferrata.org) provides maps and routes graded according to difficulty.

The *via ferrata* in Andermatt (p262) is ideal for beginners with head-spinning gorge views but minimal exertion. For a real-life game of snakes and ladders, test your nerve in Mürren (p188), offering giddying vistas of Eiger, Mönch and Jungfrau. The *vie ferrate* in Leukerbad (p160) and Kandersteg (p195) are knuckle-whitening stuff.

Vie ferrate, such as this one near Leysin (p122), are a great, safe introduction to moutain climbing

SUSY BENNETT / ALAMY

ON ICE
Skiing

Eschew glühwein-fuelled revelry in favour of low-key village charm and skiing in Switzerland becomes as affordable as neighbouring Italy and France. Well, almost. Factor in around Sfr50 to Sfr65 for a day pass plus around Sfr60 for ski hire. All major resorts have ski schools where you can take your first wobble, with half-day group lessons typically costing Sfr40 to Sfr50. **Swiss Snowsports** (www.snowsports.ch) has a clickable map of 185 ski schools across the country.

'In a land where every 10-man, 50-cow hamlet has a ski lift, the question is not *where* you can ski but *how*'

In a land where every 10-man, 50-cow hamlet has a ski lift, the question is not *where* you can ski but *how*. To spot celebrities as you slalom, make for chocolate-box Klosters (p309), which shares 315km of pistes with Davos; intermediate paradise St Moritz (p317); or ubercool Verbier (p150). Off-piste lovers dreaming of downy virgin powder will find just that in glacier-rimmed, snow-sure Saas Fee (p165), Engelberg (p257) and Andermatt (p262).

For long, eye-poppingly scenic runs with Matterhorn views, it's got to be postcard-perfect Zermatt (p161) or Crans Montana (p157). Just as oops-I-almost-tumbled-over-the-mountain-edge gorgeous are resorts in the Jungfrau region (p182) like Grindelwald, Mürren and Wengen.

Think you've skied 'em all? Well Switzerland has a few surprises tucked up its Gore-Tex sleeves. Arosa (p302) and, over the mountain, Lenzerheide (p301) are great for families.

Verbier (p150), with perfect powder and astonishing views, is just one of Switzerland's many ski resorts
GLENN VAN DER

BEHOLD THE ECO-ANGELS

Many Swiss resorts have been polishing their eco-haloes recently in a bid to offset the impact of skiing. From car-free villages to resorts running solely on renewable energy, here is our rundown of the whiter than white. For more details in planning your environmentally friendly ski trip and reducing your carbon snowprint, see **Save our Snow** (www.saveoursnow.com) and the **Association of Car-Free Swiss Resorts** (www.gast.org, in German).

Arosa (p302) Recycles diligently, runs on nearly 100% renewable energy.
Flims, Laax and **Falera** (p304) This green trio use hydroelectricity and recycled water to make snow.
Wengen (p186) Car free, generates renewable energy and implements waste reduction policies.
Verbier (p150) Uses energy-efficient snow-grooming machines with biodiesel fuel.
Mürren (p187) Car free, uses renewable energy and has biodiesel-powered snow groomers.
Saas Fee (p165) Promotes sustainable development, and has stringent eco-friendly building policies.
Bettmeralp (p168) Car free and takes active steps to reduce waste.
Zermatt (p161) Car free, and promotes sustainable skiing and eco-sound building policies.
Gstaad (p196) Has a pedestrianised centre and an excellent public transport network.
St Moritz (p317) Has a clean-energy policy, pedestrianised zones and an efficient public-transport network.

Nestled below the formidable fangs of Dents du Midi on the Swiss–French border with 650km of runs, Champéry (p146) is infamous for its black run, the Swiss Wall. Queues are few in lesser-known beauties such as Bettmeralp (p168), Arolla (p156) and Scuol (p314).

Cross-Country Skiing

Anyone with a downhill loathing, supersized skis and a fondness for spandex leggings is a serious cross-country contender. Novices can learn at the first-rate *Langlauf* ski school in Arosa (p302), then practise on groomed *Loipen* (tracks) there and in neighbouring Lenzerheide (p301). If skiing makes your legs ache, this all-over workout will make you rediscover the muscles of primary-school games. Then there's a new vernacular to learn – classic versus skating, herringbone versus diagonal strides.

Head to cross-country mecca Davos (p309) to zip along 105km of trails, or silent wonders such as Franches Montagnes in rural Jura (p141) and the remote and lovely Lötschental (p161).

Snowboarding

Those baggy trousers are madness, but they'll rock in Switzerland's freeriding hot spots. Top of the dude-licious pile is Laax (p305), which hosts the Burton European Open in January. Equally radical is Saas Fee (p166), set against an amphitheatre of monstrous glaciers. Zermatt's back country (p162) dishes up fine powdery bowls and couloirs in the shadow of Matterhorn.

There's off-piste powder to play on at Jakobshorn in Davos (p311), Andermatt (p262) and Engelberg (p257). Verbier (p150), meanwhile, has some formidable terrain for easy riders and speed freaks alike, and stages the Xtreme Freeride Contest in March. Having exhausted those opportunities, riders can catch big air at the so-called 'Hawai'i of snowboarding' around St Moritz (p317).

For tips straight from an Olympic half-pipe champion's mouth, see our interview with Gian Simmen (p303).

Switzerland, an extreme sports mecca, is full of thrills and spills, like rafting on the Rhine (p305)

KERRY WAL

ON WATER

Rafting & Hydrospeeding

White-water sports are booming in Switzerland, where the strong currents and dramatic scenery of the raging Saane, Rhine, Inn and Rhône rivers make water babies gurgle with delight. Grab your paddle, don a life jacket and you're ready to cascade down these swirling torrents. In the same white-water wonderlands, you can hydrospeed – surfing rapids solo on a glorified bodyboard. **Swissraft** (☎ 081 911 52 50; www.swissraft.ch) has bases for rafting and hydrospeeding all over the country.

Memorable splashes include the thundering Vorderrhein through the limestone Ruin' Aulta Gorge (p305) and turbulent stretches of the Saane in Pays d'Enhaut (p123) and rivers near Interlaken (p174). For a full-spin, boulder-loaded challenge, hit the foaming waters of the Inn in Scuol (p314).

Kayaking & Canoeing

Lazy summer afternoons are best spent absorbing the slow, natural rhythm of Switzerland's crystal-clear lakes and rivers. The quiet ripple as your paddle slices through the blue waters of Lake Constance (p284) or fjordlike Lake Uri (p253) of William Tell fame is hypnotically calming. If it's to be a river, make it the Doubs in Goumois (p141), which meanders through a pristine wilderness of tangled foliage to the Jura mountains.

Windsurfing & Waterskiing

So you're a dab hand with a board, eh? Excellent wind sweeps down from the heights in Silvaplana (p319), where you can you can take kitesurfing and windsurfing lessons or flaunt your skills on two wind-buffeted cobalt lakes.

The rugged mountains rearing up around Lake Thun (p191) make fascinating viewing while windsurfing and wakeboarding. It's known for its frogs, but Estavayer-le-Lac (p130) also prompts fleeting croaks of joy from waterskiers and wakeboarders.

Boat

Lake cruises (☎ 044 487 13 33; www.zsg.ch) run between April and October. They leave from Bürkliplatz (Map pp218–19). A small circular tour *(kleine Rundfahrt)* takes 1½ hours (adult/child Sfr8/4) and departs every 30 minutes from 9am to 7pm. A longer tour *(grosse Rundfahrt)* lasts four hours (adult/child Sfr23/11.50). Pick tickets up at ZVV (local transport) ticket windows.

Riverboats (Limmatschiffe; ☎ 044 487 13 33; www .zsg.ch; adult/child Sfr3.90/2.70, day passes valid; ⏰ every 30 min Easter–mid-Oct) run down the river and do a small circle around the lake (55 minutes). Your best chance of getting on board is at the Schweizerisches Landesmuseum (Map pp218–19).

Car

Parking is tricky. The two most useful **car-parking garages** (www.parkhaeuser.ch; up to Sfr40 a day) are opposite the main post office and at Uraniastrasse 3. Otherwise street meters usually have a one-hour (Sfr2) or two-hour (Sfr5) maximum.

Public Transport

Zürich's **ZVV** (www.zvv.ch) public transport system of buses, S-Bahn suburban trains and trams is completely integrated. Services run from 5.30am to midnight, and tickets must be bought in advance. Every stop has a dispenser. Either type in the four-figure code for your destination or choose your ticket type: a short single-trip *Kurzstrecke* ticket, valid for five stops (Sfr2.40); a single ticket for greater Zürich, valid for an hour (Sfr3.90); or a 24-hour city pass for the centre, Zone 10 (Sfr7.80). Tickets from dispensers don't need to be validated before travel; all others, such as the Zürichcard, must be stamped in the yellow 'Entwerters' on the platforms. A one-day pass for the whole canton costs Sfr30.40.

Weekend night services (39 bus lines and six S-Bahn lines) operate from 1am to 4am (ticket plus night supplement Sfr5, passes not valid).

Taxi

Taxis are expensive and usually unnecessary, given the quality of public transport. Pick them up at the Hauptbahnhof or other ranks, or call ☎ 044 444 44 44.

AROUND ZÜRICH

UETLIBERG
elevation 813m

A top half-day trip starts off by taking the train (line S10) to Uetliberg at 813m (23 minutes, departures every 30 minutes). From here, follow the two-hour **Planetenweg** (Planetary Path) along the mountain ridge to Felsenegg. En route you pass scale models of the planets and have lake views. At Felsenegg, a cable car descends every 10 minutes to Adliswill, from where frequent trains return to Zürich (line S4, 16 minutes). Buy the Sfr15.60 Albis-Netzkarte, which gets you to Uetliberg and back, with unlimited travel downtown.

RAPPERSWIL-JONA
pop 25,400 / elevation 405m

A pleasant excursion is to Rapperswil (part of the Rapperswil-Jona conurbation). It has a quaint old town and a children's zoo. The **tourist office** (☎ 084 881 15 00; www.zuerichsee.ch; Hintergasse 16; ⏰ 8.30am-noon & 1.30-5pm) is in the heart of the old town.

North of the train station, the old town is dominated by a 13th-century castle. Climb the hill for views and the **Polenmuseum** (Polish Museum; ☎ 055 210 18 62; www.muzeum-polskie.org; adult/child Sfr4/2; ⏰ 1-5pm daily Apr-Oct, 1-5pm Sat & Sun Nov, Dec & Mar, closed Jan & Feb), housed in the castle (a popular wedding spot). The museum details the story of Poles in Switzerland, Polish immigration, WWII and, more recently, the Solidarność trade union and Pope John Paul II.

The Swiss know Rapperswil above all for the **Circus Knie** (www.knie.ch), a family-run national circus that has been travelling the length and breadth of the country (on tour from March to November) since 1919. If you can't see the circus, drop into the **Circus Museum** (☎ 055 220 57 57; Fischmarktplatz 1; adult/under 4yr/4-12yr Sfr4/free/2; ⏰ 10am-7pm daily Jul-Aug, to 6pm Apr-Jun & Sep-Oct, 1-5pm Nov-Mar).

The circus employs about 100 animals and the Knie have another 300 at **Knies Kinderzoo** (Children's Zoo; ☎ 055 220 67 67; www.knieskinderzoo.ch; Oberseestrasse; adult/child Sfr10/4.50; ⏰ 9am-6pm early Mar-Oct), southeast of the train station (signposted). Kids can ride ponies, elephants and camels, applaud performing sea lions and learn about a host of creatures, from giraffes and apes to kangaroos and tortoises.

(Continued from page 228)

ZÜRICH

Art lovers should look at the **Kunst(zeug)haus** (☎ 055 220 20 80; www.kunstzeughaus.ch; Schönbodenstrasse 1; adult/under 6yr/concession Sfr10/free/6; ⊙ 2-8pm Wed, 2-6pm Thu-Fri, 11am-6pm Sat & Sun). Since mid-2008, this enormous art space, a converted arsenal with a very-21st-century wavy roof, has been devoted to exhibitions of contemporary Swiss art.

In 2001, a new 840m-long **wooden bridge** was laid between Rapperswil on the north side of the lake and Hurden on the south side. The last one had been taken down in 1878.

Jakob (☎ 055 220 00 50; www.jakob-hotel.ch; Hauptplatz 11; s Sfr106-121, d Sfr131-173; ⊠) is the best midrange hotel choice, with chic rooms in neutral tones. They also have a restaurant, bar (often with live music) and even a cigar lounge for inveterate puffers. Restaurants line Rapperswil's Fischmarktplatz and Hauptplatz.

Rapperswil can be reached by S5, S7 or S15 from Zürich's main train station (Sfr15.20, 40 minutes) or by boat from Bürkliplatz (two hours). Much better value for a day trip is the **9-Uhr Tagespass** (9 O'Clock Day Pass; Sfr23), valid all day from 9am Monday to Friday and all day Saturday, Sunday and holidays.

WINTERTHUR

pop 94,710 / elevation 447m

Switzerland's sixth-largest city gave its name to one of Europe's leading insurance companies and is equally known for its high-quality museums and galleries.

The greater Winterthur area counts 143,000 inhabitants, many of them young families who have fled the high prices of Zürich, a 25-minute commute away. In the 1970s, the city's heavy industry collapsed, provoking the loss of 10,000 jobs, although it has now put those dark days well behind it.

A Museumsbus shuttle (Sfr5) leaves the train station hourly between 9.45am and 4.45pm for the Sammlung Oskar Reinhart am Römerholz, the Museum Oskar Reinhart am Stadtgarten and the Kunstmuseum. On Sundays, the Fotomuseum is included in the circuit.

Information

Discount Card A museums pass costs Sfr20/30 for one/two days and gets entry to almost all the sights.
Post office (Bahnhofplatz 9; ⊙ 8.30am-7pm Mon-Sat, 9am-noon & 2.30-7pm Sun)
Tourist office (☎ 052 267 67 00; www.winterthur -tourismus.ch; near platform 1, Hauptbahnhof; ⊙ 8.30am-6.30pm Mon-Fri, 8.30am-4pm Sat)

Sights & Activities

Winterthur owes much of its eminence as an art mecca to collector Oskar Reinhart, a scion of a powerful banking and insurance family. His collection was bequeathed to the nation and entrusted to his home town when he died in 1965.

The **Sammlung Oskar Reinhart am Römerholz** (☎ 052 269 27 40; www.roemerholz.ch; Haldenstrasse 95; adult/student Sfr12/8, includes admission to Museum Oskar Reinhart am Stadtgarten; ⊙ 10am-5pm Tue & Thu-Sun, to 8pm Wed) is particularly fascinating in the way it seeks to bridge the gap between traditional and modern art, juxtaposing the likes of Cézanne, Goya, Rembrandt and Rubens with Monet, Picasso, Renoir and Van Gogh. Take bus 3 to Spital or get the Museumsbus shuttle.

Reinhart's 500-strong collection of Swiss, German and Austrian works of art is on show at the **Museum Oskar Reinhart am Stadtgarten** (☎ 052 267 51 72; www.museumoskarreinhart.ch; Stadthausstrasse; adult/student Sfr8/6 or free with Sammlung Oskar Reinhart am Römerholz ticket; ⊙ 10am-8pm Tue, 10am-5pm Wed-Sun), on the edges of the city park.

Winterthur's outstanding **Fotomuseum** (Photo Museum; ☎ 052 234 10 34; www.fotomuseum.ch; Grüzenstrasse 44; adult/concession Sfr9/7; ⊙ 11am-6pm Tue & Thu-Sun, to 8pm Wed) is another highlight among the city's total of 17 museums. The vast collection includes many great names and styles from the earliest days of this art in the 19th century to the present – although what you see may well be a temporary visiting exhibition. There's more in the **Fotostiftung** (Photo Foundation; ☎ 052 234 10 30; www.fotostiftung.ch; Grüzenstrasse 45; adult/concession Sfr7/5; ⊙ same hr as Fotomuseum) over the road. The combined price for these and other related photo exhibitions is Sfr15/11.

Another fine visit is the **Kunstmuseum** (☎ 052 267 58 00; www.kmw.ch, in German; Museumstrasse 52; adult/concession Sfr15/10; ⊙ 10am-8pm Tue, 10am-5pm Wed-Sun), with its collection of 19th- and 20th-century art. It will be closed until 2010 for renovation.

Had enough art? What about a science session? **Technorama** (☎ 052 244 08 44; www.technorama .ch; Technoramastrasse 1; adult/concession Sfr8/6; ⊙ 10am-5pm Tue-Sun) is an extraordinary voyage into the hands-on multiple worlds of science. It offers hundreds of interactive experiences that can't fail to fascinate kids, and plenty of adults too! Look into Europe's biggest plasma ball or admire the toy trains. Take bus 5 from the Hauptbahnhof.

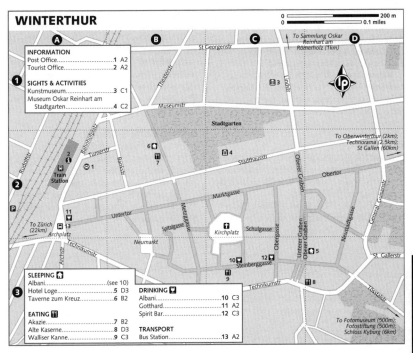

WINTERTHUR

INFORMATION
Post Office.................................1 A2
Tourist Office...........................2 A2

SIGHTS & ACTIVITIES
Kunstmuseum..........................3 C1
Museum Oskar Reinhart am
Stadtgarten...........................4 C2

SLEEPING
Albani.....................................(see 10)
Hotel Loge...............................5 D3
Taverne zum Kreuz...................6 B2

EATING
Akazie.....................................7 B2
Alte Kaserne............................8 D3
Walliser Kanne.........................9 C3

DRINKING
Albani.....................................10 C3
Gotthard..................................11 A2
Spirit Bar.................................12 C3

TRANSPORT
Bus Station...............................13 A2

Just outside the city, **Schloss Kyburg** (☎ 052 232 46 64; www.schlosskyburg.ch; adult/concession Sfr8/6; 10.30am-5.30pm Tue-Sun Mar-Oct) mixes the ancient castle buildings with some interactive fun (try on a suit of armour – but not the torture instruments!). The 15th-century murals in the castle's chapel showing Christ as the judge at the Last Judgment are especially vivid. Out the back, a vegetable and herb garden flourishes, much as in past centuries.

Take the S-Bahn to Effretikon, then the bus to Kyburg. Ask the tourist office for the Kyburg leaflet, with transport timetables. The journey takes 30 minutes each way.

Sleeping

Winterthur is an easy day trip from Zürich.

Albani (☎ 052 212 69 96; www.albani.ch; Steinberggasse 16; s/d Sfr80/100) Not only a happening bar where live music is the order of the day, this place also has nine simple but cheerful rooms. Showers and phone are in the corridor. Guests get free entry to concerts and parties in the bar downstairs. Very cool indeed.

Taverne zum Kreuz (☎ 052 269 07 20; www.taverne -zum-kreuz.ch; Stadthausstrasse 10b/lm Stadtpark; s/d

Sfr142/172) A charmingly lopsided half-timbered tavern from the 18th century, which has cosy rooms full of character. Downstairs is an equally warm restaurant and bar.

Hotel Loge (☎ 052 268 12 00; www.hotelloge.ch; Oberer Graben 6; s/d Sfr195/250) With its own bar, restaurant and even a cinema, this designer place provides all the comfort and style you will ever need. Some of the 17 spacious rooms behind the Gothic entrance offer nice views across the leafy avenue to the old town.

Eating

There's a cluster of bars and cheap restaurants along Neumarkt, offering a wide array of different ethnic cuisines.

Alte Kaserne (☎ 052 267 57 80; www.altekaserne .ch; Technikumstrasse 8; lunch menus Sfr17; 7am-midnight Mon-Fri, 3pm-midnight Sat) Set in a long, half-timbered building that was formerly a barracks, this cultural centre, as well as putting on all manner of shows and exhibitions, offers light food, including a changing menu of set lunches. Or you could pop by for one of their dawn literature readings and an early breakfast.

Akazie (☎ 052 212 17 17; Stadthausstrasse 10; menus Sfr21-32; ✆ Mon-Sat) This restaurant serves nouvelle Mediterranean cuisine that comes in old-fashioned portions, washed down with wines from as far off as Sardinia.

Walliser Kanne (☎ 052 212 81 71; Steinberggasse 25; mains Sfr24.50-37.50; ✆ lunch Mon, lunch & dinner Tue-Fri, dinner Sat) Try this rustic place for traditional Swiss specialities – they have a seemingly endless selection of fondue options.

Drinking

Gotthard (☎ 052 212 09 05; Untertor) Winterthur's student population keeps the many bars humming all hours. Indeed, Gotthard literally keeps the taps flowing 24/7.

Albani (☎ 052 212 69 96; www.albani.ch; Steinberggasse 16) Although not more than a couple of hundred punters can squeeze in, Albani is a magnet for the live gig aficionados, attracting local and international acts. The likes of Sheryl Crow and Pearl Jam have played here.

Spirit Bar (☎ 052 212 24 04; Steinberggasse 2; ✆ 4pm-late Tue-Sat) If nothing's happening at Albani, this is a good drinking alternative a short stumble away. Popular with students, they sometimes get in live music.

Getting There & Around

Four to five trains an hour run to Zürich (Sfr11.40, 19 to 25 minutes). The A1 freeway goes from Zürich, skirts Winterthur and continues to St Gallen and Austria.

As local bus tickets to Oberwinterthur cost Sfr3.90, it's better to get a 24-hour pass for Sfr7.80 instead.

ZÜRICH

Central Switzerland

If the Swiss were to nominate one canton as home, there would be no place like Central Switzerland. Green, hilly and soothingly beautiful, it is the very essence of 'Swissness'. It was here that the pact that kick-started a nation was signed in 1291; here that hero William Tell gave a rebel yell against Habsburg rule; here that in a moment of sharp brilliance Karl Elsener invented the boy scout's best friend, the Victorinox army knife. Geographically, politically, spiritually, this is Switzerland's heartland. Nowhere does the flag fly higher.

And you can see why locals swell with pride at Lake Lucerne. Still in the cold mist of morning, enigmatic in the swirling fog, molten gold in the dusky half-light – it's no wonder these waters were a source of endless fascination for the brush of Turner. Indeed the views amused Queen Victoria as she trotted up Rigi on horseback, Wagner, who knew of 'no more beautiful place on earth' and Mark Twain, who called it 'the charmingest place' he had ever lived.

Lucerne is a heart-stealer with its sparkly lake vistas, rickety bridges and Victorian curiosities. This dreamy little city is small enough to walk yet big enough to harbour red-hot designer hotels and a world-class gallery full of Picassos. From here, cruise over to resorts like Weggis and Brunnen, or hike nearby Mt Pilatus and Rigi. Northeast of Lucerne, megalomaniacal Zug has *Kirschtorte* (cherry cake) just as rich as its residents and medieval heritage.

Even on the shores of Lucerne, the Alps squeeze into the picture to demand exploration. Outdoorsy types go south to Andermatt for austere mountain-scapes close to the source of the Rhine, or angelic Engelberg for heavenly off-piste encounters in the virgin powder.

CENTRAL SWITZERLAND

HIGHLIGHTS

- Touching Lucerne's medieval past crossing the **Kapellbrücke** (p243) and clambering up the **city wall** (p243)
- Being dazzled by the blues of Lake Lucerne on the vertiginous **Bürgenstock Felsenweg** (p70) clifftop walk
- Twirling above the crevassed glacier of **Mt Titlis** (p257) on the world's first revolving cable car
- Cruising fjord-like **Lake Uri** (p253) to feel the spirit of William Tell
- Hiking to the source of the Rhine in summer, or cruising snowy backcountry in winter in **Andermatt** (p262)

City Wall;
Kapellbrücke ★

★ Bürgenstock
Felsenweg

★ Lake Uri

★ Mt Titlis

Andermatt
★

▓ POPULATION: 613,800	▓ AREA: 4484 SQ KM	▓ LANGUAGE: GERMAN

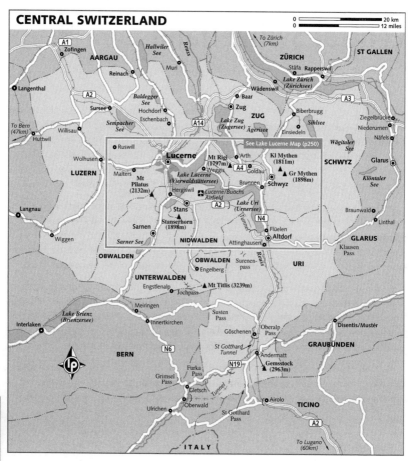

Orientation & Information

At the heart of Central Switzerland (Zentral-schweiz) is Lake Lucerne (Vierwaldstättersee in German, meaning 'Lake of the Four Forest Cantons'), surrounded by the cantons of Lucerne, Uri, Schwyz and Unterwalden (sub-divided into Nidwalden and Obwalden). Also in this region is Switzerland's smallest rural canton, Zug. Central Switzerland is fairly flat in the north and west, but a southern tip reaches into the Alps as far as the St Gotthard Pass.

For information on the entire region, con-tact the tourist office in Lucerne (opposite).

Getting There & Around

The nearest airport is Zürich, while road and rail connections are excellent in all direc-tions. An interesting way to leave the region is aboard the Wilhem Tell Express (p369).

If you don't have a Swiss or Eurail Pass (both of which are valid on lake journeys), consider purchasing the regional **Tell-Pass** (www .tell-pass.ch; per 7/15 days Sfr158/210; ☺ late Mar-Oct). Sold at Lucerne tourist office and all boat stations, the Tell-Pass provides travel for two/ five days respectively, and half-price fares for the remainder.

The handy Vierwaldstättersee Guest Card, available when you stay overnight anywhere in the region, offers benefits including dis-counts on sporting facilities and 10% to 50% off certain cable cars, as well as reduc-tions on museum admission in Lucerne and elsewhere.

LUCERNE

pop 58,380 / elevation 435m

Recipe for a gorgeous Swiss city: take a co-balt lake ringed by mountains of myth, add a well-preserved medieval Old Town, then sprinkle with covered bridges, sunny plazas, candy-coloured houses and waterfront prom-enades. Lucerne is bright, beautiful and little miss popular since the likes of Goethe, Queen Victoria and Wagner savoured her views in the 19th century. Legend has it that an angel with a light showed the first settlers where to build a chapel in Lucerne, and today it still has amazing grace.

One minute it's nostalgic, with its emo-tive lion sculpture and kitschy maze, the next highbrow, with concerts at acoustic marvel KKL and the Sammlung Rosengart's peerless Picasso collection. Though the shops are still crammed with ceramic cows and cuckoos that Mark Twain so eloquently described as 'gim-crackery of the souvenir sort', Lucerne doesn't only dwell on the past, with rock-star refuges like The Hotel and a roster of gigs keeping the vibe upbeat. Carnival capers at Fasnacht, balmy summers, golden autumns – this 'city of lights' shines in every season.

Orientation

The city perches on the western edge of its namesake lake, straddling the Reuss River. The medieval town centre is on the north-ern riverbank, within walking distance of the Hauptbahnhof (train station) on the southern side.

Information
DISCOUNT CARDS

Guest Card Stamped by your hotel, this entitles you to discounts on museum entry, some sporting facilities and lake cruises.

Lucerne Card (24-/48-/72hr Sfr19/27/33) Sold at the tourist office and train station, this offers unlimited travel on public transport (excluding SGV boats), 50% discount on museum entry, plus reductions on activities, city tours and car hire.

INTERNET ACCESS

Stadtbibliothek (Town Library; Löwenplatz 11; per hr Sfr4; ☻ 1.30-6.30pm Mon, 10am-6.30pm Tue-Fri, to 8pm Thu, 10am-4pm Sat) Free wi-fi.

Surfers Island (☎ 041 412 00 44; Weinmarkt 15; per hr Sfr10; ☻ 10am-7pm Mon-Fri, to 4pm Sat) Free 10-minute international phone call when you use the internet.

LAUNDRY

Jet Wasch (☎ 041 240 01 51; Bruchstrasse 28; ☻ 8am-noon & 2-6pm Mon-Fri, 9am-4pm Sat)

MEDICAL SERVICES

Permanence Medical Center (☎ 041 211 14 44; Base-ment, Hauptbahnhof; ☻ 24hr)

POST

Post office (cnr Bahnhofstrasse & Bahnhofplatz; ☻ 7.30am-6.30pm Mon-Fri, 8am-4pm Sat) By the train station.

TOURIST INFORMATION

Luzern Tourism (☎ enquiries 041 227 17 17, hotel reservations 041 227 17 27; www.luzern.com; Zentral-strasse 5; ☻ 8.30am-7.30pm Mon-Fri, 9am-7.30pm Sat & Sun mid-Jun–mid-Sep, 8.30am-5.30pm Mon-Fri, 9am-1pm Sat & Sun Nov-Apr, 9am-6.30pm daily rest of year) Reached from Zentralstrasse or platform 3 of the train station. Offers city walking tours.

Sights
MEDIEVAL BRIDGES

You haven't really been to Lucerne until you have strolled the creaky 14th-century **Kapellbrücke** (Chapel Bridge), spanning the Reuss River in the Old Town. The octagonal water tower is original, but its gabled roof is a modern reconstruction, rebuilt after a dis-astrous fire in 1993. As you cross the bridge, note Heinrich Wägmann's 17th-century trian-gular roof panels, showing important events from Swiss history and mythology. The icon is at its most photogenic when bathed in soft golden light at dusk.

Further down the river, the **Spreuerbrücke** (Spreuer Bridge) is darker and smaller, but its 1408 structure is entirely original. Lore has it that this was the only bridge where locals where allowed to throw *Spreu* (chaff) into the river in medieval times. The roof pan-els' theme here is artist Caspar Meglinger's movie-storyboard-style sequence of paintings, *The Dance of Death*, showing how the plague affected all levels of society.

MUSEGGMAUER

For a bird's-eye view over Lucerne's rooftops to the glittering lake and mountains beyond, wander the medieval **Museggmauer** (city wall; admission free; ☻ 8am-7pm Apr-Oct). A walkway is open between the **Schirmerturm** (tower), where you enter, and the **Wachturm**, from where you have to retrace your steps. You can also ascend

CENTRAL SWITZERLAND

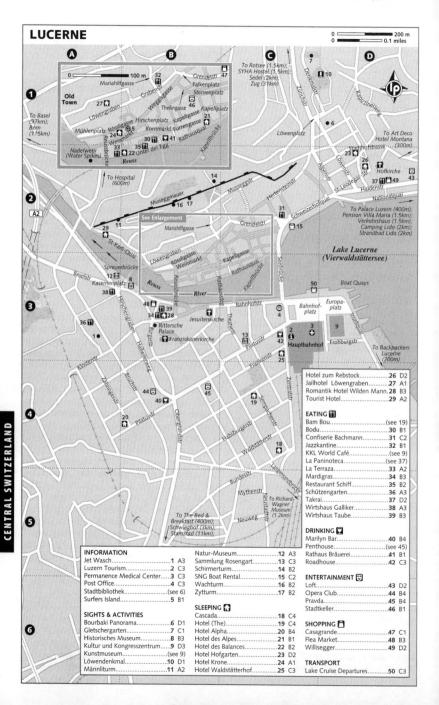

LUCERNE

and descend the **Zytturm** or **Männliturm** (the latter not connected to the ramparts walkway).

SAMMLUNG ROSENGART

Lucerne's blockbuster cultural attraction is the **Sammlung Rosengart** (Rosengart Collection; ☎ 041 220 16 60; www.rosengart.ch; Pilatusstrasse 10; adult/under 7yr/7-16yr & student/senior Sfr18/free/10/16; ☺ 10am-6pm Apr-Oct, 11am-5pm Nov-Mar), occupying a graceful neoclassical pile. It showcases the outstanding stash of Angela Rosengart, a Swiss art dealer and close friend of Picasso. Alongside works by the great Spanish master are paintings and sketches by Cézanne, Klee, Kandinsky, Miró, Matisse and Monet. Standouts include Joan Miró's electric-blue *Dancer II* (1925) and Paul Klee's childlike *X-chen* (1938).

Complementing this collection are some 200 photographs by David Douglas Duncan of the last 17 years of Picasso's life with his family in their home near Cannes, France. It's a uniquely revealing series and principally a portrait of the artist as an impish craftsman, lover and father.

VERKEHRSHAUS

It mightn't sound like an exciting way to pass an afternoon, but the interactive **Verkehrshaus** (Transport Museum; ☎ 041 370 44 44; www.verkehrshaus.ch; Lidostrasse 5; adult/under 6yr/6-16yr Sfr24/free/12; ☺ 9am-6pm Apr-Oct, 10am-5pm Nov-Mar) is actually fascinating. Alongside space rockets, steam locomotives, flying bicycles and dugout canoes are hands-on activities such as flight simulators, broadcasting studios and a shadow orchestra translating movement to music.

Switzerland's most popular museum also shelters a planetarium, an **IMAX cinema** (www .imax.ch; adult/under 6yr/child Sfr18/12/14; ☺ screenings hourly 11am-5pm Mon-Thu, to 9pm Fri-Sun) and the **Swiss Arena**, a gigantic 1:20,000 walkable map of Switzerland, taken from aerial photos, where you can delight in leaping over the Alps. Finally, there's a collection of technology-related paintings, drawings and sculptures by Swiss artist Hans Erni. Take bus 6, 8 or 24 to get here.

KULTUR UND KONGRESSZENTRUM & KUNSTMUSEUM

With striking angles and clean lines, Parisian architect Jean Nouvel's waterfront **Kultur und Kongresszentrum** (KKL; Arts & Congress Centre; www.kkl -luzern.ch; Europaplatz) is a post-modern marvel in an otherwise historic city. But don't think a pretty face implies a superficial soul: the main concert hall's acoustics are as close to perfect as humankind has ever known, according to many musicians and conductors who have performed here. The trick is that the tall, narrow concert hall, partly built below the lake's surface, is surrounded by a reverberation chamber and has an adjustable suspended ceiling, all creating a bubble of silence.

All the accolades showered upon the hall have raised the profile of the tripartite Lucerne Music Festival (see p246), increasingly one of the highlights on the global music calendar.

Inside you'll find the **Kunstmuseum** (Museum of Art; ☎ 041 226 78 00; www.kunstmuseumluzern.ch; Level K, KKL; adult/under 6yr/6-16yr & student Sfr12/free/4, Sfr4 extra for special exhibits; ☺ 10am-5pm Tue-Sun, to 8pm Wed). The permanent collection is pretty uninspiring, but keep an eye out for temporary exhibitions such as the recent retrospective of Hiroshi Sugimoto's enigmatic photography.

VICTORIAN-ERA ATTRACTIONS

Weird and wondrous Victorian attractions lure nostalgia buffs north of the Old Town. By far the most touching is the **Löwendenkmal** (Lion Monument; Denkmalstrasse). Lukas Ahorn carved this 10m-long sculpture of a dying lion into the rock face in 1820 to commemorate Swiss soldiers who died defending King Louis XVI during the French Revolution. Mark Twain once called it the 'saddest and most moving piece of rock in the world'. For Narnia fans, it often evokes Aslan at the stone table.

Next door is the **Gletschergarten** (Glacier Garden; ☎ 041 410 43 40; www.gletschergarten.ch; Denkmalstrasse 4; adult/under 6yr/6-16yr/student Sfr12/free/7/9.50; ☺ 9am-6pm Apr-Oct, 10am-5pm rest of year), a strip of rock bearing the scars (including huge potholes) inflicted on it by the glacier that slid over it some 20 million years ago. Cult kitsch fans love getting lost in the *Thousand and One Nights*–style mirror maze inspired by Spain's Alhambra Palace.

History buffs might enjoy the **Bourbaki Panorama** (☎ 041 412 30 30; www.bourbakipanorama.ch; Löwenplatz 11; adult/under 6yr/6-16yr/student & senior Sfr8/free/5/7; ☺ 1-6pm Mon, 9am-6pm Tue-Sun). This painstakingly detailed depiction of the Franco-Prussian War of 1870–71, with a moving narrative (also in English), brings to life the 1100-sq-metre circular painting of miserable-looking troops and civilians.

CENTRAL SWITZERLAND

OTHER MUSEUMS

The **Historisches Museum** (History Museum; ☎ 041 228 54 24; www.hmluzern.ch; Pfistergasse 24; adult/child/senior Sfr10/free/8; ☒ 10am-5pm Tue-Sun) is cleverly organised into a series of attention-grabbing themes, from lust and lasciviousness to government and tourism. Pick up a barcode-reading audioguide and let yourself be guided through your chosen story in German or English.

Anyone intrigued by stuffed critters and creepy crawlies shouldn't miss the hands-on **Natur-Museum** (Nature Museum; ☎ 041 228 54 11; Kasernenplatz 6; adult/under 6yr/6-16yr/student Sfr6/free/2/5; ☒ 10am-5pm Tue-Sun). Highlights feature a woodland trail with real trees and a mushroom computer (don't eat the red spotty ones). Keep your peepers open, too, for the fabled *Luzerner Drachenstein*, which, according to legend, fell from a dragon's mouth as it was flying over Mt Pilatus. Modern science suggests that the 15th century stone was probably a meteorite.

Housed in the composer's former residence in Tribschen, on the lake's southern shore, the **Richard Wagner Museum** (☎ 041 360 23 70; www.richard-wagner-museum.ch; Richard-Wagner-Weg 27; adult/under 6yr/6-12yr/student Sfr6/free/3/4; ☒ 10am-noon & 2-5pm Tue-Sun mid-Mar–Nov) harbours historic musical instruments including rarities such as a regal (portable organ). Take bus 6, 7 or 8 from the train station to Wartegg.

Activities

Perfect for a splash or sunbathe is **Strandbad Lido** (☎ 041 370 38 06; www.lido-luzern.ch; Lidostrasse 6a; adult/under 6yr/6-15yr Sfr6/free/3; ☒ 9am-8pm mid-May–Sep), a lakefront beach with a playground, volleyball court and heated outdoor pool near Camping Lido (opposite). Or you can swim for free on the other bank of the lake by Seepark, off Alpenquai.

SNG (☎ 041 368 08 08; www.sng.ch), on the northern side of Seebrücke, rents out rowing boats, pedalos and small motor boats (from Sfr22/29/55 per hour, plus deposit) and offers cheap lake cruises (Sfr15).

Outventure (☎ 041 611 14 41; www.outventure.ch; Stans) tempts adrenalin junkies with pursuits including tandem paragliding (for Sfr150), canyoning (from Sfr110), glacier trekking (Sfr150) and canoeing on Lake Lucerne (Sfr115).

There's no better way to appreciate the region's gorgeous scenery than by hitting the trail. For dizzying panoramas over Lake Lucerne,

take the ferry over to Kehrsiten-Bürgenstock for the two-hour **Bürgenstock Felsenweg** (p70). The tourist office can give details on other walks in the area, such as the gentle amble from Schwanenplatz to Sonnmatt.

If **cycling** is more your style, check out the routes circumnavigating the lake. An easy-going, scenic option is the 16km pedal to Winkel via Kastanienbaum, leading mostly along the lakefront. The train station has **bike rental** (☎ 041 51 227 32 61) costing Sfr25/33 for a half-/full day.

Festivals & Events

The world-class **Lucerne Festival** (☎ tickets 041 226 44 80, info 041 226 44 00; www.lucernefestival.ch) is divided into three separate seasons, Easter, summer and 'Piano' (in November). Concerts take place in the KKL (p245).

The **Jodlerfest Luzern** (www.jodlerfestluzern.ch) in late June is a classic Alpine shindig, welcoming some 12,000 Swiss yodellers, alphorn players and flag throwers.

Sleeping

Whether you're seeking a design-conscious hotel or a sweet and simple lakefront B&B, Lucerne has a bed to please. Visit www.luzern-hotels.ch for inspiration. Most hotels offer discounts during winter – sometimes up to one-third off, but you'll be lucky to get a bed (or any kip for that matter) at Fasnacht, so book well ahead.

BUDGET

Hostels

Backpackers Lucerne (☎ 041 360 04 20; www.backpackerslucerne.ch; Alpenquai 42; dm/d Sfr31/70; ☒ reception 7-10am & 4-11pm; ☐) Could this be backpacker heaven? Right on the lake, this is a soulful place to crash with art-slung walls, bubbly staff, a well-equipped kitchen and immaculate dorms with balconies. It's a 15-minute walk southeast of the station.

SYHA hostel (☎ 041 420 88 00; www.youthhostel.ch/luzern; Sedelstrasse 12; dm/d Sfr32.50/82; ☒ check-in 2pm-midnight in summer, from 4pm in winter; ☐ ☐) These HI digs are modern, well run and clean. Value-for-money meals are available throughout the day. Take bus 18 from the train station to Jugendherberge.

Guest Houses & Hotels

The Bed & Breakfast (☎ 041 310 15 14; www.thebandb.ch; Taubenhausstrasse 34; s/d with shared bathroom Sfr80/120;

FASNACHT FEVER

The next time someone grumbles about the Swiss being so irritatingly orderly and well behaved, send them to Lucerne for **Fasnacht** – they'll *never* use those tired clichés again. More boisterous than Basel or Bern, this six-day pre-Lenten bash is stark raving bonkers. The fun kicks off on 'Dirty Thursday' with the character 'Fritschi' greeting the crowds from the town hall and a canon signalling that hedonistic misrule can begin. Warty witches, leering ogres, jangling jesters, it doesn't matter which costume or mask you choose – dress up, drink and dance, it's tradition! Guggenmusik bands (literally) rock the bridges, acrobats and actors perform, and parades fill the streets with colour, chaos and ear-splitting music in the build up to Mardi Gras (Fat Tuesday).

⊙ Mar-Oct; P ✗) This friendly B&B feels like a private home with stylish, contemporary rooms – think crisp white bedding, scatter cushions and hot pink or lime accents. Unwind in the flowery garden or with a soak in the old-fashioned tub. Free wi-fi is another bonus. Take bus 1 to Eichof.

Tourist Hotel (☎ 041 410 24 74; www.touristhotel.ch; St-Karli-Quai 12; dm Sfr40-45, s/d Sfr80/120, with bathroom Sfr140/220; P ✗ 🖳) Don't be put off by the uninspired name and pease-pudding-green façade of this central, riverfront cheapie. Dorms are basic, but rooms cheery, with bold paintjobs, parquet floors and flat-screen TVs.

Hotel Alpha (☎ 041 240 42 80; www.hotelalpha.ch; Zähringerstrasse 24; s/d Sfr70/140; 🖳) Easy on the eye and wallet, this hotel is in a quiet residential area 10 minutes' walk from the centre. Rooms are simple, light and spotlessly clean.

Jailhotel Löwengraben (☎ 041 410 78 30; www.jailhotel.ch; Löwengraben 18; s/d Sfr118/149; ✗) This former prison has novelty value, but you might get a jailhouse shock when you enter your cell to find barred windows, bare floorboards and a prefab bathroom. It's OK for a laugh, but not for quality shut-eye, with thumping techno in the downstairs Alcatraz club to 3am. Having to pay in cash on arrival is, frankly, daylight robbery.

Camping

Camping Lido (☎ 041 370 21 46; www.camping-international.ch; Lidostrasse 19; sites per adult/child/tent Sfr10/5/10, plus Sfr5 for electricity, cabin beds Sfr25; ⊙ year-round) On the lake's northern shore, east of town, this shady ground also has four- to eight-bed wooden cabins (sleeping bag required). There's a playground, laundry, bike hire (Sfr10) and a games room with wi-fi. Take bus 6 or 8.

MIDRANGE

Hotel des Alpes (☎ 041 417 20 60; www.desalpes-luzern.ch; Furrengasse 3; s/d from Sfr128/201; ✗) Facing the river and Kapellbrücke, location is this hotel's biggest draw. The old-fashioned rooms are comfy, though light sleepers might find them noisy. Our only real gripe is the surly reception staff.

Pension Villa Maria (☎ 041 370 21 19; villamaria@bluewin.ch; Haldenstrasse 36; d Sfr150, with bathroom Sfr170; ⊙ closed Nov-Feb; P) Kindly Maria makes everyone feel at home at this granny-chic pension with clean, no-frills rooms. It's a 15-minutes lakefront stroll from the centre.

Romantik Hotel Wilden Mann (☎ 041 210 16 66; www.wilden-mann.ch; Bahnhofstrasse 30; s Sfr165-220, d Sfr215-320; 🖳) Classically elegant rooms adorned with stucco, ruby-red fabrics and antique dressers attract romantics to this 16th-century stunner near the river. The 1st-floor terrace is superb for alfresco dining.

Hotel Waldstätterhof (☎ 041 227 12 71; www.hotel-waldstaetterhof.ch; Zentralstrasse 4; s/d Sfr170/260; P ✗ 🖳) Behind its faux Gothic, red-brick exterior, this hotel has minimalist chic rooms with hardwood floors and high ceilings. Light sleepers might want to pack earplugs, though, as it's opposite the train station.

Cascada (☎ 041 226 80 88; Bundesplatz 18; www.cascada.ch; s/d Sfr175/280; P 🖳) Interiors teeter on corporate, but this is still a smart, central option close to the train station. Murals of Swiss waterfalls soften the look in spacious quarters decorated in neutral greens and blues. Courtyard-facing rooms are quieter than the others.

Hotel zum Rebstock (☎ 041 410 35 81; www.hereweare.ch; St-Leodegar-Strasse 3; s Sfr195-220, d Sfr295-320; P 🖳) When Czech novelist Franz Kafka stayed here, he bemoaned that 'rooms were dark, staff moody and fruit nonexistent'. What a difference a century makes. Today quarters skip from beamed boudoirs to arty rooms with intricate mosaic bathrooms. As for the fruit, free apples in the lobby prove they take feedback seriously.

Hotel Hofgarten (☎ 041 410 88 88; www.hofgarten
.ch; Stadthofstrasse 14; s/d Sfr205/305; **P** ✗) Rebstock's
sister hotel has striking, individually decorated
rooms, but in a more streamlined fashion. The
Mies van der Rohe furniture in room 226 sets
the tone.

Hotel Krone (☎ 041 419 44 00; www.krone-luzern.ch;
Weinmarkt 12; s/d Sfr195/310) Sleek and central,
Krone combines a historic facade with rooms
that are temples to pared-down, contemporary chic – think earthy hues, clean lines and
parquet floors. There's free wi-fi.

TOP END

Hotel des Balances (☎ 041 418 28 28; www.balances.ch;
Weinmarkt 4; s Sfr260, d Sfr360-395, ste Sfr470-550; **P** 💻)
Behind its frescoed facade, this hotel flaunts a
design lighter and frothier than Angel Delight
in ice-white rooms with gilt mirrors and inlaid parquet floors. Suites have whirlpools
and river-facing balconies. Chef Andy Fluri
interprets French cuisine imaginatively in the
chandelier-lit restaurant.

Art Deco Hotel Montana (☎ 041 419 00 00; www
.hotel-montana.ch; Adligenswilerstrasse 22; s Sfr265-390, d
Sfr330-590; ✗ 💻) Perched above the lake, this
opulent Art Deco hotel is reached by its own
funicular. The handsome rooms reveal attention to detail, from inlaid parquet floors to
period lighting. Many have fantastic views, as
do the terrace and barrel-hall entrance.

our pick **The Hotel** (☎ 041 226 86 86; www.the-hotel
.ch; Sempacherstrasse 14; ste Sfr430-570; ✗ 💻) Marilyn
Manson is among the celebrity guests at this
ubercool design hotel, bearing the imprint of
architect Jean Nouvel. Streamlined and jet-
black, the 10 vampy suites reveal stainless steel
fittings, open-plan bathrooms peeking through
to garden foliage, and stills from movie classics
gracing the ceilings. Downstairs Bam Bou is
one of Lucerne's hippest restaurants.

Palace Luzern (☎ 041 416 16 16; www.palace-luzern
.ch; Haldenstrasse 10; s Sfr400-600, d Sfr510-710, ste Sfr790-
2600; **P** 💻) This luxury belle époque hotel
on the lakefront is a favourite with the Condé
Nast set. Inside it's all gleaming marble, chandeliers and turn-of-the-century grandeur.
Given the sky-high rates, it's surprising that
guests must pay Sfr40 extra for breakfast. A
pretty expensive bowl of muesli, that.

Eating

RESTAURANTS

Jazzkantine (☎ 041 410 73 73; Grabenstrasse 8; mains
Sfr15-22; 🕑 7am-12.30am Mon-Sat, 4pm-12.30am Sun)
With its stainless-steel bar, sturdy wooden
tables and chalkboard menus, this is an arty
haunt. Go for tasty bruschetta or more am-
bitious dishes like penne vodka. Weeknight
jazz workshops are followed by gigs on
Saturday night.

La Terraza (☎ 041 410 36 31; Metzgerrainle 9; mains
Sfr17-45) Set in a 12th-century building that
has housed fishmongers, dukes and scribes
over the years, La Terraza oozes atmosphere.
High-back chairs and monochrome shots of
bella Italia give the vaulted interior urban
edge. When the sun's out, sit on the riverfront terrace for favourites like clam and
rocket spaghetti.

Wirtshaus Taube (☎ 041 210 07 47; Burgerstrasse
3; mains Sfr18-40; 🕑 daily May-Sep, Tue-Sat Jan-Apr,
Mon-Sat Oct-Dec) The mock cave and flickering
electric candles are more ghost train than
gourmet, but there are no quibbles about the
hearty cuisine served here. Standouts include
humungous 420g *Cordon bleus* and homemade veal sausages.

Bodu (☎ 041 410 01 77; Kornmarkt 5; mains Sfr18-45)
Banquettes, wood panelling and elbow-to-
elbow tables create a warm ambience at this
French bistro. Here locals huddle around bottles of Bordeaux and bowls of *bouillabaisse*
(fish stew) or succulent sirloin steaks.

Schützengarten (☎ 041 240 01 10; Bruchstrasse 20;
mains Sfr18.50-45; 🕑 Mon-Sat) This restaurant also
serves meat... As well as a cracking sense of
humour, Schützengarten has smiley service,
wood-panelled surrounds, appetising vegetarian and vegan dishes and organic wine. Sit on
the vine-strewn terrace in summer.

Restaurant Schiff (☎ 041 418 52 52; Unter der Egg
8; mains Sfr20-45) Under the waterfront arcades
and lit by tea lights at night, this restaurant
has bags of charm. Try fish from Lake Lucerne
and some of the city's most celebrated
Chögalipaschtetli (vol-au-vents stuffed with
meat and mushrooms).

Wirtshaus Galliker (☎ 041 240 10 01; Schützenstrasse
1; mains Sfr22-50; 🕑 closed Sun & Mon, Jul-mid-Aug) Don't
eat for a day before visiting this old-style tavern, passionately run by the Galliker family since 1856. It attracts a lively bunch of
regulars. Motherly waitresses dish up Lucerne
soul food (bratwurst, rösti and the like) that
is roll-me-out-the-door filling.

Bam Bou (☎ 41 226 86 86; Sempacherstrasse 14; mains
Sfr46-68) The Hotel's restaurant is an ode to
21st-century cool: black leather benches contrast strikingly with scarlet walls, gold script

and an optical illusion where slanted mirrors reflect the street outside. The cuisine is a seductive French-Asian fusion, with signatures such as coriander-crusted tuna and Scottish salmon with ginger-sake sauce.

QUICK EATS & CAFÉS

Confiserie Bachmann (☎ 041 227 70 70; Schwanenplatz 7; ⏰ 7am-7pm Mon-Sat, to 9pm Thu, 9.30am-7pm Sun) Swiss milk chocolate flows from a fountain at this sugar-coated temple. You'll find pastries, gelati and Switzerland's longest praline counter.

La Paninoteca (☎ 041 410 90 70; Haldenstrasse 9; panini & pizza Sfr7.50-17.50; ⏰ 10am-midnight Mon-Sat) Our favourite Italian job, this family-run, retro-style *paninoteca* is a relaxed spot to refuel on yummy panini such as roast beef and goat's cheese, or perfectly thin, crisp pizza.

KKL World Café (☎ 041 226 71 00; Europaplatz 1; sandwiches from Sfr8.50, mains Sfr16-19; ⏰ 9am-midnight) This sleek-looking bistro stocks muesli and sandwiches in its glass counters, but also offers wok dishes at lunch and dinner.

Mardigras (Burgerstrasse 5; light meals Sfr9-18; ⏰ 4-10.30pm Mon; 7am-10.30pm Tue-Sat, 9am-10.30pm Sun) White leather benches, monumental flower displays and soft jazz create a Parisian feel in this glam café. It's a fine spot for baguettes and Niçoise salads by day or a glass of red in the evening.

our pick **Takrai** (☎ 041 412 04 04; www.takrai.ch; Haldenstrasse 9; mains Sfr14.50-21.50) Judging by the anaconda of a queue at lunchtime, this pint-sized Thai joint is the place to be. Wafting spices and the rhythmic sizzle of woks lure you to the show kitchen. The accent here is on local organic produce and everything – from feisty papaya salads to the generously portioned curries – strikes perfect balance. Grab your chopsticks and Chang and pull up a stool. All dishes are available with tofu.

Drinking & Entertainment

Rathaus Bräuerei (☎ 041 410 52 57; Unter den Egg 2; ⏰ 8am-midnight Mon-Sat, to 11pm Sun) Sip home-brewed beer under the vaulted arches of this buzzy tavern, or nab a pavement table and watch the river flow.

Marilyn Bar (☎ 079 337 82 43; Pilatusstrasse 46) A shrine to the silver screen diva, this gallery-style bar's chilli-red walls are smothered in photos of Ms Monroe. It's a relaxed place for pre-clubbing drinks.

Roadhouse (☎ 041 220 27 27; Pilatusstrasse 1; www .roadhouse.ch; ⏰ 11am-4am) Roadhouse plays solid rock to a young, fun crowd. Check out Wednesday night's jam sessions where anyone with an instrument or voice (preferably both) can take the stand.

Penthouse (Astoria Hotel, Pilatusstrasse 29) This is a ritzy rooftop lounge where, despite great views over Lucerne, the eye-candy crowd are busier discreetly checking each other out. On the ground floor is the swanky and popular Pravda nightclub (open Wednesday to Saturday), where top DJs spin everything from bootylicious R&B to house anthems.

Opera Club (☎ 041 259 20 00; www.operaclub.ch; Pilatusplatz; ⏰ Tue-Sat) Housed in a former cinema, the Opera Club has kept its theatrical feel in the scarlet drapes and floor-length gilt mirrors. DJs keep the dance floor rammed with grooves from hip-hop to electro.

Loft (☎ 041 410 92 44; Haldenstrasse 21; ⏰ Wed-Sun) With a steel-and-concrete minimalist design, Loft attracts young, glammed-up hipsters. DJs play Latin, hip-hop and urban sounds.

Stadtkeller (☎ 041 410 47 33; Sternenplatz 3; cover Sfr15; ⏰ show 8.30pm Mar-Oct) Alphorns, cowbells, flag throwing, yodelling – name the Swiss cliché and you'll find it at this folksy haunt.

Shopping

Mosey down Haldenstrasse for art and antiques or Löwenstrasse for vintage threads and souvenirs. Fruit and vegetable stalls spring forth along the river quays every Tuesday and Saturday morning. There's also a flea market on Burgerstrasse each Saturday from May to October.

Williseger (☎ 041 410 58 81; Haldenstrasse 11; ⏰ 9am-5.30pm Mon-Fri, to 4pm Sat) Wonderfully nostalgic, this Christmas shop brims with vintage and hand-carved decorations, from Erzgebirge nutcrackers and smoking men to glitzy baubles, dinky matchbox scenes and music boxes.

Casagrande (☎ 041 418 60 70; Grendelstrasse 6; ⏰ 8am-10pm Mon-Sat, 9am-10pm Sun) Our favourite temple of kitsch might tempt you to spend on Heidi dolls, cuckoo clocks, yodelling marmots and – heaven forbid – his 'n' hers cow mugs.

Getting There & Away

Frequent trains connect Lucerne to Interlaken West (Sfr33.40, two hours, via the scenic Brünig Pass), Bern (Sfr35, 1¼ hours), Lugano (Sfr55, 2¾ hours), Geneva (Sfr72, 3¼ hours, via Olten or Langnau) and Zürich (Sfr23, one hour).

CENTRAL SWITZERLAND

The A2 freeway connecting Basel and Lugano passes by Lucerne, while the A14/A4 provides the road link to Zürich.

BOAT

For information on boat transport, see right. The departure points are the quays around Bahnhofplatz/Europaplatz.

Getting Around

Should you be going further than the largely pedestrianised Old Town, city buses leave from outside the Hauptbahnhof at Bahnhofplatz. Tickets cost Sfr2 for a short journey, Sfr2.80 for one zone and Sfr4 for two. Ticket dispensers indicate the correct fare for each destination. The 24-hour pass (Sfr10) covers all zones; Swiss Pass holders travel free. There's an underground car park at the train station.

LAKE LUCERNE

It's possible to feel the call of the mountains in Lucerne. Majestic peaks hunch conspiratorially around Vierwaldstättersee – which twists and turns as much as the tongue does when pronouncing it. Little wonder English speakers use the shorthand Lake Lucerne.

To appreciate the views, ride up to Mt Pilatus, Mt Rigi or Stanserhorn. When the clouds peel away, their precipitous lookout points reveal a crumpled tapestry of green hillsides and shimmering cobalt waters below,

and glaciated peaks beyond. It's especially atmospheric in autumn, when fog rises like dry ice from the lake, and in winter, when the craggy heights are dusted with snow.

Apart from its mountain viewpoints, the lake offers attractive tucked-away resorts, which can be reached by boat. The far eastern reach of Lake Lucerne – Lake Uri or Urnersee – has special significance for the Swiss, as it's home to the Rütli meadow where the country was supposedly born.

Getting Around

The **Lake Lucerne Navigation Company SGV** (☎ 041 367 67 67; www.lakelucerne.ch) operates boats (sometimes paddle-steamers) daily. This excludes the Lake Uri section of the lake, its most easterly finger, where services only go past Rütli in winter on Sundays and national holidays.

From Lucerne, destinations include Alpnachstad (one-way/return Sfr23/38, 1¾ hours), Weggis (Sfr16.80/31, 50 minutes), Vitznau (Sfr23/38, 1¼ hours), Brunnen (Sfr34/53, 1¾ hours) and Flüelen (Sfr39/59, 3¼ hours). Longer trips are relatively cheaper than short ones, and you can alight as often as you want. An SGV day ticket costs Sfr59 for adults and Sfr29.50 for children. Swiss Pass and Eurail (on days selected for travel only) are valid on scheduled boat trips, while InterRail entitles you to half-price. Passes will get you discounts on selected mountain railways and cable cars.

If driving, you'll find that roads run close to the shoreline most of the way around –

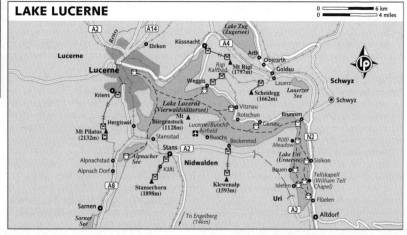

LAKE LUCERNE

excluding the stretch from Flüelen to Stansstad. Here, the A2 freeway ploughs a fairly straight line, sometimes underground and usually away from the water.

MT PILATUS

Rearing above Lucerne from the southwest, **Mt Pilatus** (www.pilatus.com) rose to fame in the 19th-century when Wagner waxed lyrical about its Alpine vistas and Queen Victoria trotted up here on horseback. Legend has it that this 2132m peak was named after Pontius Pilate, whose corpse was thrown into a lake on its summit and whose restless ghost has haunted its heights ever since. Poltergeists aside, it's more likely that the moniker derives from the Latin word *pileatus*, meaning cloud covered – as the mountain frequently is.

From May to October, you can reach Mt Pilatus on a classic 'golden round-trip'. Board the lake steamer from Lucerne to Alpnachstad, then rise with the world's steepest cog railway to Mt Pilatus. From the summit, cable cars bring you down to Kriens via Fräkmüntegg and Krienseregg, where bus 1 takes you back to Lucerne. The reverse route (Kriens–Pilatus–Alpnachstad–Lucerne) is also possible. The return trip costs Sfr88.80 (Sfr56.80/41.20/41.20 with valid Swiss/Eurail/InterRail passes).

For an above-the-treetops adventure in summer, head for **Pilatus Seilpark** (Rope Park; www.pilatus-seilpark.ch; Fräkmüntegg; adult/8–16yr Sfr26/19; 10am-5pm May-Oct, to 5.30pm Jul & Aug), where 10 head-spinning trails from high-wire bridges to tree climbs are graded according to difficulty. Fräkmüntegg is also the starting point for Switzerland's longest **summer toboggan run** (adult/under 6yr/6–16yr Sfr8/free/6; 10am-5pm May to Oct), a speedy 1.3km downhill ride.

Mt Pilatus is great for **walking**. Hikes include a steep, partially roped 2.8km scramble from Fräkmüntegg to the summit, an easy 3.5km walk through forest and moor from Krienseregg to Fräkmüntegg, and the 1.5km trudge from Pilatus-Kulm to Tomlishorn, affording views that stretch as far as the Black Forest on a clear day. Climbers can tackle the dizzying Galtigentürme rock pillars or Holzwangflue's gullies where ibex often roam.

Heaps of fun in winter is **sledging** 6km through snowy woodlands from Fräkmüntegg to Kriens. A day pass for the Kriens–Fräkmüntegg cable car cost Sfr41 for adults and Sfr20 for children. Free sledge hire is available at Fräkmüntegg station.

It's more traditional to stay overnight at Mt Rigi (p252), but there are two hotels on Pilatus. The rustic 19th-century **Pilatus-Kulm** (☎ 041 670 12 55; hotels@pilatus.ch; s/d with shared bathroom Sfr77/124) and the modern **Hotel Bellevue** (s/d Sfr111/192) share the same reception. There's also a self-service restaurant on this peak.

STANSERHORN

Looming above the lake, 1898m **Stanserhorn** (www.stanserhorn.ch) boasts the region's only revolving restaurant. Rotating once every 43 minutes, the star-shaped Rondorama offers 360-degree views looking back to Titlis and peaks which take on a watercolour dreaminess at dusk. Kids love the marmot park at the summit, where the whistling critters can be observed in a near-to-natural habitat.

The journey up is by vintage funicular from Stans to Kälti, then cable car. Both operate from mid-April to mid-November. The funicular's base station is a five-minute walk from Stans train station. The single/return trip from Stans to Stanserhorn costs Sfr29/58 for adults and Sfr7.30/14.50 for children. If you're driving, you can save an hour by parking at Kälti.

Come in August and you may well be surprised to see competitors legging it up the mountain backwards with rear-view mirrors, as they compete in the 11km **Retro Running** sprint. See the Stanserhorn website for details of this bizarre race in reverse.

Stans is on the Lucerne–Engelberg railway (one-way from Lucerne Sfr7.60). The **tourist office** (☎ 041 610 88 33; www.lakeluzern.ch; Bahnhofplatz 4; 9am-noon & 2-5pm Mon-Fri) can help out with accommodation. Dorfplatz, the hub of the charming town centre, is located behind the station, overlooked by an early baroque church. Here, too, is the well-regarded **Hotel Engel** (☎ 041 619 10 10; www.engelstans.ch; Dorfplatz 1; s/d Sfr90/150;), hiding sleek minimalist rooms behind its historic facade.

BECKENRIED

Beckenried, on the southern shore, is a bus ride from Stans. Just a few minutes' walk from the boat station is a cable car to **Klewenalp** (www.klewenalp.ch; one-way/return Sfr22/35), a much-underrated skiing destination, with 40km of well-prepared red and blue runs, which become hiking, climbing and mountain biking trails in summer. A map at the top outlines the options. Bike hire is available at the base station for Sfr33 per day.

CENTRAL SWITZERLAND

MT RIGI

Blue, no red, no dark… Turner couldn't quite make up his mind about how he preferred 1797m **Rigi** (www.rigi.ch), so in 1842 the genius painted the mountain in three different lights to reflect its changing moods. On a clear day, there are impressive views to a jagged spine of peaks including Mt Titlis and the Jungfrau giants. To the north and west, you overlook Arth-Goldau and the Zugersee, curving around until it almost joins Küssnacht and an arm of Lake Lucerne.

Sunrise is prime-time viewing around here. Since Victorian times, tourists have been staying at the **Rigi Kulm Hotel** (☎ 041 880 18 88; www.rigikulm.ch; s/d from Sfr140/220) and getting up before the crack of dawn to see the blazing sun light up the sky. Today's hotel, a 20th-century re-creation of the original, is the only major establishment at the summit, and has a restaurant and snack kiosk.

Rigi is a magnet to hikers; for recommended routes, check www.rigi.ch. There are several easy walks (1½ to two hours) down from Rigi Kulm to Rigi Kaltbad, with wonderful views. Or ask the tourist offices in Lucerne or Weggis for information on the Rigi Lehnenweg, a scenic 17.5km trek around the mountain.

Hiking up the mountain is another story. It's at least a 4½-hour walk from Weggis, but you could take the cable car from Küssnacht to Seeboldenalp (one-way/return Sfr13/22), where a steepish path leads to the summit in just over two hours. While hiking on Rigi, watch out for the *Chlyni Lüüt*, tiny 'wild folk' with supernatural powers who in mythology once inhabited Rigi!

For those of a less energetic bent, two rival railways carry passengers to the top. One runs from Arth-Goldau, the other from Vitznau. Either costs Sfr37/62 one-way/return. The Vitznau track gives the option of diverting at Rigi Kaltbad and taking the cable car to/from Weggis instead. Holders of Swiss, Eurail and InterRail passes receive a 50% discount on fares, and children under 16 travel free when accompanied by a parent.

Weggis

pop 4020 / elevation 440m

Sheltered from cold northerlies by Mt Rigi, Weggis enjoys an unusually mild climate, sprouting a few palm and fig trees by the lakefront. It's hard to believe this genteel resort was the birthplace of the rebellious 'Moderner Bund' art movement, the forerunner of Dada. Its small-town friendliness is extremely welcoming, but a few days' stopover usually suffices. A cable car runs from here up to Rigi Kaltbad (one-way/return Sfr27/45).

The **tourist office** (☎ 041 390 11 55; www.the-best-of-lake-lucerne.ch; Seestrasse 5; 8am-noon & 1-5.30pm Mon-Fri, 9am-4pm Sat & Sun) is next to the boat station.

Budget-Hotel Weggis (☎ 041 390 11 31; www.budgethotel.ch; Parkstrasse 29; s/d/tr Sfr53/101/129, with bathroom Sfr68/126/149; reception 3-9pm) Doing what it says on the label well, this cheapie keeps even pernickety customers happy with clean, simple rooms. It's up the hill from the boat station.

SeeHotel Gotthard (☎ 041 390 21 14; www.gotthard-weggis.ch; s/d from Sfr142/230; closed mid-Oct–mid-Dec) This friendly waterfront hotel has comfy, spotless rooms with tea-making facilities; the best have lake views. There's free wi-fi, bike hire and you can use the spa at the adjacent hotel.

Park Hotel Weggis (☎ 041 392 05 05; www.phw.ch; Herteinsteinstrasse 34; s/d from Sfr340/515; P ☒ ▣) Brazil's national football team stayed at this lavish lakefront pad, framed by manicured gardens. Understated elegance sums up the lavender-green rooms, as bright and breezy as Provençal meadows in summer. All come with mosaic-tiled bathrooms and five-star gadgets like espresso makers and DVD players. When you tire of those lake views, there's the Zen-inspired spa, the private beach and Michelin-starred restaurant, Annex, serving French-Asian cuisine.

Lüücht Türmli (☎ 041 390 04 04, Seestrasse 27; snacks & mains Sfr6-22; 11am-11pm Tue-Sun, daily summer high season) Ahoy there! Jazzed up with mini lighthouses and homespun art, this shipshape café is a jolly spot for fish or calamari fried to crunchy perfection. Wobble across to the jetty to chomp. They also rent pedalos/hydrobikes for Sfr28/18 per hour.

Tiffany's (☎ 041 390 18 12; Seestrasse 48; snacks Sfr10-18; Wed-Mon) You can almost picture the waves lapping and bouzouki playing at this Greek-style café. The owner has recreated a Paros taverna to a tee – from the blue-white paint job to the plastic fish nets and sunny terrace. Nibble on dolmades, aubergines and syrupy baklava. There's free wi-fi.

Grape (☎ 041 392 07 07; Seestrasse 60; mains Sfr17-30; 10am-12.30am) Weggis' California dreamer is this too-cool haunt, where you can sip Chardonnay and gaze up at Golden Gate

Bridge murals gracing brushed gold walls. The globetrotting menu skips from wood-fired pizza to Thai noodles to Caesar salads.

LAKE URI

Scything through rugged mountains, the fjord-like Lake Uri (Urnersee) finger of Lake Lucerne mirrors the country's medieval past in its glassy turquoise waters. Take the ferry from Brunnen towards Flüelen and you'll glimpse a near 30m-high natural obelisk protruding from the water. Its gold inscription pays homage to Friedrich Schiller, the author of the play *Wilhelm Tell,* so instrumental in creating the Tell legend.

Next stop is the **Rütli Meadow**, the cradle of Swiss democracy. This is where the Oath of Eternal Alliance was allegedly signed by the three cantons of Uri, Schwyz and Nidwalden in 1291 and later when General Guisan gathered the Swiss army during WWII in a show of force against potential invaders. As such, this is hallowed ground to Swiss patriots and the focus of national day celebrations on 1 August. As well as an almighty flag, there's an obligatory souvenir shop doubling as a café.

An important port of call is the serene **Tellskapelle** (William Tell Chapel), covered in murals depicting four episodes in the Tell legend, including the one that's supposed to have occurred on this spot, his escape from Gessler's boat. There's a huge carillon that chimes behind the chapel. Approaching from land instead of water, you pass – would you Adam and Eve it – apple orchards, which might make your crossbow twitch if you had one.

After crossing into another founding canton, Uri, the boat finally chugs into Flüelen; historically a staging post for the mule trains crossing the St Gotthard Pass and today a stop on the main road and rail route. Near the town is **Altdorf**, where William Tell is reputed to have performed his apple-shooting stunt. A statue of the man himself stands in the main square, and Schiller's play is sometimes performed in Altdorf's Tellspielhaus.

BRUNNEN
pop 8250 / elevation 435m
Tucked into the folds of mountains, where Lake Lucerne and Lake Uri meet at right angles, Brunnen enjoys mesmerising views south and west. A regular guest, Turner was so impressed by the vista that he whipped out his watercolours to paint *The Bay of Uri from Brunnen* (1841). As the local föhn wind rushes down from the mountains, it creates perfect conditions for sailing and paragliding. Not to forget the folkloric hot air of the weekly alphorn concerts in summer.

Information
The **tourist office** (☎ 041 825 00 40; www.brunnen tourismus.ch; Bahnhofstrasse 15; ⌚ 8.30am-6pm Mon-Fri, 9am-3pm Sat & Sun Jul & Aug, 8.30am-6pm Mon-Fri, 9am-1pm Sat Jun & Sep, 8.30am-noon & 1.30-5.30pm Mon-Fri Oct-May) has information and internet access (per hour Sfr10). The office is five minutes from the train station (following the signs), which has bike rental available for Sfr50 per day. Don't forget to ask about the Guest Card.

Activities
Glide over the treetops to **Urmiberg** (cable car one-way/return Sfr11/19) for views over the pointy peaks ringing Lake Uri and Lucerne. If you want to get even higher, contact **Touch and Go** (☎ 041 820 54 31; www.paragliding.ch; Parkstrasse 14), which offers tandem paragliding flights from Sfr150. In winter, you can rent snowshoes at the cable car station (Sfr10 per day) to stomp through twinkling woodlands.

A first-rate way of discovering the different facets of the lake is by paddling around it. **Adventure Point** (☎ 079 247 74 72; www.adventure point.ch) arranges guided canoe and kayak tours (Sfr95), or you can go it alone for around Sfr50 per person. For adrenalin-charged thrills, check out its canyoning (from Sfr99) excursions in the area.

Sleeping
Two attractive campsites in west Brunnen are open from Easter to September: family-run **Camping Urmiberg** (☎ 041 820 33 27; sites per adult/child/tent/car Sfr5.80/2.70/5.20/2.70) and lakefront **Camping Hopfreben** (☎ 041 820 18 73; sites per adult/child/tent/car Sfr5.50/3/8/3).

Schlaf im Stroh (☎ 041 820 06 70; Schulstrasse 26a; adult Sfr25, child Sfr14-19; ⌚ May-Oct; **P**) Who's the scarecrow in the mirror? You, after spending a night in the straw at the Bucheli family's farmhouse. Kids love the farmyard animals. A hearty breakfast is included and they'll even rustle up an evening meal on request.

Hotel Alfa + Schmid (☎ 041 820 18 82; www.schmid alfa.ch; Axenstrasse 5-7; s Sfr70-90, d Sfr130-220) Spread

---

SEPP STEINER (AKA WILLIAM TELL), CROSSBOW MAKER

Ever since he was a child, Sepp Steiner has been absolutely fascinated by crossbows and William Tell. Today he keeps medieval crafts and the spirit of Tell alive at his workshop **Tells Armbrust Werkstatt** (☎ 079 414 63 19; www.armbrustwerkstatt.ch; Gersau; ☿ May-Oct) on the banks of Lake Lucerne.

Is William Tell fact or fiction? Most definitely fact. He lived in Uri canton in the early 14th century and was an expert crossbow marksman. In reality he probably drowned in the lake after refusing to bow to Habsburg rule. Goethe, however, persuaded Schiller to dramatise the story and his 1804 play became famous for the apple-shooting stunt. Really we have Schiller to thank for drawing tourists to the area in the 19th century.

In your opinion, what does William Tell represent? Tell is Gotthard and its four passes, medieval craftsmanship and Lake Lucerne. He symbolises freedom from political oppression, the struggle between the aristocracy and the church and the strength of Swiss character.

How did you become interested in William Tell and crossbows? People have always called me William Tell because of my size. I've been handcrafting crossbows for 24 years and they are my favourite weapons – faster and more accurate than longbows. Four years ago, I gave up farming to fulfil my dream of making crossbows full time at this workshop. I use the same techniques and materials (cherry wood, horn and sinew) as would have been used in Tell's day. Visitors can see the crossbows and the craftsmanship required to produce one. It's important to keep these skills and crafts alive before they die completely.

What do you love about Lake Lucerne? Steamboats on the lake, Rigi, Lucerne Old Town and the wilderness of Gotthard. The feeling of independence is also more tangible in Uri than anywhere else in Switzerland because it has been self-governed since 1352. To me it's the most beautiful place in the world because it's home.

---

across two lakefront buildings, this hotel has inviting rooms with citrusy paint jobs, parquet floors and wrought-iron balconies. Budget rooms forgo the best views. The restaurant (mains Sfr17.50 to Sfr38) is renowned for its fresh lake fish.

Weisses Rössli (☎ 041 825 13 00; www.weisses-roessli -brunnen.ch; Bahnhofstrasse 8; s/d Sfr100/160; P) Rössli's spacious rooms were recently revamped and now sport shiny parquet floors, modern tiled bathrooms and flat-screen TVs. The nicest have balconies.

ourpick Alpina (☎ 041 820 18 13; www.alpina -brunnen.ch; Gersauerstrasse 32; d Sfr145-180, apt per week Sfr850; P 💻) Stefan runs Brunnen's quirkiest and most creative hotel with passion. Daylight streams into rooms with original touches like stucco, sky-painted ceilings and slanted beams. All feature kitchenettes and welcome treats such as pralines and fresh flowers. The stairs are lined with squirrel-like collections of shells, Beatles miniatures and other curios. Try the DIY organic muesli and homemade dandelion jam at breakfast. The garden is a little oasis, nurturing palms, fruit trees and vegetables.

Waldstätterhof (☎ 041 825 06 06; www.waldstaetterhof .ch; Waldstätterquai 6; s Sfr180-220, d Sfr310-360; 💻) Queen

Victoria and Winston Churchill top the list of famous past guests at this grand waterfront hotel. First impressions are chandelier-lit palatial, but service and the rather corporate rooms are something of an anticlimax.

Eating

Gasthaus Ochsen (☎ 041 820 11 59; Bahnhofstrasse 18; mains Sfr16-22) Don't like arm-long menus? Welcome to Brunnen's oldest haunt, dating to 1740, specialising in juicy roast chickens served spicy, breadcrumbed or house-style in a basket.

Mezcalito (☎ 041 820 08 08; Axenstrasse 9; mains Sfr17-35) Sombreros, technicolour throws and a lively vibe attract locals to this Mexican-style joint by the waterfront. Cheesy nachos, fajitas and burritos are washed down with potent house cocktails.

Badhüsli (☎ 079 266 75 25; lakefront; ☿ 4pm-1am Tue-Thu, 4pm-3am Fri & Sat, 10am-2am Sun) A fun-loving Dutch team runs this cave-like den, with a plane-tree shaded terrace overlooking the lake. Theatrical red velvet benches, stone walls and classy kitsch such as the resident rubber duck and sequined parrot make it a unique spot for a drink. Don't miss the concerts at 10pm on Sundays.

Getting There & Away

By far the most pleasant way to reach Brunnen is to take a boat from Lucerne (Sfr34, 1¾ hours). The train (Sfr15.80, 45 minutes to one hour) is cheaper and quicker, although often a change in Arth-Goldau is necessary. There are also road connections from Lucerne, Zug and Flüelen.

SCHWYZ CANTON

Green and hilly Schwyz has two claims to fame: it gave Switzerland its name and together with the communities of Uri and Nidwalden signed the Oath of Eternal Alliance of 1291. This birth certificate of the Swiss Confederation is still proudly displayed in Schwyz town.

SCHWYZ

pop 14,190 / elevation 516m

The arrow-shaped Mythen mountains (1898m and 1811m) give Schwyz its edge. And not only the peaks here are jagged. Surrounded by cow-grazed pastures, this unassuming little town is the birthplace of that pocket-sized, multifunctional camping lifesaver – the Swiss army knife. As if that weren't fame enough, it's also home to the most important document in Swiss history, the 1291 charter of federation.

Orientation & Information

Schwyz train station is in Seewen district, 2km from the centre. To reach the centre, take any bus outside the station marked Schwyz Post, and alight at Postplatz. The **tourist office** (☎ 041 810 19 91; www.wbs.ch; Bahnhofstrasse 4; ☽ 6.30am-6.30pm Mon-Fri, 7.30am-noon Sat) by the bus station has stacks of info on the area.

Sights

Most action in Schwyz spirals around the gurgling fountain on cobbled **Hauptplatz** (main square), dominated by the **Rathaus** (town hall), complete with elaborate 19th-century murals depicting the Battle of Morgarten, and the baroque **St Martin's Church**.

The **Bundesbriefmuseum** (Museum of Federation; ☎ 041 819 20 64; www.bundesbriefmuseum.ch; Bahnhofstrasse 20; adult/student/child Sfr4/2.50/free; ☽ 9.30-11.30am & 1.30-5pm Mon-Fri, 9am-5pm Sat & Sun May-Oct, 9.30-11.30am & 1.30-5pm Mon-Fri, 1.30-5pm Sat & Sun Nov-Apr) is worth a visit alone to eyeball the original 1291 charter of federation signed by Nidwalden, Schwyz and Uri. It's accompanied

by some academic bickering in German and French about its authenticity, as many historians question the accuracy of Switzerland's founding 'myths'. Pick up an English booklet at the front desk.

The well-curated **Forum der Schweizer Geschichte** (Forum of Swiss History; ☎ 041 819 60 11; www.landesmuseen.ch; Hofmatt; adult/child/student Sfr8/free/6; ☽ 10am-5pm Tue-Sun) whizzes through Swiss history from 1300 to 1800 with artefacts and interactive exhibits.

Set in baroque gardens, the turreted **Ital Reding-Hofstatt** (☎ 041 811 45 05; www.irh.ch; Rickenbachstrasse 24; adult/child/student Sfr5/free/3; ☽ 2-5pm Tue-Fri, 10am-noon & 2-5pm Sat & Sun Apr-Nov) was once the home of mercenary soldiers. Roam the 17th-century manor's wood-panelled rooms and vaulted cellar for a taste of the past. Across the way lies House Bethlehem, a Lilliputian house dating from 1287.

Handy and brilliantly compact, Swiss army knives can be bought at the source at the factory shop of **Victorinox** (☎ 041 818 12 11; www.victorinox.ch; Schmiedgasse 57; ☽ 7.30am-noon & 1.15-6pm Mon-Fri, 8am-3pm Sat). Karl Elsener founded the company in 1884 and, after a shaky start, hit pay dirt with the 'Officer's Knife' in 1897.

Activities

Venture to the bowels of the earth at the eerie **Hölloch Caves** in Muotatal, some 35 minutes from Schwyz. The 190km labyrinthine caves are the longest in Europe and the fourth-biggest in the world. You'll need a guide, sturdy footwear and warm clothing to explore them. **Trekking Team** (☎ 041 390 40 40; www.trekking.ch; short tours adult/child Sfr20/10, expeditions from Sfr169, overnight tours from Sfr395) arrange everything from short tours to day expeditions penetrating further into the core of the mountain. A claustrophobe's nightmare, a troglodyte's dream, the overnight bivouac tours offer a surreal experience including (it could only happen in Switzerland) a fondue feast in the inky cavern darkness.

Adventure Point (☎ 079 247 74 72; www.adventurepoint.ch; Hirschen Hotel, Hinterdorfstrasse 14) tempts with a range of adrenalin-charged activities, from caving in Hölloch (Sfr98) to canyoning in Muotaschlucht (Sfr95) and snowshoeing tours (from Sfr65).

Plenty of hikes begin from nearby **Stoos** (www.stoos.ch) on a plateau above Vierwaldstättersee, affording long views across the Muotatal to Rütli, Rigi and Pilatus.

CENTRAL SWITZERLAND

Sleeping & Eating

Hirschen (☎ 041 811 12 76; www.hirschen-schwyz.ch; Hinterdorfstrasse 14; dm Sfr32, s/d Sfr58/92, with bathroom Sfr68/112; ⚇ reception 10am-noon & 4pm-midnight; 🖳) This cheerful pad makes up for fairly basic digs with a friendly vibe. There's a kitchen, pub and a crazy stag (Hirschen's mascot) in the jungle-themed courtyard. To get here, follow the signs from Hauptplatz.

Wysses Rössli (☎ 041 811 19 22; www.wrsz.ch; Am Hauptplatz; s/d from Sfr140/220; 🖳) Goethe once stayed at this centuries-old hotel, whose spacious rooms have been renovated in generic modern style. The restaurant (mains Sfr20 to Sfr35) serves Swiss cuisine with a Med-style twist.

My Thing (☎ 041 810 30 00; Hauptplatz 7; snacks Sfr6.50-12.50; ⚇ 6.30am-midnight Mon-Fri, 8.30am-midnight Sat & Sun) Retreat to a cosy nook in the cave-like cellar at this Boho café. Scatter cushions and candlelight make it a snug spot to munch baguettes and salads or nurse a glass of merlot. Sit on the postage-stamp terrace when the sun's out.

Kreuz & Quer (☎ 041 810 01 01; Hauptplatz 7; light meals Sfr10-25; ⚇ 11.30am-1.45pm & 6-9.45pm) This totally chilled café rustles up tasty wraps, sandwiches and salads. Browse the newspapers or kick back on the pavement terrace with a coffee.

Ratskeller (☎ 041 810 10 87; Strehlgasse 3; mains Sfr18-32; ⚇ Tue-Sat) A historic charmer with bottle windows and wood panelling, Ratskeller enjoys a fierce local following. Fresh, seasonally inspired dishes might include venison with chestnuts or bilberry risotto with goats' cheese.

Purpur (☎ 041 810 01 01; Hauptplatz 7; mains Sfr27.50-36.50; ⚇ 11.30am-2pm & 8pm-midnight Mon-Fri, dinner only Sat & Sun) Forget waving cats, this Thai newcomer above Kreuz & Quer is stylish – picture scarlet walls, fountains and flickering tea lights. Curries are deliciously spicy and signatures like tamarind-honey glazed cod divine.

Getting There & Away

Schwyz is 30 minutes away from Zug (Sfr9, 31 minutes) on the main north–south rail route (see p262 for more information); Lucerne is 40 minutes away (Sfr13.80). Schwyz centre is only a few kilometres detour off the A4 freeway, which passes through Brunnen.

EINSIEDELN

pop 13,770 / elevation 900m

Pilgrims flock to Einsiedeln, Switzerland's answer to Lourdes. The story goes that in

---

FEEL THE PRIDE

Once you cross the border into Switzerland, you'll never have a second's doubt about which country you're visiting. The Swiss fly their national flag with fervent patriotism, and the white cross on a red square flutters in gardens, halfway up mountains, even in the middle of waterfalls. One of only two square flags in the world (the Vatican has the other) its proportions are easy on the eye, like all design classics. What started life as a means of identifying Swiss mercenaries during the 1339 Battle of Laupen has become a national logo today. Teddies, toasters, postcards, Victorinox army knives, you name it – the Swiss flag is everywhere.

AD 964 the Bishop of Constance tried to consecrate the original monastery but was halted by a heavenly voice, declaring: 'Desist. God Himself has consecrated this building.' A papal order later recognised this as a genuine miracle. Even if you don't believe in miracles, the fabulously over-the-top interior of the abbey church is worth a peek.

Orientation & Information

Einsiedeln is south of Zürichsee (Lake Zürich) and west of Sihlsee (Lake Sihl). The train station and the post office are in the town centre opposite Dorfplatz; head through this square and turn left into Hauptstrasse. The church is at the end of this street, overlooking Klosterplatz (a 10-minute walk). The **tourist office** (☎ 055 418 44 88; www.einsiedeln.ch in German; Hauptstrasse 85; ⚇ 8.30am-5pm Mon-Fri, 9am-4pm Sat, 10am-1pm Sun) is near the church.

Sights & Activities

All roads lead to the **Klosterkirche** (Abbey Church; ☎ 055 418 61 11; www.kloster-einsiedeln.ch; Benzigerstrasse; ⚇ 5.30am-8.30pm); follow the crowds flowing towards this baroque edifice, the 18th-century handiwork of Caspar Moosbrugger. The interior dances with colourful frescos, stucco and gold swirls. Yet most pilgrims are oblivious to the marbled opulence, directing their prayers to the holiest of holies, the **Black Madonna**, a tiny statue in a chapel by the entrance.

Continuing the devout theme is the **Bethlehem diorama** (☎ 055 412 26 17; www.diorama.ch; Benzigerstrasse; adult/child Sfr4.50/2; ⚇ 10am-5pm Easter-Oct, 1-4pm Dec-6th Jan), claiming to be the world's largest nativity scene and, further down the street, a **panorama painting of Calvary** (☎ 055 412 11 74), which is open the same hours as the diorama and costs the same.

For a fine view over the abbey complex to the surrounding hills, wander through the monastery stables and continue uphill for 15 minutes to the **statue of St Benedikt**. Alternatively, a two-hour walk north of Einsiedeln and back will bring you to the narrow, wood-covered **Devil's Bridge** (Teufelsbrücke), also built by abbey master Caspar Moosbrugger.

Sleeping

Material comfort has taken a back seat to piety in Einsiedeln, but there are a couple of decent options if you get stuck here for the night.

Hotel Linde (☎ 055 418 48 48; www.linde-einsiedeln .ch; Schmiedenstrasse 28; s/d Sfr75/110, with bathroom Sfr120/195) The best bet in town with large, modern rooms. The restaurant (mains Sfr36 to Sfr69) serves excellent fish and game in season.

Hotel Sonne (☎ 055 412 28 21; Klosterplatz; s/d Sfr75/120; 🖳) It's not going to win any design awards, but this place scores points for its location on the square facing the abbey.

Getting There & Away

Einsiedeln is in a rail cul-de-sac, so getting there usually involves changing at Biberbrugg. It is also within range of Zürich's S-Bahn trains. Zürich itself (Sfr16.80) is one hour away (via Wädenswil). Some of the trains to Lucerne (Sfr21.60, one hour) require a change at Goldau. From Einsiedeln to Schwyz, you can take the scenic 'back route' in summer: catch a postal bus to Oberiberg, then private bus (Swiss Pass not valid) from there.

ENGELBERG

pop 3635 / elevation 1050m
Engelberg (literally 'Angel Mountain') attracts two kinds of pilgrims: those seeking spiritual enlightenment in its Benedictine monastery and those worshipping the virgin powder on its divine slopes. Framed by the glacial bulk of Mt Titlis and frosted peaks, it's little wonder the larger-than-life scenery here has inspired Bollywood dream sequences. But it's a miracle that despite its deep snow, impeccable off-piste credentials and proximity to Lucerne, Engelberg remains lesser known than other resorts of its size. A blessing, some might say.

Orientation

The main street is partially pedestrianised Dorfstrasse, lined with shops and restaurants. Many of these close in November, but the influx of Indian tourists in May and June ensures more of the village now stays open at the other end of the winter and summer seasons.

Information

The **tourist office** (☎ 041 639 77 77; www.engelberg.ch; Klosterstrasse 3; ☽ 8am-6.30pm Mon-Sat, 2-6pm Sun peak season, 8am-6.30pm Mon-Fri, 8am-5pm Sat rest of year) is a five-minute walk from the train station and can help with hotel reservations. The Guest Card is good for various discounts, including 10% off the Mt Titlis cable car.

Sights
ENGELBERG MONASTERY
The Engelberg valley was once ecclesiastically governed and the **Benedictine Monastery** (☎ 041 639 61 19; tours adult/child Sfr6/3; ☽ 1hr tour 10am & 4pm Wed-Sat Jun-Oct & Dec-Apr) was the seat of power. Now the resident monks teach instead of rule, but their 12th-century home has kept its grandeur. Rebuilt after a devastating fire in 1729, it contains rooms decorated with incredibly detailed wood inlays, and a baroque **monastery church** (admission free).

Inside the monastery, you'll find a state-of-the-art **Show Cheese Dairy** (☎ 041 638 08 88; www .schaukaeserei-engelberg.ch; admission free; ☽ 9am-6.30pm Mon-Sat, 9am-5pm Sun) where you can watch the cheesemakers, savour dairy goodies in the bistro and buy creamy silo-free cheeses in the shop.

Activities
MT TITLIS
With a name that makes English speakers titter, **Titlis** (www.titlis.ch) is Central Switzerland's tallest mountain, has its only glacier and is reached by the world's first revolving cable car, completed in 1992. However, that's the last leg of a breathtaking four-stage journey. First, you glide up to Gerschnialp (1300m), then Trübsee (1800m). Transferring to a large gondola, you head for Stand (2450m) to board the Rotair for the head-spinning journey over the dazzling **Titlis Glacier**. As you twirl above the deeply crevassed ice, peaks rise like shark fins ahead, while tarn-speckled pastures, cliffs and waterfalls lie behind.

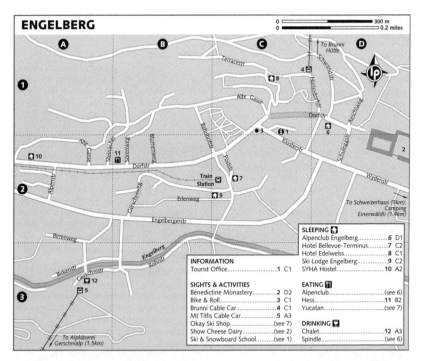

ENGELBERG

INFORMATION
Tourist Office..........................1 C1

SIGHTS & ACTIVITIES
Benedictine Monastery...........2 D2
Bike & Roll..............................3 C1
Brunni Cable Car.....................4 C1
Mt Titlis Cable Car..................5 A3
Okay Ski Shop......................(see 7)
Show Cheese Dairy.............(see 2)
Ski & Snowboard School.......(see 1)

SLEEPING
Alpenclub Engelberg................6 D1
Hotel Bellevue-Terminus..........7 C2
Hotel Edelweiss......................8 C1
Ski Lodge Engelberg................9 C2
SYHA Hostel..........................10 A2

EATING
Alpenclub............................(see 6)
Hess.....................................11 B2
Yucatan..............................(see 7)

DRINKING
Chalet..................................12 A3
Spindle...............................(see 6)

A glacial blast of air hits you at Titlis station (3020m). Inside is a kind of high-altitude theme park, with a marvellously kitsch **ice cave** where you can pick a tune (funk, an upbeat yodelling number, the Indian national anthem…) and watch neon lights make the sculpted ice tunnels sparkle. There's also an overpriced restaurant and a nostalgic **photo studio** on the 4th floor, which tries to lure you in with snaps of Bollywood stars in dirndls. Here you can strike a pose with a giant Toblerone or an alphorn against a backdrop of fake snowy mountains for as little as Sfr32.

The genuine oohs and ahs come when you step out onto the **terrace**, where the panorama of glacier-capped peaks stretches to Eiger, Mönch and Jungfrau in the Bernese Oberland. It's a 45-minute hike to the 3239m summit (wear sturdy shoes). Otherwise, enjoy the snowboarding and skiing. The **Ice Flyer chair lift** (adult/child Sfr12/6) will take you down to the glacier park where there are free snow tubes, scooters and sledges to test out. The nearby freestyle park has a half-pipe and good summer snowboarding.

The return trip to Titlis (45 minutes each way) costs Sfr82 from Engelberg. However,

in fine weather, you can walk some sections. Between Stand and Trübsee the Geologischer Wanderweg is open from July to September; it takes about two hours up and 1½ hours down. From Trübsee up to Jochpass (2207m) takes about 1½ hours, and down to Engelberg takes around the same time.

If you're hiking, destinations from Engelberg include Gerschnialp (one-way/return Sfr7/10), Trübsee (Sfr19/27) and Stand (Sfr39/55). Reductions on all fares, including to Titlis, are 50% for Swiss Pass, Eurail and InterRail. Ask about off-season reductions.

The cableway is open 8.30am to 5pm daily (last ascent/descent 3.40/4.50pm), but closes for maintenance for two weeks in early November.

HIKING

For gentle ambles and gorgeous scenery, head for Brunni on the opposite side of the valley. The cable car (one-way/return in summer Sfr14/24) goes up to Ristis at 1600m, where a chair lift takes you to the **Brunni Hütte** (☎ 041 637 37 32; www.berghuette.ch; adult Sfr62, child Sfr15-38), a recently refurbished mountain hut. From here

CENTRAL SWITZERLAND

you can watch a magnificent sunset before spending the night.

In summer, it's also possible to leave Engelberg on foot. The Surenenpass (2291m) is a great day hike to Attinghausen, where you can take a bus to Altdorf and the southern end of Lake Uri. From Jochpass a path goes to Meiringen via Engstlenalp and Tannalp. The highest point you reach is 2245m. Pick up a map and check on snow conditions before attempting these more demanding treks.

SKIING & SNOWBOARDING

Snowboarders catch big air on Titlis, Engstlenalp and the half-pipe at Jochpass, while novice and intermediate skiers slide over to family-friendly Brunni and Gerschnialp for baby blues and cruisy reds. The real thrills for powder hounds, however, lie off-piste. Backcountry legends include Laub (try to ski it in one go like the locals, if you dare), Steinberg and the biggest leg-burner of all, Galtiberg, running from Klein Titlis to the valley 2000m below. A one-day ski pass costs Sfr53 (Sfr59 on weekends and holidays).

Shops hire skiing and snowboarding equipment at fairly standard rates of about Sfr45 per day, less if you rent the equipment over a longer period.

There's a **Ski & Snowboard School** (☎ 041 639 54 54; www.skischule-engelberg.ch; Klosterstrasse 3) inside the tourist office. For off-piste skiing and snowboarding gear, stop by Dani's **Okay Ski Shop** (☎ 041 637 07 77; Hotel Bellevue), where hardcore riders hang out, exchange tips and check their email.

Engelberg hosts the **FIS Ski Jumping World Cup** (☎ 041 639 77 33; www.weltcup-engelberg.ch) in December.

ADVENTURE SPORTS

For an adrenalin rush in summer, contact **Outventure** (☎ 041 611 14 41; www.outventure.ch; Stans). They arrange glacier trekking on ice-bound Mt Titlis for Sfr150, tandem paragliding for the same price, plus other vigorous pursuits in the region including kayaking, canyoning and rock climbing.

Bike 'n' Roll (☎ 041 638 02 55; www.bikenroll.ch; Dorfstrasse 31; ☑ 8.30am-noon & 2-6.30pm Mon-Sat, closed Thu & Sun) will kit you out with a mountain bike for Sfr30 or you can join one of their two-wheel adventures for around Sfr65. They also rent out climbing gear for Sfr20, which you'll need to tackle one of Engelberg's five *vie ferrate*.

MILKY WHEY

If it is a Cleopatra-like complexion you desire, take a beautifying dip in *Molke* (whey) at **Alpkäserei Gerschnialp** (☎ 079 431 52 45; Gerschnialp; ☑ Jun-Oct) cheese dairy, nestled at the foot of Mt Titlis. Here you can soak and dream in an open-air tub, surrounded by flower-strewn meadows and serenaded by cowbells. Full of B-complex vitamins and minerals, the natural cheese by-product is said to leave the skin silky smooth. If you don't want to bathe on your lonesome for Sfr40, you can bring a friend for Sfr60, or your entire family for Sfr80. Call ahead to book.

Sleeping

The rates quoted are for the high winter season. Expect discounts of 30% to 50% in summer. Many hotels close in the shoulder seasons.

Camping Einenwäldli (☎ 041 637 19 49; www.einen waeldli.ch; sites per adult/child/small tent/car Sfr8/4/8.50/2; ☑ year-round) Attached to the Sporthotel Einenwäldli, this deluxe campsite has access to its restaurant and spa facilities. Ski and shuttle buses will drop you less than a minute from the gate.

SYHA hostel (☎ 041 637 12 92; www.familienherberge.ch; Dorfstrasse 80; dm Sfr36-41, d Sfr72; P ▣) Located 10 minutes from the station, this chalet-style hostel is clean, roomy and modern, but some dorms are impersonally large.

Hotel Bellevue-Terminus (☎ 041 639 68 68; www .bellevue-engelberg.ch; Bahnhofplatz; s/d Sfr44/88, with bathroom Sfr100/170; P ▣) Once the grand dame of Engelberg, this Victorian-era hotel is now scuffed, cracked and in desperate need of a facelift. Imperfections are, however, reflected in the price and the place has kept some character with wonderfully creaky floorboards and high-ceilinged rooms.

ourpick Ski Lodge Engelberg (☎ 041 637 35 00; www.skilodgeengelberg.com; Erlenweg 36; r per person Sfr105-120; ▣) This lodge is run by pro skiers who know what powder freaks crave – from *big* breakfasts to thigh-friendly beds. The sociable Swedes haven't cut corners on design: fusing original art-nouveau flair with 21st-century comforts in boutique-y rooms bedecked with Oskar Enander's black-and-white action shots. Après-ski here means sweltering in a Swedish sauna, gazing up at the snowy peaks in an outdoor hot tub, cocktail in hand, and sharing ski tips over Rukas' soul food.

Alpenclub Engelberg (☎ 041 637 12 43; www.alpen club.ch; Dorfstrasse 5; s/d Sfr130/180, ste 300-410; P ✗) A gem in the heart of Engelberg, the Alpenclub's 11 unique and spotlessly clean rooms echo 200 years of history – think low wood beams, textured walls and sheepskin rugs. Steinberg room has stellar Mt Titlis views. Fork out the extra francs for a suite and you'll get antique furniture, a fireplace and whirlpool.

Hotel Edelweiss (☎ 041 639 78 78; www.edelweiss engelberg.ch; Terracestrasse 10; s/d Sfr125/216; ▢) Expect a warm welcome at this turn-of-the-century hotel. Many of the high-ceilinged, classically elegant rooms afford glacier views. It's a rambling property full of quirks from stained-glass panels in the grand bar to an outdoor whirlpool for post-ski bubbles.

Eating & Drinking

Yucatan (☎ 041 637 13 24; Bahnhofplatz; mains Sfr20-32; ☾ 3pm-late) Engelberg's après-ski heavyweight is this lively Mexican joint. Mega chilli burgers and caipirinhas fuel parties with DJs, bands and jiving on the bar.

Alpenclub (☎ 041 637 12 43; Dorfstrasse 5; pizza Sfr15-26, mains Sfr28-47; ☾ 4pm-late) When the weather outside is frightful, this low-ceilinged, candlelit tavern, creaking under the weight of its 200-year history, will give you that fuzzy inner glow. Feast away on gloopy fondue, sizzling beef or thin and crisp pizza.

Schweizerhaus (☎ 041 637 12 80; Schweizerhausstrasse 41; mains Sfr25-56; ☾ Fri-Wed) Snuggle up at this traditional chalet, a local favourite for its market-fresh cuisine and fine Swiss wines. Try the tender lamb medallions with rosemary potatoes.

Hess (☎ 041 637 09 09; www.hess-restaurant.ch; Dorfstrasse 50; mains Sfr38-65; ☾ closed Mon & Tue low season) Crisp linen, hardwood floors and terracotta walls create a chic backdrop for Stephan Oberli's seasonal taste sensations. Local organic ingredients shine through in Med-style dishes like saffron-infused shellfish soup and saddle of venison with artichoke risotto, accompanied by full-bodied wines.

Chalet (Titlis base station; ☾ 3-8pm) Nowhere is better for slope-side glühwein imbibing than this cute log chalet.

Spindle (Dorfstrasse 5; ☾ 10am-4pm Wed, Fri & Sat) Revellers spill out of Yucatan and into Spindle for after-hours clubbing. It's packed to the gunnels at weekends.

Getting There & Around

Engelberg is at the end of a train line, about an hour from Lucerne (Sfr17.40). If coming on a day trip, check the Lucerne tourist office's special Mt Titlis excursion tickets. A small road off the A2 freeway near Stans leads to Engelberg.

Between early July and mid-October, a shuttle bus leaves the Engelberg train station roughly every half-hour for all the village's major hotels and attractions. It's free with a Guest Card or train ticket; Sfr1 without. In winter, there are free ski buses for getting to the slopes.

ZUG CANTON

ZUG

pop 25,500 / elevation 426m

On the face of it, Zug appears like any other cute Swiss town, lapped by a lake and ringed by mountains. Yet the hush here is the kind of entrepreneurs quietly squirreling away nest eggs in this, the richest city in one of the world's richest countries. Apart from a few flash suits and Mercedes, you'd never guess that Zug's rock-bottom tax rates (around half the national average) have lured the global moneybags. And you probably won't care as you devour cherry liqueur-drenched Kirschtorte, stroll the medieval cobbles and savour million-dollar sunsets.

Orientation

Zug hugs the northeastern shore of Zugersee. The train station lies 1km north of the Old Town (Altstadt). For the Old Town, follow the main train station exit into the roundabout at the head of Alpenstrasse (you'll see Confiserie Albert Meier to your left) and head south for another 700m.

Information

The **tourist office** (☎ 041 723 68 00; www.zug -tourismus.ch; Reisezentrum Zug, inside main train station; ☾ 9am-7pm Mon-Fri, 9am-4pm Sat, 9am-3pm Sun) has city maps and you can find money-exchange counters at the train station.

Sights & Activities

Zug Old Town is a medieval time-capsule. It starts at the town's emblem, the **Zytturm** (clock tower; Kolinplatz), whose distinctive roof is tiled in blue-and-white cantonal colours. Walking

---

BOOMTOWN RATS

Once upon a time, Zug was home to struggling farmers. But 1946 marked the start of its rags-to-riches transformation. Suddenly global multinationals bypassed Zürich to flock here; not because of the Alpine vistas and bucolic charm, but because some bright spark had the idea to create a tax haven in Central Switzerland. Today Zug's 27,000 companies outnumber its residents and include Johnson & Johnson, Kellogg, Shell, the world's largest commodities trader Glencore and hedge fund Krom River.

With personal income tax hovering between 8% and 12.5%, Zug has become a magnet to tycoons eager to save a bob. Among them is pardoned tax fugitive and aptly named billionaire Marc Rich, famous for his Iran oil dealings in the early 1980s. Wimbledon champ Boris Becker swapped his Munich pad for a Zug penthouse after receiving a fine for tax evasion in Germany in 2002. But though Zug might seem unassuming, even a modest apartment can cost Sfr1.5 million, so you need to be rich to milk this cash cow.

---

through the arch, you can veer off into the pedestrian-only lanes of Fischmarkt, Ober Altstadt and Unter Altstadt, punctuated by frescoed 15th-century townhouses and hole-in-the-wall boutiques. Keep an eye out for the fountain depicting **Gret Schell**, an old hag of a Fasnacht character, who lugs her drunken husband home in a basket.

Uphill from the clock tower, opposite St Oswald's Church, is the **Museum in der Burg** (☎ 041 728 32 97; Kirchenstrasse 11; adult/child/student Sfr9/free/5; ⏱ 2-5pm Tue-Sat, 10am-5pm Sun). This 11th-century castle exhibits paintings, costumes and a 3-D model of the town. Despite the narrative's stilted style, it's an excellent introduction to Zug – and its past tendency to partially sink into the lake.

Kunsthaus Zug (☎ 041 725 33 44; Dorfstrasse 27; www.kunsthauszug.ch; adult/child/student Sfr8/free/6; ⏱ noon-6pm Tue-Fri, 10am-5pm Sat & Sun) hides a superb collection of Viennese Modernist works of the Klimt, Kokoschka and Schiele ilk, which regularly yields to high-profile exhibitions.

On the waterfront is **Landsgemeindeplatz**. In this square there's an aviary of exotic birds, most strikingly kookaburras, hornbills and a family of scarlet ibis (looking a bit homesick in colder weather). Shaded by chestnut trees, lakefront **Seebad Seeliken** (☎ 041 711 14 56; Artherstrasse 2), just south of the Old Town, is perfect for a swim or sunbathe.

The **Schönegg funicular** rises to Zugerberg (988m), where there are impressive views and hiking trails. The Zug day pass (Sfr12) is the best deal, as it covers all bus rides and the funicular. Bus 11 gets you to the lower funicular station.

City bikes (☎ 041 761 33 55; Bundesplatz; ⏱ 9am-9pm May-Oct) are loaned out for free (ID and deposit required). On the waterfront near Landsgemeindeplatz, pedalos and rowing boats (per 30/60 minutes Sfr17/24) are for hire.

Sleeping

With city slickers often staying overnight, Zug's hotels often have a corporate feel. Guest houses offer a homelier vibe – pick up a list from the tourist office.

Camping Zugersee (☎ 041 741 84 22; Chamer Fussweg 36; sites per adult/child/tent Sfr7.80/3.90/9; ⏱ late Mar-early Oct) On the shore of the lake, 2km west of the centre, this is a very attractive site, with free swimming in the vicinity.

SYHA hostel (☎ 041 711 53 54; www.youthhostel.ch; Allmendstrasse 8; dm/d Sfr32.50/96; ⏱ reception 8-10am & 5-10pm, closed late Nov-early Mar; P 🖳) Modern and clinically clean, Zug's hostel has a communal kitchen and kiosk. It's a 10-minute walk from the station, heading right in the direction of the Sportanlagen.

Hotel Guggital (☎ 041 711 28 21; www.hotel-guggital.ch; Zugerbergstrasse 46; s Sfr118-165, d Sfr190-220) Perched above the lake with fine views to Pilatus and Rigi, this family-run hotel offers quiet and compact rooms with wi-fi and sometimes balconies. Bus 11 will get you here from the train station.

Ochsen Zug (☎ 041 729 32 32; www.ochsen-zug.ch; Am Kolinplatz; s/d/ste Sfr182/270/350; P) Although it dates from 1480 and once hosted Goethe, the Ochsen is now a business hotel and has been streamlined behind its step-gabled facade. Natural wood and fabrics dress the light-filled rooms. The junior suite, No 503, has wonderful views of the Zytturm and the lake. Ferdinand Gehr's abstract artwork adorns the bar.

CENTRAL SWITZERLAND

Hotel Löwen am See (☎ 041 725 22 22; www.loewen
-zug.ch; Landsgemeindeplatz; s/d Sfr205/280; ✖ ☐)
Sitting on a cobbled square in the Old Town
and facing the lake, this place has plain but
comfy rooms with perks like free fruit. The
Mediterranean restaurant downstairs, Domus,
is extremely popular.

Eating & Drinking
Confiserie Albert Meier (☎ 041 711 10 49; Alpenstrasse
16; cakes Sfr3-5; ☽ 7am-6.30pm Mon-Fri, 8am-4pm Sat)
Buttery smells waft from this old-style café,
specialising in *Zuger Kirschtorte* (cake made
from pastry, biscuit, almond paste and butter cream, infused with cherry liqueur). It's
sold all over town, but locals say Albert Meier
bakes the best. Individual ones cost Sfr4.50
and make scrummy gifts – if they ever make
it home, that is.

Café Platzmühle (☎ 041 711 01 10; Landsgemeindeplatz
2; pizza Sfr17-24, mains Sfr23-30; ☽ 7am-midnight Mon-Sat,
8am-midnight Sun) This one-time mill has morphed
into Zug's hippest café, with exposed brick,
granite-topped tables and a terrace strewn
with potted palms. The kitchen rustles up
salads, wood-oven pizzas and pasta.

Schiff (☎ 041 711 00 55; Graben 2; mains Sfr25-45;
☽ 11am-12.30am summer, reduced hr winter) Wood
panelling and stained glass evoke rustic
grandeur in the back room of the Schiff. The
menu fuses Swiss and world flavours, from
succulent lamb to organic Argentine beef.
After dinner, head upstairs to Panorama Bar
for dreamy views.

Gasthaus Rathauskeller (☎ 041 711 00 58; Oberer
Altstadt 1; mains in Bistro Sfr19-38, Zunftstube Sfr36-68;
☽ 11.30am-2.30pm & 3.30-10.30pm Tue-Sat) You can't
miss the late-Gothic Rathauskeller's frescoed
facade. Downstairs the art-slung bistro serves
marvellous rösti and couscous. Upstairs the
swish restaurant is a fantasy of twirling columns, creaky floors and gilt Rosenthal crockery, where delicacies such as lobster ragout with
summer truffles are married with fine wines.

Getting There & Away
Zug is on the main north–south train route
from Zürich (Sfr13.80, 25 to 45 minutes) to
Lugano, where trains from Zürich also branch
off to Lucerne (Sfr10.80, 20 to 30 minutes) and
the Bernese Oberland.

By road, the north-south N4 runs from
Zürich, sweeps around the western shore of
Zugersee and joins the A2, which continues
through Lucerne and the St Gotthard Pass and

on to Lugano and Italy. The N25 peels off the
N4 north of Zug, completes the corset around
the eastern shore of the lake, then rejoins the
A4 at Goldau.

Boats depart from Zug's Schiffsstation,
north of Landsgemeindeplatz, travelling
south to Arth in the summer and many
other destinations. Swiss Pass holders get
half-price travel.

ST GOTTHARD PASS
ANDERMATT
pop 1265 / elevation 1447m
Blessed with chocolate-box charm and austere mountains, Andermatt contrasts low-
key village charm with big wilderness. But
that's all set to change. Egyptian tycoon Samih
Sawiris, the owner of the Orascom leisure
development group, has invested Sfr1 billion
into transforming Andermatt's former army
barracks into a year-round **megaresort** (www
.andermattresort.com) complete with six five-star
hotels, a tropical spa and an 18-hole high-
altitude golf course. The creation of 2000 jobs
is expected to give a much-needed boost to
Andermatt's tourism industry. Critics, including some local farmers, say the resort will
put extra strain on the already fragile Alpine
environment, despite eco-friendly measures
including a traffic-free centre and renewable
energy policies.

Once an important staging-post on the
north–south St Gotthard route, Andermatt
is now bypassed by the tunnel, but remains
a major crossroads, with Furka Pass cork-
screwing west to Valais and the Oberalp Pass
looping east to Graubünden.

The train station is 400m north of the village centre. The **tourist office** (☎ 041 887 14 54;
www.andermatt.ch; ☽ 9am-5pm Mon-Fri, 10am-4pm Sat &
Sun), 200m to the left of the station, shares the
same hut as the postal bus ticket office.

Sights & Activities
The 2963m **Gemsstock** attracts hikers in summer and intermediate skiers with snow-sure
slopes in winter. The region is also beloved
by off-piste skiers seeking fresh powder. The
cable car from Andermatt costs Sfr32/45 one-
way/return. Ski passes cost Sfr55 per day for
Gemsstock, Sfr44 for Nätschen/Gütsch and
Sfr29 for Realp. Toboggan runs, well-prepared
walking trails and sleigh rides appeal to non-
skiers in winter.

A spectacular hike leads from the nearby Oberalp Pass to sparkly **Lai da Tuma** (p79), the source of the Rhine. For a vertigo-inducing climb, check out the Diavolo *via ferrata,* three hours of granite scrambling and clambering over grassy ledges. It affords dizzying perspectives over the **Devil's Bridge**, traversing a steep ravine. As Andermatt is situated near four major Alpine passes – Susten, Oberalp, St Gotthard and Furka – it's a terrific base for driving, cycling or bus tours. Check www .postbus.ch for the bus tours offered this year. From Realp, along the flat valley, **steam trains** (www.furka-bergstrecke.ch) run to Furka from Friday to Sunday between late June and early October (daily from mid-July to late August).

Sleeping & Eating

The tourist office can help find private rooms, but many places close between seasons.

Touristenlager Postillion (☎ 041 887 10 44; Gotthardstrasse 36; dm Sfr35; P) For skiers on a shoestring, the bare-bones dorms at this central chalet are perfectly adequate. They arrange activities from paragliding to bike tours.

Hotel Sonne (☎ 041 887 12 26; www.hotelsonne andermatt.ch; Gotthardstrasse 76; s Sfr85-110, d Sfr150-190; P) An inviting glow beckons you to this dark wood chalet. Rooms are a blast from the '70s but snug with comfy beds and loads of pine. Downstairs, the beamed restaurant (mains Sfr16 to Sfr37) is renowned for the freshness of its trout.

our pick **The River House Boutique Hotel** (☎ 041 887 00 25; www.theriverhouse.ch; Gotthardstrasse 58; d Sfr180-220, ste Sfr280-360; P 💻) Charismatic and quirky, this 250-year-old hotel is a one-off. The Swiss-American owners have used local pine and granite to handcraft beds for their beautiful rooms with inlaid parquet floors, beams and welcome baskets full of local goodies. Each has its own personality: from the bottle-lined pharmacy room to the antique door room. Breakfast is a feast of pancakes, eggs and juice. The restaurant (mains Sfr17 to Sfr42) uses market-fresh, organic produce.

Toutoune (☎ 041 887 01 76; Gotthardstrasse 91; mains Sfr20-48) Decked out with eye-catching prints of olive trees and natural stone, this Med-style restaurant has great buzz. Chow down on just-right falafel or Italian flavours like sage gnocchi, washed down with a nice glass of Chianti.

Getting There & Away

Andermatt is a stop on the Glacier Express from Zermatt to St Moritz. For north–south destinations, change at Göschenen, 15 minutes away. **Matterhorn Gotthard Bahn** (☎ 027 927 77 77) can supply details about the car-carrying trains over the Oberalp Pass to Graubünden and through the Furka Tunnel to Valais. Postal buses stop by the train station. The 17km Gotthard Tunnel is one of the busiest north–south routes across the Alps, running from Göschenen to close to Airolo in Ticino, bypassing Andermatt. Work is already underway building the new Gotthard Base Tunnel, designed for high-speed and freight trains. It should be completed in 2012.

CENTRAL SWITZERLAND

Basel & Aargau

Switzerland's northwestern cantons come as a pleasant surprise to those who take the time to visit. Experience everything from the latest in architectural creation and a buzzing art scene in good-looking, industrious Basel to Roman ruins and the canton of Aargau's proud castles, pretty medieval villages and rolling green countryside.

Basel has a slew of attractions for gallery lovers and architecture groupies. The Beyeler Foundation boasts one of the most vital collections in Switzerland, there's an absorbing museum devoted to madcap sculptor Jean Tinguely and, in nearby Weil am Rhein's Vitra Design Museum, there are showpieces by some of the world's best contemporary architects.

Basel's old city centre is a spotlessly maintained treasure chest of the past. Its 11th-century cathedral and 16th-century town hall are landmarks and strolling the narrow streets high above the Rhine is a pleasure. For ancient-history buffs, there's the best-preserved Roman remains in Switzerland at Augusta Raurica, a short train ride east of Basel on the Rhine.

Just over the cantonal border, Aargau is dotted with one-time Habsburg possessions, including Rheinfelden (of Feldschlösschen beer fame) and the castle and village, near the Aare River, that gave the family their name. A journey along the majestic Aare also takes in other gems such as coquettish Aarau, the equally fetching bath town of Baden, and various castles and villages, like charming Lenzburg. With its gentle countryside (and spectacular autumn colours), Aargau canton rewards off-the-beaten-track exploration in spades.

HIGHLIGHTS

- Being wowed by the art and architecture of the superlative **Beyeler Foundation** (p269).
- Catching interior design exhibits across the German border in the **Vitra Design Museum** (p269).
- Admiring Jean Tinguely's madcap mechanical sculptures in the **Museum Jean Tinguely** (p269).
- Wandering the enchanting streets of **Aarau** (p276), lined with centuries-old houses.
- Climbing to the mighty medieval castle in **Lenzburg** (p276) and wandering the largely baroque village below.
- Taking to the mineral-water baths in **Baden** (p276) and exploring the charming Old Town.

Vitra Design
★ Museum

★
Beyeler Foundation;
Museum Jean Tinguely

★
Baden

Aarau
★ ★
Lenzburg

■ POPULATION: 1,035,930	■ AREA: 1958 SQ KM	■ LANGUAGE: GERMAN

BASEL & AARGAU

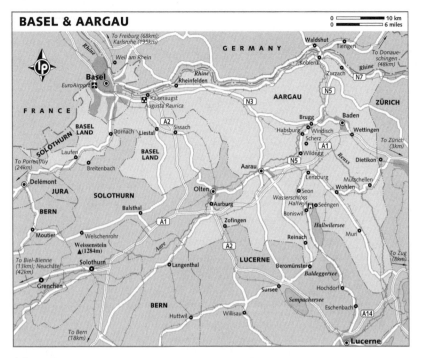

BASEL & AARGAU

0 — 10 km
0 — 6 miles

Orientation

The city-canton of Basel is tucked up in the northern corner of the country on the Rhine River, abutting France and Germany. Around it to the south and east spreads the bigger canton of Basel Land.

The much larger canton of Aargau, cut in half by the pretty Aare River, spreads out east between Basel Land and the canton of Zürich.

Along the northern edge of the cantons of Aargau and Basel Land flows the majestic Rhine River, marking the border with Germany.

The region is well connected internationally via EuroAirport in the west and Zürich's airport in the east and has excellent rail and road links to France, Germany and the rest of Switzerland. See also p273.

Information

Basel Tourismus (p267) will handle most queries for the entire region, but if you really want to get off the beaten path, ask **Aargau Tourismus** (☎ 062 824 76 24; www.aargautourismus.ch) for extra tips.

BASEL

pop 163,080 / elevation 273m
Although famous for its Fasnacht and Vogel Gryff festivals in spring and winter, perhaps the best time to visit Basel (Bâle in French, sometimes Basle in English) is in summer. The city shucks off its notorious reserve to bask in, strangely for its northerly location, some of the hottest weather in Switzerland. As locals bob along in the fast-moving Rhine (Rhein) River, whiz by on motor scooters, and dine and drink on overcrowded pavements, you could almost be in Italy, rather than on the border with both France and Germany.

Basel's year-round attractions are the engaging Old Town, some of the country's best art collections, and compelling modern buildings.

Orientation

Basel is the closest Switzerland comes to having a seaport: the Rhine, from this point until it reaches the North Sea in Holland, is navigable for decent-sized ships. It describes

BASEL & AARGAU

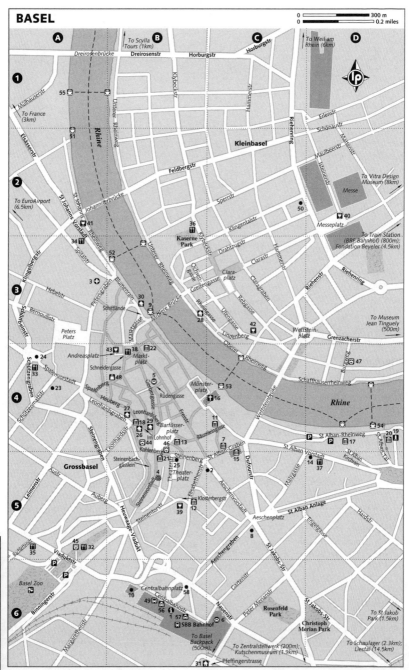

BASEL

To Scylla Tours (1km)
To Weil am Rhein (6km)

Dreirosenbrücke
Dreirosenstr
Horburgstr
Horburgstr

Kleinbasel

To France (3km)
Feldbergstr

To EuroAirport (6.5km)
Sperrstr
To Vitra Design Museum (8km)
Messe
Messeplatz
To Train Station (BBF Bahnhof) (800m); Fondation Beyeler (4.5km)

Rhine
Kaserne Park
Klingentalstr
Clara-platz

Hebelstr
Peters-graben
Schifflände

Peters Platz
Bernoullistr

Andreasplatz
Markt-platz
Schneidergasse
To Museum Jean Tinguely (500m)
Wettstein-platz
Grenzacherstr
Rheinweg

Rhine

Münster-platz
Rüdengasse
Leonhardsgraben
Barfüsser-platz
Im Lohnhof
Kohlenberg
Steinenberg
St Alban-Graben
St Alban-Rheinweg
St Alban Vorstadt
St Alban Kirchrain

Grossbasel
Steinenbach-gässlein
Theater-platz
Klosterbergstr

St Alban Anlage
Aeschenplatz

Viaduktstr
Steinentorstr
Heuwaage-Viadukt

Basel Zoo
Binningerstr

Aeschengraben

Rusenfeld Park
To St Jakob Park (1.5km)

Centralbahnplatz
Centralbahnstr
SBB Bahnhof
Christoph Merian Park
To Schaulager (2.3km); Liestal (14.5km)

To Basel Backpack (500m)
To Zentralstellwerk (200m); Kutschenmuseum (1.9km)
Pfeffingerstrasse

a gentle bend through the city, from southeast to north.

The Old Town and most sights are on the south bank in Grossbasel (Greater Basel); on the north bank is Kleinbasel (Little Basel). Historically, the 'Klein' tag was a derogatory term for the working-class locality. The relief bust of *Lällekeenig* (Tongue King) – there's a copy of the original at the crossroads at the southern end of the Mittlere Brücke – sticking his tongue out at the northern section, just about sums up the old attitude between the two.

Grossbasel has the SBB Bahnhof, the train station for travel within Switzerland. Trams 1 and 8 leave from here for the Old Town centre. In Kleinbasel is the BBF (Badischer) Bahnhof, for trains to Germany.

Information
BOOKSHOPS
Bider & Tanner (☎ 061 206 99 99; www.biderund tanner.ch; Aeschenvorstadt 2; ☼ 9am-6.30pm Mon-Wed, 9am-8pm Thu-Fri, 9am-6pm Sat) Has English-language books, travel guides and maps.

DISCOUNT CARD
BaselCard (from Sfr20/27/35 for 24/48/72hr) Offers entry to 25 museums (permanent collections only) and Basel Zoo (www.zoobasel.ch, in German), plus guided tours and ferry rides. If you don't have a mobility ticket (see p270), consider the 24-hour version for Sfr25, which includes unlimited free public transport.

INTERNET ACCESS
Internet Dome (Steinenvorstadt 53; per hr Sfr9; ☼ noon-11pm Sun-Thu, noon-1am Fri & Sat)

MEDICAL SERVICES
Cantonal Hospital (Kantonsspital; ☎ 061 265 25 25; www.kantonsspital-basel.ch; Petersgraben 2)

POST
Main post office (Rüdengasse 1; ☼ 7.30am-6.30pm Mon-Wed, 7.30am-7pm Thu-Fri, 8am-5pm Sat)
Post office (Centralbahnstrasse 20; SBB Bahnhof; ☼ 10am-1.30pm & 3-7pm daily)

TOURIST INFORMATION
Basel Tourismus (☎ 061 268 68 68; www.basel.com; ☼ 8.30am-6.30pm Mon-Fri, 9am-5pm Sat, 9am-4pm Sun) Stadtcasino (Steinenberg 14; ☼ tours 2.30-4.30pm Mon-Sat May–mid-Oct, Sat mid-Oct–Apr); SBB Bahnhof (Aeschenvorstadt 36) The Stadtcasino branch organises two-hour English-language city tours (adult/child costs Sfr15/7.50).

Sights
OLD TOWN
The medieval Old Town (*Altstadt*) in the heart of Basel is a delight. Start in Marktplatz, which is dominated by the astonishingly vivid red facade of the **Rathaus** (town hall), built in the 16th century and since restored. A walk about 400m west of Marktplatz through the former artisans' district along Spalenberg eventually leads you uphill to the 600-year-old **Spalentor**

city gate. The most beautiful of the 40 defensive gates and turrets that once dotted the protective walls, it is one of only three to survive the walls' demolition in 1866.

The narrow lanes that riddle the hillside between Marktplatz and the Spalentor form the most captivating part of Old Basel. Lined by impeccably maintained, centuries-old houses, lanes like Spalenberg, Heuberg and Leonhardsberg repay a gentle stroll.

About 400m south of Marktplatz is Barfüsserplatz, named after the eponymous church that was deconsecrated in the 18th century and has long been the seat of the **Historisches Museum Basel** (below). The lanes around here are lined with shops and eateries.

Just south of Barfüsserplatz is the zany **Tinguely Fountain** (Theaterplatz), with all sorts of wacky machines spewing and shooting forth water. It is a foretaste of the madcap moving sculptures in the Museum Jean Tinguely (opposite).

The 13th-century **Münster** (cathedral; ☎ 061 272 91 57; www.muensterbasel.ch; Münsterplatz; 10am-5pm Mon-Fri, 10am-4pm Sat, 1-5pm Sun Easter-Oct, 11am-4pm Mon-Sat, 2-4pm Sun Nov-Easter) is a mix of Gothic exteriors and Romanesque interiors and was largely rebuilt after an earthquake in 1356. The tomb of the Renaissance humanist Erasmus of Rotterdam (1466–1536), who lived in Basel, lies in the cathedral's northern aisle. In the crypt are remnants of the cathedral's 9th-century predecessor. You can climb the soaring Gothic towers (Sfr3) in groups of two or more. The two chunky, red-stone, late-Gothic cloisters, mostly from the 15th century but with Romanesque vestiges, are linked by a broad hall, whose timber ceiling was once richly decorated.

MUSEUMS & GALLERIES
For more on the city's 40-odd museums and galleries, grab the relevant tourist office booklet or check out www.museenbasel.ch.

Historisches Museum Basel
One of the most wide-ranging sight in the city, the collections of the **Historisches Museum Basel** (Basel History Museum; ☎ 061 205 86 00; www .hmb.ch; Barfüsserplatz; adult/child/student Sfr7/free/5, free 1st Sun of month; 10am-5pm Tue-Sun) include pre-Christian-era archaeological finds, a collection of religious objects from the cathedral and plenty of material documenting

the city's development. It is housed in the former Barfüsserkirche (the Barefooted Ones Church, after the barefoot Franciscan friars who founded it in the 14th century). Highlights include the fine 16th-century choir stall and 15th-century tapestries.

Further collections are spread across three other sites. The **Musikmuseum** (Im Lohnhof 9; 2-6pm Wed-Sat, 11am-5pm Sun) contains a broad collection of instruments. The star item of the **Haus zum Kirschgarten** (Elisabethenstrasse 27-29; 10am-5pm Tue-Fri, 1-5pm Sat) is a collection of fine Meissen porcelain. The **Kutschenmuseum** (Brüglingen, St Jakob im Botanischen Garten) houses 19th- and 20th-century carriages, sleighs and dog carts.

Kunstmuseum & Museum für Gegenwartskunst
The **Kunstmuseum** (Museum of Fine Arts; ☎ 061 206 62 62; www.kunstmuseumbasel.ch; St Alban-Graben 16; adult/child/student Sfr12/free/5, incl Museum für Gegenwartskunst, free 1st Sun of month; 10am-5pm Tue-Sun) concentrates on two periods: from 1400 to 1600, and from 1800 to the present day. The medieval collection includes the world's largest number of Holbein works. The smaller contemporary collection features Picassos and Rodins, and spills over into the **Museum für Gegenwartskunst** (Museum of Contemporary Art; ☎ 061 206 62 62; www .kunstmuseumbasel.ch; St Alban-Rheinweg 60; same prices as Kunstmuseum; 11am-5pm Tue-Sun).

Close by the Museum für Gegenwartskunst is the **Papiermuseum** (☎ 061 225 90 90; www.papier museum.ch; St Alban-Tal; adult/child/senior & student Sfr12/8/10; 10am-noon & 2-5pm Tue-Fri, 2-5pm Sat & Sun). Set astride a medieval canal and complete with functioning waterwheel, it evokes centuries past, in which a dozen mills operated here. This one produced paper for centuries and its museum explores that story. Just to the east stands a stretch of the old **city wall**.

Antikenmuseum Basel
Across the road from the Kunstmuseum, the **Antikenmuseum Basel** (Antiquities Museum; ☎ 061 201 12 12; www.antikenmuseumbasel.ch; St Alban-Graben 5; adult/concession Sfr7/5; 10am-5pm Tue-Sun) contains the country's most impressive collection of ancient artefacts, largely running from Egyptian to Roman times.

Puppenhausmuseum
Basel's **Puppenhausmuseum** (Doll's House Museum; ☎ 061 225 95 95; www.puppenhausmuseum.ch; Steinenvorstadt 1; adult/child/senior & student Sfr7/free/5; 10am-

6pm daily) attracts teddy-bear fans from all over the place. Indeed, the museum claims to have the world's biggest collection of teddy bears. There are doll's houses galore too.

Fondation Beyeler

Of all the private Swiss collections made public, former art dealers Hildy and Ernst Beyeler's is the most astounding. In the **Fondation Beyeler** (Beyeler Foundation; ☎ 061 645 97 00; www.beyeler.com; Baselstrasse 101, Riehen; adult/under 11yr/11-19yr/student/senior Sfr23/free/6/12/18, Sfr16/free/free/8/12 10am-6pm Mon & 5-8pm Wed; ☼ 10am-6pm Thu-Tue, to 8pm Wed), sculptures by Miró and Max Ernst are juxtaposed against tribal figures from Oceania, while 19th- and 20th-century works from the likes of Picasso and Rothko hang on the walls of this long, low, light-filled, open-plan building by leading Italian architect Renzo Piano. Take tram 6 to Riehen from Barfüsserplatz or Marktplatz.

Can't be bothered going to the 'burbs? The original **Galerie Beyeler** (☎ 061 206 97 00; www.beyeler.com; Bäumleingasse 9; admission free; ☼ 9am-noon & 2-6pm Tue-Fri, 9am-noon Sat) is worth dropping in to. You never know what you might find in their temporary exhibitions. Take a look at their website to see the impressive roll-call of artists handled by the Beyelers.

Museum Jean Tinguely

Built by leading Ticino architect Mario Botta, the **Museum Jean Tinguely** (☎ 061 681 93 20; www.tinguely.ch; Paul Sacher Anlage 1; adult/child/student

---

THE EXPLOSIVE WORLD OF JEAN TINGUELY

Raised in Basel, Jean Tinguely (1925–91) was indefatigable, working on his art, including countless installations, until shortly before his death. Known above all for his 'kinetic art', or sculptural machines, Tinguely spent much of his life in Paris, immersed in the artistic avant-garde. Not all of his machines were designed for posterity: among his more spectacular installations (at a time when installation art was in its infancy) was his self-destructible *Homage to New York*, which failed to completely self-destruct in the gardens of the MOMA in 1960. A more successful big bang was his *Study for an End of the World No 2*, in the desert near Las Vegas in 1962.

& senior Sfr15/free/10; ☼ 11am-7pm Tue-Sun) resonates with playful mischievousness. Unfortunately, you're not allowed to touch most of Tinguely's 'kinetic' sculptures (see boxed text, left), which would rattle, shake or twirl if you did, but with springs, feathers and wheels radiating at every angle, they look appealingly like the work of a mad scientist. Catch bus 31 from Claraplatz.

Vitra Design Museum

Always fancied seeing the amazing Bilbao Guggenheim Museum in Spain and find yourself in Basel? Pop across the German border to the **Vitra Design Museum** (☎ +49 7621 702 32 00; www.design-museum.de; Charles Eames Strasse 1, Weil am Rhein; adult/child/student €8/free/6.50, BaselCard valid; ☼ 10am-6pm Thu-Tue, to 8pm Wed) for a small taste of the same. Not only is the main museum building by the Guggenheim's creator, Frank Gehry, the surrounding factory complex of famous furniture manufacturer Vitra comprises buildings by other cutting-edge architects, such as Tadao Ando, Zaha Hadid and Álvaro Siza. Exhibitions cover all aspects of interior design. Catch bus 55 from Claraplatz in Kleinbasel (30 minutes) to the Vitra stop. Border checks are theoretically possible, so take your passport.

Schaulager

A kind of art bunker, **Schaulager** (☎ 061 335 32 32; www.schaulager.org; Ruchfeldstrasse 19, Münchenstein; adult/concession Sfr14/12; ☼ noon-6pm Tue, Wed & Fri, to 7pm Thu, 10am-5pm Sat & Sun Apr-Sep) was designed by Herzog & de Meuron. The sharply cornered, mostly white gallery is partly rendered in earth dug out from around the foundations. A huge video screen on the front facade gives you a foretaste of the rolling temporary exhibitions inside. Catch tram 11 from Barfüsserplatz or Marktplatz.

Activities

The tourist office's *Experiencing Basel: Five Walks across the Old Town of Basel* pamphlet lists five walks across town.

Between mid-April and mid-October **Basler Personenschiffahrt** (☎ 061 639 95 00; www.bpg.ch) operates city/harbour **boat cruises** (Sfr15; ☼ departing 2pm Tue-Sat), along with a range of options for long trips to Rheinfelden, or brunch, jazz and dinner jaunts. Cruises depart from Schifflände, near the Mittlere Brücke.

EXPLORING ARCHITECTURAL BASEL

Basel and its environs boast of having buildings by seven winners of architecture's Pritzker Prize. Four of those winners – Frank Gehry, Álvaro Siza, Tadao Ando and Zaha Hadid – have works over the German border at the **Vitra Design Museum** (p269).

Some works by Herzog & de Meuron are more central. The Basel-based duo is renowned for designing London's Tate Modern and Beijing's Olympic Stadium. In Basel, as well as the **Schaulager** (p269) and **St Jakob Park** stadium (p272), you'll find their wonderful lace-iron facade at **Schützenmattstrasse 11** and the matt-black **Zentralstellwerk** at Münchensteinerstrasse 115 – the latter is surely the only railway goods depot to be an architectural icon! Right by the main train station (SBB Bahnhof) is their surprising glass **Elsässer Tor**.

The renowned Italian architect Renzo Piano is responsible for the **Fondation Beyeler** (p269). Ticino architect Mario Botta hasn't won the Pritzker as yet, but his **Museum Jean Tinguely** (p269) and the offices of the **Bank for International Settlements** at Aeschenplatz 1 are well worth checking out.

Swimming in the Rhine River is a popular summer pastime, too.

Festivals & Events

Basel makes much of its huge **Fasnacht** spring carnival. The festival kicks off at exactly 4am on the Monday after Ash Wednesday with the **Morgestraich**. The street lights are suddenly extinguished and the procession starts to wend its way through the central district. Participants wear elaborate costumes and masks, and there's a little bit of carousing in the streets. The main parades are on the Monday and Wednesday afternoons, with Tuesday afternoon reserved for the children's parade.

It's also worth visiting **Liestal** (Sfr5, up to 16 minutes by train from Basel) on the Sunday evening before Morgestraich for the **Chienbäse**, a dramatic fire parade.

The **Vogel Gryff** festival at the end of January symbolically chases away winter from Kleinbasel. The three key figures – the griffin (*Vogel Gryff*), the savage (*Wilder Mann*) and the lion (*Leu*) – dance to the beat of drums on a raft on the Rhine and later they dance in the streets of Kleinbasel.

Leading trade events include the **MUBA** (www.muba.ch, in German & French) Swiss industries fair every spring, the **Herbstmesse** (Autumn Fair) in October, **Baselworld: The Watch and Jewellery Show** (www.baselworld.ch) in March and **ART Basel** (www.artbasel.ch), the contemporary art fair in June.

The **Swiss Indoors** (www.davidoffswissindoors.ch) tennis championship, held in Basel in October, is one of Switzerland's biggest annual sporting events. Basel-born record-breaker Roger Federer took his third home-town title there in a row in 2008.

Jazz fans should keep an eye on Basel's **Offbeat Jazz Festival** (www.jazzfestivalbasel.ch), held over two weeks in the second half of April.

Sleeping

Book ahead if coming for a convention or trade fair. There are no trade fairs in July or August, but annoyingly some Basel hotels close then. When you check in, remember to ask for your mobility ticket, which entitles you to free use of public transport.

BUDGET

For a wide range of B&Bs in the area, visit www.bbbasel.ch.

Basel Backpack (☎ 061 333 00 37; www.baselbackpack .ch; Dornacherstrasse 192; dm Sfr32, s/d Sfr80/98, breakfast Sfr8; ✗ ▯) Converted from a factory, this independent hostel has cheerful, colour-coded eight-bed dorms and more-sedate doubles and family rooms.

SYHA Basel City Youth Hostel (☎ 061 365 99 60; www.youthhostel.ch/basel.city; Pfeffingerstrasse 8; dm Sfr35.50, s/d Sfr79/95; ✦ reception 7am-noon & 3-11pm; ▯) A convenient hostel set in former post office buildings, it is just across from the SBB Bahnhof. Rooms have up to four beds and there's generally plenty of space. Hang out in the interior courtyard in summer.

Hotel Stadthof (☎ 061 261 87 11; www.stadthof.ch; Gerbergasse 84; s/d Sfr75/130) You'll need to book ahead at this Spartan but decent central hotel. Set above a pizzeria on an old town square, the nine rooms are squeaky clean (shared loo and shower) and the owners of this centuries-old building are very friendly.

MIDRANGE

our pick **Au Violon** (☎ 061 269 87 11; www.au-violon
.com; Im Lohnhof 4; s Sfr123-185, d Sfr146-208; ✗) The
doors are one of the few hints that quaint,
atmospheric Au Violon was a prison from
1835 to 1995. Most of the rooms are two cells
rolled into one and either look onto a delightful cobblestone courtyard or have views of the
Münster. Sitting on a leafy hilltop, it also has
a well-respected restaurant.

Hotel Krafft (☎ 061 690 91 30; www.hotelkrafft.ch;
Rheingasse 12; s/d from Sfr145/230, with river view Sfr185/290)
The Krafft appeals to design-savvy urbanites.
Sculptural modern chandeliers dangle in the
creaky-floored dining room (for fine food)
overlooking the Rhine, and minimalist water
bars (all stainless steel, grey and Japanese teapots) adorn each landing of the spiral stairs.
Smaller singles are bright, if tight; the doubles
have huge beds, timber floors and balconies.

Der Teufelhof (☎ 061 261 10 10; www.teufelhof.com;
Leonhardsgraben 49; s/d in Galeriehotel from Sfr180/265, r in
Kunsthotel from Sfr295; P ✗) 'The Devil's Court'
fuses two hotels into one. The Kunsthotel's
nine rooms are each decorated by a different artist. The larger Galeriehotel annexe, a
former convent, is more about stylish every-
day design, but the rooms vary considerably in
size and atmosphere. An excellent restaurant
caps it all off.

TOP END

Les Trois Rois (☎ 061 260 50 50; www.lestroisrois.com;
Blumenrain 8; s/d from Sfr365/590) Without doubt the
top address in town, The Three Kings offers
public areas and rooms that combine a digni-
fied elegance of times gone by (anyone for a
waltz in the ballroom?) with key indispensable
mod-cons, such as the state-of-the-art Bang
& Olufsen media centre in each room. Room
rates drop at weekends.

Eating

our pick **Acqua** (☎ 061 564 66 66; www.acquabasilea.ch;
Binningerstrasse 14; dishes Sfr15-42; ☯ lunch & dinner Tue-Fri,
dinner Sat) For a special experience, head to these
converted waterworks beside a quiet stream.
The atmosphere is glam postindustrial, with
brown-leather banquettes, candles and chandeliers inside bare stone and concrete walls
and floors. The food is Tuscan, and Basel's
beautiful people drink in the attached lounge
bar. Sit out in the terrace in summer.

Parterre (☎ 061 695 89 98; www.parterre.net;
Klybeckstrasse 1b; mains Sfr17-32; ☯ 8am-midnight Mon-Fri,
10am-midnight Sat) Unusual dishes, such as lake
salmon in saffron sauce with potato gratin and
cabbage, stud the menu in this slightly alternative place overlooking the Kaserne Park.

Druck Punkt (☎ 061 261 50 22; St Johanns Vorstadt 19;
menus Sfr17.50 & Sfr22.50; ☯ Mon-Fri) This converted
print shop makes an unpretentious bistro,
with chalky walls and heavy wooden tables.
Filling meals, including a super salad (Sfr19),
come at affordable prices.

Oliv (☎ 061 283 03 03; www.restaurantoliv.ch;
Bachlettenstrasse 1; mains Sfr28-39; ☯ lunch & dinner Tue-
Fri, dinner Sat) A trendy hang-out not far from
the zoo, Oliv leans towards fresh and varied
Mediterranean cooking – great for those who
can't bear the thought of more *Spätzli*. They
do a tasty Marseille-style *bouillabaisse*. You
can order half portions.

Weinstube Gifthüttli (☎ 061 261 16 56; Schneidergasse
11; mains Sfr29-57; ☯ lunch & dinner Tue-Fri, dinner Sat)
This cosy, 1st-floor eatery offers a mix of
traditional timber touches and a whiff of art
nouveau in the decor. They do various types
of *Schnitzel Cordon bleu* (stuffed veal or pork
filets) and have a set lunch for Sfr22.50.

Charon (☎ 061 261 99 80; Schützengraben 62; mains
Sfr40-49; ☯ Mon-Fri May-Sep, Tue-Sun Oct-Apr) In what
looks like someone's home, this understated restaurant with art-nouveau decorative touches offers carefully prepared dishes
leaning slightly to French tastes. One of the
house specialties is the *Seezunge gebraten mit
Minikapern* (a whole slab of sole baked with
baby capers).

St Alban Stübli (☎ 061 272 54 15; www.st-alban
-stuebli.ch; St Alban Vorstadt 74; mains Sfr40-58; ☯ Mon-Fri)
Set in a lovely quiet street, this looks for all
the world like your cosy local tavern. With
dim yellow lighting, plenty of timber and
fine linen, you are served a mix of local and
French cuisine. One of many savoury success
stories is the *Rosa gebratene Entenbrust an
Orangenpfeffersauce mit Gemüse der Saison
und Nudeln* (baked duck breast in orange-
pepper sauce with seasonal vegetables and
noodles). Just up the road at No 64, the
celebrated Basel-born art historian, Jakob
Burkhardt (1818–97) lived from 1866 to 1892.
He penned the classic *The Civilisation of the
Renaissance in Italy* (1860).

Drinking

Steinenvorstadt and Barfüsserplatz teem
with teens and 20-somethings on the weekends. A more interesting area is Kleinbasel,

around Rheingasse and Utengasse. There is a slight air of grunge, quite a few watering holes and something of a red-light zone to lend it edge.

KLEINBASEL

Bar Rouge (☎ 061 361 30 21; www.barrouge.ch; Level 31, Messeplatz 10; ☾ 5pm-1am Mon-Wed, 5pm-2am Thu, 5pm-4am Fri & Sat) This plush red bar, with panoramic views from the 31st floor of the ugly glass *Messeturm* (trade fair tower), is the city's most memorable. Hipsters, and a few suits early on weekday evenings, come to appreciate the regular DJs and films.

Kaserne (www.kaserne-basel.ch; Klybeckstrasse 1b) Opening times depend on what's on at this busy location for alternative theatre as well as drinking over in Kleinbasel.

Hirscheneck (☎ 061 692 73 33; Lindenberg 23; ☾ 9am-midnight Sun-Thu, 10am-2am Fri & Sat) A relaxed, grungy, almost knockabout place with an urban vibe (try to spot someone *without* piercings), this corner bar has tables on the footpath and regular gigs and DJs – it would be right at home in Berlin.

GROSSBASEL

Zum Roten Engel (☎ 061 261 20 08; Andreasplatz 15; ☾ 9am-midnight Mon-Sat, 10am-10pm Sun) This student-filled venue, spilling onto an irresistible, tiny cobblestone square, is great for a latte and snacks by day and a glass of wine or three in the evening. It's a temperate way to start the night.

Cargo-Bar (☎ 061 321 00 72; www.cargobar.ch; St Johanns Rheinweg 46; ☾ 4pm-1am Sun-Thu, 4pm-2.30am Fri & Sat) A nice halfway house between cool and alternative, located in a tucked-away spot on the river. There are lots of art installations, live gigs, video shows and DJs.

Atlantis (☎ 061 228 96 96; www.atlan-tis.ch; Klosterberg 13; ☾ bar 5pm-midnight Tue-Thu, 6pm-4am Fri & Sat) Leather-topped stools are strung behind the long, curving and – on DJ weekend nights – packed bar. Themes change constantly and range from funk to '90s. Maybe this is why it attracts a mostly 30-something crowd. They have a summer rooftop terrace and do lunch Monday to Friday.

Entertainment

For a comprehensive rundown on what's happening in town, pick up the monthly *Basel Live* brochure from the tourist office. The Stadtcasino and other big venues about town

like the Messe (trade fair) buildings are often used to host big musical acts.

LIVE MUSIC

The **Basel Symphony Orchestra** (www.sinfonieorchester basel.ch) and **Basel Chamber Orchestra** (www.kammer orchesterbasel.ch) both play at the Stadtcasino; ask at the tourist office for details.

Sudhaus Warteck (☎ 061 681 44 10; www.sudhaus.ch; Burgweg 15) offers a colourful cultural calendar, with anything from African percussion to '50s dance tunes on the menu.

Bird's Eye Jazz Club (☎ 061 263 33 41; www.birdseye.ch; Kohlenberg 20; ☾ 8pm-midnight Tue-Sat Sep-May, Wed-Sat Jun-Aug) is among Europe's top jazz dens. Concerts start most evenings at 9.30pm.

CLUBS

Die Kuppel (☎ 061 270 99 39; www.kuppel.ch, in German; Binningerstrasse 14; ☾ 9pm till late Tue & 10pm till late Thu-Sat) This is an atmospheric wooden dome, with a dance floor and cocktail bar, located in a secluded park. Salsa, soul, house and '70s/'80s are regularly on the bill.

SPORT

FC Basel (www.fcb.ch), one of Switzerland's top football teams, plays at St Jakob Park, 2km east of the main train station (SBB Bahnhof). The translucent skin of the stadium, by Herzog & de Meuron, looks best when lit up, which happens during games. You can pick up tickets on the team's website. Take tram 14 from Barfüsserplatz or Marktplatz.

Shopping

The area around Marktplatz and Barfüsserplatz teems with shops, selling everything from fashion to fine foods.

Long, pedestrian-only Freistrasse, which runs southeast from Marktplatz, is lined with stores of all persuasions.

Spalenberg, a lovely climbing lane to explore in its own right, is home to a line-up of intriguing boutiques. **Weihnachtshaus Johann Wanner** (☎ 061 261 48 26; Spalenberg 14) is a well-known Christmas store – pick up festive decorations year-round.

If you're in Basel in the run-up to Christmas, you'll sample plenty of the season's cheer at the Christmas markets set up in Barfüsserplatz and Marktplatz. Grab some Glühwein (mulled wine) and meander.

Marktplatz hosts a food market on the weekends year-round.

ACID HOUSE

Home to the Roche and Novartis companies, the Basel region is the epicentre of Switzerland's multibillion-franc pharmaceutical industry.

In 1943 a chemist at the Sandoz company searching for a migraine cure accidentally absorbed an experimental compound through the skin of his fingertips and (oops!) took the world's first 'acid trip'.

That chemist was Albert Hofmann (1906–2008) and the drug was lysergic acid diethylamide (LSD), which provoked a series of psychedelic hallucinations. Hofmann liked it so much, he tried it again.

Later, LSD was taken up by writers and artists, such as Aldous Huxley, who saw it as a creative force. Its mind-bending properties also made it a favourite with the 'far out' flower-power generation of the 1960s.

The drug was outlawed in most countries in the late 1960s, but whatever LSD's destructive potential, it certainly didn't do Herr Hofmann much harm – he lived to the ripe old age of 102!

Getting There & Away

AIR
EuroAirport (☎ 061 325 31 11; www.euroairport.com) serves Basel (as well as Mulhouse, in France, and Freiburg, in Germany). Located 5km north in France, it has flights to/from a host of European cities.

BOAT
An enjoyable, if slow, way to travel to/from Basel is via boat along the Rhine. The main boat landing stage is between Johanniterbrücke and Dreirosenbrücke.

Viking River Cruises (www.vikingrivers.com) runs an eight-day trip from Amsterdam starting from around UK£1150.

Also try **Scylla Tours** (☎ 061 638 81 81; www.scylla-tours.com; Uferstrasse 90).

CAR & MOTORCYCLE
The A35 freeway heads down from Strasbourg and passes by EuroAirport, and the A5 hugs the German side of the Rhine.

Rental
Several international operators have rental offices at the airport and train station (SBB Bahnhof).

A Smart ForTwo from **CityRent** (☎ 061 685 70 01; www.cityrent.ch; Hotel Alexander, Riehenring 83; per hr/day/week Sfr10/65/390, mileage extra) is a great way to zip around town.

TRAIN
Basel has two main train stations: the Swiss/French train station SBB Bahnhof, in the city's south; and the German train station BBF (Badischer) Bahnhof, in the north.

Two trains an hour run from SBB Bahnhof to Geneva (Sfr69, 2¾ hours), most involving one change en route. As many as seven, mostly direct, leave every hour for Zürich (Sfr31, 55 minutes to 1¼ hours). Trains to France also leave this station from the special SNCF section. Various train services link Paris to Basel – the fastest take 3½ hours.

Fast intercity services into Germany stop at both stations, but to reach smaller towns in southern Germany, you must board at the BBF Bahnhof.

Getting Around
Buses run every 20 to 30 minutes from 5am to around 11.30pm between the airport and the train station (SBB Bahnhof; Sfr3, 20 minutes). The trip by **taxi** (☎ 061 691 77 88, 061 271 22 22) costs around Sfr35. You'll find taxi stands outside the SBB Bahnhof.

If you're not staying in town, tickets for buses and trams cost Sfr1.90/3/8 for up to four stops/the central zone/day pass.

By 2012, tram 8 will be extended to Weil am Rhein – the first time local public transport has been extended over a national frontier in Europe since WWII.

There are several parking garages between the SBB station and the pedestrian zone. Expect to pay Sfr1.50 to Sfr3 an hour. Most street meter parking is similarly priced, with a limit of one or two hours. Down on St Alban Rheinweg, you pay Sfr0.50 per hour for a maximum of 24 hours.

You can park bicycles at **Velô** (☎ 061 272 09 10; www.veloparking.ch; Centralbahnplatz; Sfr10/18/25 3hr/half-day/full day; ☼ 8am-10pm daily), a massive underground bicycle-parking and repair station.

Small ferries cross the Rhine at four points (Sfr1.60, day passes not valid) constantly from about 9am to 5pm or dusk, whichever comes sooner.

AROUND BASEL
Augusta Raurica
By the Rhine, these **Roman ruins** (☎ 061 816 22 22; www.augustaraurica.ch; admission free; ✹ 10am-5pm) are Switzerland's largest. They're the last remnants of a colony founded in 43 BC that had grown to 20,000 citizens by the 2nd century. Today, restored features include an open-air theatre and several temples.

There's also a **Römermuseum** (Roman Museum; Giebenacherstrasse 17; adult/senior & student Sfr7/5, BaselCard valid; ✹ 1-5pm Mon, 10am-5pm Tue-Sun Mar-Oct, 1-5pm Mon, 11am-5pm Tue-Sun Nov-Feb), in the Kaiseraugst, which features an authentic Roman house among its exhibits.

The train from Basel to Kaiseraugst takes 11 minutes (Sfr5); it's then a 10-minute walk to the site.

Rheinfelden
pop 10,870 / elevation 285m
Home to Feldschlösschen beer, Rheinfelden, which is just inside Aargau canton on the south bank of the Rhine, 24km east of Basel, has a pretty, semi-circular **Altstadt** (Old Town). Several medieval city gates, defensive towers and parts of the old walls still stand. Of the towers, the triangular **Messerturm** (Knife Tower) is so named, they say, because it once contained a shaft lined with knives. Anyone thrown in would be sliced to bits!

The pedestrianised main street, Marktgasse, is lined with shops, eateries and the occasional tavern. At its western end, an early 20th-century bridge leads to the Inseli, a once-fortified island that lies in the middle of the Rhine and forms a part of the German Rheinfelden on the north bank. Bring your passport just in case.

You can visit the **Feldschlösschen brewery** (☎ 084 812 50 00; www.feldschloesschen.ch; Theophil -Roniger Strasse; tours Sfr12), housed in a 19th-century building that could be a rough imitation of Hampton Court, only with its own railway and smelling like, well, a brewery. Its name means 'little castle in the field' – a pretty accurate tag. Two-hour tours (in German) with beer tastings theoretically take place twice a day, Monday to Friday, and on alternate Saturdays. You are supposed

to book by phone but you might be able to get on the list just by wandering by in the morning – follow the signs to the *Treffpunkt* (meeting point). The brewery is a 10-minute walk from the train station.

To the west of the Old Town are some spa hotels. A couple of other lodgings are scattered about town and there's no problem getting a meal.

Rheinfelden is a short train ride from Basel (Sfr7, 15 minutes).

Dornach
The unassuming village of Dornach, 13km south of Basel, is home to the **Goetheanum** (☎ 061 706 42 42; www.goetheanum.org; tour Sfr14, ✹ 8am-10pm, tour 2pm), a rather other-worldly building that is the global headquarters of the Anthroposophical Society. Austrian philosopher and teacher Rudolf Steiner (1861–1925) developed the thinking behind anthroposophy, which proposes the possibility of apprehending a spiritual world through inner development. He also designed this 1928 building, done in reinforced concrete. Nearby, Haus Duldeck (1918) is an equally strange construction designed by Steiner, with an oddly wavy and crumpled roof (move over Antoni Gaudí!). Set in tranquil parkland, it now serves as archives.

Tram 10 (24 minutes) or local trains (Sfr3.80, 10 minutes) run from SBB Bahnhof.

AARGAU CANTON

Stretching between Zürich to the east and the canton of Basel Land to the west, Aargau is the homeland of the Habsburgs, the clan that eventually came to rule over the Austro-Hungarian Empire but lost all its territories here to the independent-minded Swiss. Pretty towns and craggy castles dot its main waterway, the Aare River. Visit **Aargau Tourismus** (www.aargautourismus.ch).

BADEN
pop 16,690 / elevation 388m
Baden is an old-school spa: people have been coming here since Roman times, either for its mineral baths' curative properties or to escape the stresses of the world. Its health-resort hotels, bunched together at a bend in the river, could come straight from Thomas Mann's *The Magic Mountain*. The medieval *Altstadt* (Old Town) is a topsy-turvy

medieval tapestry that will see you climbing narrow cobbled lanes from the river to the stony hilltop fortress ruins.

Orientation & Information

From the train station, head south for the *Altstadt* or north to the spa centre, themselves 20 minutes' walk apart.

Post office (Bahnhofstrasse 31; ☺ 7.30am-6.30pm Mon-Fri, 8am-4pm Sat)

Tourist office (☎ 056 200 83 83; www.baden.ch; Bahnhofplatz 1; ☺ noon-7pm Mon, 9.30am-7pm Tue-Fri, 9.30am-4pm Sat)

Sights & Activities

There are 19 mineral-rich **sulphur springs** in Baden, believed to be helpful in treating rheumatic, respiratory, cardiovascular and even some neurological disorders.

Pools in some of the major hotels are open to everyone; entry ranges from Sfr6 to Sfr16, but whirlpool baths, saunas, solariums and special treatments cost more. Various spas and wellness centres are also available – reckon on around Sfr40 for basic facilities.

The Old Town centre includes the covered **Holzbrücke** (timber bridge) and stepped-gabled houses. If you're feeling keen, climb the hundreds of stairs near the **Stadtturm** (city tower) for a bird's-eye view from the ruined castle on the hill. West of the spas is **Stiftung Langmatt** (☎ 056 200 86 70; www.langmatt.ch; Römerstrasse 30; adult/child/student Sfr12/free/8; ☺ 2-5pm Tue-Fri, 11am-5pm Sat & Sun Apr-Oct), a stately home full of French Impressionist art.

Sleeping & Eating

SYHA hostel (☎ 056 221 67 36; www.youthhostel.ch/baden; Kanalstrasse 7; dm Sfr33, s/d Sfr85/92; ☺ reception 7-10am & 5-9.45pm, closed mid-Dec–mid-Mar; P ✗ ▣) One of Switzerland's best-looking hostels, this has grey slate floors, earth-red walls and top-quality materials. Walk from the train station to the Old Town, cross the Limmat River at Holzbrücke, and take the first right into Kanalstrasse to find it.

Atrium-Hotel Blume (☎ 056 222 55 69; www .blume-baden.ch; Kurplatz 4; s/d Sfr180/255; ✗) An atmospheric old place featuring a wonderful inner courtyard with a fountain and plants; it also has a small thermal pool. Rooms give on to inner galleries that, on the 1st floor, are crammed with breakfast tables and sometimes rowdy diners – no matter – they have usually finished dessert by 8pm! There is wi-fi.

Roter Turm (☎ 056 222 85 25; www.restaurant -roterturm.ch; Rathausgasse 5; mains Sfr28-45; ☺ 9am-midnight Mon-Sat) A hip diner and bar in the heart of the *Altstadt*, this place offers a mix of modern European, mainly Italian, cuisine alongside more traditional dishes. It's not bad for a drink either.

our pick Rebstock (☎ 056 221 12 77; www.rebstock baden.ch; Untere Halde 21; mains Sfr30-45; ☺ lunch & dinner Tue-Fri, dinner Sat & Mon; ✗) Jazz music wafts around this 500-year-old house, a successful fusion of medieval abode (admire the giant beams, metre-thick walls and brick vaults downstairs over the loos) and chill lounge. But forget all that and concentrate on Didier's food – beautifully prepared mushrooms and game in season and the best mussels this side of Brussels (imported from northern France). People flock here from Zürich for the latter.

Drinking

Baden is a quiet town, but a few bars bring some weekend life to the centre. A relaxing place to sip wine is the Bohemian **UnvermeidBAR** (☎ 056 200 84 84; Rathausgasse 22; ☺ 9am-1pm & 7pm-1am), with its grand piano, chandelier over the bar, giant mirrors and disturbing artwork. **Rossini** (☎ 056 222 08 81; www.rossinibar.ch; Haselstrasse 29; ☺ 6pm-2am) is a somewhat livelier joint for cocktails.

Getting There & Away

Baden is 14 minutes away from Zürich by train (Sfr10.20). It is also within Zürich's S-Bahn network (lines S6 and S12, 30 minutes). By road, follow the A1 freeway to Zürich.

SOUTHWEST ALONG THE AARE

The Aare is the longest river to rise and end entirely in Switzerland. This tributary of the Rhine rises in glaciers in the Bernese Alps. Numerous captivating spots are dotted along its path through Aargau.

Brugg & Windisch

pop 15,780 / elevation 351m

Ten minutes west of Baden by train lies the Habsburg settlement of **Brugg**, basically created as a toll stop on the Aare. Hauptstrasse (Main St), lined by stepped-gabled houses and pretty facades, winds down to the one-time toll bridge, still guarded by the forbidding, 13th-century stone **Schwarzer Turm** (Black Tower). The tower was in use as a prison until 1951.

Attached at the hip to Brugg is **Windisch**, whose name stems from Roman Vindonissa. Evidence of the one-time Roman garrison town includes sparse remnants of what was thought to be Switzerland's biggest amphitheatre and of the foundations of the east gate, along the road leading out of town towards Baden. The gate stands just in front of what was a Franciscan **monastery**, originally founded by the Habsburgs in 1311. The pleasant three-sided cloister, with timber pillars and a gallery, overgrown with ivy, is home to a cafeteria. Next door stands its Gothic church, known above all for its 14th-century stained-glass windows. The whole lot is now part of a psychiatric institution, set in fields in which you are at liberty to wander.

There's a hotel and a handful of eateries on the main street in Brugg.

You can get to Brugg by regional train or the S12 of the Zürich S-Bahn network (Sfr4).

Habsburg & Wildegg

A vertical stone fortress that would not be out of place in Arthurian legend or a Monty Python sketch, the Habsburg castle was built in 1020 and gave its name to a house that would one day become one of Europe's greatest ruling dynasties.

As in Monty Python's version of Camelot, however, the Habsburgs soon tired of this particular fortress castle (in spite of the lovely views over broad green fields and nearby villages) and it changed hands many times before winding up property of Aargau canton in 1804. It houses administrative offices and a hearty **restaurant** (☎ 056 441 16 73; mains Sfr25-45; ⏰ 9am-midnight Tue-Sun May-Sep, Wed-Sun Oct-Apr).

Castle lovers have another tall stepped-gabled beauty of a **Schloss** (☎ 062 887 08 30; ⏰ 10am-5pm Tue-Sun Apr-Oct) 5.5km south atop a green hill at **Wildegg**. The location is lovely and inside the castle is a display on aspects of centuries of Swiss history, as seen through the archives and possessions of the Effinger clan, who took over the castle in 1483.

Buses run every two hours from Brugg train station to Habsburg village (Sfr3.40, 11 minutes), from where it's a 10-minute uphill walk to the fortress. If driving, it is 3km from the N5 road between Brugg and Lenzburg. You pass through the unfortunately named village of Scherz (Joke).

Trains run from Brugg to Wildegg (Sfr4, five to 10 minutes). Otherwise, local buses

run from Lenzburg train station and stop a short walk below Wildegg Schloss.

Lenzburg
pop 7700 / elevation 406m

From Lenzburg train station, a 30-minute stroll takes you through the once-medieval village, whose fine houses were rebuilt in a low-key baroque fashion in the 18th century after fire, and on up a leafy hill path to the Kyburg clan's **Schloss Lenzburg** (☎ 062 888 48 40; www.ag.ch/lenzburg; adult/under 4yr/4-16yr Sfr12/free/6, gardens only Sfr4/free/2; ⏰ 10am-5pm Tue-Sun Apr-Oct). Inside the castle's main tower and one-time dungeon are several floors of period furniture from down the centuries, ranging from medieval times to the 19th century. Take sustenance in the lovely café.

Direct trains from Baden (via Brugg) run hourly to Lenzburg (Sfr8.20, 25 minutes), from where there are occasional buses to the village and *Schloss*.

Wasserschloss Hallwyl

About 20km south of Lenzburg is one of the prettiest **castles** (☎ 062 767 60 10; www.schlosshallwyl.ch; adult/under 6yr/6-16yr Sfr12/free/6; ⏰ 10am-5pm Tue-Sun Apr-Oct) in northern Switzerland. This 'Water Castle' is so named because it is built in the middle of a river – a natural moat. It is, in fact, two modest castles joined by a bridge.

Walking paths wind out southwards towards Hallwilersee, a peaceful lake that can be criss-crossed by ferry.

An hourly S-Bahn (running between Lucerne and Lenzburg) calls in at Boniswil (Sfr4, 12 minutes from Lenzburg), from where it's a 1km walk east to the castle on the way to Seengen.

Aarau
pop 15,480 / elevation 383m

The cantonal capital is the irresistible result of medieval town planning draped on a rising spur of land overlooking the broad flow of the Aare river. Founded by the Kyburgs, the city passed for a time under Habsburg rule before being overrun by Bern canton in 1415.

Bern later lost control of Aarau in the face of revolutionary French forces. In March 1798, occupying French revolutionary authorities declared Aarau capital of the Swiss republic. This moment of glory was short-lived, as the republican government moved to Lucerne in September. In 1803, under Napoleon's reorganisation of the Swiss cantons, Aarau was made capital of Aargau.

ORIENTATION & INFORMATION

From the train station, it's about a 500m walk to Schlossplatz, at the northeast entrance to the *Altstadt*.

Post office (Metzgerstrasse 2; ☼ 8.30-11.30am & 2-6pm Mon-Fri, 8.30-11am Sat)

Tourist office (☎ 062 824 76 24; www.aargautourismus .ch; Schlossplatz 1; ☼ 1.30-6.30pm Mon, 9am-6.30pm Tue-Fri, 9am-5pm Sat)

SIGHTS

Built on a rising spur that, at its highest end (where the 15th-century church is), juts high above the Aare River, the walled Old Town of Aarau is irresistible. Its grid of streets is lined with gracious, centuries-old buildings, all quite different and diverting. Many have in common grand roofs hanging out well beyond the facades over the streets, their timber undersides gaily decorated (the city says there are more than 70 such buildings). Although there are several museums (including a contemporary art museum designed by Herzog & de Meuron), the real pleasure comes from poking your nose around the medieval centre's nooks and crannies.

SLEEPING & EATING

There are just three hotels in Aarau, all just outside the medieval core. **Gasthof zum Schützen** (☎ 062 823 01 24; www.gasthofschuetzen.ch; Schachenallee 39; s/d Sfr112/175), the cheapest, is a functional, modern place aimed in part at the business crowd. Rooms are mostly spacious and spotless.

There are plenty of restaurants and bars in the heart of town. Down from the main bustle, but still inside the Old Town, is the homey **Restaurant Halde 20** (☎ 062 823 45 65; www.halde20.ch; Halde 20; mains Sfr22-65; ☼ Mon-Sat), where you can

try anything from good pasta (Sfr22 to Sfr27) to a horsemeat steak (Sfr44).

GETTING THERE & AWAY

Direct trains run from Baden to Aarau (Sfr10.80, 25 minutes) up to three or four times an hour.

Aarburg & Zofingen

Quiet **Aarburg** is dominated by the long, gnarled finger of a *Festung* (fortress) spread over a high ridge behind Städtli, the old village. The **fortress** (☎ 062 787 01 01; ☼ tours 2pm Sat Apr-Oct) is a children's home and can be visited in guided groups (in German).

Medieval **Zofingen**, 6km south of Aarburg, is a perfectly preserved village, surrounded by its more modern 20th-century outgrowth.

The Old Town is reminiscent of Aarau and its cobblestone lanes and interlocking squares are a delight. Houses are a higgledy-piggledy mix, some half-timbered, some with baroque facades and still others, notably the 17th-century **St Urbanhof** (cnr Engelgasse & Vordere Hauptgasse), with bright frescos.

There are several hotels and eateries. The **youth hostel** (☎ 062 752 23 03; www.youthhostel.ch /zofingen; General Guisan-Strasse 10; dm Sfr29; ☼ reception 7-10am & 5-9pm, closed Mar–mid-Dec) is set in a cute little half-timbered house, just across General Guisan-Strasse from the Old Town.

At the **Wirtshaus Markthalle** (☎ 062 751 85 35; Marktgasse 8; mains Sfr29.50-35.50; ☼ lunch & dinner Mon-Fri, lunch Sat), you can tuck into hearty local fare, such as the *Zartes Rehschnitzel an Preiselbeer und Rahmsauce* (tender deer escalope in cranberry and cream sauce).

To get to Aarburg from Basel or Baden, first get to Olten train station, from where half-hourly buses run to Aarburg Städli (Sfr3.60, 15 minutes), the old village at the foot of the fortress. Trains to Zofingen run every 10 or so minutes from Olten (Sfr4, seven minutes).

Northeastern Switzerland

Away from the awe-inspiring spectacle of the Alps and the country's key cities lies a swathe of deep Switzerland that oozes a gentler beauty little touched by international tourism. It offers a wealth of opportunities for discovering the heart of the Germanic part of the nation.

Schaffhausen, St Gallen (famed for its extraordinary library) and neighbouring Germany's Konstanz, are bite-sized, centuries-old urban jewels full of surprises, from an urban castle surrounded by vineyards to hidden taverns and traditional restaurants.

The placid plains and low hill country of the north attract cyclists from all directions. Several castles and pleasant settlements dot the shores of Lake Constance and the Rhine. Vineyards producing the favoured local red, Blauburgunder (Pinot noir), abound. South of the lake, rolling hills, carefully tended pastures and manicured apple orchards keep you agog.

Several wild and powerful mountain chains stretch across the southern half of the cantons of St Gallen and Glarus. Peaks such as Säntis and the remote Piz Sardona attract hikers. Indeed, a dense web of walking trails is draped over these cantons.

Although best known for its stinky Appenzeller cheeses, this whole arc is great for comfort eating, with such favourites as rösti and *Spätzli* (boiled dough balls or egg noodles) forming the basis of many hearty meat dishes – all washed down, *natürlich*, with Blauburgunder.

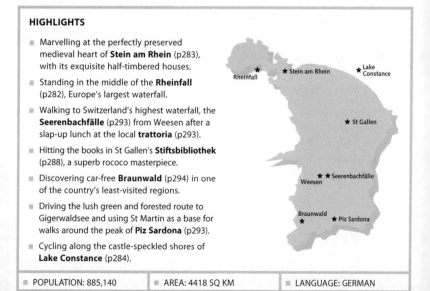

HIGHLIGHTS

- Marvelling at the perfectly preserved medieval heart of **Stein am Rhein** (p283), with its exquisite half-timbered houses.

- Standing in the middle of the **Rheinfall** (p282), Europe's largest waterfall.

- Walking to Switzerland's highest waterfall, the **Seerenbachfälle** (p293) from Weesen after a slap-up lunch at the local **trattoria** (p293).

- Hitting the books in St Gallen's **Stiftsbibliothek** (p288), a superb rococo masterpiece.

- Discovering car-free **Braunwald** (p294) in one of the country's least-visited regions.

- Driving the lush green and forested route to Gigerwaldsee and using St Martin as a base for walks around the peak of **Piz Sardona** (p293).

- Cycling along the castle-speckled shores of **Lake Constance** (p284).

★ Rheinfall ★ Stein am Rhein ★ Lake Constance

★ St Gallen

★ ★ Seerenbachfälle
Weesen

Braunwald ★ ★ Piz Sardona

■ POPULATION: 885,140　　■ AREA: 4418 SQ KM　　■ LANGUAGE: GERMAN

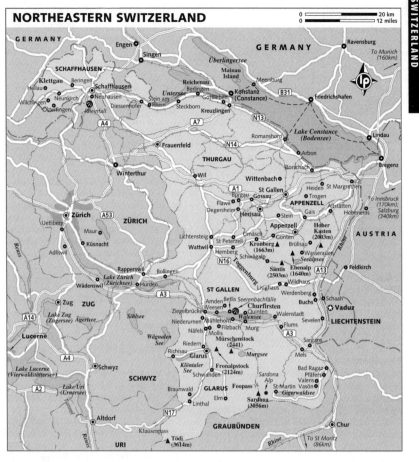

NORTHEASTERN SWITZERLAND

Orientation & Information

The tourist region of Ostschweiz (Eastern Switzerland) unites several easterly Swiss cantons and Liechtenstein (p341). Information can be found on the pages of **Switzerland Tourism** (www.myswitzerland.com) or the official website of **Ostschweiz Tourismus** (http://ostschweiz.ch). Otherwise, enquire at the St Gallen tourist office (p287).

Getting There & Around

This area lies between Zürich and Friedrichshafen (Germany) airports and can be conveniently reached from either by public or private transport. Road and rail link Zürich with Schaffhausen, Stein am Rhein, St Gallen and even Linthal

(for Braunwald). Alternatively, a ferry crosses the lake from Friedrichshafen to Romanshorn, which also has good car and train links.

Several areas, such as the Bodensee region around Lake Constance and Appenzellerland, offer regional passes. For details, see the individual sections.

SCHAFFHAUSEN CANTON

Cyclists love touring this relatively flat region and lower-end accommodation is booked up swiftly on weekends. Excellent public transport and manageable distances make it an easy day trip from Zürich (p215), too.

NORTHEASTERN SWITZERLAND

SCHAFFHAUSEN

pop 33,460 / elevation 404m

Schaffhausen is the kind of quaint medieval town one more readily associates with Germany – perhaps no coincidence, given how close it is to the border. Ornate frescos and oriel bay windows adorn the pastel-coloured houses lining the stone pavements of its pedestrian-only *Altstadt* (Old Town). The city's signature fortress, the circular Munot, lords it over a vineyard-streaked hill.

Established as a shipping base in the Middle Ages, it came under Habsburg rule for a century before joining the federated, independent Swiss cantons in 1501.

During WWII, Allied pilots 'mistook' Schaffhausen for Germany, dropping bombs on the outskirts twice in April 1944, and so giving it the dubious honour of being the only bit of Swiss soil to take a direct hit during the war.

Orientation

The train station, served by Swiss and German trains, lies parallel to one of the main streets, Vorstadt. Cross the road and head straight ahead for about 150m to find yourself in the thick of things.

Information

Main post office (☎ 052 630 03 40; Bahnhofstrasse 34; ☷ 7am-6.30pm Mon-Fri, 8am-5pm Sat) Opposite the train station.

Tourist office (☎ 052 632 40 20; www.schaffhauserland .ch; Herrenacker 15; ☷ 9.30am-6pm Mon-Fri, 9.30am-4pm Sat Jun-Sep, plus 9.30am-2pm Sun Jun-Aug, 9.30am-5pm Mon-Fri, 9.30am-2pm Sat Oct-May)

Sights & Activities

Many visitors come to Schaffhausen only for the nearby Rheinfall (Rhine Falls; see p282). However, the chocolate-box Old Town is well worth exploration. The tourist office offers one-hour **walking tours** (adult/child Sfr12/6; ☷ 10am Tue & 2pm Sat late Mar–mid-Oct), with wine-tasting tours another possibility.

Schaffhausen is often nicknamed the *Erkerstadt* because of its 170 *Erkers* (oriel bay windows), which citizens built as a display of wealth. One of the most noteworthy windows belongs to the 17th-century **Zum Goldenen Ochsen** (Vorstadt 17), whose frescoed facade displays, among other things, an eponymous Golden Ox. The 16th-century **Zum Grossen Käfig** (The Big Cage; Vorstadt 45) presents an extraordinarily

colourful tale of the parading of Turkish sultan Bajazet in a cage by the triumphant Mongol warrior leader Tamerlane. The centuries-old frescos were freshened up in 1906.

Vorstadt meanders south past the 16th-century **Mohrenbrunnen** (Moor fountain) into the old market place, Fronwagplatz, at whose southern end stands the **Metzgerbrunnen** (Butcher's Fountain), with a William Tell–type figure, and a large clock tower.

Facing the latter, the late baroque **Herrenstube** (Fronwagplatz 3) was built in 1748 and was once the drinking hole of Schaffhausen nobles.

A block east, the **Haus zum Ritter** (House of the Knight; Vordergasse 65), built in 1492, boasts a detailed Renaissance-style fresco depicting, you guessed it, a knight. This is a copy; parts of the 16th-century original are in the **Museum zu Allerheiligen** (☎ 052 633 07 77; www .allerheiligen.ch; Baumgartenstrasse 6; adult/child/student Sfr9/free/5; ☷ 11am-5pm Tue-Sun), along with all sorts of other city relics. The museum gives on to the beautifully simple Romanesque cloister of the attached **Allerheiligen Münster** (All Saints' Cathedral; ☷ 10am-noon & 2-5pm Tue-Sun). The **cloister** (☷ 7.30am-8pm Mon-Fri, 9am-8pm Sat & Sun May-Sep, 7.30am-5pm Mon-Fri, 9am-5pm Sat & Sun Oct-Apr) has gardens that seem like a tangled forest. The herbal garden out back has been tended since the Middle Ages. The church was completed in 1103 and is a rare and largely intact specimen of the Romanesque style in Switzerland.

East of the Haus zum Ritter, Vordergasse becomes Unterstadt, where you'll find stairs through vineyards to the 16th-century **Munot** (admission free; ☷ 8am-8pm May-Sep, 9am-5pm Oct-Apr). The unusual circular fortress was built with forced labour following the Reformation and affords great views.

The 45km boat trip from Schaffhausen to Konstanz is one of the Rhine's more beautiful stretches. **Untersee und Rhein** (☎ 052 634 08 88; www.urh.ch, www.riverticket.ch, both in German; Freier Platz; one-way/return Sfr21/30; ☷ 3-4 times daily May–mid-Oct, 4 times Sat, Sun & holidays late Mar-late Apr) runs boat trips to/from Konstanz via Stein am Rhein and Reichenau. The journey takes 3¾ hours downstream to Schaffhausen and 4¾ hours the other way.

Sleeping

For information on the six B&Bs in Schaffhausen, head for the tourist office

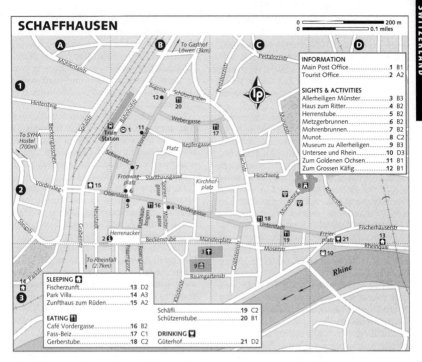

SCHAFFHAUSEN

0	200 m
0	0.1 miles

INFORMATION
Main Post Office.................**1** B1
Tourist Office......................**2** A2

SIGHTS & ACTIVITIES
Allerheiligen Münster.............**3** B3
Haus zum Ritter.....................**4** B2
Herrenstube..........................**5** B2
Metzgerbrunnen....................**6** B2
Mohrenbrunnen....................**7** B2
Munot..................................**8** C2
Museum zu Allerheiligen.........**9** B3
Untersee und Rhein...............**10** D3
Zum Goldenen Ochsen...........**11** B1
Zum Grossen Käfig................**12** B1

SLEEPING	
Fischerzunft.........................**13**	D2
Park Villa.............................**14**	A3
Zunfthaus zum Rüden............**15**	A2

EATING	
Café Vordergasse..................**16**	B2
Fass-Beiz.............................**17**	C1
Gerberstube.........................**18**	C2

Schäfli.................................**19**	C2
Schützenstube......................**20**	B1

DRINKING	
Güterhof..............................**21**	D2

(details posted in the window when closed). The cheapest of them cost Sfr45/90 for singles/doubles.

SYHA hostel (☎ 052 625 88 00; www.youthhostel .ch/schaffhausen; Randenstrasse 65; dm Sfr28; ☺ reception 8-10am & 5-9pm, closed mid-Nov–Feb; ℗ 🖳) This old pile of a mansion has clean, modern bathrooms. The bulk of dorms have six to 10 beds, although they also have a single and a double. Set in leafy grounds, it's 15 minutes by foot west of the train station, or take bus 6 to Hallenbad.

Gasthof Löwen (☎ 052 643 22 08; www.loewen-sh.ch; Im Höfli 2; s/d without bathroom Sfr80/130) About 5km north of the Old Town in Herblingen, this family-run pension has been around since the mid-17th century. The seven doubles are of a good size and comfortable, if lacking in imagination. Take bus 5 to the last stop. They don't take credit cards.

Zunfthaus zum Rüden (☎ 052 632 36 36; www.rueden.ch; Oberstadt 20; s/d from Sfr160/260; 🖳) Aimed largely at the business crowd, this solemn, grey-fronted and refurbished guildhall has a touch of character and is handily located between the medieval centre and the train station.

Park Villa (☎ 052 635 60 60; www.parkvilla.ch; Parkstrasse 18; s/d from Sfr170/180, without bathroom from Sfr80/130; ℗) The eclectic furniture in this faintly gothic house resembles a private antique collection, with a various array of four-poster beds, Persian carpets, chandeliers, patterned wallpaper and fake Ming vases in rooms. Dine in Louis XVI splendour in the banquet room.

Fischerzunft (☎ 052 632 05 05; www.fischerzunft.ch; Rheinquai 8; s/d from Sfr210/295) The sloping tiled roof and creamy-pink exterior of this low-slung Rhine-side mansion contain one of Switzerland's more-opulent hotels, known above all for its gourmet restaurant. Rooms are individually and, in some cases, rather gaudily decorated.

Eating

Café Vordergasse (☎ 052 625 42 49; Vordergasse 79; snacks & light meals Sfr10-20; ☺ 6am-7pm Mon-Fri, 7am-5pm Sat, 10am-5pm Sun) This art nouveau–style tearoom has an international flavour, with a range of sandwiches, salads, quiches and even hummus in pitta bread. Oh, and they have tea and coffee too.

Fass-Beiz (☎ 052 625 46 10; www.fassbeiz.ch; Webergasse 13; mains Sfr15.50-17.50; ☺ Mon-Sat) This tucked-away alternative café-bar enjoys a laid-back atmosphere and serves sandwiches and tasty sit-down dishes, with an excellent vegetarian selection that includes various salads. Music gigs, theatre performances and art exhibitions take place in the cellar below.

Schützenstube (☎ 052 625 42 49; www.schuetzenstube .ch; Schützengraben 27; mains Sfr16.50-42; ☺ Mon-Fri) The ornate historic exterior is a magnet. Foodwise, the emphasis is on fresh seasonal ingredients, most of them local, and the chef sometimes emerges to check diners are happy. One house speciality is *Spätzli* accompanied by anything from cheese to bacon. There's plenty of lake fish, meat and some vegetarian options.

Schäfli (☎ 052 625 11 47; Unterstadt 21; mains Sfr18-35; ☺ Tue-Sat) Since 1970 they have cooked up *Rindsfilets* (steak filets) with a range of sauces (Sfr34.50). Plenty of other Swiss classics are on offer too.

ourpick Gerberstube (☎ 052 625 21 55; www .gerberstube.ch; Bachstrasse 8; mains Sfr40-65; ☺ Tue-Sat) Behind their 1708 rococo facade, the opulent dining rooms of what in medieval times was a guildhall are a tempting setting for carefully prepared traditional cooking. Tuck into an entrecôte with Café de Paris sauce (Sfr50) or less-traditional curry scampi (Sfr65).

Drinking

The Old Town is sprinkled with several bars and the odd dance spot. Right on the Rhine is the popular **Güterhof** (☎ 052 630 40 40; www.gueterhof .ch; Freierplatz 10, ☺ 7am-midnight Sun-Wed, 7am-late Thu-Sat), once the goods depot for Rhine river transport companies and now a hip combination of bar (with outdoor seating), café, restaurant and sushi bar.

Getting There & Away

Direct hourly trains run to/from Zürich (Sfr18.20, 40 minutes). Local trains head half-hourly to Stein am Rhein (Sfr7.60, 25 minutes). Trains to St Gallen (Sfr28, one hour 20 minutes to two hours) usually involve a change at Winterthur or Romanshorn.

RHEINFALL

The **Rheinfall** (Rhine Falls; www.rhinefalls.com) might not give Niagara much competition in terms of height (23m), width (150m) or even flow of water (700 cu metre per second in summer), but it's a stunning sight nonetheless.

Two castles overlook the falls. The smaller **Schlössli Worth** is on the north bank facing the falling water and is surrounded by touristy restaurants, shops, an information centre and small ferry wharves. The more imposing **Schloss Laufen** on the south bank boasts 1000 years of history and overlooks the falls at closer quarters.

If you catch bus 1 or 6 from Schaffhausen train station to Neuhausen Zentrum (Sfr3), follow the yellow footprints to a point where you can go right towards Schlössli Worth or left across the combined train and pedestrian bridge to Schloss Laufen.

If you come by train from Schaffhausen or Winterthur to Schloss Laufen am Rheinfall (April to October only), you'll need to climb the hill to the castle. By car, you'll pull up in the car park behind it.

Most views of the falls are free, but to get close up to the rushing waters on the south side of the falls, you pay Sfr1 at the Schloss Laufen souvenir shop (open daily) to descend the staircase to the Känzeli viewing platform.

During summer, **ferries** (☎ 052 672 48 11; www .maendli.ch) flit in and out of the water at the bottom of the falls. Some merely cross from Schlössli Worth to Schloss Laufen (adult/child Sfr2.50/1.50) but the round trip that stops at the tall rock in the middle of the falls (adult/child Sfr6.50/3.50), where you can climb to the top and watch the water rush all around you, is far more fun.

On Swiss National Day, 1 August, there are spectacular fireworks over the falls.

If you're interested in the sound of the waterfall lulling you to sleep at night, there's an **SYHA hostel** (☎ 052 659 61 52; www.youthhostel.ch /dachsen; dm Sfr28.50-36; ☺ reception 8-9.30am & 5-9pm, closed mid-Oct–mid-Mar) inside Schloss Laufen.

From late 2008, Schloss Laufen and its youth hostel, restaurants and viewing platform access were shut for major overhaul works, but were set to reopen mid-2009.

KLETTGAU

West of Schaffhausen spreads the red-wine-producing territory of Klettgau, which spills over into neighbouring Germany. Like sheets of corduroy, the serried ranks of mostly Blauburgunder vineyards are draped over pea-green fields and gentle rises.

Sprinkled about this soothing countryside are engaging villages. The most striking is the medieval **Neunkirch**, 13km from

Schaffhausen. Others worth passing through include **Beringen, Hallau** and **Osterfingen**. Some of these slow-paced hamlets come to life in mid-October for wine festivals. In particular, look out for Osterfingen's **Trottenfest**, when vintners throw open their doors for tastings. If you come at any other time, head for **Bad Osterfingen** (☎ 052 681 21 21; www.badosterfingen.ch; Zollstrasse; mains Sfr30-45; ☺ Wed-Sun), where you'll be regaled with hearty local cooking and the best *Spätzli* around for miles.

Buses from Schaffhausen serve these villages.

STEIN AM RHEIN
pop 3120 / elevation 407m

Stein am Rhein is painfully picturesque. The effect is most overwhelming in its cobblestone Rathausplatz (considered by some Switzerland's most beautiful town square – no mean claim!), where houses of all shapes and sizes, some half-timbered, others covered in frescos seemed to have lined up for a permanent photo op. Why isn't this place on Unesco's World Heritage list? On the slopes up to the local castle, vineyards provide the raw material for the local reds.

Orientation & Information

The train station (which has bicycle rental) is on the south side of the Rhine and the Old Town on the north bank.

The tiny **tourist office** (☎ 052 742 20 90; www .steinamrhein.ch; Oberstadt 3; ☺ 9.30am-noon & 1.30-5pm Mon-Fri) lies east of the central Rathausplatz.

Sights & Activities

The fresco-festooned **Rathaus** (town hall) closes off the east end of **Rathausplatz**. Some of the 16th-century houses that line this elongated 'square' are named according to the pictures with which they are adorned, like *Sonne* (Sun) and *Der Weisse Adler* (The White Eagle).

The pleasure of Stein am Rhein is to wander around soaking up all this infuriatingly impossible cuteness. One four-storey house has been converted into the diverting **Museum Lindwurm** (☎ 052 741 25 12; www.museum-lindwurm.ch; Unterstadt 18; admission Sfr5; ☺ 10am-5pm Wed-Mon Mar-Oct), whose living rooms, servants' quarters and kitchen replicate the conditions enjoyed in the mid-19th century by a bourgeois family.

Also worth a look is the **Klostermuseum St Georgen** (adult/senior & student Sfr4/2; ☺ 10am-5pm

---

Tue-Sun Apr-Oct), between the Rathaus and the Rhine. A Benedictine monastery was built here in 1007, but what you see today, including the cool cloister and magnificent *Festsaal* (grand dining room), is largely a late-Gothic creation.

Watching over the city (the views alone are worth the drive up – it's a rather long walk) is the **Burg Hohenklingen** (☎ 052 741 21 37; www.burghohenklingen.ch; Hohenklingenstrasse 1; ☺ 10am-11pm Tue-Sun Apr-Oct, Wed-Sun Nov-Mar), a hilltop fortress, which recently underwent a Sfr20-million overhaul. Foodies will enjoy gourmet meals in the Rittersaal (Hall of Knights) or on the terrace.

Sleeping

SYHA hostel (☎ 052 741 12 55; www.youthhostel.ch /stein; Hemishoferstrasse 87; dm Sfr28; ☺ reception 8-10am & 5-10pm, closed Nov-Feb; ☐) About 1.5km west of the centre of town you'll find Stein am Rhein's pleasant hostel, some two minutes from the beach. Seven of the rooms are doubles.

Hotel Schiff (☎ 052 741 22 73; Schifflände 10; s/d Sfr85/130) A narrow riverfront house with a handful of smallish but welcoming rooms, this is a good little deal for rooms with a Rhine view.

Rheingerbe (☎ 052 741 29 91; www.rheingerbe .ch; Rathausplatz 2; s/d Sfr90/160) The rooms in this pretty, four-storey house are a little old fashioned, with dark timber beds and simple furniture. You need to book to get a room with river views.

Rheinfels (☎ 052 741 21 44; www.rheinfels.ch; s/d Sfr135/190) Up the creaky staircase, past the suit of armour (or, more prosaically, straight up the lift), this atmospheric hotel has generously sized rooms, decorated in an older style with lots of pink and brown, but many with river views. The hotel is right by the bridge and its restaurant is renowned for fish.

NORTHEASTERN SWITZERLAND

Eating

Badstube (☎ 052 741 20 93; www.badstube.ch, in German; Bei der Schifflände; mains Sfr19-42; ☸ Wed-Sun Feb-Oct) Several dining areas, loaded with timber and terracotta floor tiles, offer scrumptious Swiss grub in this typical half-timbered house just back from the Rhine. Sit outside on summer days and tuck into one of the many varieties of rösti, a house speciality.

ourpick **Hotel Adler** (☎ 052 742 61 61; www.adler steinamrhein.ch; Rathausplatz 2; mains Sfr29-49; ☸ Tue-Sun) Behind the frescoed exterior lies a fine eatery, especially for those looking for local fish. The dining areas have a pleasingly old-fashioned feel about them and the grub, while nothing outlandishly creative, hits the spot.

Burg Hohenklingen (p283) is a gourmand's delight with views thrown in.

Getting There & Away

Stein am Rhein is on the direct hourly train route that links Schaffhausen (Sfr7.60, 25 minutes) with St Gallen (Sfr28, 1½ hours).

LAKE CONSTANCE

Before package holidays began carrying large numbers of locals and their beach towels abroad in the '70s and '80s, Lake Constance (Bodensee) was the German Mediterranean. The 'Swabian Sea', as it's nicknamed, is still a great place to wind down for a few days and enjoy the water, the pretty countryside and enchanting locations.

Orientation

Switzerland shares Lake Constance with Germany and Austria.

Konstanz is the largest town on the lake and sits on the end of the peninsula between the two western arms, the Überlingersee and the Untersee. Konstanz proper is in Germany but adjoining Kreuzlingen is Swiss and they are part of the same conurbation.

Information

DISCOUNT CARDS

The **Bodensee Erlebniskarte** (www.bodensee -erlebniskarte.de; 3/7/14 days €69/89/121) is sold from March to October. In its most expensive version, it entitles the holder to free unlimited ferry travel, entrance to many museums, including the Zeppelin Museum in Friedrichshafen, a return journey up the

> **ROLLING AROUND THURGAU**
>
> Much of the canton of Thurgau is nice and flat, especially where it flanks Lake Constance. This makes it ideal for roller-blading, and the canton has gone to some lengths to accommodate enthusiasts. For details of three trails of between 30km and 52km, check out www.thurgau-tourismus .ch and click on Skater's Paradise.

Säntisbahn (p291), walking tours in St Gallen and more.

MONEY

Most shops, restaurants and other businesses on either side of the lake accept both euros and Swiss francs.

Getting There & Away

Ryanair (www.ryanair.com) flies from London Stansted, Liverpool and Dublin to **Friedrichshafen Airport** (www.fly-away.de) in Germany. Friedrichshafen is connected by (car) ferry to Romanshorn on the Swiss side.

Good rail services link Zürich to Konstanz. From Germany, they come south from Munich. Trains from Austria come via Bregenz and enter Switzerland at St Margrethen.

Getting Around

Various ferry companies, including Switzerland's **SBS Schifffart** (☎ 071 466 78 88; www.sbsag.ch), Austria's **Vorarlberg Lines** (☎ +43 5574 42868; www .bodenseeschifffahrt.at) and Germany's **BSB** (☎ +49 7531 3640 389; www.bsb-online.com), travel across, along and around the lake from early March to late October, with the more-frequent services starting in late May. A Swiss Pass is valid only on the Swiss side of the lake.

Trains tend to be the easiest way to get around on the Swiss side, buses on the German bank. The B31 road hugs the north shore, but can get busy. On the south shore, the N13 shadows the train line around the lake.

A 270km bike track encircles the lake and is well signposted. Most train stations in the region rent out bikes (p363).

KONSTANZ

☎ +49 7531 / pop 81,900 / elevation 397m
Konstanz (Constance) is the cosmopolitan hub of the Bodensee and one in seven inhabitants –

affectionately known as *Seehasen* (sea hares) – is a student at the university.

The **tourist office** (☎ 133 030; www.konstanz.de /tourismus; Bahnhofplatz 13; ⏰ 9am-6.30pm Mon-Fri, 9am-4pm Sat, 10am-1pm Sun Apr-Oct, 9.30am-12.30pm & 2-6pm Mon-Fri Nov-Mar) is just north of the main train station exit.

Konstanz' moment of glory came in 1414–18, when the Council of Konstanz convened here to elect a single pope and tried, unsuccessfully, to heal the schism in the Catholic Church. That council convened inside the enormous grey **Münster Unserer Lieben Frau** (Cathedral of Our Beloved Lady), which showcases various architectural styles from 1052 to 1856. In the 9th- to 10th-century crypt are four gold plates from the outside wall of the one-time choir stalls. The Gothic **bell tower** (⏰ 10am-5pm Mon-Sat, 12.30-5.30pm Sun) can be climbed for vertiginous views.

Stretching north from the cathedral to the Rhine is the old quarter of **Niederburg**, with lots of tight winding alleys.

Konstanz has several **museums**, but its most astonishing attraction is an island a little out of the centre, reached by ferry or bus 4 from the train station. **Insel Mainau** (☎ 303 0; www .mainau.de; adult/child/student Apr-Oct €14.90/free/8, adult/child/student Nov-Mar €6.50/free/3.20; ⏰ sunrise to sunset) is an island landscaped with 45 hectares of splendid gardens, including a tropical garden, an Italian garden, a butterfly enclosure and a palm house (closed winter). It can get crowded in summer. You can take bikes.

Sleeping & Eating

DJH hostel (☎ 322 60; www.jugendherberge-konstanz .de; Zur Allmannshöhe 16; dm under/over 27yr €21.90/24.90; ⏰ Mar-Oct) Although located in a converted water tower, this hostel's rooms are fairly bland, if spick and span. Catch bus 4 from the train station to Jugendherberge.

Barbarossa (☎ 128 990; www.barbarossa-hotel.com; Obermarkt 8-12; s €50-70, d €90-120) With its three categories of rooms, this labyrinthine hotel in the heart of the Old Town caters for most budgets and tastes. Documents suggest there has been a building on this spot since the early 15th century. The cheaper rooms are modern and simple; the costlier ones are more atmospheric. The hotel also offers elegant dining (mains €12 to €25, set meal €32).

** our pick** **Stephanskeller** (☎ 691 818; www .stephanskeller.com; Stephansplatz 41; mains €10-12) For those on a budget, this warm cellar is a great

option. Located beside the church of the same name, this noisy, old-fashioned diner and tavern has a broad menu, but the house speciality is a series of meat and veg mixes sizzled up in a frying pan.

KREUZLINGEN
pop 18,300 / elevation 404m

Kreuzlingen, in the Swiss canton of Thurgau, is little more than an appendage to Konstanz and is not as attractive as the larger town. There's a good **SYHA hostel** (☎ 071 688 26 63; www.youthhostel.ch/kreuzlingen; Promenadenstrasse 7; dm Sfr29.30; ⏰ Mar-Nov), but otherwise the most sensible thing is to change trains at Kreuzlingen station and head straight to Konstanz (Sfr3, three minutes); there is no passport control (unlike during WWII, when this border post was used in the exchange of prisoners and the wounded). Should you need more details, try the **tourist information counter** (☎ 071 672 38 40; www.kreuzlingen-tourismus.ch; Sonnenstrasse 4; ⏰ 9.30am-noon & 1.30-5pm Mon-Fri). Direct trains run every 30 minutes between Kreuzlingen and Schaffhausen (Sfr16.80, 55 minutes).

The lakeside road between Kreuzlingen and Stein am Rhein (p283) is dotted with attractive Thurgau villages, such as **Gottlieben**, **Steckborn** and **Berlingen**. Near the latter is **Schloss Arenenberg** (☎ 071 663 32 60; www.napoleon museum.tg.ch; Salenstein; adult/under 6yr/6-16yr/senior & student Sfr10/free/5/8; ⏰ 1-5pm Mon, 10am-5pm Tue-Sun mid-Apr–mid-Oct, 10am-5pm Tue-Sun mid-Jan–mid-Apr & mid-Oct–mid-Dec), where France's Napoleon III grew up.

FRIEDRICHSHAFEN
☎ +49 7541 / pop 58,300 / elevation 400m

Friedrichshafen, in Germany, will forever be associated with the Zeppelin, the early cigar-shaped craft of the skies. The first of Graf (Duke) Zeppelin's airships made its inaugural flight over Lake Constance in 1900: these rigid-framed 'blimps' have been resurrected here as a tourist attraction. The town itself is otherwise hardly bubbling over with charm.

The **tourist office** (☎ 19412, 24hr hotel booking 30010; www.friedrichshafen.info; Bahnhofplatz 2; ⏰ 9am-6pm Mon-Fri, 9am-1pm Sat May-Sep, 9am-noon & 2-5pm Mon-Thu, 9am-noon Fri Apr & Oct, 9am-noon & 2-4pm Mon-Thu, 9am-noon Fri Nov-Mar) is just outside the Friedrichshafen Stadt train station.

The **Zeppelin Museum** (☎ 38010; www.zeppelin -museum.de; Seestrasse 22; adult/student & child/senior €7.50/3/6.50; ⏰ 9am-5pm daily Jul-Sep, 9am-5pm Tue-Sun

May, Jun & Oct, 10am-5pm Tue-Sun Nov-Apr), wedged between the Old Town and the ferry docks, traces the history of this majestic, but ill-fated, means of air transport, including a reconstruction of part of the *Hindenburg*, which went down in history for all the wrong reasons, collapsing in flames on arrival in New Jersey after a trans-Atlantic flight from Frankfurt in 1937, killing 36 crew and passengers.

Deutsche Zeppelin Reederei (☎ 59000; www.zeppelin flug.de; 30min/1hr/2hr from €200/335/715; ☼ Apr-Nov) offers sightseeing Zeppelin flights over Lake Constance or Friedrichshafen, and as far inland as Schaffhausen and the Rheinfall.

Two BOB trains an hour (€1.70, 15 minutes) run from the **airport** (www.fly-away.de) to Friedrichshafen Stadt and Friedrichshafen Hafen, where you'll find the Zeppelin Museum and ferries. A **car ferry** (☎ 9238 389; www.bsb-online.com; adult/child/family €7/3.50/25.40, car €16) runs between Friedrichshafen and Romanshorn hourly from at least 8.30am to 5.30pm.

ROMANSHORN & ARBON

Romanshorn pop 9230 / elevation 406m
Arbon pop 13,070 / elevation 398m

Despite its one prominent church spire, **Romanshorn** is of minimal sightseeing interest – little more than a staging point as you go to/ from Friedrichshafen on the ferry.

The medieval town centre of **Arbon**, 8km southeast, is much prettier, with its half-timbered houses and ancient chapels. It's about a 1km walk from the train station to the **tourist office** (☎ 071 440 13 80; www.arbon.ch; Schmiedgasse 5; ☼ 9-11.30am & 2-6pm Mon-Fri, plus 9-11.30am Sat mid-Jun–Aug) in the historic centre, watched over by its 16th-century castle, **Schloss Arbon**. The castle's **Historisches Museum** (History Museum; ☎ 071 446 60 10; Alemannenstrasse 4; adult/child Sfr4/2; ☼ 2-5pm May-Sep, Sun only Mar-Apr & Oct-Nov) is worth a visit. On one lane, centuries-old houses bear frescos depicting trades of yore.

There's a good range of places to stay, from the cheerful **Hotel Altstadt** (☎ 071 446 12 93; www.altstadttarbon.ch; Schäfligasse 4; d Sfr120, s/d without bathroom Sfr57/96). The more-upmarket **Gasthof Frohsinn** (☎ 071 447 84 84; www.frohsinn -arbon.ch; Romanshornerstrasse 15; s/d Sfr120/180) is set in a pretty partly timbered house. Most hotels have their own restaurants and the Frohsinn has its own microbrewery.

Romanshorn and Arbon are on the train line between Zürich and Rorschach.

RORSCHACH

pop 8460 / elevation 398m

Nothing to do with the psychiatric ink-blot tests of the same name, the quiet waterfront resort of Rorschach is backed by a wooded hill. Although something of a faded beauty, the town has some fine 16th- to 18th-century houses with oriel windows.

There are three train stations: Rorschach Stadt, Rorschach Hafen and Rorschach Hauptbahnhof. If coming from St Gallen, alight at Rorschach Stadt station (Sfr6.20, 15 to 20 minutes) and walk 500m northeast through the centre to Rorschach Hafen station (on the line from Arbon and Schaffhausen), the nearby **tourist office** (☎ 071 841 70 34; www.tourist -rorschach.ch; Hauptstrasse 63; ☼ 8.30-noon & 1.30-6pm Mon-Fri year-round, plus 10am-4pm Sat May–mid-Sep) and the cogwheel train (Bergbahn Rorschach-Heiden) that leaves to the health resort of **Heiden**.

Rorschach Hafen station is handily located on Haupstrasse, in the heart of the Old Town. Walk left (east) from the station to see some fine oriel windows, particularly at Nos 33, 31 and the town hall, No 29. There are more on Mariabergstrasse. Out on the lake is the 19th-century **Badhütte** (Bathing Hut), attached to land by a little covered bridge, which is a pleasant place for a drink.

Walk right from the train station to find the main hotels, including the modest **Hotel Rössli** (☎ 071 844 68 68; www.hotel-roessli.ch; Hauptstrasse 88; s/d from Sfr85/140), which offers perfectly comfortable rooms and an acceptable restaurant.

ourpick Schloss Wartegg (☎ 071 858 62 62; http:// wartegg.ch; Rorschacherberg; s Sfr145-155, d Sfr220-270; ⓟ ⊠) For an exceptional escape, book into this magnificent fantasy palace a 10-minute drive from central Rorschach on the hillside above town. This 16th-century former royal Austrian castle, set in leafy grounds with towering sequoias, underwent several overhauls before being converted into a sleek hotel in 1999.

BREGENZ

☎ +43 5574 / pop 27,300 / elevation 405m

Bregenz is an untidy-looking, provincial Austrian capital at its busiest during the spectacular annual **Bregenz Festival** (☎ 407-0; www .bregenzerfestspiele.com; ☼ Aug), when opera, rock and classical music are performed on a vast water-borne stage.

There are spectacular views and **hiking** atop the nearby Pfänder mountain (1064m).

A **cable car** (☎ 42 16 00; www.pfaenderbahn.at; adult/
child/senior return €10.40/5.20/9.40; ☻ 8am-7pm, closed 2
weeks in Nov) carries you up and back.

The **tourist office** (☎ 495 90; www.bregenz.ws;
Rathausstrasse 35a; ☻ 8.30am-6pm Mon-Fri & 9am-noon
Sat) is just back from the waterfront in the
Old Town.

A huddle of cobbled streets heading inland around and beyond Kaiserstrasse reward a little wandering, but there's little
specific to see.

Hotels are in good supply (but book
ahead during the festival). **Pension Sonne**
(☎ 425 72; www.bbn.at/sonne; Kaiserstrasse 8; d €35-55)
is a straight-up-and-down, no-nonsense digs
in the heart of town.

For a slap-up meal in traditional Austrian
style, head for the delightfully timeless, half-
timbered **Gaststätte Zum Goldenen Hirschen**
(☎ 428 15; Kirchstrasse 8, mains €9-28; ☻ Wed-Mon).
Every imaginable cut of beef is available
here in a long list of options known as
Rindfleischtöpfli (beef pots).

ST GALLEN & APPENZELL CANTONS

The cultural high point of a journey around
the extreme northeast of the country is a
visit to St Gallen's legendary abbey, with its
extraordinary rococo library. To explore the
surrounding territory is to dive into a deeply
Germanic, rural world.

The canton of St Gallen stretches
from Zürich in the west to Austria and
Liechtenstein in the east. To the north
it joins with Thurgau and touches Lake
Constance. To the southwest it joins Glarus
canton (aka Glarnerland) and Graubünden
to the south. The two half-cantons of
Appenzell (Innerrhoden and Ausserrhoden),
huddle together within St Gallen.

The Appenzellers are the butt of many a
cruel joke by their fellow Swiss, a little like
Tasmanians in Australia or Newfoundlanders
in Canada. As Swiss Germans say,
Appenzellers *hätte ä langi Laitig* (have a very
long cable): it takes a while after you tug for
them to get the message.

There is no denying that these cantons are
rooted in tradition. Innerrhoden still holds a
yearly open-air parliament and didn't permit
women to vote until 1991.

Such devotion to rural tradition has an
upside. Locals go to great lengths to preserve
their heritage and this area of impossibly
green valleys, thick forests and impressive
mountains is dotted with beautiful, timeless
villages.

These cantons are criss-crossed by endless
hiking, cycling and mountain-biking trails.

ST GALLEN
pop 70,380 / elevation 670m
St Gallen's history as the 'writing room of
Europe' is evident in its principal attraction
today: the rococo library of its huge Catholic
abbey, which remains its central focus.

The Old Town forms an attractive core,
perfect for wandering, while the outdoor 'City
Lounge' provides a modern counterpoint.

Orientation
The pedestrian-only *Altstadt*, containing most
major sights, is a 10-minute walk east of the
train station.

Information
Main post office (Bahnhofplatz 5; ☻ 7am-7.30pm
Mon-Wed & Fri, to 8pm Thu, 7am-4pm Sat, 3-6pm Sun)
Tourist office (☎ 071 227 37 37; www.stgallen-bodensee
.ch; Bahnhofplatz 1a; ☻ 9am-6pm Mon-Fri, 9am-3pm Sat
May-Oct, 9am-6pm Mon-Fri, 10am-1pm Sat Nov-Apr). There's
another self-service information point, where you can pick
up brochures, in the Chocolaterie (p290).

Sights
Many houses of Old St Gallen boast elabo-
rate *Erker*, especially around Gallusplatz,
Spisergasse, Schmiedgasse and Kugelgasse.
The city's tourism folk have counted them all
up and reckon there are 111 oriel windows!
Some bear the most extraordinary timber

THE LEGEND OF ST GALLEN

St Gallen all began with a bush, a bear and
an Irish monk, who should have watched
where he was going. In AD 612, the tale
goes, itinerant Gallus fell into a briar and
considered the stumble a calling from God.
After a fortuitous encounter with a bear, in
which he persuaded it to bring him a log,
take some bread in return and leave him in
peace, he used the log to begin building a
hermitage that would one day morph into
St Gallen's cathedral.

NORTHEASTERN SWITZERLAND

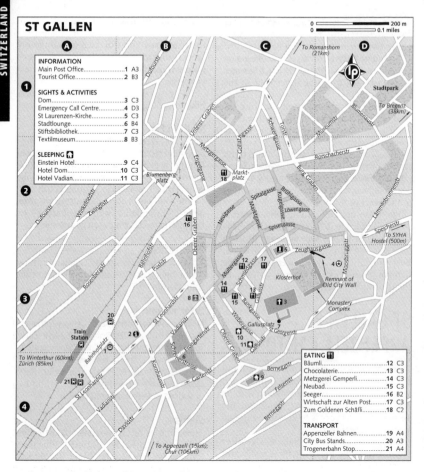

ST GALLEN

0   200 m
0   0.1 miles

INFORMATION
Main Post Office...................1 A3
Tourist Office........................2 B3

SIGHTS & ACTIVITIES
Dom..3 C3
Emergency Call Centre.............4 D3
St Laurenzen-Kirche.................5 C3
Stadtlounge............................6 B4
Stiftsbibliothek......................7 C3
Textilmuseum.........................8 B3

SLEEPING
Einstein Hotel.........................9 C4
Hotel Dom.............................10 C3
Hotel Vadian.........................11 C3

EATING
Bäumli..................................12 C3
Chocolaterie.........................13 C3
Metzgerei Gemperli...............14 C3
Neubad.................................15 C3
Seeger..................................16 B2
Wirtschaft zur Alten Post........17 C3
Zum Goldenen Schäfli.............18 C2

TRANSPORT
Appenzeller Bahnen...............19 A4
City Bus Stands.....................20 A3
Trogenerbahn Stop................21 A4

sculptures – a reflection of the wealth of their one-time owners, mostly textile barons.

STIFTSBIBLIOTHEK & CATHEDRAL

St Gallen's 16th-century **Stiftsbibliothek** (abbey library; ☎ 071 227 34 16; www.stiftsbibliothek.ch; Klosterhof 6d; adult/child/student & senior Sfr7/free/5; ☑ 10am-5pm Mon-Sat, to 4pm Sun) is one of the world's oldest libraries and the finest example of rococo architecture in Switzerland. Along with the rest of the monastery complex surrounding it, the library forms a Unesco World Heritage Site.

Filled with priceless books and manuscripts painstakingly handwritten by monks during the Middle Ages, it's a dimly lit confection of ceiling frescos, stucco, cherubs and parquetry.

Only 30,000 of the total 150,000 volumes are in the library at any one time, and only a handful in display cases, arranged into special exhibitions. If there's a tour guide in the library at the time, you might see the monks' filing system, hidden in the wall panels.

Kids are enthralled by the 2700-year-old mummified corpse in the far right corner.

The twin-towered **Dom** (cathedral; ☑ 9am-6pm Mon, Tue, Thu & Fri, 10am-6pm Wed, 9am-4pm Sat, noon-5.30pm Sun, closed during services) is only slightly less ornate than its library, with dark and stormy frescos and aqua-green stucco embellishments. Oddly, entry is by two modest doors on the north flank – there is no door in the main facade, which is actually the cathedral's apse! Concerts are sometimes held – consult www.kirchenmusik.ch. Concerts are also frequently held in the 16th-century (but largely rebuilt in 1850–54) Protestant neo-Gothic **St Laurenzen-Kirche**, north across Zeughausgasse from the cathedral. There are great views from its **tower** (9.30-11.30am & 2-4pm Apr-Oct).

The cantonal police **emergency call centre** on Moosbruggstrasse presents a daring, modern contrast to its medieval surroundings. Designed by Spanish architect Santiago Calatrava, it resembles a menacing metallic bug.

STADTLOUNGE

Quite astonishingly, part of historic St Gallen is covered by a rubberised red tennis-court coating, in place since 2005. This 'carpet' covers Gartenstrasse, Schreinerstrasse and Vadianstrasse, as well as a range of in-situ outdoor-furniture-like chairs, sofas, tables and even a car. This zany art installation project by Pipilotti Rist and Carlos Martínez goes by the name of **Stadtlounge** (City Lounge; www.stadtlounge.ch) and is intended as an 'outdoor living room', where people are encouraged to linger and chat.

TEXTILMUSEUM

St Gallen has long been an important hub of the Swiss textile industry, and the **Textilmuseum** (071 222 17 44; www.textilmuseum.ch; Vadianstrasse 2; adult/child/student Sfr12/free/7; 10am-5pm) is the most interesting of the town's several museums (which cover everything from beer to 18th-century music boxes). It traces the town's history of cloth making.

Festivals & Events

The city has a busy calendar, but one of the key events is the **St Galler Festspiele**, a two-week outdoor opera season (from about 20 June to the end of the first week of July), held in the square behind the cathedral.

Sleeping

St Gallen is a business town, and frequent exhibitions and conferences can make beds scarce and prices high.

SYHA Hostel (071 245 47 77; www.youthhostel .ch/st.gallen; Jüchstrasse 25; dm Sfr30.50, s/d/q per person Sfr58/43/35; reception 7.30-10am & 5-10pm, closed mid-Dec–Feb) This modern hillside hostel, set in leafy grounds with good views and outdoor eating areas, is a 15-minute walk from the Old Town (or take the Trogenerbahn from outside the

train station to 'Schülerhaus', Sfr3). Rooms are simple, bare brick affairs.

Hotel Vadian (071 228 18 78; www.hotel-vadian.com; Gallusstrasse 36; s/d without bathroom from Sfr80/120, with bathroom Sfr115/190) You can't get much closer to the heart of St Gallen at these prices. The hotel was given an overhaul in 2006 and varied modern rooms are in perfect nick. Some have nice touches, like ceiling beams.

Hotel Dom (071 227 71 71; www.hoteldom.ch; Webergasse 22; s/d Sfr90/120, with bathroom Sfr155/205; P) An almost startlingly modern hotel has been plonked in the middle of the Old Town. Rooms have clean lines, are comfortable, and come with different budgets in mind. The staff are all people with minor disabilities, who put a lot of loving care into their work – including the hotel art. Rooms have wi-fi.

Einstein Hotel (071 227 55 55; www.einstein.ch; Berneggstrasse 2; s/d from Sfr300/350; P) Even demanding rich Russians seem mollified by the levels of service and luxury at St Gallen's premier hotel. One wing contains the slightly older standard rooms. The superior rooms are brighter, airier, more hi-tech and spacious. Silk curtains, cherry-wood furnishings and woollen throw rugs are among the touches of comfort in rooms.

Eating
FIRST-FLOOR RESTAURANTS

St Gallen is noted for its *Erststock-Beizli*, traditional taverns situated on the 1st floor of half-timbered houses.

Wirtschaft zur Alten Post (071 222 66 01; Gallusstrasse 4; mains Sfr20-39; Tue-Sat) Things are a little ritzy at this upmarket but historical *Beizl*, where Swiss dishes are complemented with more-original creations such as the *Fischvariation in Limonenöl gebraten auf Kürbisrisotto mit Gartengemüse* (a selection of fish baked in lemon oil on a bed of pumpkin rice and mixed vegetables).

Bäumli (071 222 11 74; Schmiedgasse 18; mains Sfr22-47; Tue-Sat Aug-Jun) A late-medieval building houses a timeless eatery that showcases all the typical 1st-floor specialities, from bratwurst with fried onions (Sfr12.80) to lamb cutlets, Wiener schnitzel, *Cordon bleus* (pork schnitzel stuffed with ham and cheese), *Geschnetzeltes* (a sliced pork or veal dish) and *Mostbröggli* (smoked beef jerky).

Zum Goldenen Schäfli (071 223 27 27; Metzgergasse 5; mains Sfr25-43; closed Sun in summer;) This delightfully cosy 1st-floor restaurant has a distinctly sloping floor and eye-catching, sloping aperitif glasses to match. The glasses, silverware and flowers crowd the white tablecloths and a tiled medieval oven sits in the corner.

OTHER CUISINE

Inexpensive restaurants are strung out along Marktplatz. St Gallen is also known for its OLMA-Bratwurst, served plain in a *Bürli* (bun). Sausage stands are ubiquitous, but the best outlet is at **Metzgerei Gemperli** (cnr Schmiedgasse & Webergasse; sausages from Sfr6).

our pick **Neubad** (☎ 071 222 86 83; www.restaurant -neubad.ch; Bankgasse 6; mains Sfr18.50-30.50; ☺ Mon-Fri) A crisp but welcoming interior draws you in for some classic local cooking. Especially tempting are the set lunch menu options (10 in all, from Sfr21.50 to Sfr36.50), including classics like *St Galler Bratwurst vom Metzger Schmid mit Zwiebelsauce und Rösti* (a fat veal sausage in onion sauce with rösti).

Chocolaterie (☎ 071 222 57 70; Gallusstrasse 20; ☺ 1-6.30pm Mon, 9am-6.30pm Tue-Fri, 9am-5pm Sat) For exquisite chocolate in liquid and solid forms, this place opposite the cathedral is surely the devil's work.

Getting There & Away

It's a short train or bus ride to/from Romanshorn (Sfr10.80, 25 minutes). There are also regular trains (only four of them direct) to Bregenz in Austria (Sfr19), Chur (Sfr32, 1½ hours) and Zürich (Sfr28, 65 minutes via Winterthur).

By car, the main link is the A1 freeway, which runs from Zürich and Winterthur to the Austrian border.

Getting Around

Single journeys on the local city buses cost Sfr2.50, or Sfr9 for a day pass. Individual bus tickets are not valid on the Trogenerbahn, where the fare depends upon distance, but the general day passes *are* valid (as far as Rank station).

ST GALLEN TO APPENZELL

The most picturesque route to Appenzell from St Gallen takes you east on a winding country road through high mountain pastures and the village of **Trogen**. The scenery is lovely and, about 5km east of Trogen, starts a steep drop down to the Rhine valley plains town of **Altstätten**. From there, wind back 15km westwards via Gais to reach Appenzell.

APPENZELL

pop 5710 / elevation 785m

Appenzell is a feast for both the eyes and the stomach. Behind the gaily decorative pastel-coloured facades of its traditional buildings lie cafés, *confiseries* (sweets and cake shops), cheese shops, delicatessens, butchers and restaurants offering local specialities. It's absolutely perfect for a long lunch and a lazy wander.

Orientation & Information

The train station (with money-exchange facilities and bike rental) is 400m from the centre. Take the exit marked 'Ortszentrum' and continue north to Hauptgasse. The Landsgemeindeplatz is to your left (west); to your right (east), 100m or so along, is the **tourist office** (☎ 071 788 96 41; www.appenzell.ch; Hauptgasse 4; ☺ 9am-noon & 1.30-6pm Mon-Fri, 10am-noon & 2-5pm Sat & Sun Apr-Oct, 9am-noon & 2-5pm Mon-Fri, 2-5pm Sat & Sun Nov-Mar).

People who stay three days or longer in the region are eligible for the free Appenzeller Ferienkarte, which offers transport, sporting and museum discounts; ask at the tourist office.

Sights & Activities

Appenzell's main focus is the **Landsgemeindeplatz**, the square where the open-air parliament takes place on the last Sunday of every April, with locals wearing traditional dress and voting (in the case of the men, by raising a short dagger). It's one of the most picturesque spots in town, with elaborately painted hotels and restaurants around its edges.

The buildings along Hauptgasse are also admirable. The village **church** has gold and silver figures flanking a baroque altar. Nearby, beside the tourist office, is the **Appenzell Museum** (adult/student Sfr6/4; ☺ closed Mon in winter), which will fill you in on traditional customs – although you'll learn more at the museum in Stein (p292).

On the other side of the train station from the town, the **Museum Liner** (☎ 071 788 18 00; www .museumliner.ch; Unterrainstrasse 5; adult/concession Sfr9/6; ☺ 10am-noon & 2-5pm Tue-Fri, 11am-5pm Sat & Sun Apr-Oct; 2-5pm Tue-Fri, 11am-5pm Sat & Sun Nov-Mar) is Appenzell's contemporary art gallery. The building (whose metallic sheen gives it the appearance, in profile, of a saw) is more interesting than the collection, dedicated to local artists Carl August Liner and his son Carl Walter.

SAY CHEESE

Appenzell is known for its **strong-smelling cheeses** (www.appenzeller.ch). They make excellent fondues when mixed with fresh herbs and alcohol, and restaurants also dish them up in the form of *Käseschnitte/Chässchnitte* (cheese on toast), *Chäshörnli* (irregularly formed cheese dumplings with fried onions) or *Chäsmageroone* (macaroni cheese).

An Appenzell *Chäsflade* is a savoury cheese tart with coriander, and a *Chäshappech* is a pancake made with cheese, flour, milk, beer and eggs, and fried in oil. With Raclette also popular, vegans might want to drown their sorrows in *Saurer Most* (local cider) or *Alpenbitter*, a herbal alcoholic drink à la Jägermeister.

Local menus also feature lots of rösti, pork cutlets, veal, calf's liver and rabbit, but change regularly to accommodate seasonal specialities (eg venison and pumpkin in autumn). Appenzell produces a wide range of its own confectionery.

Many hiking trails in the area around Appenzell are lined with mountain restaurants. One unusual trail is the **Barefoot Path** from Appenzell to Gonten, where you really don't need shoes. In Gontenbad there's the **Natur-Moorbad** (natural moor bath; ☎ 071 795 31 23; www.naturmoorbad.ch; Gontenbad, Appenzellerland), dating to 1740, where you can dip in mud-laden water from the moors (Sfr20) to help with stress or skin conditions (adding in nettles, ferns and other plants), or luxuriate in a pampering rose bath (Sfr80 for two).

Sleeping & Eating

Many of the best restaurants are in the hotels, most of which are within a few minutes' walk of one another. Most restaurants charge roughly Sfr12 to Sfr14 for *Käseschnitte* (cheese on toast) and other snacks, and Sfr20 to Sfr40 for main courses.

Gasthaus Hof (☎ 071 787 40 30; www.gasthaus-hof.ch; Engelgasse 4; s/d/tr/q Sfr85/130/180/220) Just off Landsgemeindeplatz, this cheap-sleep option has simple but spacious rooms with timber-clad walls. The smoky old-school restaurant comes with plenty of local bonhomie.

Hotel Appenzell (☎ 071 788 15 15; www.hotel-appenzell.ch; Landsgemeindeplatz; s/d Sfr130/220, discounts for long stays; ✗) With its broad, brightly decorated facade, this typical Appenzeller building houses generously sized rooms with wooden beds. Decor combines gentle pinks and blues and frilly lace on the picture windows. The restaurant offers a wide-ranging seasonal menu that includes vegetarian dishes.

Hotel Freudenberg (☎ 071 787 12 40; Riedstrasse 57; ✓ Tue-Mon Dec-Oct) Ten minutes' walk up the hill from the train station, in the opposite direction from the town, this family-run restaurant (with rooms costing Sfr100/170 for a single/double) has a terrace with panoramic views of Appenzell and around.

Getting There & Away

From St Gallen, the narrow-gauge train to Appenzell (Sfr10.80, 50 minutes) leaves from the front and to the right of the main train station. There are two routes, so you can go back a different way. Departures from St Gallen are approximately every half-hour, via Gais or Herisau (where you must occasionally change trains).

SÄNTIS

Small in Swiss terms, the jagged Säntis peak (2503m) is the highest in this part of Switzerland. It offers a marvellous panorama encompassing Bodensee, Zürichsee, the Alps and the Vorarlberg Mountains. Take the train from Appenzell to Urnäsch and transfer to the bus (approximately hourly) to Schwägalp (total fare Sfr16). From Schwägalp, the cable car, **Säntisbahn** (☎ 071 365 65 65; www.saentisbahn.ch; one-way/return Sfr27/38; ✓ 7.30am-6pm Jun–mid-Oct, 8.30am-5pm mid-Oct–May) ascends to the summit every 30 minutes.

From Säntis, you can walk along the ridge to the neighbouring peak of Ebenalp (1640m) in about 3½ hours. At Wildkirchli on Ebenalp there are prehistoric caves showing traces of Stone Age habitation.

The descent to Seealpsee on foot takes 1½ hours. Alternatively, a **cable car** (☎ 071 799 12 12; www.ebenalp.ch, in German; one-way/return in summer Sfr18/25, half-/full day in winter Sfr25/33) runs between the summit and Wasserauen approximately every 30 minutes. Wasserauen and Appenzell are connected by rail (Sfr4, 10 minutes).

APPENZELL TO TOGGENBURG

Two driving routes west to the Toggenburg mountain range suggest themselves from Appenzell.

The first leads initially 15km northwest towards Herisau, the capital of Appenzell Ausserrhoden. Don't race straight there, however. At Hundwil, turn north a few kilometres to **Stein**, where you can visit its **Volkskunde Museum** (Folklore Museum; ☎ 071 368 50 56; www .appenzeller-museum-stein.ch; adult/child/student Sfr7/3.50/6; 🕙 10am-5pm Tue-Sat), which provides a comprehensive rundown on traditional Appenzell life and the occasional weaving demonstration. Cheese-lovers could pop into the nearby **Appenzeller Schaukäserie** (Appenzell Showcase Cheese Dairy; ☎ 071 368 50 70; www.showcheese.ch; admission free; 🕙 8.30am-6.30pm May-Oct, to 5.30pm Nov-Apr), which runs through the manufacturing process, explaining how cheeses like the famous Räss get their sweaty-socks smell (a coating of herbs and brine). Not much goes on after 2pm. Buses run directly to Stein from St Gallen. From Appenzell, you must first take a train to Herisau and pick up a bus.

Herisau (population 15,200) is a city that grew on the basis of its textile wealth. Aside from attractive houses around the centre (among them a handful of timber ones), and a museum in the Altes Rathaus (Old Town Hall), there's not much to hold you up. You may well just pass through on your way elsewhere especially to change train or bus.

From Herisau, you could move north 4km to Gossau and then west. About 2km before Flawil, take the turn-off for **Burgau**. This 1000-year-old hamlet hides among its timber and shingle houses a remarkable decorated, half-timbered house that long served as Burgau's town hall. A pretty minor route across hill and dale leads south via rural centres like Degersheim to **St Peterzell**. Here, head west 9km along an equally picturesque route for **Lichtensteig**, a curious medieval town whose cobbled lanes and central, porticoed main street are lined by tall, traditional houses, a 15th-century town hall and a local museum. From Appenzell, trains via St Gallen or Herisau to Lichtensteig take about 1½ hours (Sfr19).

The second route is shorter but just as pretty. Head out of town for Gonten. This narrow country road wiggles its way west through picture-postcard country via the villages of Urnäsch and Hemberg to Wattwil, just south of Lichtensteig.

The N16 road heads southeast from Wattwil along the valley lining the south flank of the **Toggenburg** mountain range. One kilometre short of the small ski resort of **Wildhaus**, the modest timber house where Huldrych Zwingli (p29) was born stands preserved (it is thought to be one of the oldest such houses in the country) in **Lisighaus** (signposted).

Just before entering Buchs, you'd miss **Werdenberg** if you blinked. That would be a shame! Founded in 1289, it is said to be the oldest settlement of timber houses in Switzerland. This huddle of some 40-odd houses lies between an oversized pond and a grapevine-covered hill topped by the Werdenberg **Schloss** (adult/under 6yr/6-16yr/student Sfr4/free/2/3; 🕙 9.30am-5pm Tue-Sun Apr-Oct). From St Gallen, it takes about an hour by train to Buchs and then local bus (Sfr19 in total). You can enter Schaan in Liechtenstein (p341) from Buchs by local bus.

Backpackers with a taste for the bizarre could head 6km south of Buchs to **Sevelen**, where a nuclear civil-defence bunker has been converted into a cheap sleep, **Null Stern Hotel** (Zero Star Hotel; www.null-stern-hotel.ch). The opening of this windowless (look at the monitors instead) subterranean lodgings is planned for January 2009, pending local government approval. Two artists have let their imaginations rip, turning the collective shower into a fountain. They already have their eyes on other bunkers up and down the country.

WALENSEE

Walensee is a long finger of a lake along the A3 freeway (and railway line) that connects Zürich with Graubünden. Along its north flank rises the abrupt stone wall of the Churfirsten mountains, occasionally interrupted by a coastal hamlet or upland pasture and, about halfway along the lakefront, seemingly cracked open by Switzerland's highest waterfall.

From St Gallen, there are roughly equidistant routes to the lake. One takes you southeast via Altstätten to the A13 freeway along the Rhine, which you follow south the length of Liechtenstein to pick up the A3 at Sargans, then head northwest to **Walenstadt**, on the east end of the lake. Otherwise, head for Wattwil via Herisau and Lichtensteig (see above), from where it's 27km south to **Weesen**. Both are also handily located on the A3 freeway from Zürich. By train from Zürich, get off at Ziegelbrücke (Sfr20.60, 45 minutes by direct train), which is a 15-minute walk from central Weesen, or change for trains on to Walenstadt.

Of the two towns, Weesen is smaller and a prettier place to stay, with just one hotel just back from the lake (which has a Geneva-style fountain shooting high into the air): **Parkhotel Schwert** (☎ 055 616 14 74; www.parkhotelschwert.ch; Hauptstrasse 23; s/d Sfr125/190) has a variety of rooms, from wheelchair-adapted to five-bed jobs. They have nice timber floors and all the mod cons. There are a few cheaper places further away from the lake, outside Weesen. The **Hotel Walensee Trattoria** (☎ 055 616 16 04; www.hotel-walensee .ch; Hauptstrasse 27; mains Sfr22-36; ☺ lunch & dinner daily) is no hotel but host to one of the best Italian restaurants this side of the Alps, with excellent and abundant pasta dishes.

A relatively easy hike leads along the north shore from Weesen to Walenstadt (about 6½ hours) or vice versa. The walk takes you along the lake shore, through dense forest, green pastureland and past a smattering of houses.

The highlight of the hike lies about two hours east of Weesen. The **Seerenbachfälle** is a series of three colossal waterfalls thundering down 585m from top to bottom, fuelled by a complex network of underground rivers running through the mountain rock from as far away as the peak of Säntis (p291). The middle waterfall, a 305m drop, is considered the highest in the land.

The closest you can reach by car is **Betlis**, a 30-minute hike away. In upper Betlis, there's a wonderful lodge, the **Landgasthof Paradiesli** (☎ 055 611 11 79; s/d Sfr75/140). A beautiful spot, where the silence is broken by the distant roar of the waterfalls, birdsong and the occasional cowbell, this place offers rustic rooms, a fine garden (not to mention the pet llamas) and views south to the shore and mountains beyond, like the **Mürtschenstock** (2441m) and, to the west, the **Fronalpstock** (2124m), both capped in snow most of the year.

About 1½ hour's walk shy of Walenstadt is **Quinten**, a tiny and pretty settlement with vineyards and a couple of guest houses.

A 6km drive northeast of Weesen leads to the high pasture plateau of **Amden**. It seems like Zeus himself scattered the houses and barns here. There's some nice walking amid the green fields and a bit of snow activity in winter (check out www.amden.ch).

A minor road along the south shore makes for a worthwhile drive. From Weesen, head south to Mollis, from where the road winds up east above the plain. Even before you reach **Filzbach**, you get some wonderful high-up views north over the lake. That story continues as far as **Mühlehorn**, from where the road descends to the lake and **Murg**. Aside from the boat to Quinten (see below), a walking trail leads four hours (15km) south of Murg to the **Murgsee** lakes.

Schiffsbetrieb Walensee (☎ 081 738 12 08; www .walenseeschiff.ch) boats cross regularly between Quinten and Murg. From March to October there are also regular boats between Weesen and Walenstadt, calling in at various spots along the way (including Betlis and Quinten).

About 6km southeast of Walenstadt, the town of **Flums** opens the way to a little Alpine fun. A mountain road winds up westward from Flums to a series of villages and some gentle winter skiing in the area of **Flumserberg** (www.flumserberg.ch). A warm and friendly family-run sleeping option is **Hotel Siesta** (☎ 081 733 00 13; www.hotel-siesta.ch; Tannenboden; s/d from Sfr140/190). Prices drop in summer.

TAMINATAL & SARDONA

The peak of **Sardona** (3056m) is the highest in St Gallen (to be fair, it straddles the cantonal boundary with Glarus). Few foreigners have the pleasure of exploring this Alpine area, spread out along the boundary with Graubünden.

To get there, take one of two minor roads southwest from Bad Ragaz (p308). Both climb rapidly, one passing via Pfäfers and the other via Valens and Vasön. Where they join, you enter the **Taminatal**, a spectacular valley, mixing high pastureland with dense forest (the autumn colours are nearly as vivid as in Maine in the USA).

After 20km you reach the foot of the dam of **Gigerwaldsee** (look out for the restaurant). Another 7km sees you climbing up to the dam and skirting its southern shore through a series of spooky tunnels to reach **St Martin**, a Walser-speaking hamlet. You can stay at **our pick** Restaurant St Martin (☎ 081 306 12 34, 081 723 63 07; dm/s/d Sfr36/70/120; meal Sfr40-50; ☺ May–mid-Oct), the perfect base for a couple of days' majestic walking. An easy trail heads two hours west to **Sardona Alp**. Another hour is needed to reach the simple mountain refuge **Sardona**

TECTONIC COLLISIONS

Since mid-2008, the Sardona tectonic area, at the heart of the Glarus Alps that straddle the cantons of St Gallen, Glarus and Graubünden, has been a Unesco World Heritage Site. It takes in seven peaks above 3000m that clearly show how older rock layers have been pushed up over younger layers in the process of tectonic thrust. A key site for geological study since the 18th century, the Sardona area is rare because of the clarity with which the layers can be distinguished.

Hütte (☎ 081 306 13 88; ◷ daily late Jul–late August, Sat & Sun Jun–late Jul, late Aug–mid-Oct). A nine-hour hike would take you from St Martin past the peak of Piz Sardona and over **Foopass** (2225m) to the village of Elm (below).

GLARUS CANTON

Connected to the centre of the country by the high Klausenpass, this canton (aka Glarnerland) is a little-explored but quite-beautiful pocket of the country. Its northern boundary touches Walensee (p292) and provides much of the Alpine beauty that can be observed from the lake's north shore. It also harbours a handful of stunning secrets of its own. For more information, contact **Glarner Tourismus** (☎ 055 610 21 25; www.glarusnet.ch; Niederurnen).

WALENSEE TO GLARUS

Roads weave their way south from Weesen, at the western end of Walensee, 14km to Glarus, the capital of the eponymous canton. They pass through the twin towns of **Näfels** and **Mollis**, both pleasant to wander about, with intriguing old houses and the occasional cosy eatery.

Glarus (population 5840) itself is a curious affair. Two-thirds destroyed by fire in 1861, it is a graceful 19th-century creation with some fine residential buildings and the occasional typical old timber rural house that survived the flames. It could make a pleasant base. A couple of hotels overlook the park in front of the main train station. **Hotel Stadthof** (☎ 055 640 63 66; www.stadthof.ch; Kirchstrasse 2; s/d Sfr90/140; ✗) is handy to the train station and has 12

rather-plain but clean brightly whitewashed rooms with parquet flooring, some of which look over the park. There's no shortage of eateries in Glarus.

Some trains from Zürich (Sfr24, 55 to 65 minutes) require a change at Rapperswil or Ziegelbrücke (a 15-minute walk from Weesen). From St Gallen (Sfr26, one hour 25 minutes) the trip is longer.

KLÖNTAL

A 12km escape into one of the country's least touched valleys (and back-door route into Schwyz canton), Klöntal, leads west of Glarus to **Klöntaler See**, a mirror-still lake backed on its south side by the sheer walls of the Glärnisch mountains. A couple of majestic waterfalls open up clefts in this massif. At the lake's west end you'll find a camping ground and a couple of hotels. **Hotel Vorauen** (☎ 055 640 13 83; www.vorauen.ch; dm/s/d Sfr45/60/110) has a handful of timber-lined rooms and primary-colour dorms.

The road then climbs steeply away from the lake to pass through **Richisau**, little more than a smattering of farmhouses (and one hotel), to proceed over the cantonal frontier with Schwyz. Occasional buses run between Glarus and Richisau.

SOUTH OF GLARUS

Six kilometres south of central Glarus, the road splits at Schwanden. One branch proceeds down a broad valley to **Elm**, once famous for its slate quarries and still known locally for its mineral water. It is a peaceful centre for hiking in summer and even a little skiing in winter. In this rural backwater, it is hard to believe that only about 20km southeast as the (Alpine) crow flies is the megatrendy snowboarders' resort of Flims (p304). Elm has a couple of hotels and eateries. Buses run from Glarus.

The southwest branch leads to **Linthal** (17km from Glarus), from where you can reach the attractive car-free mountain resort of **Braunwald** (1256m). Braunwald basks in sunshine on the side of a steep hill, gazing at the snow-capped Tödi Mountain (3614m) and overlooking valley pastures below.

The **Braunwaldbahn** (one-way/return Sfr7.60/15.20, Swiss Pass holders free, seven minutes) climbs the hill from the Linthal Braunwaldbahn station. **Braunwald Tourism** (☎ 055 653 65 65; www.braunwald.ch; ◷ 8am-noon &

1.30-5pm Mon-Fri, plus Sat Jul-Aug) is on the top floor of the funicular station.

Braunwald is a hiker's paradise, and you'll find pamphlets at the funicular station outlining several routes, including to the **Oberblegisee**, a well-known local lake. Mountain climbing, skiing and snowboarding are all popular.

Hostel Adrenalin (☎ 079 347 29 05; www.adrenalin.gl; Braunwald; r per person Sfr35, bedding & towels each extra Sfr5, breakfast Sfr8, Sfr20 surcharge for one-night stay in r with shower) Less than two minutes from the funicular station, this hostel is the hub of the young snowboarding and adventure-sports community in winter, with video games, cycle storage and repair, and lots of parties. It consists of 50% singles and doubles, and 50% dorms (up to six beds).

Märchenhotel Bellevue (☎ 055 653 71 71; www .maerchenhotel.ch; r per person from Sfr135, child under 6yr free, various discounts & weekly packages available; P) A converted grand Victorian 'fairy-tale' hotel, the Bellevue combines elegant modern rooms, with saunas and bars for parents and all manner of playthings for children. Adults can relax in the rooftop spa area while kids are looked after in the play area.

Most hotels in Braunwald have their own restaurants.

The **Glarner Sprinter train** (www.glarnersprinter.ch) runs hourly to Linthal Braunwaldbahn from Ziegelbrücke (40 minutes) via Glarus. There are handy connections in Ziegelbrücke to Zürich (Sfr28, 1¾ hours from Linthal Braunwaldbahn). Some of the connections to/from Zürich involve a change of train in Rapperswil instead.

It's a one-hour drive to/from Zürich along the A3.

KLAUSENPASS

A spectacular start or finale to a jaunt around Glarus canton is the breathtaking drive along the N17 road, which takes you over the vertiginous **Klausenpass** (about 10km into Uri canton), an attraction in its own right. Postal buses run between Linthal and Altdorf (p253) from July to mid-October, on some days as many as five times (two to 2½ hours). Bad weather can close the pass in winter.

Graubünden

Ask locals what they love about their canton and they'll gush about how, well, wild it is. In a country blessed with supermodel looks, Graubünden seduces with raw natural beauty. Whether it's wind-battered plateaux in Engadine where clouds roll over big-shouldered mountains, the Rhine gouging out knife-edge ravines near Flims, or the inky-blue tarns and sylvan dewiness of the Swiss National Park, one word says it all: wow.

Don't be fooled by Graubünden's diminutive size on a map. This is topographic origami at its finest. Unfold the rippled landscape to find roads winding to lonesome passes, Engadine's idiosyncratic stone dwellings and effervescent spa towns like Vals. A cultural one-off, Graubünden thrives on contradictions: one minute it's Heidi cheese and fondue in the Alps, the next high culture in Chur and risotto near the Italian border. Linguistically wired to flick from Italian to German to Romansch, locals keep you guessing too.

No matter the season, this is an outdoorsy wonderland of gigantic proportions. Come summer, you can scramble up *vie ferrate* in Unterengadin or trudge through meadows blushing with *Alpenrosen* near Lenzerheide before snoozing in a barn. Autumn invites romps through moorland and sun-dappled larch forests tinged russet and gold.

With the first icy breath of winter, Graubünden becomes the playground of the glitterati. Prince Charles regularly gives the powder a royal pounding in Klosters, celebrities in salopettes flash Prada and snow-white porcelain smiles in St Moritz' swanky bars, while freestylers crank up the slope-side partying in Flims. Escapists, meanwhile, can ponder Davos' mountains with a twilight shuffle through virgin snow to their igloo – magic.

HIGHLIGHTS

- Discovering your inner Eskimo at the igloo village at 2620m in **Davos** (p313).
- Taking a walk on the wild side through the sublime **Swiss National Park** (p315).
- Soaking in the therapeutic waters of Peter Zumthor's quartzite wonder **Therme Vals** (p306).
- Gawping at the weird limestone pinnacles of **Ruin' Aulta** (p305), or thrashing past them white-water rafting on the Vorderrhein.
- Slaloming with celebs and royals on the majestic pistes of **St Moritz** (p317) and **Klosters** (p310).

- POPULATION: 188,800
- AREA: 7106 SQ KM
- LANGUAGES: GERMAN, ROMANSCH & ITALIAN

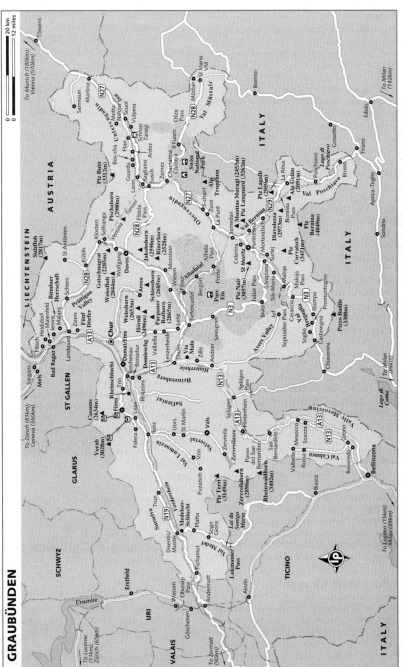

GRAUBÜNDEN

History

The canton's openness to all comers today is a far cry from its inward-looking, diffident past. Throughout the centuries, the people of this rugged area lived largely in isolated, rural pockets, mistrustful of outsiders and, aided by the near impregnable mountain terrain, able to resist most would-be conquerors.

In medieval times the region was known as Rhaetia, and was loosely bound by an association of three leagues *(Drei Bünde)*. The modern name for the canton derives from the *Grauer Bund* (Grey League). Graubünden joined the Swiss Confederation in 1803.

However, much more important was the year 1864, when a hotel owner in St Moritz invited summer guests to stay for the winter – for free. In this way, winter tourism in Graubünden, and later all of Switzerland, was launched.

Orientation & Information

Two major rivers traverse the rugged terrain: the Rhine (with two main source rivers in the canton) and the Inn. The Alps dominate most of the region, which explains why the canton is so sparsely populated. The Julier Pass and Maloja Pass have been key transit routes across the Alps since Roman times.

Chur, the capital, houses the cantonal tourist office, **Graubünden Ferien** (☎ 081 254 24 24; www.graubuenden.ch; Alexanderstrasse 24; ⏰ 8am-noon & 1-5pm Mon-Fri), located in the building marked 'Publicitas', 200m east of the train station.

Language

In the north (around Chur and Davos) German is spoken, in the south Italian, and in between (in St Moritz, Lower Engadine and parts of the Vorderrhein Valley) mostly Romansch. German speakers account for 68% of the Graubünden population, while roughly 11% speak Italian and around 14% Romansch. Other languages make up the remaining 7%.

Getting There & Around

Three main passes lead from northern and western Graubünden into the southeast Engadine region: Julier (open year-round), Albula (summer only) and Flüela (year-round subject to weather). These approximately correspond to three exit points into Italy: Maloja, Bernina and Fuorn/Ofen (all

open year-round). The Oberalp Pass west to Andermatt is closed in winter but, as at Albula, there's the option of taking the car-carrying train instead. In winter, carry snow chains or use winter tyres.

Graubünden offers a regional transport pass (Sfr124/155) valid for seven/14 days from May to October. You get two/four days of unlimited free travel on all Rhätische Bahn (RhB) trains serving the canton, the SBB line between Chur and Bad Ragaz, the RhB bus between Tirano and Lugano and cantonal postal buses. For the remaining days you pay half-price. The pass also offers half-price on most cable cars and funiculars, the Furka-Oberalp line between Disentis/Mustér and Brig, and Davos city buses.

CHUR

pop 32,500 / elevation 585m

The Alps rise like an amphitheatre around Chur, Switzerland's oldest city, inhabited since 3000 BC. Linger more than a few minutes on your way to St Moritz, Davos or Arosa and you'll soon warm to the capital of Graubünden. After a stint in the mountains, its gallery showcasing Alberto Giacometti originals, futuristic Giger Bar, arty boutiques, appetising restaurants and vibrant bars are a refreshing tonic.

When the city was almost destroyed by fire in 1464, German-speaking artisans arrived to rebuild and, in the process, inadvertently suppressed the local lingo. So it was *abunansvair* Romansch and *Guten Tag* German.

Information

INTERNET ACCESS

Street Café (☎ 081 253 79 14; Grabenstrasse 47; per 20min Sfr5; ⏰ 9am-midnight Sun-Thu, 9am-2am Fri & Sat)

LAUNDRY

Malteser's Wäsch-Egga (Grabenstrasse; wash/dry Sfr7/4; ⏰ 24 hr) Self-service laundry.

MONEY

You can change money (from 7am to 8pm) at the train station. The UBS bank has a handy central branch with ATMs on Poststrasse.

POST

Post office (Postplatz; ⏰ 7.30am-6.30pm Mon-Fri, 8am-noon Sat) Just outside the Old Town.

TOURIST INFORMATION

Tourist office (☎ 081 252 18 18; www.churtourismus.ch; Bahnhofplatz 3; ⏱ 7am-8pm Mon-Fri, 8am-6pm Sat & Sun) Has stacks of info and maps on the region and can arrange city tours.

Sights & Activities

To appreciate Chur's charm, saunter the cobblestone lanes of the pedestrianised Old Town (*Altstadt*), dotted with frescoed 16th-century facades, gurgling fountains and lofty towers. Near the Plessur River, the **Obertor** marks the main medieval entrance. Alongside the stout, stone **Maltesertor** (once the medieval munitions tower), and the **Sennhofturm** (nowadays the city's prison), it's all that remains of the city's defensive walls.

Unassuming outside, the 12th-century **Kathedrale** (cathedral; ☎ 081 258 60 00; Hof; ⏱ 6am-7pm) hides striking stained-glass windows and Jakob Russ' late 15th-century high altar containing a splendid triptych.

Housed in a baroque patrician residence, the **Rätisches Museum** (☎ 081 254 16 40; www.raetischesmuseum.gr.ch; Hofstrasse 1; adult/child/student & senior Sfr6/free/4; ⏱ 10am-5pm Tue-Sun) spells out the canton's history in artefacts, with Roman relics, coins, weapons, armour and a section on rural Alpine tools and gizmos.

For an insight into the artistic legacy of Graubünden-born Alberto Giacometti (1877–1947) and his equally talented relatives, visit the **Bündner Kunstmuseum** (Museum of Fine Arts; ☎ 081 257 28 68; www.buendner-kunstmuseum.ch;

GRAUBÜNDEN

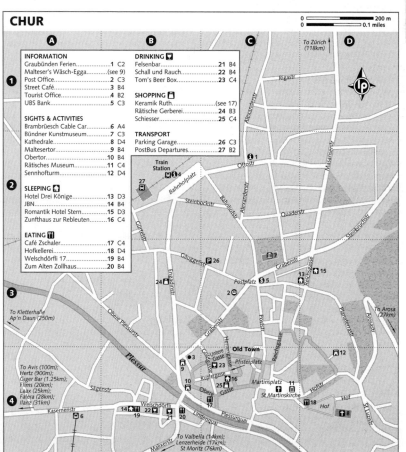

CHUR

INFORMATION	
Graubünden Ferien	1 C2
Malteser's Wäsch-Egga	(see 9)
Post Office	2 C3
Street Café	3 B4
Tourist Office	4 B2
UBS Bank	5 C3

SIGHTS & ACTIVITIES	
Brambrüesch Cable Car	6 A4
Bündner Kunstmuseum	7 C3
Kathedrale	8 D4
Maltesertor	9 B4
Obertor	10 B4
Rätisches Museum	11 C4
Sennhofturm	12 D4

SLEEPING	
Hotel Drei Könige	13 D3
JBN	14 B4
Romantik Hotel Stern	15 D3
Zunfthaus zur Rebleuten	16 C4

EATING	
Café Zschaler	17 C4
Hofkellerei	18 D4
Welschdörfli 17	19 B4
Zum Alten Zollhaus	20 B4

DRINKING	
Felsenbar	21 B4
Schall und Rauch	22 B4
Tom's Beer Box	23 C4

SHOPPING	
Keramik Ruth	(see 17)
Rätische Gerberei	24 B3
Schiesser	25 C4

TRANSPORT	
Parking Garage	26 C3
PostBus Departures	27 B2

To Zürich (118km)

Rigastr

To Kletterhalle
Ap'n Daun (250m)

Train Station

Bahnhofplatz

Steinbockstr

Ottostr

Alexanderstr

Masanserstr

Quaderstr

Steinbruchstr

Gäuggelistr

Postplatz

To Arosa (27km)

To Avis (100m);
Hertz (900m);
Giger Bar (1.25km);
Flims (20km);
Laax (25km);
Falera (28km);
Ilanz (31km)

Sägenstr

Plessur

Obere Plessurstr

Kasernenstr

Welschdörfli

Grabenstr

Untere Gasse

Pfisterplatz

Old Town

Kupfergasse

Obere Gasse

Martinsplatz

St.Martinskirche

Martinsgasse

Hofstr

Hof

St.Luzistr

Reichsgasse

Planterrastr

Arosastr

Lindenquai

Plessurquai

Malixerstr

To Valbella (14km);
Lenzerheide (17km);
St Moritz (76km)

0 ——— 200 m
0 ——— 0.1 miles

Postplatz; adult/child/student Sfr8/free/6; 🕑 10am-5pm Tue-Sun) occupying the neoclassical Villa Planta. The biggest crowd-puller is the Giacometti collection on the top floor. Other star pieces include Chur-born Angelika Kaufmann's enigmatic *Self Portrait* (1780).

Had enough of enclosed spaces? Take the **Brambrüesch cable car** (☎ 081 250 55 90; Kasernenstrasse 15; return fare adult/under 6yr/6-16yr Sfr24/free/5; 🕑 8.30am-5pm mid-Jun–late Oct & mid-Dec–mid-Mar) to Brambrüesch at 1600m for a summer hike through wildflower-strewn heights. It's in action again in winter, together with a couple of lifts, allowing locals to warm up for more-serious downhill skiing elsewhere in Graubünden.

Rock climbers limber up at **Kletterhalle Ap'n Daun** (☎ 081 284 02 84; www.kletterhallechur.ch; Pulvermühlestrasse 20; adult/student Sfr10/8; 🕑 9am-10.30pm Mon-Fri, 10am-7pm Sat & Sun Nov-Apr, 5-10pm Mon-Thu & 1-7pm Sat & Sun May-Oct), where courses and equipment rental are available.

Festivals & Events

Sway to jazz and world music on Pfisterplatz at the **Jazz Welt Festival** (www.jazzwelt.ch) in June. Careless whiskers make barbers' razor blades twitch at the **Internationales Alpenbarttreffen** (International Alpine Beard Festival) in August, where the hairiest men of the mountain do battle. The big summer bash is the **Churer Fest** (www.churerfest.org) in mid-August, three days of concerts, feasting, cow-milking marathons and kiddie fun.

Sleeping

our pick JBN (☎ 081 284 10 10; www.justbenice.ch; Welschdörfli 19; dm Sfr33-40, d Sfr108-138, ste Sfr178; ✗ 🖳) Hurrah! Finally there's a backpacker gem in Chur's buzzy Welschdörfli district. JBN offers spacious dorms, glammed up with original photography and quirky touches like dog's-backside coat hangers. The club pumps up the volume at weekends, so choose a mountain-facing room if decibels affect your slumber. Breakfast is worth the extra Sfr7 with cereals, juice and strong espresso. There's free internet.

Hotel Drei Könige (☎ 081 354 90 90; www.dreikoenige.ch; Reichsgasse 18; s/d Sfr70/160; P) Despite crying out for a makeover in the hospital-ward-like corridors, this 18th-century hotel is a central, good-value pick. The humble but comfy rooms vary from timber lined to bright white. Free wi-fi is a bonus.

Zunfthaus zur Rebleuten (☎ 081 255 11 44; Pfisterplatz 1; s/d Sfr85/140) It oozes 500 years of history, but never fear, this classic has been redecorated once or twice since it was built! The 12 rooms are fresh and inviting. Especially romantic (watch your head) are those in the loft.

Romantik Hotel Stern (☎ 081 258 57 57; www.stern-chur.ch; Reichsgasse 11; s/d Sfr150/290; P 🖳) Part of Switzerland's romantic clan, this centuries-old hotel has kept its flair with vaulted corridors and low-ceilinged, pine-filled rooms. Enjoy regional dishes or a glass of Grisons wine on the restaurant's cobbled terrace. Call ahead and they'll pick you up from the station in a 1933 Buick.

Eating

Café Zschaler (☎ 081 252 35 76; Obere Gasse 31; 🕑 8am-5.30pm, closed Wed & Sun) Behind Chur's most eye-catching frescoed facade, this cheery café rustles up toasties, cakes and speciality teas. Bag a seat on the river-facing terrace when the sun's out.

Hofkellerei (☎ 081 252 32 30; Hof 1; mains Sfr19-36; 🕑 Tue-Sun) Ye olde inn has been sizzling and stirring since 1522. Wooden floorboards creak as you enter the vaulted Gothic restaurant to feast away on regional flavours like *Pizokel* (noodles) with plums and *capuns* (silverbeet rolls) under the wrought-iron chandeliers.

Welschdörfli 17 (☎ 081 534 14 41; Welschdörfli 17; stir-fries Sfr19.50; 🕑 11am-2pm Tue-Fri, 5pm-late Sat) Scarlet walls and scatter cushions give this café an arty feel. Compose your own stir-fry, slurp curry macchiatos or munch scrummy tapas and salads.

Zum Alten Zollhaus (☎ 081 252 33 98; Malixerstrasse 1; mains Sfr25-40) On frosty winter nights, this tavern's soft lantern glow is a beacon to locals. Waiters bustle beneath low timber beams, serving freshly hunted game, rösti and other hearty favourites.

Drinking

A restless student population keeps the after-dark vibe lively in Chur, especially around bar-lined Untere Gasse and Welschdörfli, where lap-dancing clubs sidle up to bars heaving with (fully clothed) party-goers. Visit www.churbynight.ch for up-to-date listings.

Felsenbar (☎ 081 284 50 50; Welschdörfli 1; 🕑 8pm-2am Tue-Thu, 8pm-3am Fri & Sat) DJs working the decks and themed parties from single nights to cooking duels attract a vivacious bunch to this all-black haunt, set around a horseshoe bar.

ALIEN ENCOUNTERS

'In space, no one can hear you scream…' Born in Chur in 1940, Swiss surrealist HR Giger was the creative brains behind the other-worldly terror portrayed in Ridley Scott's 1979 film *Alien*. The artist's fantastical painting *Necronom IV* (1976) inspired the set design and the life cycle of the alien, and his subsequent work on the film won him an Oscar for Achievement in Visual Effects in 1980. For sci-fi encounters today, visit the space-age **Giger Bar** (☎ 081 253 75 06; www.hrgiger.com; Kalchbühl Center, Comercialstrasse 23; ☷ 8am-8pm Mon-Fri, 8am-late Sat), a silver-black phantasmagoria of biomechanical artwork with chairs like ribcages, tendril-like mirrors and the odd extraterrestrial where you least expect it…

Schall und Rauch (www.schallundrau.ch, in German; Welschdörfli; ☷ 5pm-2am Wed-Sat, 3pm-2am Sun) Lounge lizard music wafts across the red and orange stage-lit bar at 'Sound and Smoke'. At one end is a mezzanine, at the other a flat-screen TV with a loop fireplace sequence to give you a warm feeling even without imbibing.

Street Café (☎ 081 253 79 14; Grabenstrasse 47; ☷ 9am-midnight Sun-Thu, 9am-2am Fri & Sat) Among the trendier hang-outs to begin an evening, Street Café has a perfect people-watching terrace.

Tom's Beer Box (☎ 081 252 77 57; Untere Gasse 11; ☷ 5pm-midnight Mon-Thu, 3pm-1am Fri & Sat) The bottle-top window is a shrine to beer at this chilled haunt, where locals spill outside to socialise and guzzle one of 140 brews. Wacky events include ciggie-rolling and air-guitar contests.

Shopping

Keramik Ruth (☎ 081 253 58 01; Obere Gasse 31) Ruth displays her sweet-shop bright pottery at this hobbit-sized shop – from hand-thrown pots to polka-dotty teapots.

Rätische Gerberei (☎ 081 252 52 42; Engadinstrasse 30) This well-hidden tannery is worth seeking. Downstairs are mountains of fluffy sheepskins and genuine cowbells for a fraction of the price you'd pay elsewhere. Check if they're handmade by looking for the seam inside.

Schiesser (☎ 081 252 35 43; Obere Gasse 22) Impressed by local meat specialities? Head for Schiesser, where there is *Bündnerfleisch* (air-dried beef), *Rohschinken* (cured ham) and all sorts of *Salsiz* (sausage) to salivate over.

Getting There & Away

There are rail connections to Klosters (Sfr20.60, 1¼ hours) and Davos (Sfr27, 1½ hours), and fast trains to Sargans for Liechtenstein (Sfr10.20, 20 to 25 minutes) and Zürich (Sfr37, 1¼ to 1½ hours). Postal buses leave from the terminus above the train station. The A13 freeway runs north from Chur to Zürich and Lake Constance.

Getting Around

Bahnhofplatz is the hub for all local buses, which cost Sfr2.50 per journey (valid for changes for 30 minutes). Services become less frequent after 8pm.

The Old Town is mostly pedestrians only. Look for signs to several parking garages on the edge of the Old Town (eg on Gäuggelistrasse), charging around Sfr2 per hour.

CAR RENTAL

If you plan to hire a car, try **Avis** (☎ 081 300 33 77; Kasernenstrasse 37), in the Carrosserie Claus car body shop, or **Hertz** (☎ 081 252 32 22; Triststrasse 15).

AROUND CHUR

LENZERHEIDE & VALBELLA
elevation 1470m & 1540m

Straddling the petrol-blue Heidsee, these linked resorts bombard you with mountainous wooded splendour. And such beauty doesn't only appeal to humans: in early 2008 a bear paid Lenzerheide a visit. Sadly his appetite for sheep, nocturnal campsite escapades and (living up to those clichés) the honey of local beehives sealed his fate.

Among the area's 170km of hiking trails, the five- to seven-hour trek to 2865m **Parpaner Rothorn** (p77) stands out as one of the best. Kids let off excess energy on the **Globi Trail**, with activities from pine-cone throwing to splashy water games. The tourist office has free maps.

In summer, Lenzerheide morphs into a **mountain biking** centre, with 305km of marked routes and 920km of self-guided GPS tours.

GRAUBÜNDEN

The latter are available from the tourist office and cost Sfr24/34 for one/two days. **Activ Sport Baselgia** (☎ 081 384 25 34; Voa Sporz 19; ✆ 8.30am-noon & 2-6.30pm Mon-Fri, to 5pm Sat) rents mountain bikes/downhill bikes/kids bikes for Sfr38/50/18 per day.

Skiing on the 155km of slopes is mostly geared towards beginners and intermediates. A one-day ski pass costs Sfr62 for adults and Sfr20 for children. **Cross-country** skiers can glissade along 50km of tracks. Twinkling off-piste and family-oriented fun includes 80km of **winter walking trails** and a 3km **toboggan run**.

The **Lenzerheide tourist office** (☎ 081 385 11 20; www.lenzerheide.ch; Voa Principala; ✆ 8.30am-noon & 1.30-6pm Mon-Fri, 8.30am-noon Sat) is on the main road.

Sleeping & Eating

Pop into the tourist office for a list of holiday apartments and chalets.

Camping St Cassian (☎ 081 384 24 72; www .st-cassian.ch, in German; Lenz; sites per adult/child/tent/car Sfr8/4.50/7/2.50; ✆ year-round) Popular with cyclists, this tree-shaded campsite is 3km south of town. Expect pin-drop peace, mountain vistas and first-rate facilities, including barbecue areas, a restaurant and wi-fi. Mr Nadig, the affable owner, is a mine of local knowledge.

ourpick Bauernhof Tgantieni (☎ 081 384 24 30; Maiensäss; per adult/child Sfr20/10, ✆ Jun-Sep) If you've ever fancied exchanging your bed for a shed, here's your chance. High on a hill above Lenzerheide, this rural idyll is ideal for those willing to swap creature comforts for a night in the straw. Brave an icy wash at the spring before a hearty breakfast of homemade bread and preserves. Tots love the resident cats, rabbits and goats. Bring your own sleeping bag.

Hotel Pöstli (☎ 081 384 11 60; www.stall-lenzerheide .ch, in German; Hauptstrasse 37, Lenzerheide; s/d Sfr90/170) These cosy Lenzerheide digs have timberfilled rooms. Downstairs, the restaurant dishes up tasty fondue and Raclette, and sometimes cranks up the après-ski music (light sleepers beware!).

Seerestaurant Forellenstube (☎ 081 384 11 41; Am Heidsee; mains Sfr16-49) Hailed for the freshness of its trout, this lakefront restaurant is worth the 2km toddle north of Lenzerheide. Go for the fish or specialities such as homemade venison sausage. Gracing the wall is the head of a *Wolpertinger*, a fictional critter said to roam Alpine forests.

Getting There & Away

Either resort is easily reached by an hourly bus from Chur (Sfr10.20, 40 minutes). They're on the route from Chur to St Moritz spanning the Julier Pass. In the high summer and winter seasons, a free bus operates between Lenzerheide and Valbella.

AROSA

pop 2250 / elevation 1800m

Framed by the peaks of Weisshorn, Hörnli and moraine-streaked Schiesshorn, Arosa is a great Alpine all-rounder: perfect for downhill and cross-country skiers in winter, hikers and downhill bikers in summer, and families yearround with heaps of activities to amuse kids.

Although only 30km southeast of Chur, getting here is nothing short of spectacular. The road zigzags up from Chur in a series of 365 hairpin bends so challenging that Arosa cannot be reached by postal buses. The scenic train ride from Chur makes an excellent alternative.

Orientation & Information

Arosa has two parts: the main resort Ausserarosa (Outer Arosa), huddled on the shores of Obersee (Upper Lake) at the train terminus; and the older village Innerarosa. The train station has money-exchange counters, luggage storage and scooter rental.

From Oberseeplatz, head uphill along Poststrasse towards Innerarosa. Within five minutes you'll reach the **tourist office** (☎ 081 378 70 20; www.arosa.ch; Poststrasse; ✆ 8am-noon & 1.30-6pm Mon-Fri, 9am-1pm Sat, 9am-noon Sun May-Nov, 8am-6pm Mon-Fri, 9am-5pm Sat, 4-5.30pm Sun Dec-Apr).

If you stay here in summer, you'll receive the free all-inclusive card giving unlimited access to lifts, local buses, pedalos and rowing boats on Obersee, and the lido at Untersee.

Activities

WINTER SPORTS

Arosa attracts beginner and intermediate skiers with 60km of red and blue runs, rising as high as Weisshorn at 2653m. Big air fans should check out the half-pipe and fun park. Contact the **ski school** (☎ 081 378 75 00; www.sssa.ch; Seeblickstrasse; ✆ 8.30am-5.30pm) for lessons. Ski passes cost Sfr58 for one day and Sfr295 for one week (there are senior/youth reductions).

Cross-country skiing is equally superb, with 30km of prepared *Loipen* (tracks)

GIAN SIMMEN, OLYMPIC HALF-PIPE CHAMPION

Gian has been passionate about snowboarding since he was 12. With the mountains on his door-step in Arosa and Davos, he'd be out building kickers and ramps straight after school. He's learned a few tricks since then, picking up the first-ever Olympic gold medal for half-pipe in 1998.

What do you love about snowboarding?
Everything! The feeling of catching air when you jump, especially freestyle. It's like flying as you glide over the powder and land supersoftly. I love the speed, the rush, the scenery, the weight-lessness, the freedom to rotate. It's such a buzz when you get all the moves right.

What did winning gold at the 1998 Olympics mean to you?
It was both a career highlight and the start of my career. Apart from the 1996 Swiss Championships, it was the first time I'd won anything major. I jumped in at the deep end [laughs]. I'm now 31 and one of the oldest guys on the slopes, but I keep up.

Favourite places to snowboard in Switzerland?
For freeriding and freestyle, Laax (p304), Davos (p311), Meiringen (p193) and Andermatt (p262). Davos really looks after their parks and half-pipes, and the Riders Palace in Laax has a great off-snow program with DJs and concerts. Arosa is an alternative if you don't want to ride with the pros, as it's relaxed and attitude free. I know almost every rock here…

Any snowboarding tips?
Have fun and don't give up. Respect your own limits but don't be afraid to fall with freestyle. If you're prepared to hike, you will always find good snow. Get up early in the morning and walk.

---

stretching from Maran's gentle forest trails to challenging routes at La Isla and Ochsenalp. **Langlauf- und Skiwanderschule Geeser** (☎ 081 377 22 15; www.geeser-arosa.ch; ☷ 9am-noon & 1-6pm) offers equipment rental and instruction, with cross-country and snowshoe taster sessions starting at Sfr50.

There's plenty to amuse families and nonskiers in winter. Prätschli is the start of a floodlit 1km **toboggan run** through twinkling woodlands. Otherwise, you can stomp through the snow on 40km of prepared **winter walking trails**, twirl across an open-air ice rink, or rock up for a game of curling.

SUMMER ACTIVITIES
Arosa's backyard has 200km of maintained **hiking trails**, such as the 3½-hour uphill trudge to Weisshorn, affording far-reaching vistas. Footpaths fan out from the top station of **Hörnli** (2513m). You can even hike west to Lenzerheide (p301) in around three hours. Shorter rambles include forest trails shadowing the Plessur to Litzirüti (one hour) and Langwies (two hours). Get up early for mountain reflections in the aquamarine lakes of Schwellisee and Älpisee. Kids enjoy spotting red squirrels on the Eichhörnchenweg.

For knuckle-whitening thrills, hire a downhill bike at **Obersee** (☎ 081 377 23 77; ☷ 10am-5pm) to race from Mittelstation to Litzirüti or from

Hörnli to Arosa; both tracks involve descents of more than 500m.

Sleeping
Many hotels and restaurants close in shoulder seasons (mid-April to early June and mid-October to early December).

Hotel Erzhorn (☎ 081 377 15 26; www.erzhorn.ch; Kirchweg; s 97-117, d 210-260; ⓟ) Up near Arosa's 500-year-old Bergkirchli chapel, this timber chalet is in a silent part of town. The Nau family run the place like (Swiss) clockwork and the bright, pine-ceilinged rooms with balconies are kept spotless.

Praval (☎ 081 377 11 40; www.praval.ch, in German; Innere Poststrasse; s/d Sfr125/250; ⓟ) Expect a smiley welcome at this mountain chalet, where the all-pine rooms have comfy beds. Easily the best are south-facing doubles with balconies and long views over the valley. It's near Hörnli Express ski lift.

Hotel Arlenwald (☎ 081 377 18 38; www.arlenwald hotel.ch; Prätschli; s/d/ste Sfr130/220/300; ⓟ) Direct access to Burestübli restaurant (p304) is just one of the perks of staying at this hotel. The spacious, light-flooded rooms feature loads of chunky pine, antique family heirlooms and wi-fi. The sauna overlooks the fir-brushed peaks.

Waldhotel (☎ 081 378 55 55; www.waldhotel.ch; s/d/ste Sfr235/520/670; ⓟ ☐ ☗) Deep in the forest, this is the kind of hideaway where you pray for flakes to fall. Nobel Prize–winning German novelist Thomas Mann spent the first weeks of his exile here. The luxurious hotel is an old-world charmer with its intricately carved ceilings, elegant rooms and guests arriving by horse-drawn carriage. Get scrubbed or rubbed with hot chocolate in the spa, or sip a glass of red as the pianist plays in the lounge.

Eating & Drinking

Grishuna (☎ 081 377 17 01; Poststrasse; mains Sfr16.50-38.50; ☺ closed mid-Sep–Oct, Tue year-round) The enormous cowbells hanging in the window of this low-beamed, antique-filled tavern grab your attention. It's a convivial spot for delicacies such as thinly sliced home-smoked salmon and fresh game in season.

ourpick Burestübli (☎ 081 377 18 38; Arlenwald Hotel, Prätschli; mains Sfr17-32; ☺ closed Thu Sep-Nov) This woodsy chalet on the forest edge affords magical above-the-treetop views. Come winter, it's beloved by ruddy-faced sledders who huddle around pots of gooey fondue, buttersoft steaks and mugs of glühwein before a floodlit dash through the snow. Book a sled by calling a day ahead. The marvellously eccentric chef prides himself on using first-rate local produce.

Alpenblick (☎ 081 377 14 28; 3-course meals Sfr40-50) Sitting below Hörnli Express cable car, this country-style chalet offers dreamy Alpine vistas from its terrace. It serves warming snacks like goulash soup, specialities such as herby Bündner lamb and cracking homemade apple strudel.

Los Café (☎ 081 356 56 10; www.losbar.ch; Haus Madrisa) Slope-side imbibing aside, this is where the party is in winter. The gallery-style bar attracts a laid-back crowd with DJs, table football and shots aplenty.

Getting There & Away

The only way to reach Arosa is from Chur: take the hourly narrow-gauge train that leaves from in front of the train station (Sfr13.80, one hour). It's a winding, scenic journey chugging past mountains, pine trees, streams and bridges. The train crosses the oldest steel-and-concrete rail bridge ever built. At 62m high, it is a dizzying engineering feat, completed in 1914.

Buses in the resort are free. Drivers should note a traffic ban from midnight to 6am.

WEST OF CHUR

The mainly Romansch-speaking Surselva area west of Chur stretches out along the lonely N19 highway snaking west towards the canton of Uri and, not far beyond, to Valais. Beyond the twinkling cheer of Flims, Laax and Falera, the pickings are slim along this road, although a few points along the Vorderrhein River are worth a stop. More compelling are a couple of wild valleys extending south of the road, which itself trails out in Alpine wilderness as it rises to the wind-chilled **Oberalp Pass** (2044m) that separates Graubünden from Uri. About 4km south of the pass, near the tiny Lai da Tuma, lies hidden the source of the Vorderrhein River, best explored on the high-level Lai da Tuma Circuit (p79).

FLIMS, LAAX & FALERA

They say that if the snow ain't falling anywhere else, you'll surely find some around Flims, Laax and Falera. These three towns, 20km west of Chur, form the Weisse Arena (White Arena) ski area, with 220km of slopes catering for all levels. Host of the Burton European Open in January, Laax is a mecca for snowboarders, who spice up the nightlife too. The resort is barely two hours by train and bus (less by car) from Zürich airport.

Orientation & Information

The three towns forming the backbone of the resort are strung northeast to southwest over 15km. Flims is the biggest, divided into the larger, residential Flims Dorf to the north, and the leafier Flims Waldhaus, 1km away. Ski lifts lie between the two. Laax is also divided into two. The sleepy Old Town, Lag Grond, with its pretty chalets and lake, lies to the south; Laax Murschetg, where the lifts are located, is 1km to the north. The third town, Falera, is the smallest and quietest. There are tourist offices in all three, but the **main tourist office** (☎ 081 920 92 00; summer information www.flims.com, winter information www.laax.com; Via Nova, Flims; ☺ 8am-6pm Mon-Fri, 8am-noon Sat mid-Jun–mid-Aug, 8am-5pm Mon-Sat mid-Dec–mid-Apr) is in Flims.

Sights
FALERA
History buffs will be drawn to the Romanesque **St Remigiuskirche** in Falera, perched on a hill that has been a site of worship since prehistoric times, as attested by the line-up of

modest menhirs leading up to it. Inside the shingle-roofed church is a striking mid-17th-century fresco depicting the Last Supper. From the cemetery you can see deep into the Vorderrhein Valley.

CAUMASEE
Ringed by thick woods, this exquisitely turquoise lake is a 15-minute hike or five-minute stroll and then ride by lift south of Flims Waldhaus. It's an attractive spot for a cool summer swim. You can hire a row boat and eat at a restaurant terrace overlooking the lake.

Activities
SKIING & SNOWBOARDING
Ask clued-up snowboarders to rattle off their top Swiss resorts and Laax will invariably make the grade. The riders' mecca boasts both Europe's smallest and largest half-pipe, excellent freestyle parks and many off-piste opportunities. Skiers are equally content to bash the pistes in the interlinked resorts, with 220km of varied slopes (most above 2000m) to suit all but the most hard-core black-run freaks. Slaloming downhill, you'll probably spy the unfortunately named Crap da Flem (*crap* means 'peak' in Romansch). The season starts in late October on the 3018m Vorab glacier and mid-December elsewhere. A one-day ski pass includes ski buses and costs Sfr66 (plus Sfr5 for the KeyCard that you use to access the lifts). There are 60km of cross-country skiing trails.

HIKING
In summer, the hiking network spans 250km. The *Naturlehrpfad* circuit at the summit of Cassons is brilliant for spotting wild Alpine flowers and critters. Even more dramatic is the half-day trek **Ruin' Aulta** (p75) through the glacier-gouged **Rheinschlucht** (Rhine Gorge), where limestone cliffs have been eroded into bizarre pinnacles and columns. Seeking a tougher challenge? Traverse soaring rock faces and get an eagle's-eye view of the valley on the **Pinut** *via ferrata*. It costs around Sfr25 to hire the gear from sports shops or the tourist office in Flims.

RIVER RAFTING
Taking you through the Rheinschlucht, the turbulent 17km stretch of the Vorderrhein between Ilanz and Reichenau is white-water-rafting heaven. **Swissraft** (☎ 081 911 52 50;

www.swissraft.ch) offers half-/full day rafting for Sfr109/160. The meeting spot is Ilanz train station. You can get the same dramatic views of the gorge on westward-bound trains, but without the thrills and spills.

Sleeping & Eating
Ask the tourist office for a list of good-value holiday houses and apartments. Hotels, restaurants and bars generally close from mid-April to June and late September to mid-November.

Riders Palace (☎ 081 927 97 00; www.riderspalace .ch; Laax Murschetg; dm Sfr30-60; d Sfr180-280) Sleep? Dream on. This oversized Rubik's cube draws party-hearty boarders. It's a curious slice of designer cool, with bare concrete walls and fluorescent lighting. Choose between basic five-bed dorms, slick rooms with Philippe Starck tubs, or hi-tech suites complete with PlayStation and Dolby surround sound. It's 200m from the Laax lifts.

Posta Veglia (☎ 081 921 44 66; www.postaveglia.ch; Via Principala 54, Laax; s/d/ste Sfr150/250/330; P) Today this 19th-century post office delivers discreet service and rustic flavour. The seven country-cottage-style rooms and suites are filled with beams, antiques and mod cons like DVD players and free wi-fi.

Hotel Cresta (☎ 081 911 35 35; www.cresta.ch; Via Passadi, Flims Waldhaus; s/d Sfr158/286; P ⛲) Tucked away in the wooded back lanes of Waldhaus, these contemporary digs are a beauty-conscious diva's dream, with saunas, steam baths, whirlpools and pampering treatments. Oh, and they have rather nice rooms too.

Clavau Vegl (☎ 081 911 36 44; Via Nova 29, Flims Dorf; mains Sfr19-30; ⏲ 8.30am-9.30pm Tue-Sat) All pine and giant cowbells, this one-time stable has kept its on-the-farm feel. Join locals for well-prepared regional staples such as *capuns* and *Pizokel*.

Cavigilli (☎ 081 911 01 25; www.cavigilli.ch; Via Arviul 1, Flims Dorf; mains 19-45; ⏲ closed Wed) Your kindly hosts are Stefanie und Rüdiger Szimba at Flims' oldest house, dating to 1453, comprising a Gothic parlour, a dining room bearing the imprint of Swiss artist Alois Carigiet and a bulging wine cellar. The accent is on market-fresh produce, from homemade ravioli to hearty stews.

Restaurant Pöstli (☎ 081 921 44 66; Via Principala 54, Laax; mains Sfr28-40; ⏲ closed Mon) Posta Veglia's wood-panelled restaurant and vaulted cellar please even pernickety foodies with creative, attractively presented dishes such as venison schnitzel with chocolate-balsamic jus.

La Vacca (☎ 081 927 99 62; Plaun Station, Laax-Murschetg lifts; mains Sfr40-70; ☯ late Dec–mid-Apr) *Rawhide* meets the Alps at this funky tepee, where cowhide-draped chairs surround a roaring open fire. Forget stringy fondue, the menu here is as exciting as the design – think melt-in-your-mouth bison steaks paired with full-bodied Argentine wines.

Drinking

Riders Palace (☎ 081 927 97 00; www.riderspalace.ch; Laax Murschetg; ☯ 4pm-4am) The favourite hang-out of freestyle dudes, this too-cool bar in the lobby of the eponymous hostel (p305) rocks to gigs and DJs spinning beats into the blurry-eyed hours.

Crap Bar (☎ 081 927 99 45; Laax-Murschetg lifts; ☯ 4pm-2am) Crap by name but not by nature, this après-ski hot spot is shaped from 24 tonnes of granite. It's the place to slam shots, check your email and shimmy in your snow boots after a day pounding powder.

Getting There & Away

Postal buses run to Flims and the other villages in the White Arena area hourly from Chur (Sfr12.80 to Flims Dorf, 30 minutes). A free local shuttle bus connects the three villages.

ILANZ

A bustling town with a pleasant-enough Old Town, Ilanz is, for most visitors, a transport hub. The main N19 road ribbons westward, passing through quaint towns in the predominantly German-speaking Obersaxen area before reaching the Romansch monastery village of Disentis/Mustér. Ilanz is also the departure point for two enchanting southern valleys.

VALSERTAL & VAL LUMNEZIA

Shadowing the course of the babbling Glogn (Glenner) stream south, the luxuriantly green Valsertal (Vals Valley) is full of sylvan beauty, sleepy hamlets and thundering waterfalls. The delightful drive passes Uors and St Martin before arriving at the star attraction, **Vals** (1252m). After St Martin, the valley tightens and deepens, with forest canopy folding over the narrow, serpentine road. About 2km short of the village, you emerge into verdant Alpine pastures, liberally scattered with chalets and shepherds' huts.

Vals, home to Valser mineral water, stretches 2km along its glittering stream. The secret of this chocolate-box village and its soothing waters is out since Basel-born architect Peter Zumthor worked architectural magic to transform Therme Vals' thermal baths into a temple of cutting-edge cool.

Sights & Activities

Using 60,000 slabs of local quartzite and playing on light to amplify the feeling of space, Zumthor created one of the country's most enchanting thermal spas, **Therme Vals** (☎ 081 926 89 61; www.therme-vals.ch; Vals; adult/child Sfr40/26, treatments Sfr55-255; ☯ 11am-8pm Jun-Mar). Aside from heated indoor and outdoor pools, this grey-stone labyrinth hides all sorts of watery nooks and crannies, cleverly lit and full of cavernous atmosphere. Try the deep-heat Feuerbad (42°C), the perfumed Blütenbad or the escapist Grottenbad. Have a hum in the latter and enjoy the other-worldly acoustics! Sweat out all those impurities in the steam rooms.

Less well known than the baths is an exhilarating 8km trip south to the turquoise lake of **Zervreilasee**, overshadowed by the frosted 3402m peak of Rheinwaldhorn. Access is usually only possible from June to October. From above the lake, various hiking options present themselves. There is some modest downhill skiing in the heights above Vals in winter.

Running parallel to the Valsertal from Ilanz, and then gradually branching away to the southwest, is the **Val Lumnezia**, as broad and sunlit green as the Valsertal is deep and narrow. The road runs high along the west flank of the valley. Where it dips out of sight of the valley, you arrive in **Vrin**, a cheerful huddle of rural houses gathered around a brightly frescoed church. The asphalt peters out 8km further on in Puzatsch.

Sleeping

Apart from holiday houses for rent, Vals offers a handful of hotel options.

Gasthaus Edelweiss (☎ 081 935 11 33; www.edelweiss-vals.ch; Dorfsplatz, Vals; s/d Sfr49/118) Right on the village square, this century-old guest house has humble timber-lined rooms. The restaurant whips up local grub like *capuns*. The hotel can get you Sfr5 off entry to the baths.

Hotel Glenner (☎ 081 935 11 15; www.glenner.ch; Vals; d Sfr170-190) Ablaze with red geraniums in summer, this dark wooden chalet shelters cosy, if slightly old-fashioned, rooms with

---

MAGIC MUSHROOMS

There was a time when there were customs stations on the passes that lead from Graubünden to Ticino. They are long gone but, come autumn, cantonal police are again stationed on passes such as the Lukmanier Pass, 15km south of Disentis, on the lookout for 'bandits' sneaking out kilos of luscious mushrooms.

No, it's not drug trafficking. The magic of these mushrooms is the flavour they bring to a risotto. The people of Ticino and their Italian cousins can't get enough of them and they pour across the cantonal border to fill their picnic baskets with the autumn crop. There's just one hitch. The legal limit is 2kg per person per day. And the police take a dim view of cheats. On one September weekend, 30 people were fined for excessive picking – one mushroomer was caught with 70kg of tasty tubers!

---

pine trappings and squeaky-clean bathrooms. Chomp on hearty regional fare in the restaurant downstairs.

Hotel Therme (☎ 081 926 80 80; www.therme-vals.ch; Vals; s/d Sfr265/450; 💻) In this 1960s colossus, Peter Zumthor has revamped many of the rooms; the newest sport stucco lustro, parquet floors and satin sheets. Some of the hotel's annexes have not been given the Zumthor treatment and are cheaper and, frankly, ugly. Urs Dietrich emphasises market-fresh cuisine in the restaurant.

Getting There & Away

Postal buses run more or less hourly to Vrin (Sfr12.80, 47 minutes) and Vals (Sfr11.80, 36 minutes) from Ilanz (itself reached by regular train from Chur, Sfr14.80, 40 minutes). The Vals bus goes on to Zervreila from June to October, taking an extra 30 minutes.

DISENTIS/MUSTÉR & VAL MEDEL

Rising like a vision above Disentis/Mustér is a baubly Benedictine monastery with a lavishly stuccoed baroque church attached. A monastery has stood here since the 8th century, but the present immense complex dates to the 18th century. Left of the church entrance is a door that leads you down a corridor to the **Klostermuseum** (admission Sfr6; 🕑 2-5pm Tue, Thu & Sat Jun-Oct, 2-5pm Wed Christmas-Easter), crammed with memorabilia on the history of the monastery. Head left upstairs to the **Marienkirche**, a Romanesque-rooted chapel filled with ex-voto images from people in need of (or giving thanks for) some miraculous intervention from the Virgin Mary.

Smack in the middle of Disentis, **Hotel Alpsu** (☎ 081 947 51 17; s/d Sfr72/136; 🅿) is a gem. With lots of woodwork, each room is quite unique. In one you find a four-poster, in another

exposed beams and a bubble bath opposite the bed. The restaurant does fine renditions of *capuns* and *Pizokel*.

South of Disentis, the **Val Medel** starts in dramatic style with the **Medelser-Schlucht** (Medel Gorge). You pass through several villages, of which **Platta** is noteworthy for its shingle-roofed Romanesque church. About 20km on, by the petrol-blue **Lai da Sontga Maria** lake and surrounded by 3000m peaks, the road hits the **Lukmanier Pass** (Passo di Lucomagno, 1914m) and crosses into Ticino.

Disentis/Mustér is where Matterhorn–Gotthard trains from Brig via Andermatt (Sfr19, one hour) terminate, and local RhB trains heading to Chur (Sfr27, 1¼ hours) start. Trains leave in both directions every hour. Five buses a day rumble over the Lukmanier Pass, four of them heading on to Biasca in Ticino.

SOUTH OF CHUR

Remote wilderness, vertiginous castle ruins, cascading falls and one of Switzerland's most breathtaking gorges, Via Mala, are standouts along the main route south of Chur. An important north–south trade route since Roman times, the road heads on into the forlorn Italian-speaking Valle Mesolcina en route to Ticino.

VIA MALA & AVERS VALLEY

The A13 freeway and railway south of Chur first veer west to Reichenau before swinging south along the Hinterrhein River between the Domleschg mountain range to the east and the Heinzenberg to the west. A string of villages and ruined robber-knight castles dot the way to **Thusis**, a bustling town whose main draw lies in the far-reaching views from ruined **Obertagstein** castle about an hour's walk from the centre. Trains from Chur en route for St Moritz call in here, before heading east toward the ski resort via Tiefencastel.

South of Thusis, take the N13 rather than the freeway to explore the narrow, breathtakingly sheer gorge **Via Mala** (Evil Rd), once part of a pack-mule trail to Italy. Starting in Thusis, the 7km Veia Traversina hike takes in the ravine in all its giddy splendour; see the website www.viamala.ch for route descriptions in German. The deep chasm opens out just before **Zillis**, famed for its **St Martinskirche** (adult/child Sfr4/2; ☉ 9am-6pm late Mar-Oct), whose wooden Romanesque ceiling bears 153 extraordinarily vivid panels depicting the lives of Christ and St Martin.

To really get out into the wild, head south another 8km past **Andeer** (known for its thermal baths and home to several hotels and a camping ground) for the junction with the road into the remote **Avers Valley**. This lonely trail wriggles 24km south through thick forests, a stark Alpine valley and tiny hamlets to reach escapist fantasy **Juf** (2126m), claiming to be Europe's highest permanently inhabited village. With a population of just 30, it's more likely you'll meet resident marmots and cudchewing cows than locals.

Postal buses trundle between Thusis and Bellinzona in Ticino (Sfr39, two to 2½ hours), stopping at Zillis, Andeer, Splügen and towns along the Valle Mesolcina. Buses from Andeer run to Juf (Sfr15.80, 52 minutes).

SPLÜGEN & VALLE MESOLCINA

From the Avers turn-off, the main roads, the A13 and the N13, branch west into the pine-brushed Rheinwald (Rhine Forest), leading to the 1460m-high town of **Splügen**. The Via Mala website (www.viamala.ch, in German) covers Splügen, the Avers area, Andeer and Zillis. Splügen intrigues with its mix of dark timber, slate-roofed Walser (Valais-style) farmhouses and mansions of trading families made wealthy by 19th-century commerce with Italy over the nearby Splügen and San Bernardino passes. Apart from the riverside camping ground, you could stay in one of the simple, pine-furnished rooms at **Haus Teuriblick** (☎ 081 664 16 56; s/d Sfr60/120; P).

South of Splügen, a dizzying road loops 9km to the like-named pass into Italy,

while the main roads continue west 8km before dropping south to the Passo del San Bernardino (take the tunnel when the pass is closed) and the rugged **Valle Mesolcina**, an Italian-infused corner of Graubünden. The main towns are Mesocco, where towering castle ruins will grab your attention, and low-key Soazza and Roveredo.

Just north of Roveredo, the wild, barely visited **Val Calanca** opens up to the north, with a 19km road that terminates in the hamlet of **Rossa**, from where a dirt track continues another 5km north past **Valbella**. Several peaceful hiking trails roll out in the heights above the narrow valley. From Roveredo, it is about 10km to Bellinzona (p324), the capital of Ticino.

See Via Mala & Avers Valley (p307) for transport information. In addition, buses run roughly every 1½ hours up the Val Calanca to Rossa from Bellinzona (Sfr16.80, 1½ hours) via Rovoredo (change at Grono).

NORTH OF CHUR

Eager to act out Heidi fantasies skipping down flowery slopes or sip full-bodied Pinot noirs amongst the vines? Welcome to the Bündner Herrschaft, Graubünden's chief wine region and home to the fabulously kitsch delights of Heidiland. You can also take to the thermal waters at nearby Bad Ragaz.

BÜNDNER HERRSCHAFT

The A13 freeway blasts northward from Chur, through the wine-growing region called **Fünf Dörfer** (Five Villages), of which bucolic **Zizers** is probably the prettiest. Follow the country lane out of industrial Landquart for Malans, which takes you into the Bündner Herrschaft. This is the canton's premier wine region, dominated by the Blauburgunder (Pinot noir) grape variety that yields some memorable reds. This is also, rather unforgettably, Heidiland.

Malans & Jenins

Through vineyards and woods you arrive in **Malans**, dominated by the private castle of the Salis dynasty, a name in local wine and historic rivals to the Planta clan, whose town houses line the village square. A few kilometres north is **Jenins**, a less-noble-looking village, worth a stop for a glass or three of the local wine and perhaps a snooze in homey **Gasthaus Zur Traube** (☎ 081 302 18 26; www.traube -jenins.ch; Unterdorf 1; s/d Sfr48/96).

Some trains from Chur to Malans (Sfr7, 22 to 32 minutes) require a change in Landquart. To push on to Jenins (from Sfr9.60, 36 minutes from Chur) get a connecting postal bus from Landquart, Malans or Maienfeld.

Maienfeld & Heididorf

The most impressive of these wine villages is **Maienfeld**, another 2km through lush woods and vineyards. Dominated by a colourfully frescoed **Rathaus** (town hall) and haughty church, it's worth hanging out for the local cuisine. Make for **Schloss Brandis** (☎ 081 302 24 23; mains Sfr20-40), a lofty 15th-century tower housing one of the canton's best restaurants. You can almost picture the hog-roast feasting of yore in the beamed, lantern-lit dining room, where folk tuck into Maienfeld riesling soup and meatier specialities. For wine tasting, head to convivial **Vinothek von Salis** (☎ 081 302 50 57; Kruseckgasse 3; ⏰ 2-6pm Mon-Fri, 9.30am-4pm Sat), where Frau Möhr will tell you everything you need to know about the local tipples if your German is up to it.

Each year the four Bündner Herrschaft towns (Maienfeld, Malans, Jenins and Fläsch) take turns to celebrate the **Herbstfest** on the first weekend of October. This autumnal wine fest brings much drinking, eating and merrymaking to the normally quiet streets.

OK, we've held out till now – Maienfeld is where to start your Heidiland experience. Johanna Spyri (1827–1901) had the idea of basing the story of Heidi in the countryside around Maienfeld, and the locals had the worse idea of identifying one local village as Heidi's. It is now called – oh dear! – **Heididorf**, a 20-minute signposted walk from Maienfeld across idyllic country. In peak periods you might be able to get the Heidi Express bus, which will pass by the Heidihof Hotel. Apart from the **Heidihaus** (☎ 081 330 19 12; www.heidi -swiss.ch; adult/under 6yr/6-16yr Sfr7/free/3; ⏰ 10am-5pm mid-Mar–mid-Nov), where of course she never lived because she never existed, you could visit the Heidishop to buy Heidi colouring-in books, Heidi videos or just plain Heidikitsch. For little-girl-of-the-Alps overkill, you could follow the Heidiweg into the surrounding hills (Heidialp). When you're done, you might be in need of some Heidiwein for your Heidiheadache…or perhaps just hit the

A13 road and Heiditail it out of here north into Liechtenstein.

Maienfeld is on the Chur–Bad Ragaz train line.

Bad Ragaz

pop 5041 / elevation 502m

The perfect cure for a bad case of Heidiness could be spa town Bad Ragaz, a couple of kilometres west of Maienfeld, which opened in 1840 and has attracted the bath-loving likes of Douglas Fairbanks and Mary Pickford. **Tamina Therme** (☎ 081 303 27 41; www.resortragaz.ch), a couple of kilometres south of town, was getting a makeover at the time of writing, but should reopen in summer 2009; call ahead or check online for times and prices. Bad Ragaz is on the Chur–Zürich train line. Trains from Chur via Maienfeld run hourly (Sfr8.20, 15 minutes).

KLOSTERS & DAVOS

Following the N28 road east from Landquart, you enter the broad Prättigau Valley, which stretches east to celebrity magnet Klosters. Several valley roads spike off the highway before Klosters, and the one leading to **St Antönien** is the most attractive. There are no specific sights, just high Alpine country dotted by villages and burned-wood Walser houses raised by this rural folk since migrating here from eastern Valais from the 13th century onward.

KLOSTERS

pop 3860 / elevation 1194m

Klosters coined the phrase Royal Ski, as the place where Prince Charles first wobbled on planks at age 14 and today carves the powder with Wills and Harry. Neither flash nor brash, this picture-perfect resort manages (well, usually) to keep the paparazzi out and blue-blooded snow babies in with its hushed sophistication and arresting beauty. Classy Klosters is more Champagne cocktails than Jägermeister shots, more wooden toys than won't-stop-yodelling kitsch, and more understated elegance than bling-bling.

Orientation & Information

Klosters is split into two sections. Klosters Platz is the main resort, grouped around the train station. Right of the station is the

GRAUBÜNDEN

tourist office (☎ 081 410 20 20; www.klosters.ch; Alte Bahnhofstrasse 6; ☻ 9am-noon & 2-6pm daily Dec-Mar, 9am-noon & 2-5pm Mon-Fri, 9am-noon & 2-5pm Sat Jun-Oct, 9am-noon & 2-5pm Mon-Fri rest of year). The post office is opposite the station.

Two kilometres to the left of the station is smaller Klosters Dorf, with several hotels and the Madrisa cable car. Klosters buses are free with a Guest Card (which also gives discounts on local sport activities and other items) or ski pass.

Activities

Davos and Klosters share 315km of **ski runs**, covered by the Regionalpass (adult/child/youth Sfr65/23/46 a day). One-day passes for specific areas are marginally cheaper.

Parsenn beckons confidence-building novices and Madrisa intermediates, with long, sunny runs, mostly above the treeline. Knee-trembling black runs include panoramic Schlappin and off-piste Gotschnawang. The chance of rubbing shoulders with royalty on the slopes adds a spritz of glamour to carving. **Snowboarders** can catch big air at Madrisa or the freestyle park at Selfranga lift. If the thought of gliding noiselessly through pine forest appeals, Klosters has 35km of **cross-country** trails to test out. For more details on skiing in the resorts, visit www.davosklosters.ch.

Kid-friendly winter activities include the 8.5km **toboggan run** (☻ 8.15am-4pm Dec-Apr) from Madrisa to Saas; sleds are available for hire at the mountain station for Sfr8 plus Sfr10 deposit. Another means of dashing through the snow is on a **horse-drawn sleigh ride** (☎ 081 422 18 73; www.pferdekutschen.ch), which costs around Sfr80 per hour.

In summer, the region's vast **hiking** network covers the entire spectrum from gentle Alpine strolls to tough day hikes. Mountain and downhill **biking** are equally popular in Klosters and you can hire wheels from **Bertram's Bike Shop** (☎ 076 318 42 64; Bahnhofstrasse 16; ☻ 9am-noon & 1.30-6.30pm Mon-Fri, 9am-4pm Sat). Check the tourist office's website for inspiration for routes.

Sleeping

Pick up a list of private rooms and apartments from the tourist office. As in neighbouring Davos, most places close in shoulder seasons. Prices are 30% to 50% cheaper in summer.

Soldanella (☎ 081 422 13 16; www.youthhostel.ch /klosters; Talstrasse 73; dm Sfr45; ☻ reception 8-10am & 5-9pm; ☐) Even the HI hostel in Klosters has Alpine appeal, spanning two mountain chalets. Dorms are clean and bright, and there's a sun-drenched terrace for chilling. It's a 12-minute amble from the station.

Hotel Chesa Grischuna (☎ 081 422 22 22; www .chesagrischuna.ch; Bahnhofstrasse 12; s/d/ste 240/410/550) An archetypal vision of a Swiss chalet, this family-run pad has toasty pine rooms with antique flourishes and ornately carved ceilings. The wood-panelled, lantern-lit restaurant is an Alpine charmer, too, with dirndl-clad waitresses bringing local treats to the table.

Rustico (☎ 081 410 22 88; www.rusticohotel.com; Landstrasse 194; d Sfr265-365; Ⓟ) Near Gotschnabahn ski lift in Klosters Platz, this intimate hotel's doubles are spacious, with parquet floors and plump beds. Timber-ceilinged loft rooms are the cosiest. Warm up by the lobby fire or with a steam in the sauna. The art-slung restaurant rustles up international titbits with an Asian twist.

Eating & Drinking

Gasthaus Bargis (☎ 081 422 55 77; Kantonsstrasse 8; mains Sfr17.50-50; ☻ Wed-Sun) This snug timber-fronted house on the road into Klosters Dorf is a top nosh spot for substantial grub, from humongous schnitzels to wintry stews. When the sun's out, eat on the terrace overlooking the mountains. (

Salzi's Sonne (☎ 081 422 13 49; Landstrasse 155; mains Sfr20-50; ☻ Wed-Sun) Expect a homely welcome in this wood-panelled, family-run tavern. Among the calorie-laden favourites are fondue (from Sfr28 per person), porcini ravioli, beef stroganoff and crisp apple strudel crowned with whipped cream.

Prättiger Huschi (☎ 081 410 22 88; Landstrasse 192; fondue Sfr28-49; ☻ 6-10pm winter only) Sidling up to Rustico, this 200-year-old chalet gives you that inner glow in winter, when ruddy-cheeked folk fill its cowhide benches to devour bubbling fondue.

It's Bar (☎ 081 422 40 61; Landstrasse 195; ☻ 5pm-1am Tue-Sat) Giving Klosters Platz an injection of cool, this chichi cocktail bar plays soft lounge tunes and flaunts a razor-sharp design with spidery metal lights and high-back chairs. How clever: gilt-framed pictures, which, on closer inspection, reveal (real) bubbling goldfish.

Getting There & Away

See Davos (p313), as Klosters is on the same train route between Landquart and Filisur.

Klosters and Davos are linked by free buses for those with Guest Cards or ski passes.

DAVOS
pop 10,700 / elevation 1560m

OK, so Davos isn't a pretty face – that honour belongs to sibling rival Klosters. But what the resort lacks in chocolate-box looks, it makes up for with seductive skiing, including monster runs descending up to 2000m, and Europop-fuelled après-ski parties. It is also the annual meeting point for the crème de la crème of world capitalism, the World Economic Forum. Global chat fests aside, Davos inspired Sir Arthur Conan Doyle (of *Sherlock Holmes* fame) to don skis and Thomas Mann to pen *The Magic Mountain*.

Orientation & Information

Davos stretches 4km beside the train line and the Landwasser River. It comprises two contiguous areas, each with a train station: Davos Platz and the older Davos Dorf. The main branch of the **tourist office** (☎ 081 415 21 21; www.davos.ch; Promenade 67; ☙ 8.30am-6.30pm Mon-Fri, 9am-5pm Sat, 10am-noon & 3-5.30pm Sun) is in

Platz. Hours are reduced in low season (spring and autumn). The **post office** (Bahnhofstrasse 9; ☙ 8.30am-noon & 2pm-6pm Mon-Fri, 8.30-11am Sat) is in Davos Dorf.

The Guest Card allows free travel on local buses and trains, as does the general ski pass (and the Swiss Pass). **Expert RoRo** (☎ 081 420 11 11; Promenade 123; per 20/60min Sfr5/12) has Internet access.

Sights

Davos is mostly an outdoor experience, but if you're craving a culture fix, quirky museums include the ski-obsessed **Wintersportmuseum** (☎ 081 413 24 84; Promenade 43; adult/child Sfr5/3; ☙ 4.30-6.30pm Tue & Thu Dec-Mar & Jul-Oct), catapulting you back to an age where men were as tough as hobnail boots.

Kirchner Museum (☎ 081 413 22 02; Ernst-Ludwig-Kirchner-Platz; adult/child/senior & student Sfr10/5/8; ☙ 10am-6pm Tue-Sun Christmas-Easter & 15 Jul-late Sep, 2-6pm Tue-Sun rest of year) displays the world's largest collection of works by the German expressionist painter Ernst Ludwig Kirchner (1880–1938), who painted extraordinary scenes of the area. When the Nazis classified

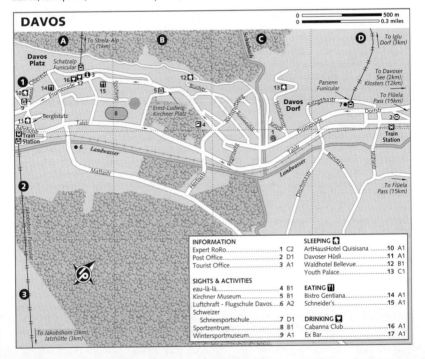

DAVOS

0 — 500 m
0 — 0.3 miles

Kirchner a 'degenerate artist' and emptied galleries of his works, he was overcome with despair and took his own life in 1938.

Activities

WINTER SPORTS

Naturally blessed with awesome scenery and great powder, Davos has carved out a name for itself as a first-class **skiing** destination, offering varied runs in five different areas. The vast **Parsenn** area reaches as high as Weissfluhjoch (2844m), from where you can ski to Küblis, more than 2000m lower and 12km away. Alternatively, take the demanding run to Wolfgang (1629m) or the scenic slopes to Klosters. Across the valley, **Jakobshorn** is a favourite **snowboarding** playground with its half-pipe, terrain park and excellent off-piste opportunities. See p310 for ski-pass prices.

One of the best ski and snowboard schools is the **Schweizer Schneesportschule** (☎ 081 416 24 54; www.ssd.ch; Promenade 157). Davos is a **cross-country skiing** hot spot, with 75km of well-groomed trails, including classic and skating options, plus a floodlit track for starlit swishing. It is also laced with **toboggan** runs, such as the 2.5km floodlit track from Schatzalp to Davos Platz; hire your sled at base station Schatzalp.

SUMMER ACTIVITIES

Together Davos and Klosters provide 700km of marked **hiking** paths and 600km of **mountain bike** tracks. Summertime water sports include windsurfing and sailing on **Davoser See** (Davos Lake). At the **Sportzentrum** (☎ 081 415 36 00; Talstrasse 41), you can get into handball, volleyball and more – it is free for overnight guests. Daredevils eager to leap off Jakobshorn can book tandem flights for around Sfr175 by contacting **Luftchraft – Flugschule Davos** (☎ 079 623 19 70; www.luftchraft.ch; Mattastrasse 9). If you prefer horizontal sightseeing to vertical drops, try **eau-là-là** (☎ 081 413 64 63; www.eau-la-la.ch; Promenade 90; pool adult/child Sfr9/5, day spa Sfr26; 🕑 10am-10pm Mon-Sat, 10am-6pm Sun), with heated outdoor pools and a spa affording mountain views.

Festivals & Events

Classical music dominates the **Davos Festival**, from late July to early August. It's preceded by a week-long jazz festival. Swiss craziness peaks at **Sertig Schwinget** in August, with *Schwingen* (Alpine wrestling) champs doing battle in the sawdust. Davos hosts the **FIS Cross-Country World Cup** in December.

Sleeping

Davoser Hüsli (☎ 081 417 67 77; Berglistutz 2; dm/s/d Sfr45/50/100) A cheap 'n cheerful choice in Davos Platz, the traditional Hüsli chalet offers a mix of cosy, low-ceilinged dorms and rooms with shared bathrooms. Claustrophobics may find them a trifle stifling, however.

Youth Palace (☎ 081 410 19 20; www.youthhostel.ch/davos; Horlaubenstrasse 27; dm/d/tr with half-board Sfr51/162/213; 🅿) Near Parsenn funicular, this one-time sanatorium has been transformed into a groovy backpacker palace. Party-loving, budget-conscious skiers dig the bright, modern dorms with pine bunks (balconies cost a few francs extra). There's a relaxed lounge, ski storage and wi-fi.

ArtHausHotel Quisisana (☎ 081 410 05 10; www.arthaushotel.ch; Platzstrasse 5; s/d Sfr150/260) Sprinkled liberally with owner Diego do Clavadetscher's abstract acrylics, this self-defined art hotel shelters modern and fairly spacious rooms (miniscule bathrooms aside).

Waldhotel Bellevue (☎ 081 415 37 47; www.waldhotel-bellevue.ch; Buolstrasse 3; s/d Sfr240/440; 🅿 💻 🏊) Once a sanatorium (which became the Magic Mountain in Thomas Mann's eponymous 1924 novel), this hotel has recently been given a stylish facelift. Rooms are comfy, if a tad on the standard side. When you tire of mountain views from your balcony, spoil yourself in the spa's saltwater pools and saunas. The restaurant specialises in Grisons cuisine.

Eating

Strela-Alp (☎ 081 413 56 83; mains Sfr15-30; 🕑 9am-5pm May-Oct, 9am-11pm Tue-Sat & 9am-5pm Sun & Mon Dec-Apr) The stunning mountain views from the terrace are just as moreish as the menu at this rustic haunt near Schatzalp funicular top station. Work up an appetite for rösti and apple strudel with a bracing forest hike.

Schneider's (☎ 081 420 00 00; Promenade 68; pastries Sfr3-6, mains Sfr20-35; 🕑 patisserie 7am-6.30pm, restaurant 8am-7pm) Crumbly pastries, beer-filled truffles and *Bündner Nüsstorte* (nut tart) lure the sweet toothed to this patisserie and tearoom. They serve regional dishes too, but personally we'd skip them and go straight for dessert!

Bistro Gentiana (☎ 081 413 56 49; Promenade 53; mains Sfr28-42; 🕑 closed May, Wed in summer) This art-deco bistro specialises in snails *(Schnecken)* and rich cheese fondues. A dish of six juicy snails ovencooked in mushroom heads costs Sfr29.80.

BABY IT'S COLD INSIDE...

Brace yourself for a frosty welcome at Davos' **Iglu Dorf** (☎ 041 612 27 28; www.iglu-dorf.com; Parsenn/Hauptertäli; per person Sfr149-179; ☷ late Dec–mid-Apr), an igloo village at 2620m for those keen to live out Inuit fantasies. The thought alone of kipping in a dome-shaped ice dwelling might make your teeth chatter, but snuggle down in your expedition sleeping bag and pull over the sheepskins and you'll soon forget those subzero temps. Gloopy fondue served in a communal pot and pre-bedtime schnapps at the ice bar also help pave the way to slumber land. And few experiences can match snowshoeing through the starry night with iridescent peaks all around apart from, that is, shelling out the extra for an igloo suite with private whirlpool. How cool is that?

Drinking

Cabanna Club (☎ 081 415 42 01; Promenade 63; ☷ 8pm-3am Dec-Apr) Techno dominates the decks of this ever-popular club in Hotel Europe. It's heaven for those seeking life after après-ski.

Ex Bar (☎ 081 413 56 45; Promenade 63; ☷ 5pm-6am daily winter, 5pm-2am Mon-Thu, 5pm-5am Fri & Sat summer) Europop tunes, free salty popcorn and a huge toy reindeer hanging over the door sum up this crowded party den.

Jatzhütte (☎ 081 413 73 61; Jakobshorn) Perched at 2530m, this is Davos' wackiest après-ski joint. Those who dare to partially bare can soak in a 39°C whirlpool framed by icy peaks. Prefer to keep your thermals on? Grab a flame-grilled burger, try the sex coffee (the mind boggles!) or take your ski boots grooving inside.

Getting There & Away

For trains to Chur (Sfr28, 1½ hours) or Zürich (Sfr51, 2½ hours), you will change at Landquart. For St Moritz (Sfr29, 1½ hours), take the train at Davos Platz and change at Filisur. For the hourly service to Scuol (Sfr28, 1¼ hours) in the Unterengadin, take the train from Davos Dorf and change at Klosters.

PARC ELA

Dropping southwest of Davos towards Tiefencastel, you enter the wilderness of Switzerland's biggest nature park, **Parc Ela** (☎ 081 407 11 18; www.parc-ela.ch, in German), which opened in 2006 to protect the region's biotope and boost its weak economy. Spanning 600 sq km and encompassing 21 communities in the Albula–Bergün and Savognin–Bivio areas, the park is three and a half times the size of the Swiss National Park.

Driving through the **Albulatal** (Albula Valley), you'll pass flower-strewn pastures, thick pine and larch forests, lonely moors, bizarre rock formations and tiny hamlets with Italianate churches. Near family-friendly Wiesen (www.wiesen.ch), a superb base for hikers, mountains rise abruptly above the valley floor and make the stone railway arches of the early 20th-century, Unesco-listed **Albulabahn** (www.rhb-unesco.ch) appear toytown tiny.

THE ENGADINE

The almost-3000km-long Inn River (En in Romansch) springs up from the snowy Graubünden Alps around the Maloja Pass and gives its name to its long valley, the Engadine (Engadin in German, Engiadina in Romansch).

The valley is carved into two: the Oberengadin (Upper Engadine), from Maloja to Zernez; and the Unterengadin (Lower Engadine), stretching from Zernez to Martina, by the Austrian border.

Oberengadin is dominated by the ritzy ski resort of St Moritz and the windsurfing mecca of Silvaplana, while Unterengadin, comprising two valleys and home to the country's only national park, is characterised by quaint villages with sgraffito-decorated houses and pristine countryside. It's one of the best places to hear Romansch spoken, although the lingua franca is German.

Chalandamarz, a spring and youth festival, is celebrated in the Engadine on 1 March. During **Schlitteda**, lads on flamboyant horse-drawn sleds whisk girls (to their delight or dismay) on rides through the snow. This age-old custom takes place in St Moritz, Pontresina and Silvaplana in January.

UNTERENGADIN

The thickly wooded Unterengadin (Lower Engadine in English, Bassa Engiadina in Romansch) in eastern Switzerland juts like a wolf's snout into neighbouring Austria and Italy. From Davos, the N28 highway climbs up to the barren Flüela Pass (2383m) in a series of loops before dropping over the other side, opening up majestic vistas of Alpine crags, valleys and silvery mountain streams.

The road descends to **Susch**, close to the exit point of Sagliains for the car train through the Vereina Tunnel from Selfranga (just outside Klosters), the only way to make the trip when snow blocks the pass. Trains run every 30 to 60 minutes during the day and cost Sfr27 to Sfr40 per car, depending on the season.

From Susch you can head 6km south to Zernez and then east into the Swiss National Park and Val Müstair, or further southwest to the Oberengadin. Or you can follow the Inn on its gradual eastern progress to Austria.

Guarda and around

pop 180 / elevation 1653m

With its twisting cobbled streets and hobbit-like houses in candy shades, serene **Guarda**, 6km east of Susch, has story-book appeal. Guarda is 30 minutes' uphill trudge from its valley-floor train station, or take the postal bus (Sfr3), which runs roughly hourly during the day. A trail leads 8km north to the foothills of 3312m Piz Buin (of sunscreen fame), dominating the glaciated Silvretta range on the Swiss-Austrian border.

Guarda has plenty of lodgings in its traditional houses, including family-run, flower-bedecked **Hotel Piz Buin** (☎ 081 861 30 00; www.pizbuin.ch; s/d Sfr95/176), where many of the cosy, immaculate rooms are clad in Swiss stone pine. Take breakfast on the terrace to the backbeat of cowbells before a bubble in the outdoor hot tub overlooking the mountains.

A couple of wooded kilometres east lies the hamlet of **Bos-cha**, but by car you can't get any further. To continue, return to the low road and follow the signs up to **Ardez**, a tiny village with a ruined medieval tower, well-preserved oriels and 17th-century Chesa Claglüna, decorated with elaborate sgraffito. Another 8km brings you to **Ftan**, where forested slopes rise gently to brooding pinnacles. From here, the narrow road slithers down to Scuol.

Scuol

pop 2180 / elevation 1250m

Surrounded by rippling peaks and dense forests, Scuol is a seasoned people pleaser – ideal for remote Alpine hikes in summer, crowd-free cruising in winter and blissful relaxation in its thermal baths year-round. Scuol's cobbled heart is a loveable jumble of centuries-old houses embellished with sgraffito.

ORIENTATION & INFORMATION

The train station is 1km west of the village centre. For info on outdoor activities in the region, nip into the **tourist office** (☎ 081 861 22 22; www.scuol.ch; Stradun; ☉ 8am-6.30pm Mon-Fri, 9am-12.30pm & 1-5.30pm Sat, 9am-noon Sun, reduced hr btwn seasons) in the town centre.

SIGHTS & ACTIVITIES

The Old Town (Lower Scuol) is made for languid saunters, and is peppered with quaint Engadine dwellings and cobbled squares, where fountains spout mineral water, tapped from one of 20 springs in the region. Slung high on a clifftop, 11th-century **Schloss Tarasp** (☎ 081 864 93 68; www.schloss-tarasp.ch; tour adult/child Sfr7.20/3.20; ☉ guided visits 2.30pm & 3.30pm Jun–mid-Jul & Sep–mid-Oct, 11am, 2.30pm, 3.30pm & 4.30pm mid-Jul–Aug) is fairy-tale stuff. It's a 6km drive to the southwest.

Scuol's biggest stunner is **Engadin Bad Scuol** (☎ 081 861 20 00; www.engadinbadscuol.ch; Stradun; adult/under 6yr/6-15yr Sfr25/5/16; ☉ 8am-9.45pm), one of Switzerland's finest thermal baths. Standard entry gives 2½ hours in the saunas, pools with massage jets, waterfalls and whirlpools. The snail-shaped outdoor pool is especially atmospheric by night, when you can enjoy a starlit soak. For full-on pampering, book a 2¼-hour Roman-Irish bath (Sfr66), combining different baths, massages and relaxation, all done naked.

There's **skiing** above Scuol up to 2800m, with a total of 80km of runs. A one-day pass costs Sfr51/26/41 for adults/children/students. **Engadin Adventure** (☎ 081 861 14 19; www.engadin-adventure.ch) offers **white-water rafting** for Sfr95 and knuckle-whitening **downhill bike tours** from Motta Naluns to Scuol for Sfr96 including equipment.

SLEEPING & EATING

Scuol has a campsite, apartments and several attractive hotels in the Old Town and Stradun, the main drag in the modern town.

Hotel Traube (☎ 081 861 07 00; www.traube.ch; Stradun; s/d 120/210) This peach-fronted hotel has light, spacious rooms, a sauna and even its own mineral spring. The pine-panelled restaurant tempts with Swiss-Italian fare such as porcini risotto.

ourpick **Hotel Engiadina** (☎ 081 864 14 21; www
.engiadina-scuol.ch, in German; d Sfr178-264) Boutiquey
Engiadina offers silent slumber in the Old
Town. Beautifully decorated in Swiss stone
pine and drenched with light, rooms vary –
some are whitewashed, some vaulted, some
feature intricate timber ceilings. Best of all
is the award-winning restaurant (mains
Sfr25 to Sfr54), serving specialities like rack
of Alpine venison with hazelnut *Pizokel* by
candlelight.

GETTING THERE & AWAY
The train from St Moritz (Sfr26, 1½ hours),
with a change at Samedan, terminates at
Scuol-Tarasp station. There are direct trains
from Klosters (Sfr21.60, 45 minutes). From
Scuol, the train to Guarda (Sfr7) takes 17
minutes. Postal buses from the station operate year-round to Tarasp (Sfr4, 15 minutes),
Samnaun (Sfr19, 1¼ hours), and Austria (as
far as Landeck).

Samnaun
pop 819 / elevation 1377m
The drive east along the Inn to the Austrian
border is beautiful, if otherwise eventless. You
could detour briefly into Austria and then
back into a remote corner of Switzerland to
the duty-free town of Samnaun. Part of the
Silvretta Arena, Samnaun has access to 230km
of groomed pistes in winter, but most locals
pour in for the tax-free goods. Its crazier claim
to fame is as the host of the Santa Claus World
Championships (see boxed text, right).

Müstair
pop 765 / elevation 1375m
Squirreled away in a remote corner of
Switzerland, Müstair is one of Europe's early
Christian treasures. When Charlemagne supposedly founded a monastery and a church
here in the 9th century, this was a strategically
placed spot below the Ofen Pass, separating
northern Europe from Italy and the heart
of Christendom.

For information on lodgings along the Val
Müstair, check with the village **tourist office**
(☎ 081 858 50 00; www.val-muestair.ch; 9am-6pm Mon-
Fri, 1.30-6pm Sat & Sun May-Oct, 10am-noon & 1.30-4.30pm
Mon-Fri, 1.30-4.30pm Sat & Sun Nov-Apr).

Vibrant Carolingian (9th century) and
Romanesque (12th century) frescos smother
the interior of the church of **Kloster St Johann**
(St John's Monastery; ☎ 081 851 62 28; www.muestair.ch;

YOU BETTER WATCH OUT

For most of the year Samnaun is but a
sleepy little town. Yet on the first weekend in December, it steals Lapland's reigns
by staging **Clau Wau** (www.clauwau.com),
aka the Santa Claus World Championships.
Some 100 pseudo–Father Christmases
gather to compete for the title of world's
best Santa. The men in red prove their Xmas
factor in disciplines like chimney climbing,
gingerbread decorating, gift-laden donkey
racing (for want of reindeer) and sledding.
It's an event full of Yuletide cheer and ho-
ho-ho-ing overkill.

---

admission free; 7am-8pm May-Oct & 7am-5pm Nov-
Apr). Beneath Carolingian representations of
Christ in Glory in the apses are Romanesque
stories depicting the grisly ends of St Peter
(crucified), St Paul (decapitated) and St Steven
(stoned). Above all reign images of Christ
in Heavenly Majesty. Next door, the **museum**
(adult/child Sfr12/6; 9am-noon & 1.30-5pm Mon-Sat,
1.30-5pm Sun May-Oct, 10am-noon & 1.30-4.30pm Mon-Sat,
1.30-4.30pm Sun Nov-Apr) takes you through part of
the monastery complex, with Carolingian art
and other relics.

Located just before the Italian border at the
end of Val Müstair, Müstair can be reached
from Samnaun by dropping down through
Austria and Italy, or Zernez through the national park (see below). Postal buses run along
the valley between Zernez and Müstair (Sfr19,
one hour).

Swiss National Park (Parc Naziunal Svizzer)
Created in 1914 and spanning 172 sq km,
Switzerland's only national park is a nature-gone-wild swathe of dolomitic peaks,
shimmering glaciers, larch woodlands, gen-
tian-flecked pastures, clear waterfalls, and
high moors strung with topaz-blue lakes.
Don walking boots to hit trails where you're
just as likely to encounter ibexes, burrowing
marmots and golden eagles as other walkers.
A fabulous day hike is the tough yet rewarding
Lakes of Macun (p80).

At the national park's core lies **Zernez**, home
to the brand-new, hands-on **Swiss National Park
Centre** (☎ 081 851 41 41; www.nationalpark.ch; adult/
under 6yr/6-16yr Sfr7/free/3; 8.30am-6pm Jun-Oct, 9am-
noon & 2-5pm Nov-May), where you can explore a

GRAUBÜNDEN

NO LIONS, NO TIGERS, BUT BEARS – OH MY!

In recent years, brown bears with wanderlust and an appetite for tasty Swiss sheep have frequently crossed the border from Italy into the Engadine. Their favourite place to cause havoc? The Swiss National Park, naturally, where they have less chance of being spotted. Bears made several cameo appearances in summer 2007, sticking their paws into beehives near Zernez and upsetting locals by killing a dozen or more sheep around the Albula Pass. One was captured and given a tracking device, which should at least put a stop to his Swiss escapades.

---

marmot hole, eyeball adders in the vivarium and learn about conservation and environmental change. The tourist office here can provide details on hikes in the park, including the three-hour trudge from S-chanf to Alp Trupchun, particularly popular in autumn, when you might spy rutting deer; and the Naturlehrpfad circuit near Il Fuorn, where bearded vultures are often sighted.

Entry to the park and its car parks is free. Walkers can enter by trails from Zernez, S-chanf and Scuol. Conservation is paramount here, so stick to footpaths and respect regulations prohibiting camping, littering, lighting fires, cycling, picking flowers and disturbing the animals.

SLEEPING & EATING

There are several hotels and restaurants in Zernez and a couple in the park itself.

Chamanna Cluozza (☎ 081 856 12 35; cluozza@hotmail .com; dm/d with half-board Sfr58/136; ☼ late Jun–mid-Oct) For peace and a cracking location, you can't beat this forest hideaway. The dorms are great for walkers eager to hit the trail first thing. It's about a three-hour hike southeast from Zernez.

Hotel Bär & Post (☎ 081 851 55 00; www.baer-post.ch; Zernez; dm/s/d Sfr18/85/170) Welcoming all-comers since 1905, these central digs have inviting rooms with lots of stone pine and downy duvets, plus basic bunk rooms. There's also a sauna and a rustic restaurant, dishing up good steaks and pasta.

Il Fuorn (☎ 081 856 12 26; www.ilfuorn.ch; Il Fuorn; s/d from Sfr80/140, half-board extra Sfr30; ☼ May-Oct) Bang in the heart of the national park, this guest

house shelters light, comfy rooms with pine furnishings. Trout and game are big on the *Stübli* menu.

GETTING THERE & AWAY

Trains run regularly from Zernez to St Moritz (Sfr17.40, 50 minutes), stopping at S-chanf, Zuoz and Celerina. For the latter and St Moritz, change at Samedan.

OBERENGADIN

Just as the Unterengadin is loaded with rural charm, the Oberengadin is charged with skiing adrenalin. St Moritz, possibly the slickest resort of the lot in Switzerland, is joined by a string of other piste-pounding hot spots along the Oberengadin Valley and nearby Pontresina. The regional ski pass covers 350km of runs.

Zuoz
pop 1245 / elevation 1750m

Zuoz, 13km southwest of Zernez, is a quintessential Engadine town, with colourful sgraffito houses, flower boxes bursting with geraniums and Augusto Giacometti stained-glass windows illuminating the church chancel. Though skiing is fairly limited, the town is unquestionably one of the Oberengadin's prettiest.

Overlooking the central plaza is **Hotel Crusch Alva** (☎ 081 854 13 19; www.hotelcruschalva.ch; Via Maistra 26; s/d Sfr115/230; ☼ closed Nov & May). The 12 rooms in this beautiful 500-year-old Engadine house are full of timber-flavoured rustic charm. Savour fondue or fish in the little *Stüva* (parlour) on the 1st floor.

Design trailblazer **Castell** (☎ 081 851 52 53; www.hotelcastell.ch; d/ste 300/470; P 🖳) gets rave reviews for its nature-meets-minimalist interiors. Some of Europe's leading architects have pooled their creativity to transform this turn-of-the-century hotel, which now boasts art-slung spaces, chic and colourful rooms and a restaurant serving Asian-inspired cuisine. Unwind with a steam or a soapy massage in the ultra-cool *hammam* (Turkish bath).

Celerina

Hugging the banks of the Inn River, sunny Celerina is a 45-minute amble northeast of St Moritz and shares the same ski slopes. It's often mentioned in the same breath as its 1.6km Olympic **bob run** (☎ 081 830 02 00; www .olympia-bobrun.ch), which is the world's oldest and made from natural ice. A hair-raising

135km/h 'taxi ride' trip costs a cool Sfr250, but the buzz is priceless. Equally heart-stopping is the head-first 1km **Cresta Run** (☎ 081 833 46 09; www.cresta-run.com), created by British tourists in 1885, which starts near the Schiefer Turm in St Moritz. A set of five rides costs Sfr600 (and Sfr50 a ride thereafter).

The **tourist office** (☎ 081 830 00 11; www.celerina.ch; cnr Via Maistra & Via da la Staziun; ☜ 8.30am-6pm Mon-Fri, 9am-noon & 2-6pm Sat, 4-6pm Sun high season, 8.30am-noon & 2-6pm Mon-Fri, 9am-noon Sat low season) is in the village centre.

Hotel Cresta Run (☎ 081 833 09 19; www.hotel-cresta -run.ch; Via Maistra; d/tr/q Sfr170/210/260; **P**) is on a minor road linking Celerina and St Moritz, about 500m south of Celerina's town centre. It's a simple family hotel, with its own pizzeria, located by the finish of the Cresta bob run.

Celerina is easily reached from St Moritz by train (Sfr3, three minutes) or by local bus.

ST MORITZ
pop 5060 / elevation 1856m
Switzerland's original winter wonderland and the cradle of Alpine tourism, St Moritz (San Murezzan in Romansch) has been luring royals, the filthy rich and moneyed wannabes since 1864. With its smugly perfect lake and aloof mountains, the town looks a million dollars. Those still waiting to make their first billion usually stay in St Moritz Bad.

Yet despite the Gucci set propping up the bars and celebs bashing the pistes (Kate Moss and George Clooney included), this resort isn't all show. The real riches lie outdoors with superb carving on Corviglia, hairy black runs on Diavolezza and miles of hiking trails when the powder melts.

Orientation & Information
Uphill from the lakeside train station on Via Serlas is the post office and five minutes further on is the **tourist office** (☎ 081 837 33 33; www .stmoritz.ch; Via Maistra 12; ☜ 9am-6.30pm Mon-Fri, 9am-noon & 1.30-6pm Sat, 4-6pm Sun Dec-Easter & mid-Jun–mid-Sep, 9am-noon & 2-6pm Mon-Fri, 9am-noon Sat rest of the year). St Moritz Bad is about 2km southwest of the main town, St Moritz Dorf. Local buses and postal buses shuttle between the two. Not much stays open during November, May and early June.

Sights
For a peek at the archetypal dwellings and humble interiors of the Engadine Valley, visit the **Engadiner Museum** (☎ 081 833 43 33; Via dal Bagn 39; adult/child Sfr5/2.50; ☜ 10am-noon & 2-5pm Mon-Fri, 10am-noon Sun Dec-Apr & Jun-Oct), showing traditional stoves and archaeological finds.

Giovanni Segantini (1858–99) beautifully captured the dramatic light and ambience of the Alps on canvas. His paintings are shown at the **Segantini Museum** (☎ 081 833 44 54; www .segantini-museum.ch; Via Somplaz 30; adult/child/student Sfr10/3/7; ☜ 10am-noon & 2-6pm Tue-Sun Dec-Apr & mid-May–mid-Oct).

Activities
SKIING
Downhill skiing concentrates on three key areas: Corviglia, Corvatsch and Diavolezza. For groomed slopes with big mountain vistas, head to Corviglia (2486m), accessible by funicular from Dorf. From Bad a cable car goes to Signal (shorter queues), giving access to the slopes of Piz Nair. A ski pass for both areas costs Sfr67 (child/youth Sfr23/45) for one day. There's varied skiing at Corvatsch (3303m), above nearby Silvaplana, including spectacular glacier descents and the gentle black run Hahnensee. Silhouetted by glaciated four-thousanders, Diavolezza (2978m) is a must-ski for freeriders and fans of jaw-dropping descents. Avid cross-country skiers can glide through snow-dusted woodlands and plains on 160km of groomed trails.

The first Swiss ski school was founded in St Moritz in 1929. Today you can arrange skiing or snowboarding tuition (Sfr70 per day) at the **Schweizer Skischule** (☎ 081 830 01 01; www .skischool.ch; Via Stredas 14; ☜ 8am-6pm Mon-Sat, 8-9am & 3.30-6pm Sun Dec-Apr).

A general ski pass covering all the slopes, including Silvaplana, Sils-Maria, Celerina, Zuoz, Pontresina and Diavolezza costs Sfr384/131/257 for adults/children/youths for seven days in high season. Visit the website www.skiengadin.ch for the low-down on skiing facilities and services.

HIKING & OTHER ACTIVITIES
In summer, get out and stride one of the region's excellent **hiking** trails, such as the Corvatsch *Wasserweg* (water trail) linking six mountain lakes. Soaring above St Moritz, Piz Nair (3057m) affords panoramic vistas of Alpine peaks and the lakes and valley below. For a cliff-hanger moment, tackle the vertiginous **Piz Trovat** *via ferrata* at Diavolezza; equipment rental is available at the base

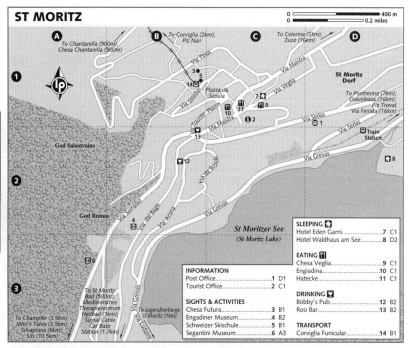

ST MORITZ

To Chantarella (900m);
Chesa Chantarella (900m)

To Corviglia (2km);
Piz Nair

To Celerina (2km);
Zuoz (16km)

St Moritz
Dorf

To Pontresina (7km);
Diavolezza (16km);
Piz Trovat
Via Ferrata (16km)

God Salastrains

Train
Station

God Ruinas

St Moritzer See
(St Moritz Lake)

To St Moritz
Bad (500m);
Medizinisches
Therapiezentrum
Heilbad (1km);
Signal Cable
Car Base
Station (1.7km)

To Champfèr (3.5km);
Jöhri's Talvo (3.5km);
Silvaplana (6km);
Sils (10.5km)

To Jugendherberge
St Moritz (1km)

SLEEPING	
Hotel Eden Garni	7 C1
Hotel Waldhaus am See	8 D2

EATING	
Chesa Veglia	9 C1
Engiadina	10 C1
Hatecke	11 C1

DRINKING	
Bobby's Pub	12 B2
Roo Bar	13 B2

TRANSPORT	
Corviglia Funicular	14 B1

INFORMATION	
Post Office	1 D1
Tourist Office	2 C1

SIGHTS & ACTIVITIES	
Chesa Futura	3 B1
Engadiner Museum	4 B2
Schweizer Skischule	5 B1
Segantini Museum	6 A3

station. The tourist office has a map providing more suggestions (in English) for walking in Oberengadin.

St Moritz has recently boosted its eco-credentials with the 2½-hour **Clean Energy Tour** (www.clean-energy.ch, in German). Showcasing different kinds of renewable energy in natural settings, the green tour whisks you up to Piz Nair via Chantarella and Corviglia. You'll hike down from Chantarella along the flower-speckled Heidi Blumenweg, then Schellenurslisweg past Lord Norman Foster's eco-sound, wood-tiled Chesa Futura.

After all that exertion, rest in a mineral bath or with a mud pack at **Medizinisches Therapiezentrum Heilbad** (☎ 081 833 30 62; www.heilbad -stmoritz.ch; Plazza Paracelsus 2; admission to mineral baths Sfr35; ☻ 8am-noon & 2-7pm Mon-Fri, 8am-noon Sat).

Festivals & Events
St Moritz hosts the notoriously gruelling **Engadine Ski Marathon** (www.engadin-skimarathon.ch) in early March, where cross-country skiers skate 42km from Maloja to S-chanf. The frozen lake is the centre of attention again in late January for the **Cartier Polo World Cup on**

Snow (www.polostmoritz.com) and in early February for the **White Turf** (www.whiteturf.ch) winter horse races.

Sleeping
Jugendherberge St Moritz (☎ 081 836 61 11; Stille Via Surpunt 60; www.youthhostel.ch/st.moritz; dm/d Sfr55/137; ☐) Budget beds are gold-dust rare in St Moritz, but you'll find one at this hostel edging the forest. The four-bed dorms and doubles are quiet and clean. There's a kiosk, games room and laundrette.

Chesa Chantarella (☎ 081 833 33 55; www.chesa chantarella.ch; Via Salastrains; s/d Sfr95/190; ☻ Jun-Sep & Dec-Apr; ℗) Sitting above the town, this is a lively choice with bright, modern rooms. Sip hot chocolate on the terrace, venture down to the wine cellar or dine on hearty local fare in the restaurant.

Hotel Eden Garni (☎ 081 830 81 00; www.edenst moritz.ch; Via Veglia 12; s/d Sfr169/318; ℗ ☐) Smack in the heart of St Moritz Dorf, this is a decent midrange pick with an attractive central atrium. The old-style, pine-panelled rooms are cosy and those on the top floor afford terrific lake and mountain views.

Hotel Waldhaus am See (☎ 081 836 60 00; www .waldhaus-am-see.ch; s/d Sfr170/320; P 🖳) Overlooking the lake, this friendly pad has light-flooded rooms with pine furnishings and floral fabrics, many with enticing lake and mountain views. There's a sauna and a restaurant serving appetising grill specialities.

Eating

our pick **Hatecke** (☎ 081 864 11 75; www.hatecke.ch; Via Maistra 16; snacks & mains Sfr15-25; 🕙 9am-6.30pm Mon-Fri, 9am-6pm Sat) Edible art is the only way to describe the organic, locally sourced delicacies at Hatecke. *Bündnerfleisch* (air-dried beef) and melt-in-your-mouth venison ham are carved into wafer-thin slices on a century-old slicing machine in this speciality shop. Take a seat on a sheepskin stool in the funky café next door to lunch on delicious Engadine beef carpaccio or *Bündnerfleisch* with truffle oil.

Chesa Veglia (☎ 081 837 28 00; Via Veglia 2; pizza Sfr22-36, mains Sfr40-60, 🕙 daily Dec-Mar & Jul-Sep) This slate-roofed, chalk-white chalet is St Moritz' oldest restaurant, dating from 1658. The rustic interior is all low beams and creaking wood floors, while the terrace affords great views. Thin and crisp wood-oven pizzas are a good pick, as are the herby lamb cutlets.

Engiadina (☎ 081 833 32 65; Plazza da Scuola 2; fondue Sfr29-46; 🕙 Mon-Sat) A proper locals' place, Engiadina is famous for fondue, and that's the best thing to eat here. Champagne gives the melted cheese a kick. It's open year-round.

Jöhri's Talvo (☎ 081 833 44 55; Via Gunels 15; 4-course tasting menu lunch/dinner Sfr148/230; 🕙 Tue-Sun) Set in a converted 17th-century Engadine farmhouse in nearby Champfér, this gourmet haunt shines with two Michelin stars. Light pine, crisp white linen and candles create a backdrop for French taste sensations, such as Pyrenean milk-fed lamb and *bouillabaisse* (fish stew).

Drinking

Around 20 bars and clubs pulsate in winter. While you shuffle to the beat, your wallet might waltz itself wafer-thin, because nights out in St Moritz can be nasty on the banknotes.

Bobby's Pub (☎ 081 834 42 83; Via dal Bagn 50a; 🕙 9.30am-1.30am) Laid-back and friendly, this English-style watering hole serves 30 different brews and attracts young snowboarders in season. It's among the few places open year-round.

Roo Bar (☎ 081 837 50 50; Via Traunter Plazzas 7; 🕙 2-8pm Dec-Apr) After a hard day's skiing or boarding, snow bums fill the terrace of this après-ski joint at Hauser's Hotel. Hip hop, techno and copious quantities of schnapps fuel the party.

Getting There & Away

The **Glacier Express** (www.glacierexpress.ch) links St Moritz to Zermatt (Sfr133, plus Sfr10 reservation fee) via the 2033m Oberalp Pass. The majestic route takes 7½ hours to cover the 290km and crosses 291 bridges. In summer you pay Sfr15 or Sfr30 reservation fee, depending on the train.

Regular trains, as many as one every 30 minutes, run from Zürich to St Moritz (Sfr69, 3½ hours) with one change (at Landquart or Chur). Those via Landquart pass through Klosters, Zernez, Zuoz and Samedan. Via Chur they take a different route, passing through Reichenau, Thusis, Tiefencastel and Celerina.

Postal buses run every 30 to 60 minutes in high season from St Moritz southwest to Maloja (Sfr10.60, 35 minutes) with stops at Silvaplana (Sfr5, 14 minutes) and Sils-Maria (Sfr7.60, 21 minutes). For Pontresina and beyond, see Bernina Pass Rd (p320).

SILVAPLANA, SILS-MARIA & MALOJA

With two cobalt, wind-buffeted lakes framed by densely forested slopes, Silvaplana (Silvaplauna in Romansch), 7.5km southwest of St Moritz, is a kitesurfing and windsurfing mecca. Slip into a wetsuit at **Sportzentrum Mulets** (☎ 081 828 97 67; Silvaplana; intro/2-day/5-day course Sfr190/300/500; 🕙 10am-6pm), offering instruction and equipment rental. Four-hour introductory lessons take place on Thursdays from June to September.

A virtual ode to surfing, **Julier Palace** (☎ 081 828 96 44, www.julierpalace.com; Via Maistra 6, Silvaplana; r per person Sfr90-150; 🖳) has a party vibe, chill-out lounge and free internet. The retro-style rooms stretch from bare-bones noisy ones with futons to larger deluxe pads with snazzy paint jobs. All rooms have TVs and DVD players. The restaurant rolls out decent pizza and pasta dishes.

Another 4km brings you to picture-book **Sils-Maria** (Segl in Romansch) at the foot of the mountains. A cable car ascends to Furtschellas (2312m), where there is a network of hiking trails and ski slopes.

Sils might be a sleepy lakeside village now, but the rumble of existential philosophy once reverberated around these peaks, courtesy of Friedrich Nietzsche who spent his summers here from 1881 to 1888 writing texts concerning the travails of modern man, including *Thus Spake Zarathustra*. The **Nietzsche Haus** (☎ 081 826 53 69; www.nietzschehaus.ch; adult/child/student & senior Sfr6/free/3; ☒ 3-6pm Tue-Sun mid-Jun–mid-Oct & late Dec–mid-Apr) showcases photos, memorabilia, and letters penned by the German giant.

If you want to overnight in Sils, a terrific choice is family-run **Pensiun Privata** (☎ 081 832 62 00; www.pensiunprivata.ch; s/d Sfr190/340), a dreamy country-style hotel with huge pine-clad rooms, antique-style furniture and forest views from the herb and flower garden. For gregarious grandeur, try the palatial **Hotel Waldhaus** (☎ 081 838 51 00; www.waldhaus-sils.ch; s/d with half-board Sfr440/870; ☒ mid-Jun–Oct & mid-Dec–mid-Apr; ☒ ☒), set on a rise amid the woods. Along with modern comforts (pool, Turkish baths, tennis courts), the owners have carefully maintained the charm of the lavish public areas.

At hole-in-the-wall **Dada's Creparia** (☎ 081 826 51 04; crêpes Sfr5.50-17; ☒ 11.11am-10.10pm Thu-Mon), the chirpy staff whips up some of the lightest crêpes this side of the Alps – try nectarine and cream, organic cheese or chestnut and chocolate. Otherwise, head across to **Chesa Marchetta** (☎ 081 826 52 32; cakes Sfr5-6; ☒ 3.30-11pm), where you can sample delicious Engadine nut tart under the beams. The little shop at the front sells preserves made with home-grown fruit.

The road from Sils follows the north shore of its lake to the one-street village of **Maloja** and, shortly after, the **Maloja Pass**, which separates the Engadine from the Val Bregaglia. The artist Giovanni Segantini lived in the village from 1894. His **studio** (atelier; adult/child Sfr3/1.50; ☒ 3-5pm Wed & Sun mid-Jun–mid-Oct & Jan–mid-Apr) can be visited. Paintings are also on display in the **Belvedere Tower** (admission free; ☒ 9am-5pm daily Jun–mid-Oct & Jan-Apr). There are also several places to stay and eat.

All these towns are on the postal-bus route from St Moritz.

BERNINA PASS ROAD

Bare, brooding mountains and glaciers that sweep down to farmland give the landscape around the Bernina Pass (2323m; Passo del Bernina in Italian) austere grandeur. The road

twists spectacularly from Celerina southeast to Tirano in Italy, linking Val Bernina and Val Poschiavo. There is some great hiking in these heights, shown in detail on walking maps available from Pontresina tourist office.

From St Moritz, as many as 10 trains run via Pontresina (Sfr5, 11 minutes) direct to Tirano (Sfr29, 2½ hours) in northern Italy. This stretch of track, known as the **Bernina Line** (www.rhb-unesco .ch), was added to the Unesco World Heritage list in 2008 along with the Albula Pass (p313). Constructed in 1910, it is one of world's steepest narrow-gauge railways, negotiating the highest rail crossing in Europe and taking in spectacular glaciers, gorges and rock pinnacles.

PONTRESINA & AROUND
pop 1940 / elevation 1800m

At the mouth of the Val Bernina and licked by the ice-white tongue of Morteratsch Glacier, Pontresina is a relaxed alternative to St Moritz. Check out the pentagonal Moorish tower and the Santa Maria Chapel, with frescos dating from the 13th and 15th centuries.

From the train station, west of the village, cross the two rivers, Rosegg and Bernina, for the centre and the **tourist office** (☎ 081 838 83 00; www.pontresina.ch; Rondo Bldg, Via Maistra; ☒ 8.30am-6pm Mon-Fri, 8.30am-noon & 3-6pm Sat & 3-6pm Sun, closed Sun mid-Oct–mid-Dec).

Pontresina's own mountain, Piz Languard (3262m), is well suited to families and novice skiers. Use the resort as a base to explore slopes further down the valley at **Piz Lagalb** (2959m) and **Diavolezza** (2973m), with its phenomenal 10km glacier descent. Combined ski passes for the two cost Sfr58/20/39 per adult/child/ student (or get the Engadine skiing pass, p317). In summer, it's worth taking the cable cars to either for views. For striking glacier close-ups, walk from Diavolezza to Morteratsch.

Pontresina's dramatic cliffs and glaciated summits create a backdrop for other vigorous pursuits too. **GoVertical** (☎ 081 834 57 58; www.govertical .ch; Chesa Curtinatsch) covers the entire adventure spectrum from rock climbing and canyoning in summer to freeriding and snowshoeing in winter. Call ahead for times and prices.

Sleeping
Pension Hauser (☎ 081 842 63 26; www.hotelpension -hauser.ch; Cruscheda 165; s/d 85/170; ☒) Quiet and welcoming, this century-old Engadine house has rooms in Swiss stone pine that overlook Pontresina's rooftops. You'll find solid home

cooking and possibly accordion-playing locals in the restaurant.

Hotel Albris (☎ 081 838 80 40; www.albris.ch; Via Maistra; s/d Sfr155/280; **P** **🖳**) On Pontresina's main drag, Albris' well-appointed rooms feature lots of timber and squeaky-clean bathrooms. Downstairs there's a feng shui–inspired wellness centre. The restaurant is famous for its fish specialities and the bakery for its Engadine nut tart.

VAL POSCHIAVO

Once over the **Bernina Pass** (2328m), you drop into the sunny Italian-speaking Val Poschiavo. A fine lookout is Alp Grüm (2091m), reached on foot (two hours) from Ospizio Bernina restaurant at the pass.

Fourteen kilometres south of the pass lies **Poschiavo**, 15km from the border with Italy. At its heart is Plazza da Cumün, framed by pastel-hued mansions and pavement cafés. Right on the square, **Hotel Albrici** (☎ 081 844 01 73; www.hotelalbrici.ch; Plazza da Cumün; s/d Sfr85/150; **P**) is a 17th-century lodging, whose spacious rooms have polished-timber floors, antique furniture and plenty of charm. Sit on the restaurant terrace to munch crisp wood-fired pizza

You could pop down from St Moritz one day for a change of speed. Just past the glittering **Lago di Poschiavo**, the town of **Brusio** is known for its distinctive circular train viaduct. Another 5km and you reach **Tirano**, just over the Italian border.

VAL BREGAGLIA

From the Maloja Pass (1815m), the road spirals down into the rugged Val Bregaglia (Bergell in German), cutting a course south-west into Italy. The road then splits, with one arm leading north and back into Switzerland via the Splügen Pass, and the other going south to Lago di Como and on to Milan. The postal bus from St Moritz to Lugano branches off from the Milan road to circle the western shore of the lake.

As you proceed down the valley, the villages reveal an increasing Italian influence. **Stampa** was the home of the artist Alberto Giacometti (1901–66), and is the location of the valley's **tourist office** (☎ 081 822 15 55; www.bregaglia.ch; ⌚ 9-11.30am & 3-5.30pm Mon-Fri, 9-11.30am Sat).

Soglio (1090m), a hamlet near the Italian border, faces the smooth-sided Pizzo Badile (3308m) on a south-facing ledge, reached from the valley floor by a narrow road. The village, a warren of lanes and stone houses, lies at the end of a steep, thickly wooded trail off the main road and is the starting point for **hiking** trails, most notably the historic 11km La Panoramica route to Casaccia down in the valley.

There are several modest guest houses in Soglio alongside the dazzling white four-storey **Palazzo Salis** (☎ 081 822 12 08; www.palazzosalis.ch; Soglio; s Sfr100, d Sfr210-290; ⌚ early Mar-late Nov), a truly regal resting place with portraits gracing the walls, coats of armour and ornate furniture. Built in 1630, it has rooms with stucco or wooden ceilings, centuries-old antique furniture and oodles of charm. It also has a restaurant (mains Sfr20 to Sfr35) and mature gardens shaded by giant sequoias.

Buses from St Moritz to Castasegna travel along Val Bregaglia. Alight at the post office at Promontogno and take the bus to Soglio from there (Sfr3.40, six to 10 departures daily, 12 minutes).

GRAUBÜNDEN

Ticino

The summer air is rich and hot. The peacock-proud posers propel their scooters in and out of traffic. Italian weather. Italian style. And that's not to mention the Italian ice cream, Italian pizza, Italian architecture, Italian language. But this isn't Rome, Florence or Naples. It's the Switzerland that Heidi never mentioned.

Ticino (Tessin in German and French) is a strange mix. Classic, dark-haired Latin lookers rub shoulders with equally style-conscious blue-eyed blondes. There is a certain vibrant snappiness in the air of towns like Lugano. But this is Switzerland, after all, and the temperament is tamer than further south. A lusty love for Italian comfort food and full-bodied wines (mostly merlot) is balanced by a healthy respect for rules and regulations. And in the scattered valley hamlets the Italian spoken has a halting lilt that marks its distance from the honeyed heat of southern Italian conversation. The very manner of the people is demonstrative of how the canton manages a blend of Swiss cool and Italian passion.

The region offers a little of everything. A touch of the shimmering lake life can be had in Lugano and Locarno. Their mirror-like lakes, studded with pastel-coloured villages sporting mansions and palm trees, are framed by grand, verdant mountains. To the north, Bellinzona, the region's capital, is a quieter but stunning medieval fortress town.

Those in search of rural quiet have come to the right place. Various valleys spread across the length of the northern half of the canton, blessed by homely hamlets, Romanesque chapels and endless hiking options past lakes and roaring mountain streams.

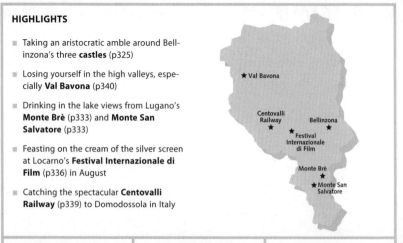

HIGHLIGHTS

- Taking an aristocratic amble around Bellinzona's three **castles** (p325)

- Losing yourself in the high valleys, especially **Val Bavona** (p340)

- Drinking in the lake views from Lugano's **Monte Brè** (p333) and **Monte San Salvatore** (p333)

- Feasting on the cream of the silver screen at Locarno's **Festival Internazionale di Film** (p336) in August

- Catching the spectacular **Centovalli Railway** (p339) to Domodossola in Italy

★ Val Bavona

Centovalli Railway ★ Bellinzona ★

★ Festival Internazionale di Film

Monte Brè ★

★ Monte San Salvatore

| ▪ POPULATION: 328,580 | ▪ AREA: 2812.5 SQ KM | ▪ LANGUAGE: ITALIAN |

History

Ticino, long a poor, rural buffer between the Swiss German cantons north of the Alps and Italy to the south, was absorbed by the Swiss in the late 15th century after centuries of changing hands between the lords of Como and the dukes of Milan.

The founding cantons of the Swiss confederation, Uri, Scwhyz and Unterwalden, defeated a superior Milanese force at Giornico in the Valle Levantina in 1478 and took Bellinzona in 1503, thus securing the confederation's vulnerable underbelly. In 1803, Ticino entered the new Swiss Confederation, concocted by Napoleon, as a free and equal canton.

Nowadays, the region thrives as a services (mostly banking) centre and tourist attraction,

especially for Swiss Germans looking for a little Italian style without leaving home. The establishment of a university at Lugano in 1996 was a significant step, as the Italian-speaking population had long been caught between two hard options: study elsewhere in Switzerland in another language, or overcome bureaucratic hell to gain admission to Italian universities.

With such a small percentage of the Swiss population, the canton counts for little in big national decisions. Wages are lower (as much as 25%) than in most of the rest of Switzerland and unemployment (at more than 4%) is above the national average (2.6%). Ticinesi are attracted by big brother Italy, but often suffer a sense of indifference, when not inferiority

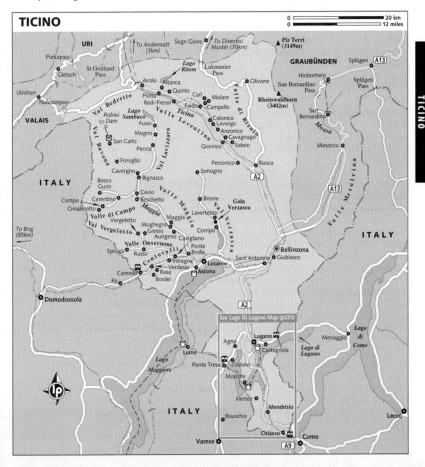

TICINO

(not aided by the parading Prada brigade from Milan), next to their southern cousins.

Ticino followed Italy's lead with an outright ban on smoking in all public places in 2007. It was the first canton to do so.

Orientation & Information

Ticino is the country's fourth-largest canton, bordering with Graubünden to the north and east, a small stretch of the Valais to the west, and with Italy to west, south and southeast. The climate is mild on the lakes and a little more extreme in the rural valleys. Average afternoon temperatures for Lugano are around 28°C in July and August, 17°C in April and September and 7°C in December and January. Locarno gets more than 2300 hours of sunshine per year.

In addition to the normal Swiss national holidays, the following public holidays are taken in Ticino:

Epiphany (Epifania or La Befana) 6 January
St Joseph's Day (Festa di San Giuseppe) 19 March
Labour Day (Festa del Lavoro) 1 May
Corpus Christi variable date
Sts Peter and Paul Day (Festa di SS Pietro e Paolo) 29 June
Feast of the Assumption (Assunzione or Ferragosto) 15 August
All Saints' Day (Ognissanti) 1 November
Feast of the Immaculate Conception (Immaculata Concezione) 8 December

The regional tourist office is the **Ente Ticinese per il Turismo** (☎ 091 825 70 56; www.ticino.ch; Villa Turrita, Via Lugano 12, Bellinzona; ⏱ 8.15am-noon & 1.30-5.30pm Mon-Fri). An administrative office, they have general information for the public too.

Pick up a *Ticino Camping* brochure, which details the canton's 39 camping grounds (you can also check them out online at www.ticino .ch). Ask about the 29 mountain huts run by the **Federazione Alpinistica Ticinese** (FAT; www.fat-ti.ch) along hiking trails. They and other huts (often unstaffed) are listed at www.capanneti.ch.

Wine is a big part of the Ticino experience. Get *Le Strade del Vino* map-guide, which details wineries around the canton. To learn more about Ticino Merlot mania, see www.ticinowine.ch.

Getting There & Around

The Lugano Regional Pass gives free travel on Lago di Lugano and on regional public transport in and around Lugano (including the funiculars up Monte Brè and San Salvatore).

It also gives free or reduced rides on the cable cars and rack and pinion railways in the area, as well as half-price transport to and around Locarno and on Lago Maggiore. The price is Sfr88/108 for three/seven days. It is available for 2nd class only and issued from around Easter to October.

BELLINZONA

pop 16,980 / elevation 230m
Placed at the convergence point of several valleys leading down from the Alps, Bellinzona is visually unique. Inhabited since Neolithic times, it is dominated by three grey-stone medieval castles that have attracted everyone from Swiss invaders to painters like William Turner. Turner may have liked the place, but Bellinzona has a surprisingly low tourist profile, in spite of its castles forming one of only nine World Heritage sites in Switzerland.

The rocky central hill upon which rises the main castle, Castelgrande, was a Roman frontier post and Lombard defensive tower, and was later developed as a heavily fortified town controlled by Milan. The three castles and valley walls could not stop the Swiss German confederate troops from overwhelming the city in 1503, thus deciding Ticino's fate for the following three centuries.

Information

Bisi (☎ 091 210 60 40; Via Magoria 10; per hr Sfr5; ⏱ 10am-7pm Mon-Fri) Internet access with eight computers in this Intercultural Library.
Post office (Viale della Stazione 18; ⏱ 7.30am-6.30pm Mon-Fri, 9am-noon Sat)
Tourist office (☎ 091 825 21 31; www.bellinzona turismo.ch; Piazza Nosetto; ⏱ 9am-6pm Mon-Fri, to noon Sat) In the restored Renaissance Palazzo Civico (town hall).

Sights & Activities

A stroll around the cobblestoned old town is a treat. Keep an eye out for fresco-adorned churches and close-knit townhouses. South of Piazza dell'Indipendenza, the medieval huddle gives way to elegant, if ageing, villas.

CASTLES

The city's three imposing castles are the main draw. Read up on them at www.bellinzona unesco.ch. To visit all three, get a general ticket (adult/concession Sfr10/4), valid indefinitely.

TICINO

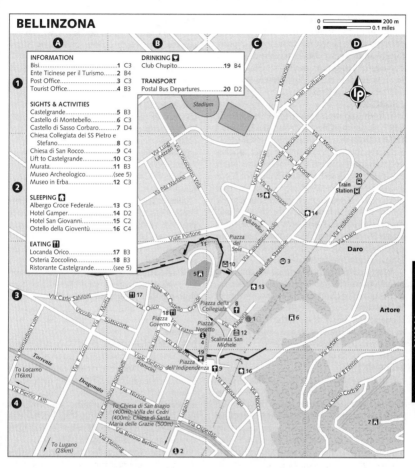

BELLINZONA

0 ——— 200 m
0 ——— 0.1 miles

INFORMATION	
Bisi	1 C3
Ente Ticinese per il Turismo	2 B4
Post Office	3 C3
Tourist Office	4 B3

SIGHTS & ACTIVITIES	
Castelgrande	5 B3
Castello di Montebello	6 C3
Castello di Sasso Corbaro	7 D4
Chiesa Collegiata dei SS Pietro e Stefano	8 C3
Chiesa di San Rocco	9 C4
Lift to Castelgrande	10 C3
Murata	11 B3
Museo Archeologico	(see 5)
Museo in Erba	12 C3

SLEEPING	
Albergo Croce Federale	13 C3
Hotel Gamper	14 D2
Hotel San Giovanni	15 C2
Ostello della Gioventù	16 C4

EATING	
Locanda Orico	17 B3
Osteria Zoccolino	18 B3
Ristorante Castelgrande	(see 5)

DRINKING	
Club Chupito	19 B4

TRANSPORT	
Postal Bus Departures	20 D2

Castelgrande (☎ 091 825 81 45; Monte San Michele; admission to grounds free; ⏰ 9am-10pm Tue-Sun, 10am-6pm Mon), dating from the 6th century, is the biggest fortification and is in the town centre. You can walk (head up Scalinata San Michele from Piazza della Collegiata) or take the lift, buried deep in the rocky hill in an extraordinary concrete bunker-style construction, from Piazza del Sole. The castle's **Museo Archeologico** (Archaeological Museum; adult/concession Sfr5/2; ⏰ 10am-6pm mid-Mar–Oct, to 5pm Nov–mid-Mar) has a modest collection of finds from the hill dating to prehistoric times. More engaging is the display of 15th-century decorations taken from the ceiling of a former noble house in central Bellinzona. The pictures range from weird animals (late medieval ideas on

what a camel looked like were curious) to a humorous series on the 'world upside down'. Examples of the latter include an ox driving a man-pulled plough and a sex-crazed woman chasing a chaste man (!). The uncomfortable black seats you sit on for the 12-minute audiovisual on the castle's history were designed by Mario Botta (see p330) and cost around Sfr1000 a pop!

After wandering the grounds and the museum, head west along the **Murata** (Walls; admission free; ⏰ 9am-7pm Apr-Sep, 10am-5pm Oct-Mar).

Castello di Montebello (☎ 091 825 13 42; Salita ai Castelli; admission to castle free; museum adult/concession Sfr5/2; ⏰ castle 8am-8pm mid-Mar–Oct, museum 10am-6pm mid-Mar–Oct) is slightly above the town and has a smaller museum that continues the study of

TICINO

medieval Bellinzona. From here it's a 3.5km climb uphill to **Castello di Sasso Corbaro**. At this point you should be too exhausted to explore the grounds. Lucky you – there are none. The castle hosts temporary **exhibitions** (☎ 091 825 59 06; adult/concession Sfr5/2; ✆ 10am-6pm mid-Mar–Oct).

CHURCHES

Wandering south from the train station, you will first see the **Chiesa Collegiata dei SS Pietro e Stefano** (Piazza della Collegiata; ✆ 8am-1pm & 4-6pm), a Renaissance church with baroque touches and rich in frescos inside. More immediately eye-catching is the **Chiesa di San Rocco** (Piazza dell'Indipendenza; ✆ 7-11am & 2-5pm), with its huge fresco of St Christopher and a smaller one of the Virgin Mary and Christ. Similarly decorated is the 14th-century **Chiesa di San Biagio** (Piazza San Biagio; ✆ 7am-noon & 2-5pm), the difference being that these frescos are not 20th-century restorations.

West over the railway line stands the **Chiesa di Santa Maria delle Grazie** (Via Convento; ✆ 7am-6pm), a 15th-century church with an extraordinary fresco cycle (recently restored after being damaged by fire in 1996) of the life and death of Christ. The centrepiece is a panel depicting Christ's Crucifixion.

MUSEUMS

Off the same square is the elegant **Villa dei Cedri**, set in lush **gardens** (admission free; ✆ 8am-8pm Apr-Sep, 9am-5pm Oct-Mar) and home to the city's **art collection** (☎ 091 821 85 20; www.villacedri.ch; Piazza San Biagio 9; adult/concession Sfr8/5; ✆ 2-6pm Tue-Fri, 11am-6pm Sat, Sun & hols), mostly local and northern Italian works of the 19th and 20th centuries.

From Paris comes an original idea in the **Museo in Erba** (☎ 091 835 52 54; www.museoinerba .com; Piazza Magoria 8; admission €5; ✆ 8.30-11.30am & 1.30-4.30pm Mon-Fri, 2-5pm Sat & Sun), an interactive museum for kids launched in the French capital as the Musée en Herbe. Aimed at children aged four to 11, the idea is to stimulate an interest in art through games and usually two exhibitions are put on each year.

Festivals & Events

Rabadan (www.rabadan.ch), Bellinzona's rowdy carnival, starts on a Thursday seven-and-a-half weeks before Easter Sunday. **Piazza Blues Festival** (www.piazzablues.ch; ✆ Jun-Jul) brings four days of international blues to the city in summer. Entry is free except to the main stage on the last two days (Sfr15).

Sleeping

None of the functional hotels will win charm awards. Most are strung out along Viale della Stazione.

Ostello della Gioventù (☎ 091 825 15 22; www.youth hostel.ch/bellinzona; Via Nocca 4; dm Sfr36.50, s/d Sfr65/90; ✆ reception closed 10am-3pm; hostel closed last two weeks of December; 🖳) Housed in Villa Montebello, at the foot of the eponymous castle, the youth hostel occupies what for 100 years was a high-class girls' school.

Hotel San Giovanni (☎ 091 825 19 19; Via San Giovanni 5-7; s/d Sfr50/90, d with shower Sfr120) The single main quality of this place is the low price of the cluttered rooms (with shared bathroom).

Albergo Croce Federale (☎ 091 825 16 67; Viale della Stazione 12; s/d Sfr100/140) The only place just inside the Old Town (a hefty tower of the old city wall looms behind it), this is a pleasant stop. Rooms are straightforward but light, and the restaurant downstairs is cheerful.

Hotel Gamper (☎ 091 825 37 92; www.hotel-gamper .com; Viale della Stazione 29; s/d Sfr110/160) The top-floor box-like rooms offer good views. Rooms are functional and clean.

Eating

Osteria Zoccolino (☎ 091 825 06 70; Piazza Governo 5; mains Sfr14-20; ✆ Mon-Sat) A photographer runs this slightly chaotic but cheery eatery that fills at lunchtime especially. You never quite know what to expect here: a set lunch of Indian food, concerts on Thursday nights…and you may find he opens at night only if he has enough bookings. Don't worry, there are several alternatives along Via Teatro and Via Orico.

Ristorante Castelgrande (☎ 091 826 23 53; www .castelgrande.ch; Castelgrande; mains Sfr35-60; ✆ Tue-Sun) It's not often you get the chance to eat inside a Unesco World Heritage Site. The medieval castle setting alone is enough to bewitch. Elegantly presented Italian- and Ticino-style cuisine will help too. You can opt for a set dinner menu at Sfr68.

our pick **Locanda Orico** (☎ 091 825 15 18; Via Orico 13; pasta Sfr30-40, mains Sfr45-62; ✆ Tue-Sat) Behind the lace curtains in this low-slung temple to good food you come across such creations as *gnocchetti di patate alla zucca in una dadolat di camoscio in salmì* (little pumpkin gnocchi in jugged chamois meat).

Drinking

For a night with Bellinzona's young and restless, head for **Club Chupito** (Via Dogana; ✆ 11pm-3am

TICINO

Sun-Thu, to 4am Fri & Sat), a fairly basic downstairs dance den where you can knock back cocktails for Sfr15. It's just on the right inside the medieval city gate.

Getting There & Away

Bellinzona is on the train route connecting Locarno (Sfr8.20, 20 to 25 minutes) and Lugano (Sfr11.80, 26 to 30 minutes). It is also on the Zürich–Milan route. Up to six postal buses head northeast to Chur (Sfr48, 2½ hours). Postal buses depart from beside the train station.

NORTH OF BELLINZONA
Biasca & Valle di Blenio

Biasca is, with the vague exception of its 13th-century **Chiesa di SS Pietro e Paolo**, of little interest, but is an important transport junction. Trains run twice an hour from Bellinzona (Sfr7.60, 12 to 14 minutes).

If you pass through, head for the series of *grotti* on Via ai Grotti, a series of simple, traditional eateries huddled around simple stone huts backing into the rocky mountain wall. Although not quite the case here, *grotti* (the original stone buildings once used as houses and storage) are often built right into the rock of hillsides and generally open around Easter to early October. **Grotto Greina** (☎ 091 862 15 27; Via ai Grotti 36; mains Sfr20-30; 11am-11pm Tue-Sun Mar-Jan) is a good example, serving up lashings of grilled meats with polenta. You can hang around as late as 1am over a grappa.

Directly north of Biasca, the Valle di Blenio splits off the main route and heads for the Lukmanier Pass (Passo di Lucomagno). It is a barren-looking valley, laced with potential hiking options and modest skiing near the pass.

The main town along the way is **Olivone**, where you will find a **tourist office** (☎ 091 872 14 87; www.blenioturismo.ch; 8.30am-noon & 2-6pm Mon-Fri, 8.30am-12.30pm Sat May-Oct, 9am-noon & 1.30-5.30pm Mon-Fri Nov-Apr). Staff can help with hiking tips in the surrounding mountains, among the least explored in the country. **Albergo Olivone e Posta** (☎ 091 872 13 66; www.hotel-olivone.ch; Via Lucomagno; s/d Sfr85/140, without bathroom Sfr60/110) is the most enticing hotel, a sturdy establishment at the northern entrance to town. It has a decent restaurant (closed Sunday). Try the *pappardelle al ragù di lepre* (Sfr18), ribbon pasta drenched in a thick hare sauce.

From Bellinzona get the train to Biasca and change to the postal bus (Sfr21.40, one hour).

Valle Leventina

From Biasca, the freeway powers on northwest to Airolo and then on to the St Gotthard Pass into central Switzerland. Taking this road you'd never know that high above it is strung a series of mountain hamlets offering superlative views, great walking (the Strada Alta, partly asphalted, runs about 45km from Biasca to Airolo) and the occasional fine feed.

A **walking route** (www.gottardo-wanderweg.ch, in German and Italian) that runs from the Reuss valley in Uri (starting at Erstfeld) and then in bits (bus connections between each stage from Airolo on are suggested) down the Valle Leventina follows the railway line and, with informative panels (in Italian and German), explains the history of the line and the valleys.

About 7km northwest of Biasca, head for Personico for its **Grotto Val d'Ambra** (☎ 091 864 18 29; mains Sfr15-28; daily Jun-Aug, Tue-Sun Easter-May & Sep), 500m outside the village. More than a century old, this is one of the most traditional of Ticino's *grotti*. The main restaurant building has a cosy dining area full of timber furniture. Outside, on balmy summer days, up to 100 people gather around the rough granite tables scattered about the dozen or so shaded *grotti*.

About 4km further, **Giornico** (site of a major defeat of the Milanese by Swiss Confederate forces in 1478) boasts two Romanesque bridges, the finest example of a Romanesque church in Ticino (**Chiesa di San Nicolao**, on the south bank of the Ticino river), a picturesque old centre and a couple of decent places to stay and eat. For the latter, follow the signs to **Grotto Rodai** (☎ 091 864 21 48; mains Sfr16-30; Tue-Sun Apr–mid-Oct), a typical *grotto*.

If driving, you can head up to the Strada Alta, high up on the north flank of the Ticino river valley, at several locations. From Lavorgo, 4km northwest of Giornico, a road winds up to the hamlets of **Anzonico**, **Cavagnago** and **Sobrio**. About 7km further on, another road leads from Faido to high points like **Campello**, **Molare** and **Carì**.

At **Rodi-Fiesso**, the broad valley floor narrows to a claustrophobic gorge. Just outside the eastern entry to town, a Swiss customs and control point has guarded the way to the St Gotthard Pass since the 16th century. Today the restored **Dazio Grande** (☎ 091 874 60

TICINO

60; www.daziogrande.ch; Via San Gottardo; s/d Sfr120/180; ♥ May-Oct) has pleasant, modern rooms, a small museum on the post's history and a **restaurant** (set menu Sfr39, ♥ Tue-Sun May-Sep, Wed-Sun Oct). The museum contains a small permanent display on the *Via delle Genti*, the transalpine route that followed this valley since medieval times.

About 7km northwest of Rodi-Fiesso, you reach the sleepy valley town of Piotta. On the north side of the freeway here, Europe's steepest **funicular** (adult/child/senior return Sfr22/10/19; ♥ May-Oct) heads up above the Strada Alta to **Lago Ritom**, a high dam from where walkers can head into the mountains. Behind the dam, **Ristorante Lago Ritom** (☎ 091 868 14 24; www.lagoritom .com; dm Sfr45; ♥ Apr-Oct) offers simple meals and dorm beds.

Airolo is a surprisingly big settlement at the head of the Valle Leventina, but not of great interest. If you want to cross the Alps into central Switzerland, this is the easiest route to follow.

The Passo di San Gottardo (St Gotthard Pass) lies 7km north of Airolo. You can opt for the 17km tunnel or, when snow doesn't close it, the mountain road.

The hourly train (the rail tunnel, opened in 1882, cost 177 lives) to Airolo from Bellinzona (Sfr21.40, 55 minutes) continues as far as Zürich and passes through the valley towns. From these you can connect by occasional postal bus to the hamlets of the Strada Alta.

You can sleep deep below the pass, underground! **La Claustra** (☎ 091 880 50 55; www .claustra.ch; San Gottardo; s/d Sfr245/490; ♥ May-Oct) is a combination of Wellness hotel, restaurant, library, wine cellar and seminar centre, all at 2050m above sea level buried deep in the rock beneath the St Gotthard Pass in what was once one of the most impregnable of Swiss army bunkers, the San Carlo artillery base. Clearly, none of the 17 rooms, all individually decorated, come with views. Water comes from underground sources. Take a postal bus from Airolo to the pass. Booking ahead is essential. Groups of 10 or more can also book one-hour visits.

West of Airolo, the quiet **Val Bedretto** climbs, slowly at first and then in sweeping curves, through the bald Alpine terrain to reach another mountain crossing, the Nufenen Pass in eastern Valais (see p169). The area is beloved of hikers in search of tranquillity.

LUGANO

pop 49,720 / elevation 270m

Ticino's lush lake isn't its only liquid asset. The largest city in the canton is also the country's third most important banking centre.

Visitors can only wonder how so many locals can work in stuffy banks when they could be wandering the spaghetti maze of steep cobblestone streets that untangle themselves at the edge of the lake. And how can they resist the water sports and hill-walking opportunities available to them?

Orientation

Lugano rests on the northern shore of pretty Lago di Lugano. The train station stands above and to the west of the Centro Storico (Old Town). Take the stairs or the funicular (Sfr1.10, open 5.20am to 11.50pm) down to the centre, a patchwork of interlocking *piazze*. The most important one, Piazza della Riforma, is presided over by the 1844 neoclassical Municipio (town hall).

Paradiso, a southern suburb, is the departure point for the funicular to Monte San Salvatore. The other mountain looming over the town, Monte Brè, is to the east. The airport is 3km west of the train station.

Information

INTERNET ACCESS
Mondialplay (☎ 091 922 25 69; Via Canova 9; per 15min/1hr Sfr3/8; ♥ 9am-6.30pm Mon-Fri, 10am-5pm)

MEDICAL SERVICES
Emergency doctor/dentist (☎ 1811)
Ospedale Civico (☎ 091 811 61 11; Via Tesserete 46) Hospital north of the city centre.

POST
Post office (Via Della Posta 7; ♥ 7.30am-6.15pm Mon-Fri, 8am-4pm Sat) In centre of Old Town.

TOURIST INFORMATION
Tourist office Municipio (☎ 091 913 32 32; www .lugano-tourism.ch; Riva Giocondo Albertolli; ♥ 9am-7pm Mon-Fri, 9am-5pm Sat, 10am-5pm Sun & hols Apr-Oct, 9am-noon & 2-5.30pm Mon-Fri, 10am-12.30pm & 1.30-5pm Sat Nov-Mar), Train Station (♥ 2-7pm Mon-Sat).

Sights
OLD TOWN & CHURCHES
Wander through the porticoed lanes woven around the busy main square, Piazza della

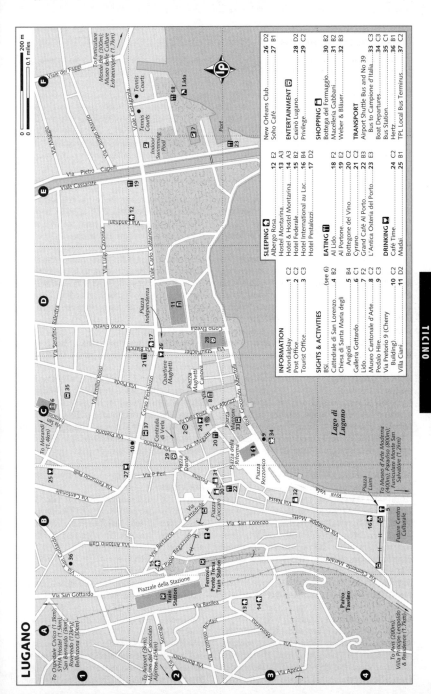

LUGANO

TICINO

INFORMATION
BSI..**1** C2
Mondialplay........................**2** C2
Post Office..........................**3** C3
Tourist Office.....................(see 6)

SIGHTS & ACTIVITIES
Cattedrale di San Lorenzo.....**4** B2
Chiesa di Santa Maria degli
Angioli...............................**5** B4
Galleria Gottardo..................**6** C1
Lido....................................**7** F2
Museo Cantonale d'Arte.......**8** C2
Pedalo Hire.........................**9** C3
Via Pretorio 9 (Cherry
Building)............................**10** C2
Villa Ciani............................**11** D2

SLEEPING
Albergo Rosa.......................**12** E2
Hostel Montarina..................**13** A3
Hotel & Hostel Montarina......**14** A3
Hotel Federale.....................**15** B2
Hotel International au Lac......**16** B4
Hotel Pestalozzi...................**17** D2

EATING
Al Lido................................**18** F2
Al Portone...........................**19** E2
Bottegone del Vino...............**20** C2
Cyrano................................**21** C2
Grand Café Al Porto..............**22** B3
L'Antica Osteria del Porto......**23** E3

DRINKING
Café Time...........................**24** C2
Madai.................................**25** B1

ENTERTAINMENT
New Orleans Club.................**26** D2
Soho Café............................**27** B1
Casinò Lugano.....................**28** D2
Privilege..............................**29** C2

SHOPPING
Bottega del Formaggio.........**30** B2
Macelleria Gabbani...............**31** B2
Weber & Bläuer....................**32** B3

TRANSPORT
Airport Shuttle Bus and No 39
Bus to Campione d'Italia.......**33** C3
Boat Departures...................**34** C3
Bus Station..........................**35** C1
Hertz..................................**36** B1
TPL Local Bus Terminus.........**37** C2

TICINO

MARIO BOTTA IN THE PINK

Lugano's Mario Botta (born 1943 in nearby Mendrisio) has made a name for himself as a leading light in contemporary architecture. Best known for his work abroad (like San Francisco's Museum of Modern Art, the Kyobo Tower in Seoul, the Santo Volto church in Turin and restoration of the La Scala opera theatre in Milan), Botta has also left an indelible mark on and around Lugano. The 12-storey Casino in Campione d'Italia is one example. Botta seems to have a thing about right angles and the colour pink. In the centre of town, his landmarks include the **BSI** (Via San Franscini 12), a series of interconnected monoliths formerly known as the Banca del Gottardo; the pink brick office block at **Via Pretorio 9** (known to locals as the Cherry Building because of the cherry tree planted on the roof); and the roof of the TPL local bus terminal on Corso Pestalozzi. At night it is illuminated…in light pink.

Riforma (which is even more lively when the Tuesday and Friday morning markets are held).

The simple Romanesque **Chiesa di Santa Maria degli Angioli** (St Mary of the Angels; Piazza Luini; 7am-6pm), against which a now crumbling former hotel was built, contains two frescos by Bernardino Luini dating from 1529. Covering the entire wall that divides the church in two is a grand didactic illustration of the Crucifixion. The closer you look, the more scenes of Christ's Passion are revealed, along with others of him being taken down from the cross and his resurrection. The power and vivacity of the colours are astounding. Less alive is Luini's depiction of the Last Supper on the left wall.

Below the train station, the early 16th-century **Cattedrale di San Lorenzo** (St Lawrence Cathedral; 6.30am-6pm) boasts a Renaissance facade and contains some fine frescos and ornately decorated baroque statues.

MUSEUMS & GALLERIES

The **Museo Cantonale d'Arte** (Cantonal Art Museum; 091 910 47 80; www.museo-cantonale-arte.ch; Via Canova 10; adult/student Sfr7/5, special exhibitions Sfr10/7; 2-5pm Tue, 10am-5pm Wed-Sun) celebrates the work of modern artists (mostly 19th and 20th century masters) from the region. There's more creativity from the cutting edge at the **Museo d'Arte Moderna** (Modern Art Museum; 058 866 72 14; www.mdam.ch; Riva Antonio Caccia 5; adult/under 11yr/11-14yr/15-18yr/student & senior Sfr12/free/3/5/8; 9am-7pm Tue-Sun). Housed in Villa Malpensata, it is one of the city's main art spaces.

Another is **Galleria Gottardo** (091 808 19 88; www.galleria-gottardo.org; Via San Franscini 12; admission free; 2-5pm Tue, 11am-5pm Wed-Sat), the private foundation of the BSI (formerly Banca del Gottardo) bank, which puts on exhibitions

ranging from sculpture to photography. The ochre-hued **Villa Ciani** (091 800 72 01; Parco Civico; 10am-6pm Tue-Sun), just in from the lake, is also the site of regular art exhibitions.

About 1.7km from central Lugano, in Villa Heleneum, is the **Museo delle Culture Extraeuropee** (Museum of Non-European Cultures; 058 866 69 09; www.lugano.ch/museoculture; Via Cortivo 24-28; adult/child/senior & student Sfr12/free/8; 10am-6pm Tue-Sun). The brew of tribal relics from far-off countries includes a collection of masks and statues soaked in sexuality. Take bus 1.

Chomp into some cocoa culture at the **Museo del Cioccolato Alprose** (091 611 88 88; www.alprose.ch; Via Rompada 36, Caslano; adult/under 6yr/7-16yr Sfr3/free/1; 9am-5.30pm Mon-Fri, to 4.30pm Sat & Sun). This is a great place to take the children or anyone with a sweet tooth. As well as getting a chocolate-coated history lesson, you can watch the sugary substance being made and enjoy a free tasting. The shop, cunningly, stays open half an hour longer. Take the Ferrovia Ponte Tresa train (Sfr7).

Activities

East of the Cassarate stream is the **Lido** (058 866 68 80; Viale Castagnola; per day Sfr9; 9am-7pm May & Sep, to 7.30pm Jun-Aug), with beaches and a swimming pool. You can hire pedalos (Sfr18 per hour) by the boat landing.

Festivals & Events

This classy town takes in some classical tunes during the **Lugano Festival** (www.luganofestival.ch) from April to May in the Palazzo dei Congressi. Free open-air music festivals include **Estival Jazz** (www.estivaljazz.ch) for three days in early July (plus two days in Mendrisio at the end of June) and the **Blues to Bop Festival** (www.bluestobop.ch) over the last three days of August. The lake explodes in a display of pyrotechnical wizardry around midnight on 1 August, Switzerland's **National Day**.

Sleeping

Many hotels close for at least part of the winter.

BUDGET

Hostel Montarina (☎ 091 966 72 72; www.montarina .ch; Via Montarina 1; dm Sfr26) The Hostel Montarina has simple rooms with four to 16 bunk beds. A buffet breakfast is available for Sfr12. There is also a hotel on the site (see below).

SYHA hostel (☎ 091 966 27 28; www.luganoyouthhostel .ch; Via Cantonale 13, Savosa; dm/s/d Sfr26/68/96; ☺ reception 7am-noon & 3-10pm mid-Mar–Oct; ☎) Housed in the Villa Savosa, this is one of the more enticing youth hostels in the country. The dorms have up to eight bunk beds. Take bus 5 to Crocifisso.

Hotel Montarina (☎ 091 966 72 72; www.montarina.ch; Via Montarina 1; s/d Sfr85/125; ☎ P) Behind the train station is this charming hotel, whose best rooms are airy, with timber floors and antiques. Some rooms have private kitchen. The pool is set in pleasant gardens.

MIDRANGE

Hotel Pestalozzi (☎ 091 921 46 46; www.pestalozzi -lugano.ch; Piazza Independenza 9; s/d Sfr106/188, s/d without bathroom Sfr64/108; ☒) A renovated art-nouveau building is home to rooms with reds, blues and creams dominating the decor. Cheaper ones have a shared bathroom in the corridor. The restaurant downstairs is a no-alcohol establishment.

Albergo Rosa (☎ 091 922 92 86; www.albergorosa .ch; Via Landriani 2-4; s/d Sfr125/175, s/d without bathroom Sfr72/124; P) A cheerful little four-storey retreat in a nice spot near the Parco Civico, this family-run hotel is gathered around a courtyard and offers clean rooms (shame about the carpet in some). Singles are small. Prices drop about a quarter in slower moments.

Hotel Federale (☎ 091 910 08 08; www.hotel-federale.ch; Via Paolo Regazzoni 8; s/d Sfr165/230; ☺ Feb-Dec; P) If you can afford the grand top floor doubles with lake views, this curiously shaped pink place beats many multi-stellar places hands down. A short luggage-laden stumble from the train station, it is in a quiet spot with immaculately kept rooms. There is wi-fi in the lobby.

Hotel International au Lac (☎ 091 922 75 41; www .hotel-international.ch; Via Nassa 88; s Sfr125-185, d Sfr220-310; ☺ Apr-Oct; P ☒ ☎) From the balconies of

the front rooms you look straight out over Lago di Lugano. These are the best, but other cheaper rooms are scattered about the hotel. Rooms are comfortable, with a smattering of antique furniture.

TOP END

Villa Principe Leopoldo & Residence (☎ 091 985 88 55; www.leopoldohotel.com; Via Montalbano 5; s/d up to Sfr500/590; P ☒ ☎) This red-tiled residence set in sculptured gardens was built in 1926 for Prince Leopold von Hohenzollern, of the exiled German royal family. It oozes a regal, nostalgic atmosphere. The gardens and many splendid rooms offer lake views. Prices of suites reach for the stars. They have wi-fi.

Eating

For pizza or overpriced pasta, any of the places around Piazza della Riforma are pleasant and lively enough.

Grand Café Al Porto (☎ 091 910 51 30; Via Pessina 3; ☺ 8am-6.30pm Mon-Sat) This café, which began life way back in 1803, has several fine rooms for dining too. Be sure to take a look at the frescoed Cenacolo Fiorentino, once a monastery dining hall, upstairs. It's used for private functions.

Al Lido (☎ 091 971 55 00; Viale Castagnola; ☺ brunch 11am-6pm; dinner Wed-Sat) Lugano's lakeside beach restaurant is especially popular for its Sunday buffet brunch (Sfr36.50). They also do a Wednesday evening version, Lunar (6.30pm to 1am), for the same price and with DJ thrown in.

L'Antica Osteria del Porto (☎ 091 971 42 00; Via Foce 9; mains Sfr22-39; ☺ Wed-Mon) Set back from Lugano's sailing club, this is the place for savouring local fish and Ticinese dishes. It's hard to resist the *grigliata mista di pesci di mare e crostacei* (mixed fish and shellfish grill). The terrace overlooking the Cassarate stream is pleasant, and you also have lake views.

Cyrano (☎ 091 922 21 82; Via Bianchi; pasta Sfr19.50-22.50, mains Sfr25.50-38.50; ☺ Mon-Fri) Try to ignore the horrendous orange building and be soothed by the crisp interior and white linen. Out of the kitchen comes a mix of local cooking with broader Swiss and Mediterranean strands. The *spadellata di camoscio al ginepro e sugo di caccia con spätzli al burro e cavolo rosso alle mele* (pan-cooked chamois with juniper and game sauce, butter *spätzli* and red cabbage with apple) is a mouth-watering autumn Swiss country feast.

TICINO

our pick **Bottegone del Vino** (☎ 091 922 76 89; Via Magatti 3; mains Sfr28-42; Mon-Sat) Favoured by the local banking brigade at lunchtime, this is a great place to taste fine local wines over a well-prepared meal. The menu changes daily and might include a *filetto di rombo al vapore* (steamed turbot fillet) or ravioli stuffed with fine Tuscan Chianina beef. Knowledgeable waiters fuss around the tables and are only too happy to suggest the perfect Ticino tipple.

Al Portone (☎ 091 923 55 11; Viale Cassarate 3; mains Sfr30-50; Tue-Sat) For an upmarket meal, this place remains a sure bet for gourmands. It has a lunchtime set menu (Sfr58) and a tasting feast menu at night (Sfr120). How about the *filetto di manzo gratinato alle cipolle rosse di Tropea e purea di patate* (steak fillet au gratin with south Italian red onions and mashed potato)?

Drinking

Soho Café (☎ 091 922 60 80; Corso Pestalozzi 3; 7am-1am Mon-Fri, 4pm-1am Sat) So that's where they are! All those good-looking Lugano townies crowd in to this long, orange-lit bar for cocktails. Chilled DJ music creates a pleasant buzz. The problem might be squeezing through to the bar!

For Italian-style aperitif time, **Café Time** (☎ 091 922 56 06; Via Canova 9; 8am-1am Mon-Sat), buried inside an unlikely little shopping arcade, attracts the local movers and shakers. Relax against the high-backed burgundy leather benches over a fine wine or cocktail with tasty bar snacks.

Madai (☎ 091 922 56 37; www.luganodinotte.ch; Via Ferruccio Pelli 13; 7pm-3am Wed-Sat) A cool cocktail bar with reddish hues, lounges and dance music. At 10pm, the aperitif phase gives way to a club-style ambience.

Another lively spot from Thursday to Saturday nights is **New Orleans Club** (☎ 091 921 44 77; www.neworleansclublugano.com; Piazza Indipendenza 1; 5pm-1am Mon-Sat), with Latin, hip-hop and disco nights. Deeply dark inside, there's also room for a smoko outside.

Entertainment

Privilege (☎ 091 922 94 38; www.privilegelugano.ch; Piazza Dante 8; admission Sfr20; Wed-Sat) Downstairs from street level and easily missed, this is the most central club in town. There are a couple of separate areas, including one for smokers! With go-go girls and guys, and the occasional spurt of live music, it attracts a pretty mixed crowd.

Morandi (☎ 076 508 32 25; Via Trevano 56; admission Sfr25; midnight-5am Fri & Sat) A stalwart of Lugano's dance scene, this multi-space club (including asphyxiating smoking room) places a fairly steady house diet and attracts a crowd that ranges from 17 to 47. Pink is the dominating hue.

Can't be bothered going to the huge casino in Campione d'Italia (p334)? No problem, you can lose your money in the rather lurid **Casinò Lugano** (☎ 091 973 7111; www.casinolugano.ch; Via Stauffacher 1; admission free; noon-4am Sun-Thu, to 5am Fri & Sat).

Shopping

One of the main shopping strips is Via Nassa, lined with purveyors of Swiss watches (what else?!), Italian fashion, cigar shops and jewellery stores. An intriguing store is the timeless **Weber & Bläuer** (☎ 091 922 70 30; Via Nassa 7; Tue-Sat), which sells antiques and old jewellery.

Macelleria Gabbani (☎ 091 911 30 80; www.gabbani.com; Via Pessina 12) You'll find it hard to miss the giant sausages hanging out the front of this irresistible delicatessen. The same people operate a tempting cheese shop, the Bottega del Formaggio, across the road at No 13.

Getting There & Away

AIR

From **Agno airport** (☎ 091 612 11 11; www.lugano-airport.ch), **Darwin Airline** (www.darwinairline.com) flies to Rome (Fiumicino), Geneva and Olbia (in Sardinia). **Flybaboo** (www.flybaboo.com) flies regularly to Geneva and **Swiss** (www.swiss.com) to Zürich.

BUS

Lugano is on the same road and rail route as Bellinzona. To St Moritz, one postal bus runs direct via Italy at least Friday to Sunday (Sfr69, four hours, daily late June to mid-October and late December to early January). Reserve at the bus station, the train station information office or on ☎ 091 807 85 20. All postal buses leave from the main bus depot at Via Serafino Balestra, but you can pick up the St Moritz and some other buses outside the train station 15 minutes later.

TRAIN & BOAT

For further train and boat information, see p327.

CAR & MOTORCYCLE

You can hire cars at **Hertz** (☎ 091 923 46 75; Via San Gottardo 13) and **Avis** (☎ 091 913 41 51; Via Clemente Maraini 14).

Getting Around

A shuttle bus runs to the airport from Piazza Manzoni (one-way/return Sfr10/18) and the train station (Sfr8/15). Get timetables from the tourist office. A **taxi** (☎ 091 605 25 10) to the airport costs Sfr25 to Sfr30.

Bus 1 runs from Castagnola in the east through the centre to Paradiso, while bus 2 runs from central Lugano to Paradiso via the train station. A single trip costs Sfr1.20 to Sfr2 (ticket dispensers at stops indicate the appropriate rate) or it's Sfr5 for a one-day pass. The main local bus terminus is on Corso Pestalozzi.

AROUND LUGANO

The tourist office has guides on the best lakeside walks. If you'd rather float than use your feet, relaxing in a boat can be a blast.

For a bird's-eye view of Lugano and the lake, head for the hills. The **funicular** (☎ 091 971 31 71; www.montebre.ch; one-way/return Sfr14/20, Swiss Pass valid; ☽ Mar-Dec) from Cassarate (walk or take bus 1 from central Lugano) scales Monte Brè (925m). From Cassarate a first funicular takes you to Suvigliana (free up, Sfr1.60 down) to connect with the main funicular. Or take bus 12 from the main post office to Brè village and walk about 15 minutes.

From Paradiso, the **funicular** (☎ 091 985 28 28; www.montesansalvatore.ch; one-way/return Sfr19/26; ☽ mid-Mar–early Nov) to Monte San Salvatore operates from mid-March to mid-November. Aside from the views, the walk down to Paradiso or Melide is an hour well spent.

A lovely place to stay is the `ourpick` **Locanda del Giglio** (☎ 091 930 09 33; www.locandadelgiglio.ch; dm Sfr40, s/d Sfr95/150), in Roveredo, Capriasca, 12km north of Lugano. It is a warm timber building powered on solar energy. Rooms have balconies offering mountain views and even lake glimpses. Take a bus from Lugano to Tesserete (30 minutes) and change there for another to Roveredo (about 10 minutes).

LAGO DI LUGANO

Much can be seen in one day if you don't fancy a longer excursion. Boats are operated by the **Società Navigazione del Lago di Lugano** (☎ 091 971

52 23; www.lakelugano.ch). Examples of return fares from Lugano are Melide (Sfr21.60), Morcote (Sfr30.80) and Ponte Tresa (Sfr37.40). If you want to visit several places, buy a pass: one/three days cost Sfr38/58 and one week costs Sfr68. There are reduced fares for children.

The departure point from Lugano is by Piazza della Riforma. Boats sail year-round, but the service is more frequent from late March to late October. During this time some boats go as far as Ponte Tresa, so you could go one-way by boat and return to Lugano on the Ponte Tresa train.

Trains run to Melide (Sfr3.40, six minutes). For Morcote, get bus 431 from Piazza Rezzonico (30 to 35 minutes).

GANDRIA

Gandria is an attractive, compact village almost dipping into the water. A popular trip is to take the boat from Lugano and walk back along the shore to Castagnola (around 40 minutes), where you can visit Villa Heleneum and/or Villa Favorita, or simply continue back to Lugano by foot or bus 1.

Across the lake from Gandria is the **Museo delle Dogane Svizzere** (Swiss Customs Museum; ☎ 091 923 98 43; admission free; ☼ 1.30-5.30pm late Mar-early Oct), at Cantine di Gandria, and accessible by boat. It tells the history of customs (and more interestingly smuggling) in this border area. On display are confiscated smugglers' boats that once operated on the lake.

CAMPIONE D'ITALIA

It's hard to tell, but this really is a part of Italy surrounded by Switzerland. There are no border formalities (but take your passport anyway); many cars in the village have Swiss number plates and they use Swiss telephones and Swiss francs.

Euros (and any other hard currency), however, are equally welcome as there are none of the Swiss restrictions on gambling in Campione d'Italia. The 12-storey **casino** (☎ 091 640 11 11; www.nuovocasinodicampione.it; admission free; ☼ 10.30am-5am Sun-Thu, to 6am Fri & Sat), converted by Lugano's favourite architect, Mario Botta, into Europe's biggest in 2005, does a brisk business. Smart dress is required. From noon to midnight you can take bus 39 from Lugano's Piazza Manzoni (one-way/return Sfr6.80/13.60) to Campione d'Italia. The last return bus leaves at 12.40am, and then there's one at 6.39am.

MONTE GENEROSO

The fine panorama provided by this summit (1701m) includes lakes, Alps and the Apennines on a clear day. It can be reached by boat (except in winter), train (Sfr5.60, 17 minutes) or car to Capolago, then the rack and pinion **train** (☎ 091 630 51 11; www.montegeneroso.ch; adult/child/under 5yr return Sfr39/19.50/free; ☼ up to 10 daily Apr-Oct & early Dec-early Jan).

CERESIO PENINSULA

South of Lugano, this peninsula is created by the looping shoreline of Lake Lugano. Walking trails dissect the interior and small villages dot the lakeside. The postal bus from Lugano to Morcote goes via either Melide or Figino, and departs approximately hourly. Year-round boats also connect Morcote and Melide to Lugano.

Montagnola

The German novelist Hermann Hesse (1877–1962) chose to live in this small town in 1919 after the horrors of WWI had separated him from his family. As crisis followed crisis in Germany, topped by the rise of the Nazis, he saw little reason to return home. He wrote some of his greatest works here, at first in an apartment in Casa Camuzzi. Nearby, in Torre Camuzzi, is the **Museo Hermann Hesse** (☎ 091 993 37 70; www.hessemontagnola.ch; Torre Camuzzi; adult/under 12yr/student & senior Sfr7.50/free/6; ☼ 10am-12.30pm & 2-6.30pm Tue-Sun Mar-Oct, Sat & Sun Nov-Feb). Personal objects, some of the thousands of watercolours he painted in Ticino, books and other odds and ends help re-create something of Hesse's life. From Lugano, get the Ferrovia Ponte Tresa train to Sorengo and change for a postal bus (Sfr3.40, 20 minutes).

Melide

Melide is a bulge of shore from which the A2 freeway slices across the lake. The main attraction is **Swissminiatur** (☎ 091 640 10 60; www.swissminiatur.ch; Via Cantonale; adult/child/senior Sfr15/10/13; ☼ 9am-6pm mid-Mar–mid-Nov), where you'll find 1:25 scale models of more than 120 national attractions. It's the quick way to see Switzerland in a day.

Morcote

With its narrow cobbled lanes and endless nooks and crannies, this peaceful former fishing village (population 740) clusters at the foot of Monte Abostora. Narrow stairways lead to **Chiesa di Santa Maria del Sasso**, a 15-minute climb. Views are excellent and the church has frescos (16th century) and carved faces on the organ. From there continue another 15 minutes upstairs to **Vico di Morcote**, a pleasant high-altitude hamlet. About 5km further is Carona, worth a visit for the **Parco Botanico San Grato** (admission free).

Parco Scherrer (☎ 091 996 21 25; adult/under 6yr/6-10yr/student & senior Sfr7/free/2/6; ☼ 10am-5pm mid-Mar–Oct, to 6pm Jul-Aug), 400m left (west) from the boat stop, offers a bustling range of architectural styles, including copies of famous buildings and generic types (eg Temple of Nefertiti, Siamese teahouse). It's all set in subtropical parkland.

There are several lakeside sleeping options. **Albergo della Posta** (☎ 091 996 11 27; www.hotelmorcote .com; Piazza Grande; s/d Sfr135/190; ☼ Mar-Nov) has charming little rooms (10 in all), with timber floors and most with views across the lake. It has its own restaurant.

The walk along the shore to Melide takes around 50 minutes.

WHAT'S COOKING IN TICINO?

If eating and drinking is your idea of a great time, Ticino is a must-visit. Some of your most satisfying eating experiences in Ticino will happen in *grotti* –rustic, out-of-the-way eateries, where in the warmer months you can sit outside at granite tables for wholesome local fare. Some are mentioned in this chapter, but fan(atic)s might want to track down the trilingual *Guida a Grotti e Osterie*.

What rösti is to the Swiss Germans, polenta is to the Ticinesi. This maize-based staple alone is stodgy, but coupled with other ingredients becomes another ball game. You might find it with *brasato* (braised beef) or *capretto in umido alla Mesolcinese*, a tangy kid meat stew with a touch of cinnamon and cooked in red wine. Polenta is good served with any game meat (*cacciagione*) in autumn.

Cazzöla is a meat dish with a savoury selection teaming up on one plate, served with cabbage and potatoes. More delicate dishes include *cicitt* (small sausages) and *mazza casalinga* (a selection of delicatessen cuts).

Plenty of enticing dishes from Italy have found their way over the border. Indeed, many restaurants in Ticino are run by Italians. Risotto (rice-based) dishes are common. A good version is with *funghi* (mushrooms).

Down on lakes Lugano and Maggiore, expect to find fish, especially *persico* (perch), *coregone* (whitefish) and *salmerino* (a cross between salmon and trout, only smaller).

Various cheeses are produced in Ticino. *Robiola* is a soft cow's milk cheese that comes in small discs. A cool, fresh alternative is *robiolino* (tubes of cow's milk cheese). Goats' cheese can also be found, along with various types of *formaggella*, a harder, crusty cheese.

Portions in general tend to be very generous in Ticino, so the Italian habit of eating a *primo* (first course, generally of pasta) followed by a *secondo* (main course) is by no means obligatory. High prices often make such gluttony onerous anyway. Another common alternative to the full two courses is to have *mezza porzione* (half-serving) of a first course and then a full serve of a second course.

For broader tips on Swiss food and wine, see p42.

MENDRISIO & AROUND
pop 6760 / elevation 354m

South of Lago di Lugano is the Mendrisiotto and Lower Ceresio. It is a fine area for walking tours around the rolling valleys and unspoilt villages. Mendrisio is the district capital and has a useful **tourist office** (☎ 091 641 30 50; www .mendrisiotourism.ch; Via Lavizzari 2; ☼ 9am-noon & 2-6pm Mon-Fri, 9am-noon Sat), near the central Piazza alla Valle. The town has several interesting old churches and buildings, and is worth a visit for the **Maundy Thursday Procession** or the **Wine Harvest** in September.

For big serves of good food, sit down in **Ristorante Stella** (☎ 091 646 72 28; Via Stella 13; pizza Sfr11-19, mains Sfr25-40; ☼ Mon-Sat), an old-style place that won't win any design prizes but will hit the spot. Try the autumn pasta specials, like *pappardelle con cantarelli e pancetta affumicata* (ribbon pasta with chanterelle mushrooms and bacon). In summer, sit out in the cobblestone courtyard.

Trains run here from Lugano (Sfr7, 20 minutes).

Exiting southeast from Mendrisio, a side road leads about 15km uphill and north along the **Valle di Muggio**, known for its cheese. This pretty drive ends abruptly in the hamlet of **Roncapiano**. Hiking enthusiasts could start a climb of 2½ hours to **Monte Generoso** from here.

MERIDE
pop 320 / elevation 583m

The **Museo dei Fossili** (Fossil Museum; ☎ 091 646 37 80; www.montesangiorgio.ch; admission free; ☼ 8am-6pm) in Meride, northwest of Mendrisio, displays vestiges of the first creatures to inhabit the region – reptiles and fish dating back more than 200 million years. It may sound dry but the finds are important enough to warrant Unesco recognition of the area around Monte San Giorgio (where they were uncovered) as a World Heritage Site.

Near the town is a circular **nature trail.** You can reach Meride from Lugano by taking the train to Mendrisio and then the postal bus (Sfr11).

TICINO

LOCARNO

pop 14,680 / elevation 205m

With its palm trees and much-vaunted 2300 hours of sunshine a year, Locarno has attracted northern tourists to its warm, Mediterranean-style setting since the late 19th century. The lowest town in Switzerland, it seemed like a soothing spot to host the 1925 peace conference intended to bring stability to Europe after WWI. Long before, the Romans appreciated its strategic position on the lake and Maggia river.

Orientation & Information

Five minutes' walk west of the train station is the town's core, Piazza Grande. The **tourist office** (☎ 091 791 00 91; www.maggiore.ch; Largo Zorzi 1; 🕙 9am-6pm Mon-Fri, 10am-6pm Sat & holidays, 10am-1.30pm & 2.30-5pm Sun mid-Mar–Oct, 9.30am-noon & 1.30-5pm Mon-Fri, 10am-noon & 1.30-5pm Sat Nov–mid-Mar) is nearby. Ask about the Lago Maggiore Guest Card and its discounts.

Piazza Grande is home to the post office, a shopping arcade and cafés. North and west of the piazza is the Old Town (*città vecchia*).

Sights

SANTUARIO DELLA MADONNA DEL SASSO

Overlooking the town, this sanctuary was built after the Virgin Mary supposedly appeared in a vision to a monk, Bartolomeo d'Ivrea, in 1480. There's a small **museum** (☎ 091 743 62 65; Via del Santuario 2; adult/student & child Sfr2.50/1.50; 🕙 2-5pm), a **church** (🕙 8am-6.45pm) and several rather rough, near-life-size statue groups (including one of the Last Supper) in niches on the stairway. The best-known painting in the church is *La Fuga in Egitto* (Flight to Egypt), painted in 1522 by Bramantino.

Contrasting in style are the naive votive paintings by the church entrance, where the Madonna and Child appear as ghostly apparitions in life-and-death situations.

A funicular runs every 15 to 30 minutes from the town centre (Sfr4.50 up, Sfr6.60 return) past the sanctuary to Orselina, but the 20-minute walk up is not all that demanding (take Via al Sasso off Via Cappuccini) in spite of being a chapel-lined path known as the Via Crucis.

OLD TOWN

Plod the Italianate piazzas and arcades, and admire the Lombard houses. There are some interesting churches. Built in the 17th century,

the **Chiesa Nuova** (New Church; Via Cittadella) has an almost sickeningly ornate baroque ceiling. Outside, left of the entrance, stands a giant statue of St Christopher with disproportionately tiny feet. The 16th-century **Chiesa di San Francesco** (Piazza San Francesco) has frescos by Baldassare Orelli, while the **Chiesa di Sant'Antonio** is best known for its altar to the *Cristo Morto* (Dead Christ).

Castello Visconteo (☎ 091 756 31 70; Piazza Castello; adult/student Sfr7/5; 🕙 10am-noon & 2-5pm Tue-Fri, 10am-5pm Sat & Sun Apr–mid-Nov), dating from the 15th century and named after the Visconti clan that long ruled Milan, today houses a museum with Roman and Bronze Age exhibits. Locarno is believed to have been a glass-manufacturing town in Roman times, which accounts for the strong showing of glass artefacts in the museum. This labyrinth of a castle, whose nucleus was raised around the 10th century, also hosts a small display (in Italian) on the Locarno Treaty.

Activities

From the Orselina funicular stop, a cable car goes to **Cardada** (🕙 8am-8pm Jun-Sep, 9am-6pm Mon-Thu, 8am-8pm Fri-Sun Mar-May & Oct-Nov), and then a chair lift soars to **Cimetta** (www.cardada.ch; return adult/under 6yr/6-16yr/senior Sfr33/free/11/25; 🕙 9.15am-12.30pm & 1.30-4.50pm daily Mar-Nov) at 1672m. From either stop there are fine views and walking trails. Paragliding is possible at Cimetta, as is skiing in winter.

Locarno's climate is perfect for lolling about the lake. **Giardini Jean Arp** (Jean Arp Gardens) is a lakeside park off Lungolago Motta, with sculptures by the surrealist artist scattered among the palm trees. It is free to swim in various convenient spots around the lake.

Kids will love the displays of falconry at **Falconeria Locarno** (☎ 091 751 95 86; www.falconeria .ch; Via delle Scuole 12; adult/under 5yr/5-16yr Sfr20/free/15; 🕙 10am-noon & 1.30-4.30pm Tue-Sun mid-Mar–Oct).

Festivals & Events

Locarno has hosted the two-week **Festival Internazionale di Film** (International Film Festival; ☎ 091 756 21 21; www.pardo.ch; Via Ciseri 23, CH-6600 Locarno) in August since 1948. Cinemas are used during the day but, at night, films are screened on a giant screen in Piazza Grande.

Sleeping

During the film festival in August, room prices soar by 50% to 100%.

TICINO

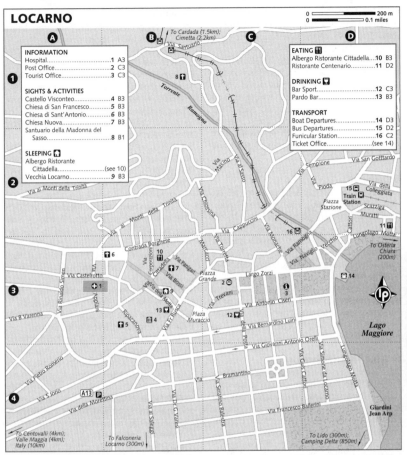

LOCARNO

INFORMATION	
Hospital....................................1 A3	
Post Office...............................2 C3	
Tourist Office..........................3 C3	
SIGHTS & ACTIVITIES	
Castello Visconteo...................4 B3	
Chiesa di San Francesco..........5 B3	
Chiesa di Sant'Antonio............6 B3	
Chiesa Nuova...........................7 B3	
Santuario della Madonna del	
Sasso......................................8 B1	
SLEEPING	
Albergo Ristorante	
Cittadella..........................(see 10)	
Vecchia Locarno.....................9 B3	

EATING	
Albergo Ristorante Cittadella...10 B3	
Ristorante Centenario............11 D2	
DRINKING	
Bar Sport................................12 C3	
Pardo Bar................................13 B3	
TRANSPORT	
Boat Departures......................14 D3	
Bus Departures.......................15 D2	
Funicular Station....................16 C2	
Ticket Office........................(see 14)	

Camping Delta (☎ 091 751 60 81; www.campingdelta .com; Via Respini 7; campsites Sfr47-57, plus per adult/child/ senior & student Sfr18/6/16; ☼ Mar-Oct) Although pricey, this camping ground has great facilities and is brilliantly located between the shores of Lago Maggiore and the Maggia river.

Vecchia Locarno (☎ 091 751 65 02; www.hotel-vecchia -locarno.ch; Via della Motta 10; s/d Sfr55/100) Rooms are gathered around a sunny internal courtyard, evoking a Mediterranean mood, and some have views over the Old Town centre and hills. The digs are simple enough, but comfortable (heaters are provided in the colder months). Bathrooms are in the corridor.

Albergo Ristorante Cittadella (☎ 091 751 58 85; www.cittadella.ch; Via Cittadella 18; s/d Sfr100/170) Aside from its well-known restaurant, this spot has

a handful of pretty little rooms, individually decorated with chessboard tile floors. The attic rooms with sloping timber ceilings are especially snug.

Eating

Albergo Ristorante Cittadella (☎ 091 751 58 85; Via Cittadella 18; mains Sfr15-25; ☼ Tue-Sun) This is the place to go if you enjoy fine fish – the upstairs section does not serve anything else. Downstairs the menu is not quite so focused on the aquatic and includes pizza from Sfr6 to Sfr8.50.

ourpick Osteria Chiara (☎ 091 743 32 96; Vicolo della Chiara 1; pasta & mains Sfr16-32; ☼ Tue-Sat) Tucked away on a cobbled lane, this has all the cosy feel of a *grotto*. Sit at granite tables beneath the pergola or at timber tables by the fireplace for chunky pasta and mostly meat dishes. From the lake follow the signs up Vicolo dei Nessi.

Ristorante Centenario (☎ 091 743 82 22; Lungolago Motta 17; mains Sfr41-62; ♥ Tue-Sat) This lakeside gem seems to have left behind a trifle of its former French-inspired snobbery but remains a top culinary address, turning out such clever dishes as *filetto di vitello con cuore di cantucci alle mandorle e scaloppa di fegato d'anatra scottata* (veal fillet with almond biscuit and roast duck liver).

Drinking

Bar Sport (Via della Posta 4; ♥ 8am-1am Mon-Fri, 10am-1am Sat, 2pm-1am Sun) A fairly run-of-the-mill place by day, this rough-and-tumble bar with the red-walled dance space out the back and beer garden on the side is an extremely popular hang-out with Locarno's night owls. There are a few other bars in the immediate vicinity.

Pardo Bar (☎ 091 752 21 23; www.pardobar.com; Via della Motta 3; ♥ 4pm-1am daily) With its background music, scattered timber tables (a couple of computers on one) and wine and cocktails on offer, Pardo Bar attracts a relaxed and mixed crowd.

Getting There & Away

Trains run every one to two hours from Brig (Sfr51, 2½ to three hours), passing through Italy (bring your passport). Change trains at Domodossola. There are also runs to/from Lucerne, usually involving one or two changes en route (Sfr53, 2¾ to 3¼ hours). Similarly, various trains head to Zürich, following different routes (Sfr57, three to 3½ hours). Most go via Bellinzona.

Postal buses to the surrounding valleys leave from outside the train station, and boats (see below) from near Piazza Grande. There is cheap street parking (Sfr3 for 10 hours) along Via della Morettina.

AROUND LOCARNO
Lago Maggiore

Only the northeast corner of Lago Maggiore is in Switzerland; the rest slices into Italy's Lombardy region. **Navigazione Lago Maggiore** (NLM; ☎ 091 751 61 40; www.navigazionelaghi.it) operates boats across the entire lake. Limited day passes cost Sfr13.80, but the Sfr24 version is valid for the entire Swiss basin. There are various options for visiting the Italian side.

Ascona

Ascona is Locarno's smaller twin (population 5430) across the Maggia river delta.

SIGHTS & ACTIVITIES

The late 19th century saw the arrival of 'back to nature' utopians, anarchists and sexual libertarians from northern Europe in Ascona. Their aspirations and eccentricities are the subject of the **Museo Casa Anatta** (☎ 091 785 40 40; www.monteverita.org; Via Collina 78; adult/student & senior Sfr6/4; ♥ 3-7pm Tue-Sun Jul & Aug, 2.30-6pm Tue-Sun Apr-Jun & Sep-Oct) on Monte Verità (take the small bus to Buxi from the post office; Sfr1). All sorts of characters, including Herman Hesse, dropped by to look at the goings on.

The **Museo Comunale d'Arte Moderna** (☎ 091 759 81 40; www.museoascona.ch, in Italian; Via Borgo 34; adult/concession Sfr7/5; ♥ 10am-noon & 3-6pm Tue-Sat, 4-6pm Sun), in Palazzo Pancaldi, includes paintings by artists connected with the town, among them Paul Klee, Ben Nicholson, Alexej Jawlensky and Hans Arp.

The **Collegio Papio** (Via Cappelle), now a high school, boasts a fine Lombard courtyard and includes the 15th-century **Chiesa Santa Maria della Misericordia**, with medieval frescos.

Since 1946, Ascona has hosted **Settimane Musicali** (www.settimane-musicali.ch), an international classical music festival lasting from the end of August to mid-October.

SLEEPING & EATING

Ascona is bursting with hotels and eateries, especially along the lakefront.

Ristorante Antica Posta (☎ 091 791 04 26; www .ti-gastro.ch/anticaposta; Via Borgo; s Sfr90-100, d Sfr160-220) Aside from having a pleasant restaurant gathered around an internal courtyard, this place offers 10 simple rooms in the heart of town.

Castello Seeschloss (☎ 091 791 01 61; www.castello-see schloss.ch; Piazza Motta; standard s/d Sfr184/348; P ♣ ♨) A 13th-century castle/palace that never saw military action but has undergone numerous overhauls, this spot is now a romantic waterfront hotel in the southeast corner of the old town centre. Standard rooms are in the main building. The most extraordinary rooms, some full of frescos, are in the ivy-covered tower.

Antica Osteria Vacchini (☎ 091 791 13 96; Contrada Maggiore 23; mains Sfr18-36; ♥ Mon-Sat) Diners find no shortage of pasta, meat and fish options in this old-time eatery (with outdoor section across the lane) but the house special is *piodadella della Vallamaggia*, a set of three kinds of cold meats with three matching sauces, salad and fried – a filling and tasty summer option.

GETTING THERE & AWAY
Bus 31 from Locarno's train station and Piazza Grande stops at Ascona's post office with departures every 15 minutes (Sfr2.80). Boat services on Lago Maggiore stop at Ascona.

WESTERN VALLEYS

The valleys ranging to the north and west of Locarno team with grey stone villages, gushing mountain streams, cosy retreats, traditional *grotti* and there are endless walking opportunities.

CENTOVALLI
The 'hundred valleys' is the westward valley route to Domodossola in Italy, known on the Italian side as Val Vigezzo. As you head west of the busy traffic junction of Ponte Brolla (with several fine eateries), 4km west of Locarno, the road winds out in a string of tight curves, often with surprisingly heavy traffic, high on the north flank of the Melezzo stream, which is largely held in check by a dam.

The quiet towns with their stone houses and heavy slate roofs, mostly high above the road and railway line on either side of the valley, make tranquil bases for mountain hikes. Among the best stops are **Verdasio**, **Rasa** and **Bordei**. Rasa is only accessible by cable car from Verdasio. **Ristorante al Pentolino** (☎ 091 780 81 00; d Sfr120; restaurant ⏲ Wed-Sun), in the heart of Verdasio, offers a couple of nice doubles (the owners also have three apartments for rent). You can enjoy hearty cooking at any time of the day (11.30am to 10.30pm, Sfr30 to Sfr35) at the granite tables beneath the pergola.

At **Re**, on the Italian side, there is a procession of pilgrims on 30 April each year, a tradition that originated when a painting of the Madonna was reported to have started bleeding when struck by a ball in 1480. More startling than the legend is the bulbous basilica built in the name of the Madonna del Sangue (Madonna of the Blood) in 1922–50.

The picturesque **Centovalli Railway**, trundling across numerous viaducts, leaves from Locarno for Domodossola (adult/under six years old/six to 16 years old Sfr32/free/16 one-way, one hour and 50 minutes). There are up to 11 departures a day. Take your passport.

VALLE ONSERNONE
Once known for its granite mines, this is one of the least visited of Ticino's valleys. About 10km west of Locarno along the Centovalli route, take a right at Cavigliano and swing northwest into barely inhabited territory. Clusters of stone houses form attractive hamlets along the way.

Shortly after Russo, a west branch road leads to **Spruga** (a popular starting point for walks with Swiss German visitors). The main road curves further north into the **Val Vergeletto**, whose main town bears the same name. It is a quiet, old place, except for the roar of the mountain stream past its houses and church. About 2km further west is the delightful **Locanda Zott** (☎ 091 797 10 98; r per person Sfr55 or Sfr60 with shower), with its child-friendly atmosphere, busy downstairs restaurant and renovated rooms upstairs, some with their own shower. The road peters out 6km west and the territory is great for hiking.

Make the excursion to nearby **Gresso**, perched high above Vergeletto at 999m. The views are great from this unadorned, close-knit hamlet where you may find a lone *osteria* open for lunch.

Up to five daily buses run from Locarno to Spruga (Sfr16.80, 1¼ hours). Change at Russo for Vergeletto and Gresso.

VALLE MAGGIA
This mostly broad, sunny valley follows the river of the same name from Ponte Brolla, passing small villages, until at Cevio (the valley's main town) it splits, the first of several divisions into smaller valleys. The valley's **tourist office** (☎ 091 753 18 85; www.vallemaggia.ch) is in Maggia.

Among the earlier villages, **Moghegno** and **Aurigeno** are worth a stop and look around. The former is a quiet conglomeration of grey stone houses, while the latter is known for its colourful frescos. **Maggia** itself is handy for stocking up at the supermarket, but otherwise without great charm.

Cevio, 12km northwest, holds more interest. Admire the colourful facade of the 16th-century **Pretorio**, covered in the family coats-of-arms of many of the town's rulers, mostly in the 17th century. About 1km away, the core of the old town is graced with 16th-century mansions. A short walk away (signposted) are *grotti*, cellars carved out of great blocks of granite that tumbled onto the town here

TICINO

in a landslide. There is a handful of hotels and eateries here.

Take the road for Bosco Gurin and after 1km, a side road to **Boschetto** that leads over a stream (note the riverside *grotti* of **Rovana**). This mostly abandoned hamlet is a starting point for local walks and has a haunting quality.

The road to Bosco Gurin slices up in seemingly endless hairpin bends to **Cerentino**, where the road forks. You can stay at the cute **Osteria Centrale** (☎ 091 754 12 62; s/d Sfr50/100; ☺ Apr–mid-Oct), which has a handful of simple rooms (available only in summer, as there is no heating) and a restaurant with a fine local reputation.

The right fork leads 5.5km to **Bosco Gurin**, a minor ski centre (with a couple of hotels) and pleasantly sun-kissed high pasture village of slate-roofed, white-washed houses. It is the only town in Ticino where the majority language is German, a heritage of Valais immigrants. The other fork from Cerentino leads up the 8km-long **Valle di Campo** along a winding forest road to another broad, sunny, upland valley. The prettiest of its towns is **Campo**, with its scattered houses and Romanesque belltower. The valley is closed off by **Cimalmotto**, which offers great views.

Back in Cevio, the Valle Maggia road continues 3km to Bignasco, where you turn west for the **Val Bavona**, the prettiest of them all. A smooth road follows a mountain stream on its course through narrow meadows cradled between steep rocky walls. Its series of tightly huddled stone and slate-roofed hamlets is protected by a local foundation, but only inhabited from April to October. The valley sees no direct sunlight from November to February. For all that, its hamlets are irresistible. **Foroglio** is dominated by a powerful waterfall (a 10-minute walk away) and home to our pick **Ristorante La Froda** (☎ 091 754 11 81; meal Sfr45-50; ☺ daily Apr-Oct). Sit at one of five timber tables by a crackling fire for heaped serves of melt-in-the-mouth *stinco di maiale* (pork shank), served with the best polenta you are likely to taste. Wash down with a glass of Merlot.

At the end of the valley, just after San Carlo, a **cable car** (adult/child return Sfr20/10; ☺ mid-Jun–early Oct) rides up to the **Robiei dam** and nearby lakes, great for a day's hiking. A bus runs four times a day from Bignasco to San Carlo (Sfr10.80, 30 minutes), from April to October.

From Bignasco it is 17km to **Fusio**, another pretty town surrounded by woods at the head of the **Val Lavizzara**. Stop in **Mogno** on the way to see the extraordinary 1996 cylindrical church designed by Mario Botta. The grey (Maggia granite) and white (marble from Peccia) interior doorway has a strangely neo-Romanesque air. From Fusio the road leads to the dam holding back the emerald **Lago Sambuco**, from where you can hike on to other artificial lakes as well as north over the mountains into Valle Leventina. In Fusio, the **Antica Osteria Dazio** (☎ 091 755 11 62; www.hats.ch; dm Sfr16, s Sfr130, d Sfr150-260; ☺ Mar-Nov; ⓟ) is a beautifully renovated place to sleep, with loads of timber and Alpine charm. The more you spend on the doubles, the more charming the room. It has a restaurant, too.

Regular buses run from Locarno to Cevio and Bignasco (Sfr15.80, 50 minutes), from where you make less regular connections into the side valleys.

VAL VERZASCA

About 4km northeast of Locarno, this rugged 26km valley snakes north past the impressive Vogorno dam, which is fed by the gushing Verzasca (Green Waters), a delightful river whose white stones lend the transparent mountain water a scintillating emerald hue.

Just beyond the Vogorno lake, look to the left and you will see the picture-postcard hamlet of **Corripo** seemingly pasted on to the thickly wooded mountain flank. To reach it you cross the **Gola Verzasca**, a delightful little gorge. Up in Corripo you can eat at the basic **Osteria Corripo** (☎ 091 745 18 71; pasta Sfr12-15; ☺ Wed-Mon Apr-Oct). From June on you're likely to find it open on Tuesday too.

About 5km upstream, **Lavertezzo** is known for its narrow, double-humped, Romanesque bridge (rebuilt from scratch after the 1951 floods destroyed it) and natural pools in the icy stream. Be careful, as storms upstream can turn the river into a raging torrent in no time. Stay at riverside **Osteria Vittoria** (☎ 091 746 15 81; www.osteriavittoria.ch; s Sfr70-100, d Sfr120-140), a bustling family lodge with its own restaurant and garden. Most rooms have balconies with views over the Verzasca.

Another 12km takes you to **Sonogno**, a once abandoned hamlet at the head of the valley that has been resuscitated largely due to tourism.

Postal buses operate to Sonogno from Locarno as often as once hourly (Sfr17.60, 70 minutes).

Liechtenstein

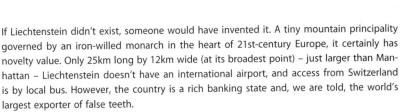

If Liechtenstein didn't exist, someone would have invented it. A tiny mountain principality governed by an iron-willed monarch in the heart of 21st-century Europe, it certainly has novelty value. Only 25km long by 12km wide (at its broadest point) – just larger than Manhattan – Liechtenstein doesn't have an international airport, and access from Switzerland is by local bus. However, the country is a rich banking state and, we are told, the world's largest exporter of false teeth.

Liechtensteiners sing German lyrics to the tune of God Save the Queen in their national anthem and they sure hope the Lord preserves their royals. Head of state Prince Hans Adam II and his son, Crown Prince Alois, have constitutional powers unmatched in modern Europe but most locals accept this situation gladly, as their monarchs' business nous and, perhaps also, tourist appeal, help keep this landlocked sliver of a micro-nation extremely prosperous.

Most come to Liechtenstein just to say they've been, and tour buses disgorge day-trippers in search of souvenir passport stamps. If you're going to make the effort to come this way, however, it's pointless not to venture further, even briefly. With friendly locals and magnificent views, the place comes into its own away from soulless Vaduz.

In fact, the more you read about Fürstentum Liechtenstein (FL) the easier it is to see it as the model for Ruritania – the mythical kingdom conjured up in fiction as diverse as *The Prisoner of Zenda* and Evelyn Waugh's *Vile Bodies*.

LIECHTENSTEIN

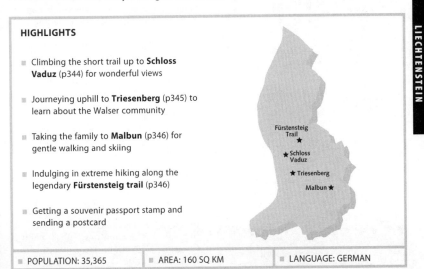

HIGHLIGHTS

- Climbing the short trail up to **Schloss Vaduz** (p344) for wonderful views

- Journeying uphill to **Triesenberg** (p345) to learn about the Walser community

- Taking the family to **Malbun** (p346) for gentle walking and skiing

- Indulging in extreme hiking along the legendary **Fürstensteig trail** (p346)

- Getting a souvenir passport stamp and sending a postcard

Fürstensteig Trail ★

★ Schloss Vaduz

★ Triesenberg

Malbun ★

| POPULATION: 35,365 | AREA: 160 SQ KM | LANGUAGE: GERMAN |

History

Austrian prince Johann Adam Von Liechtenstein purchased the counties of Schellenberg (1699) and Vaduz (1712) from impoverished German nobles and gave them his name. Long a principality under the Holy Roman Empire, Liechtenstein gained independence in 1866. In 1923, it formed a customs union with Switzerland.

Even then, none of the ruling Liechtensteins had bothered to leave their Viennese palace to see their acquisitions. It wasn't until 1938, in the wake of the Anschluss (Nazi Germany's takeover of Austria) that Prince Franz Josef II became the first monarch to live in the principality, when he and his much-loved wife, Gina, began transforming a poor rural nation into today's rich banking state. Their son, Prince Hans Adam II, ascended the throne on the prince's death in 1989.

The Liechtenstein clan lost considerable territories and possessions (including various castles and palaces) in Poland and the then Czechoslovakia after WWII, when the authorities of those countries seized them. The family has been trying, unsuccessfully,

to recover these possessions in international courts ever since.

The country's use of the Swiss franc encourages people to see it as a mere extension of its neighbour, but Liechtenstein has very different foreign policies, having joined the UN and the European Economic Area (EEA) relatively early, in 1990 and 1995 respectively.

Known as a tax haven, the principality banned customers from banking money anonymously in 2000. However, it remains under pressure (mainly from the European Union) to introduce more reforms.

In 2003, Hans Adam won sweeping powers to dismiss the elected government, appoint judges and reject proposed laws. The following year, he handed the day-to-day running of the country to his son Alois.

Orientation

Liechtenstein feels small because two-thirds is mountainous. A thin plain – the basin of the River Rhine separating Liechtenstein from Switzerland – runs down the country's western edge. The main north–south thoroughfare follows this.

The plain is wider and lower in the north, an area called Unterland (lowland), while the south is described as the Oberland (highland). The country's highest point is Grauspitz (2599m), on the southern border with Switzerland.

IT'S LIECHTENSTEIN TRIVIA TIME!

- Liechtenstein is the only country in the world named after the people who purchased it.

- In its last military engagement in 1866, none of its 80 soldiers was killed. In fact, 81 returned, including a new Italian 'friend'. The army was disbanded soon afterwards.

- Low business taxes means around 75,000 firms, many of them so-called 'letter box companies', with nominal head offices, are registered here – about twice the number of the principality's inhabitants.

- Liechtenstein is Europe's fourth-smallest nation (only the Vatican, Monaco and San Marino are smaller).

Entering the country from Buchs, you first reach Schaan, which virtually merges into Vaduz and then Triesen further south. Further south still is Balzers.

From Triesen, you can take the steep, winding road west up to Triesenberg and Malbun (1600m).

North of Schaan are quiet villages like Planken and Schellenberg.

Information

For general information on the country, have a look at www.liechtenstein.li. For more tourism-related information, check out www .tourismus.li. Liechtenstein's international phone prefix is ☎ 423.

Prices are comparable with those in Switzerland. Shops usually open 8am to noon and 1.30pm to 6.30pm Monday to Friday, and 8am to 4pm Saturday, although souvenir shops also open on high-season Sundays. Banks open from 8am to noon and 1.30pm to 4.30pm, Monday to Friday. The country uses Swiss currency.

Devoutly Catholic, Liechtenstein takes off all the main religious feast days, plus Labour Day (1 May) and National Day (August 15), totalling a healthy 22 public holidays annually.

The official language is German, although most speak an Alemannic dialect. The Austrian 'Grüss Gott' is as common as the Swiss 'Grüezi'. English is widely spoken.

Getting There & Away

The nearest airports are Friedrichshafen (Germany) and Zürich, with train connections to the Swiss border towns of Buchs and Sargans. From each of these towns there are usually three buses to Vaduz (Sfr2.40/3.60 from Buchs/Sargans, Swiss Pass valid). Buses run every 30 minutes from the Austrian border town of Feldkirch; you sometimes have to change at Schaan to reach Vaduz.

A few Buchs–Feldkirch trains stop at Schaan (bus tickets are valid).

By road, the A16 from Switzerland passes through Liechtenstein via Schaan and ends at Feldkirch. The N13 follows the Rhine along the border; minor roads cross into Liechtenstein at each freeway exit.

Getting Around

Buses traverse the country. Single fares (buy tickets on the bus) are Sfr2.40/3.60 for two/three zones, while a weekly bus pass costs

---

> **THE INSIDE READ**
>
> Liechtenstein sounds quite wacky but it is really like a small village where everyone knows everyone else's business. Liechtensteiners are warm-hearted folk who know what's important in life, as you soon realise reading Charlie Connelly's amusing *Stamping Grounds: Liechtenstein's Quest for the World Cup*, possibly the longest and most engrossing read ever about Liechtenstein.

Sfr13/6.50 per adult/child. The latter is available from post offices and tourist offices. Swiss travel passes are valid on all main routes. Timetables are posted at stops.

For bicycle hire, try the Swiss train stations in Buchs or Sargans, or **Sigi's Velo Shop** (☎ 384 27 50; www.sigis-veloshop.li; Balzers; per day from Sfr30; ⏲ 8.30am-noon & 1.30-6pm Mon, Wed-Fri, 8.30am-noon Tue & Sat). For a taxi, try calling ☎ 233 35 35 or ☎ 231 20 41.

VADUZ

pop 5150 / elevation 455m

Poor Vaduz. It's all that most visitors to Liechtenstein see, and it feels like its soul has been sold to cater to the whims of its banks and the hordes of whirlwind tourists who alight for 17 minutes on guided bus tours. Souvenir shops, tax-free luxury-goods stores and cube-shaped concrete buildings dominate the antiseptic pedestrian centre beneath the steep castle hill.

Don't be disheartened. Traces of the quaint village that existed just 50 years ago still exist, there are a couple of good museums and the rest of the country awaits exploration.

Orientation

Two streets, Städtle and Äulestrasse, diverge and then rejoin, making up the town centre. Everything of practical importance is near this small area.

Information

The **Liechtenstein Center** (☎ 239 63 00; www.tourismus .li; Städtle; ⏲ 9am-5pm) offers brochures, souvenir passport stamps (Sfr3) and multi-video screens with scenes from all over the country. Philatelie Liechtenstein will interest stamp collectors. The **post office** (Äulestrasse 38; ⏲ 7.45am-6pm Mon-Fri, 8-11am Sat) is nearby.

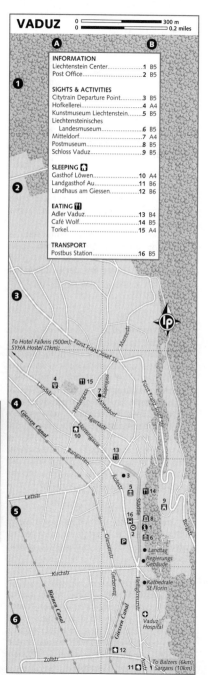

VADUZ

INFORMATION	
Liechtenstein Center	**1** B5
Post Office	**2** B5

SIGHTS & ACTIVITIES	
Citytrain Departure Point	**3** B5
Hofkellerei	**4** A4
Kunstmuseum Liechtenstein	**5** B5
Liechtensteinisches Landesmuseum	**6** B5
Mitteldorf	**7** A4
Postmuseum	**8** B5
Schloss Vaduz	**9** B5

SLEEPING	
Gasthof Löwen	**10** A4
Landgasthof Au	**11** B6
Landhaus am Giessen	**12** B6

EATING	
Adler Vaduz	**13** B4
Café Wolf	**14** B5
Torkel	**15** A4

TRANSPORT	
Postbus Station	**16** B5

Sights & Activities

Schloss Vaduz (Vaduz Castle) looms over the capital from the hill above and, although closed to the public, is worth the climb for the vistas. Trails climb the hill from the end of Egertastrasse.

For a rare peek inside the castle grounds, arrive on 15 August, Liechtenstein's National Day, when there are magnificent fireworks and the prince invites all 35,365 Liechtensteiners over to his place for a glass of wine or beer.

In the centre, the well-designed **Liechtensteinisches Landesmuseum** (National Museum; ☎ 239 68 20; www.landesmuseum.li; Städtle 43; adult/concession Sfr8/5, combined with Kunstmuseum Sfr18/8; ☉ 10am-5pm Tue-Sun, to 8pm Wed) provides a surprisingly interesting romp through the principality's history, from medieval witch-trials and burnings to the manufacture of false teeth.

The mainstay of the **Kunstmuseum Liechtenstein** (☎ 235 03 00; www.kunstmuseum.li; Städtle 32; adult/concession Sfr12/8, combined with Landesmuseum Sfr18/8; ☉ 10am-5pm Tue-Sun, to 8pm Thu) is temporary exhibitions of contemporary art, not the prince's collection of old masters, which was relocated to the Liechtenstein Museum in Vienna. There are some 20th-century classics on the ground floor.

The **Postmuseum** (Post Museum; ☎ 236 61 05; Städtle 37; admission free; ☉ 10am-noon & 1-5pm), on the 1st floor, is mildly diverting. Liechtenstein once made a packet producing souvenir stamps for enthusiasts, but that market has been hit by the rise of email. Here you'll find all national stamps issued since 1912.

To see how Vaduz once looked, head northeast from the pedestrian zone to **Mitteldorf**. This and the surrounding streets form a charming quarter of traditional houses and verdant gardens.

Nearby lies the prince's wine cellar, the **Hofkellerei** (☎ 232 10 18; www.hofkellerei.li; Feldstrasse 4). It is possible to sample the wines here only in a large group and if you have booked ahead.

Every afternoon from May to October at 4.30pm, a touristy **Citytrain** (☎ 777 34 90; www.citytrain.li; adult/child Sfr10.50/7) makes a 35-minute circuit of Vaduz.

Sleeping & Eating

Vaduz is the most convenient base, but other towns are more charming for longer stays, so ask at the tourist office.

A TAXING RELATIONSHIP

Says one journalist in Liechtenstein: the 'Swiss are our brothers, the Austrians our friends and the Germans our customers.' The cosiness of that latter relationship was shaken in February 2008, when a tax evasion scandal revealed that some of those 'customers' had been less than honest with Germany's taxman. More than 1000 high-flying Germans, including the Deutsche Post (national post office) chief, Klaus Zumwinkel, were found to have evaded tax by depositing large sums of money in trusts run by the principality's LGT bank, partly owned by the princely family.

The German Bundesnachrichtendienst (BND, foreign intelligence service) allegedly paid a disgruntled former bank employee, Heinrich Kieber, €5 million for blowing the whistle. The total amount secreted away was estimated at €4 billion. Kieber's CD contained information on tax evaders from as many as 15 other European countries.

Liechtenstein, while not disputing that such money could have wound up in its banks (the principality doesn't consider tax evasion a crime), accused Germany of spying. Kieber, who also sold confidential information to the USA, hoofed it out of the country. Liechtenstein views him as an informer and traitor.

The entire storm, according to some, was also meant as a shot across the bows of more important Swiss banks. The EU and Switzerland have long been at loggerheads over the latter's perceived attachment to banking confidentiality.

Hotel Falknis (☎ 232 63 77; Landstrasse 92; s/d with shared bathroom Sfr55/110; **P**) Basic rooms some 15 minutes on foot north of the centre – or take the bus.

Landgasthof Au (☎ 232 11 17; Austrasse 2; s/d without bathroom Sfr68/110, s/d with bathroom Sfr90/140; **P**) A couple of bus stops south of Vaduz town centre (about a 10-minute walk), this simple, family-run place is a reasonable budget option. A couple of the bigger doubles have a terrace. Note that they only accept cash. The garden restaurant (mains Sfr18 to Sfr35, Wednesday to Sunday) has a good name for local grub: anything from a ham omelette to a couple of vegetarian dishes and a kids' menu.

Landhaus am Giessen (☎ 235 00 35; www.giessen.li; Zollstrasse 16; s/d Sfr100/150; **P** **⊞**) Virtually around the corner from the Landgasthof Au, this is a fairly modern affair with comfortable and good-sized, if comparatively charmless, rooms. They have a sauna and offer massages. There is wi-fi throughout.

ourpick Gasthof Löwen (☎ 238 11 41; www .hotel-loewen.li; Herrengasse 35; s/d from Sfr199/299; **P**) Historic and creakily elegant, this six-century old guest house has eight spacious rooms with antique furniture and modern bathrooms. There's a cosy bar, fine-dining restaurant and a rear outdoor terrace overlooking grapevines.

Café Wolf (☎ 232 23 21; Städtle 29; mains Sfr12.50-19.50) This relaxed café and restaurant has pavement tables in summer and a menu that mixes Swiss and international cuisine – anything from pizza to pseudo-Asian dishes.

Adler Vaduz (☎ 232 21 31; Herrengasse 2; dishes Sfr17.50-46; ⊗ Mon-Fri) A pleasant restaurant in the Hotel Adler, the Adler offers a broad selection, from pasta to *Rindsfilet vom Grill auf Steinpilzrisotto mit Trüffel-Rotweinsauce nappiert* (beef steak filet with mushroom risotto and a truffle-red wine sauce).

Torkel (☎ 232 44 10; Hintergasse 9; dishes Sfr42-58; ⊗ lunch & dinner Mon-Fri, dinner Sat) Just above the prince's vineyards sits His Majesty's ivy-clad restaurant. The garden terrace enjoys a wonderful perspective of the castle above, while the ancient, wood-lined interior is cosy in winter. Food mixes classic with modern. The set lunch menu (Sfr64) gives a good overview.

AROUND VADUZ
Sights

Away from the capital, one's impression of Liechtenstein swiftly improves, thanks to magnificent Alpine scenery.

Triesenberg (bus 21 from Vaduz) is perched on a terrace above the Rhine Valley. The **Walsermuseum** (☎ 262 19 26; www.triesenberg.li; Jonaboda 2; adult/concession Sfr2/1; 7.45-11.45am & 1.30-5.45pm Mon-Fri, 7.45-11am & 1.30-5pm Sat) tells the intriguing story of the Walsers and contains some curious carvings out of twisted tree trunks and branches. The Walsers were a German-speaking 'tribe' from the Valais (Wallis in German) that emigrated across Europe in the 13th century and settled in many places, including Liechtenstein, where they still speak their own dialect. Ask at the museum about visiting the nearby Walserhaus (Hag 19), a 400-year-old house furnished in 19th century fashion.

Hinterschellenberg (bus 11 from Vaduz to Mauren and then bus 33) briefly entered the stream of world history when about 500 Russian soldiers who had fought on the German side in WWII crossed the border in search of asylum in 1945. They remained for about two-and-a-half years, after which most made for Argentina. Liechtenstein was the only country not to cede to the Soviet Union's demands that such soldiers (considered traitors) be extradited to the USSR – which generally meant death. A memorial about 100m from the Austrian border marks the event.

Asylum talks were held in the **Wirtschaft zum Löwen** (mains Sfr16-35; ☽ Fri-Tue), just behind the memorial and still a great tavern for local goodies. It's across the road from the bus 33 terminus stop.

In **Balzers** (bus 12 from Vaduz Post), the now state-owned, hilltop 13th-century **Burg Gutenberg** castle only opens for concerts. It cuts a striking figure on the horizon and boasts nice strolls in the vicinity. The area was settled as early as the Neolithic period and Roman elements have been found in the castle foundations. Much of the original castle's stonework was used to rebuild the village below after fire in 1795. The castle was restored in the early 20th century.

Hiking

Some 400km of hiking trails criss-cross the principality. For some ideas, check out www.wanderwege-llv.li.

The country's most famous trail is the **Fürstensteig**, a rite of passage for nearly every Liechtensteiner. You must be fit and not suffer from vertigo, as in places the path is narrow, reinforced with rope handholds and/or falls away to a sheer drop. The hike (up to four hours) begins at the **Berggasthaus Gaflei** (bus 22 from Triesenberg). Travel light and wear good shoes.

A steep two-hour climb from **Planken** (bus 26 from Schaan Post) brings you to the panoramic **Gafadurahütte** (☎ 262 89 27; www.alpenverein.li; ☽ mid-May–mid-Oct). From here, over the **Drei Schwestern (Three Sisters)** mountain, you can meet up with the Fürstensteig.

Sleeping

Camping Mittagspitze (☎ 392 36 77; www.camping triesen.li; camping 2 adults, car & tent Sfr29, dm adult/child Sfr22/13; ☒) This well-equipped camp site in a leafy spot is excellent for families, with a playground and pool as well as a restaurant, TV lounge and kiosk. It's south of Triesen on the road to Balzers.

SYHA Hostel (☎ 232 50 22; www.youthhostel.ch /schaan; Untere Rütigasse 6; dm Sfr31.40, d Sfr82.80; ☽ mid-Mar-Oct, reception closed 10am-5pm) This hostel caters particularly to cyclists and families. Halfway between Schaan and Vaduz, it's within easy walking distance of either.

Hotel Garni Säga (☎ 392 43 77; www.saega.li; Alte Landstrasse 17; s Sfr89-115, d Sfr170; P) This modern family-run pension, next door to the camping ground, has pleasant, sunny rooms.

MALBUN
pop 35 / elevation 1600m

At the end of the road from Vaduz, the 1600m-high resort of Malbun feels – in the nicest possible sense – like the edge of the earth.

It's not really as remote as it seems and in high season Malbun is mobbed. However, generally it's perfect for unwinding, especially with the family. The skiing is inexpensive, if not too extensive, while the hiking is relaxing and beautiful. The place is dead out of season.

Information

The **tourist office** (☎ 263 65 77; www.malbun.li; ☽ 9am-noon & 1-4.30pm Mon-Sat Jun-Oct & mid-Dec–mid-Apr) is on the main street, not far from Hotel Walserhof. There's an ATM by the lower bus stop, accepting all major cards.

Activities

Skiing is aimed at beginners, with a few intermediate and cross-country runs thrown in. Indeed, older British royals like Prince Charles learnt to ski here. A general ski pass (including the Sareis chairlift) for a day/week costs Sfr45/205 for adults and Sfr29/127 for children. One day's equipment rental from **Malbun Sport** (☎ 263 37 55; www.malbunsport.li; ☽ 8am-6pm Mon-Fri, plus Sat & Sun high season) costs Sfr58 including skis, shoes and poles.

Some hiking trails, including to **Sassfürkle**, stay open during the winter. During the summer, other treks include the **Furstin-Gina Path**, with views over Austria, Switzerland and Liechtenstein. This walk starts at the top of

LIECHTENSTEIN

the Sareis chairlift (Sfr8.30/12.90 single/return in summer) and returns to Malbun.

Sleeping & Eating

Hotel Walserhof (☎ 264 43 23; d Sfr140) A simple mountain house with four doubles, the Walserhof is a friendly place with cheerful outdoor dining. The rooms are a little dated but perfectly comfortable.

Alpenhotel Malbun (☎ 263 11 81; www.alpenhotel.li; s/d to Sfr110/180; P ⊠) Rooms in the sienna-coloured main chalet are cute if cramped, with traditional painted doors and plenty of timber, but only shared bathrooms (these rooms are a little cheaper). En-suite rooms in the nearby annexe are larger and comfier but straight from the 1970s. Enjoy the kitschy Alpine decor and hearty food in the hotel restaurant.

For gob-smacking mountain views while eating, it is hard to beat the **Bergrestaurant**

Sareiserjoch (☎ 268 21 01; www.sareis.li; mains Sfr20-35; ⏱ Jun-mid-Oct & mid-Dec-Apr), at the end of the Sareis chairlift. *Käsknöpfli* (cheese-filled dumplings) and rösti are on the menu. Thursday in winter is Raclette night.

Getting There & Around

Bus 21 travels more or less hourly from Vaduz to Malbun between 7.03am and 8.33pm every day (Sfr3.60, Swiss Pass valid, 30 minutes), returning between 8.20am and 7.20pm.

AROUND MALBUN

Two kilometres before Malbun is the Väluna Valley, the main **cross-country skiing** area. The trail, illuminated in winter, starts at Steg. Nearby is the simple but charming **Berggasthaus Sücka** (☎ 263 25 79; www.suecka-erlebnis.li; dm Sfr25, d Sfr80; P), which also has a restaurant open from Tuesday to Sunday. The dorm area is simply a row of mattresses.

Directory

CONTENTS

ACCOMMODATION

From palatial palaces and castles to a mountain refuge, nuclear bunker or simple hayloft, Switzerland sports traditional and creative accommodation in every price range. Moreover, an increasing number of places are green when it comes to eco-friendly heating, lighting, waste disposal and so on; see p403 and p19.

This guidebook runs the gamut from budget to midrange and top-end accommodation. Budget accommodation includes campsites, dormitories, farm stays, hostels and simple hotels, many of which offer rooms with shared bathroom facilities. These generally cost up to Sfr150 for a double, although this can differ slightly, depending on whether you're staying in a city or the countryside. Midrange accommodation – with all the comforts of private bathroom, TV, telephone and more – rises

to approximately Sfr350 for a double, again depending on where you're staying. Over and above this price, wallow in pure unadulterated, time-honoured Swiss luxury.

Rates in cities and most towns stay constant throughout the year bar the immediate Christmas and New Year periods, when rates rise. In mountain resorts prices are strictly seasonal: low season (mid-September to mid-December and mid-April to mid-June) is the cheapest time to visit; mid-season (January to mid-February and mid-June to early July and September) begins to get pricy; while high season (July-August, Christmas, and mid-February to Easter) is the busy period, when you pay full whack. Seasonal differences are less marked with budget hotels.

Local tourist offices have accommodation listings and most will make a hotel reservation for you, for as little as Sfr5 or no commission. In this guide we list high-season prices, and review accommodation in price ascending order, that is budget first, deluxe last. Unless noted otherwise, hotel prices include breakfast. Online, MySwitzerland. com is a fabulous resource for tracking down accommodation.

B&Bs

Some of Switzerland's most charming accommodation comes in the form of bed and breakfast – a room in a private home which can be anything from a castle to a farm, Alpine chalet or urban guest house and includes a feisty breakfast, often of homemade produce, in the price. Some hosts will also, assuming you order in advance, cook up a delicious evening meal served around a shared table for an additional charge of Sfr20 to Sfr30 per person, including wine.

WHAT THE COMPUTER ICON MEANS

Throughout this guide, only accommodation that provides an actual computer that guests can use to access the internet is flagged with a computer icon like this: 🖳 ; those that offer wi-fi access, but have no computer, carry no icon but are reviewed as wi-fi friendly.

PRACTICALITIES

■ Major newspapers include Zürich's *Neue Zürcher Zeitung* (www.nzz.ch, in German) and *Tages Anzeiger* (www.tagesanzeiger.ch, in German); Geneva's *Le Temps* (www.letemps.ch, in French) and *La Tribune de Genève* (www.tdg.ch, in French); and Lugano-based *Corriere del Ticino* (www.cdt.ch, in Italian). More populist papers include free tabloid *20 Minuten* (www.20min.ch, in German and French) and right-wing *Blick* (www.blick.ch, in German). *Facts* (http://facts.ch, in German) is a monthly news magazine.

■ Public broadcast media is largely broken down along linguistic lines: German-language SF-DRS operates three TV and five radio stations; French and Italian TV operators are TSR and RTSI respectively, with RSR and RSI being their radio equivalents; and TvR and Radio Rumantsch (RR; www.rtr.ch) are Switzerland's respective Romansch TV and radio stations.

■ Swissinfo (www.swissinfo.org) is a national news website available in several languages, including English; while WRS (FM 88.4; www.worldradio.ch) is a Geneva-based English-language station broadcasting music and news country-wide.

■ Electrical supply is 220V, 50Hz. Swiss sockets are recessed, hexagonally shaped and incompatible with most plugs from abroad (including 'universal' adapters). Fortunately, you will also usually find at least one standard, three-pin continental socket in every building.

■ Metric measurements are used. Like other continental Europeans, the Swiss indicate decimals with commas and thousands with full points.

Tourist offices have lists of B&Bs in their areas – urban rarities but plentiful in the countryside areas – and 800-odd can be tracked through **BnB** (www.bnb.ch), which also publishes an annual guide (Sfr25). For B&Bs on farms see p353.

In rural areas private houses frequently offer inexpensive 'room(s) vacant' (*Zimmer frei/chambres libres/camere libere* in German/French/Italian), with or without breakfast.

Camping

Camp sites brandish one to five stars depending on their amenities and convenience of location. They are often scenically situated in an out-of-the-way place by a river or lake, so having your own transport is useful. Charges per night are from around Sfr8 per person plus Sfr6 to Sfr12 for a tent, and from an additional Sfr4 for a car. Telephone ahead, as in the high season camps might be full, and at the start or end of the season camps may close if demand is low or the weather poor.

Wild camping (*wildes camping/camping sauvage* in German/French) is not strictly allowed and should be discreet, but it is perfectly viable in the wide-open mountain spaces, and is fairly common in places like Ticino. If the police come across you, they may not do anything (especially if you've been responsible with your rubbish) or they

may move you on. A fine is theoretically possible.

For more on camping in Switzerland contact **Schweizerischer Camping und Caravanning Verband** (Swiss Camping & Caravanning Federation, SCCV; ☎ 062 777 40 08; www.sccv.ch) or surf **Verband Schweizer Campings** (Swiss Camping Association; www.swisscamps.ch) and **Camping NET** (www.camping.ch).

The **Touring Club der Schweiz** (Swiss Touring Club, TCS; ☎ 022 417 22 20; www.tcs.ch, in German, French & Italian; Chemin de Blandonnet, CP 820, CH-1214 Geneva) publishes a comprehensive guide to Swiss camp sites.

Dorms, Jails & Igloos

Dormitory accommodation (*Touristenlager* or *Massenlager* in German, *dortoir* in French) has been well established for years in ski and other resorts. Take care in studying accommodation lists, as dormitories may only take groups. Mattresses are often crammed side by side in massive bunks in these places; however, there are usually no curfews and the doors aren't usually locked during the day. Some camp sites offer simple dorm beds too.

Then, of course, there is the increasingly trendy swath of eclectic and creative accommodation options, all of which, depending on your viewpoint, involve some sort of roughing it: fancy sleeping in a wine barrel (p157), a tree-trunk bed (p192), a one-time jail (p247), a nuclear bunker (p292) or an ice-cold igloo (p197 & p313)?

For the low-down on Alpine huts and refuges see p57.

Hostels

Swiss hostels (*Jugendherberge* in German, *auberge de jeunesse* in French, *alloggio per giovanni* in Italian) range from older, institutional affairs to modern establishments bordering on designer accommodation. Most charge between Sfr29.50 and Sfr47 for a dorm bed, including breakfast and sheets (sleeping bags are no longer allowed in hostels), and are run by Switzerland's HI-affiliated, national hostelling organisation **Schweizer Jugendherbergen** (Swiss Youth Hostel Association, SYHA; ☎ 044 360 14 14; www.youth hostel.ch). Non-HI members who want to stay in one of its 58 hostels can become a member straight away (Sfr33/22 per adult/under 18yr) or pay a nightly 'guest fee' of Sfr6 on top of the bed price – six overnights equal a fully-fledged annual HI membership.

Hostels do get full; telephone reservations are not accepted but bookings can be made via the website. During busy times a three-day maximum stay may apply.

Then there are backpacker hostels. These tend to be more flexible in their regulations, reception times and opening hours, and are usually free of school or youth groups. Membership is not required; 33 such hostels are loosely affiliated under **Swiss Backpackers** (☎ 033 823 46 46; www.swissbackpackers.ch).

Another 80 or so hostels in the shape of an Alpine chalet or rural farmhouse offer hostel-style accommodation under the green umbrella group **Naturfreundehaus** (Friends of Nature; www.nfhouse.org).

Hotels & Pensions

Despite the great reputation of Swiss hotels, some historic, some downright decadent, the standard at the lower end of the market

---

BOOK ACCOMMODATION ONLINE

For more accommodation reviews and recommendations by Lonely Planet authors, check out www.lonelyplanet.com/hotels. You'll find the true, insider lowdown on the best places to stay. Reviews are thorough and independent. Best of all, you can book online.

---

varies. Cheapest are rooms with sink and shared toilet and shower in the corridor, costing around Sfr50/80 for a single/double in a small town, or around Sfr90/100 in cities or mountain resorts. Pop in a private shower and the nightly rate rises by Sfr10 to Sfr20 per person at least.

If you're staying in mostly one- or two-star hotels, **Swiss Budget Hotels** (☎ 084 880 55 08; www.rooms.ch) produces a national booklet of good-quality cheaper hotels and has regular special offers.

A *Frühstückspension* or *Hotel-Garni* serves only breakfast; no half- or full board. Small pensions with a restaurant often have a 'rest day' when check-in may not be possible, unless by prior arrangement (so telephone ahead).

Once in the realm of three- and four-star pensions and hotels, a decent level of comfort is assured, telephone, TV and oftentimes minibar in the room included.

Swiss excellence comes into its own with five-star hotels which are palatial, luxurious, often historic and impeccable in service. Several – Zürich's Baur au Lac, Gstaad's Palace hotel and the Schatzalp in Davos – are legendary.

To sleep sustainably opt for one of Switzerland's **Steinbock Label** (www.steinbock-label .ch, in German) hotels – places recognised as eco-hotels and labelled with one to five *Steinböcke* (ibexes) to reflect their sustainability.

Rental Accommodation

Self-caterers can opt for a chalet or apartment, both of which need booking in advance; for peak periods, reserve six to 12 months ahead. A minimum stay of one week (usually Saturday to Saturday) is common.

Tourist offices send lists of rental-accommodation. Useful online resources for bargain-basement deals, particularly out of high season or for last-minute bookings, include **REKA** (Schweizer Reisekasse; ☎ 031 329 66 33; www.reka.ch); **Interhome** (Zürich ☎ 01 497 22 22; www .interhome.ch; USA ☎ 305-940 2299; Australia ☎ 02-9453 2744; UK ☎ 020-8891 1294); and **Switzerland Tourism** (www.myswitzerland.com).

BUSINESS HOURS

Most shops are open from 8am to 6.30pm Monday to Friday, sometimes with a one- to two-hour break for lunch at noon in smaller towns. In larger cities, there's often a late

---

TOP PICKS: KIDDING AROUND

- Tour the Jura by horse and cart; sleep in straw and search for dinosaurs at Prehisto Parc (p143)
- Learn cow herding, bobbin-lace making and other traditional farm skills at Ballenberg's Open-Air Museum (p193)
- Get hands mucky in the name of art at a children's workshop in Bern's Zentrum Paul Klee (p203)
- Dash beneath Geneva's iconic Jet d'Eau (p87)
- Fly a plane, whiz to the moon and drive a lorry at Lucerne's interactive Transport Museum (p245)
- Dodge clouds aboard a hot-air balloon over Château-d'Œx (p123)
- Throw pine cones and play water games along Lenzerheide's kid-themed Globi Trail (p301)
- Cuddle the world's biggest collection of teddy bears at Basel's Doll's House Museum (p267) and play games at Vevey's Swiss Games Museum (p113)
- Pet tame marmots at Spielboden near Saas Fee (p166)
- See Switzerland in a day at Swissminiatur (p334)
- Fly down Switzerland's longest summer toboggan run (p251)

---

shopping day until 9pm, typically Thursday or Friday. Closing times on Saturday are usually 4pm or 5pm. Sunday sees some souvenir shops and supermarkets at some train stations open, but little else.

Offices are typically open from about 8am to noon and 2pm to 5pm Monday to Friday. Banks are open from 8.30am to 4.30pm Monday to Friday, with late opening usually one day a week.

CHILDREN

Orderly, clean and not overly commercial, Switzerland is a dream for family travel and promotes itself heavily as such: the meaty Swiss tourist board *Families* brochure (order it online at www.myswitzerland.com) is jam-packed with ideas, as is its website which lists kid-friendly accommodation, family offers and so on.

Family train travel is good-value. Kids under six years travel for free with **Swiss Railways** (www.rail.ch) and those aged six to 16 years revel in free unlimited rail travel with its annual Junior Card (Sfr20) or – should it be grandparents travelling with the kids – Grandparent Card (Sfr60). Switzerland's mountain of scenic journeys by train and boat (p368) enchant children of all ages. Upon arrival at point B, dozens of segments of the perfectly-signposted hiking/biking/rollerblading/canoeing trails designed strictly for non-

motorised traffic by **SwitzerlandMobility** (p18) are flagged as suitable for younger children.

Staying in a B&B (p348) is family fabulous: little kids can sweetly slumber upstairs while weary parents wine and dine in peace downstairs (don't forget your baby monitor!). Pick a B&B on a farm or kip on straw in the hay barn (p353) for adventurous kids to have the time of their life.

Those with kids aged six to 12 years should buy Diana Dicks' *Ticking Along with Swiss Kids,* part children's book about Switzerland, part guide for parents on what to see, where to eat and so on.

CLIMATE

Be prepared for a range of temperatures given that the mountains create a variety of local and regional microclimates: Jura, the coldest area, can be bitterly cold in winter, while Ticino in the south has a hot Mediterranean climate. This said, Switzerland generally has a central European climate with daytime temperatures hovering between 18° and 28°C in summer, -2° to 7°C in winter.

Watch out for the Föhn, a hot, dry wind that sweeps down into the valleys and can be oppressively uncomfortable (though some find its warming effect refreshing). It strikes any time of the year, but most frequently in spring and autumn.

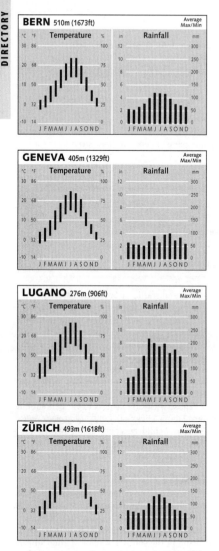

To check the weather forecast call **MeteoSwiss** (☎ 162, from abroad +41 848 800 162; www.meteosuisse .admin.ch).

For more on when to visit, see p17.

CUSTOMS

Visitors from Europe may import 200 cigarettes, 50 cigars or 250g of pipe tobacco. Visitors from non-European countries may import twice as much. The allowance for alcoholic beverages is the same for everyone: 1L for beverages containing more than 15% alcohol by volume, and 2L for beverages containing less than 15%. Alcohol and tobacco may only be brought in by people aged 17 or over. Gifts up to the value of Sfr100 may also be imported, as well as food provisions for one day.

DANGERS & ANNOYANCES

Street crime is fairly uncommon. However, do watch your belongings; pickpockets thrive in city crowds. The Swiss police aren't very visible, but when they do appear, they have a poor reputation for their treatment of people of non-European descent or appearance, with some suggesting that they perform random street searches of questionable necessity etc.

Several cities, such as Zürich and Bern, have a heroin problem, but these days you generally have to be way off the main thoroughfares to notice it.

Avalanches

On average, 25 people a year are killed in the Swiss Alps by avalanches, of which there are about 10,000 annually. Despite modern measures to help prevent them, such as crisscross metal barriers above resorts to prevent snow slips, controlled explosions to prevent dangerous build-up of snow and resorts' warning systems involving flags or flashing lights – skiers and boarders should never be complacent. Avalanche warnings should be heeded, and local advice sought before detouring from prepared runs.

Research suggests that most fatal avalanches are caused by the victims. So if you're going off-piste or hiking in snowy areas, never go alone, take an avalanche shovel to dig out injured companions and be careful around narrow valleys below or close to ridges. Before setting foot in the mountains check the day's **avalanche bulletin** (☎ 187, from abroad +41 848 800 162/3; connection charge 50c plus 50c per min).

People's chances of being found and rescued are improved if they carry – and most importantly know how to use – a special avalanche radio transceiver. Such equipment is expensive, but it's foolhardy to forget it. Many boarders and off-piste skiers also now take a self-inflating avalanche balloon, which, if the worst happens, is designed to keep its owner above or close to the surface of the snow.

DISCOUNT CARDS
Senior Cards
Senior citizens are not entitled to discounts on Swiss railways, but they do get many discounts on museum admission, ski passes and some cable cars.

Numerous hotels also offer low-season discounts; **Switzerland Tourism** (www.myswitzerland.com) can send you a list.

Proof of age is needed for museum and transport discounts. The discounts often start for those as young as 62, although sometimes a higher limit is observed. The abbreviation for senior citizens is AHV in German and AVS in French.

Student & Youth Cards
An International Student Identity Card (ISIC) yields discounts on admission prices, air and international train tickets and even some ski passes.

If you're under 26 but not a student, apply for the IYTC (International Youth Travel Card). Both cards should be issued by student unions and by youth-oriented travel agencies in your home country.

Travel agencies **STA Travel** (www.statravel.ch) and **Globetrotter** (www.globetrotter.ch, in German) issue ISIC cards (Sfr20).

Visitors' Cards
In many resorts and a few cities there's a visitors' card, sometimes called a guest card (Gästekarte), which provides various useful benefits such as reduced prices for museums, swimming pools or cable cars. Cards are issued by your accommodation (even hostels and camp sites), though if you're in a holiday apartment you'll need to get one from the tourist office. They're well worth having, so if your hotel doesn't supply one automatically, ask if such a scheme exists.

Swiss Museum Pass
Regular or long-term visitors to Switzerland might want to consider buying a **Swiss Museum Pass** (www.museumspass.ch; adult/family Sfr144/255) which covers entry to the permanent collection (only) of 440 museums. See the website for details.

EMBASSIES & CONSULATES
For a comprehensive list of Swiss embassies abroad and embassies in Switzerland, go to www.eda.admin.ch.

Embassies & Consulates in Switzerland
Embassies are in Bern while cities such as Zürich and Geneva have several consulates.

KIP WITH THE COWS

No other European country does it…encourage travellers to bunk up with the cows in haylofts, that is. A fabulous way to experience life on a Swiss farm close up, Switzerland's **Aventure sur la paille/Schlaf im Stroh** (☎ 041 678 12 86; www.abenteuer-stroh.ch) is the ultimate adventure in the straw.

When their cows are out to pasture in summer or indeed, even after they've been brought in for the winter come early October, Swiss farmers charge travellers Sfr20 to Sfr30 per adult and Sfr10 to Sfr20 per child to sleep on straw in their hay barns or lofts (listen to the jangle of cow or goat bells beneath your head!). Farmers provide cotton undersheets (to avoid straw pricks) and woolly blankets for extra warmth, but guests need their own sleeping bags and – strongly advisable – pocket torch. Nightly rates include a farmhouse breakfast, and a morning shower and evening meal are usually available for an extra Sfr2 and Sfr20 to Sfr30 respectively. Advance reservations are particularly recommended in summer. A comprehensive listing of the 200-odd farms across Switzerland offering straw accommodation is online.

Should you prefer a room in the farmhouse rather than above the cows, try **Swiss Holidays Farms** (☎ 031 329 66 99; www.bauernhof-ferien.ch), an association of 250 farms countrywide that open their doors to both overnight B&B guests and self-caterers keen to rent a renovated barn or farmhouse cottage etc for a week or longer; or **Rural Tourism** (☎ 021 619 44 37; www.tourisme-rural.ch) which allows you to search its countryside-property listings by Alpine or vineyard location, chalet, farmhouse, hut, hay barn and so on, and lists plenty of ideas for outdoor rural activities and gourmet discoveries. Both have online catalogues.

To go the whole hog and work on the farm as well as kip there, see p358. Should it be or become an emotional affair, try mothering a cow or baby calf; see p53.

Australia and New Zealand have no embassy in Switzerland, but each a consulate in Geneva.

Australia (☎ 022 799 91 00; www.australia.ch; Chemin des Fins 2, CH-1121 Geneva)

Austria (Map p200; ☎ 031 356 52 52; www.aussen ministerium.at/bern, in German; Kirchenfeldstrasse 77-79, Bern)

Canada Bern (Map p200; ☎ 031 357 32 00; www .canada-ambassade.ch; Kirchenfeldstrasse 88); Geneva (Map p88; ☎ 022 919 92 00; 5 Ave de l'Ariana)

France Bern (☎ 031 359 21 11; www.ambafrance-ch .org, in German & French; Schosshaldenstrasse 46); Geneva (☎ 022 319 00 00; www.consulfrance-geneve.org, in French; 2 Cours des Bastiona)

Germany Bern (☎ 031-359 41 11; www.bern.diplo.de, in German & French; Willadingweg 83); Basel (☎ 061 693 33 03; Schwarzwaldallee 200); Geneva (☎ 022 730 11 11; Chemin du Petit-Saconnex 28c)

Italy (Map p200; ☎ 031 350 07 77; www.ambitalia.ch; Elfenstrasse 14, Bern)

New Zealand (Map p88; ☎ 022 929 03 50; Chemin des Fins 2, Grand-Saconnex, Geneva)

UK Bern (Map p200; ☎ 031 359 77 00; www.britain-in -switzerland.ch; Thunstrasse 50); Geneva (☎ 022 918 24 00; Ave Louis Casai 50); Zürich (☎ 01 383 65 60; Hegi-bachstrasse 47)

USA Bern (☎ 031 357 70 11; http://bern.usembassy.gov; Sulgeneckstrasse 19); Geneva (☎ 022 840 51 60; Rue François Versonnex 7); Zürich (☎ 043 499 29 60; Dufourstrasse 101)

FOOD

This guide includes options for all tastes and budgets, reviewed in ascending price – ie cheapest first – in Eating sections of respective town and city sections. Expect to dine for less than Sfr30 per person in budget restaurants and between Sfr30 and Sfr80 a head in midrange places. The bill in fine-dining restaurants rises to Sfr200 per person or more. See p42 for more.

GAY & LESBIAN TRAVELLERS

Attitudes to homosexuality are progressive. Gay marriage is recognised (although gay couples are not permitted to adopt children or have fertility treatment) and the age of consent for gay sex is the same as for heterosexuals, at 16 years.

All major cities have gay and lesbian bars. **Cruiser magazine** (☎ 044 388 41 54; www.cruiser.ch, in German) has extensive listings of organisations, places and events and a searchable online agenda. Other useful websites include: www .gay.ch (in German), www.pinkcross.ch (in German and French) and www.lesbian.ch (in German). Pride marches are held in Geneva (early July) and Zürich (mid-July).

HOLIDAYS

National holidays:
New Year's Day 1 January
Easter March/April; Good Friday, Easter Sunday and Monday
Ascension Day 40th day after Easter
Whit Sunday & Monday 7th week after Easter
National Day 1 August
Christmas Day 25 December
St Stephen's Day 26 December

Some cantons observe their own special holidays and religious days, eg 2 January, 1 May (Labour Day), Corpus Christi, 15 August (Assumption) and 1 November (All Saints' Day). Ticino and Lucerne are the luckiest cantons, enjoying an extra eight/seven public holidays respectively. The third Sunday in September is a federal fast day, and some cantons (eg Vaud and Neuchâtel) take the following Monday as a holiday.

INSURANCE

Not only is free health treatment in Switzerland very limited; healthcare generally is very expensive, making it vital to have the correct travel insurance.

If you're skiing/snowboarding or trekking in the mountains, check whether your policy covers helicopter rescue and emergency repatriation. Mountain rescue is remortgage-the-house expensive and most normal policies don't cover many outdoor activities; you'll need to pay a premium for winter-sports cover. Further premiums are necessary for adventure sports like bungee jumping, skydiving, rafting and canyoning.

The majority of adventures pass without injury. However, there's always a risk and it's worth backing up your insurance and enquiring about the safety standards of the company you choose.

Worldwide travel insurance is available at www.lonelyplanet.com/bookings/insurance .do. Buy, extend and claim online anytime, even if you're already on the road.

For more on health insurance, see p370.

INTERNET ACCESS

Public wireless access points can be found at major airports, at 30-odd Swiss train stations, in business seats of some 1st-class train carriages, in most hotels (many of which provide the service for free), and at lots of cafés and other public spaces. Most, like those provided by **Swisscom** (☎ 080 055 64 64; www.swisscom-mobile.ch) are paying and cost around Sfr4 per hour on top of provider charges (around Sfr5/20/30 per 30 minutes/four hours/24 hours), payable by credit card or prepaid card sold at Swisscom's 1200 hot spots; locate where they are with its online hot-spot locator.

Internet cafés, listed under Information in the regional chapters, can be found in larger towns and cities, but are practically nonexistent in most small towns and remote areas. And surfing is pricy: prices range from Sfr5 to Sfr15 per hour.

If it is just a short email you need to send, nip into a Swisscom phone box (p357), equipped with an electronic phonebook allowing users to send short emails (240 characters) and SMS text messages (120 characters) worldwide.

For useful national Swiss websites, see p20.

LEGAL MATTERS

Swiss police have wide-ranging powers of detention, allowing them to hold a person without charges or a trial – so stay on the right side of the law! If approached by them, you will be required to show your passport, so carry it at all times.

There are some minor legal variations between the 26 cantons: in Zürich women are not allowed to use or carry pepper spray (*Pfefferspray*) to deter attackers, but in neighbouring Aargau, they are. Similarly, busking (playing music in the streets) is allowed in some places and not in others. If in doubt, ask.

Drugs

Moves to decriminalise cannabis in Switzerland were abandoned in October 2003, but you will still notice a fair bit of dope around. In the cities, police tend not to do much about it, but if they do decide to enforce the law you face a fine of several hundred francs. Possession of over about 30g of cannabis, or any amount of a harder drug, may mean being looked upon as a dealer, and you'll possibly be liable for a larger fine, jail or deportation.

MAPS

Hallwag, Kümmerly + Frey (☎ 031 850 31 31; www .swisstravelcenter.ch; Grubenstrasse 109, CH-3322 Schönbühl) has a vast range of road atlases, city maps and hiking maps, which can be bought online. Swiss Hiking Federation maps and maps produced by the Bundesamt for Topographie (sometimes down to 1:15,000 scale) are also found in most travel bookshops. The *Swiss Travel System* brochure, free from Switzerland Tourism and major train stations, has a clear A3 map of bus and train routes. For more detail, buy the Swiss Federal Railway rail map from any Swiss train station.

In Swiss cities and towns, tourist offices have free maps and brochures.

MONEY

Swiss francs are divided into 100 centimes (*Rappen* in German-speaking Switzerland). There are notes for 10, 20, 50, 100, 200 and 1000 francs, and coins for five, 10, 20 and 50 centimes, as well as for one, two and five francs.

See p17 for costs in Switzerland.

ATMs

Automated teller machines (ATMs) – called Bancomats in banks and Postomats in post offices – are common, and are accessible 24 hours. They can be used with most international bank or credit cards to withdraw Swiss francs, and they have English instructions. Your bank or credit-card company will usually charge a 1% to 2.5% fee, and there may also be a small charge at the ATM end.

Cash

Many businesses throughout Switzerland, including most hotels, some restaurants and souvenir shops, will accept payment in euros. However, any change will be given in Swiss francs, at the rate of exchange calculated on the day.

Credit Cards

The use of credit cards is less widespread than in the UK or USA and not all shops, hotels or restaurants accept them. EuroCard/MasterCard and Visa are the most popular.

Moneychangers

Change money at banks, airports and nearly every train station daily until late into the evening. Whereas banks tend to charge about 5% commission, some money-exchange bureaus don't charge commission at all. Exchange rates are *slightly* better for travellers cheques than for cash, but there's not much difference.

For bank opening hours and exchange rates, see the inside front cover of this guidebook.

Tipping

Tipping is not necessary, given hotels, restaurants, bars and even some taxis are legally required to include a 15% service charge in bills. However, if you've been very happy with a meal or service round up the bill as locals do; hotel and railway porters expect a franc or two per bag. Bargaining is nonexistent.

POST

Post office opening times vary, but they're usually open from at least 8am to noon and 2pm to 5pm Monday to Friday, and from 8.30am to noon on Saturday. Larger post offices stay open over lunch and have an emergency counter *(Dringlichschalter)* outside normal operating hours (eg lunchtime, evening, Saturday afternoon, Sunday evening), but transactions are subject to a Sfr1 to Sfr2 surcharge. Many post offices have an ATM.

Postal Rates

Within Switzerland, deliveries are by A-Post (delivered next working day) or B-Post (taking three working days). Standard letters (up to 100g) and postcards sent A-Post cost Sfr1 and by B-Post, Sfr0.85.

Internationally, priority *(prioritaire)* deliveries to Europe take two to four days, and to elsewhere roughly seven days. Economy *(economique)* service to Europe takes four to eight days and seven to 12 days to other destinations,. Rates for priority/economy letters under 20g to Europe are Sfr1.30/1.20. Equivalent rates to countries outside Europe are Sfr1.80/1.40.

Parcel post *(Paketpost)* are cheaper for heavier items than for regular letter post *(Briefpost)*. An 'Urgent' service is also available for same-day or next-day international deliveries; for prices and other details contact **Swiss Post** (☎ 084 845 45 45; www.post.ch).

SHOPPING

The souvenir cowbells, cuckoo clocks, chocolate bars and Matterhorn snow globes are unavoidable. A cut above the rest is **Schweizer Heimatwerk** (www.heimatwerk.ch), an upmarket and exclusive chain selling strictly Swiss-made, beautifully crafted wooden toys, games for children and adults, ceramics, textiles, jewellery and so on. Find boutiques at Zürich

and Geneva airports, and in Zürich and Basel town centres.

The land of brands, Switzerland oozes shopping opportunities:

Bags & satchels Switzerland is home to Freitag (www .freitag.ch), the manufacturer of trendy, courier-style satchels made from recycled materials.

Colouring pencils The world's first water-soluble brand of pencil was Switzerland's Caran d'Ache (www .carandache.ch).

Footwear Bally (www.bally.ch) is known abroad, but the stay-at-home national chain Navyboot (www.navyboot.ch) also does great high-stepping boots and shoes.

Swiss army knives The leading and original brand is Victorinox (www.victorinox.ch), although Wenger (www .wenger-knife.ch) also does a decent cut. Knives can cost anything from Sfr7.50 to Sfr200 or more, depending on functionality.

Watches A TAG Heuer, Rolex, Cartier or Patek Philippe might break the bank, but a Swatch (www.swatch.ch) won't.

Water bottles Sigg (www.sigg.ch) is a world leader in its field; one of its brightly coloured, aluminium-coated flasks is even immortalised in New York's Museum of Modern Art.

Taxes & Refunds

VAT (MWST in German, TVA in French) is levied on goods and services at a rate of 7.6%, except on hotel bills, when it's only 3.6%. Nonresidents can claim the tax back on purchases over Sfr400. (This doesn't apply to services or hotel/restaurant bills.) Before making a purchase, ensure that the shop has the required paperwork for you to make a claim. Refunds are given at main border crossings and at Geneva and Zürich airports, or claim later by post.

SOLO TRAVELLERS

Solo travellers should experience no particular problems and will be safe. You'll meet people staying in hostels, of course; however, the Swiss are also pretty chatty and friendly, and will often strike up impromptu conversations.

TRAVELLERS WITH DISABILITIES

Despite all its mountainous regions, Switzerland ranks among the world's most easily navigable countries for travellers with physical disabilities. Most train stations have a mobile lift for boarding trains, and many hotels have disabled access (although budget pensions tend not to have lifts).

Switzerland Tourism (www.myswitzerland.com) and tourist offices can offer travel tips for people

> **WARNING: DIAL ALL NUMBERS**
>
> Area codes do not exist in Switzerland. Although the numbers for a particular city or town share the same three-digit prefix (for example Bern 031, Geneva 022), numbers always must be dialled in full, even when calling from next door – literally.

with physical disabilities, as can **Mobility International Schweiz** (☎ 062 206 88 35; www.mis-ch.ch; Froburgstrasse 4, CH-4600 Olten).

TELEPHONE

National telephone provider **Swisscom** (☎ 080 080 08 00, from abroad +41 848 800 811; http://fr.swisscom.ch) is the proud operator of the world's densest network of public phone booths – 8500 countrywide! The minimum charge for a call is 50c and phones take coins (Swiss francs or euros) and 'taxcards' (phonecards), sold in values of Sfr5, Sfr10 and Sfr20 at post offices, newsagencies and so on. Many booths also accept major credit cards.

To find a phone number in Switzerland check the phone book – searchable online at http://tel.local.ch/en; dial ☎ 1812 (connection charge 80c plus 10c a minute) to speak to an automated machine; or the pricier ☎ 1811 (connection charge Sfr1.50, Sfr0.70 for the first minute and Sfr0.22 per minute thereafter) to speak to a real person; the latter can also find international telephone numbers for you.

Phone Codes

The country code for Switzerland is ☎ 41. When calling Switzerland from abroad drop the initial zero from the number, hence to call Bern dial ☎ 41 31 (preceded by the overseas access code of the country you're dialling from).

The international access code from Switzerland is ☎ 00. To call Britain (country code ☎ 44), start by dialling ☎ 00 44

Telephone numbers with the code 0800 are toll-free; those with 0848 are charged at the local rate. Numbers beginning with 156 or 157 are always charged at the premium rate.

Mobile phone numbers start with the code 079.

Tariffs & International Phonecards

There are two national tariffs to fixed line phones: Sfr0.08 per minute for daytime calls

Monday to Friday, anywhere in Switzerland, and Sfr0.04 per minute after 5pm, before 8am and on weekends. To call Swisscom mobiles or other mobiles, equivalent rates are Sfr0.37/0.27 and Sfr0.55/0.45 respectively.

The normal/cheap tariff for international dialling to fixed-line phones is Sfr0.12/0.10 per minute for a range of countries including Australia, Britain, Canada, New Zealand and the USA, and Sfr0.25/0.20 to countries including Ireland, Japan and the Netherlands. Naturally many hotels add a hefty premium to these rates.

Save money on the normal international tariff by buying a prepaid Swisscom card worth Sfr10, Sfr20, Sfr50 and Sfr100. Or look for prepaid cards from rival operators such as **Mobile Zone** (www.mobilezone.ch, in German, French & Italian).

Mobile Phones

Most phones on European GSM networks work in Switzerland perfectly, though you should check with your provider about costs. Alternatively, prepay local SIM cards (from Sfr30 to Sfr100) are available from the three network operators: **Orange** (www.orange.ch), **Sunrise** (www.sunrise.ch) and **Swisscom Mobile** (www.swisscom-mobile.ch). Buy these via the nationwide **Mobile Zone** (www.mobilezone.ch, in German, French & Italian) chain of shops; check the website for the nearest branch. All prepay cards must be officially registered, so take your passport when you go to buy.

TIME

Swiss time is GMT/UTC plus one hour. If it's noon in Bern it's 11am in London, 6am in New York and Toronto, 3am in San Francisco, 9pm in Sydney and 11pm in Auckland. Daylight-saving time comes into effect at midnight on the last Saturday in March, when the clocks are moved forward one hour; they go back again on the last Saturday in October. The Swiss use the 24-hour clock when writing times.

Note that in German *halb* is used to indicate the half-hour before the hour, hence *halb acht* (half eight) means 7.30, not 8.30.

TOILETS

Public toilets are clean. Urinals are often free, and many cubicles are too, but some of the latter may have a charge of between Sfr0.20 and Sfr0.50. The spotless Mr Clean range of facilities in most train stations is more expensive – about Sfr2 to pee.

DIRECTORY

TOURIST INFORMATION

Make the Swiss tourist board **Switzerland Tourism** (www.myswitzerland.com) your first port of call.

Local Tourist Offices

Next step, for detailed resort information, contact the local tourist office, listed under Tourist Information in the town and city sections of this guide. Information and maps are free and somebody invariably speaks English; and many book hotel rooms, tours and excursions for you. In German-speaking Switzerland tourist offices are called *Verkehrsbüro*, or *Kurverein* in some resorts. In French they are called *office du tourisme* and in Italian, *ufficio turistico*.

Tourist Offices Abroad

Swiss tourist offices abroad include the following:

France (☎ 00800 100 200 30; info@myswitzerland.com; 11bis Rue Scribe, F-75009 Paris) Only provides information by phone, email or post.

UK (☎ 020 7420 4900, 00800 100 200 30; info.uk@switzerland.com; 30 Bedford St, London WC2E 9ED)

USA (☎ 1877 794 8037; info.usa@switzerland.com; Swiss Center, 608 Fifth Ave, New York, NY 10020)

VISAS

For up-to-date details on visa requirements, go to the **Swiss Federal Office for Migration** (www.eda.admin.ch) and click 'Services'.

Visas are not required if you hold a passport from the UK, Ireland, the USA, Canada, Australia, New Zealand or South Africa, whether visiting as a tourist or on business. Citizens of the EU, Norwegians and Icelanders may also enter Switzerland without a visa. A maximum three-month stay applies, although passports are rarely stamped.

Other people wishing to come to Switzerland have to apply for a **Schengen Visa**, named after the agreements that abolished passport controls between 15 European countries: Austria, Belgium, Denmark, Finland, France, Germany, Greece, Iceland, Italy, Luxembourg, the Netherlands, Norway, Portugal, Spain and Sweden. It allows unlimited travel throughout the entire zone for a 90-day period. Application should be made to the consulate of the country you are entering first, or that will be your main destination. Among other things, you will need travel and repatriation insurance and be able to show that you have sufficient funds to support yourself.

In Switzerland, carry your passport at all times and guard it carefully. Swiss citizens are required always to carry personal identification, so you will also need to be able to identify yourself at any time.

WOMEN TRAVELLERS

Minor sexual harassment (catcalls and the like) is much less common than in some neighbouring countries, such as Italy and France, but, in our experience at least, it's a teensy bit more common than in others, like Germany and Austria. Common sense is the best guide to dealing with potentially dangerous situations such as hitching or walking alone at night.

WORK

Work Permits

Citizens of the EU, plus Norwegians and Icelanders, may work in Switzerland for up to 90 days a year without a permit. However, these workers still have to register with the Swiss cantonal authorities before arrival.

Other foreigners and EU citizens on longer assignments will need a permit. For details visit online the **Swiss Federal Office for Migration** (www.eda.admin.ch). If you get caught working illegally you can be fined and deported.

These rules can change at any time, so do some research beforehand.

Types of Work

Language skills are particularly crucial for work in service industries. Generally, the ski resorts are the most likely places to find a position. *Working in Ski Resorts – Europe* (paperback) by Victoria Pybus provides detailed information. Within Switzerland, check through ads for hotel and restaurant positions in the weekly newspaper *hotel + tourismus revue* (Sfr4.30), mostly in German. A useful web resource for service-industry jobs is www.gastronet.ch.

In October, work is available in vineyards in Vaud and Valais. Conditions are usually better than in other countries.

WWOOF (Worldwide Opportunities on Organic Farms; http://zapfig.com/wwoof) finds people volunteer work on small organic farms throughout Switzerland. Those aged 14 to 25yr keen to lend a farm hand can also contact **Landdienst** (www.landdienst.ch, in French & German).

Transport

CONTENTS

GETTING THERE & AWAY

When visiting Switzerland from outside Europe, check if it's cheaper to fly to a European 'gateway' city, such as London or Frankfurt, and travel on from there. Flights, tours and rail tickets can be booked online at www.lonelyplanet.com/travel_services.

ENTERING THE COUNTRY

Formalities are minimal when entering Switzerland by air, rail or road. Since December 2008, when Switzerland implemented the Schengen Agreements, those arriving from the EU do not need to show a passport.

Arriving from a non-EU country, you have to show your passport or EU identity card, and visa if you need one (see opposite), plus clear customs.

Passport

Ensure your passport is valid until well after you plan to end your trip – six months is a safe minimum. Swiss citizens are required to always carry personal ID, so carry your passport at all times and guard it carefully.

AIR
Airports

The main airports are **Zürich Airport** (☎ 043 816 22 11; flight information by SMS send message ZRH plus flight number to ☎ 9292; www.zurich-airport.com), **Geneva International Airport** (☎ 0900 57 15 00; www.gva.ch), and increasingly France-based **EuroAirport** (☎ +33 3 89 90 31 11; www.euroairport.com), serving Basel (as well as Mulhouse in France and Freiburg, Germany).

Bern-Belp (☎ 031 960 21 11; www.flughafenbern.ch) and **Lugano Airport** (☎ 091 610 11 11; www.lugano -airport.ch) are secondary airports, but growing.

Friedrichshafen (www.fly-away.de) in Germany and Milano's **Linate and Malpensa airports** (www .sea-aeroportimilano.it) in Italy are other handy airports close to the Swiss border.

Airlines

More than 100 scheduled airlines fly to/from Switzerland, including:

Air France (☎ 044 439 18 18; www.airfrance.com; airline code AF; hub Paris)

Alitalia (☎ 044 828 45 40; www.alitalia.com; airline code AZ; hub Rome)

American Airlines (☎ 044 654 52 56; www.aa.com; airline code AA; hub Dallas)

Austrian Airlines (☎ 044 286 80 80; www.austrianair lines.com; airline code OS; hub Vienna)

British Airways (☎ 084 884 58 45; www.ba.com; airline code BA; hub London)

Continental Airlines (☎ 044 800 91 12; www .continental.com; airline code CO; hub Houston)

Lufthansa (☎ 0900 900 922; www.lufthansa.com; airline code LH; hub Frankfurt)

Qantas Airways (☎ 043 888 78 78; www.qantas.com; airline code QF; hub Sydney)

Swiss International Air Lines (☎ 084 885 20 00; www.swiss.com) Switzerland's national carrier, commonly known as Swiss Air.

THINGS CHANGE...

The information in this chapter is particularly vulnerable to change. Check directly with the airline or a travel agent to make sure you understand how a fare (and ticket you may buy) works and be aware of the security requirements for international travel. Shop carefully. The details given in this chapter should be regarded as pointers and are not a substitute for your own careful, up-to-date research.

United Airlines (☎ 044 212 47 17; www.ual.com; airline code UAL; hub Denver)

Budget Airlines

This market is constantly changing; watch for new entrants and new/defunct routes.

Air Berlin (www.airberlin.com) Links EuroAirport (Basel) and Zürich with dozens of destinations in Germany, Italy, Spain and Portugal.

Air Transat (www.airtransat.com) Flights from Canada to/from EuroAirport (Basel).

Atlas Blue (www.atlas-blue.com) Moroccan budget airline flying Geneva–Marrekech.

Baboo (www.flybaboo.com) Swiss carrier linking Geneva with dozens of destinations in Spain, France, Italy and further east.

Bmibaby (www.bmibaby.com) Flights to Geneva from Birmingham, Cardiff, East Midlands and Manchester, and from Zürich to/from Edinburgh.

easyJet (www.easyjet.com) UK budget carrier flying into Zürich, Geneva and EuroAirport (Basel) from dozens of European destinations.

Flybe (www.flybe.com) Links Geneva with a dozen cities in the UK, and Bern-Belp with Southampton.

Flyglobespan (www.flyglobespan.com) Scottish budget carrier serving Geneva–Edinburgh route.

Germanwings (www.germanwings.com) Cologne-based German budget carrier flying to/from Zürich from Cologne-Bonn.

Helvetic (www.helvetic.com) Swiss budget carrier hubbed in Zürich and flying to/from Italy, Portugal, Spain, the Czech Republic and Hungary.

Jet2.com (www.jet2.com) Links Geneva with northern cities in the UK.

Ryanair (www.ryanair.com) Flies from EuroAirport (Basel) to Dublin, London, Alicante, Barcelona, Stockholm and Valencia.

Transavia.com (www.transavia.com) Budget subsidiary of the Air France–KLM Group linking Geneva and Rotterdam.

Tickets

Checking internet sites and scouring major newspapers' travel sections can result in significant savings on your air ticket. Start early: some of the cheapest tickets have to be bought well in advance.

Africa

South Africa is the best place on the continent to buy tickets to Switzerland. **Swiss International Air Lines** (☎ 086 004 05 06; www.swiss.com; 2nd fl, Grosvenor Gate, Hyde Park Lane, Hyde Park POB 299, Parklands 2121, Johannesburg) has direct flights daily from Johannesburg to Zürich.

Asia

With tourism from India the fastest-growing sector of the Swiss tourism market, **Swiss International Air Lines** (Delhi ☎ toll-free 1-800 209 7240, 022-6713 7240; 5th fl, World Trade Tower, Barakhamba Lane; Mumbai ☎ 022-6713 7240; Vashani Chambers, 1st fl, 9 New Marine Lines) has plenty of offices in the country and flies directly to Zürich from Mumbai.

Direct flights also go to Zürich from Bangkok, Hong Kong, Singapore, Shanghai and Tokyo.

Australia

Sydney-based **Swiss Travel Centre** (☎ 02 8270 4866; www.swisstravel.com.au; Level 3, 332 Kent St) has specially negotiated airfares to Switzerland.

Swiss International Air Lines (☎ 1300-724 666; Walshes World Agencies, Level 2, Macquarie St, Sydney 2000) has linked services with Air New Zealand, British Airways, Qantas and Singapore Airlines.

Canada

Swiss International Air Lines (☎ 1-877 359 7947; www.swiss.com) has direct daily flights between Montreal and Zürich, and code-share services via New York.

Budget airline Air Transat (www.airtransat.com) operates cheap flights to EuroAirport (Basel) from Montreal.

Continental Europe

Advertisements for travel agencies appear in the travel pages of the weekend broadsheet newspapers, *Time Out*, the *Evening Standard* and the

---

FLY-RAIL BAGGAGE SERVICE

Travellers bound for Geneva and Zürich airports can send their luggage directly on to any one of 50-odd Swiss train stations, without having to wait for their bags at the airport. Upon departure, similarly, they can check their luggage in any of these train stations up to 24 hours before their flight and collect it upon arrival at their destination airport. The charge is Sfr20 per item of luggage; 32kg is the maximum weight per item and bulky stuff like bicycles and surfboards are no go. For details, surf www.sbb.ch or www.myswitzerland.com. Similar back-saving luggage forwarding is likewise possible within Switzerland (see p369).

CLIMATE CHANGE & TRAVEL

Climate change is a serious threat to the ecosystems that humans rely upon, and air travel is the fastest-growing contributor to the problem. Lonely Planet regards travel, overall, as a global benefit, but believes we all have a responsibility to limit our personal impact on global warming.

Flying & climate change

Pretty much every form of motorized travel generates CO_2 (the main cause of human-induced climate change) but planes are far and away the worst offenders, not just because of the sheer distances they allow us to travel, but because they release greenhouse gases high into the atmosphere. The statistics are frightening: two people taking a return flight between Europe and the US will contribute as much to climate change as an average household's gas and electricity consumption over a whole year.

Carbon offset schemes

Climatecare.org and other websites use 'carbon calculators' that allow travellers to offset the level of greenhouse gases they are responsible for with financial contributions to sustainable travel schemes that reduce global warming – including projects in India, Honduras, Kazakhstan and Uganda.

Lonely Planet, together with Rough Guides and other concerned partners in the travel industry, support the carbon offset scheme run by climatecare.org. Lonely Planet offsets all of its staff and author travel.

For more information see www.lonelyplanet.com.

---

free online magazine **TNT** (www.tntmagazine.com), but most of the best deals are direct from budget airlines. For a list of these airlines, their websites and where they fly see opposite.

Regional Ticino-based Swiss carrier **Darwin Airline** (☎ 091 612 45 00; www.darwin-airline.com) flies year-round from Geneva and Lugano to Rome; and seasonally to/from Olbia and Cagliari (Sardinia).

Austrian airline **Robin Hood** (www.robinhood.aero) jets predominantly business travellers into Zürich from Stuttgart (Germany) and Graz (Austria).

UK

The two main scheduled carriers are **British Airways** (☎ 0845-773 3377; www.ba.com) and **Swiss International Air Lines** (☎ 0845-601 0956; www.swiss.com), with services from Heathrow and London City airports.

Several low-cost carriers travel between the UK and Switzerland; see opposite. Budget flights are particularly rampant from the UK between mid-December and April, during the winter ski season.

Useful websites:
www.ebookers.com
www.flightcentre.co.uk
www.trailfinders.com
www.usit.ie

USA

Swiss International Air Lines (☎ 1 877 359 7947; www.swiss.com) code-shares with **American Airlines** (www.aa.com) on several nonstop daily flights to Zürich from New York, Boston, Chicago, Los Angeles, Miami and Washington, as well as direct flights to/from Geneva.

San Francisco is *the* ticket consolidator capital of America, although some good deals can be found in Los Angeles, New York and other big cities. Useful agencies:
www.cheaptickets.com
www.expedia.com
www.itn.net
www.lowestfare.com
www.orbitz.com
www.statravel.com
www.travelocity.com

Other rock-bottom options for discounted trans-Atlantic air travel include stand-by and courier flights:
www.airhitch.org
www.couriertravel.org
www.courier.org

LAND
Bus

Eurolines (www.eurolines.com), via local operator **Alsa+Eggman** (☎ 0900 573 747, Geneva 022 716 91 10,

Zürich 043 444 65 20; www.alsa-eggmann.ch), operates services on some 35 routes to/from Austria, Croatia, Hungary, Germany, Montenegro, Poland, Portugal, Romania, Serbia, Slovakia and Spain.

See p368 for further bus services.

Car & Motorcycle

There are fast, well-maintained freeways to Switzerland through all surrounding countries. German freeways (*Autobahnen*) have no tolls, whereas the Austrian, Czech, French (*autoroutes*) and Italian (*autostrade*) and Slovak freeways do.

The Alps present a natural barrier to entering Switzerland, so main roads generally head through tunnels (see the boxed text Road Tolls, p365 for information about the costs involved). Smaller roads are scenically more interesting, but special care is needed when negotiating mountain passes. Some, like the N5 route from Champagnole in the French Jura to Geneva, aren't recommended if you have no previous experience driving in the mountains. See p364 for more on getting around using this mode of transport.

PAPERWORK & PREPARATIONS

An EU driving licence is acceptable throughout Europe for up to a year. Third-party motor insurance is a minimum requirement: get proof of this in the form of a Green Card, issued by your insurers. Also ask for a 'European Accident Statement' form. Taking out a European breakdown assistance policy is a good investment.

A warning triangle, to be displayed in the event of a breakdown, is compulsory almost everywhere in Europe, including Switzerland. Recommended accessories include a first-aid kit (compulsory in Austria, Slovenia, Croatia and Greece), a spare bulb kit and a fire extinguisher. In the UK, contact the **RAC** (www.rac.co.uk) or the **AA** (www.theaa.com) for travel information.

Train

Within Europe taking the train might be more expensive and a tad more time-consuming than flying, but sheer joy can be found in arriving in eco-friendly Switzerland by such a relatively green mode of transport. Contact www.raileurope.co.uk, www.raileurope.com or your local European rail operator.

From the UK, the quickest rail route is aboard the **Eurostar** (☎ 08705-186 186 in UK, 0892 35 35 39 in France; www.eurostar.com) from London (St Pancras International) to Paris–Gare du Nord (hourly), then onwards by super-speedy, dead-comfy French TGV from Paris-Est to Geneva (nine hours, UK£150 to UK£200) and beyond; passengers aged under 26 and over 60 get slight discounts. Typical adult one-way TGV fares from Paris include Lausanne (3½ to four hours, €92 to €120), Bern (4½ hours, €106 to €132), Basel (3¾ hours, €91), Zermatt via Lausanne and Visp (7¼ hours, €153 to €170).

Eurostar offers a bewildering array of fares. A standard 2nd-class one-way/return ticket from London to Paris costs a whopping UK£154.50/309 (€232.50/435), but super-discount returns go for as little as UK£59. The best deal is a non-exchangeable, non-refundable return ticket, booked months in advance (the cheapest fares sell out early) and which include a Saturday night.

Zürich, 4¼ hours (€105) from Paris by TGV, is Switzerland's busiest international terminus. Four daily trains connect with Munich (4¼ hours, Sfr104). Two daytime trains and one night train leave for Vienna (8¾ to 9½ hours, Sfr146), from where there are extensive onward connections to/from cities in Eastern Europe.

Most connections from Germany pass through Zürich or Basel. Nearly all connections from Italy pass through Milan before branching off to Zürich, Lucerne, Bern or Lausanne.

SEA & RIVER

Switzerland can be reached by steamer from several lakes, although it's a slightly more unusual option. From Germany, arrive via Lake Constance (p284); from Italy via Lago Maggiore (p338); and from France along Lake Geneva (p111).

Or cruise down the River Rhine to Basel (p273).

GETTING AROUND

Switzerland's fully integrated public transport system is among the world's most efficient. Indeed, the Swiss think nothing of coordinating schedules with just a few minutes' leeway between arrivals and departures – missing a connection through a late arrival is rare.

But travel within Switzerland is expensive and visitors planning to use public transport on inter-city routes should consider investing in a Swiss travel pass; see p367.

Timetables often refer to *Werktags* (work days), which means Monday to Saturday, unless there is the qualification *'ausser Samstag'* (except Saturday).

AIR

Internal flights are of little interest to most visitors, owing to Switzerland's compact size and excellent rail transport. However, **Swiss International Air Lines** (www.swiss.com) serves the major hubs of EuroAirport (Basel), Geneva and Zürich airports, with return fares fluctuating wildly – anything from Sfr70 to Sfr300; and Swiss no-frills carrier **Fly Baboo** (www.flybaboo .com) flies Geneva–Lugano.

Some mountain resorts have helicopter operators offering flights around the Alps. There are also scenic Zeppelin airship rides over Lake Constance (p285).

BICYCLE

For information on the experience of biking around Switzerland and national cycle routes, see p232.

Hire

Rent a Bike (☎ 041 925 11 70; www.rent-a-bike.ch, in German & French) hires bikes at 100-odd train stations. Prices start at Sfr25/33 per half-/full day or Sfr40 per day if you rent your wheels at one train station and drop them off at another; Swiss travel pass-holders and those aged under 16 years pay half-price. Counters are open daily, usually from the crack of dawn until some time in the evening. In summer particularly, there's huge demand for these bikes, plus some smaller stations only have a handful of wheels to rent; reserve your bike at least a day or two ahead.

Revel in free bike rental in Bern (p207), Geneva (p100), Zug (p260) and Zürich (p228).

Transport

One bike per passenger can be taken on slower trains (for the price of a regular adult 2nd-class ticket), and sometimes even on InterCity (IC) or EuroCity (EC) trains, when there is enough room in the luggage carriage (one-/six-day bike ticket Sfr15/60, one-day ticket with Swiss Travel Pass Sfr10). Between 31 March and 31 October, you must book (SFr5) to take your bike on ICN (inter-city tilting) trains.

Trains that don't permit accompanied bikes are marked with a crossed-out pictogram in the timetable. Sending a standard bike unaccompanied costs Sfr16.

BOAT

All the larger lakes are serviced by steamers operated by Swiss Federal Railways (SBB/CFF/ FFS), or allied private companies for which national travel passes are valid. Lakes covered include Geneva, Constance, Lucerne, Lugano, Neuchâtel, Biel, Murten, Thun, Brienz and Zug, but not Lago Maggiore. Rail passes are not valid for cruises offered by smaller boat companies.

BUS

Yellow 'postal buses' (Postbus in German, Car Postal in French, Auto Postale in Italian; www .postbus.ch) supplement the rail network, following postal routes and linking towns to the more inaccessible mountain regions. They are extremely regular, and departures tie in with train arrivals. Bus stations are invariably next to train stations. Travel is one class only.

For a flat fee of Sfr12, your luggage can be sent ahead to a post office and picked up later – especially useful for hikers relying on the postal bus network.

For those schlepping home late from a club or rushing to make a red-eye flight, there are several **Nightbuses** (☎ 0900 100 201; http://mct.sbb .ch/mct/nightbird, in German & French) on weekends.

Bus Passes

Swiss national travel passes (see p367) are valid on postal buses, although a few tourist-oriented Alpine routes levy a surcharge of Sfr15 to Sfr25. Details are given in the relevant chapters.

Costs

Postal bus fares are comparable to train fares (see p368).

Reservations

Tickets are usually purchased from the driver, though on some scenic routes over the Alps (eg the Lugano–St Moritz run) advance reservations are necessary. See www.postbus.ch for details.

TRANSPORT

TRANSPORT

ROAD DISTANCES (KM)

	Basel	Bellinzona	Bern	Biel-Bienne	Brig	Chur	Fribourg	Geneva	Interlaken	Lausanne	Lucerne	Lugano	Neuchâtel	St Gallen	St Moritz	Schaffhausen	Sion
Bellinzona	241																
Bern	97	253															
Biel-Bienne	93	247	41														
Brig	190	161	91	129													
Chur	228	115	242	237	174												
Fribourg	132	285	34	71	179	274											
Geneva	267	420	171	209	214	409	138										
Interlaken	153	195	57	92	73	209	92	230									
Lausanne	203	359	107	146	151	346	72	62	167								
Lucerne	103	140	115	107	149	140	147	280	71	218							
Lugano	267	28	279	273	187	141	331	446	221	383	166						
Neuchâtel	141	294	46	31	141	283	43	123	104	73	156	320					
St Gallen	191	217	204	197	288	102	236	371	225	307	138	243	244				
St Moritz	313	150	327	321	241	85	359	494	294	430	225	176	368	178			
Schaffhausen	161	246	173	167	259	182	205	340	228	276	108	272	214	80	266		
Sion	252	214	160	195	53	399	128	161	86	98	271	240	166	356	294	329	
Zürich	113	195	125	119	208	118	157	292	177	229	57	221	166	81	203	51	281

CAR & MOTORCYCLE

If you're deciding whether to travel by car or motorcycle, consider the effect your exhaust emissions will have on the Alpine environment. You might also find it frustrating to have to concentrate on the road while magnificent scenery unfolds all around.

Public transport is generally excellent in city centres, where parking can make cars an inconvenience.

Automobile Associations

The **Swiss Touring Club** (TCS; ☎ 022 417 22 20; www .tcs.ch, in German, French & Italian; Chemin de Blandonnet, Case Postale 820, CH-1214 Geneva) and **Swiss Automobile Club** (Automobil-Club der Schweiz, ACS; ☎ 031 328 31 11; www.acs.ch, in German, French & Italian; Wasserwerkgasse 39, CH-3000, Bern 13) provide details on driving in Switzerland.

The larger TCS operates the national **24-hour emergency breakdown service** (☎ 140), free for members of the Swiss motoring clubs and their affiliates.

Bring Your Own Vehicle

For information on bringing your own transport into Switzerland, see p362.

Driving Licence

European Union (EU) and US licences are accepted in Switzerland for up to one year. Otherwise, you should obtain an International Driving Permit (IDP).

Fuel

Unleaded (*bleifrei, sans plomb, senza piombo*) petrol is standard, found at green pumps, but diesel is also widely available (black pumps). At the time of writing, unleaded fuel cost Sfr1.78 per litre, diesel Sfr1.99. For the latest prices, go to www.theaa.com and search for 'fuel'.

Hire

Car rental is expensive, especially if hiring from a multinational firm. It's cheaper to book ahead from your own country, but you're still looking at Sfr350 to Sfr500 per week. For travellers flying into Geneva airport, it is cheaper to rent a car on the French rather than Swiss side. Minimum rental age is usually 25, but falls to 20 with some local firms and you always need a credit card. Rental cars are automatically equipped with winter tyres…in winter.

TRANSPORT

ROAD TOLLS

There's an annual one-off charge of Sfr40 to use Swiss freeways and semi-freeways, identified by green signs. The charge is payable at the border (in cash, including euros), at petrol stations, from Swiss tourist offices abroad (p358) and online for UK£21 plus UK£5 booking fee at www .swisstravelsystem.com. The sticker (*vignette* in French and German, *contrassegno* in Italian) you receive upon paying the tax can also be bought at post offices and petrol stations. It must be displayed on the windscreen and is valid for a calendar year, with one month's leeway. If you're caught without it, you'll be fined Sfr100. A separate *vignette* is required for trailers and caravans. Motorcyclists are also charged the Sfr40. For more details, see www.vignette.ch.

Generally, it's easy enough to avoid freeways and hence not bother with the *vignette*. However, note a *vignette* is also necessary to use either the Gotthard Tunnel (between Ticino and Uri) or the San Bernardino Tunnel (between Ticino and Graubünden).

On the Swiss-Italian border you'll need to pay an additional toll if using the Grand St Bernard Tunnel between Aosta, Italy, and Valais (car and passengers one-way/return Sfr30.50/48.50, motorcycles Sfr17/24).

Companies include:

Avis (☎ 084 881 18 18; www.avis.ch)
Europcar (☎ 084 880 80 99; www.europcar.ch)
Hertz (☎ 084 881 10 10; www.hertz.ch)
Holiday Autos Australia (☎ 1300 554 507, www .holidayautos.co.au); Switzerland (☎ 056 675 75 85; www .holidayautos.ch); UK (☎ 0871-472 5229; www.holiday autos.co.uk); USA (☎ 888 392 9288; www.holidayautos.com)
Sixt (☎ 084 888 44 44; www.sixt.ch)
Thrifty (Australia ☎ 1300 367 227; www.thrifty.com.au; New Zealand ☎ 0800 737 070; www.thrifty.co.nz; UK ☎ 01494 751 500; www.thrifty.co.uk).

Insurance
See p362.

Road Conditions
Predictably Swiss roads are well built, well signposted and well maintained, but you should stay in low gear on steep stretches and carry snow chains in winter.

Most major Alpine passes are negotiable year-round, depending on the current weather. However, you will often have to use a tunnel instead at the Great St Bernard, St Gotthard and San Bernardino passes. Passes that are open only June to October are Albula, Furka, Grimsel, Klausen, Oberalp, Susten and Umbrail. Other passes are Lukmanier (open May to November), Nufenen (June to September), and Splügen (May to October).

Phone ☎ 163 for up-to-the-hour traffic conditions (recorded information in French, German, Italian and English).

Take your car on trains through these tunnels and passes, open year-round:

Lötschberg Tunnel (☎ 0900 553 333; www.bls.ch) From Kandersteg to Goppenstein (car and passengers Monday to Thursday/Friday to Sunday Sfr20/25, journey time 15 minutes) or Iselle in Italy (car and passengers Sfr90; book in advance).
Furka Pass (☎ 027 927 77 71; www.mgbahn.ch) From Oberwald to Realp.
Vereina Tunnel (☎ 081 288 37 37; www.rhb.ch) Alternative to the Flüela Pass, closed in winter; from Klosters-Selfranga to Sagliains-Engadine (car and passengers low/mid-/high season Sfr27/35/40)

Road Rules
A handbook on Swiss traffic regulations (in English) is available from cantonal registration offices and at some customs posts. The minimum driving age for cars and motorcycles is 18, and for mopeds it's 14.

The Swiss drive on the right-hand side of the road. If in doubt, always give priority to traffic approaching from the right. On mountain roads, the ascending vehicle has priority, unless a postal bus is involved, as it always has right of way. Postal bus drivers let rip a multitone bugle when approaching blind corners. In towns, allow trams plenty of respect, and stop behind a halted tram to give way to disembarking passengers.

The speed limit is 50km/h in towns (though certain stretches may be as low as 30km/h), 80km/h on main roads outside towns, 100km/h on single-lane freeways and 120km/h on dual-lane freeways. Car occupants must wear a seatbelt at all times where fitted, and vehicles must carry a breakdown-warning triangle, which must be readily accessible (ie not in the boot).

TRANSPORT

ROUND-TRIP TICKETS

If you have a specific itinerary and are certain you won't be changing your route, a *Rundfahrt* (*billet circulaire* in French) ticket is worth investigating as a sometimes cheaper alternative to a Swiss travel pass. Such tickets allow you to journey in a circular loop and, because they are valid for a month, it's possible to break your journey for several days at various cities and towns along the way.

Dipped headlights must be turned on in all tunnels, and are recommended for motorcyclists during the day. Headlights must be used in rain or poor visibility. Both motorcyclists and their passengers must wear crash helmets.

Switzerland is tough on drink-driving. The blood alcohol content (BAC) limit is 0.05%, and if caught exceeding this limit you may face a heavy fine, a driving ban or even imprisonment. If you're involved in a car accident, the police must be called if anyone receives more than superficial injuries.

Proof of ownership of a private vehicle should always be carried. Within Switzerland, you can drive a vehicle registered abroad for up to 12 months, but its plates should be clearly visible.

Road Signs

Almost all road signs use internationally recognised conventions. Signs you may not

have seen before are: a crisscrossed white tyre on a blue circular background, which means snow chains are compulsory; and a yellow bugle on a square blue background, which indicates a mountain postal road where you must obey instructions given by postal bus drivers.

Urban Parking

Street parking in the centre (assuming traffic isn't banned, as it often is) is controlled by parking meters during working hours (8am to 7pm Monday to Saturday). Parking costs Sfr1.50 to Sfr2 per hour, with maximum time limits from 30 minutes to two hours. Central streets outside these metered areas are usually marked as blue zones, allowing a 1½-hour stay during working hours, or as (increasingly rare) red zones, with a 15-hour maximum. In either of the latter two cases, you need to display a parking disc in your window indicating the time you first parked. Discs are available for free from tourist offices, car-rental companies and police stations.

LOCAL TRANSPORT
Public Transport

All local city transport is linked via the same ticketing system, so you can change lines on one ticket. Usually you must buy tickets before boarding, from ticket dispensers at stops. Very occasionally you can also buy from machines on board.

In some Swiss towns, single tickets may give a time limit (eg one hour) for travel within a

MAJOR SWISS RAIL ROUTES

SWISS TRAVEL PASSES

The following national travel passes generally offer betters savings than Eurail or Inter Rail passes (see p369) on extensive travel within Switzerland. Before arriving in Switzerland passes can be purchased in the UK from the **Switzerland Travel Centre** (☎ 0207 420 49 00; www.swisstravelsystem.com; 30 Bedford St, London WC2E 9ED) or online from its hugely informative website. In Switzerland larger train-station offices sell travel passes.

Find comprehensive information on all of them at http://traintickets.myswitzerland.com.

Swiss Pass

The Swiss Pass entitles the holder to unlimited travel on almost every train, boat and bus service in the country, and on trams and buses in 38 towns. Reductions of 50% apply on funiculars, cable cars and private railways such as Pilatus Railways. The following prices are for 2nd-class passes; 1st class is 50% higher. If you are under 26, you are entitled to a Swiss Youth Pass, 25% cheaper in each instance.

- four days (Sfr260)
- eight days (Sfr376)
- 15 days (Sfr455)
- 22 days (Sfr525)
- one month (Sfr578)

Swiss Flexi Pass

This pass allows you to nominate a certain number of days (anywhere from three to eight) during a month in which you can enjoy unlimited travel.

- three days (Sfr249)
- four days (Sfr302)
- five days (Sfr349)
- six days (Sfr397)

Half-Fare Card

Almost every Swiss person owns one of these. As the name suggests, you pay only half-fare on trains with this card, plus you get some discounts on local-network buses, trams and cable cars. The card, valid for one year, costs Sfr150/92 per adult/16-18 years (photo necessary).

Family Card

A free Family Card gets you free travel (on trains, buses and boats – even on some cable cars) for those aged six to 15 years when travelling with at least one of their parents. Children within that age bracket and travelling with an adult, not a relative, get 50% off.

Regional Passes

Network passes valid only within a particular region are available in several parts of the country. Such passes are available from train stations in the region and more details can be found in individual destination chapters.

particular zone, and you can only break the journey within that time. Multistrip tickets may be available at a discount (validate them in the on-board machine at the outset of the journey), or one-day passes are even better value.

Inspectors regularly check for people travelling without tickets. Those found without a ticket pay an on-the-spot fine.

Taxi

Metered taxis can be found outside train stations or can be called; see individual chapters for details.

MOUNTAIN TRANSPORT

The Swiss have many words to describe mountain transport: funicular (*Standseilbahn* in

TRANSPORT

SCENIC JOURNEYS

Swiss trains, buses and boats are more than a means of getting from A to B. Stunning views invariably make the journey in itself the destination. Switzerland boasts the following routes among its classic sightseeing journeys. Bear in mind that you can choose just one leg of the trip, and that scheduled services ply the same routes for standard fares. In addition to these journeys, almost any train in the Jungfrau region (p179) provides beautiful views.

Panorama Trains

The following have panoramic coaches with extended-height windows:

The **Glacier Express** (Brig ☎ 027 927 77 77, Chur 081 288 43 40; www.glacierexpress.ch; 2nd/1st class Sfr133/221, obligatory seat-reservation supplement Sfr9-17, obligatory surcharge mid-Dec–mid-May Sfr51/10 with/without lunch, mid-May–mid-Dec Sfr71/30 with/without lunch; ☻ 7½hr, daily) runs between Zermatt and St Moritz, Chur or Davos. It's a spectacular journey over the Alps, past the lakes of central Switzerland and on to the rolling countryside of Graubünden. The Brig–Zermatt Alpine leg makes for pretty powerful viewing, as does the area between Disentis/Mustér and Brig. See p24.

The **Golden Pass Route** (☎ 0900 245 245, from abroad +41 840 245 245; www.goldenpass.ch; one-way 2nd/1st class Sfr69/114; ☻ 5hr, 4 trips daily) travels between Lucerne and Montreux, from the wonderful landscape of central Switzerland over the Brünig Pass to Gstaad and then down to the waters and vineyards of the Lake Geneva area. The journey is in three legs, and you must change trains twice. The Lucerne–Interlaken leg (2nd/1st class Sfr31/52, two hours) is best around the Brünig Pass, while the Montreux–Zweisimmen section (Sfr30/50; two hours) comes to life from Montreux to Château-d'Œx, especially on the climb/descent from Lake Geneva. The Interlaken–Zweisimmen section (Sfr25/42) takes an hour. Regular trains, without panoramic windows, work the whole route hourly.

German, *funiculaire* in French, *funicolare* in Italian), cable car (*Luftseilbahn, téléphérique, funivia*), gondola (*Gondelbahn, télécabine, telecabinoia*) and chair lift (*Sesselbahn, télésiège, seggiovia*). All are subject to regular safety inspections and are generally plain sailing to use. Always check what time the last cable car goes down the mountain; even in the height of summer this can be as early as 4pm in some resorts.

TRAIN

The Swiss rail network combines state-run and private operations. The **Swiss Federal Railway** (www.rail.ch, www.sbb.ch/en) is abbreviated to SBB in German, CFF in French and FFS in Italian. All major train stations are connected to each other by hourly departures, at least between 6am and midnight.

Most long-distance trains have a dining car and some, a family car for kids to play around in. Smoking is banned on all trains and train stations.

Classes

Most travellers will find spick-and-span 2nd-class compartments perfectly acceptable. However, these carriages can be fairly full sometimes, especially when the army is on the move, and occasionally you'll have to stand.

In 1st class, carriages are even more comfortable, spacious and have less passengers. Power points for laptops let you work aboard and some lucky seats sit in a wi-fi hotspot.

Costs

Ordinary fares are relatively expensive, about Sfr35 per 100km; best buy a rail pass – see (p367). Return fares are only cheaper than two singles for longer trips. Special deals are sometimes available in the low season.

All fares quoted in this guide are for 2nd-class travel unless stated otherwise; 1st-class fares average 50% to 65% higher.

Information

All stations can provide advice in English and free timetable booklets. Timetables are also available online and can be personalised and downloaded onto your mobile. See www.sbb.ch for more information or call the number for all **train information & reservations** (☎ 0900 300 300); calls cost Sfr1.19 per minute.

Train schedules are revised every December; always double-check fares and frequencies quoted here.

The **Bernina Express** (☎ 081 288 63 26; www.rhb.ch; one-way 2nd/1st class Sfr57/95, reservations obligatory winter/summer Sfr7/9; 🕑 2½hr, daily) cuts 145km through Engadine from Chur to Tirano. The train travels through viaducts and switchback tunnels, past glaciers, streams and Alpine flowers and up through the 2253m Bernina Pass without a rack and pinion system. May and October, you can opt to continue onwards from Tirano to Lugano by bus.

Other scenic rail routes include:

Chocolate train (www.mob.ch) Return trip in a Pullman car from Montreux to the chocolate factory at Broc.

Mont Blanc/St Bernard Expresses (www.tmrsa.ch) From Martigny to Chamonix, France, or over St Bernard Pass.

Voralpen Express (www.voralpen-express.ch) Lake Constance to Lake Lucerne, through St Gallen, Rapperswil and Romanshorn.

Rail/Boat

Or you could combine a panorama train with a lake steamer...

The **Wilhem Tell Express** (Lucerne ☎ 041 367 67 67, Locarno ☎ 027 922 81 51; www.lakelucerne.ch; 2nd/1st class Sfr73/111, Swiss Pass free, obligatory reservation Sfr47; 🕑 May-Oct) starts with a wonderful three-hour cruise across Lake Lucerne to Flüelen, from where a train wends its way through ravines and past mountains to Locarno.

Postal Bus

The **Palm Express** (☎ 058 386 31 66; www.palmexpress.ch; ticket Sfr69, obligatory reservation Sfr20) travels between Lugano and St Moritz, skirting the Mediterranean-style Lakes Lugano and Como (in Italy) before rising into the mountains via the Maloja Pass into Engadine.

Another half a dozen scenic Alpine routes can be found at www.postbus.ch.

TRANSPORT

Luggage

Most train stations offer luggage storage at a staffed counter (Sfr10 per item) or in 24-hour lockers (small/medium/large Sfr5/8/10), usually accessible 6am to midnight.

Nearly every station allows ticket-holders to send their luggage ahead (Sfr20 per item up to 25kg) where you can dispatch your bag before 9am and collect it at your destination station after 6pm – useful if you're stopping off en route at other places before your overnight stop.

Reservations & Tickets

Seat reservations (Sfr5) are advisable for longer journeys, particularly in high season.

Some smaller, rural rail routes, marked with a yellow eye pictogram, have a 'self-control' ticketing system. On these routes, buy a ticket before boarding or risk a fine. Ticket inspectors appear quite frequently.

Single train tickets for journeys over 80km are valid for two days. Return tickets over 160km are valid for a month and allow you to break your journey.

Train Passes

European rail passes (www.raileurope.co.uk, www.raileurope.com), including Eurail and Inter Rail passes, are valid on Swiss national railways. However, you cannot use them on postal buses, city transport, cable cars or private train lines (eg the Zermatt route and the Jungfraubahn routes at the heart of the Bernese Oberland). So, while they're practical if you're covering several countries in one journey, they're less useful than Swiss travel passes (p367) for exploring scenic Switzerland.

Health

CONTENTS

Travel health depends on your pre-departure preparations, your daily health care while travelling and how well you handle any medical problem that does develop. In Switzerland, you face no unusual threats to your health.

BEFORE YOU GO

Make sure you're healthy before you start travelling. If you require a particular medication take an adequate supply, as it may not be available locally. Take part of the packaging showing the generic name rather than the brand, which will make getting replacements easier. It's a good idea to have a legible prescription or letter from your doctor to show that you legally use the medication, to avoid any problems.

INSURANCE

Make sure that you have adequate health insurance (see p354). Although there is a public system in Switzerland, it is not really free, as all residents in Switzerland have to pay for health insurance. EU members are covered to an extent, but should take out private travel/health cover. Treatment in a public ward of a public hospital is covered by the European Health Insurance Card (EHIC), the card European citizens use to obtain reciprocal health care in other EU member states. There is a nonrefundable excess charge for every 30-day period in hospital. EU citizens with the EHIC pay half of the full cost of ambulances (road and air). Go to any doctor registered with the Swiss health system. Dental care, except emergency accident treatment, is not covered at all. You will generally have to pay up front and claim a refund from **Gemeinsame Einrichtung KVG** (☎ +41 32 625 48 20; Gibelinstrasse 25, Postfach CH-4503 Solothurn).

RECOMMENDED VACCINATIONS

No immunisations are required to enter Switzerland, but generally it's a good idea to make sure your tetanus, diphtheria and polio vaccinations are up to date before travelling. You may also like to consider immunisation against tick-borne encephalitis if you are going to be in rural areas. Check with your doctor and leave plenty of time for shots – ideally six weeks before travel. The **World Health Organization** (www.who.int) and the US-based **Centers for Disease Control & Prevention** (www.cdc.gov) also have information.

Although there is no risk of yellow fever in Switzerland, if you are arriving from a yellow fever-infected area (ie most of sub-Saharan Africa and parts of South America) you'll need proof of yellow fever vaccination before you will be allowed to enter the country.

INTERNET RESOURCES

EU citizens should see the website of their national health system for travel advice and what the European Health Insurance Card (EHIC) entitles them to in Switzerland. In the case of the UK, check the NHS website (www.dh.gov.uk).

IN TRANSIT

DEEP VEIN THROMBOSIS (DVT)

Blood clots may form in the legs during plane flights, chiefly because of prolonged immobility (the longer the flight, the greater the risk). The chief symptom of DVT is swelling or pain of the foot, ankle or calf, usually but not always on just one side. When a blood clot travels to the lungs, it may cause chest pain and breathing difficulties. Travellers with any of these symptoms should immediately seek medical attention. To prevent the development of DVT on long flights you should walk about the cabin, contract the leg muscles while sitting, drink plenty of fluids and avoid alcohol and tobacco.

JET LAG & MOTION SICKNESS

To avoid jet lag try drinking plenty of non-alcoholic fluids and eating light meals. Upon arrival, get exposure to natural sunlight and readjust your schedule (for meals, sleep etc) as soon as possible.

IN SWITZERLAND

Self-diagnosis and treatment can be risky, so you should always seek medical help. An embassy, consulate or five-star hotel can usually recommend a local doctor or clinic. The quality of health care in Switzerland is generally very high, whether in public or private hospitals. See opposite for more information.

TRAVELLER'S DIARRHOEA

Simple things like a change of water, food or climate can all cause a mild bout of diarrhoea, but a few rushed toilet trips with no other symptoms is not indicative of a major problem.

Dehydration is the main danger with any diarrhoea, particularly in children or the elderly as dehydration can occur quite quickly. Under all circumstances *fluid replacement* (at least equal to the volume being lost) is the most important thing to remember. Weak black tea with a little sugar, soda water, or soft drinks allowed to go flat and diluted 50% with clean water, are all good. Stick to a bland diet as you recover.

Swiss restaurants generally have very high standards of hygiene, and food poisoning is rare – although, naturally, always possible. Some of the country's dairy products have very high levels of fat, however.

ENVIRONMENTAL HAZARDS
Altitude Sickness

This disorder can occur above 3000m, but very few treks or ski runs in the Austrian, French, Italian or Swiss Alps reach heights of 3000m or more – Mont Blanc is one exception – so altitude sickness is unlikely. Headache, vomiting, dizziness, extreme faintness, and difficulty in breathing and sleeping are all signs to heed. Treat mild symptoms with rest and simple painkillers. If mild symptoms persist or get worse, descend to a lower altitude and seek medical advice.

Bites & Stings
SNAKES

Switzerland is home to several types of snakes, a couple of which can deliver a nasty, although not fatal, bite. They are more prevalent in the mountains. To minimise your chances of being bitten always wear boots, socks and long trousers when walking through undergrowth where snakes may be present. Don't put your hands into holes and crevices, and be careful when collecting firewood.

If bitten by a snake that could be venomous, immediately wrap the bitten limb tightly, as you would for a sprained ankle, and then attach a splint to immobilise it. Keep the victim still and seek medical help. Tourniquets and sucking out the poison are now comprehensively discredited.

TICKS

These small creatures can be found throughout Switzerland up to an altitude of 1200m, and typically live in underbrush at the forest edge or beside walking tracks. A tiny proportion carry viral encephalitis, which may become serious if not detected early (see p372).

You should always check all over your body if you have been walking through a potentially tick-infested area, as ticks can cause skin infections and other more serious diseases. If a tick is found attached, press down around the tick's head with tweezers, grab the head and gently pull upwards. Avoid pulling the rear of the body as this may squeeze the tick's gut contents through the attached mouth-parts into the skin, increasing the risk of infection and disease. Smearing chemicals on the tick will not make it let go and is not recommended.

Lyme Disease

This is an infection transmitted by ticks that may be acquired in Europe. The illness usually begins with a spreading rash at the site of the tick bite and is accompanied by fever, headache, extreme fatigue, aching joints and muscles, and mild neck stiffness. If untreated, these symptoms usually resolve over several weeks, but over subsequent weeks or months, disorders of the nervous system, heart and joints may develop. Treatment works best early in the illness. Medical help should be sought.

HEALTH

Tick-Borne Encephalitis

This disease is a cerebral inflammation carried by a virus. Tick-borne encephalitis can occur in most forest and rural areas of Switzerland. If you have been bitten, even having removed the tick, you should keep an eye out for symptoms, including blotches around the bite, which is sometimes pale in the middle. Headache, stiffness and other flu-like symptoms, as well as extreme tiredness, appearing a week or two after the bite, can progress to more serious problems. Medical help must be sought. A vaccination is available and is the best protection.

Hypothermia

The weather in Europe's mountains can be extremely changeable at any time of the year. Skiers and hikers should always be prepared for very cold and wet weather.

Hypothermia will occur when the body loses heat faster than it can produce it and the core temperature of the body falls. It is surprisingly easy to progress from very cold to dangerously cold due to a combination of wind, wet clothing, fatigue and hunger, even if the air temperature is above freezing. It is best to dress in layers; silk, wool and some of the new artificial fibres are all good insulating materials. A hat is important, as a lot of heat is lost through the head. A strong, waterproof outer layer (and a 'space' blanket for emergencies) is essential. Carry basic supplies, including food containing simple sugars to generate heat quickly and fluid to drink.

Symptoms of hypothermia are exhaustion, numb skin (particularly toes and fingers), shivering, slurred speech, irrational or violent behaviour, lethargy, stumbling, dizzy spells, muscle cramps and violent bursts of energy. Irrationality may take the form of sufferers claiming they are warm and trying to take off their clothes.

To treat mild hypothermia, first get the person out of the wind and/or rain, remove their clothing if it's wet and replace it with dry, warm clothing. Give them hot liquids – not alcohol – and high-kilojoule, easily digestible food. Do not rub victims; instead, allow them to slowly warm themselves. This should be enough to treat the early stages of hypothermia. The early recognition and treatment of mild hypothermia is the only way to prevent severe hypothermia, which is a critical condition.

Sunburn

You can get sunburnt surprisingly quickly, even through cloud, and particularly at high altitude. Use a sunscreen, a hat and a barrier cream for your nose and lips. Calamine lotion or a commercial after-sun preparation are good for mild sunburn. Protect your eyes with good-quality sunglasses, particularly if you will be near water, sand or snow.

Water

You rely on tap water in Switzerland, and the water from most of the country's tens of thousands of fountains is also drinkable. Occasionally you will come across a tap or fountain labelled *Kein Trinkwasser* or *eau non potable*, meaning it's *not* drinking quality.

If you will be drinking water from rivers, lakes or streams – even crystal-clear Alpine streams – you should take steps to purify it. The simplest way of purifying water is to boil it thoroughly. Vigorous boiling should be satisfactory; however, at high altitude water boils at a lower temperature, so germs are less likely to be killed. Boil it for longer in these environments. Consider purchasing a water filter for a long trip. Alternatively, iodine is effective in purifying water and is available in tablet form. Follow the directions carefully and remember that too much iodine can be harmful.

Language

CONTENTS

In the corner of Europe where the German, French and Italian language areas meet, Switzerland (Schweiz, Suisse, Svizzera) has three official federal languages: German (the native language of about 64% of the population), French (19%) and Italian (8%). A fourth language (from the Rhaeto-Romanic language family), Romansch, is spoken by less than 1% of the population, mainly in the canton of Graubünden. Derived from Latin, Romansch is a linguistic relic that, along with Friulian and Ladin across the border in Italy, has survived in the isolation of the

> **TALK OF THE TOWN**
>
> Occasionally, it's hard to remember there's a language divide in Switzerland, when the person at the next table flits from German to French and a widespread form of thanks, *merci vielmals*, mixes the two. Undoubtedly, the much-vaunted Röstigraben (Rösti Ditch) still divides French- and German-speaking parts of the country, both in language and culture, but visitors will more often be charmed by the country's linguistic ambidexterity. By the time you leave Switzerland, you might well be in thrall of the way many Swiss Germans say *Salut* as if it were 'Sally' or bid you farewell with *Adieu* rather than *Tschüss*. You might relish the drawn-out, sing-song vowels of the Swiss German greeting *Grüezi wohl*. However, don't worry if you don't even begin to understand anything more complicated in Schwyzertütsch, not even many French or Italian Swiss do.

mountain valleys. Since 1996, Romansch has enjoyed status as a semi-official federal language, together with guarantees for its preservation and promotion.

Being Understood in English

Day-to-day language use is somewhat different to how the list of official languages reads. In order of predominance, the country's spoken languages are German, English, French and Italian. Surprising as it is, English is increasingly the lingua franca in Swiss companies spanning several of the country's language regions. Children in Zürich and seven other German-speaking cantons are, controversially, starting to learn English in school before they're even taught French.

Most Swiss, particularly those working in service industries (tourist-office staff, telephone operators, hotel and office receptionists, restaurant staff and shopkeepers), already speak excellent English. In German-speaking Switzerland, you'll also meet many fluent English speakers in other walks of life, especially in the cities. To a

LANGUAGE

LANGUAGE AREAS

- Romansch
- German
- French
- Italian

progressively lesser extent, the same is true in French-, Italian- and Romansch-speaking Switzerland. You'll rarely get stuck, but that's no excuse not to have a go at the local lingo.

FRENCH

SWISS FRENCH

Neuchâtel is where the form closest to standard French is spoken, yet you won't find much difference from standard French wherever you go. Of course there are some local expressions and regional accents. A female waitress is a *sommelière*, not a *serveuse*, and a postal box is a *case postale*, not a *boîte postale*. Although the regular French numbers are understood, most locals use *septante* for 70, *huitante* for 80, and *nonante* for 90. *La Suisse romande* is a term used to refer to French-speaking Switzerland.

PRONUNCIATION

Most letters in the French alphabet are pronounced more or less the same as their English counterparts; a few that may cause confusion are listed below. The combinations *un* and *on* in the pronunciation guides are nasal sounds – the 'n' is not pronounced; *zh* is pronounced as the 's' in 'measure'.

c	before **e** and **i**, as the 's' in 'sit'; before **a**, **o** and **u** it's pronounced like English 'k'
ç	always the 's' in 'sit'
h	always silent
j	as the 's' in 'leisure'
n, m,	where a syllable ends in a single **n** or **m**, these letters are not pronounced, but the preceding vowel is given a nasal pronunciation
r	from the back of the throat while constricting the muscles to restrict the flow of air
s	often not pronounced in plurals or at the end of words

GENDER

All nouns in French are either masculine or feminine and adjectives reflect the gender of the noun they modify. The feminine form of many nouns and adjectives is indicated by a silent **e** added to the masculine form, as in *ami* and *amie* (the masculine and feminine for 'friend'). In the following phrases both masculine and feminine forms have been indicated where necessary. The masculine form comes first and is separated from the feminine by a slash. The gender of a noun is often indicated by a preceding article: 'the/a/some' or *le/un/du* (m), *la/une/de la* (f) in French.

ACCOMMODATION

I'm looking for a ...	Je cherche ...	zher shairsh ...
guest house	une pension (de famille)	ewn pon·syon (der fa·mee·yer)
hotel	un hôtel	un o·tel
youth hostel	une auberge de jeunesse	ewn o·bairzh der zher·nes

What is the address?
Quelle est l'adresse?
kel ay la·dres
Could you write the address, please?
Est-ce que vous pourriez écrire l'adresse, s'il vous plaît?
es·ker voo poo·ryay ay·kreer la·dres seel voo play
Do you have any rooms available?
Est-ce que vous avez des chambres libres?
es ker voo za·vay day shom·brer lee·brer
May I see it?
Est-ce que je peux voir la chambre?
es ker zher per vwa la shom·brer
Where is the bathroom?
Où est la salle de bains?
oo ay la sal der bun

I'd like (a) ...	Je voudrais ...	zher voo·dray ...
single room	une chambre simple	ewn shom·brer sum·pler
double-bed room	une chambre double	ewn shom·brer doo·bler
twin room (with two beds)	une chambre avec des lits jumeaux	ewn shom·brer a·vek day lee zhew·mo

How much is it ...?	*Quel est le prix ...?*	kel ay ler pree ...
per night	*par nuit*	par nwee
per person	*par personne*	par pair·son

CONVERSATION & ESSENTIALS

You'll find any attempt to communicate in French very much appreciated. Even if the only sentence you can muster is *Pardon, madame/monsieur/mademoiselle, parlez-vous anglais?* (Excuse me, Madam/Sir/Miss, do you speak English?), you're sure to be more warmly received than if you blindly address a stranger in English.

An important distinction is made in French between *tu* and *vous*, which both mean 'you'; *tu* is only used when addressing people you know well, children or animals. If you're addressing an adult who isn't a personal friend, *vous* should be used unless the person invites you to use *tu*.

Hello.	*Bonjour.*	bon·zhoor
Goodbye.	*Au revoir.*	o rer·vwa
Yes.	*Oui.*	wee
No.	*Non.*	non
Please.	*S'il vous plaît.*	seel voo play
Thank you.	*Merci.*	mair·see
You're welcome.	*Je vous en prie.*	zher voo zon pree
	De rien. (inf)	der ree·en
Excuse me.	*Excusez-moi.*	ek·skew·zay·mwa
Sorry. (forgive me)	*Pardon.*	par·don

What's your name?
Comment vous appelez-vous?
ko·mon voo za·pay·lay voo
My name is ...
Je m'appelle ...
zher ma·pel ...
Do you speak English?
Parlez-vous anglais?
par·lay·voo ong·glay
I don't understand.
Je ne comprends pas.
zher ner kom·pron pa
Could you write it down, please?
Est-ce que vous pourriez l'écrire, s'il vous plaît?
es ker voo poo·ryay lay·kreer seel voo play

NUMBERS

0	*zero*	zay·ro
1	*un*	un
2	*deux*	der
3	*trois*	trwa
4	*quatre*	ka·trer
5	*cinq*	sungk

EMERGENCIES

Help!
  Au secours!   o skoor
There's been an accident!
  Il y a eu un accident!   eel ee a ew un ak·see·don
I'm lost.
  Je me suis égaré/e. (m/f)   zhe me swee zay·ga·ray
Leave me alone!
  Fichez-moi la paix!   fee·shay·mwa la pay

Call ... !	*Appelez ... !*	a·play ...
a doctor	*un médecin*	un mayd·sun
the police	*la police*	la po·lees

6	*six*	sees
7	*sept*	set
8	*huit*	weet
9	*neuf*	nerf
10	*dix*	dees
11	*onze*	onz
12	*douze*	dooz
13	*treize*	trez
14	*quatorze*	ka·torz
15	*quinze*	kunz
16	*seize*	sez
17	*dix-sept*	dee·set
18	*dix-huit*	deez·weet
19	*dix-neuf*	deez·nerf
20	*vingt*	vun
21	*vingt et un*	vun tay un
22	*vingt-deux*	vun·der
30	*trente*	tront
40	*quarante*	ka·ront
50	*cinquante*	sung·kont
60	*soixante*	swa·sont
70	*septante*	se·tont
80	*huitante*	wee·tont
90	*nonante*	no·nont
100	*cent*	son
1000	*mille*	meel

SHOPPING & SERVICES

I'd like to buy ...
  Je voudrais acheter ...   zher voo·dray zash·tay ...
How much is it?
  C'est combien?   say kom·byun

Can I pay by ...?
Est-ce que je peux payer avec ...?
es ker zher per pay·yay a·vek ...
  credit card
    ma carte de crédit   ma kart der kray·dee
  travellers cheques
    des chèques de voyage   day shek der vwa·yazh

LANGUAGE

SIGNS	
Entrée	Entrance
Sortie	Exit
Ouvert	Open
Fermé	Closed
Interdit	Prohibited
Toilettes/WC	Toilets
Hommes/Femmes	Men/Women

I'm looking for ...	*Je cherche ...*	zhe shairsh ...
a bank	*une banque*	ewn bonk
the ... embassy	*l'ambassade de ...*	lam·ba·sad der ...
the hospital	*l'hôpital*	lo·pee·tal
the market	*le marché*	ler mar·shay
the police	*la police*	la po·lees
the post office	*la poste*	la post
a public phone	*une cabine téléphonique*	ewn ka·been tay·lay·fo·neek
a public toilet	*les toilettes publiques*	lay twa·let pewb·leek
the tourist office	*l'office de tourisme*	lo·fees der too·rees·mer

TIME & DATES

What time is it?	*Quelle heure est-il?*	kel er ay·til
It's (eight) o'clock.	*Il est (huit) heures.*	il ay (weet) er
It's half past ...	*Il est ... heures et demie.*	il ay ... er ay der·mee
in the morning	*du matin*	dew ma·tun
in the afternoon	*de l'après-midi*	der la·pray·mee·dee
in the evening	*du soir*	dew swar
Monday	*lundi*	lun·dee
Tuesday	*mardi*	mar·dee
Wednesday	*mercredi*	mair·krer·dee
Thursday	*jeudi*	zher·dee
Friday	*vendredi*	von·drer·dee
Saturday	*samedi*	sam·dee
Sunday	*dimanche*	dee·monsh
January	*janvier*	zhon·vyay
February	*février*	fayv·ryay
March	*mars*	mars
April	*avril*	av·reel
May	*mai*	may
June	*juin*	zhwun
July	*juillet*	zhwee·yay
August	*août*	oot
September	*septembre*	sep·tom·brer
October	*octobre*	ok·to·brer
November	*novembre*	no·vom·brer
December	*décembre*	day·som·brer

TRANSPORT

What time does the ... leave/arrive?	*À quelle heure part/arrive ...?*	a kel er par/a·reev ...
bus	*le bus*	ler bews
train	*le train*	ler trun
I'd like a ... ticket.	*Je voudrais un ... billet*	zher voo·dray zun bee·yay ...
one-way	*simple*	sum·pler
return	*aller-retour*	a·lay·rer·toor
1st class	*de première classe*	der prem·yair klas
2nd class	*de deuxième classe*	der der·zyem klas
the first	*le premier* (m)	ler prer·myay
	la première (f)	la prer·myair
the last	*le dernier* (m)	ler dair·nyay
	la dernière (f)	la dair·nyair
train station	*la gare*	la gar

Directions

I want to go to ...	*Je voudrais aller à ...*	zher voo·dray a·lay a ...
Where is ...?	*Où est ...?*	oo ay ...
Go straight ahead.	*Continuez tout droit.*	kon·teen·way too drwa
Turn left/right.	*Tournez à gauche/droite.*	toor·nay a gosh/drwat
near (to)/far (from)	*près (de)/loin (de)*	pray (der)/lwun (der)
Can you show me (on the map)?	*Pouvez-vous m'indiquer (sur la carte)?*	poo·vay·voo mun·dee·kay (sewr la kart)

GERMAN

SWISS GERMAN

Though German-speaking Swiss have little trouble with standard High German, they use Swiss German (Schwyzertütsch) in private conversation and in most unofficial situations. Contrary to the worldwide trend of erosion of dialects, its usage is actually increasing. Swiss German covers a wide variety of melodic dialects that can differ quite markedly from High German, often more closely resembling the German of hundreds of years ago than the modern version. It's as different to High German as Dutch is.

Swiss German is an oral language, rarely written down, and indeed there is no standard written form – they can't even agree on how to spell 'Schwyzertütsch'! While newspapers and books almost invariably use High German, also used in news broadcasts, schools and the parliament, people are more comfortable with their own Swiss German, and may even attempt a completely different language when speaking to foreigners rather than resort to High German.

Germans themselves often have trouble understanding Schwyzertütsch. To English speakers' ears High German sounds like it's full of rasping 'ch' sounds, but even Germans will joke that *Schwyzertütsch ist keine Sprache, sondern eine Halsentzündung* (Swiss German isn't really a language, it's a throat infection). To make matters even more complicated, regional dialects are strongly differentiated for such a small country, thanks to the isolating effect of mountain ranges (and the lack of a written standard).

With no written form and so many dialects, it's impossible to provide a proper vocabulary for Swiss German. The commonly used greeting is *Grüezi* (hello) and 'tram' is *Tram*, not *Strassenbahn*. Versions of French words are often used: 'thank you' is not *danke* but *merci* (though pronounced as 'mur·see' rather than the correct French, 'mair·see'); 'bicycle' is *vélo*, not *Fahrrad*; 'ice cream' is *glace*, not *Sahneneis*. In pronunciation, double vowel sounds are common – 'good' sounds more like 'gu·et' than the High German *gut*. Visitors might also note the frequent use of the suffix *-li* to indicate the diminutive or a term of endearment.

For more information, read *Dialect and High German in German-Speaking Switzerland*, published by Pro Helvetia, the Arts Council of Switzerland. For a more in-depth guide to High German, get a copy of Lonely Planet's *German Phrasebook*.

PRONUNCIATION
Vowels

German	Pronunciation Guide
hat	**a** (eg the 'u' in 'run')
habe	**ah** (eg 'father')
mein	**ai** (eg 'aisle')
Bär	**air** (eg 'hair', with no 'r' sound)
Boot	**aw** (eg 'saw')
leben	**ay** (eg 'say')

Bett/Männer	**e** (eg 'bed')
fliegen	**ee** (eg 'thief')
schön	**er** (eg 'her', with no 'r' sound)
mit	**i** (eg 'bit')
Koffer	**o** (eg 'pot')
Leute/Häuser	**oy** (eg 'toy')
Schuhe	**oo** (eg 'moon')
Haus	**ow** (eg 'how')
züruck	**ü** ('ee' said with rounded lips)
unter	**u** (eg 'put')

Consonants

The only two tricky consonant sounds in German are **ch** and **r**. All other consonants are pronounced much the same as their English counterparts (except **sch**, which is always as the 'sh' in 'shoe'). The **ch** sound is generally like the 'ch' in Bach or Scottish *loch* – like a hiss from the back of the throat. When **ch** occurs after the vowels **e** and **i**, it's more like a 'sh' sound, produced with the tongue more forward in the mouth. In this book we've simplified things by using the one symbol **kh** for both sounds. The **r** sound is different from English, and it isn't rolled like in Italian or Spanish. It's pronounced like the French 'r', at the back of the throat, almost like saying a 'g' sound, but with some friction – it's a bit like gargling.

Word Stress

As a general rule, word stress in German mostly falls on the first syllable. In the pronunciation guides for the following words and phrases, the stressed syllable is shown in italics.

ACCOMMODATION

Where's a ...?	*Wo ist ...?*	vaw ist ...
guest house	*eine*	ai·ne
	Pension	pahng·*zyawn*
hotel	*ein Hotel*	ain ho·*tel*
inn	*ein Gasthof*	ain *gast*·hawf
youth hostel	*eine Jugend-*	ai·ne yoo·gent·
	herberge	her·ber·ge

Do you have a ... room?	*Haben Sie ein ...?*	hah·ben zee ain ...
single	*Einzelzimmer*	ain·tsel·tsi·mer
double	*Doppelzimmer*	do·pel·tsi·mer
	mit einem	mit ai·nem
	Doppelbett	do·pel·bet
twin	*Doppelzimmer*	do·pel·tsi·mer
	mit zwei	mit tsvai
	Einzelbetten	ain·tsel·be·ten

LANGUAGE

EMERGENCIES

Help!	*Hilfe!*	*hil*·fe
I'm sick.	*Ich bin krank.*	ikh bin krangk
Go away!	*Gehen Sie weg!*	*gay*·en zee vek

Call a doctor!		
	Rufen Sie einen Arzt!	*roo*·fen zee *ai*·nen artst
Call the police!		
	Rufen Sie die Polizei!	*roo*·fen zee dee po·li·*tsai*
I'm lost.		
	Ich habe mich verirrt.	ikh *hah*·be mikh fer·*irt*

What's the address?

Wie ist die Adresse?	vee ist dee a·*dre*·se
May I see it?	
Kann ich es sehen?	kan ikh es *zay*·en

How much is it	*Wie viel kostet es*	vee feel *kos*·tet es
per ...?	*pro ...?*	praw ...
night	*Nacht*	nakht
person	*Person*	per·*zawn*

CONVERSATION & ESSENTIALS

You should be aware that German uses polite and informal forms for 'you' (*Sie* and *du* respectively). When addressing people you don't know well, you should always use the polite form (though younger people will be less inclined to expect it). In this language guide we use the polite form unless indicated by 'inf' (for 'informal') in brackets.

If you need to ask for assistance from a stranger, remember to always introduce your request with a simple *Entschuldigung* (Excuse me).

Good ...	*Guten ...*	*goo*·ten ...
morning	*Morgen*	*mor*·gen
afternoon	*Tag*	tahk
evening	*Abend*	*ah*·bent

Hello.	*Guten Tag.*	*goo*·ten tahk
Goodbye.	*Auf Wiedersehen.*	owf *vee*·der·*zay*·en
Yes.	*Ja.*	yah
No.	*Nein.*	nain
Please.	*Bitte.*	*bi*·te
Thank you.	*Danke.*	*dang*·ke
Thank you very much.	*Vielen Dank.*	*fee*·len dangk
You're welcome.	*Bitte (sehr).*	*bi*·te (zair)
Sorry.	*Entschuldigung.*	ent·*shul*·di·gung
Excuse me, ...	*Entschuldigung.*	ent·*shul*·di·gung
(before asking for help or directions)		

What's your name?

Wie ist Ihr Name? (pol)	vee ist eer *nah*·me
Wie heisst du? (inf)	vee haist doo
My name is ...	
Mein Name ist .../	main *nah*·me ist .../
Ich heisse ...	ikh *hai*·se ...
Do you speak English?	
Sprechen Sie Englisch?	*shpre*·khen zee *eng*·lish
I (don't) understand.	
Ich verstehe (nicht).	ikh fer·*shtay*·e (nikht)
Could you please write it down?	
Könnten Sie das bitte aufschreiben?	*kern*·ten zee das *bi*·te owf·*shrai*·ben

NUMBERS

1	*eins*	aints
2	*zwei*	tsvai
3	*drei*	drai
4	*vier*	feer
5	*fünf*	fünf
6	*sechs*	zeks
7	*sieben*	*zee*·ben
8	*acht*	akht
9	*neun*	noyn
10	*zehn*	tsayn
11	*elf*	elf
12	*zwölf*	zverlf
13	*dreizehn*	drai·tsayn
14	*vierzehn*	feer·tsayn
15	*fünfzehn*	fünf·tsayn
16	*sechzehn*	zeks·tsayn
17	*siebzehn*	zeep·tsayn
18	*achtzehn*	akh·tsayn
19	*neunzehn*	noyn·tsayn
20	*zwanzig*	tsvan·tsikh
21	*einundzwanzig*	ain·unt·tsvan·tsikh
30	*dreissig*	drai·sikh
40	*vierzig*	feer·tsikh
50	*fünfzig*	fünf·tsikh
60	*sechzig*	zekh·tsikh
70	*siebzig*	zeep·tsikh
80	*achtzig*	akh·tsikh
90	*neunzig*	noyn·tsikh
100	*hundert*	*hun*·dert
1000	*tausend*	*tow*·sent

SHOPPING & SERVICES

I'm looking for ...

Ich suche ...	ikh *zoo*·khe ...
How much (is this)?	
Wie viel (kostet das)?	vee feel (*kos*·tet das)
What time does it open/close?	
Wann macht (er/sie/es) auf/zu? (m/f/n)	van makht (air/zee/es) owf/tsoo

SIGNS	
Polizei	Police
Eingang	Entrance
Ausgang	Exit
Offen	Open
Geschlossen	Closed
Kein Zutritt	No Entry
Rauchen Verboten	No Smoking
Verboten	Prohibited
Toiletten (WC)	Toilets
Herren	Men
Damen	Women

Do you accept ...?	*Nehmen Sie ...?*	*nay*·men zee ...
credit cards	*Kreditkarten*	kre·*deet*·kar·ten
travellers cheques	*Reiseschecks*	*rai*·ze·sheks

a bank	*eine Bank*	*ai*·ne bangk
a chemist	*eine Apotheke*	*ai*·ne a·po·*tay*·ke
the ... embassy	*die ... Botschaft*	dee ... *bot*·shaft
the hospital	*das Krankenhaus*	das *krang*·ken·hows
the market	*der Markt*	dair markt
the police	*die Polizei*	dee po·li·*tsai*
the post office	*das Postamt*	das *post*·amt
a public phone	*ein öffentliches Telefon*	ain er·fent·li·khes te·le·*fawn*
a public toilet	*eine öffentliche Toilette*	*ai*·ne er·fent·li·khe te·le·*fawn*

TIME & DATES

What time is it?	*Wie spät ist es?*	vee shpayt ist es
It's (one) o'clock.	*Es ist (ein) Uhr.*	es ist (ain) oor
Twenty past one.	*Zwanzig nach eins.*	*tsvan*·tsikh nahkh ains
am	*morgens/ vormittags*	*mor*·gens/ *fawr*·mi·tahks
pm	*nachmittags/ abends*	*nahkh*·mi·tahks/ *ah*·bents

Monday	*Montag*	*mawn*·tahk
Tuesday	*Dienstag*	*deens*·tahk
Wednesday	*Mittwoch*	*mit*·vokh
Thursday	*Donnerstag*	*do*·ners·tahk
Friday	*Freitag*	*frai*·tahk
Saturday	*Samstag*	*zams*·tahk
Sunday	*Sonntag*	*zon*·tahk

January	*Januar*	*yan*·u·ahr
February	*Februar*	*fay*·bru·ahr
March	*März*	merts
April	*April*	a·*pril*
May	*Mai*	mai
June	*Juni*	*yoo*·ni
July	*Juli*	*yoo*·li
August	*August*	ow·*gust*
September	*September*	zep·*tem*·ber
October	*Oktober*	ok·*taw*·ber
November	*November*	no·*vem*·ber
December	*Dezember*	de·*tsem*·ber

TRANSPORT

What time does the ... leave?	*Wann fährt ... ab?*	van fairt ... ap
bus	*der Bus*	dair bus
train	*der Zug*	dair tsook

What time's the ... bus?	*Wann fährt der ... Bus?*	van fairt dair ... bus
first	*erste*	*ers*·te
last	*letzte*	*lets*·te
next	*nächste*	*naykhs*·te

A ... ticket to ...	*Eine ... nach ...*	*ai*·ne ... nahkh ...
one-way	*einfache Fahrkarte*	*ain*·fa·khe *fahr*·kar·te
return	*Rückfahrkarte*	*rük*·fahr·kar·te
1st-class	*Fahrkarte erster Klasse*	*fahr*·kar·te *ers*·ter *kla*·se
2nd-class	*Fahrkarte zweiter Klasse*	*fahr*·kar·te *tsvai*·ter *kla*·se

Directions

Where's (a bank)?
Wo ist (eine Bank)? vaw ist (*ai*·ne bangk)
Can you show me (on the map)?
Können Sie mir (auf der Karte) zeigen? ker·nen zee es meer (owf dair *kar*·te) *tsai*·gen

Turn ...	*Biegen Sie ... ab.*	*bee*·gen zee ... ap
at the corner	*an der Ecke*	an dair *e*·ke
left	*links*	lingks
right	*rechts*	rekhts

straight ahead	*geradeaus*	ge·rah·de·*ows*
near	*nahe*	*nah*·e
far away	*weit weg*	vait vek

ITALIAN

SWISS ITALIAN

There are differences between Ticinese and standard Italian, but they aren't very significant. You may come across people saying *bun di* instead of *buon giorno* (good day), and *buona noc* (pronounced 'nockh') instead of *buona notte* (goodnight).

PRONUNCIATION
Vowels
Vowels are more clipped than in English:

a	as in 'art', eg *caro* (dear); sometimes short, eg *amico/a* (friend)
e	short, as in 'let', eg *mettere* (to put); long, as in 'there', eg *mela* (apple)
i	short, as in 'it', eg *inizio* (start); long, as in 'marine', eg *vino* (wine)
o	short, as in 'dot', eg *donna* (woman); long, as in 'port', eg *ora* (hour)
u	as the 'oo' in 'book', eg *puro* (pure)

Consonants
A double consonant is a longer, more forceful sound than a single consonant.

c	as the 'k' in 'kit' before **a**, **o**, **u**, and **h**; as the 'ch' in 'choose' before **e** and **i**
g	as the 'g' in 'get' before **a**, **o**, **u** and **h**; as the 'j' in 'jet' before **e** and **i**
gli	as the 'lli' in 'million'
gn	as the 'ny' in 'canyon'
h	always silent
r	a rolled 'rr' sound
sc	as the 'sh' in 'sheep' before **e** and **i**; as 'sk' before **a**, **o**, **u** and **h**
z	as the 'ts' in 'lights'; at the beginning of a word, as the 'ds' in 'suds'

Word Stress
Stress is indicated in our pronunciation guide by italics. Word stress generally falls on the second-last syllable, as in 'spa·*ghet*·ti', but when a word has an accent, the stress falls on that syllable, as in 'cit·*tà*' (city).

ACCOMMODATION

I'm looking for a ...	*Cerco ...*	*cher*·ko ...
guest house	*una pensione*	oo·na pen·*syo*·ne
hotel	*un albergo*	oon al·*ber*·go
youth hostel	*un ostello per la gioventù*	oon os·*te*·lo per la jo·ven·*too*

What is the address?
Qual'è l'indirizzo?   kwa·*le* leen·dee·*ree*·tso
Could you write the address, please?
Può scrivere l'indirizzo,   pwo *skree*·ve·re leen·dee·*ree*·tso
per favore?   per fa·*vo*·re
Do you have any rooms available?
Avete camere libere?   a·*ve*·te *ka*·me·re *lee*·be·re
May I see it?
Posso vederla?   *po*·so ve·*der*·la

EMERGENCIES

Help!		
Aiuto!		a·*yoo*·to
I'm ill.		
Mi sento male.		mee *sen*·to *ma*·le
I'm lost.		
Mi sono perso/a. (m/f)		mee *so*·no *per*·so/a
Go away!		
Lasciami in pace!		la·*sha*·mi een *pa*·che
Vai via! (inf)		va·ee *vee*·a
Call ...!	*Chiami ...!*	*kee*·ya·mee ...
a doctor	*un dottore/*	oon do·*to*·re/
	un medico	oon *me*·dee·ko
the police	*la polizia*	la po·lee·*tsee*·ya

I'd like a ... room.	*Vorrei una camera ...*	vo·*ray* oo·na *ka*·me·ra ...
single	*singola*	*seen*·go·la
double	*matrimoniale*	ma·tree·mo·*nya*·le
twin	*doppia*	*do*·pya

How much is it ...?	*Quanto costa ...?*	*kwan*·to *ko*·sta ...
per night	*per la notte*	per la *no*·te
per person	*per persona*	per per·*so*·na

CONVERSATION & ESSENTIALS

Hello.	*Buongiorno./*	bwon·*jor*·no
	Ciao. (inf)	chow
Goodbye.	*Arrivederci./*	a·ree·ve·*der*·chee
	Ciao. (inf)	chow
Good evening.	*Buonasera.*	bwo·na·*se*·ra
(from early afternoon onwards)		
Good night.	*Buonanotte.*	bwo·na·*no*·te
Yes.	*Sì.*	see
No.	*No.*	no
Please.	*Per favore./*	per fa·*vo*·re
	Per piacere.	per pya·*che*·re
Thank you.	*Grazie.*	*gra*·tsye
That's fine./ You're welcome.	*Prego.*	*pre*·go
Excuse me.	*Mi scusi.*	mee *skoo*·zee
Sorry. (forgive me)	*Mi scusi./*	mee *skoo*·zee/
	Mi perdoni.	mee per·*do*·nee

What's your name?
Come si chiama?   *ko*·me see *kya*·ma
My name is ...
Mi chiamo ...   mee *kya*·mo ...
Do you speak English?
Parla inglese?   *par*·la een·*gle*·ze

I don't understand.
Non capisco. non ka-*pee*-sko

Please write it down.
Può scriverlo, per pwo skree-ver-lo per
favore? fa-*vo*-re

NUMBERS

0	*zero*	dze-ro
1	*uno*	oo-no
2	*due*	doo-e
3	*tre*	tre
4	*quattro*	kwa-tro
5	*cinque*	cheen-kwe
6	*sei*	say
7	*sette*	se-te
8	*otto*	o-to
9	*nove*	no-ve
10	*dieci*	dye-chee
11	*undici*	oon-dee-chee
12	*dodici*	do-dee-chee
13	*tredici*	tre-dee-chee
14	*quattordici*	kwa-*tor*-dee-chee
15	*quindici*	kween-dee-chee
16	*sedici*	se-dee-chee
17	*diciassette*	dee-cha-*se*-te
18	*diciotto*	dee-*cho*-to
19	*diciannove*	dee-cha-*no*-ve
20	*venti*	ven-tee
21	*ventuno*	ven-*too*-no
22	*ventidue*	ven-tee-*doo*-e
30	*trenta*	tren-ta
40	*quaranta*	kwa-*ran*-ta
50	*cinquanta*	cheen-*kwan*-ta
60	*sessanta*	se-*san*-ta
70	*settanta*	se-*tan*-ta
80	*ottanta*	o-*tan*-ta
90	*novanta*	no-*van*-ta
100	*cento*	chen-*to*
1000	*mille*	mee-*le*

SHOPPING & SERVICES

I'd like to buy ...
Vorrei comprare ... vo-*ray* kom-*pra*-re ...

How much is it?
Quanto costa? kwan-to *ko*-sta

Do you accept credit cards?
Accettate carte a-che-*ta*-te *kar*-te
di credito? dee kre-dee-to

I want to	*Voglio*	vo-lyo
change ...	*cambiare ...*	kam-*bya*-re ...
money	*del denaro*	del de-*na*-ro
travellers	*assegni di*	a-*se*-nyee dee
cheques	*viaggio*	vee-*a*-jo

I'm looking for ...	*Cerco ...*	cher-ko ...
a bank	*un banco*	oon *ban*-ko
the ... embassy	*l'ambasciata di ...*	lam-ba-*sha*-ta dee ...
the market	*il mercato*	eel mer-*ka*-to
the post office	*la posta*	la *po*-sta
a public toilet	*un gabinetto*	oon ga-bee-*ne*-to
the tourist	*l'ufficio*	loo-*fee*-cho
office	*di turismo*	dee too-*reez*-mo

TIME & DATES

What time is it? *Che ore sono?* ke o-re *so*-no
It's (eight o'clock). *Sono (le otto).* *so*-no (le o-to)
in the morning *di mattina* dee ma-*tee*-na
in the afternoon *di pomeriggio* dee po-me-*ree*-jo
in the evening *di sera* dee *se*-ra

Monday	*lunedì*	loo-ne-*dee*
Tuesday	*martedì*	mar-te-*dee*
Wednesday	*mercoledì*	mer-ko-le-*dee*
Thursday	*giovedì*	jo-ve-*dee*
Friday	*venerdì*	ve-ner-*dee*
Saturday	*sabato*	*sa*-ba-to
Sunday	*domenica*	do-*me*-nee-ka

January	*gennaio*	je-*na*-yo
February	*febbraio*	fe-*bra*-yo
March	*marzo*	*mar*-tso
April	*aprile*	a-*pree*-le
May	*maggio*	*ma*-jo
June	*giugno*	*joo*-nyo
July	*luglio*	*loo*-lyo
August	*agosto*	a-*gos*-to
September	*settembre*	se-*tem*-bre
October	*ottobre*	o-*to*-bre
November	*novembre*	no-*vem*-bre
December	*dicembre*	dee-*chem*-bre

TRANSPORT

What time does	*A che ora parte/*	a ke o-ra *par*-te/
the ... leave/	*arriva ...?*	a-*ree*-va ...
arrive?		
(city) bus	*l'autobus*	low-to-boos
(intercity) bus	*il pullman*	eel *pool*-man
train	*il treno*	eel *tre*-no

I'd like a ...	*Vorrei un*	vo-*ray* oon
ticket.	*biglietto ...*	bee-*lye*-to ...
one-way	*di solo andata*	dee *so*-lo an-*da*-ta
return	*di andata e*	dee an-*da*-ta e
	ritorno	ree-*toor*-no
1st class	*di prima*	dee *pree*-ma
	classe	*kla*-se
2nd class	*di seconda*	dee se-*kon*-da
	classe	*kla*-se

SIGNS

Ingresso/Entrata	Entrance
Uscita	Exit
Informazione	Information
Aperto	Open
Chiuso	Closed
Proibito/Vietato	Prohibited
Polizia/Carabinieri	Police
Gabinetti/Bagni	Toilets
Uomini	Men
Donne	Women

the first	*il primo*	eel *pree*·mo
the last	*l'ultimo*	lool·tee·mo
train station	*stazione*	sta·*tsyo*·ne

Directions

Where is ...?	*Dov'è ...?*	do·*ve* ...
Turn left.	*Giri a sinistra.*	*jee*·ree a see·*nee*·stra
Turn right.	*Giri a destra.*	*jee*·ree a *de*·stra

Go straight ahead.
Si va sempre diritto./   see va *sem*·pre dee·*ree*·to
Vai sempre diritto. (inf)   va·ee *sem*·pre dee·*ree*·to
Can you show me (on the map)?
Può mostrarmelo   pwo mos·*trar*·me·lo
(sulla pianta)?   (soo·la *pyan*·ta)

ROMANSCH

Romansch dialects tend to be restricted to their own particular mountain valley. Usage is gradually being undermined by the steady encroachment of German, and linguists fear that the language may eventually disappear altogether. There are so many dialects that not all the Romansch words listed here will be understood. The main street in villages is usually called Via Maistra.

BASIC WORDS & PHRASES

Please.	*Anzi.*
Thank you.	*Grazia.*
Hello.	*Allegra.*
Goodbye.	*Adieu/Abunansvair.*
Good morning.	*Bun di.*
Good evening.	*Buna saira.*
Good night.	*Buna notg.*
bed	*letg*
room	*chombra*
left	*sanester*
right	*dretg*
tourist office	*societad da traffic*
closed	*serrà*
cross-country skiing	*passlung*
man	*um*
woman	*dunna*
food	*mangiar*
bread	*paun*
cheese	*chaschiel*
fish	*pesch*
ham	*schambun*
milk	*latg*
wine	*vin*
Monday	*Lündeschdi*
Tuesday	*Mardi*
Wednesday	*Marculdi*
Thursday	*Gievgia*
Friday	*Venderdi*
Saturday	*Sanda*
Sunday	*Dumengia*

1	*in*
2	*dus*
3	*trais*
4	*quatter*
5	*tschinch*
6	*ses*
7	*set*
8	*och*
9	*nouv*
10	*diesch*

LANGUAGE

Alternative Place Names

Basel (E, G) – Basle (E), Bâle (F), Basilea (I)
Bern (E, G) – Berne (E, F), Berna (I)
Bernese Mittelland (E) – Berner Mittelland (G), Le Plateau Bernois (F)
Bernese Oberland (E) – Berner Oberland (G)
Biel (G) – Bienne (F)
Bodensee (G) – Lake Constance (E)
Brienzersee (G) – Lake Brienz (E)
Brig (E, G) – Brigue (F)
Bündner Oberland – older term for Graubünden's Surselva region

Chur (E, G) – Coire (F)

Fribourg (E, F) – Freiburg (G), Friburgo (I)

Geneva (E) – Genève (F), Genf (G), Ginevra (I)
Glarnerland – Glarus Canton
Graubünden (E, G) – Grisons (F), Grigioni (I), Grishun (R)

Lake Geneva (E) – Lac Léman or Lac du Genève (F), Genfersee (G)
Lake Geneva Region (E) – Région du Léman (F), Genferseegebiet (G)
Lago Maggiore (I) – Lake Maggiore (E)
Leuk (E,G) – Loeche (F)

Leukerbad (E,G) – Loeche-les-Bains (F)
Lower Valais (E) – Unterwallis (G), Bas Valais (F)
Lucerne (E, F) – Luzern (G), Lucerna (I)

Matterhorn (E, G) – Cervino (I)
Mont Blanc (F) – Monte Bianco (I)

Neuchâtel (E, F) – Neuenburg (G)

Rhine River (E) – Rhein (G), Rhin (F)

St Gallen (E, G) – St Gall (F), San Gallo (I)
St Moritz (E, G, F) – San Murezzan (R)
St Peter's Island (E) – St Petersinsel (G), Île de St Pierre (F)
Sarine River (E) – Saane (G), Sarine (F)
Schaffhausen (E, G) – Schaffhouse (F), Sciafusa (I)
Sierre (E, F) – Siders (G)
Sion (E, F) – Sitten (G)
Solothurn (E, G) – Soleure (F), Soletta (I)
Switzerland (E) – Suisse (F), Schweiz (G), Svizzerra (I), Svizzra (R)

Thunersee (G) – Lake Thun (E), Lac de Thoune (F)
Ticino (E, I) – Tessin (G, F)

Upper Valais (E) – Oberwallis (G), Haut Valais (F)

Valais (E, F) – Wallis (G)
Vaud (E, F) – Waadt (G)
Vierwaldstättersee (G) – Lake Lucerne (E)
Visp (E,G) – Viège (F)

Winterthur (E, G) – Winterthour (F)

Zug (E, G) – Zoug (F)
Zugersee (G) – Lake Zug (E), Lac de Zoug (F)
Zürich (G) – Zurich (E, F), Zurigo (I)

GLOSSARY

Glossary

The language of origin of non-English terms is noted in brackets: French (F), High German (G), Italian (I), Romansch (R) and Swiss German (S).

abbaye – (F/G) abbey
AOC – (F) Appellation d'Origine Contrôlée; food and wine products that have met stringent government regulations governing where, how and under what conditions the ingredients and final product are produced
albergo – (I) hotel
Altstadt – (G) old town
auberge – (F) inn, guest house
auberge de jeunesse – (F) youth hostel

Bach – (G) stream; often in compound nouns such as Milibach
Bad – (G) spa, bath
Bahnhof – (G) train station
belvédère/belvedere (F/I) – 'beautiful view'; scenic high point
Berg – (G) mountain
Berggasthaus, Berghaus – (G) mountain inn
billetterie – (F) box office
bisse – (F) mountain aqueduct in the Valais
Brücke – (G) bridge
Burg– (G) castle, also *Schloss*

cabane/capanna– (F/I) mountain hut offering basic accommodation
cairn – piles of stones, often used to mark a route or path junction
cantons – the self-governing regions within the Swiss Confederation
castello – (I) castle
cave – (F) wine or cheese cellar
château – (F) castle
chiesa – (I) church
cirque – a rounded high precipice formed by the action of ice in the high-Alpine zone
col/passo – (F/I) a mountain pass

dégustation – (F) the fine art of tasting wine or cheese
domaine – (F) wine-producing estate
dortoir – (F/I) dormitory

église – (F) church

föhn – warm southerly wind

gare – (F) train station
gare routière – (F) bus station
Garni – (G) B&B
Gasthaus – (G) guest house
Gletscher – (G/I) glacier
Grat – (G) ridge
grotto – (I) rustic Ticino-style restaurant

Hauptbahnhof – (G) central train station
haute route/Höhenweg – (F/G) literally 'high route', a high-level mountain route; also the classic Chamonix to Zermatt skiing and walking route through the Valais
Hütte – (G) hut, usually used in compounds, eg Zwinglihütte

Kathedrale – (G) cathedral
Kirche – (G) church
Kunstmuseum – (G) fine-arts museum

lac/lago/lai – (F/I/R) lake
lido – (I) beach
locanda – (I) inn serving food, small hotel

maison d'hôte – (F) upmarket B&B
Markt – (G) market, covered market
menu – (F) meal at a fixed price with two or more courses
murata – (I) city walls
musée des beaux arts – (F) fine-arts museum

Oberland – (G) a term used to describe the regional 'uplands' of various cantons, eg Bernese Oberland
ostello della gioventù – (I) youth hostel
osteria – (I) cheap restaurant, snack bar

pizzo – (I) peak, summit
place/platz/piazza – (F/G/I) square
plat du jour – (F) dish of the day
pont – (F) bridge
postal bus – regional public bus network run by Swiss Post

Röstigraben – French–German linguistic divide
rustico/rustici – (I; singular/plural) rustic Ticino-style cottage(s) built of stone

SAC – Swiss Alpine Club; Schweizer Alpen-Club
SAW – Swiss Hiking Federation; Schweizer Wanderwege
SBB/CFF/FSS – (G/F/I) Swiss Federal Railways
Scheidegg – (S) watershed
Schloss – (G) palace, castle

See – (G) lake
sentier du viticole/vin – (F) wine-themed walking path, often through vineyards
Stadt – (G) city or town
strada alta – (I) literally 'high route', a high-level mountain route
strade del vino – (I) wine-themed tourist routes around wineries

Tal – (G) valley; often in compound place names, eg Mattertal
tarn – tiny Alpine lake

trattoria – (I) traditional, inexpensive, often family-run restaurant
trottinette – (F) microscooter

val – (I/R) valley
valle/vallée – (I/F) valley
vieille ville – (F) old town
ville – (F) city or town
Voralpen – (G) Pre-Alps

Wald – (G) forest
Weg – (G) way, path

The Authors

NICOLA WILLIAMS
Coordinating Author, Geneva, Fribourg, Neuchâtel & Jura, Mittelland

Ever since Nicola moved to a village on the southern side of Lake Geneva, she has never quite been able to shake off the feeling that she is on holiday – waking up to a garden tumbling down the hillside towards the lake and Switzerland's mysterious Jura mountains beyond. Nicola has lived and worked in France since 1997 and when not flitting to Geneva, skiing or dipping into the Swiss countryside, she can be found at her desk writing. Previous Lonely Planet titles include *France; Provence & the Côte d'Azur; Languedoc-Roussillon; Tuscany & Umbria; Milan, Turin & Genoa;* and *Piedmont.*

DAMIEN SIMONIS
Lake Geneva, Zürich, Basel & Aargau, Northeastern Switzerland, Ticino, Liechtenstein

The kaleidoscopic fare on offer in Switzerland would probably have passed Damien by had his other half not decided on moving to Lausanne on Lake Geneva. It might have seemed an obvious place for him to be, speaking as he does French, German (but alas, not Schwyzertütsch!) and Italian (not to mention the unofficial lingua franca, er, English!). The further he explores the place, from Italian eateries in Ticino to the ski runs of Zermatt, the more he fails to understand how he could have failed to cotton on to the place earlier. Better late than never! Nowhere else in Europe has he found such breathtaking natural beauty and cultural variety.

KERRY WALKER
Walking in Switzerland, Valais, Bernese Oberland, Central Switzerland, Graubünden

Born in pancake-flat Essex, Kerry has always been fascinated by mountains and (true to her name) quickly discovered walking boots were more her style than stilettos. In 2000 she arrived penniless at a vegetable farm near Bern. After exerting herself digging up metre-high weeds and carrying courgettes by the kilo, she decided this was a country after her own heart and returned with salopettes for seasonal stints in Arosa and Wengen. Realising post-MA that she was lost in translation, Kerry turned to travel writing and has authored some 15 books and scores of online guides. When not trotting the globe, Kerry lives in the Black Forest, Germany.

LONELY PLANET AUTHORS

Why is our travel information the best in the world? It's simple: our authors are passionate, dedicated travellers. They don't take freebies in exchange for positive coverage so you can be sure the advice you're given is impartial. They travel widely to all the popular spots, and off the beaten track. They don't research using just the internet or phone. They discover new places not included in any other guidebook. They personally visit thousands of hotels, restaurants, palaces, trails, galleries, temples and more. They speak with dozens of locals every day to make sure you get the kind of insider knowledge only a local could tell you. They take pride in getting all the details right, and in telling it how it is. Think you can do it? Find out how at **lonelyplanet.com**.

Behind the Scenes

THIS BOOK

The 6th edition of Switzerland was written and re-
searched by Nicola Williams, Damien Simonis and
Kerry Walker. Damien and Nicola also wrote the
5th edition with some contributions from Sarah
Johnstone. This guidebook was commissioned by
Lonely Planet's London office, and produced by
the following:

Commissioning Editors Paula Hardy, Sally Schafer
Coordinating Editor Robyn Loughnane
Coordinating Cartographer Ross Butler
Coordinating Layout Designers Carlos Solarte, Clara
Monitto
Managing Editor Bruce Evans
Managing Cartographers Mark Griffiths, Herman So,
Shahara Ahmed
Managing Layout Designers Sally Darmody, Laura
Jane
Assisting Editors Sally O'Brien, Diana Saad, Cathryn Game
Assisting Cartographers Andy Rojas
Cover Designer Marika Mercer
Project Manager Glenn van der Knijff
Language Content Coordinator Quentin Frayne,
Branislava Vladisavljevic

Thanks to Jessica Boland, Melanie Dankel, Jennifer
Garrett, James Hardy, Alex Leung, Trent Paton, Darren
O'Connell, Amanda Rogerson, Lyahna Spencer

THANKS
NICOLA WILLIAMS

Several friends and acquaintances recommended
places to eat, things to do, places to go, not least
my efficient army of Geneva-savvy volunteers
from the World Economic Forum in Cologny:
Carine Benetti, Danielle Boiston, Lena Hagelstein,
Sophie Lux, Stéphanie Nassenstein, Juraj Ondrejk-
ovic and Tessema Tesfachew. Special thanks in
Geneva to party gal Ciara Browne for opening
her address book to me and to man-around-town
Alan Turner for his sterling drinking-'n-dancing-
till-dawn pointers. Appreciation in equal measure
to Sarah Garner for putting me in touch; temporary New Yorker Claudia Rosiny for Bern talk;
Elizabeth and Nicolas at Ferme Montavon for
Jurassic farm pleasures; all the Messery gals and
guys (Lee, Michael et al) for keeping me posted
on their Geneva *sorties;* the ever dependable Nana
and Omi for domestic reinforcement; and last but
far from least the lovely Lüfkens boys Niko, Mischa
and Matthias for always travelling with so much
relish and gusto.

DAMIEN SIMONIS

Thanks in general go to tourist office staff in Vaud,
Basel, Aargau, Zürich, Schaffhausen, Thurgau, St
Gallen, Glarus and Ticino.

THE LONELY PLANET STORY

Fresh from an epic journey across Europe, Asia and Australia in 1972, Tony and Maureen Wheeler
sat at their kitchen table stapling together notes. The first Lonely Planet guidebook, *Across Asia
on the Cheap,* was born.

Travellers snapped up the guides. Inspired by their success, the Wheelers began publishing
books to Southeast Asia, India and beyond. Demand was prodigious, and the Wheelers expanded
the business rapidly to keep up. Over the years, Lonely Planet extended its coverage to every
country and into the virtual world via lonelyplanet.com and the Thorn Tree message board.

As Lonely Planet became a globally loved brand, Tony and Maureen received several offers for
the company. But it wasn't until 2007 that they found a partner whom they trusted to remain true
to the company's principles of travelling widely, treading lightly and giving sustainably. In October
of that year, BBC Worldwide acquired a 75% share in the company, pledging to uphold Lonely
Planet's commitment to independent travel, trustworthy advice and editorial independence.

Today, Lonely Planet has offices in Melbourne, London and Oakland, with over 500 staff members and 300 authors. Tony and Maureen are still actively involved with Lonely Planet. They're
travelling more often than ever, and they're devoting their spare time to charitable projects. And
the company is still driven by the philosophy of *Across Asia on the Cheap*: 'All you've got to do
is decide to go and the hardest part is over. So go!'

In Zürich, Thierry Délèze rolled out the welcome mat, providing contacts and ideas and participating in the consumption of some soothing beers! It would be hard to find a more enthusiastic Welshländer resident of Zürich!

In Ticino, I owe a big *grazie* to Monica Bonetti and her family in Lugano, who welcomed me into their home. Monica introduced me to *gente molto simpatica,* like Gaia Francesconi, Simona Candela, Tommaso di Caro and co. *Grazie anche a* Nicole della Pietra and Andrea Muehle.

A special *merci vielmal* goes to the little boy who pointed out the Seerenbachfälle waterfalls to us across the lake from Mühlehorn and calmly informed us of their significance. When he grows up, I will owe him a big beer.

Judith Bongard in Lausanne had some excellent tips – hopefully we'll catch up for that coffee before this is published!

I owe a *gracias* to Helena Ramírez for her bunker tip.

The modest results of this Swiss tour are dedicated to Janique LeBlanc, who provided endlessly patient company on a protracted jaunt across the northeast – and that with a crook hip!

KERRY WALKER

Heartfelt thanks to my fiancé and travel companion Andy for his support and skilful driving up those dizzying mountain passes. Special thanks to Evelyne Binsack, Gian Simmen, Sepp Steiner, Damian Cina and Thomas Kernen for the interviews. *Vielen Dank* to the tourism professionals who made the road to research silky smooth, particularly Sibylle Gerardi in Lucerne, Daniela Fuchs in Jungfrau Region, Susanne Daxelhoffer in Interlaken, Nicole Steindl in Zermatt, David Graefen in Leukerbad, Maria Ferretti in Engelberg, Katharina Schreiber in Chur and Claudia Kleinbrod

in Lenzerheide. *Merci* also to Fiona Buchan for the gig, as well as Paula Hardy, Mark Griffiths, co-authors Nicola and Damien, and everyone at Lonely Planet.

OUR READERS

Many thanks to the travellers who used the last edition and wrote to us with helpful hints, useful advice and interesting anecdotes:

Sara Alereza, Jon Barker, Regina Caputo, Clare Carmody, Rachel Cassidy, Donald Casson, Angie Clark, Christine Cooper, David Cory, Julien Dubois, Tim Dunk, Judy East, Sveinung Eikenes, Krista Eleftheriou, Fabio Fabbiano, Roy Freere, Lilani Goonesena, Anna Lisa Grech, Yunhee Ha, Friederike Haass, Olivier Hartmann, Nadia Hashmi, Tom Hughes, Trout Johnson, Lizanne Joubert, Michael Kaiser-Nyman, Miles Cary Leahey, To Nhu Ly, Kim Lyons, John Madden, Hugh and Eileen Morton, David Polmantuin, Sanat Raiturcar, Flavio Renzetti, Cedric Roserens, Daniel Ryan, Stefan Schmidlin, Keith Siddel, Markus Spring, Alyson Stoakley, Dorien Terpstra, Eva Toia, Jonathan Toker, Bert Van Der Neut, Janneke Van Hardeveld, Matt and Sheryl Vincent, Lizzie Wright

ACKNOWLEDGMENTS

Internal photographs p8 (#1), p9 (#7) by Arcaid/ Alamy; p11 (#6) Arco Images GmbH/Alamy; p12 (#4) Travelstock44/Alamy; p8 (#3) Yvonne Bischofberger. All other photographs by Lonely Planet Images, and by Glenn van der Knijff p7 (#2); Karl Lehman p6 (#4); Martin Moos p5, p10 (#1), p11 (#3), Witold Skrypczak p6 (#1).

All images are the copyright of the photographers unless otherwise indicated. Many of the images in this guide are available for licensing from Lonely Planet Images: www.lonelyplanetimages.com.

Many thanks to the following for the use of their content:

Globe on title page ©Mountain High Maps 1993 Digital Wisdom, Inc.

BEHIND THE SCENES

Index

INDEX

INDEX

GreenDex

The following have been selected by Lonely Planet authors because they demonstrate a commitment to sustainability. We've selected cafés and restaurants for their support of local producers – so they might serve only seasonal, locally sourced produce on their menus. We've also highlighted farmers markets and the local producers themselves. In addition, we've covered accommodation that we deem to be environmentally friendly, for example for their commitment to recycling or energy conservation. Attractions are listed because they're involved in conservation or environmental education or have been given an ecological award. For more tips about travelling sustainably in Switzerland, turn to the Getting Started chapter (p17). We want to keep developing our sustainable-travel content. If you think we've omitted someone who should be listed here, email us at http://www.lonelyplanet.com/contact. For more information about sustainable tourism and Lonely Planet, see www.lonelyplanet.com/responsibletravel.

MAP LEGEND

ROUTES

Tollway	Mall/Steps
Freeway	Tunnel
Primary	Pedestrian Overpass
Secondary	Walking Tour
Tertiary	Walking Tour Detour
Lane	Walking Trail
Unsealed Road	Walking Path
One-Way Street	Track

TRANSPORT

Ferry	Rail
Metro	Rail (Underground)
Monorail	Tram
Bus Route	Cable Car, Funicular

HYDROGRAPHY

River, Creek	Canal
Intermittent River	Water
Swamp	Glacier

BOUNDARIES

International	Regional, Suburb
State, Provincial	Ancient Wall
Marine Park	Cliff

AREA FEATURES

Airport	Land
Area of Interest	Market
Beach, Desert	Park
Building	Rocks
Campus	Sports
Cemetery, Christian	Urban
Forest	

POPULATION

◎ **CAPITAL (NATIONAL)**	◉ CAPITAL (STATE)
● **Large City**	◉ Medium City
● Small City	◦ Town, Village

SYMBOLS

Sights/Activities
- Beach
- Canoeing, Kayaking
- Castle, Fortress
- Christian
- Jewish
- Monument
- Museum, Gallery
- Point of Interest
- Pool
- Ruin
- Skiing
- Trail Head
- Winery, Vineyard
- Zoo, Bird Sanctuary

Eating
- Eating

Drinking
- Drinking
- Café

Entertainment
- Entertainment

Shopping
- Shopping

Sleeping
- Sleeping
- Camping

Transport
- Airport, Airfield
- Bus Station
- General Transport
- Parking Area
- Petrol Station
- Taxi Rank

Information
- Bank, ATM
- Embassy/Consulate
- Hospital, Medical
- Information
- Internet Facilities
- Police Station
- Post Office, GPO
- Telephone
- Toilets

Geographic
- Lookout
- Mountain, Volcano
- National Park
- Pass, Canyon
- Picnic Area
- River Flow
- Shelter, Hut
- Spot Height
- Waterfall

LONELY PLANET OFFICES

Australia
Head Office
Locked Bag 1, Footscray, Victoria 3011
☎ 03 8379 8000, fax 03 8379 8111
talk2us@lonelyplanet.com.au

USA
150 Linden St, Oakland, CA 94607
☎ 510 250 6400, toll free 800 275 8555
fax 510 893 8572
info@lonelyplanet.com

UK
2nd fl, 186 City Rd,
London EC1V 2NT
☎ 020 7106 2100, fax 020 7106 2101
go@lonelyplanet.co.uk

Published by Lonely Planet Publications Pty Ltd
ABN 36 005 607 983

© Lonely Planet Publications Pty Ltd 2009

© photographers as indicated 2009

Cover photograph: Man fishing in Goschener Tal, Winterberg, Karl Lehmann/Lonely Planet Images. Many of the images in this guide are available for licensing from Lonely Planet Images: www.lonelyplanet images.com.

Mixed Sources
Product group from well-managed forests and other controlled sources
www.fsc.org Cert no. SGS-COC-005002
© 1996 Forest Stewardship Council
FSC